19th Nordic Conference of Computational Linguistics (NODALIDA 2013)

NEALT Proceedings Series Volume 16

Oslo, Norway
22 – 24 May 2013

Editors:

Stephan Oepen
Kristin Hagen
Janne Bondi Johannessen

ISBN: 978-1-5108-3335-7

Proceedings of the 19th Nordic Conference of Computational Linguistics (NODALIDA 2013)

Stephan Oepen, Kristin Hagen, and
Janne Bondi Johannessen (Editors)

May 22–24, 2013

Oslo University (Norway)

Preface

The tradition of bi-annual Nordic conferences in Computational Linguistics and related disciplines dates back to 1977, well before our professional organization—The Northern European Association for Language Technology (NEALT; `http://omilia.uio.no/nealt/`)—was formally established. With a sense of tradition as well as pride, this volume comprises the proceedings of the 19th Nordic Conference on Computational Linguistics (NODALIDA 2013), held on the campus of the University of Oslo, Norway, between May 22 and May 24, 2013. On the first day of NODALIDA 2013, four topical worshops are held, each with its own set of organizers and programme committee; these workshops have compiled their own proceedings volumes, which are published in the same series and included on the media distributed at the conference.

NODALIDA addresses all aspects of speech recognition and synthesis, natural language processing, and computational linguistics—including work in closely related neighbouring disciplines (such as, for example, linguistics or psychology) that is sufficiently formalized or applied to bear relevance to speech and language technologies. Following the pattern of previous years, the Programme Committee invited paper submissions in four distinct tracks:

- *regular papers* on substantial, original, and unpublished research, including empirical evaluation results, where appropriate;

- *student papers* on completed or ongoing work, where at least the first author is a Master- or PhD-level student;

- *short papers* on smaller, focused contributions, work in progress, negative results, surveys, or opinion pieces; and

- *demonstration papers* summarizing a software system or language resource, to be accompanied by a live demonstration at the conference.

The conference received 60 submissions from all over Europe (and one each from Mexico and the US), of which 38 are collected in this volume and will be presented at the conference: 13 regular, 6 student, 12 short, and 7 demonstration papers. All submissions were reviewed by at least three experts in the field (two for demonstration papers), and the final selection was made by the Programme Committee. We are indebted to everyone who contributed to the reviewing and selection process. The conference programme is complemented by three invited keynotes by distinguished researchers from Denmark, Germany, and the US, as well as by a special session on High-Performance Computing for Natural Language Processing.

NODALIDA 2013 is made possible by the joint work of many dedicated individuals, in particular the Programme and Organizing Committees; we warmly acknowledge their enthusiasm and community spirit. From the Organizing Committee, Kristin Hagen deserves a special note of gratitude, as the untiring 'heart and soul' of the conference logistics. We are grateful to the Department of Linguistics and Scandinavian Studies and the Department of Informatics at the University of Oslo for generously making available infrastructure and staff time. The conference is financially supported by organizations listed on the back cover, who thus make an important contribution to keeping participation fees at quite reasonable leves (by Norwegian standards).

With just about two more weeks to go, we expect some 150 participants at the conference and much look forward to welcoming our colleagues and peers to Oslo.

Stephan Oepen (Programme Chair), Janne Bondi Johannessen (Organizing Chair)

Programme Committee

- Lars Ahrenberg, Linköping University, Sweden

- Heiki-Jaan Kaalep, University of Tartu, Estonia

- Mikko Kurimo, Aalto University, Finland

- Stephan Oepen (Programme Chair), University of Oslo, Norway

- Eva Pettersson, Uppsala University, Sweden

- Bolette Sandford Pedersen, University of Copenhagen, Denmark

- Victoria Rosén, University of Bergen, Norway

Organizing Committee

- Ruth Vatvedt Fjeld

- Kristin Hagen

- Janne Bondi Johannessen (Organizing Chair)

- Anders Nøklestad

- Erik Velldal

- Lilja Øvrelid

Reviewers

- Szymon Acedański, Poland

- Tanel Alumäe, Estonia

- Miguel Ballesteros, Spain

- Emily M. Bender, USA

- Gosse Bouma, Netherlands

- Johan Boye, Sweden

- Aoife Cahill, USA

- Stefanie Dipper, Germany

- Helge Dyvik, Norway

- Jakob Elming, Denmark

- Tomaž Erjavec, Slovenia

- Peter Exner, Sweden

- Mark Fishel, Estonia

- Victoria Fossum, USA

- Jennifer Foster, Irland

- Tatiana Gornostay, Latvia

- Gintarė Grigonytė, Switzerland

- Christian Hardmeier, Sweden

- Petter Haugereid, Norway

- Anna Hjalmarsson, Sweden

- Sofie Johansson Kokkinakis, Sweden

- Arne Jönsson, Sweden

- Reima Karhila, Finland

- Mare Koit, Estonia

- Jan Tore Lønning, Norway

- Bente Maegaard, Denmark

- Diana McCarthy, United Kingdom

- Beata Megyesi, Sweden

- Einar Meister, Estonia

- Magnus Merkel, Sweden

- Paul Meurer Norway

- Costanza Navarretta, Denmark

- Mattias Nilsson, Sweden

- Joakim Nivre, Sweden

- Pierre Nugues Lund, Sweden

- Petya Osenova, Bulgaria

- Patrizia Paggio, Denmark

- Barbara Plank, Italy

- Adam Przepiórkowsk, Poland

- Jonathon Read, Norway

- Trial Reviewer, Norway

- Inguna Skadiņa, Latvia

- Anders Søgaard, Denmark

- Sara Stymne, Sweden

- Jörg Tiedemann, Sweden

- Andrius Utka, Lithuania

- Erik Velldal, Norway

- Sumithra Velupillai, Sweden

- Yi Zhang, Germany

- Heike Zinsmeister, Germany

Table of Contents

Student Papers

Short Papers

Demonstration Papers

The Conversational User Interface

Ron Kaplan

Nuance Communications & Stanford University

`ron.kaplan@nuance.com`

ABSTRACT

Work on both the graphical user interface (GUI) and the conversational user interface (CUI) started at about the same time, about 40 years ago. The GUI was a lot easier to implement, and it made computing and information resources available to ordinary people—but over the years it has lost much of its simplicity and charm. The CUI has taken many more years to develop, requiring major scientific and engineering advances in speech, natural language processing, user-modeling, and reasoning, not to mention increases in cost-effective computation. But the infrastructure is now in place for the widespread distribution of conversational interfaces, and we have begun to imagine and create sophisticated ways of exploiting this new mode of interaction. This may well be the "killer app" for deep natural language processing and complex reasoning.

KEYWORDS: Conversational User Interface, Deep Natural Language Processing, Reasoning.

Detecting and Processing Figurative Language in Discourse

Caroline Sporleder

Universität Trier

`sporledc@uni-trier.de`

ABSTRACT

Figurative language poses a serious challenge to NLP systems. The use of idiomatic and metaphoric expressions is not only extremely widespread in natural language; many figurative expressions, in particular idioms, also behave idiosyncratically. These idiosyncrasies are not restricted to a non-compositional meaning but often also extend to syntactic properties, selectional preferences etc. To deal appropriately with such expressions, NLP tools need to detect figurative language and assign the correct analyses to non-literal expressions. While there has been quite a bit of work on determining the general 'idiomaticity' of an expression (type-based approaches), this only solves part of the problem as many expressions, such as *break the ice* or *play with fire*, can also have a literal, perfectly compositional meaning (e.g. *break the ice on the duck pond*). Such expressions have to be disambiguated in context (token-based approaches). Token-based approaches have received increased attention recently. In this talk, I will present an unsupervised method for token-based idiom detection. The method exploits the fact that well-formed texts exhibit lexical cohesion, i.e. words are semantically related to other words in the context. I will show how cohesion can be modelled and how the cohesive structure can be used to distinguish literal and idiomatic usages and even detect newly coined figurative expressions.

KEYWORDS: Discourse, Figurative Language, Token-Based Idiom Detection.

6,909 Reasons to Mess Up Your Data

Anders Søgaard

Københavns Universitet

`soegaard@hum.ku.dk`

ABSTRACT

In computational linguistics we develop tools and on-line services for everything from literature to social media data, but our tools are often optimized to minimize expected error on a single annotated dataset, typically newspaper articles—and evaluated on held-out data sampled from the same dataset. Significance testing across data points randomly sampled from a standard dataset only tells us how likely we are to see better performance on more data points sampled this way, but says nothing about performance on other datasets. This talk discusses how to modify learning algorithms to minimize expected error on future, unseen datasets, with applications to PoS tagging and dependency parsing, including cross-language learning problems. It also discusses the related issue of how to best evaluate NLP tools (intrinsically) taking their possible out-of-domain applications into account.

KEYWORDS: Domain Variation, PoS Tagging, Dependency Parsing, Evaluation.

The Nordic e-Infrastucture Collaboration: Opportunities for Synergy Without Borders

Gudmund Høst

NordForsk, Nordic e-Infrastructure Collaboration

`gudmund.host@nordforsk.org`

ABSTRACT

The Nordic e-Infrastructure Collaboration (NeIC) is a distributed organization of IT-experts working at various national HPC centers throughout the Nordic region. The mission of NeIC is to facilitate the development of high-quality e-Infrastructure solutions in areas of joint Nordic interest. It is owned by the research councils and national e-Infrastructure provider organisations from Denmark, Finland, Iceland, Norway, and Sweden. NeIC is hosted by NordForsk in Oslo. Current collaboration areas include high-energy physics (CERN-related) and life sciences. A call for Letters of Interest in 2012 elicited several opportunities within the humanities, including fields such as computational analysis of language and semantic annotation. This presentation will give an overview of the NeIC and its modus operandi, and aims to provide a basis for discussions at NoDaLiDa on how NeIC may be put into use as a vehicle for facilitating development of common e-Infrastructure services for linguistics and related fields.

KEYWORDS: Nordic e-Infrastructure Collaboration, NeIC, Cross-Border HPC Collaboration.

Tidying up the Basement:
A Tale of Large-Scale Parsing on National eInfrastructure

Stephan Oepen

Universitetet i Oslo

`oe@ifi.uio.no`

ABSTRACT

Until about six years ago, our research group used non-trivial amounts of project funds and researcher time on maintaining a dedicated server farm in the basement of our department. Rack space and cooling (just as much as funds and time) were in short supply, and we never quite got around to implementing automated load balancing across compute nodes, tuning the Linux kernel and filesystem for optimum performance, or connecting to the uninterruptible power supply. When pointed to the Norwegian National High-Performance Computing Initiative, we were intially doubtful that Natural Language Processing should be among their target user groups. Also, we were a tad hesitant to give up control of our own equipment and of course worried we would miss what we thought were our fancy toys. Today, any member of the group can access thousands of cpus simultaneously, we have about five terabytes of project data on-line, and our research has scaled to dataset sizes and turn-around times that would be just inconceivable on group-local hardware—at no charge to our project funds and no administrator responsibilities. For example, 'deep' semantic parsing of the about 900 million words of the English Wikipedia we can typically complete in less than one day (while expending what would be about eight sequential years of computation). Or, when searching for the best-performing features and hyper-parameters in a machine learning problem, we can explore a large 'grid' of possible configurations in parallel, without much need for a staged, partly manual, 'coarse-to-fine' search strategy. Access to the very large-scale Norwegian National eInfrastructure and its high-quality technical support have enabled a comparatively computation-heavy research profile of our group and has thus contributed to its international competitiveness. In this presentation, I will review some of our experiences in establishing a dialogue with the HPC crowd and propose *HPC for the Masses* as a candidate vision in the on-going development trend towards more and more large-scale computational sciences.

KEYWORDS: Parsing Wikipedia, HPC for the Masses, National eInfrastructure.

Experiences in Building the *Let's MT!* Portal on Amazon EC2

Jörg Tiedemann

Uppsala Universitet

`jorg.tiedemann@lingfil.uu.se`

ABSTRACT

In this presentation I will discuss the design and implementation of *Let's MT!*, a collaborative platform for building statistical machine translation systems. The goal of this platform is to make MT technology, that has been developed in academia, accessible for professional translators, freelancers and every-day users without requiring technical skills and deep background knowledge of the approaches used in the backend of the translation engine. The main challenge in this project was the development of a robust environment that can serve a growing community and large numbers of user requests. The key for success is a distributed environment that allows a maximum of scalability and robustness. With this in mind, we developed a modular platform that can be scaled by adding new nodes to the different components of the system. We opted for a cloud-based solution based on Amazon EC2 to create a cost-efficient environment that can dynamically be adjusted to user needs and system load. In the presentation I will explain our design of the distributed resource repository, the SMT training facilities and the actual translation service. I will mention issues of data security and optimization of the training procedures in order to fit our setup and the expected usage of the system.

KEYWORDS: Let's MT!, Statistical Machine Translation, Distributed Computing.

Using Constraint Grammar for Chunking

Eckhard Bick

University of Southern Denmark, Odense

`eckhard.bick@mail.dk`

ABSTRACT

This paper presents and evaluates a novel and flexible chunking method using Constraint Grammar (CG) rules to introduce chunk edges in corpus annotation. Our method exploits pre-existing (non-constituent) morphosyntactic annotation such as part-of-speech or function tags, but can also be made to work on raw text, integrated with other CG modules. The first version of the chunker was developed for German CG-annotated interview data, with a parallel English version derived from the German one, indicating a high degree of language-independence of the rules in the presence of generalized syntactic-functional tags (e.g. subject, object, modifier). Two different approaches are discussed, one for minimal, flat chunking, the other for deep, nested chunking. The system has a reasonable performance and robustness for both, achieving F-scores of 89.1 and 97.4 for nested and minimal chunking, respectively. Xml markup is supported, and with a full set of rules, the tool can be used to convert CG annotation into complete constituent trees in VISL or TIGER format.

KEYWORDS: Chunking, Constraint Grammar, Syntactic Constituent Trees

1   Introduction and related research

In its simplest NLP meaning, chunking can be defined as a shallow parsing method where the edges of syntactic groups are marked, but where the internal structure, head-dependent relations and syntactic function is ignored. When defining the term, Abney (1991) cited psychological (processing) evidence for the linguistic relevance of chunks and used the expression "a single content word surrounded by a constellation of function words, matching a fixed template". In the original sense, chunks are minimal syntactic units with a recursivity restriction, and chunks of different syntactic type will be shown as chained rather than layered - in particular, no (simple) chunk type will be allowed to span across a (more complex) daughter chunk, and subclauses are not made explicit as chunks. Thus, in minimal chunking np's will not contain postnominal pp's or relative clauses. If a chunk does swallow another chunk, the latter will lose its edges. Depending on linguistic design, this may occur in the handling of prepositions or quantifying adverbials.

Minimal chunking is often used as an intermediate step in NLP, after part-of-speech (POS) tagging, and before deeper structural or functional analysis. Thus, Abney's chunk parser would first create a stream of such minimal chunks, then use an "attacher" to link words within chunks, and chunks to each other in order to create a complete parse tree. Kübler & Hinrichs (2001) use a similar 2-step method, but focus on syntactic function assignment as a vehicle to extend non-recursive chunks to full parse structures on the background of a treebank instance database. In our own approach, we implement a third strategy, where (syntactic) function comes before (syntactic) form, and links are created before chunks. Chunk edges are assigned based on functional relations, and chunking depth becomes a design option rather than a clear, methodologically desired, processing stage distinction. In the context of this paper, we will therefore extend the meaning of chunking to include progressively layered chunking, where nesting is allowed e.g. for np's or object clauses, and where a fully chunked sentence will ultimately be structurally equivalent to a PSG constituent tree.

Chunking is useful for tasks such as term and name extraction (Carreras and Màrquez 2005), information retrieval (Banko et al. 2007), topic screening and others. In such automatic analysis applications, minimal chunking has the obvious advantage of being more robust than layered chunking, being able to avoid complexity issues such as discontinuity, coordination and ellipsis, as well as circumventing free-word-order problems, while still supporting most aspects of the applicative tasks mentioned above. Unlike Abney's original system, the majority of automatic chunkers today are based on machine learning (ML) and trained on manually revised gold annotations such as treebanks. In a CoNLL shared task in 2000, the highest F-score for chunking was 93.5 (Tjong Kim Sang and Buchholz 2000), with relatively little performance variation across different ML techniques. There is evidence that with sufficient training data, similar results can be achieved with ML techniques even without the use of POS information (van den Bosch and Buchholz 2002), while finite state transducers (FST) have an upper bound F-score of 92 for the same task (Jurafsky and Martin 2009). The only rule-based systems in the CoNNL evaluation performed at the bottom of the field, with F-scores of 85.8 and 87.2.

Contrary to these findings, we believe rule-based chunking to have a considerable potential, and have chosen Constraint Grammar for the experiments reported here, a versatile and modular methodology based entirely on linguist-written rules. It is reasonable to assume that differences between rules sets, the expressive power of the rule formalism itself as well as its lexical support may amount to huge performance differences - maybe bigger differences than can be expected from different machine learners using the same training data, and this will be further compounded by the fact that rule-based approaches require a great deal of specialist labour and hence may suffer from project time and manpower constraints. Thus, when writing a chunking grammar, performance will crucially depend on the existence and quality of a morphosyntactic tagger to provide annotated input. What we intend to show and evaluate in this paper is exactly this - how rule-based chunking can mash with and exploit output from a CG tagger, in this case the morphosyntactic stage of the EngGram parser (available online at http://beta.visl.sdu.dk/visl/en/). Since it has already been shown that morphosyntactic CG tagging does support syntactic trees, either through a PSG layer (Bick 2003, for English) or an added external dependency grammar (Bick 2005, for Danish), it is not CG-*based* constituent bracketing as such that is the focus here, but rather the efficiency of our method and the fact that we are exploiting a novel CG feature (relational tags) to perform both dependency-linking and chunking *within* the CG formalism itself rather than as a hybrid add-on technique. This way, all types of existing CG annotation can be seamlessly exploited without loss of information, and with the full expressivity of contextual CG rules.

2   Adding Chunk Edges

Both the output and input of our chunkers follow the verticalized, 1-token-per-line format common in Constraint Grammar annotation. We have developed two different methods to add chunking information to this format, with different methodological advantages, which can then both be filtered into a common xml-style format. Both methods exploit recent improvements in the open-source CG3 compiler (http://beta.visl.sdu.dk/cg3.html), allowing so-called cohort insertion and named, bidirectional relational tags.

2.1   The Cohort Insertion Method

Constraint Grammar compilers traditionally use a fixed tokenization, where each token may have several readings (a so-called cohort), but without the possibility of changing the number, order or span of the tokens themselves. In our own implementation, however, we provide for the possibility of adding, moving and removing tokens, exploiting this feature for the insertion of chunk edges. In its simplest version, our insertion chunker uses 20 CG rules, first 12 rules (a,b) to insert different types of chunk-opening brackets (named for phrase type), then 8 rules (c) to insert matching chunk-closing brackets.

The first two examples open np chunks by adding a marker cohort before (left of) the first np element. Rule (a) looks for prenominal modifiers (@>N) or potential np-heads, i.e. nouns or pronouns/numbers provided that the latter do not have a function marking as prenominals (@>N) or predicatives (@PRED, @SC, @OC) which would indicate an adjectival reading. In order to make sure that the found np-element is in fact the np's left edge, there is a NOT condition excluding further prenominals (@>N) to the left, as well as adverbial pre-adjects (@>A) that might pre-modify the premodifiers themselves (e.g. *'very @>A high @>N taxes'*). The NEGATE condition, finally, provides for the exception of coordinated premodifiers[1]. Rule (b) addresses np-

---

[1] In this version of the chunker, we follow the principle, applied in the CoNLL 2000 shared task on chunking, that lower level coordination within a phrase is treated as chunk-internal, while coordination of phrase heads is treated as chunk-external.

internal adverbial adjects (@>A) in a similar way, again taking into account possible coordination of pre-modifiers.

(a) ADDCOHORT ("<$np>" "CHUNK" NP) BEFORE @>N OR N/PROP/PRON OR DET/NUM/PERS - @>N - @PRED - @SC - @OC (NOT -1 @>A OR @>N) (NEGATE -1 IT LINK -1 @>N) ;

(b) ADDCOHORT ("<$np>" "CHUNK" NP) BEFORE @>A (*1 @>N BARRIER NON-ADV - KC) (NOT -1 @>A OR @>N) (NEGATE -1 IT LINK -1 @>A - PRP OR @>N) ;

Similar rules exist for the other chunk types: adjective phrase (adjp), adverbial phrase (advp), prepositional phrase (pp), verb phrase (vp) and the minor classes of conjp (conjunction phrase), prt (particles), intj (interjection) that usually contain only a single word. Once a chunk is opened, a corresponding rule can insert an ENDCHUNK marker token after the last element in the chunk. Thus, rule (c) looks for potential np-heads with a NOT condition against them functioning as pre-modifiers (@>N) themselves (as would be the case in English noun chain compounds). To ensure exact bracket matching and as a safety measure, there is a condition looking left (*-1) for the corresponding chunk-opening token with a BARRIER condition for overlaps, i.e. other CHUNK markers.

(c) ADDCOHORT ("<$/np>" "ENDCHUNK" NP) AFTER N/PROP/PRON OR N/PROP/PRON OR DET/NUM/PERS - @>N - @PRED - @SC - @OC (NOT 0 @>N) (*-1 CHUNK-NP BARRIER CHUNK) ;

2.2   The Relation-Adding Method

The cohort insertion method is a very simple method, and works well and robustly for minimal chunking. However, in the face of more complex annotation needs, it has the shortcoming of not marking chunk heads as opposed to other chunk elements, and it is less well-suited for layered chunking, because of the risk of crossing brackets. The CG-compiler may lack sufficient structural information simply because opening and closing brackets are only inserted and not paired by links. Thus, in layered chunking, closing brackets in particular may accumulate after the same token, and bracket order will simply be by (inverse) rule order, making it very difficult for the grammarian to control this order, not least because CG rules can be reiterated if contexts change from false to true due to other rules being applied, and because opening and closing brackets have opposite ordering needs. To further complicate things, a more fine-grained, head-marking chunking scheme may run into cases of discontinuity, with a need for partial closing and re-opening bracket types raising ambiguity issues in complex cases.

All of these problems can be addressed simultaneously by exploiting another non-traditional CG feature, named relations, which we originally added for the sake of anaphora treatment and discourse structure. Using relational tags, chunk edges can either be linked to each other or to the chunk head, and in principle carry all information needed to configure a complete, classical constituent tree. In this approach, given sufficient structural information in the CG input annotation, chunking provides a conversion method between different functional dependency grammar on the one hand, and labeled constituent trees on the other. Users will be able to apply standard xml tools to manipulate, search, evaluate or visualize the resulting chunk structures because chunk brackets can be expressed as xml opening and closing markers.

We developed the relation chunker in the context of a joined annotation project for German and English transcribed speech corpora, and some design options are therefore project-specific, such as the decision to allow discontinuity (crossing branches), to provide for separate coordination chunks, and to only mark multi-word chunks. However, it has to be borne in mind that in a rule-based CG system, it is relatively easy to change such design parameters, without the need of manual re-annotation of a training corpus. In particular, the chunk type of single-word constituents is implicit in their word-class, and could be added with one rule per type.

The relations chunker uses 59 rules to establish relations between a constituent head and its leftmost and rightmost descendents (dependents, dependents of dependents etc.). A typical rule pair is shown below:

(a) ADDRELATIONS (np-head-l) (np-start) TARGET (*) (c @>N OR @N<&) TO (llScc (*)) ;

(b) ADDRELATIONS (np-head-r) (np-stop) TARGET (*) (c @>N OR @N<&) (r:np-head-l (*)) TO (rrScc (*)) ;

Rule (a) adds a left-edge relation between any (*) target word with a pre-nominal (@>N) or postnominal (@N<) modifier child (c), and the leftmost (ll) of its descendents[2] (cc - children & children's children). The S (self) provision allows for the head itself forming the chunk's edge, and the modifier condition prevents 1-word chunks. An ADDRELATIONS rule allows for two asymmetric relation names, given in the first two brackets of the rule. Here, *np-head-l* (np-head-leftlooking) is the relation name tagged on the head, and *np-start* is the name for the same relation seen from, and tagged on, the leftmost dependent.

Rule (b) adds the corresponding right-edge relation to the rightmost (rr) descendents (cc) of np-heads. Matching bracket counts are ensured by adding the condition that the target already has to carry a pre-existing *np-head-l* tag.

2.2.1 Discontinuity

The rules described above will identify external chunk edges by locating leftmost and rightmost descendents of a given head, but they cannot cope with internal edges caused by crossing dependency branches (constituent discontinuity). Therefore, further rules are needed, like the np-examples below. Rule (a) marks the end of a discontinuity "hole", with a head-edge relation named *np-head-ld* (left-oriented discontinuity edge) on the head, and *np-stop-d* (discontinuity stop edge) on the (right-located) internal edge dependent. The rule works by identifying existing, ordinary right edges (r:np-head-r (*)) and looks left of these (LINK *-1) for arguments, adverbials (@ARG/ADVL) or verbs (VV), implying that such function tags would break the continuity of an np chunk if they are not explicitly marked as embedded, i.e. if neither the break candidate itself (S) or any of its ancestors or parent (*p) is identical with the rule target (NOT *pS _TARGET_). If a chunk-breaker is found, the rule backtracks (x) to the outer edge and from there looks left (**-1xA) for the *last* word (**) that *does* have the rule target as parent-ancestor, or is identical with it (*pS), and attaches (A) the relation here.

(a) ADDRELATIONS (np-head-ld) (np-stop-d) TARGET (*) (c @>N OR @N<&) (r:np-head-r (*) LINK *-1 @ARG/ADVL OR VV LINK NOT *pS _TARGET_) TO (r:np-head-r (*) LINK *-1X @ARG/ADVL OR VV LINK **-1xA ALL-ORD LINK *pS _TARGET_) ;

---

[2] In principle, a leftmost ancestor dependency chain (llcc) can be quite complex because a right daughter dependent may have crossing left granddaughter dependents that are further left than the head itself or its left daughters.

Correspondingly, rule (b) marks a relation between a head and a left-located internal edge, named *np-head-rd* (right-oriented discontinuity edge) on the head, and *np-start-d* (discontinuity start edge) on the edge dependent. Again, to ensure matching bracket counts, the rule checks if the matching *head-ld* relation tag is already present on the head. This way, the head accumulates information about all edges controlled by it, while the chunk edge tokens themselves carry only one tag containing chunk type and head ID[3].

(b) ADDRELATIONS (np-head-rd) (np-start-d) TARGET (*) (c @>N OR @N<&) TO (r:np-head-ld (*) LINK **1A ALL LINK *pS _TARGET_) ;

2.3   Language independence

It is an interesting question to what degree a function-first, linking-before-chunking approach will lead to a higher degree of language independence in a chunking grammar. We believe this to be the case because the use of higher-level categories, at least if notationally unified, insulates the chunking grammar from language specific differences such as agreement features and word order. Though we do not yet have data for less related languages, our German and English grammars provide empirical support for this assumption. Thus, the original German layered chunker did work without rule modifications for English, and even the final, optimized English grammar (59 rules) needed rule changes or additions almost exclusively in areas, where the German grammar still had coverage problems, specifically coordination (10 rules) and vp discontinuity (6 rules). Only one rule had to be amended in a truly language-specific way, to account for discontinuous, fronted arguments of stranded prepositions in English, and 8 default bracket closing rules were added to check for matching brackets. Most importantly, all of the above English changes could be reexported into the German grammar almost as is, and even the language-specific stranded-preposition rule would do no harm - rather, it would simply not apply. As long as function tags and dependencies are defined in a unified way, this might be true for many other language pairs, too: Unimpeded by morphological or topological constraints, a pure function/relation reference in a chunking rule will either have the desired effect in the other language, or none at all.

3   Format conversions

Because all information is encoded locally as tags on tokens, Constraint Grammar output is easy to parse for format conversion programs, allowing such filters to extract information from several levels of tagging at the same time, with only one regular expression match. This way information can be made explicit that would otherwise be stated only implicitly, and html tags (for visualization), sgml tags (for corpus segmentation) or xml tags (for external tools) can be inserted before or after certain trigger tags or tag combinations. For the speech corpus annotation project, xml-style encoding of chunking information was the desired target format. With the cohort insertion method this amounted to simply turning chunk edge cohorts into <...> lines (Fig. 1), while the filter program for the relation-adding method had to insert xml tags before or after tokens carrying chunk edge labels (Fig. 3). Because this method was used to produce multi-layered chunking, the filter program also had to keep track of the xml tag nesting, i.e. arrange brackets in correct matching order, whereas the minimal chunks produced with the insertion

---

[3] Of course, if a head is situated leftmost or rightmost in its chunk, it will carry both types of tags.

method were simply defined - following CoNLL conventions - as non-overlapping and non-recursive, avoiding any bracketing complexities:

```
<chunk form="advp">                      <chunk form="np">
  So [so] <*> <aquant> ADV @ADVL>          different [different] ADJ POS @>N
<chunk form="/advp">                       types [type] <ac-cat> <idf> N P NOM @<ACC
<chunk form="np">                        <chunk form="/np">
  anyone [anyone] INDP S NOM @SUBJ>      <chunk form="pp">
<chunk form="/np">                         of [of] PRP @N<
<chunk form="np">                        <chunk form="/pp">
  who_ [who] <sam-> <rel> INDP S/P @SUBJ>  <chunk form="np">
<chunk form="/np">                         games [game] <game> <idf> N P NOM @P<
<chunk form="vp">                        <chunk form="/np">
  _s [be] <-sam> <mv> V PR 3S @FS-N<     <chunk form="pp">
<chunk form="/vp">                         through [through] PRP @<ADVL
<chunk form="adjp">                      <chunk form="/pp">
  familiar [familiar] ADJ POS @<SC       <chunk form="np">
<chunk form="/adjp">                        a [a] <indef> ART S @>N
<chunk form="pp">                          console [console] <tool> <idf> N S NOM @P<
  with [with] PRP @A<                    <chunk form="/np">
<chunk form="/pp">                        <chunk form="vp">
<chunk form="vp">                          will [will] <aux> V PR @FS-STA
  playing [play] <mv> V PCP1 @ICL-P<       be [be] <mv> V INF @ICL-AUX<
<chunk form="/vp">                        <chunk form="/vp">
                                         ...
```

FIGURE 1: Minimal chunks, insertion method, xml format

The format does not explicitly mark heads, but because we followed the CoNLL standard in only allowing left dependents, this does not amount to any loss of information - the head is simply the rightmost/last constituent of a multi-word minimal chunk.

For the sake of evaluation and comparability, we also provide a denser, non-xml format, with the <B> (beginning-of) and <I> (inside-of) tags used in the CoNLL evaluation. This is achieved by a couple of short CG rules, where (a) extracts the chunk type ("<.(.+)>"r) as a bracketed regular expression variable from an immediately preceding (-1) CHUNK opening cohort and remaps it as a <B> tag (<C:B-$1>), while rule (b) adds <I> tags with chunk type-information extracted from immediately preceding <B>- or <I>-tagged words. A third rule (c) maps an <O> tag (outside-of-chunk) to all remaining words. Since minimal chunking regards 1-word constituents as chunks, and all word classes are mapped onto chunk types, all instances of <O> amount to annotation errors in the CG input.

```
So           <C:B-advp> ADV @ADVL>                near         <C:B-pp> PRP @<ADVL
you          <C:B-np> PERS 2S/P NOM @SUBJ>        completely   <C:B-np> ADV @>A
might        <C:B-vp> V IMPF @FS-STA              *different    <C:I-np> ADJ POS @>N
*be          <C:I-vp> V INF @ICL-AUX<            *things       <C:I-np> N P NOM @P<
near         <C:B-pp> PRP @<SA                    that         <C:B-np> INDP P @SUBJ>
some         <C:B-np> DET S/P @>N                 are          <C:B-vp> V PR -1/3S @FS-N<
*universities <C:I-np> N P NOM @P<                completely   <C:B-adjp> ADV @>A
but          <C:B-conjp> KC @CO                   *unrelated    <C:I-adjp> ADJ POS @<SC
you          <C:B-np> PERS 2S/P NOM @SUBJ>        to           <C:B-pp> PRP @A<
```

could	<C:B-vp> V IMPF @FS-STA	you	<C:B-np> PERS 2S/P ACC @P<
*end	<C:I-vp> V INF @ICL-AUX<	as=well	<C:B-advp> ADV @<ADVL
up	<C:B-prt> ADV @MV<	.	

FIGURE 2: Minimal chunks, insertion method, B/I/O format

Like most Constraint Grammars, our input CG marks a number of multi-word expressions (MWEs) as tokens, in particular certain complex prepositions, conjunctions and adverbs, as well as MWEs in the productive category of names. An example is the last word in Fig. 2 ('as well'), which however could simply be expanded by splitting on space, letting the first part of the MWE inherit the MWE tag, and adding <I> tags to all other MWE parts.

Fig. 3 shows a fully layered chunk tree for the same data used in Fig. 1, with layering depth shown as indented dots (. . .), to improve readability. CG lemma, inflexion, pos, function and dependency tags are retained, the latter employing a sentence-internal numbering scheme (#n->m tags). The relational, chunk edge-linking CG tags would be redundant, and are not shown after conversion into xml-format. In order to facilitate linguistic corpus searches, the xml chunk lines carry explicit feature-attribute pairs for (chunk) form, (head) function and head ID. The latter are - unlike dependency IDs - numbered across the whole corpus, because our CG compiler in principle allows relations across sentence boundaries, allowing for co-referent resolution, discourse annotation or text-level chunking.

```
<chunk form="fcl" function="STA" head="167">
. So        [so] <*> <aquant> ADV @ADVL> #1->16 ID:153
. <chunk form="np" function="SUBJ" head="154">
.. anyone [anyone] INDP S NOM @SUBJ> #2->15 ID:154
.. <chunk form="fcl" function="N<" head="156">
... who_ [who] <clb> <sam-> <rel> INDP S/P @SUBJ> #3->4 ID:155
...._s   [be] <-sam> <mv> V PR 3S @FS-N< #4->2 ID:156
... <chunk form="adjp" function="SC" head="157">
.... familiar       [familiar] <close-2> <acquainted> ADJ POS @<SC #5->4 ID:157
.... <chunk form="pp" function="A<" head="158">
..... with       [with] PRP @A< #6->5 ID:158
..... <chunk form="icl" function="P<" head="159">
...... playing       [play] <mv> V PCP1 @ICL-P< #7->6 ID:159
...... <chunk form="np" function="ACC" head="161">
....... different  [different] ADJ POS @>N #8->9 ID:160
....... types      [type] <ac-cat> <idf> <nhead> N P NOM @<ACC #9->7 ID:161
....... <chunk form="pp" function="N<" head="162">
........ of        [of] PRP @N< #10->9 ID:162
........ games     [game] <game> <idf> <nhead> N P NOM @P< #11->10 ID:163
...... </chunk form="pp" function="N<" head="162">
...... </chunk form="np" function="ACC" head="161">
...... <chunk form="pp" function="ADVL" head="164">
....... through    [through] <advl-fs> PRP @<ADVL #12->7 ID:164
...... <chunk form="np" function="P<" head="166">
........ a         [a] <indef> ART S @>N #13->14 ID:165
........ console   [console] <tool> <idf> <nhead> N S NOM @P< #14->12 ID:166
...... </chunk form="np" function="P<" head="166">
..... </chunk form="pp" function="ADVL" head="164">
.... </chunk form="icl" function="P<" head="159">
.... </chunk form="pp" function="A<" head="158">
```

```
. . . </chunk form="adjp" function="SC" head="157">
. . </chunk form="fcl" function="N<" head="156">
. </chunk form="np" function="SUBJ" head="154">
. <chunk form="vp" function="P" head="167">
. . will      [will] <aux> <cjt-first> V PR @FS-STA #15->0 ID:167
. . be        [be] <mv> V INF @ICL-AUX< #16->15 ID:168
. </chunk form="vp" function="P" head="167">
... (37 lines)
</chunk form="fcl" function="STA" head="167">
```

FIGURE 3: Layered "maximal" chunking, relational method, xml format

As can be seen from the example, this implementation of layered chunking does provide for right branching (e.g. postnominal pp's), and it can also handle discontinuity, marking left and right halves of a discontinuous chunk by adding right or left hyphens, respectively, to the chunk's form attribute:

```
<chunk form="fcl" function="STA" headid="2" head="does">
. <chunk form="pp-" function="SA" headid="5" head="from">
. . Where [where] <clb> <*> <interr> <aloc> ADV @>>P #1->5 ID:1
. </chunk form="pp-" function="SA" head="5" head="from">
. <chunk form="vp-" function="STA" headid="2" head="does">
. . does   [do] <chunk-head> <aux> V PR 3S @FS-STA #2->0 ID:2
. </chunk form="vp-" function="P" head="2" head="does">
. it       [it] PERS NEU 3S NOM @<SUBJ #3->4 ID:3
. <chunk form="-vp" function="STA" headid="2" head="does">
. . come   [come] <move> <mv> V INF @ICL-AUX< #4->2 ID:4
. </chunk form="-vp" function="STA" head="2" head="does">
. <chunk form="-pp" function="SA" headid="5" head="from">
. . from   [from] <chunk-head> <prp-strand> PRP @<SA #5->4 ID:5
. </chunk form="-pp" function="SA" head="5" head="from">
</chunk form="fcl" function="STA" head="2" head="does">
$?        [?] PU @PU #6->0 ID:6
```

FIGURE 4: Layered chunking, discontinuity

For the layered, maximal chunking we followed the VISL convention, avoiding non-branching nodes and bracketing 1-word chunks only in the case of discontinuity (http://beta.visl.sdu.dk/VTB-design.html). If, for instance for np extraction purposes, single nouns were to be bracketed, this could be easily achieved by adding one simple rule applying to all nouns without an np head relation tag, mimicking the behavior of the minimal chunker on this point[4]. Because our layered bracketing de facto amounts to complete constituent trees, we were able to build conversion filters for both the VISL and TIGER formats[5] (figures 5 & 6), allowing corpus users to take advantage of the numerous tools available for these formats, such as visualizers, editors and search tools.

```
A1                                =======DN:adj("different" POS) different
STA:fcl                           =======H:n("type" <idf> P NOM) types
```

---

[4] Likewise, all other word classes could of course be made to spawn 1-word chunks of a corresponding type.
[5] For clarity, a number of secondary tags was removed from the VISL non-terminal brackets. Similarly, the lemma, morphology and extra fields were removed from the TIGER non-terminal lines.

```
=fA:adv("so" <aquant>) So                 =======DN:pp
=S:np                                      ========H:prp("of") of
==H:pron-indef("anyone" S NOM) anyone      =======DP:n("game" <idf> P NOM) games
==DN:fcl                                    ======fA:pp
===S:pron-rel("who" <sam-> <rel> S) who_   =======H:prp("through") through
===P:v-fin("be" <-sam> PR 3S) _s           ======DP:np
===Cs:adjp                                  ========DN:art("a" <indef> S) a
====H:adj("familiar" POS) familiar          =======H:n("console" <idf> S NOM) console
====DA:pp                                   =,
=====H:prp("with") with                     =P:vp
=====DP:icl                                 ==Vaux:v-fin("will" <cli> PR) will
======P:v-pcp1("play") playing             ==Vm:v-inf("be") be
======Od:np                                 =Cs:adj("content" POS) content
```

FIGURE 5: VISL constituent trees

```
<terminals>                                     <nonterminals>
  <t id="s1_1" word="So" pos="adv"/>              <nt id="s1_500" cat="s">
  <t id="s1_2" word="anyone" pos="pron-indef" />    <edge label="STA" idref="s1_501"/></nt>
  <t id="s1_3" word="who_" pos="pron-rel"/>       <nt id="s1_501" cat="fcl">
  <t id="s1_4" word="_s" pos="v-fin"/>              <edge label="PU" idref="s1_19"/></nt>
  <t id="s1_5" word="familiar" pos="adj"/>        <nt id="s1_502" cat="np">
  <t id="s1_6" word="with" pos="prp"/>              <edge label="H" idref="s1_2"/>
  <t id="s1_7" word="playing" pos="v-pcp1"/>        <edge label="DN" idref="s1_503"/></nt>
  <t id="s1_8" word="different" pos="adj"/>       <nt id="s1_503" cat="fcl">
  <t id="s1_9" word="types" pos="n"/>               <edge label="S" idref="s1_3"/>
  <t id="s1_10" word="of" pos="prp"/>               <edge label="P" idref="s1_4"/>
  <t id="s1_11" word="games" pos="n"/>              <edge label="Cs" idref="s1_504"/></nt>
  <t id="s1_12" word="through" pos="prp"/>        <nt id="s1_504" cat="adjp">
  <t id="s1_13" word="a" pos="art"/>                <edge label="H" idref="s1_5"/>
  <t id="s1_14" word="console" pos="n"/>            <edge label="DA" idref="s1_505"/></nt>
  <t id="s1_15" word="," pos="pu"/>               <nt id="s1_505" cat="pp">
  <t id="s1_16" word="will" pos="v-fin"/>           <edge label="H" idref="s1_6"/>
  <t id="s1_17" word="be" pos="v-inf"/>             <edge label="DP" idref="s1_506"/></nt>
  <t id="s1_18" word="content" pos="adj"/>        <nt id="s1_506" cat="icl">
  <t id="s1_19" word="." pos="pu"/>                 <edge label="P" idref="s1_7"/></nt>
</terminals>                                     </nonterminals>
```

FIGURE 6: TIGER treebank format

4   Evaluation

4.1   Minimal Chunker evaluation

There are several aspects in the evaluation of a CG-based chunker. First of all, in descriptive terms, it is interesting to see how well a function-based medium-level CG annotation can be converted into a constituent-based chunking parse which basically amounts to the task of computing (syntactic) form from (syntactic) function. Second, because a CG rule set is malleable and allows incremental improvements, it is important for development to identify specific error patterns and error triggers. For minimal chunking in particular, which as a shallow parsing technique will usually be performed on raw input rather than on corpora with linguist-revised grammatical tagging, it is important to evaluate the annotation chain as a whole, not just the chunker as such, and to identify error triggers at all levels.

We therefore evaluated the minimal chunker together with a morphosyntactic (POS and function) run of the underlying CG, on a 3563-word section of the English interview corpus, in the B/I/O format. Since error inspection was important for us, and no funding was available to create a multi-annotator gold standard, evaluation was done by output correction alone, with a corresponding risk of parser-friendly bias. For the complete run, recall was 97.4% and precision 97.5%, the difference being due to 3 MWE tokenization errors and 5 <O> (out-of-chunk) errors. While the latter are caused by the chunking grammar itself, the former is partly triggered by transcription conventions in the corpus, where noun-verb contractions were not recognized (persona's = persona is, who've = who have). Of the main body of errors, i.e. <B> and <I> errors, about 25% were pure chunking errors, where chunk form was correct, but segmentation faulty, caused almost always by function tag errors in the underlying CG. In the remaining 75%, chunk form was wrong, indicating underlying POS errors. Table 1 shows a confusion matrix for this error type.

gold: tagged:	np	adjp	advp	vp	pp	conjp	intj	prt
np	-	4	2	5	0	1	3	0
adjp	6	-	3	0	0	0	3	0
advp	5	8	-	0	0	1	0	0
vp	4	3	1	-	0	0	0	0
pp	0	0	3	0	-	1	0	0
conjp	3	0	1	0	1	-	0	0
intj	0	0	0	0	0	0	-	0
prt	0	0	0	0	0	0	0	-
sum/all	18/1630	15/101	10/254	5/956	1/316	3/236	6/50	0/21
relative	1.1%	14.9%	3.9%	0.5%	0.3%	1.3%	12.0%	0%

TABLE 1: Confusion table for chunk form types, minimal chunking

As can be seen, the most common form error was adjective phrases tagged as adverb phrases. Across confusion types, as a class, np's had the highest error frequency, but in relative terms the most error-prone classes were adjp's and interjections. Particles (verb-integrated adverbs) were recognized 100%, and vp and pp errors were very rare.

4.2   Maximal Chunker evaluation

For the the maximal/layered chunker (constituent tree generator), two evaluation runs were performed, one with a complete analysis chain, the other with a morphosyntactic gold corpus as input, where PoS and function tags had been hand-corrected, and where only dependency links had to be added automatically. For the former, the same (interview) data were used as for the minimal chunking evaluation, the latter consisted of 102 random Journalese sentences (1817 words) from the Leipzig Corpora Collection (http://corpora.informatik.uni-leipzig.de/download.html)[6].

With errors in only 12 out of 1055 multi-word[7] chunks (1,1%), the gold input run demonstrated the effectiveness of the CG chunking method in isolation, especially when taking into account that 3/4 of the errors were attachment errors directly attributable to (live) dependency grammar rather than the chunker itself. The only chunk missing outright was a coordination chunk, and 2 of the 3 chunk bracketing errors that were not due to attachment problems, also involved coordination chunks. In a certain sense, it can be concluded that CG chunking on top of syntactic CG analysis is more a format conversion than an independent layer of annotation - in other words, it is (almost) information-equivalent to CG dependency annotation, with most new information being contained in the latter already, making performance a direct function of the performance of the underlying morphosyntactic CG parser. Thus, the only chunk type in our grammar that does not really "trust" its dependency input, is coordination, where rules work with matching form and function tags rather than dependency links alone, taking into account the relatively high dependency error rate for this category.

In the raw text run, the maximal chunker suffered from the accumulated error rate of all CG analysis modules, and did not perform as well. A 1389 word section was used, containing 635 (multi-word) chunks. 17 chunks were not recognized, 4 chunks were in excess and 58 chunks had wrong bracketing[8]. This amounts to a recall of 88.2%, a precision of 90.0% and a balanced F-score[9] of 89.1.

Because both the CG dependency grammar and the chunk form assignment relied on morphosyntactic tags, erroneous head PoS or erroneous dependent function will lead to both wrong attachment and wrong form assignment, so form tag errors in correctly bracketed chunks were extremely rare, and category confusion was otherwise mainly triggered by wrong morphosyntactic tagging. Again, coordination errors figured prominently, and over 50% of undetected chunks were coordination chunks.

5   Conclusions

We have shown that Constraint Grammar rules constitute an efficient method for syntactic chunking. In a full CG suite, together with a morphosyntactic annotation module, between 89% and 97.5% of chunks will be correctly recovered for raw English text, representing the extremes of minimal chunking (no right np-branching and no nesting) on the one hand, and full layered constituent chunking on the other. While both chunking modules are quite rule-efficient (with 20 and 59 rules, respectively), only the minimal chunker works on morphosyntactic tags alone, while the layered chunker (which in its deepest version is a constituent parser rather than a chunker in the traditional sense of the word) uses an intermediate step of dependency attachment (279 rules). Still, even the combined error percentage of dependency and chunker is very low

---

[6] A direct comparison on the same data could have been interesting, but within the timeframe of the project, it was not possible to create a CG gold corpus for the Interview data.

[7] If single words were counted as chunks, no new error information would be added because all errors would constitute integration into multi-word chunks and should thus already be marked as multi-word chunk errors.

[8] For discontinuous chunks, both parts were counted as chunks, and the only discontinuity error was therefore counted as two.

[9] Defined as the harmonic mean of recall and precision.

(just over 1%) if seen in isolation, i.e. on correct function tag input, so the performance gap between minimal and layered chunking seems to be caused not so much by the chunking rules themselves, but rather by the fact that the deeper the nesting, the more morphosyntactic errors will trigger bracketing errors.

We believe, from a grammar writer's perspective, that the chunkers - especially the minimal chunker - are fairly language independent, because they run on an input level where syntactic function categories provide a "language-insulating" level of abstraction (provided a common notational system is used), but this assumption needs to be verified by future evaluation with generic rules and a larger set of languages, including languages that are typologically more different than English and German.

For practical reasons of availability, we tested gold input performance on a different genre (news) than the raw input runs (interview data), but optimally both runs and both chunking levels should be evaluated across different genre in a comparable way. This could also shed light on the question whether rule-based chunking is either more or less genre-sensitive than machine learning methods, and - if relevant - how much individual rules contribute to genre sensitivity, allowing the use of limited, genre-specific grammar patches.

References

Abney, Steven (1991). Parsing by Chunks. In: *Principle-Based Parsing*. Kluwer Academic Publishers, pp. 257-278

Banko, M., M.J. Cafarella, S. Soderland, M. Broadhead and O. Etzioni (2007). Open Information Extraction from the Web. In: *Proceedings of the 20th IJCAI*, pp. 2670-2676

Bick, Eckhard (2003). A CG & PSG Hybrid Approach to Automatic Corpus Annotation. In: Kiril Simow & Petya Osenova (eds.), *Proceedings of SProLaC2003* (at Corpus Linguistics 2003, Lancaster), pp. 1-12

Bick, Eckhard (2005). Turning Constraint Grammar Data into Running Dependency Treebanks, In: Civit, Montserrat & Kübler, Sandra & Martí, Ma. Antònia (red.), *Proceedings of TLT 2005 (4th Workshop on Treebanks and Linguistic Theory, Barcelona, December 9th - 10th, 2005)*, pp. 19-27

Carreras, X and L. Màrquez (2003). Phrase Recognition by Filtering and Ranking with Perceptrons. In: *Proceedings of RANLP-2003*, pp. 78-85.

Jurafsky, D. and J. H. Martin (2009). *Speech and Language Technology*, Pearson Education, p. 490.

Kübler, Sandra and Erhard W. Hinrichs (2001). From chunks to function-argument structure: A similarity- based approach. In *Proceedings of ACL-EACL 2001* (Tolouse, France), pp. 338-345.

Tjong Kim Sang, E. and S. Buchholz. (2000). Introduction to the CoNLL-2000 shared task: Chunking. In *Proceedings of CoNLL-2000 and LLL-2000* (Lisbon, Portugal), pp. 127– 132.

Van den Bosch, Antal and Sabine Buchholz (2002). Shallow parsing on the basis of words only: A case study . In *Proceedings of the 40th Meeting of the Association for Computational Linguistics* (ACL'02), pp. 433-440.

Features indicating readability in Swedish text

Johan Falkenjack[1], Katarina Heimann Mühlenbock[2], Arne Jönsson[3]

(1) Department of Information and Computer Science, Linköping University, Linköping, Sweden
(2) Språkbanken, University of Gothenburg, Gothenburg
(3) SICS East Swedish ICT AB

`johan.falkenjack@liu.se, katarina.heimann.muhlenbock@gu.se, arne.jonsson@liu.se`

ABSTRACT

Studies have shown that modern methods of readability assessment, using automated linguistic analysis and machine learning (ML), is a viable road forward for readability classification and ranking. In this paper we present a study of different levels of analysis and a large number of features and how they affect an ML-system's accuracy when it comes to readability assessment. We test a large number of features proposed for different languages (mainly English) and evaluate their usefulness for readability assessment for Swedish as well as comparing their performance to that of established metrics. We find that the best performing features are language models based on part-of-speech and dependency type.

KEYWORDS: Readability assessment, Machine learning, Dependency parsing, Weka.

1 Introduction

The problem of readability assessment is the problem of mapping from a text to some unit representing the text's degree of readability. Measures of readability are mostly used to inform a reader how difficult a text is to read, either to give them a hint that they may try to find an easier to read text on the same topic or simply to inform them that a text may take some time to comprehend. Readability measures are mainly used to inform persons with reading disabilities on the complexity of a text, but can also be used to, for instance, assist teachers with assessing the reading ability of a student. By measuring the reading abilities of a person, it might also be possible to automatically find texts that fits that persons reading ability. It has further been shown that readability is a useful measure for finding a corpus for training vector space models (Smith et al., 2012).

Readability gives rise to a number of problems. For instance, readability is not a function of text only but a function of both text and reader, as defined by Dale and Chall (1949): "[Readability is] the sum total (including all the interactions) of all those elements within a given piece of printed material that affect the success a group of readers have with it. The success is the extent to which they understand it, read it at optimal speed, and find it interesting." However, in this study we make the assumption that a function of text only can be a useful approximation. This assumption is supported by and related to the practice of American researchers to normalize their metrics to the U.S. grade level. Resources for such a normalisation for Swedish are not yet readily available and until they are we focus on the problem of classifying texts as either easy-to-read or not.

Readability assessment has been a field of interest for linguists since the 1920s but intensive research begun in the U.S. in the late 1940s (Sjöholm, 2012). This research resulted in the introduction of the first version of the Flesch Reading Ease test (Flesch, 1948) and the Dale-Chall formula, versions of which are still used today.

A number of easily calculated readability metrics (consisting of a small number of easily counted features such as average word length, lexical variation and frequency of "simple words") were introduced for English during the following three decades. Some examples are the Coleman-Liau index, which was specifically designed for automated assessment of readability (Coleman and Liau, 1975), the SMOG formula (McLaughlin, 1969) and the Fry readability formula (Fry, 1968). All of these metrics were designed to output a score corresponding to the U.S. grade level thought necessary for full comprehension of a text. In 1975 the Flesch Reading Ease test was reinvented as the Flesch-Kincaid Grade Level with the same principle in mind (Kincaid et al., 1975).

This way of constructing readability metrics was widely accepted as good enough for a long time. However, in the 1980's research questioning the performance of these traditional metrics was being published (Davison and Kantor, 1982).

Readability assessment for Swedish has mostly been done using metrics similar to the ones constructed for English. The most utilized readability metric for Swedish is LIX, Läsbarhetsindex (Readability index) (Björnsson, 1968), which is formulated in a way similar to that of the Flesch metric. Today the LIX metric is basically the standard metric for readability in Swedish. However, in recent years new research has shown that the metric is not always sufficient (Mühlenbock and Johansson Kokkinakis, 2009; Heimann Mühlenbock, 2013).

The OVIX Ordvariationsindex (Word variation index) and Nominal Ratio metrics (Hultman and Westman, 1977) have been used in research to complement LIX as they are assumed to correlate with degree of readability viewed from other linguistic levels.

Since the early 2000s the speed and accuracy of text analysis tools such as lemmatizers, part-of-speech taggers and syntax parsers have made new text features available for readability assessment. By using machine learning a number of researchers have devised innovative ways of assessing readability. For instance, phrase grammar parsing has been used to find the average number of sub-clauses, verb phrases, noun phrases and average tree depth (Schwarm and Ostendorf, 2005).

The use of language models to assess the degree of readability was also introduced in the early 2000s (Collins-Thompson and Callan, 2004) and later combined with classification algorithms such as support vector machines to further increase accuracy (Petersen, 2007; Feng, 2010)

In this paper we present a study on the problem of finding and evaluating features relevant for classification. Such classifiers have previously been experimented with for Italian (Dell'Orletta et al., 2011). An extension of such a classifier has been proposed as an alternative to regression or detectors when it comes to ordering documents based on degree of readability (Falkenjack and Heimann Mühlenbock, 2012). The present approach is experimental in the sense that several feature models, simple as well as complex, are tested and compared. The models are based on text properties acting at various language levels, and the task is to identify the best-performing feature model for readability assessment viewed from one or several specific aspects of written language. An even more complex model where also the semantic aspect is taken into account would demand language resources supplied with information on concepts and meaning as for instance WordNet (Miller, 1995). Such an approach is presented in Heimann Mühlenbock (2013), where readability is regarded as the totality of features acting at five different levels of language representation, including the idea density level.

2 Study

In the study presented in this paper we evaluate a number of models for readability on a variety of corpora to assess the models' ability to classify a text as easy-to-read or not.

2.1 Corpora

To train and test our classifier we use one easy-to-read corpus and five corpora representing ordinary language in different text genres. The latter corpora will further on be labeled as non-easy-to-read. For each category we use 700 texts.

Our source of easy-to-read material is the LäSBarT corpus (Mühlenbock, 2008). LäSBarT consists of manually created easy-to-read texts from a variety of sources and genres.

The non-easy-to-read material comprise texts from a variety of corpora to make sure that what we are classifying is readability rather than genre. This material consists of 215 articles from GP2007 (news text), 34 whole issues of Forskning och Framsteg (popular science), 214 articles from Läkartidningen 05 (professional news), 214 public information notices from Smittskyddsinstitutet (government text) and 23 full novels from the Norstedts publishing house (fiction).

By using a corpus with such a variety of documents we will get texts that have different degree of readability which is important as we want to be able to use the same model on all types of text.

The texts are preprocessed using the Korp corpus import tool (Borin et al., 2012). Steps in the preprocessing chain relevant for this study are tokenization, lemmatisation, part-of-speech tagging and dependency grammar parsing. The Korp tool is publicly available for testing.

2.2 Classification

We use the Waikato Environment for Knowledge Analysis (Weka) suite and its implementation of the popular classification algorithm Support Vector Machine (SVM). Support Vector Machines has been increasingly popular in Computational Linguistics in recent years and have, among other uses, been used for readability assessment with good results (Petersen, 2007; Feng, 2010).

The SVM algorithm is an algebraic approach to the classification problem. Objects with a known class are represented as points in an n-dimensional space, where n is the number of attributes. An algorithm then attempts to find a maximum margin hyperplane separating the objects by their class (Witten et al., 2011). New objects are classified by calculating on which side of this hyperplane the object's corresponding point occurs.

The version of SVM-learning (finding the separating hyperplane) we use is the SMO, Sequential Minimal Optimization, algorithm (Platt, 1998). A Java implementation of a SMO-based SVM is included in the standard Weka toolkit.

We chose the SVM-approach as prior research has shown that it is one of the best performing algorithms for degree of readability classification using the full set, or subsets, of features we evaluate in this study (Sjöholm, 2012).

2.3 Models

We have constructed a total of 34 models. First we have three models representing the established Swedish metrics used to measure, or assumed to correlate with some aspect of readability, namely LIX, OVIX and Nominal ratio (NR).

We also use 21 single feature models. These models represent features proposed for readability assessment in prior research, mainly on English texts. As the primary aim of this study is to evaluate these feature models' ability to predict readability these models are the most important.

As many of the single feature models result from the same kind of preprocessing, we have also decided to create ten compound models. We divide the features into four levels similar to the four levels used by the READ-IT system for Italian (Dell'Orletta et al., 2011). These levels are Shallow (requires tokenization), Lexical (requires lemmatisation), morpho-syntactic (requires part-of-speech tagging) and Syntactic (requires parsing, in our case with a dependency grammar parser).

Seven models based on these levels are constructed, four which covers only a single level each; Shallow, Lexical, Morpho and Syntactic. Three models incrementally add levels to the analysis; the LexicalInc model which consists of all features from the Lexical and Shallow models, the MorphoInc model which consists of all features from the LexicalInc and Morpho models and the SyntacticInc model which consists of all features from the MorphoInc and the Syntactic models. These models are used to evaluate to what degree each level of linguistic analysis improves our model's ability to predict readability.

We also create three models combining the established metrics, LIX, OVIX and NR. The first, called TradComb, comprise only the three established metrics. The other two combine TradComb with SyntacticInc (Total) and MorphoInc (NoDep) respectively.

2.3.1 Shallow features

The shallow text features are the main features traditionally used for simple readability metrics. They occur in the "shallow" surface structure of the text and can be extracted after tokenization by simply counting words and characters. They include:

AvgWordLengthChars Average word length calculated as the average number of characters per word.

AvgWordLengthSylls Average word length calculated as the average number of syllables per word. The number of syllables is approximated by counting the number of vowels.

AvgSentLength Average sentence length calculated as the average number of words per sentence.

Longer sentences, as well as longer words, tend to predict a more difficult text as exemplified by the performance of the LIX metric and related metrics for English. These types of features have been used in a number of readability studies based on machine learning (Feng, 2010) and as baseline when evaluating new features (Pitler and Nenkova, 2008).

2.3.2 Lexical features

Our lexical features are based on categorical word frequencies. The word frequencies are extracted after lemmatization and are calculated using the basic Swedish vocabulary SweVoc (Heimann Mühlenbock, 2013). SweVoc is comparable to the list used in the classic Dale-Chall formula (Dale and Chall, 1949) for English and developed for similar purposes, however special sub-categories have been added (of which three are specifically considered). The following frequencies are calculated, based on different categories in SweVoc:

SweVocC SweVoc lemmas fundamental for communication (category C).

SweVocD SweVoc lemmas for everyday use (category D).

SweVocH SweVoc other highly frequent lemmas (category H).

SweVocTotal Unique, per lemma, SweVoc words (all categories, including some not mentioned above) per sentence.

A high ratio of SweVoc words should indicate a more easy-to-read text. The Dale-Chall metric (Chall and Dale, 1995) has been used as a similar feature in a number of machine learning based studies of text readability for English (Feng, 2010; Pitler and Nenkova, 2008). The SweVoc metrics are also related to the language model features used in a number of studies (Schwarm and Ostendorf, 2005; Heilman et al., 2008).

2.3.3 Morpho-syntactic features

The morpho-syntactic features concern a morphology based analysis of text. For the purposes of this study the analysis relies on previously part-of-speech annotated text, which is investigated with regard to the following features:

UnigramPOS Unigram probabilities for 26 different parts-of-speech in the document, that is, the ratio of each part-of-speech, on a per token basis, as individual attributes. Such a unigram language model based on part-of-speech, and similar metrics, has shown to be a relevant feature for readability assessment for English (Heilman et al., 2007; Petersen, 2007; Dell'Orletta et al., 2011).

RatioContent The ratio of content words (nouns, verbs, adjectives and adverbs), on a per token basis, in the text. Such a metric has been used in a number of related studies (Alusio et al., 2010).

2.3.4 Syntactic features

These features are estimable after syntactic parsing of the text. The syntactic feature set is extracted after dependency parsing using the Maltparser (Nivre et al., 2006). Such parsers has been used for preprocessing texts for readability assessment for Italian (Dell'Orletta et al., 2011). The dependency based features consist of:

AvgDepDistDep The average dependency distance in the document on a per dependent basis. A longer average dependency distance could indicate a more complex text (Liu, 2008).

AvgDepDistSent The average dependency distance in the document on a per sentence basis. A longer average total dependency distance per sentence could indicate a more complex text (Liu, 2008).

RightDeps The ratio of right dependencies to total number of dependencies in the document. A high ratio of right dependencies could indicate a more complex text.

SentenceDepth The average sentence depth. Sentences with deeper dependency trees could be indicative of a more complex text in the same way as phrase grammar trees has been shown to be (Petersen and Ostendorf, 2009).

UnigramDepType Unigram probabilities for the 63 dependency types resulting from the dependency parsing, on a per token basis. These features are comparable to the part-of-speech unigram probabilities and to the phrase type rate based on phrase grammar parsing used in earlier research (Nenkova et al., 2010).

VerbalRoots The ratio of sentences with a verbal root, that is, the ratio of sentences where the root word is a verb to the total number of sentences (Dell'Orletta et al., 2011).

AvgVerbArity The average arity of verbs in the document, calculated as the average number of dependents per verb (Dell'Orletta et al., 2011).

UnigramVerbArity The ratios of verbs with an arity of 0-7 as distinct features (Dell'Orletta et al., 2011).

We also propose the following four syntactic features:

TokensPerClause The average number of tokens per clause in the document. This is related to the shallow feature average number of tokens per sentence.

PreModifiers The average number of nominal pre-modifiers per sentence.

PostModifiers The average number of nominal post-modifiers per sentence.

PrepComp The average number of prepositional complements per sentence in the document.

2.4 Evaluation

We evaluated the 21 single feature models presented above, three traditional metric models and the ten compound models presented above. Some features, rendered in italics in Table 2, consist of more than one concrete attribute and a few attributes are considered both as features in themselves and as attributes in larger feature models.

To test our models we use 7-fold cross validation over a set of 1400 documents. Each chunk consists of 100 easy-to-read texts and 100 non-easy-to-read texts. The corpora used to make up the non-easy-to-read set are shuffled and might therefore not be evenly distributed among the chunks (if this is a problem it should show up as a generally high standard deviation for all accuracies).

The result of the evaluation represents each model's ability to correctly identify easy-to-read texts. The accuracy of a model represents the proportion of the documents which are correctly classified as either easy-to-read or non-easy-to-read. A higher accuracy implies that the model, and its underlying features, more strongly predict degree of readability. To complement the accuracy we also provide precision and recall for the sets of easy-to-read texts and non-easy-to-read texts respectively, this to better understand where low performing models might go wrong.

In addition we present the standard deviation for each percentage based on the 7 folds of the cross validation. A high standard deviation implies inconsistent performance.

3   Results and discussion

The results of our test runs are presented below. We present the average values for the 7-fold cross validation in percent as well as the standard deviation in percentage points.

3.1   Traditional metrics

Among the traditional metrics (see Table 1) OVIX actually seems to perform about as well as LIX. This is somewhat surprising as LIX is designed to directly measure readability while OVIX is only assumed to indirectly measure readability. As OVIX considers totally different features from LIX, it does, perhaps, strengthen the point that LIX, as the standard readability metric for Swedish, might be overly simplistic.

Nominal ratio, NR, is the worst performing of the traditional metrics. It seems that the NR model tend to over-classify documents as easy to read, demonstrated by high recall but low precision for LäSBarT. As NR and ratio of content words, RatioContent, (see Table 2) both

Table 1: Performance of the three traditional metrics. The accuracy represents the average percentage of texts classified correctly, with the standard deviation within parentheses. Precision and Recall are also provided, with standard deviations within parenthesis, for both easy-to-read (LäSBarT) and non-easy-to-read (Other) sets.

Model	Accuracy	LäSBarT		Other	
		Precision	Recall	Precision	Recall
LIX	84.6 (1.9)	87.9 (2.9)	80.4 (2.8)	82.0 (2.1)	88.9 (3.0)
OVIX	85.6 (2.3)	86.8 (4.3)	84.4 (3.1)	84.9 (2.4)	86.9 (5.0)
NR	55.3 (9.1)	53.5 (6.8)	99.1 (1.9)	96.0 (7.7)	11.4 (20.1)

perform badly, it seems that only a more complex part-of-speech based feature, such as the multi-attribute feature consisting of unigrams for all POS-types is sufficient. Further analysis of single POS-type models might yield interesting results though.

3.2 Single feature models

Looking at Table 2 we see that most single feature models provide some indication on degree of text readability. There are however some models which perform a lot worse than anticipated.

It seems that the average dependency distance per sentence, AvgDepDistSent, is more or less useless, it might be that this is nothing more than a convoluted way to talk about sentence length, AvgSentLength, which in itself appears to be a highly inconsistent feature. Both these metrics over-classify documents as easy-to-read to a very high degree.

Also surprising is that the ratio of content words, RatioContent, does not seem to be a good indicator of readability. However, this does not seem to be a problem of over-classification, rather the model seems to be equally bad at classifying both sets, based on precision and recall close to 50 % for both sets. It might be that a high ratio of content words indicate a higher information density and therefore a more complex text while at the same time a low ratio might instead indicate a syntactically complex text. In such cases a simple SVM classification is not sufficient. Also, for an inflecting language like Swedish, the ratio of content words might yield different results than for languages with a more modest morphology, as for instance English. As with the nominal ratio metric, a closer inspection of single POS-type ratios might yield some further clues.

The average number of tokens per clause, TokensPerClause, and the ratio of nominal post-modifiers also seem to have a tendency to over-classify documents as easy-to-read having high LäSBarT recall but relatively low precision. Nominal pre-modifiers, however, while still suffering from slight easy-to-read over-classification, perform almost as well as LIX or OVIX when only accuracy is considered.

Best performing of the single feature models are the unigram models for part-of-speech, UnigramPOS, and dependency type, UnigramDepType. This is not surprising as these features represent simple language models and language models are often very powerful when compared to single attribute features.

It is only the unigram language models, UnigramPOS and UnigramDepType, and the average

Table 2: Performance of the single feature models, italicised models consist of more than one concrete attribute. The accuracy represents the average percentage of texts classified correctly, with the standard deviation within parentheses. Precision and Recall are also provided, with standard deviations within parenthesis, for both easy-to-read (LäSBarT) and non-easy-to-read (Other) sets.

		LäSBarT		Other	
Model	Accuracy	Precision	Recall	Precision	Recall
AvgWordLengthChars	79.6 (2.6)	82.3 (5.0)	75.7 (1.4)	77.4 (1.3)	83.4 (5.5)
AvgWordLengthSylls	75.6 (2.6)	78.7 (4.0)	70.3 (2.8)	73.1 (2.1)	80.9 (4.4)
AvgSentLength	62.4 (8.1)	58.0 (7.5)	98.7 (3.0)	97.8 (4.0)	26.1 (19.2)
SweVocC	79.3 (0.8)	84.3 (1.1)	72.0 (2.1)	75.6 (1.2)	86.6 (1.3)
SweVocD	57.6 (3.8)	63.1 (7.4)	37.9 (5.2)	55.5 (2.7)	77.4 (6.3)
SweVocH	63.1 (4.5)	63.1 (4.6)	63.4 (5.1)	63.2 (4.5)	62.9 (5.4)
SweVocTotal	75.2 (1.4)	80.6 (3.4)	66.7 (2.3)	71.6 (0.8)	83.7 (4.2)
UnigramPOS	*96.8 (1.6)*	*96.9 (2.5)*	*96.7 (1.1)*	*96.7 (1.1)*	*96.9 (2.6)*
RatioContent	50.4 (1.8)	50.4 (1.7)	52.7 (3.1)	50.4 (1.9)	48.1 (3.6)
AvgDepDistDep	88.5 (2.0)	88.5 (2.3)	88.6 (2.2)	88.6 (2.1)	88.4 (2.4)
AvgDepDistSent	53.9 (10.2)	52.8 (7.2)	99.7 (0.8)	28.1 (48.0)	8.1 (21.1)
RightDeps	68.9 (2.1)	70.6 (3.2)	65.1 (4.0)	67.7 (2.1)	72.7 (4.6)
SentenceDepth	75.1 (3.5)	79.1 (4.3)	68.4 (4.6)	72.2 (3.4)	81.9 (4.2)
UnigramDepType	*97.9 (0.8)*	*97.7 (1.1)*	*98.0 (1.3)*	*98.0 (1.3)*	*97.7 (1.1)*
VerbalRoots	72.6 (2.0)	77.0 (3.4)	64.6 (3.3)	69.5 (1.7)	80.6 (4.3)
AvgVerbArity	63.4 (3.0)	64.9 (3.2)	58.4 (4.9)	62.3 (3.0)	68.4 (3.2)
UnigramVerbArity	68.6 (1.7)	70.2 (2.6)	65.0 (2.8)	67.4 (1.5)	72.3 (4.0)
TokensPerClause	71.4 (4.7)	64.2 (4.4)	98.6 (1.0)	97.0 (1.8)	44.3 (10.0)
PreModifiers	83.4 (2.9)	78.1 (3.1)	93.0 (2.2)	91.3 (2.6)	73.9 (4.5)
PostModifiers	57.4 (4.3)	54.1 (2.7)	99.9 (0.4)	98.4 (4.2)	15.0 (8.5)
PrepComp	83.5 (3.5)	80.1 (2.4)	89.1 (5.9)	88.1 (5.8)	77.9 (2.7)

dependency distance per dependency, AvgDepDistDep, that outperform the traditional metrics OVIX and LIX. However, the average number of prepositional complements per sentence, PrepComp, and nominal pre-modifiers per sentence, PreModifiers, respectively do come close.

3.3   Compound models

When we look at the compound models, Table 3 we can see highly improved performance. Not surprisingly, we get the best performance from the Total model consisting of all features that the system is able to extract.

All compound metrics except for the Shallow and Lexical models outperform the traditional metrics. However, combining these two, the LexicalInc model, does outperform the traditional metrics LIX, OVIX and NR.

Interestingly the UnigramPOS feature model seems to perform slightly better than the Morpho model (which actually consists of UnigramPOS and RatioContent). The bad performance of the ratio of content words model, RatioContent, might introduce some performance-decreasing

Table 3: Performance of the ten compound models. The accuracy represents the average percentage of texts classified correctly, with the standard deviation within parentheses. Precision and Recall are also provided, with standard deviations within parenthesis, for both easy-to-read (LäSBarT) and non-easy-to-read (Other) sets.

Model	Accuracy	LäSBarT		Other	
		Precision	Recall	Precision	Recall
TradComb	91.4 (3.0)	92.0 (4.6)	91.0 (2.1)	91.1 (2.2)	91.9 (4.9)
Shallow	81.6 (2.7)	83.3 (4.4)	79.4 (3.1)	80.3 (2.5)	83.9 (4.9)
Lexical	78.4 (2.2)	81.8 (2.9)	73.0 (2.9)	75.6 (2.1)	83.7 (3.0)
Morpho	96.7 (1.6)	96.8 (2.6)	96.7 (1.4)	96.7 (1.3)	96.7 (2.7)
Syntactic	98.0 (1.1)	97.9 (1.7)	98.1 (1.2)	98.1 (1.2)	97.9 (1.8)
LexicalInc	90.1 (2.9)	87.1 (4.1)	94.3 (2.6)	93.8 (2.7)	85.9 (4.9)
MorphoInc	97.3 (0.8)	96.9 (1.6)	97.7 (1.6)	97.7 (1.5)	96.9 (1.7)
SyntacticInc	98.4 (0.9)	98.3 (1.4)	98.6 (1.0)	98.6 (1.0)	98.3 (1.4)
NoDep	98.3 (1.0)	97.4 (1.9)	99.3 (1.3)	99.3 (1.2)	97.3 (2.0)
Total	98.9 (1.0)	98.9 (1.1)	98.9 (1.1)	98.9 (1.1)	98.9 (1.1)

confusion though.

The Morpho and Syntactic models both more or less equal the UnigramPOS and UnigramDepType models respectively implying that these are by far the most important features in the respective models.

4 Conclusions

In this study we have presented a large number of feature models proposed for readability assessment. Most of these models have previously been shown to be useful for assessing readability of English texts. Our results show that many of them are also relevant for Swedish, however some models are less relevant, most notably the ratio of content words, RatioContent, for which we have no simple explanation. Contrary to, for instance, NR which erroneously classify many texts as readable and consequentially achieves a very low accuracy, RatioContent does not have a high recall on any category in the corpora.

The best performing features seem to be part-of-speech or dependency type based language models, especially the compound models that require parsing using a dependency parser; Syntactic, SyntacticInc and Total. These models all have high Accuracy, more than 98% and a fairly low standard deviation showing a stable performance.

We also show that a combination of the three established metrics outperform the standard LIX metric but also that the use of the raw data necessary to calculate those metrics (the data in the MorphoInc model) might possibly be put to even better use. Dependency grammar parsing seems to provide very useful data for identifying easy-to-read texts but in an environment where such heavy calculations are infeasible a very good result might be found without it as demonstrated by the NoDep model.

We propose that future research look further into the language models represented by the UnigramPOS and UnigramDepType models. It might be possible to construct relatively simple metrics based on only a few of the attributes in these models. It might also be possible to construct even better performing models by looking at bigrams or trigrams instead of just unigrams.

Acknowledgments

We would like to thank Santa Anna IT Research Institute AB for funding this research as well as the staff members at Språkbanken who created and let us use the Korp corpus import tool.

References

Alusio, S., Specia, L., Gasperin, C., and Scarton, C. (2010). Readability assessment for text simplification. In *Proceedings of the NAACL HLT 2010 Fifth Workshop on Innovative Use of NLP for Building Educational Applications*, pages 1–9.

Björnsson, C. H. (1968). *Läsbarhet*. Liber, Stockholm.

Borin, L., Forsberg, M., and Roxendal, J. (2012). Korp – the corpus infrastructure of språkbanken. In *Proceedings of the Eighth International Conference on Language Resources and Evaluation (LREC'12)*.

Chall, J. S. and Dale, E. (1995). *Readability revisited: The new Dale–Chall readability formula*. Brookline Books, Cambride, MA.

Coleman, M. and Liau, T. L. (1975). A computer readability formula designed for machine scoring. *Journal of Applied Psychology*, 60:283–284.

Collins-Thompson, K. and Callan, J. (2004). A Language Modeling Approach to Predicting Reading Difficulty. In *Proceedings of the Human Language Technology Conference of the North American Chapter of the Association for Computational Linguistics*.

Dale, E. and Chall, J. S. (1949). The concept of readability. *Elementary English*, 26(23).

Davison, A. and Kantor, R. N. (1982). On the failure of readability formulas to define readable texts: A case study from adaptations. *Reading Research Quarterly*, 17(2):187–209.

Dell'Orletta, F., Montemagni, S., and Venturi, G. (2011). READ-IT: Assessing Readability of Italian Texts with a View to Text Simplification. In *Proceedings of the 2nd Workshop on Speech and Language Processing for Assistive Technologies*, pages 73–83.

Falkenjack, J. and Heimann Mühlenbock, K. (2012). Readability as probability. In *Proceedings of The Fourth Swedish Language Technology Conference*, pages 27–28.

Feng, L. (2010). *Automatic Readability Assessment*. PhD thesis, City University of New York.

Flesch, R. (1948). A new readibility yardstick. *Journal of Applied Psychology*, 32(3):221–233.

Fry, E. B. (1968). A readability formula that saves time. *Journal of Reading*, 11:513–516.

Heilman, M. J., Collins-Thompson, K., Callan, J., and Eskenazi, M. (2007). Combining Lexical and Grammatical Features to Improve Readability Measures for First and Second Language Texts. In *Proceedings of NAACL HLT 2007*, pages 460–467.

Heilman, M. J., Collins-Thompson, K., and Eskenazi, M. (2008). An Analysis of Statistical Models and Features for Reading Difficulty Prediction. In *Proceedings of the Third ACL Workshop on Innovative Use of NLP for Building Educational Applications*, pages 71–79.

Heimann Mühlenbock, K. (2013). *I see what you mean. Assessing readability for specific target groups*. Dissertation, Språkbanken, Dept of Swedish, University of Gothenburg.

Hultman, T. G. and Westman, M. (1977). *Gymnasistsvenska*. LiberLäromedel, Lund.

Kincaid, J. P., Fishburne, R. P., Rogers, R. L., and Chissom, B. S. (1975). Derivation of new readability formulas (Automated Readability Index, Fog Count, and Flesch Reading Ease Formula) for Navy enlisted personnel. Technical report, U.S. Naval Air Station, Millington, TN.

Liu, H. (2008). Dependency distance as a metric of language comprehension difficulty. *Journal of Cognitive Science*, 9(2):169–191.

McLaughlin, G. H. (1969). SMOG grading - a new readability formula. *Journal of Reading*, 22:639–646.

Miller, G. A. (1995). WordNet: A Lexical Database for English. *Communications of the ACM*, 38(11):39–41.

Mühlenbock, K. (2008). Readable, Legible or Plain Words – Presentation of an easy-to-read Swedish corpus. In Saxena, A. and Viberg, Å., editors, *Multilingualism: Proceedings of the 23rd Scandinavian Conference of Linguistics*, volume 8 of *Acta Universitatis Upsaliensis*, pages 327–329, Uppsala, Sweden. Acta Universitatis Upsaliensis.

Mühlenbock, K. and Johansson Kokkinakis, S. (2009). LIX 68 revisited - An extended readability measure. In Mahlberg, M., González-Díaz, V., and Smith, C., editors, *Proceedings of the Corpus Linguistics Conference CL2009*, Liverpool, UK.

Nenkova, A., Chae, J., Louis, A., and Pitler, E. (2010). *Structural Features for Predicting the Linguistic Quality of Text Applications to Machine Translation, Automatic Summarization and Human–Authored Text.*, pages 222–241. Empirical Methods in NLG. Springer-Verlag.

Nivre, J., Hall, J., and Nilsson, J. (2006). MaltParser: A Data-Driven Parser-Generator for Dependency Parsing. In *Proceedings of the fifth international conference on Language Resources and Evaluation (LREC2006)*, pages 2216–2219.

Petersen, S. (2007). *Natural language processing tools for reading level assessment and text simplification for bilingual education*. PhD thesis, University of Washington, Seattle, WA.

Petersen, S. and Ostendorf, M. (2009). A machine learning approach toreading level assessment. *Computer Speech and Language*, 23:89–106.

Pitler, E. and Nenkova, A. (2008). Revisiting Readability: A Unified Framework for Predicting Text Quality. In *Proceedings of the 2008 Conference on Empirical Methods in Natural Language Processing*, pages 186–195, Honolulu, HI.

Platt, J. C. (1998). Sequential Minimal Optimization: A Fast Algorithm for Training Support Vector Machines. Technical Report MSR-TR-98-14, Microsoft Research.

Schwarm, S. E. and Ostendorf, M. (2005). Reading level assessment using support vector machines and statistical language models. In *Proceedings of the 43rd Annual Meeting of the Association for Computational Linguistics*.

Sjöholm, J. (2012). Probability as readability: A new machine learning approach to readability assessment for written Swedish. Master's thesis, Linköping University.

Smith, C., Danielsson, H., and Jönsson, A. (2012). A good space: Lexical predictors in vector space evaluation. In *Proceedings of the eighth international conference on Language Resources and Evaluation (LREC), Istanbul, Turkey*.

Witten, I. H., Frank, E., and Hall, M. A. (2011). *Data Mining: Practical Machine Learning Tools and Techniques*. The Morgan Kaufmann series in data management system. Morgan Kaufmann Publishers, third edition.

Towards a Dependency-based PropBank of General Finnish

Katri Haverinen,[1,2] *Veronika Laippala,*[3] *Samuel Kohonen,*[2] *Anna Missilä,*[2]
Jenna Nyblom,[2] *Stina Ojala,*[2] *Timo Viljanen,*[2]
Tapio Salakoski[1,2] *and Filip Ginter*[2]

(1) Turku Centre for Computer Science (TUCS), Turku, Finland
(2) Department of Information Technology, University of Turku, Finland
(3) Department of Languages and Translation Studies, University of Turku, Finland

`first.last@utu.fi`

ABSTRACT

In this work, we present the first results of a project aiming at a Finnish Proposition Bank, an annotated corpus of semantic roles. The annotation is based on an existing treebank of Finnish, the Turku Dependency Treebank, annotated using the well-known Stanford Dependency scheme. We describe the use of the dependency treebank for PropBanking purposes and show that both annotation layers present in the treebank are highly useful for the annotation of semantic roles. We also discuss the specific features of Finnish influencing the development of a PropBank as well as the methods employed in the annotation, and finally, we present preliminary evaluation of the annotation quality.

KEYWORDS: PropBank, Finnish, dependency.

1   Introduction

Semantic role labeling (SRL) is one of the fundamental tasks of natural language processing. In a sense, it continues from where syntactic parsing ends: it identifies the events and participants, such as agents and patients, present in a sentence, and therefore it is an essential step in automatically processing the sentence semantics. SRL can be applied in, for example, text generation, text understanding, machine translation and fact retrieval (Palmer et al., 2005).

There have been several different efforts to capture and annotate semantic roles, the best-known projects being FrameNet (Baker et al., 1998), VerbNet (Dang et al., 1998) and PropBank (Palmer et al., 2005), all built for the English language. Out of the three resources, FrameNet is the most fine-grained one, defining roles for specific classes of verbs, such as *Cook* and *Food* for verbs relating to cooking. PropBank, in contrast, uses very generic labels, and is the only one of the three intended for corpus annotation rather than as a lexical resource. VerbNet, in turn, is between FrameNet and PropBank in granularity, and somewhat like PropBank, has close ties to syntactic structure. For a more thorough comparison of the three schemes, see the overview by Palmer et al. (2010).

The PropBank scheme in particular has become popular for semantic role labeling resources: after the initial effort on English, PropBanks for different languages have emerged, including, among others, PropBanks for Chinese (Xue and Palmer, 2009), Arabic (Zaghouani et al., 2010), Hindi (Palmer et al., 2009) and Brazilian Portuguese (Duran and Aluísio, 2011). As a PropBank is intended for corpus annotation purposes, and as the annotation scheme is closely tied to syntax, PropBanks are annotated on top of existing treebanks.

For Finnish, a freely available general language treebank has recently become available (Haverinen et al., 2010b, 2011), but no corpus annotated for semantic roles exists in the general domain. Haverinen et al. (2010a) have previously made available a small-scale PropBank of clinical Finnish, and thus shown that in principle, the PropBank scheme is suitable for Finnish and combinable with the Stanford Dependency (SD) scheme (de Marneffe and Manning, 2008a,b), the annotation scheme of both the clinical treebank and the general language treebank of Haverinen et al.

In this work, we present the first results of a project that aims to create a general language PropBank for Finnish, built on top of the existing Turku Dependency Treebank. This paper describes the methodology used for constructing the PropBank in a dependency-based manner, as well as shows the utility of the two different annotation layers present in the treebank. We also discuss the ways in which the Finnish PropBank relates to the English PropBank, our efforts to provide links between the two resources and the specific features of the Finnish language that require attention in the annotation process. Finally, we discuss the employed annotation methods and present preliminary evaluation.

2   PropBank Terminology

The purpose of a *Proposition Bank* or *PropBank*, as originally developed for English by Palmer et al. (2005), is to provide running text annotation of *semantic roles*, that is, the participants of the events described. For instance, the participants may include an *agent* who actively causes the event, or a *patient*, someone to whom the event happens. As defining a single set of roles that would cover all possible predicates is difficult, the PropBank annotation scheme defines roles on a verb-by-verb basis. Each verb receives a number of *framesets*, which can be thought of as coarse-grained senses for the verb. Each frameset consists of a *roleset*, which is a set of

act.01: to play a role, to behave	act.02: to do something
arg0 Player	arg0 Actor
arg1 Role	arg1 Grounds for action

Figure 1: Two framesets for the verb *to act*. The frameset *act.01* is intended for usages such as *He acted as her trustee* and the frameset *act.02* for usages such as *He acted on the knowledge that she betrayed him.*

semantic roles associated with this sense of the verb, and in addition, a set of syntactic frames that describe the allowable syntactic variations.

The *roles* or *arguments* in each roleset are numbered from zero onwards. A verb can have up to six numbered arguments, although according to Palmer et al. most verbs have two to four. The arguments zero and one (Arg0 and Arg1) have specific, predefined meanings: Arg0 is reserved for *agents*, *causers* and *experiencers*, and Arg1 is used for *patients* and *themes*. The arguments Arg2 to Arg5 have no predefined meanings, but rather they are specified separately for each verb. The original PropBank project makes an effort, however, to keep also these arguments consistent within classes of verbs defined in VerbNet (Dang et al., 1998). Figure 1 illustrates two framesets for the English verb *to act*.

In addition to numbered arguments, the PropBank scheme defines so called *adjunct-like arguments* or *ArgMs*. These, unlike the numbered arguments, are not verb-specific, but rather can be applied to any verb. The original PropBank defines a set of 11 different ArgMs: *location (LOC)*, *extent (EXT)*, *discourse (DIS)*, *negation (NEG)*, *modal verb (MOD)*, *cause (CAU)*, *time (TMP)*, *purpose (PNC)*, *manner (MNR)*, *direction (DIR)* and *general purpose adverbial (ADV)*. The distinction between numbered arguments and ArgMs is made on the basis of frequency: roles that occur frequently with a particular verb sense are given numbered argument status, and less frequent roles are left as ArgMs.

PropBanks are constructed in a data-driven manner using an underlying treebank. For each different verb present in the corpus, the verb senses observed are assigned framesets in a process called *framing*, and after the framesets have been created, the occurrences in the treebank are annotated accordingly. For each verb occurrence, the annotator must select the correct frameset and mark the arguments as defined in this frameset as well as the ArgMs.

3   The Turku Dependency Treebank

This work builds on top of the previously established Turku Dependency Treebank (TDT) (Haverinen et al., 2010b, 2011), which consists of 204,399 tokens (15,126 sentences) from 10 different genres of written Finnish. The text sources of the treebank are the Finnish Wikipedia and Wikinews, popular blogs, a university online magazine, student magazines, the Finnish sections of the Europarl and JRC-Acquis corpora, a financial newspaper, grammar examples from a Finnish reference grammar and amateur fiction from various web-sources.

The syntax annotation scheme of the treebank is a Finnish-specific version of the well-known Stanford Dependency (SD) scheme (de Marneffe and Manning, 2008a,b). The SD scheme represents the syntactic structure of a sentence as a directed graph, where the nodes represent the words of the sentence and the edges represent pairwise dependencies between them. Each dependency has a direction, meaning that one of the two words connected is the *head* or *governor* and the other is the *dependent*. Each dependency also has a *type* or *label*, which describes the syntactic function of the dependent.

Figure 2: The SD scheme on a Finnish sentence. The example can be translated as *The actor has earlier lived in Italy, and moved from there to Germany*.

Figure 3: Conjunct propagation and coordination scope ambiguity. Left: the reading where only the cars are old. Right: The reading where both the cars and the bikes are old.

The original SD scheme contains 55 dependency types arranged in a hierarchy, where each type is a direct or indirect subtype of the most general dependency type *dependent* (*dep*). The scheme has four different *variants*, each using a different subset of the dependency types and giving a different amount of information on the sentence structure. The *basic* variant of the scheme restricts the sentence structures to trees, and the dependency types convey mostly syntactic information. The other variants add further dependencies on top of the tree structure, making the structures graphs rather than trees.

TDT uses a Finnish-specific version of the scheme, which defines a total of 53 dependency types and is described in detail in the annotation manual by Haverinen (2012). The annotation consists of two different layers of dependencies. The first annotation layer is grounded on the *basic* variant of the SD scheme, and hence the structures of the sentences in this layer are trees. The base layer of annotation is illustrated in Figure 2. The second annotation layer, termed *Conjunct propagation and additional dependencies*, adds on top of the first layer additional dependencies describing the following phenomena: *propagation of conjunct dependencies, external subjects* and *syntactic functions of relativizers*.

Conjunct propagation in the SD scheme provides further information on coordinations. The *basic* variant of the scheme considers the first coordinated element the head, and all other coordinated elements and the coordinating conjunction depend on it. Therefore, if a phrase modifies the first element of a coordination, it may in fact also modify all or some of the other conjuncts, and it should be *propagated* to those conjuncts that it modifies. Similarly, it is possible that all or some of the coordinated elements modify another sentence element. Conjunct propagation is used to resolve some (not all) *coordination scope ambiguities*; for instance, whether the adjective *old* modifies both *cars* and *bikes* or only *cars* in the phrase *old cars and bikes* (see Figure 3).

External subjects occur with *open clausal complements*, where a verb and its complement verb share a subject (*subject control*). The fact that the subject of the first verb is also the subject of the second verb cannot be marked in the first layer due to treeness restrictions, leaving it part of the second layer. *Relativizers*, or the phrases containing the relative word, such as *which* or *who*, are only marked as relativizers in the first layer of the treebank annotation, again in order to preserve the treeness of the structure. However, they also always have a secondary syntactic function, which in turn is annotated in the second layer of TDT. For instance, in *The man who stood at the door was tall*, the pronoun *who* acts as the subject of the verb *stood*. All of the phenomena addressed in the second layer of TDT are illustrated in Figure 4.

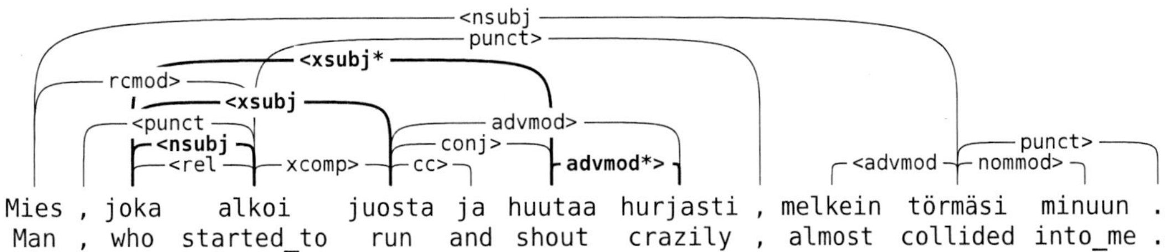

Figure 4: The second annotation layer of TDT. The example can be translated as *The man, who started to run and shout crazily, almost collided with me*. All second layer dependencies are in bold, and propagated dependencies are marked by an asterisk. The relative pronoun *joka* (*who*) also acts as the subject of the relative clause, as well an external subject to an open clausal complement. The external subject of the verb *juosta* (*run*) is also the external subject of the second coordinated verb, *huutaa* (*shout*) and is therefore propagated to the second conjunct. Similarly, the adverb modifier *hurjasti* (*crazily*) is shared between the two coordinated verbs. None of these phenomena can be accounted for in the first layer of annotation due to the treeness restriction.

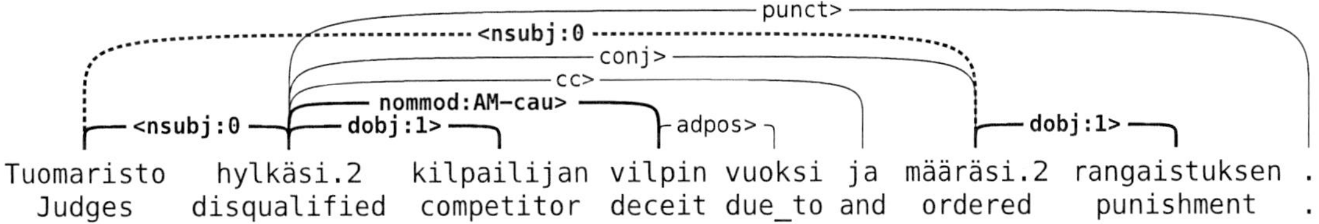

Figure 5: PropBank annotation on top of the dependency treebank. Dependencies with an associated PropBank argument are marked in bold. Note how one of the arguments (Arg0) of the latter verb in the sentence is associated with a second-layer dependency. The example sentence can be translated as *The judges disqualified the competitor due to deceit and ordered a punishment.*

4 Dependency-based PropBanking

The PropBank annotation of this work is built on top of the dependency syntax annotation of TDT, including both the first and second annotation layer. This is in contrast to the English PropBank, which has been built on top of the constituency-based Penn Treebank (Marcus et al., 1993). In the Finnish PropBank, each argument of a verb is associated with a dependency (be it first or second layer) in the underlying treebank, which means that the subtree of the dependent word, as defined by the dependencies of the first annotation layer, acts as the argument. For an illustration of the dependency-based PropBank annotation, see Figure 5.

In contrast to the original PropBank (Palmer et al., 2005) where in theory any constituent could be an argument, we make use of a heuristic: in most cases, the arguments of a verb will be its direct dependents. However, unlike the clinical language pilot study of Haverinen et al. (2010a), we do annotate all arguments, whether direct dependents of the verb or not. The heuristic of direct dependents being the likeliest arguments is only used to increase the speed of annotation by highlighting likely argument candidates for the annotator in the annotation software. In cases where an argument is found outside the dependents of the verb, we allow an extra dependency of the type *xarg* (*external argument*) to be added to any non-dependent word at annotation time, so that the argument can be attached to this dependency. For an illustration of external arguments, see Figure 6.

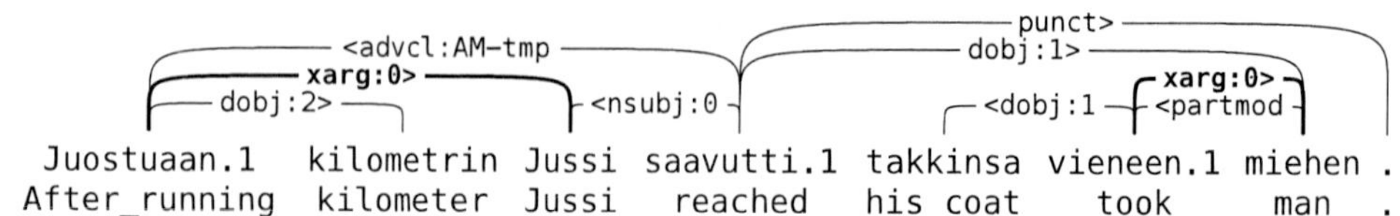

Figure 6: Arguments that are not direct dependents of the verb. On the left, the third person singular possessive suffix of the verb *juostuaan* (*after running, after he ran*) shows that it shares the subject of *saavutti* (*reached*), although this is not marked in the syntax annotation as the structure is not a case of subject control. On the right, semantically the noun *miehen* (*man*) is an argument to the verb *vieneen* (*took*), although syntactically, the verb participle modifies the noun. Note how by the assumption of whole subtrees forming arguments, the verb *vieneen* itself is incorrectly included in its own argument (Arg0) in the rightmost case. The example can be translated as *After running a kilometer, Jussi reached the man who took his coat.*

In the currently complete portion of the PropBank, 81.0% of all arguments, including both numbered arguments and ArgMs, are associated with a dependency of the first syntactic layer. If one takes into account dependencies of the second layer as well as the first, 93.1% of the arguments are covered, leaving a portion of 6.9% as external arguments. This shows that while the first layer of annotation does not suffice to cover an adequate proportion of the arguments, the second layer, which was annotated exactly for the purpose of finding semantic arguments falling outside the base-syntactic dependents of a verb, covers the majority of the remaining arguments.

As Choi and Palmer (2010) have shown, when using a dependency treebank for constructing a PropBank, in some cases the assumption that arguments are the dependents of the verb and their full subtrees results in some missing arguments that are directly due to the dependency structure of the sentence, as well as incorrect argument boundaries. In our work, the missing arguments are remedied by the *xarg* strategy, for instance in the case of a participal modifier, which is syntactically a dependent of the noun, although in fact the noun is its semantic argument. This is illustrated in Figure 6. In the case of a participal modifier, however, the addition of an *xarg* dependency leads to an incorrect argument boundary, as by the full subtree assumption the verb itself becomes part of its own argument. It should be noted that using the SD scheme already prevents some of the boundary issues mentioned by Choi and Palmer. For instance, in their work, modal verbs are problematic, as they are marked as the head of the main verb, whereas in the PropBank, the modal verb should be marked as an *ArgM-mod* for the main verb. In SD, however, the main verb is made the head and the auxiliary depends on it, which is unproblematic for PropBank annotation. A principled solution for the remaining boundary issues is not proposed in this paper, but is left as future work — perhaps using a rule-based approach, seeing that the boundary issues consist mostly of clear, regular cases.

5   Specific Features of Finnish Verbs

In the development of the Finnish PropBank, we have followed the same design principles as were used in the original PropBank: the arguments are numbered similarly from zero onwards, and the principles on which the framesets are created and distinguished are the same. We also use the same set of adjunct-like arguments, *ArgMs*, only adding two new subtypes, *consequence* (*CSQ*) and *phrasal marker* (*PRT*).

In order to expand the application potential of the Finnish PropBank to multilingual settings,

erota.2: leave a job		quit.01: leave a job	
Arg0	Person quitting	Arg0	Person quitting
Arg1	Job or position	Arg1	Job or position

Figure 7: Finnish and English verbs with corresponding framesets. The Finnish verb *erota* can be translated as *to quit*, and the framesets of this verb sense define identical argument structures. Therefore, the Finnish frameset is assigned the English as its corresponding frameset.

we assign to the Finnish frameset a corresponding frameset from the English PropBank where possible. Naturally, not all Finnish framesets have a corresponding English frameset, due to differences between the two languages. In this section, we discuss the specific features of the Finnish language influencing the creation of a PropBank, as well as the assignment of a corresponding English frameset and cases where no such frameset exists.

5.1   Frameset Correspondences and Non-correspondences

A frameset is assigned a corresponding English PropBank frameset when two conditions apply. The English verb must be a valid translation for the sense of the Finnish verb under consideration, and the two framesets must have the same arguments present, with matching argument numbers as well as argument descriptions. Occasionally, the argument descriptions of a corresponding English frameset are slightly rephrased in order to maximize the internal consistency of the Finnish PropBank.

As an example of corresponding framesets, one of the senses of the Finnish verb *erota* can be translated as *to quit* and it is used in contexts such as quitting a job or a position. This sense of the verb has its own frameset in the Finnish PropBank, and it is assigned a corresponding frameset in the English PropBank. The two framesets are illustrated in Figure 7.

For some verbs, however, the specific features of Finnish and the usages of the verbs being different to English do not allow assigning corresponding framesets. For instance, the frameset for the Finnish verb *korjata* meaning *to fix* or *to repair*, corresponds to neither of the English framesets, which, in turn, are also different from each other. The framesets for the three verbs are illustrated in Figure 8.

The difference between the two English framesets lies in the Arg2 argument; *to fix* includes an argument described as *benefactive*, which is absent in the description of *to repair*. The Finnish frameset, in contrast, contains an Arg2 describing an *instrument*, which is absent in both of the English framesets. Therefore it cannot be assigned either of them as the corresponding frameset. The addition of the *instrument* argument was necessary, however, as it is frequently found in the instances of the verb in the underlying treebank.

The corpus-based development of the framesets implies, naturally, that the non-correspondence of framesets does not necessarily indicate a difference between the languages. As the framesets are based on the treebank texts, they do not reflect all possible meanings and argument structures that a verb can have. This means that a non-correspondence can be caused merely by the limited and possibly different topics and text sources of the underlying treebanks. For example, the non-correspondence of the verb *korjata* with its English equivalents may be, at least partly, caused by contextual differences in the treebank texts.

A clear example of contextual differences causing non-correspondence of framesets is the Finnish

fix.02: to repair	korjata.1: to fix, to repair
arg0 Fixer	arg0 Entity repairing something
arg1 Thing fixed	arg1 Entity repaired
arg2 Benefactive	arg2 Instrument, thing repaired with
repair.01: to restore after damage or injury	
arg0 Repairer, agent	
arg1 Entity repaired	

Figure 8: Framesets of Finnish and English verbs with the meaning *to repair*. The Finnish frameset contains an argument describing the instrument of fixing, which is not present in either of the English framesets. Note that also the two English framesets differ in that the frameset for *to fix* contains a benefactive argument, whereas the frameset for *to repair* does not.

run.02: walk quickly, course or contest	juosta.1: move rapidly on foot
arg0 Runner	arg0 Creature running, agent
arg1 Course, race, distance	arg2 EXT, distance
arg2 Opponent	arg3 Start point
	arg4 End point

Figure 9: Framesets of Finnish and English verbs describing *running*, the rapid movement of an agent on foot. The English frameset describes running a competition or a course, as in *John ran a marathon*, and the Finnish frameset describes running from one location to another, as in *John ran from home to work*. The abbreviation *EXT* on the Finnish frameset refers to *extent*, which is one of the ArgM subtypes defined in the PropBank scheme.

verb *juosta* and its English counterpart, *to run*, both of which describe the rapid movement of an agent. In the underlying Finnish treebank, the majority of examples describe an agent running from one location to another. However, the English PropBank does not contain a frameset for such a use of the verb *to run*, but rather only a frameset describing running a competition, distance or course. This is presumably due to the Penn Treebank only containing such examples, as the English *to run* can perfectly well be used for describing movement between two locations (see for instance the Collins English dictionary (2009)). As the examples present in the Finnish treebank require a frameset whose equivalent does not exist in the English PropBank, the framesets for these two verbs are necessarily different, as illustrated in Figure 9.

5.2   Finnish Causative Verbs and Polysemous Verbs in English

In addition to verbs differing by virtue of different usages, a more systematic difference between English and Finnish verbs is caused by the verb derivation system in Finnish. In English, many verbs, especially those of movement, are polysemous and can be used in different syntactic configurations. These verbs, also termed *variable behavior verbs* (see the work of Levin and Hovav (1994) and Perlmutter (1978)), can take as their syntactic subject either an agent actively causing an event or a patient merely undergoing it. For instance, the verb *to move* can have both subject types, as in *I move* versus *The chair moves*. In addition, the verb can also be used transitively, as in *I move the chair*, where the agent causes the event undergone by the patient.

In contrast, Finnish expresses the transitive meaning using a separate verb, typically formed by adding a morpheme to the root verb. For example, from the verb *liikkua (to move, intransitive)*, it is possible to derive *liikuttaa (to make something move)*, as illustrated in Figure 10. These *causative* verbs can be formed both from originally transitive, such as *syödä (to eat)*, the

$$
\begin{array}{lll}
(1) & \textit{I move} & \textit{Minä liikun} \\
(2) & \textit{The chair moves} & \textit{Tuoli liikkuu} \\
(3) & \textit{I move the chair} & \textit{*Minä liikun tuolia} \\
 & & \textit{Minä liikutan tuolia}
\end{array}
$$

Figure 10: Verbs taking both agents and patients as subjects in English and in Finnish. In English, the verb *to move* has three different uses: two intransitive uses and one transitive, where the agent causes the event occurring to the patient. In Finnish, this last sense, the transitive one, is expressed by a causative verb derived from the root verb.

liikkua.1: to move, be moved		liikuttaa.1: to move something	
arg0	Entity moving actively	arg0	Entity moving arg1
arg1	Entity whose movement something causes **if not arg0**	arg1	Entity moved
arg2	Place	arg2	Place
move.01: change location			
arg0	Mover		
arg1	Moved		
arg2	Destination		

Figure 11: Framesets of Finnish and English verbs with the meaning *to move*. Top left: Finnish, intransitive verb that takes as its subject either an agent or a patient. Top right: Finnish, transitive causative verb for moving. Bottom left: English, transitive and intransitive uses. Despite appearances, the frameset *liikuttaa.1* does not correspond to the frameset *move.01*, as the English verb is allowed to take either an Arg0 or an Arg1 as its subject, whereas the Finnish verb is not.

causative being *syöttää (to feed)*, and intransitive verbs, such as *nukkua (to sleep)*, where the causative is *nukuttaa (to make someone sleep)* (Hakulinen et al., 2004, §311). For causatives and causativity in general, see for instance the work of Shibatani (1976) and Itkonen (1996), and the introduction by Paulsen (2011).

For the English PropBank, all three usages of the verb *to move* can be defined by a single frameset that includes both argument zero and argument one. Depending on the arguments present in a sentence, one or both arguments can be annotated, as PropBank does not require that all arguments are present in all examples. The formulation of the Finnish framesets and the assignment of corresponding framesets is, however, more challenging.

Because of its specific argument structure, the frameset for the Finnish causative derivation *liikuttaa (to make something move)* cannot be assigned the English *to move* as its corresponding frameset; *to move* can take either an Arg0 or an Arg1 as its subject, while *liikuttaa* can not. Despite this, the verb can still have the same arguments as the English frameset. As the Finnish intransitive *liikkua (to move)* is able to take either an agent or a patient as a subject, we assign it a single frameset that contains both an Arg0 and an Arg1, and explicitly mark that these arguments are mutually exclusive, meaning that only one of them should be annotated in any given example. Figure 11 illustrates the framesets of the two Finnish verbs and for comparison, the English verb *to move*.

It is also possible, although less common, for a Finnish verb taking alternatively an agent or a patient as its subject to allow a transitive usage. An example of this is the verb *lentää (to fly)*, where the intransitive with an agent (*lintu lentää, the bird flies*), the intransitive with a patient (*lentokone lentää, the plane flies*) and the transitive (*pilotti lentää lentokonetta, the pilot flies the plane*) all use the same verb. These verbs are treated similarly to the original PropBank as they are not problematic in the same way as the verbs described above, but they are nevertheless marked as variable behavior verbs in the frameset.

6   Annotation Protocol

The annotation of the Finnish PropBank, similarly to the English one, consists of two main phases. In the first phase, each verb is given a number of framesets that describe the different senses of the verb as they occur in the underlying corpus, and in the second phase, all the occurrences of the verb are annotated according to the framesets given.

In order to recognize tokens that require PropBank annotation, we use the open source morphological analyzer OMorFi (Pirinen, 2008; Lindén et al., 2009), which gives each token all of its possible readings with no disambiguation between them. In order to ensure the annotation of all verbs in the treebank, all tokens that receive a verbal reading, or a reading indicating that the word can be a *minen*-derivation (resembles the English *ing*-participle), are selected for annotation. Calculated in this manner, the Turku Dependency Treebank contains 49,727 potential verb tokens that require annotation, and 2,946 possible different verb lemmas. At this stage, 335 lemmas have been fully annotated, resulting in a total of 9,051 annotated tokens. This means that with respect to lemmas, approximately 11.4% of the work has been completed, and with respect to tokens, the estimate is 18.2%. It should be noted that when advancing from the common verbs towards verbs with less occurrences, the annotation becomes gradually more laborious. As illustrated in Figure 12, the amount of verbs with a large amount of occurrences is fairly small as compared to the amount of verbs with only few occurrences. The framing and annotation in this project commenced not from the most common verbs but rather those with a middle range occurrence rate, in order to settle the annotation scheme before moving to the most common verbs. Thus at this stage, the verbs with the most occurrences are in fact not yet annotated.

In total six different annotators, with different amounts of previous experience and different backgrounds, contribute to the PropBank, and the same annotators also act as framers. The verbs present in the treebank are framed and annotated one lemma at a time. In the beginning of the annotation process, all occurrences of each lemma were double annotated, in order to ensure high annotation quality even in the beginning phases of the project. As the work has progressed, we have gradually moved towards single annotation; high-frequency lemmas are partially double annotated, while low-frequency lemmas are single annotated. This is to increase the annotation speed while still being able to measure and control the annotation quality even after the initial learning phase.

In the case of double annotation, the two annotators assigned to a lemma create the framesets jointly, after which both of them independently annotate all occurrences using these framesets. At this stage, the annotator is required to mark both the numbered arguments and the adjunct-like arguments present in each example. Afterwards, the two analyses of each example are automatically merged, so that all disagreements can easily be seen, and in a meeting between all annotators, a single correct analysis is decided upon. Partially double annotated lemmas are framed in co-operation, and a portion of the occurrences is double annotated while the rest are divided between the annotators. In single annotation, each lemma is given to one annotator, and additionally, one annotator is assigned as a *consultant*, whom the annotator of the lemma

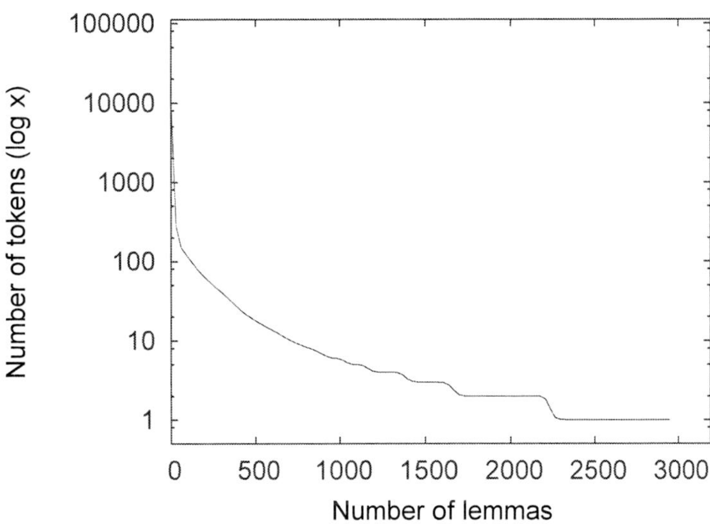

Figure 12: Numbers of verb lemmas of different frequencies as sorted from the highest number of occurrences to the lowest. High-frequency lemmas are relatively few, while many different low-frequency lemmas occur in the treebank text.

can turn to if facing problems with the framing. If unsure in the annotation phase, be it double or single annotation, an annotator can mark any argument as unsure. This function can also be used to signal suspected syntax-level errors in the treebank, as annotators are not allowed to alter the syntax at this stage.

In order to alleviate the labor-intensity of creating the framesets, *batches* of similar verbs are given their framesets simultaneously. When creating a new frameset for a lemma, the annotator is to consider whether there are other verbs that should also receive the same frameset, if such verbs are easily found. (The opposite is also possible: when considering a lemma, if the annotator finds that an existing frameset from another lemma can be re-used, they may copy the desired frameset for the verb under consideration.) For instance, if an annotator is considering the verb *to like*, possible other verbs that could receive the same frameset would be *to love*, *to care* or other verbs expressing affection that may have the same arguments. However, simply having the same arguments as in numbered arguments is not sufficient to be included in the same batch: for instance, verbs of dislike, although they also receive arguments describing the experiencer and the object of the feeling, should not be assigned to the same batch as the verbs of affection. In order to be included in the same batch, the verbs must have the same numbered arguments, and also the argument descriptions are required to be suitable for all verbs included.

This strategy has two benefits: in addition to saving time by creating framesets practically with no additional cost, it can enforce some consistency across the verbs. As a minor drawback, it requires additional care, as annotators should always make sure that the lemma they are considering does not already have the intended frameset as a side product of some other lemma. Also, if making a frameset for several verbs at once, care should be taken that verbs assigned simultaneously to other annotators do not receive framesets without these annotators' knowledge.

The distinctions between different framesets are made according to guidelines similar to those used in the English PropBank, that is, the verb senses that the framesets correspond to are fairly coarse-grained. The main criterion used is that if two potential framesets have the same arguments (including the descriptions), or the arguments of one are a subset of the arguments of the other, only one frameset should be created.

The annotation is done using a custom software (see Figure 13) that allows the annotator to select a lemma to be annotated and then displays each occurrence as a separate case. The annotator must first select the correct frameset for the occurrence under consideration, and then assign the numbered arguments and adjunct-like arguments. All dependents of the verb occurrence are highlighted as default options for arguments, except for certain dependency types, such as punctuation, which never act as arguments. In case a dependency does not correspond to an argument, it is possible to leave the dependency unmarked. In addition, it is possible to mark a sentence element not depending on the verb as an argument using the *external argument* dependency. In addition to choosing one of the framesets defined, it is also possible to take one of the following actions. First, the annotator can mark an occurrence as *not a verb*, where the token is not in fact a verb but rather another part-of-speech, despite having a verbal reading assigned by OMorFi. Second, similarly it is possible mark the token to have a *wrong lemma*, where the token is a verb, but not of the lemma currently under consideration. Third, it is possible to mark the occurrence as an *auxiliary*, as in the PropBank scheme auxiliaries do not receive framesets or arguments.

7 Evaluation

In order to evaluate the performance of the annotators, we measure their *annotator accuracy* against the *merged* annotation. The accuracy is calculated using F_1-score, which is defined as $F_1 = \frac{2PR}{P+R}$. *Precision* (P) is the percentage of arguments in the individual annotation that are also present in the merged annotation, and *recall* (R) the percentage of arguments in the merged annotation that are also present in the individual annotation. For an argument to be considered correct, both its dependent word (the head word is the verb and thus always correct) and the argument number or the ArgM type must be correct. If the frameset of a verb is incorrect, then all numbered arguments of this verb token are considered incorrect as well. An ArgM of the correct type is judged correct regardless of the frameset of the verb, as ArgMs are verb-independent. For comparison, we also calculate *inter-annotator agreement* using *Cohen's kappa*, defined as $\kappa = \frac{P(A)-P(E)}{1-P(E)}$, where *P(A)* is the observed agreement and *P(E)* is the agreement expected by chance.

The overall annotator accuracy on the whole task is 94.1%, and the overall inter-annotator agreement in Kappa is 89.7%. While the F_1-score measures the accuracy of an annotator against the merged gold-standard, the Kappa-score measures the agreement between the annotators. It should also be noted that as the Kappa-score can only reasonably be calculated for labeling tasks, the external arguments, that is, arguments that are not syntactically direct dependents of the verb, are only taken into account in the F_1-score and not in Kappa. The per-annotator accuracies in F_1-score are listed in Table 1. The Table lists both overall scores and scores on numbered arguments and adjunct-like arguments separately, as well as the external arguments. These results show that overall, the accuracy is high, and that the adjunct-like arguments are more difficult to annotate than the numbered arguments, which is an expected result based on the figures previously reported by Palmer et al. (2005). The external arguments also seem to be more difficult than the numbered arguments in general. Some annotators show a large difference between precision and recall on the external arguments, indicating that these

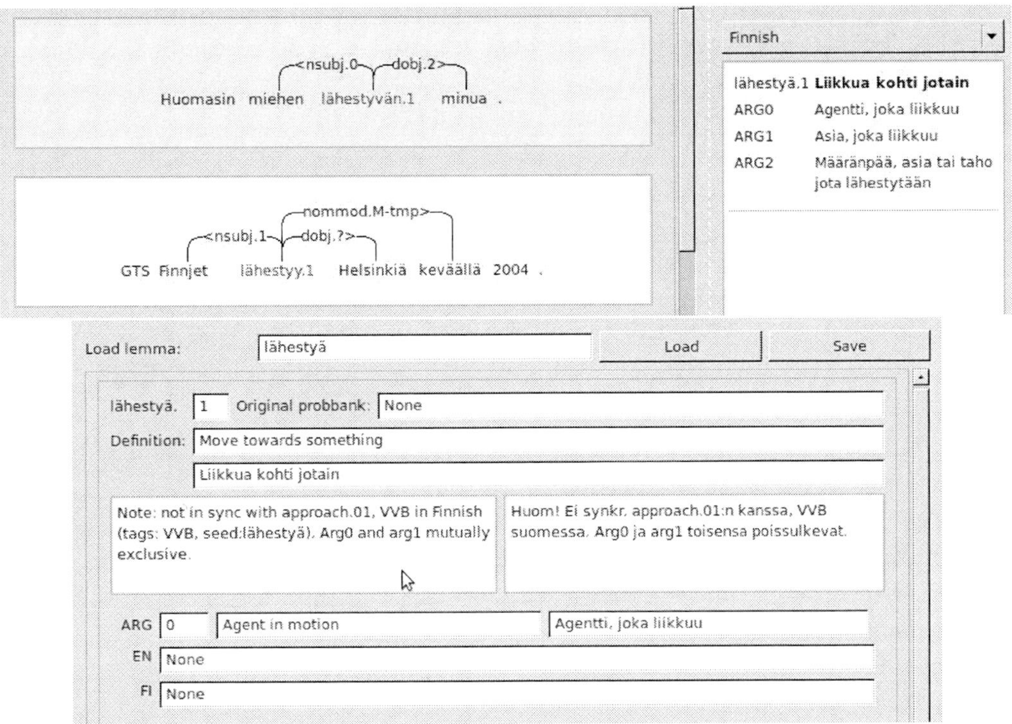

Figure 13: The annotation tool. Top: occurrence annotation. Two occurrences to be annotated are shown on the left, one marked as ready and one in mid-annotation. The direct dependents of the verb are shown as default alternatives for the arguments, and the question mark in the latter example indicates a dependency that has not been assigned with an argument. The framesets that have been created for the verb currently being annotated are shown on the right. Bottom: frameset editor. Each frameset has a number, a description, a field for the corresponding English PropBank frameset (not set in this example), as well as a free comment field. Similarly, each argument has a number, a description and a comment field. The comment fields may be used, for instance, for case requirements or use examples.

	Ann. 1	Ann. 2	Ann. 3	Ann. 4	Ann. 5	Ann. 6	All
Numbered (n=29,076)							
Recall	98.1	96.5	96.5	94.9	97.8	95.6	96.9
Precision	98.5	98.0	98.0	95.1	98.1	94.5	97.4
F-score	98.3	97.2	97.3	95.0	97.9	95.1	97.1
ArgM (n=15,771)							
Recall	92.5	86.6	87.3	83.7	90.1	82.8	87.8
Precision	92.9	87.3	86.6	85.2	92.6	82.0	88.2
F-score	92.7	86.9	87.0	84.4	91.3	82.4	88.0
xarg (n=3,118)							
Recall	93.3	80.8	79.3	70.3	87.4	85.9	86.0
Precision	97.8	97.8	92.3	70.3	94.7	84.3	92.7
F-score	95.5	88.5	85.3	70.3	90.9	85.1	89.2
overall (n=44,847)							
Recall	96.3	93.0	93.4	90.9	95.2	91.6	93.9
Precision	96.7	94.2	94.1	91.5	96.3	90.6	94.3
F-score	96.5	93.6	93.7	91.2	95.8	91.1	94.1

Table 1: Annotator accuracy results per annotator, both overall and separately for numbered arguments and ArgMs. Also a separate evaluation of the external arguments (*xarg*) is given. Note that for the F_1-scores the external arguments are also included in the counts of numbered arguments and ArgMs, seeing that each external argument is also one of these two argument types.

annotators forget to mark an external argument more often than mark an extraneous one. In addition to the possibility of overlooking an external argument, the task is made more difficult by the fact that with *xargs*, unlike the other arguments, the annotator is required to identify the correct token to act as the dependent.

Further, we evaluate the correctness of the frameset selections. Out of all frameset choices (including the possible choices of *not a verb*, *wrong lemma* and *auxiliary*), 88.4% were correct as measured against the final annotation result. Measured on only those instances where the frameset was correctly selected, the overall F_1-score was 94.6%.

8 Conclusions

In this work, we have presented the first results from a project aiming at a general Finnish PropBank. This PropBank is built on top of the previously existing Turku Dependency Treebank and utilizes both the first and second layers of syntax annotation present in the treebank, which are annotated according to the Stanford Dependency scheme.

We confirm the preliminary finding of the clinical language pilot study by Haverinen et al. (2010a) that the PropBank scheme can be used for Finnish and is compatible with the SD scheme. We also find that a large number of arguments are covered by the simplifying assumption that arguments are syntactic dependents of the verb; 81.0% of all arguments are accounted for when only considering the first layer of syntax annotation in TDT, and 93.1% if also the second layer is taken into consideration.

Regarding the quality of annotation, we find that the overall annotator accuracy of all six different annotators is 94.1% in F_1-score, and the accuracy on adjunct-like arguments (ArgMs) alone is 88.0%. The inter-annotator agreement in Cohen's kappa on the overall task disregarding external arguments is 89.7%. From these figures we conclude that overall the quality of annotation is high, and that as expected, the adjunct-like arguments are more difficult to annotate than the numbered arguments. External arguments, with an overall F_1-score of 89.2%, are also more difficult than numbered arguments in general, due to the possibility of overlooking an external argument as well as the fact that for these arguments, the annotator also needs to identify the correct dependent word.

As future work, in addition to increasing the coverage of the PropBank, it would be beneficial to build rules to treat cases where the full subtree assumption of arguments fails, as well as enhance the annotation towards noun argument structures, that is, a NomBank (Meyers et al., 2004). The annotation could also be enhanced in several ways in order to accommodate, for instance, text generation, along the guidelines suggested by Wanner et al. (2012).

Acknowledgments

This work has been supported by the Academy of Finland and the Emil Aaltonen Foundation.

References

(2009). *Collins English Dictionary — 30th Anniversary Edition*. HarperCollins Publishers.

Baker, C. F., Fillmore, C. J., and Lowe, J. B. (1998). The Berkeley FrameNet project. In *Proceedings of COLING-ACL'98*, pages 86–90.

Choi, J. and Palmer, M. (2010). Retrieving correct semantic boundaries in dependency structure. In *Proceedings of LAW IV*, pages 91–99.

Dang, H. T., Kipper, K., Palmer, M., and Rosenzweig, J. (1998). Investigating regular sense extensions based on intersective Levin classes. In *Proceedings of COLING-ACL'98*, pages 293–299.

Duran, M. S. and Aluísio, S. M. (2011). Propbank-br: a Brazilian treebank annotated with semantic role labels. In *Proceedings of STIL'11*, pages 1862–1867.

Hakulinen, A., Vilkuna, M., Korhonen, R., Koivisto, V., Heinonen, T.-R., and Alho, I. (2004). *Iso suomen kielioppi / Grammar of Finnish*. Suomalaisen kirjallisuuden seura.

Haverinen, K. (2012). Syntax annotation guidelines for the Turku Dependency Treebank. Technical Report 1034, Turku Centre for Computer Science.

Haverinen, K., Ginter, F., Laippala, V., Kohonen, S., Viljanen, T., Nyblom, J., and Salakoski, T. (2011). A dependency-based analysis of treebank annotation errors. In *Proceedings of Depling'11*, pages 115–124.

Haverinen, K., Ginter, F., Laippala, V., Viljanen, T., and Salakoski, T. (2010a). Dependency-based propbanking of clinical Finnish. In *Proceedings of LAW IV*, pages 137–141.

Haverinen, K., Viljanen, T., Laippala, V., Kohonen, S., Ginter, F., and Salakoski, T. (2010b). Treebanking Finnish. In Dickinson, M., Müürisep, K., and Passarotti, M., editors, *Proceedings of The ninth International Workshop on Treebanks and Linguistic Theories (TLT9)*, pages 79–90.

Itkonen, E. (1996). *Maailman kielten erilaisuus ja samuus / Differences and Similarities of the World Languages*. Gaudeamus.

Levin, B. and Hovav, M. R. (1994). *Unaccusativity: At the syntax–lexical semantics interface*, volume 26 of *Linguistic Inquiry*. MIT Press.

Lindén, K., Silfverberg, M., and Pirinen, T. (2009). HFST tools for morphology — an efficient open-source package for construction of morphological analyzers. In *State of the Art in Computational Morphology*, volume 41 of *Communications in Computer and Information Science*, pages 28–47.

Marcus, M., Marcinkiwicz, M. A., and Santorini, B. (1993). Building a large annotated corpus of English: The Penn Treebank. *Computational Linguistics*, 19(2):313–330.

de Marneffe, M.-C. and Manning, C. (2008a). Stanford typed dependencies manual. Technical report, Stanford University.

de Marneffe, M.-C. and Manning, C. (2008b). Stanford typed dependencies representation. In *Proceedings of COLING'08, Workshop on Cross-Framework and Cross-Domain Parser Evaluation*, pages 1–8.

Meyers, A., Reeves, R., Macleod, C., Szekely, R., Zielinska, V., Young, B., and Grishman, R. (2004). The NomBank project: An interim report. In *In Proceedings of the NAACL/HLT Workshop on Frontiers in Corpus Annotation*.

Palmer, M., Bhatt, R., Narasimhan, B., Rambow, O., Sharma, D. M., and Xia, F. (2009). Hindi syntax: annotating dependency, lexical predicate–argument structure, and phrase structure. In *Proceedings of ICON'09*.

Palmer, M., Gildea, D., and Kingsbury, P. (2005). The Proposition Bank: An annotated corpus of semantic roles. *Computational Linguistics*, 31(1):71–106.

Palmer, M., Gildea, D., and Xue, N. (2010). *Semantic Role Labeling*. Synthesis Lectures on Human Language Technologies. Morgan & Claypool Publishers.

Paulsen, G. (2011). *Causation and Dominance*. PhD thesis.

Perlmutter, D. (1978). Impersonal passives and the unaccusative hypothesis. In *Proceedings of the Fourth Annual Meeting of the Berkeley Linguistic Society*, pages 157–189.

Pirinen, T. (2008). Suomen kielen äärellistilainen automaattinen morfologinen jäsennin avoimen lähdekoodin resurssein. Master's thesis, University of Helsinki.

Shibatani, M., editor (1976). *The Grammar of Causative Constructions*, volume 6 of *Syntax and Semantics*. Seminar Press.

Wanner, L., Mille, S., and Bohnet, B. (2012). Towards a surface realization-oriented corpus annotation. In *Proceedings of INLG '12*, pages 22–30.

Xue, N. and Palmer, M. (2009). Adding semantic roles to the Chinese treebank. *Natural Language Engineering*, 15(Special issue 01):143–172.

Zaghouani, W., Diab, M., Mansouri, A., Pradhan, S., and Palmer, M. (2010). The revised Arabic PropBank. In *Proceedings of LAW IV*, pages 222–226.

Using Finite State Transducers for Making Efficient Reading Comprehension Dictionaries

Ryan Johnson, Lene Antonsen, Trond Trosterud

University of Tromsø, Norway

`ryan.txanson@gmail.com, lene.antonsen@uit.no, trond.trosterud@uit.no`

ABSTRACT

This article presents a novel way of combining finite-state transducers (FSTs) with electronic dictionaries, thereby creating efficient reading comprehension dictionaries. We compare a North Saami - Norwegian and a South Saami - Norwegian dictionary, both enriched with an FST, with existing, available dictionaries containing pre-generated paradigms, and show the advantages of our approach. Being more flexible, the FSTs may also adjust the dictionary to different contexts. The finite state transducer analyses the word to be looked up, and the dictionary itself conducts the actual lookup. The FST part is crucial for morphology-rich languages, where as little as 10 % of the wordforms in running text actually consists of lemma forms. If a compound or derived word, or a word with an enclitic particle is not found in the dictionary, the FST will give the stems and derivation affixes of the wordform, and each of the stems will be given a separate translation. In this way, the coverage of the FST-dictionary will be far larger than an ordinary dictionary of the same size.

KEYWORDS: Lexicography, Computational Morphology, Orthographic Variation, Finite-state Transducers, Electronic Dictionaries.

1　Introduction

The article presents work on enriching bilingual dictionaries with existing finite state transducers (FST). There is a need for reading comprehension dictionaries of morphology-rich languages like the Saami languages. They are also members of the North European Sprachbund, and contain dynamic compounds.

All of the Saami languages are minority languages. An effective digital dictionary is a necessity for language learners, but it is also important for Saami speakers: when they write in Saami, they are often met with complaints from those who do not understand the language well enough, and are asked to write in the majority language instead. This repeatedly appears in discussions in the Facebook group of one of the Saami organisations in Norway (Facebook-group, 2012).

The paper is structured as follows: in Section 2, we look at why we need dictionaries with morphology and dynamic compounding for highly inflected languages. Section 3 describes how we produce dictionaries by combining lexical resources, finite-state transducers, and open-source software. In Section 4, we evaluate the North Saami and South Saami FST-dictionaries and compare their performance with wordform dictionaries. In Section 5, we look at more possibilities that this gives us, by adjusting the FST for special needs. Our conclusion is presented in Section 6.

2　Saami Lexicography and its Challenges

Saami lexicography boasts a history spanning over 250 years, and contains several multi-volume works of high quality (for overview and discussion, see (Larsson, 1997) and (Magga, 2012)). During the first 200 years, the goal in Saami lexicography was to present the Saami languages to scientific audiences. In recent decades, an increasing use of Saami in writing has posed new challenges for Saami lexicography. For a discussion on how to present Saami in dictionaries with Saami as a target language, see (Trosterud, 2000); and for a discussion on the source language vocabulary behind Norwegian - Saami dictionaries, see (Trosterud and Eskonsipo, 2012).

Electronic North Saami dictionaries are a fairly recent phenomenon. Apart from the work presented here, there are two such dictionaries available offering lemma pairs: a small (5500 lemma) North Saami <-> English dictionary, by Renato B. Figueiredo[1]; and in 2013 a larger dictionary between Norwegian and North Saami was released from the publisher Davvi girji[2], presenting the lemma pairs from their large paper dictionaries. Giellatekno, at the University of Tromsø, has published wordform dictionaries for North and South Saami[3]. These are discussed in Section 4 below.

The idea of using FSTs for making passive dictionaries is not new. One version similar to ours is (Maxwell and Poser, 2004). It elaborates upon the idea of unifying dictionaries with FSTs, but does not cite any actual implemetation. A simpler non-FST approach would be to create a static list of every inflected form, combined with their respective lemmas, or articles in the dictionary which these forms relate to. Commercial products rarely present their methodology,

---

[1]`http://www.freelang.net/online/sami.php`

[2]`http://533.davvi.no/ordbok_samnor.php?lang=sam`

[3]Vuosttaš Digisánit for North Saami in 2008 (`http://giellatekno.uit.no/words/dicts/index.eng.html`) and Voestes Digibaakoeh (`http://giellatekno.uit.no/words/dicts/index-sma.eng.html` for South Saami in 2010.

but this is probably the method underlying dictionaries for morphology-poor languages like English and German.

The Saami languages are morphologically complex, suffixing languages with much non-concatenative morphology. Most lemmas have large inflection paradigms: North Saami verbs have about 55 different wordforms, with more than 40 of these being finite forms. Nouns have about 80 different wordforms, 70 of which include possessive suffixes. Adjectives have about 30 wordforms. In addition, variants of these forms exist within the normative orthography. Many of the word forms are transparent, but others are not. For example, the North Saami wordforms *gullái* and *boðii* are the first person singular past tense form of the verbs *gullát* 'to start to wake up' and *boahtit* 'to come', the latter of which has a less obvious basic form, due to diphthong simplification and consonant gradation, frequent phonological processes in the language.

The Saami languages also rely heavily on derivation. Lexical aspects like continuative and inchoative, the causative, and even the passive voice are the result of derivation. North Saami compounding causes vowel changes in the stem vowel, so it is not possible to split a compound mechanically into two parts. For example, *bargojoavku* 'work team' is a compound of the nouns *bargu* 'work' and *joavku* 'team', but a noun like **bargo* does not exist. This is also very common: in a corpus of 1.1 million words, 26.7% are noun compounds, comprising 7.0% of all of the words (Antonsen et al., 2009). In addition, the Saami languages have clitic particles. In North Saami for instance, there is a question enclitic and 11 focus enclitics which can be written as a part of almost all words.

The conclusion is that we need comprehension dictionaries with inflectional word forms, as well as dynamic derivation, compounding and enclitisation. Used as an electronic dictionary, a dictionary containing only lemmas is simply not sufficient, particularly because only 7.9% of the word forms in North Saami running text are identical to the lemma form, as in Table 2. Another possibility would be to use *stemming*, but as shown in (Antonsen and Trosterud, 2010), a stemmer containing all North Saami inflectional suffixes still assigns the wrong stem to 31% of a large test corpus. The reason for this poor result is wide range of non-concatenative morphological processes in North Saami: consonant gradation, and root and stem vowel changes require an approach beyond concatenative affixation.

	North Saami	Finnish	Norwegian
Wordforms in test material	252,461	45,144	64,994
Lemmata in automaton	99,071	94,111	38,983
Coverage	7.9%	10.0%	30.5%

Table 1: Coverage of dictionary without a morphological component, (Antonsen et al., 2009).

Our previous approach for a morphological dictionary was presented in (Antonsen et al., 2009) and consists of lemmas and wordforms for each lemma. The last version for North Saami was compiled in 2012 and contains 252,787 wordforms referring to 9,999 lemma articles, and the South Saami dictionary contains 180,352 wordforms referring to 10,657 lemma articles. The wordforms are generated ahead of time with the same FST as is used in the implementation in this article. In Section 4, we will compare the performance of this wordform dictionary to the FST dictionary described in 3.

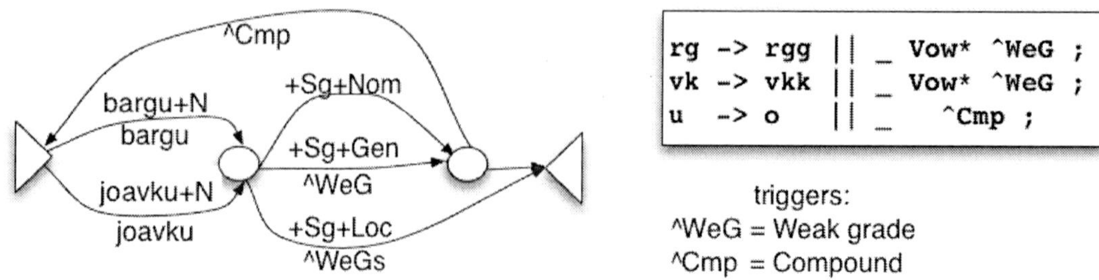

Figure 1: The finite-state transducer produces the word forms *bargu, barggu, barggus* ('work.N') and *joavku, joavkku, joavkkus* ('team.N') and it maps between the wordform and the grammatical word. There is a compound path for both the genitive and the nominative form, so the FST can produce e.g. *boargojoavku, joavkobargu* ('work team, team work') (cfr. Section 2). Changes in the stem are carried out simultaneously in another transducer `twolc` by means of triggers.

3 Morphologically Sensitive Dictionaries

3.1 Building an FST-dictionary on Existing Resources

Our FST-dictionary, which we call *Neahttadigisánit* (http://sanit.oahpa.no) , takes existing lexical resources and morphological resources and combines them to produce a dictionary which is able to look up a larger set of possible inputs, by analysing wordforms and finding lemmas, but also by splitting up compound words to provide either lemmas that combine to make the compound, or either the whole compound word if a translation is available. The application also runs without need for relational databases, as linguistic resources are all contained within static files and external command-line tools.

In this system, we use bilingual lexicons for different language pairs, which we will evaluate later in this article. Currently, the dictionaries are built on a North Saami dictlexicon containing 9,999 lemmas, and a South Saami dictlexicon containing 10,657 lemmas. The lexicons are stored in XML and combined with existing FSTs for these two languages.

Both the North Saami and South Saami FSTs consist of lexical transducers written in `lexc` with respectively 110,000 and 85,000 entries, and phonological transducers implemented in `twolc` for the suprasegmental processes (Koskenniemi, 1983) and (Moshagen et al., 2004). They may be compiled with both the Xerox (Beesley and Karttunen, 2003) and HFST (Lindén et al., 2009) compilers, and are available as open-source [4] under the terms of the GNU General Public License.

Instead of compiling what is essentially a list of all word forms in a language, the FST approach involves listing the stems and affixes separately, and combining them to individual word forms by means of finite-state automata. A finite-state transducer is a finite-state automaton that maps between two strings of characters: the word form itself and the grammatical word, as in Figure 1: *girjin* (the lower level) and *girji+N+Ess* (the upper level). An FST can run both ways: giving the grammatical word from a wordform, or generating a wordform from the grammatical word.

Using an FST to generate paradigms for the dictionary demands some adaptations to make it

---

[4] https://victorio.uit.no/langtech/trunk/gt/

possible to generate the correct paradigm for each lemma, because there are certain considerations that are not present from the perspective of a morphological analyser, which may simply accept any and all input in a descriptive manner. Instead, generation requires attention to lexicalisation of certain word forms as their own individual words. For example, some lemmas have different meanings in singular or plural, such as *gaskabeaivi* 'midday (sg.)', and *gaskabeaivvit* 'dinner (pl.)'. Some lemmas also have a homonymous basic form, but have different paradigms and different translations. Some extra tags in the FST are used to keep these apart.

The FSTs already build the backbone to pedagogical systems for new beginners and heritage speakers, spellchecking and grammar checking systems for text proofing, and machine translation systems. As such, some modifications are also required in order to mark certain words or word forms for inclusion or exclusion from individual systems, to control for normative outputs, or to compensate for specific kinds of input from second-language learners.

3.2 Software

3.2.1 User Interface

Thanks to the open-source community, there are numerous resources available which make it easy to produce designs with good cross-browser compatibility. Previously, troubleshooting these issues for each individual browser would take time, when one would rather focus on implementation and basically, producing usable software.

In this case, we used Twitter Bootstrap[5] to get the most for less, and it has resulted in an easy to use and very minimal layout, see Figure 2. The layout works simultaneously on all the major browsers for desktop operating systems, as well as the most popular mobile browsers, see Figure 2. Thus, there is no real need to produce code specific to Apple's iOS or the Android operating system, or pay for the licensing setup involved with iOS development, and we get all of these things for free.

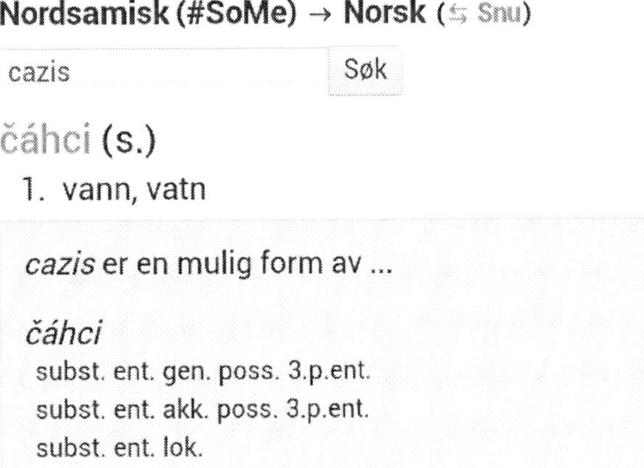

Figure 2: The FST-dictionary on the mobile.

3.2.2 Server Architecture

Having to not worry about the design meant that there was more time left for developing functionality. Our dictionary is based on Flask[6], a light, and flexible web framework for Python.

---

[5] http://twitter.github.com/bootstrap/
[6] http://flask.pocoo.org/

As mentioned above, the lexical data used in this application is stored in an XML format, with one file per language pair, per direction (thus making separate files for language 1 to language 2, and language 2 to language 1). These files range in size from 2MB to 5MB, and are used in the live site, without the need for a relational database to store the data. On our server, queries end up being quite fast, but to ensure that this continues to be true for larger dictionaries, we have also used one of the quickest XML libraries for Python currently available, *lxml*[7] benchmarks[8] This allows us to simply update the files, and restart the service, and any new lexical entries are immediately available to users.

Our previous wordform dictionaries demanded installation in two steps: installing a separate dictionary program (StarDict for Windows and Linux; and the preinstalled Dictionary.app for Mac OS X), and then downloading and installing the linguistic files in the dictionary program. New and updated dictionary versions demanded new downloading and installing. Our new, web-based approach naturally avoids all of this, as users only require the URL. The web dictionary may also be updated by the providers at any time, without the need for users to be aware of and perform the updates themselves.

Compared to our web dictionary, the wordform dictionaries had one major advantage: they could be used to click on words in any application running within the operating system in order to get an analysis and definition, whereas the similar functionality provided in the web dictionary only works on web pages within the browser. However, newer versions of Mac OSX have lost a user-friendly means of installing additional dictionaries to the preinstalled dictionary application, as such, this has become a point in favor of web-based solutions.

There is also an advantage for the providers of the dictionary, programmers and linguists alike. With the previous wordform dictionaries, new versions of the software (such as with StarDict), required adjustments in the format of the dictionary files, and we would often find ourselves concerned over whether we should add more linguistic content, or aim for smaller file sizes. As such, running the dictionary on a server with already existing lexicons is a big step forward.

Having a server-based system also allows us to pay attention to actual usage of the systems. As such, we log all incoming queries along with their results, in order to detect areas where the dictionary needs expansion, and these updates are then available to users as they are made.

3.3   Dictionary API

In addition to being searchable via a form in the web interface, we provide detailed lexical entries in an easily linkable HTML format, and in a more bare-bones format, JSON (JavaScript Object Notation). JSON is a widely adopted, and open standard for communication between applications, specifically with a focus on web applications. The intent here is that data is provided not just for our web-based dictionary via the interface that we provide, but that it may also be used within external applications, on other websites, and even potentially in mobile services.

The data is exposed in a couple of public-facing API endpoints or URL paths, more or less following REST (Representational State Transfer) architecture. One of the endpoints, which provides detailed word entries with inflectional paradigms has already been included in MultiDict's

---

[7]`http://lxml.de/`
[8]`http://lxml.de/performance.html`

Wordlink[9], a reading comprehension tool that includes many other languages and dictionaries. WordLink is quite nice, but naturally, we had some of our own designs for how to use this API.

3.4 Example Applications

3.4.1 Wordpress Plugin and Cross-browser Bookmarklet

Two of the learning tools already constructed for North Saami are *Kursa* and *Oahpa*. *Kursa* is a free, multimedia-rich set of online course materials in North Saami, containing lessons with text, and audio recordings, which are implemented in WordPress[10], a free and open-source blogging tool. There is another version on the way for South Saami.

To go with these learning materials, we have created a plugin for WordPress written in JavaScript, jQuery, and Twitter Bootstrap, which provides access to lemmatisation, compound analysis and lexicon lookup. Users simply `Alt/Opt+Double Click` a word, and it is highlighted with a text-bubble appearing below that contains word translations and wordform analysis 2. Users can quickly and easily look up as many words as they need to comprehend a text, which erases one of the barriers to reading in a new language, namely: the need to frequently look up words in a dictionary, while being unacquainted with potential "dictionary" word forms.

The modular nature of the core library within the plugin allows it to be inserted into several other potential situations with ease. For example, it could be included on a specific page or website, or inserted via a web browser plugin in any page. We have ensured that the library works in the most commonly used, and current web browsers, as such, this functionality is available on Windows, Mac OS X and Linux; in Internet Explorer, Firefox, Chrome, Opera, and Safari.

In addition to plugin for *Kursa*, we have produced a cross-browser solution which is similar to a browser extension, but instead, is accessible via a *bookmarklet*, which is a bookmark providing functionality, instead of a link to a website. As it turns out, this option has been much more preferable to developing (and also convincing users to install) browser specific plugins, and "installation" is simply a drag-and-drop affair. Thus, when on a page they wish to read, users may simply click the bookmarklet, which downloads and includes the plugin source in the HTML document structure facing the user. Now the world of news, blogs, or even Facebook, is accessible in all of the language pairs that we support.

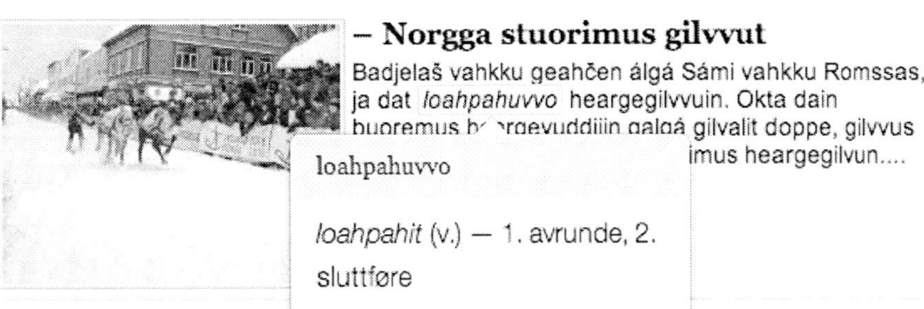

Figure 3: Reading a text with the FST-dictionary on the Saami news website site *Avvir.no*.

---

[9]`http://multidict.net/multidict/`
[10]`http://www.wordpress.org/`

4 Evaluation

The evaluation was run against two separate corpora, one North Saami corpus, containing 44,256 words, and one South Saami corpus, containing 60,037 words (excluding Arabic numerals, punctuation, web-addresses, and proper nouns). Since the task was to evaluate web dictionaries, the test corpora contain a balanced selection of the main text genres found online: web sites of official institutions, news texts, and political blogs. Note that Saami text on the Internet is poorly proofread, and 4.4% of the North Saami corpus (Antonsen, 2013) are words not written according to normative orthography. A part of them are misspellings, a part are subforms which are included in the FST. This should be taken into account when evaluating the data in Table 4.

The corpora were tested with both the FST-dictionary and the wordform dictionary in order to compare performance. The wordform dictionary can only recognise whole words based on sets of pre-generated word forms; while the FST-dictionary also recognises individual parts of compound words, so these translations are categorised as partial translations in Table 4.

	Translation		Partly transl.		No transl.		100%
FST-dict: all wds	39,920	90.2%	549	1.2%	3787	8.6%	44,256
wf-dict: all wds	36,231	81.9%	–	–	8025	18.1%	44,256
FST-dict: unique wds	10,862	79.7%	448	3.3%	2322	17.0%	13,632
wf-dict: unique wds	7874	57.8%	–	–	5758	42.2%	13,632

Table 2: Coverage of an North Saami FST-dictionary compared to a wordform-dictionary.

In Table 4, the coverage of the FST-dictionary is as high as 91.4% (90.2% + 1.2%) for all words in the running text. The numbers for unique words in the corpus give a more realistic picture of the usefulness of the dictionary for a language learner. The FST-dictionary leaves 17% of the unique words without any translation, while the wordform dictionary is unable to translate three times as many. If we look closer at the words that are not translated by the wordform dictionary, there are derivations such as *bivnnutvuođa*, which receives the analysis *bivnnut+A+Der/vuohta+N+Sg+Acc*. The FST-dictionary finds the lemma *bivnnut* with 'popular', while the whole word together means 'popularity'. There are also compounds which get all parts translated by the FST-dictionary, such as *sáhpánjagiid sáhpán+N+SgNomCmp+Cmp#jahki+N+Pl+Gen*, translations: *sáhpán* 'mouse', *jahki* 'year'. And, there are compounds with partial translations, such as *divamávssu diva+N+SgNomCmp+Cmp#máksu+N+Sg+Acc*. Here, only one of the lemmas is translated: *máksu* 'payment, signification'.

The FST-dictionary also manages to translate words with an enclitic, like *oidnoge oidnot+V+Ind+Prs+ConNeg+Foc/ge*. The lemma is translated: *oidnot* 'to show', *ge* is an enclitic. And the FST-dictionary is more tolerant to non-normative forms, such as *eandalit*, which is recognised by the FST as *eandalii+Adv* 'absolutely'. Among the unique 2,322 words for which the FST-dictionary does not give any translation to at all, 47.6% are unknown for the FST, mostly misspellings, or even Norwegian or Finnish quotes. 52.4% are missing in the dictionary.

In Table 4, a similar evaluation was performed with a South Saami corpus and dictionaries. The South Saami wordform dictionary leaves more words without translation than the North Saami wordform dictionary, which correlates to the fact that the South Saami dictionary has a smaller

	Translation		Partly transl.		No transl.		100%
FST-dict: all wds	53,295	88.8%	475	0.8%	6266	10.4%	60,037
wf-dict: all wds	44,989	74.7%	–	–	15,268	25.3%	60,257
FST-dict: unique wds	8039	67.0%	308	2.6%	3660	30.5%	12,008
wf-dict: unique wds	4945	41.1%	–	–	7085	58.9%	12,030

Table 3: Coverage of a South Saami FST-dictionary compared to a wordform-dictionary. Data for partly translation is relevant only for the FST dictionary, the wordform dictionary is not able to handle compounds.

amount of wordforms (180,352 vs. 252,787). The FST-dictionary leaves as much as 30.5% of the unique words without translation. Of these 3,660 words, 78.4% are lacking in the FST. This is due to the fact that the South Saami FST is not as good as the North Saami ones, and also that there are even more misspellings in South Saami than in North Saami. Note that even though the amount of lemmas in the South Saami dictionary is slightly higher than for North Saami, they are not as relevant for the corpus as the lemmas in the North Saami dictionary are for the corpus.

South Saami also has some additional orthographic challenges not present in North Saami: namely, the orthography lacks a single norm that is used in the whole of the South Saami speaking region. Generally, one can expect certain sounds to be represented with characters that are found in each region's majority language, such as Swedish ä and ö, compared to Norwegian æ and ø, however these are often found mixed in single texts; thus the FSTs take into account certain "spelling relaxations" to handle this. In addition, there is a character, ï, which does not exist in either Norwegian or Swedish, and is not obligatory to write since its distribution is phonologically predictable.

5 More FST possibilites

5.1 Modularising the North Saami FST-dictionary

Using finite state transducers makes it possible to make more flexible dictionaries. Many text genres are written outside the written norm, or using input devices with keyboard restrictions. A case in point is the North Saami Facebook group *Ártegis ságat*[11]. The group is open, and has over 1800 registered members, a number equivalent to approximately 10% of the whole speaker community. Many Facebook users read and write using smartphones. Smartphones come without preinstalled Saami keyboards, and for iPhone and Nokia smartphones there also are no such keyboards available at all. An investigation of the discussion during a three months' period, measuring the 30 most frequent words containing North Saami characters, revealed that almost 20% of the text was written without a Saami keyboard. In a North Saami running text, 38% of the words contain North Saami characters, and are thus the remainder are outside of the reach of electronic dictionaries.

Table 5.1 shows the performance of the dictionary combined with the ordinary FST and with a Facebook-FST with spell relax, thus allowing it to accept letters without diacritics as North Saami letters (e.g. the characters *acdsz* are accepted as representatives of *áčdšž*). The corpus

---

[11] https://www.facebook.com/groups/336300756303/?fref=ts

is taken from *Ártegis ságat* during the period 24.10.2012 – 21.01.2013 and contains 67,265 words (excluding Arabic numerals, punctuation, web-addresses and proper nouns).

	Translation		Partly transl.		No transl.		100%
Fb-FST: all wds	54,197	80.6%	315	0.5%	12,753	19.0%	67,265
ord. FST: all wds	50,263	76.3%	250	0.4%	15,364	23.3%	65,877
Fb-FST: unique wds	10,596	59.8%	286	1.6%	6825	38.5%	17,707
ord. FST: unique wds	8813	50.8%	224	1.3%	8326	48.0%	17,363

Table 4: Coverage of a North Saami FST-dictionary. The corpus is analysed with the ordinary FST and an FST adapted to the Facebook orthography.

The overall results shown in Table 5.1 are worse than the results given in Table 4 above, but this is due to the nature of the Facebook corpus, containing a higher amount of orthographic errors and non-Saami text than is found in published text. The important point when reading Table 5.1 is the difference between the ordinary and the adjusted dictionaries. For unique words, the adapted FST recognises 59.8% of the words, as opposed to 50.8% with the ordinary FST.

Finite state transducers are flexible tools, not only for analysing wordforms, but also for changing their shapes. In this way, we are able to adjust the dictionary to different types of input. In an ordinary dictionary, the preference will still be to show the lexicalised words, while filtering out other analyses, however in a student dictionary it would be useful to show all the potential analyses. A Facebook-oriented dictionary will be like the ordinary dictionary, but in addition be able to understand letters lacking the proper diacritics.

5.2 Flexible FSTs: Nynorsk and Bokmål in one

Most bilingual Norwegian-L1 dictionaries are made with Bokmål as the source language. There are lexical differences between Bokmål and Nynorsk (*ikke/ikkje* 'not', *forskjell/skilnad* 'difference'), but the main difference between Nynorsk and Bokmål is morphological. In the nominal morphology, Nynorsk masculines have *-ar, -ane*, whereas Bokmål has *-er, -ene*. Similar differences are to be found in other parts of speech. In order to deal with this, we have made a special dictionary transducer. At the outset, it was an ordinary Bokmål transducer, but we added the main lexical differences between Bokmål and Nynorsk, as well as the Nynorsk morphology. Thus, rather than adding *ikkje* to the dictionary, we made *ikke* the lemma form of *ikkje*, which is then used in lexicon lookups. Nynorsk forms like *handlingar, diskusjonar*, were recognised as plural forms of *handling* 'action', *diskusjon* 'discussion' on par with Bokmål *handlinger, diskusjoner*. For a paper dictionary user, such plural forms do not pose problems, but the electronic comprehension dictionary needs a mechanism for coping with it.

In Table 5.2, we analyse two corpora of 10,606,263 words from the Nynorsk and Bokmål Wikipedia (excluding words containing capital letters or symbols outside of the Norwegian alphabet). The reference Bokmål transducer is not of outstanding quality: it recognised only 93.36% of the Bokmål test corpus. Analysing the Nynorsk corpus with the same transducer resulted in coverage of 79.34% of the wordforms, but minor changes to the analyser (referred to above) to include Nynorsk forms improves the coverage to 89.62%, cf. 5.2[12].

---

[12]The dictionary coverage is poorer than the FST coverage, this reflects the size of the Norwegian - North Saami dictionary, and is irrelevant to the discussion on FST flexibility.

Text		FST coverage		dictionary coverage	
Nynorsk text	Conservative Bokmål	2,191,428	79.34%	3,504,733	66.96%
	All Bokmål varieties	1,849,654	82.56%	3,206,796	69.77%
	Bokmål with Nynorsk	1,101,116	89.62%	2,530,995	76.14%
Bokmål text	All Bokmål varieties	703,950	93.36%	1,644,286	84.50%

Table 5: Coverage of an Bokmål - North Saami FST-dictionary on Nynorsk text.

5.3 Reuse of FSTs for Reading Comprehension Dictionaries

FSTs are in use in many areas apart from lexicography, such as in parsing and spellchecking. The demands on a FST when used for electronic dictionaries are very different from these other usages, however. In order to be efficient for spellchecking and parsing, the FST must have an accuracy rate very close to 100%. If it drops to, say 95%, there will, on average, be one error in almost every sentence. For sentence analysis and syntactic disambiguation, every error has the potential of destroying larger parts of the sentence analysis, and for a spellchecker, one false alarm in each sentence will make the spellchecker useless. For an e-dictionary, on the other hand, 95% correct implies that 19 out of 20 words will have a relevant analysis. Since the individual errors will not destroy the overall result, the dictionary is much more tolerant to errors, and even an FST recognising two thirds of the wordforms would result in a great improvement over an e-dictionary without any FST.

There are openly available finite state transducers for all Nordic languages, for all languages taught as foreign languages in Nordic schools, for all official EU languages except for Greek, and for most of the minority languages in Europe. With an increasing amount of parallel texts online, the number of bilingual dictionary resources is increasing rapidly. Given the dictionary setup described here, the missing link is a finite state transducer, which will turn a bilingual dictionary into a useful comprehension dictionary for reading of online texts.

Although our example evaluations have shown high quality FSTs in use in comprehension dictionaries, even a low quality FST would result in a drastic improvement for morphologically complex languages, where a running text contains a relatively small percentage of word forms that are also the lemma. Adding one more noun to such an FST system where each noun may have upwards of 40 word forms would thus result in coverage of 40 additional tokens in a text, as opposed to just one word form as with a non-morphologically sensitive dictionary. Gains to text coverage by adding more frequent words to such a system would result in dramatic gains to coverage. Thus, one does not need a high quality morphology or a high quality lexicon to gain the benefits that come from connecting these two things.

5.4 FSTs for Vacillating Norms

Several literary languages have vacillating norms, for one reason or another. The reason may be purely technical, as is the case for Romanian, where the Turkic ş (s with cedilla) is used more often than the correct Romanian ș (s with comma below); or when users of minority languages in Russia use Latin letters instead of modified Cyrillic ones. Writers may also lack access to keyboard layouts for their language, as demonstrated with North Saami above, or alternatively writers may just write without need or attention to detail.

In cases where there are several dialects competing for the status of being the written standard, or where the standard is new or otherwise not yet firmly rooted in the language community, the variation within written text may be considerable. To the extent that one may predict the variation, it is a trivial matter to use an FST to reduce the varying forms to a common lemma, thus increasing the coverage of a dictionary drastically.

6 Conclusion

The present article has focused upon the role that FSTs may play in coping with linguistic variation of one type or another with the goal of building reading comprehension dictionaries. Written language occurs in many varieties and in many contexts, and FSTs provide dictionaries that are flexible enough to cope with this variation, while at the same time maintaining the integrity of the dictionary itself. This article gave one example using a North Saami Facebook corpus, but many other settings may be envisaged, and coped with in a similar way.

Here, we presented bilingual dictionaries combined with finite-state transducers for morphology-rich languages. In our evaluation, we compared our existing wordform dictionaries with this finite-state solution, and found that use of an FST improves the coverage of the dictionary tremendously, from 57.8 % to 83.3 % for North Saami, and from 41.4 % to 69.6 % for South Saami.

In addition, there are other ways of analysing the linguistic inputs. For instance, words do not occur in isolation, but in sentences, so with morphological analysis as a starting point, one might also disambiguate the word grammatically, syntactically, and lexically, in order to pick a verbal reading rather than a nominal one, and to give word-sense disambiguation based upon context. These perspectives are left to future research, but it is also worth note that given the availability of FSTs in many other highly inflected languages, these possibilities are also available for many more languages than just those presented here.

Running the dictionary on a server is also a far better user experience to providing users with a dictionary to install on their computers, and has the added benefit of providing a mobile-friendly dictionary for users on the go. The implementation has also resulted in a means for reading running texts on any website without having to look away from the text itself, with a high success rate for text coverage. Together, these solutions strike down one of the larger barriers to text comprehension for language learners, who will no longer need to spend their time looking up words in dictionaries, and can instead use it for reading more texts.

Acknowledgments

Our thanks go to Norway Open Universities for funding the project "Interactive Saami Instruction on the Internet", which this work is a part of, to Berit Merete N. Eskonsipo and Inger Ellen Márjá Eira for working on the North Saami dictionary content, and to our other collegues at Giellatekno, Divvun and Aajege for participating in the project as a whole.

References

Antonsen, L. (2013). Čállinmeattáhusaid guorran. [English summary: Tracking misspellings.]. University of Tromsø.

Antonsen, L. and Trosterud, T. (2010). Manne dihtor galgá máhttit grammatihka? [English summary: Why the computer should know its Sami grammar.]. *Sámi dieđalaš áigečála*, 1:3–28.

Antonsen, L., Trosterud, T., Gerstenberger, C.-V., and Moshagen, S. N. (2009). Ei intelligent ordbok for samisk. *LexicoNordica*, 16:271–283.

Beesley, K. R. and Karttunen, L. (2003). *Finite State Morphology*. CSLI publications in Computational Linguistics, USA.

Facebook-group (2012). Discussions in NSR – a Norwegian Saami Organisation's facebook group. `https://www.facebook.com/groups/norskesamersriksforbund/?fref=ts`. [last visited on 25/01/2013].

Koskenniemi, K. (1983). *Two-level morphology : a general computational model for word-form recognition and production*. Helsingin yliopisto, Helsinki.

Larsson, L.-G. (1997). Prästen och ordet. Ur den samiska lexikografins historia. *LexicoNordica*, 4:101–117.

Lindén, K., Silfverberg, M., and Pirinen, T. (2009). HFST tools for morphology – An Efficient Open-Source Package for Construction of Morphological Analyzers. In *Proceedings of the Workshop on Systems and Frameworks for Computational Morphology*, Zürich, Switzerland.

Magga, O. H. (2012). Lexicography and indigenous languages. In Fjeld, R. V. and Torjusen, J. M., editors, *Proceedings of the 15th EURALEX International Congress*, pages 3–18, Oslo, Norway. Department of Linguistics and Scandinavian Studies, University of Oslo.

Maxwell, M. and Poser, W. (2004). Morphological interfaces to dictionaries. In Zock, M., editor, *COLING 2004 Enhancing and using electronic dictionaries*, pages 65–68, Geneva, Switzerland. COLING.

Moshagen, S., Sammallahti, P., and Trosterud, T. (2004). Twol at work. In Arppe, A., Carlson, L., Lindén, K., Piitulainen, J., Suominen, M., Vainio, M., Westerlund, H., and Yli-Jyrä, A., editors, *Inquiries into Words, Constraints and Contexts*, pages 94–105, Stanford, CA. CSLI.

Trosterud, T. (2000). Kåven, Brita E. (red) 2000: Stor norsk-samisk ordbok [book review]. *LexicoNordica*, 8:283–306.

Trosterud, T. and Eskonsipo, B. N. (2012). A North Sami translator's mailing list seen as a key to minority language lexicography. In Fjeld, R. V. and Torjusen, J. M., editors, *Proceedings of the 15th EURALEX International Congress*, pages 250–256, Oslo, Norway. Department of Linguistics and Scandinavian Studies, University of Oslo.

Exploring Features for Named Entity Recognition in Lithuanian Text Corpus

Jurgita Kapočiūtė-Dzikienė[1], Anders Nøklestad[2],

Janne Bondi Johannessen[2], Algis Krupavičius[1]

(1) KAUNAS UNIVERSITY OF TECHNOLOGY, K. Donelaičio 73, LT-44249, Kaunas, Lithuania
(2) UNIVERSITY OF OSLO, P.O. Box 1102, Blindern, N-0317 Oslo, Norway

Jurgita.Kapociute-Dzikiene@ktu.lt, Anders.Noklestad@iln.uio.no,
J.B.Johannessen@iln.uio.no, pvai@ktu.lt

ABSTRACT

Despite the existence of effective methods that solve named entity recognition tasks for such widely used languages as English, there is no clear answer which methods are the most suitable for languages that are substantially different. In this paper we attempt to solve a named entity recognition task for Lithuanian, using a supervised machine learning approach and exploring different sets of features in terms of orthographic and grammatical information, different windows, etc. Although the performance is significantly higher when language dependent features based on gazetteer lookup and automatic grammatical tools (part-of-speech tagger, lemmatizer or stemmer) are taken into account; we demonstrate that the performance does not degrade when features based on grammatical tools are replaced with affix information only. The best results (micro-averaged F-score=0.895) were obtained using all available features, but the results decreased by only 0.002 when features based on grammatical tools were omitted.

KEYWORDS: Named entity recognition and classification, supervised machine learning, Lithuanian.

1   Introduction

The objective of Named Entity Recognition (NER) is to allocate and classify tokens in texts into predefined categories, such as person names, location names, organizations, etc. NER is a subtask of many natural language processing applications, i.e. in information extraction, machine translation, question answering, etc.

The methods used to solve NER task fall into three main categories: hand-crafted, machine learning and hybrid. Hand-crafted approaches are based on an analysis of the application domain and the manual construction of gazetteers and sets of patterns capable of taking named entity recognition and classification decisions. Hand-crafted methods assure high accuracy, but at the same time they have low portability to new domains: i.e. changing domains require expert intervention and manual re-creation of rules. Thus, very often machine learning methods are selected instead of the rule-based ones. For machine learning approaches NER is usually interpreted as classification task, where tokens are classified into categories with non-named and different named entity types. Rules (defined as the model) by these methods are built automatically after observation and generalization over the characteristics extracted from the text. Supervised machine learning methods for model creation use texts prepared by the domain experts with manually assigned classes (identifying particular named entity type or not a named entity) to all tokens. Semi-supervised machine learning methods for NER are usually based on a bootstrapping learning scheme: an initial small set of tokens with predefined categories (types of named entities) is used as the seed to build initial model, then all tokens in the texts are classified using that seed model and the most confident classifications (recognized named entities) are added to the training data and the process is iterated. Supervised machine learning methods outperform semi-supervised methods in terms of accuracy, but the strongest point of semi-supervised methods is that they do not require large annotated corpora. Hybrid methods usually combine the strongest points of both hand-crafted and machine learning methods.

In this paper we are solving the named entity recognition task using a supervised machine learning technique. Our focus is to find the most informative features for the Standard Lithuanian language yielding the best named entity classification results for person, location and organization names. Our experiments include different sets of language independent and dependent features based on orthographic and grammatical information, different windows (tokens before and after a current one), etc. We also assess whether it is possible to perform named entity classification effectively without resorting to external grammatical tools such as part-of-speech taggers, lemmatizers or stemmers, because they have limited availability, and are slow and unreliable when identifying proper names in Lithuanian texts.

Section 2 contains an overview of related work. In Section 3, we describe the Lithuanian language and its properties. We outline the methodology of our named entity classification experiments in Section 4 and present the results in Section 5. We discuss these results in Section 6 and conclude in Section 7.

2   Related work

The NER research for English started in early 1990s and this task was successfully solved (for a review see Nadeu & Sekine, 2007), because NER achieved human annotation performance (Sundheim, 1995) in terms of accuracy. Thus current works for English mostly focus on the improvement of other important metrics, e.g. speed: i.e. Al-Rfou' & Skiena (2012) demonstrated that the speed of a NER tagger can be increased after improvement of tokenizer and part-of-speech tagger that are used as the sub-modules in NER pipeline.

The reason why methods achieve very high accuracy on English texts is because they are based on rich external resources (such as wide range of annotated corpora and gazetteers, accurate part-of-speech taggers, etc.) that are not always available for the other languages. Besides, the English language is not as complex as highly inflective, morphologically rich and ambiguous languages; moreover it does not suffer from lack of capitalization problems for proper nouns. Thus, it can be concluded that NER task for each language requires its detailed analysis and adaptation.

However, some generalizations can be made, e.g. language dependent features (based on gazetteers or morphological information) always increase NER accuracy; morphological information is inevitable for morphologically rich languages in order for the NER method to be comparable to the state-of-the-art methods for English. The importance of accurate morphological analyzers in NER task was revealed by Hasan et al. (2009): NER results for Bengali were significantly improved by simple refining non-accurate part-of-speech tagger (the part-of-speech tagger was improved during extraction of information from Wikipedia that in turn improved recognizer). Morphological information in NER methods can be either incorporated into rules or used as features (part-of-speech tags, lemmas). Examples of such methods are: rule-based methods for Arabic (Elsebai et al., 2009), Danish and Norwegian (Johannessen et al., 2005), Russian (Popov et al., 2004), and Urdu (Singh et al., 2012); supervised machine learning methods for Bulgarian (Georgiev et al., 2009), Dutch (Desmet & Hoste, 2010), Norwegian (Haaland, 2008; Nøklestad, 2009), and Polish (Marcinczuk et al., 2011; Marcinczuk & Janicki, 2012); hybrid method for Arabic (Mai & Khaled, 2012). Hasan et al. (2009) also proved that affixes are very important in solving NER task for morphologically rich languages. Affixes helped to increase NER results for Bengali, Bulgarian, Polish, etc.

NER task for Lithuanian was previously solved using two different methods: rule-based (for person and location names, abbreviations, date and time) (Kapočiūtė & Raškinis, 2005) and semi-supervised machine learning (bootstrapping) (for person, location and organization names, product, date, time and money) (Pinnis, 2012). Unfortunately, we cannot give any examples of experiments based on supervised machine learning techniques for NER. Consequently, this paper will be the first attempt at finding an accurate supervised machine learning method (in terms of the most informative features) for NER in Lithuanian texts.

3   Lithuanian language challenges

Of all living Indo-European languages, Lithuanian has the richest inflectional morphology, making it more complex than even Latvian or Slavic languages (Savickienė et al., 2009). Lithuanian nominal words (nouns or adjectives that are used as person, location or organization names) can be inflected by 7 cases, 2 genders, and 2 numbers. Various inflection forms are expressed by different endings. Person names can have either masculine or feminine gender and are inflected by case and number. To exemplify: the possible inflection forms of masculine person name *Jonas* (John) are: *Jonas* (singular nominative), *Jono* (singular genitive), *Jonui* (singular dative), *Joną* (singular accusative), *Jonu* (singular ablative), *Jone* (singular locative), *Jonai* (singular and plural vocative; plural nominative), *Jonų* (plural genitive), *Jonams* (plural dative), *Jonus* (plural accusative), *Jonais* (plural ablative), *Jonuose* (plural locative). The location names or organizations can have either masculine or feminine gender and singular or plural number, and are inflected by case. E.g. *Lietuva* (Lithuania) is singular feminine noun; *Aukštieji Tatrai* (High Tatres) is composed of plural masculine adjective *Aukštieji* (High) and plural masculine noun *Tatrai* (Tatres), where all words are inflected only by 7 cases. In the Lithuanian language there are 12 inflection paradigms for nouns, and 9 inflection paradigms for adjectives.

The same inflection rules are used to inflect foreign person names in Standard Lithuanian texts. Endings can either be directly attached to the end of the noun e.g. *Tonis Blairas* (Tony Blair) or can be added after an apostrophe e.g. *Tony'is Blair'as* (Tony Blair).

In Lithuanian, male and female surnames are different; moreover, in the surnames of married and unmarried women the suffixes are also different. For example, given the male surname *Karalius*, the appropriate female surname of an unmarried woman is *Karaliūtė*, and of a married woman – *Karalienė*. Besides, women can have surnames that do not reveal their marital status, e.g. *Karalė*, or keep both surnames – typically written with a hyphen, e.g. *Petraitytė-Karalienė* or *Petraitytė-Karalė*.

In Lithuanian organization names only the first word is capitalized in organization names (the other words are capitalized only if they happen to be a person or location name). E.g. *Lietuvos mokslo taryba* (Research Council of Lithuania), *Kauno Maironio gimnazija* (Kaunas Maironis Gymnasium) *Maironio* is a person name that is capitalized. The names of the companies in Lithuanian texts are written in quotation-marks. Despite the fact that the words in organization names are written in lower case (starting from the second word); acronyms are written in upper case, e.g. the acronym for *Kauno technologijos universitetas* (Kaunas University of Technology) is abbreviated to *KTU*.

Lithuanian is a synthetic language; and the word order in the sentence is absolutely free. As in ancient Indo-European languages, in Lithuanian the word order does not perform a grammatical, but a notional, function: i.e., the same sentence will be grammatically correct regardless of word order, but the meaning (things that have to be highlighted) will be a bit different. Thus, any named entity can appear in any place of the sentence. Despite this, the words that act as triggers (words that directly signal a named entity) or modifiers (words that limit or qualify the sense of named entity) are located close to the named entity they describe. E.g. in *dr. Jonas Basanavičius* (dr. Jonas Basanavičius) *dr.* is the trigger that identifies the following word as the person name; in *gyventi Lietuvoje* or *Lietuvoje gyventi* (to live in Lithuania) *gyventi* (to live in) is the modifier that qualifies the named entity *Lietuvoje* as a location name.

47% of Lithuanian words or word forms are ambiguous (Zinkevičius et al., 2005); named entities are no exception. Ambiguities are often between common nouns/adjectives written at the beginning of a sentence and person/location/organization names, e.g. *Raudonoji* (Red) can be either a common word in *Raudonoji arbata* (Red tea) or a location name in *Raudonoji jūra* (Red sea); *Rūta* can be either the name of the person or the common word "rue". Ambiguities can also emerge between person names and location names, e.g. *Roma* is the name of the person or location name "Rome"). Depending on the meaning, named entities can change their type, e.g. *Maironis* is a person name, but in *Maironio gatvė* (Maironis street) the word is treated as a location; *Vilnius* is a location name, but in *Vilniaus universitetas* (Vilnius University) it is treated as part of an organization name. This analysis reflects what is called "Function over Form" in Johannessen et al. (2005).

4　Methodology

4.1　Feature extraction

Supervised machine learning systems cannot be directly trained on a corpus annotated with named entities. The corpus has to be transformed into a collection of instances. Usually instances are generated for consecutive tokens excluding punctuation marks (e.g. from string *J. Petraitytė-Karalienė* would be generated three instances "J", "Petraitytė", and "Karalienė"), sometimes punctuation marks are stored as part of tokens (e.g. from string *J. Petraitytė-Karalienė* would be generated: "J.", "Petraitytė-", and "Karalienė"). Since punctuation marks carry a lot of information about named entities in Lithuanian language and their loss would be harmful (e.g. when recognizing classified named entities in plain text) in our experiments we treat punctuation marks as tokens, too – i.e. as separate instances (thus, e.g. from string *J. Petraitytė-Karalienė* would be generated five instances: "J", ".", "Petraitytė", "-", and "Karalienė"). During such transformation the order of tokens and punctuation marks in the collection is not changed.

All instances that are used in the classification process are represented as vectors, each composed of the class label (identifying none or a particular type of named entity) and the list of features (where the first one describes original token – "J", "Petraitytė", "Karalė" or punctuation mark – ".", "-"). Considering Lithuanian language properties and available resources, we have made the list of features that should be effective in solving named entity classification task. All features can be grouped into two main categories: language independent and language dependent. Language independent features are very general, based only on the orthographic information directly available in the corpus; language dependent features resort to external resources such as special purpose grammatical tools (part-of-speech tagger, lemmatizer, stemmer) or gazetteers (gazetteer of person names, gazetteer of location names).

Below we present a list of all the features that were used in our experiments.

Language independent (basic and orthographic) features:

- t – the original token or punctuation mark.
- *Lowercase* (t) – t in lower case letters (e.g. *Lowercase* (*Lietuva*) = *lietuva*). The usage of this feature decreases the number of tokens that can be treated differently because of case sensitivity (especially relevant for common words at the beginning of the sentence).
- *IsFirstUpper*(t) – Boolean indicator that determines if the first character of t is capitalized (e.g. *IsFirstUpper*(*Lietuva*) = *true*).
- *Acronym*(t) – Boolean indicator that determines if all characters in t are capitalized (e.g. *Acronym*(*KTU*) = *true*). This feature should help to identify organizations abbreviated as acronyms.
- *Number*(t) – Boolean indicator that determines if t is a number (e.g. *Number*(*Sk1*) = *false*).
- *Length* (t) – numeral indicator that determines the length of t.
- *Prefix-n*(t) – affix that determines the first n (in our experiments $3 \leq n \leq 5$) characters of t in lower case (e.g. *Prefix*-5(*Šiauliai*) = *šiaul*). This feature should help to extract stable parts of tokens and thus get rid of inflectional Lithuanian endings.
- *Suffix-n*(t) – affix that determines the last n (in our experiments $3 \leq n \leq 5$) characters of t in lower case (e.g. *Suffix*-5(*Šiauliuose*) = *iuose*; *Suffix*-5(*Šakiuose*) = *iuose*). This feature should help to extract inflectional Lithuanian endings. E.g. the roots in "Šiauliuose" and "Šakiuose" are different, but they share the same ending in locative case "iuose".

Language dependent features:

- *Lemma(t)* – the lemma of *t* (e.g. *Lemma(Lietuvoje)* = *Lietuva*). The lemmatizer transforms recognized words into their major form (by replacing appropriate endings, but not touching affixes); the common words also are transformed into lower-case letters.
- *POS(t)* – the part-of-speech tag of *t* (e.g. *POS(Lietuvoje)* = *noun*).
- *Stem(t)* – the stem of *t* (e.g. *Stem(Lietuvoje)* = *Lietuv*). The stemmer eliminates inflectional ending (and some other suffixes) of the input word.
- *IsPERGaz(t)* – A Boolean indicator that determines if *t* is in the gazetteer of person names.
- *IsLOCGaz(t)* – A string indicator that determines if *t* is in the gazetteer of location names, and if so, then if it is the beginning or any other word in the location name (e.g. for *gyvenu Didžiojoje Britanijoje* (I live in Great Britain), *IsLOCGaz(gyvenu)* = *no*; *IsLOCGaz(Didžiojoje)* = *yesB*; *IsLOCGaz(Britanijoje)* = *yesI*).

Class labels:

The corpus contains three types of named entities for person names, location names and organizations. Class labels are represented in BIO notation, thus B-PER, B-LOC, B-ORG indicate the first token in person, location, organization named entity, respectively; I-PER, I-LOC, I-ORG indicate any other token (except the first one) in person, location, organization named entity, respectively; O indicates any other token (not in named entities).

4.2   Dataset

All the texts for the NER task were taken from the Vytautas Magnus University corpus (Marcinkevičienė, 2000). We aimed to avoid domain adaptation problem, thus texts were taken from several domains (as it was done by Kitoogo et al. (2008)). The created dataset in total contained ~ 0.5 million running words and was composed from the texts representing Standard Lithuanian and taken from 5 different domains: popular periodic, local newspapers, republican newspapers, parliamentary transcripts and legislative texts (the distribution of running words over different domains is presented in FIGURE 1).

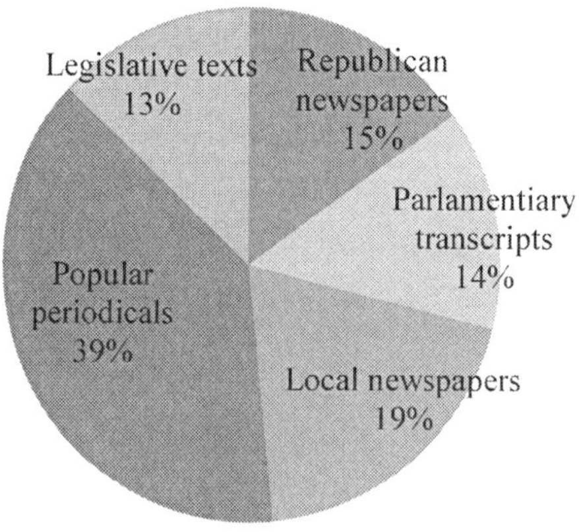

FIGURE 1 – The distribution of words (used in our NER experiments) over 5 different domains.

All texts used in our named entity classification experiments were manually annotated with person, location and organization names (the distribution of words into named entities over different domains is presented in FIGURE 2.). Named entities were annotated considering "Function over Form" annotation manner, thus the same named entity could be tagged differently in different context, e.g. in *Maironis skaito savo poeziją* (Maironis reads his poetry) *Maironis* is annotated as person name; in *gyvenu Maironio gatvėje* (live in Maironis street) *Maironio* is annotated as location name; in *Skaitau knygą "Apie Maironį"* (I read the book "About Maironis") *Maironį* is not annotated as named entity because it is neither person, nor location, nor organization name, but it is the title of the book. Besides, inner named entities were not annotated. E.g. in *Vilniaus universitetas* (Vilnius University) inner location name *Vilniaus* was ignored; instead of it both words were annotated as single organization name.

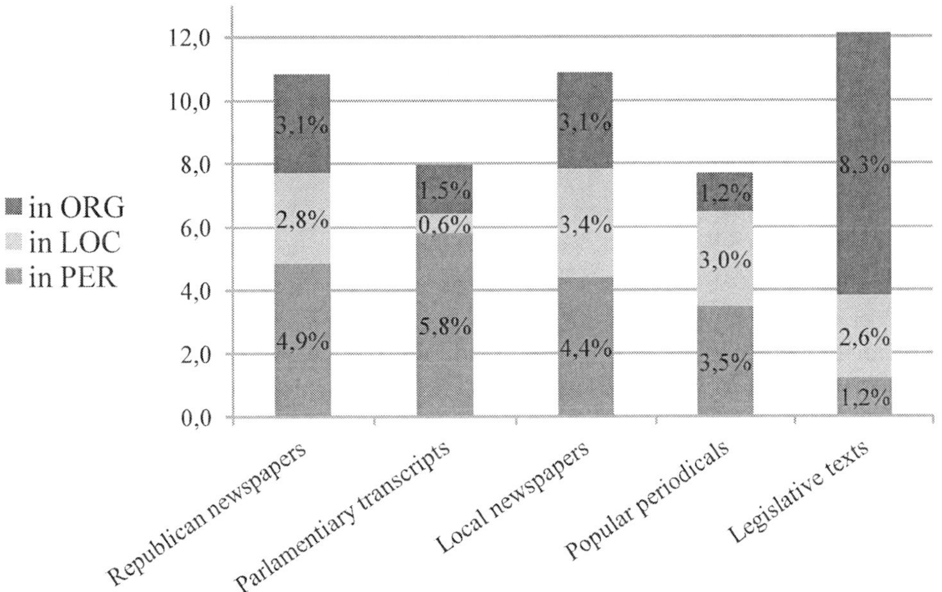

FIGURE 2 – The distribution of words into named entities (person names – *in PER*, location names – *in LOC*, organization names – *in ORG*) over 5 different domains.

Annotated texts were transformed into collection of instances. Statistics about number of instances (tokens/punctuation marks) belonging to their appropriate classes is presented in TABLE 1.

Class label	Number of instances
B-PER	10902
I-PER	13861
B-LOC	12152
I-LOC	1322
B-ORG	5937
I-ORG	10482
All NEs	54656
O	577771
Total	632427

TABLE 1 – Number of instances for all classes in the dataset used in our NER experiments.

4.3   Formal description of the task

The mathematical formulation of the named entity classification task we are attempting to solve is given below.

Let D be our dataset containing instances I, where $\forall I \in D$.

Let C be a finite set of classes: $C = \{c_1, c_2, \ldots, c_N\}$. In our case $2 < N << \infty$ – i.e. we have a multi-class classification problem, because $C = \{$B-PER, I-PER, B-LOC, I-LOC, B-ORG, I-ORG, O$\}$ and $N=7$.

Let I be the instance described by feature vector v with the appropriate class label c, thus all instances in the dataset are represented as $I=\langle v, c\rangle$. We do not consider inner named entities; therefore our dataset contains single-labeled instances only: i.e. any instance cannot be attached to more than one class c.

Let function γ be a classification function mapping instances to classes, $\gamma : I \rightarrow C$. Function γ determines how I was labeled with c. In our dataset annotation of named entities was performed by the domain expert.

Let Γ denote a supervised learning method which given D as the input, could return a learned classification function γ' (defined as a model) as the output: $\Gamma(D) \rightarrow \gamma'$.

4.4   Experimental setup

In order to find the most informative features for the NER task on Lithuanian texts, we performed experiments based on:

- Different windows $[t_{x-m}, t_{x+m}]$. E.g. window $[t_{x=0}]$ contains only one element – current instance $t_{x=0}$; window $[t_{x-1}, t_{x=0}]$ contains current instance $t_{x=0}$ and instance t_{x-1} that is before $t_{x=0}$; window $[t_{x=0}, t_{x+1}]$ contains current instance $t_{x=0}$ and instance t_{x+1} that is after $t_{x=0}$, etc. We restricted m to 3 and thus experimented with 12 different windows in total.
- 9 different sets of features (see TABLE 2). The sets of features No. 1 and No. 5 contain only language independent features; all other sets of features contain both language independent and language dependent features.
  Sets No. 2 and No. 6 – No. 9 also contain gazetteer lookup features. These feature values were generated considering information stored in the gazetteers. To avoid redundancy when storing named entities in all their inflectional forms as separate instances, distinct named entities were represented by stem and their appropriate inflectional paradigm identifier. Thus, the gazetteer of person names consists of ~7 thousand individual person names (e.g. *Jon:*1 retains named entity in all its inflectional forms: *Jonas, Jono, Jonui,* etc.); the gazetteer of location names consists of ~2.2 thousand location names: individual (the same as for person names) or compound (e.g. *Didži:*2 *Britanij:* 3 retains this named entity in all its inflectional forms: *Didžioji Britanija, Didžiosios Britanijos, Didžiajai Britanijai,* etc.).
  Sets No. 3, No. 6, and No. 9 also contain part-of-speech tags and lemmas as features. The tokens were part-of-speech tagged and lemmatized using the dictionary-based morphological analyzer-lemmatizer "Lemuoklis" (Zinkevičius, 2000; Daudaravičius et al., 2007). "Lemuoklis" also solves morphological disambiguation problems and achieves ~95% accuracy on standard texts. Despite "Lemuoklis" being very accurate on common words; its weakness is unknown proper names (Zinkevičius et al., 2005). In our experiments "Lemuoklis" was unable to recognize 30.6% of the words as either named entities or common words, and classified them as "unknown"; it recognized only 34.4% of words as proper names, the rest 35% words it recognized as common words (for the detailed statistics see FIGURE 3).

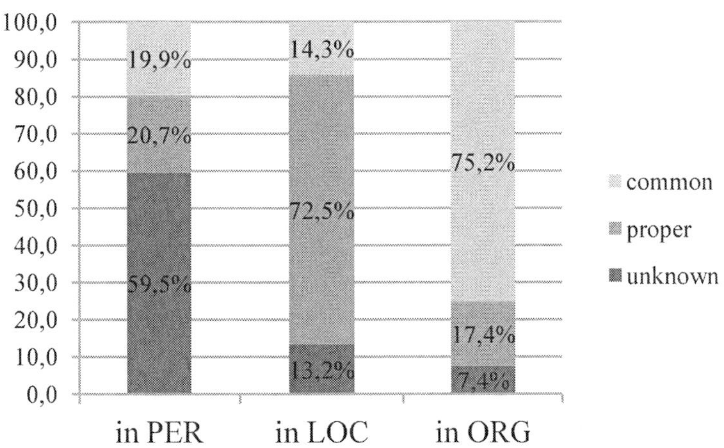

FIGURE 3 – The percentage distribution of words in named entities (person names – *in PER*, location names – *in LOC*, organization names – *in ORG*) that were recognized by "Lemuoklis" as proper names (*proper*), common words (*common*) or not recognized at all (*unknown*).

| | | **Feature sets** | | | | | | | |
		No.1	*No.2*	*No.3*	*No.4*	*No.5*	*No.6*	*No.7*	*No.8*	*No.9*
Features	*t*	×	×	×	×	×	×	×	×	×
	Lowercase(t)	×	×	×	×	×	×	×	×	×
	IsFirstUpper(t)	×	×	×	×	×	×	×	×	×
	Acronym(t)	×	×	×	×	×	×	×	×	×
	Number(t)	×	×	×	×	×	×	×	×	×
	Length(t)	×	×	×	×	×	×	×	×	×
	Prefix-3-5(t)					×			×	×
	Suffix-3-5(t)					×			×	×
	Lemma(t)			×			×			×
	POS(t)			×			×			×
	Stem(t)				×			×		×
	IsPERGaz(t)		×				×	×	×	×
	IsLOCGaz(t)		×				×	×	×	×

TABLE 2 – Different sets of features used in our NER experiments.

Sets No. 4, No. 7, and No. 9 also contain stems of tokens as features. The tokens were stemmed using a Lithuanian stemmer (Krilavičius & Medelis, 2010) based on the Porter stemming algorithm (Willet, 2006). The Lithuanian stemmer eliminates all endings and also some suffixes (but do not touch prefixes). The stemmer is rule-based, thus it can cope with proper names as well as with the other words. But in some cases stemming can cause the loss of meaning and ambiguity, e.g. *Lietuva* (Lithuania), *Lietuvis* (Lithuanian) will both be stemmed to the same *Lietuv*.

Sets No. 5, No. 8, and No. 9 contain affix features: the first and the last 3, 4 and 5 characters of each token.

As previously described, in our experiments we used 9 sets of features and 12 windows, that is 9×12=108 different experiments in total.

Before the experiments we made two hypotheses.

Our first hypothesis is that language dependent features (morphological and gazetteer lookup) should increase the accuracy of NER on Lithuanian texts (the same as for Bengali ((Hasan et al., 2009), Polish (Marcinczuk & Janicki, 2012), and other languages). We expect that gazetteers should solve the disambiguation problems between named entities and not named entities or between different types of named entities; and grammatical tools (part-of-speech tagger/lemmatizer and stemmer) will cope with the inflections of the Lithuanian language (that in turn should reduce the sparseness of feature space and should lead to the construction of more reliable model).

The grammatical tools seem necessary due to the importance of inflection in Lithuanian, but they are unreliable when identifying proper names (Zinkevičius et al., 2005). Therefore, our second hypothesis is that the stable parts of the words and the influence of inflection can be captured in a different way – i.e. by affix information. We expect that with affix features (*Prefix*-3-5(t) and *Suffix*-3-5(t)), the NER method will achieve similar accuracy as with features based on part-of-speech information, lemmas or stems.

4.5   Classification

Our attempt was to find a method Γ which could create the model γ' the best approximating γ. Since a NER task using supervised machine learning approach has never been undertaken for Lithuanian, we had no knowledge which method is the most appropriate. Therefore we selected Conditional Random Fields (CRFs) method (a detailed description of CRFs is presented in Lafferty et al., 2001) as Γ, because it is one of the popular techniques utilized for the NER task (Nadeau & Sekine, 2007) outperforming many other popular methods, such as Hidden Markov Models (HMMs), Maximum Entropy Markov Models (MEMMs), and etc.

The implementation of CRFs we used in our experiments is CRF++ version 0.57[1], which requires a template file (with the determined features that are considered) and datasets for training and testing.

5   Results

All results reported below are based on 10 fold cross-validation (the biggest class O for non-named entities is treated as the negative class in all calculations).

The experiments with different windows revealed that the best results are obtained with window $[t_{x-2}; t_{x+1}]$, except for the feature sets No. 2 and No. 3, where the best results were obtained with $[t_{x-1}; t_{x+1}]$. Despite that, the improvement on micro-averaged F-scores was less than 0.0006. FIGURE 4 reports the results obtained using different windows with the feature set No. 1.

We experimented with different n values of *Prefix*-n(t) and *Suffix*-n(t) also, but the best results were reported with $3 \leq n \leq 5$: with feature set No. 5 micro-averaged F-score using n=3 was 0.8556, with $3 \leq n \leq 4$ – 0.8614, the peak 0.8645 was with $3 \leq n \leq 5$, the higher n values degraded the results. Besides, using only *Prefix*-3-5(t) or only *Suffix*-3-5(t) was not effective also: e.g. with the feature set No. 5 micro-averaged F-score when using only *Prefix*-3-5(t) was 0.8549, when using only *Suffix*-3-5(t) – 0.8517, when using both – 0.8645.

---

[1] http://crfpp.sourceforge.net

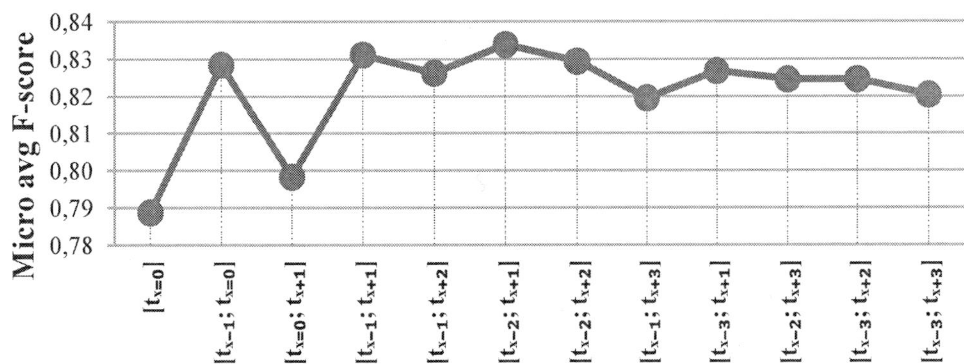

FIGURE 4 – Micro-averaged F-scores obtained with different windows when feature set No. 1.

The results obtained using window $[t_{x\text{-}2}; t_{x+1}]$ and $3 \leq n \leq 5$ for all 9 feature sets are reported in TABLE 3.

		Precision		Recall		F-score	
		micro avg	*macro avg*	*micro avg*	*macro avg*	*micro avg*	*macro avg*
	No.1	0.8655	0.8648	0.8043	0.8061	0.8338	0.8342
	No.2	0.9159	0.9174	0.8587	0.8643	0.8864	0.8897
	No.3	0.8738	0.8745	0.8353	0.8380	0.8541	0.8556
	No.4	0.8748	0.8744	0.8122	0.8141	0.8424	0.8429
Feature sets	*No.5*	0.8933	0.8923	0.8375	0.8391	0.8645	0.8647
	No.6	0.9141	0.9169	0.8732	0.8785	0.8932	0.8970
	No.7	*0.9177*	*0.9195*	0.8636	0.8691	0.8899	0.8933
	No.8	0.9168	0.9176	0.8708	0.8754	0.8932	0.8957
	No.9	0.9140	0.9161	*0.8773*	*0.8817*	*0.8953*	*0.8984*

TABLE 3 – Micro/macro averaged precision/recall/f-scores for all sets of features with window $[t_{x\text{-}2}; t_{x+1}]$ and $3 \leq n \leq 5$.

To determine whether the performances of the classifier trained on different feature sets were significantly different from each other, we performed approximate randomization testing (Yeh, 2000). In all approximate randomization testing experiments we used 1000 shuffles.

The differences between many experiments are statistically significant to a very high degree ($p = 0.00099$) with some exceptions, presented in FIGURE 5: i.e. differences are statistically significant to a high degree when $0.00099 < p \leq 0.01$; statistically significant when $0.01 < p \leq 0.05$; and not significant when $p > 0.05$.

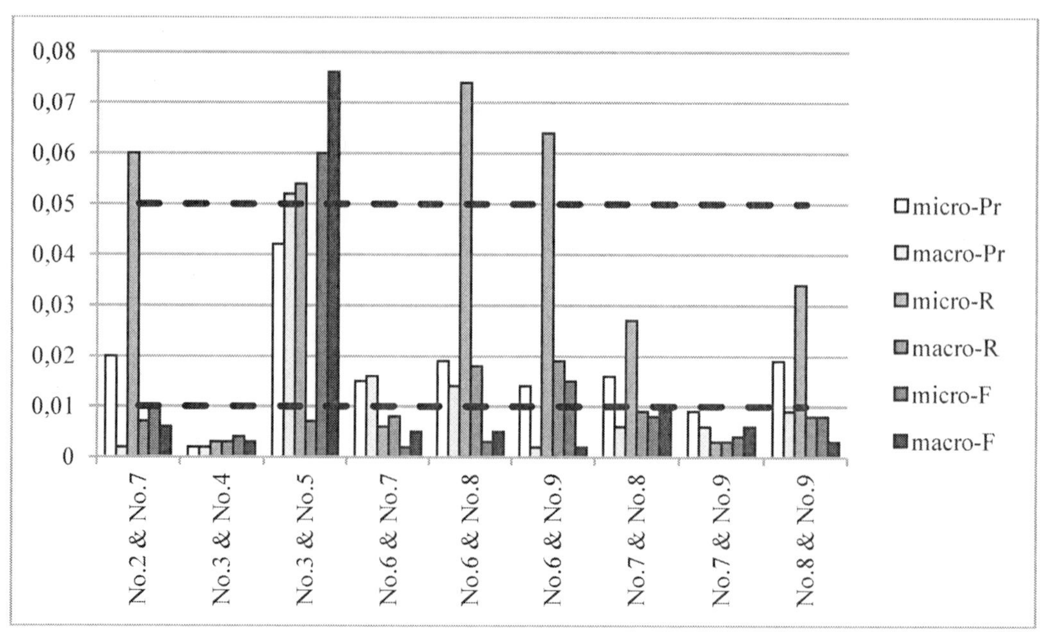

FIGURE 5 – *p* scores indicating statistical differences between the results (micro/macro precision (Pr)/recall (R)/F-score (F)) obtained on different feature sets.

6   Discussion

A glance at TABLE 3 in Section 5 shows that our first hypothesis is confirmed: language independent features are easily beaten with language dependent features. These findings agree with the findings obtained for other languages: Bengali (Hasan et al., 2009), Bulgarian (Georgiev et al., 2009), etc.

As it is presented in TABLE 3, the usage of gazetteer lookup features in No. 2 increased the results of No. 1 by 0.0526 in micro-averaged F-score, despite the fact that a gazetteer of organization names is not available for Lithuanian (only of person and location names). The features obtained using grammatical tools also increased NER results (compared with No. 1 which is based on orthographic information only): the increment in micro-averaged F-score using part-of-speech tagger/lemmatizer in No. 3 is 0.0203; whereas stemmer in No. 4 caused only a small boost in performance – increment in micro-average F-score is only 0.0086. The lemmatizer and stemmer cope with inflectional endings of Lithuanian language by reducing the number of distinct tokens. Thus a reduced number of feature values leads to the construction of more reliable and, as it can be concluded from the results, to more accurate models. The reason why part-of-speech tagging/lemmatization improves performance over stemming is that the part-of-speech tagger/lemmatizer is more accurate compared with stemmer, besides it preserves inflectional information that is important in Lithuanian language (the ending is not lost during lemmatization, only changed into the major form). The results obtained in No. 3 (with the part-of-speech tagger/lemmatizer) are worse than in No. 2 (with the gazetteer lookup), because the part-of-speech tagger/lemmatizer is not robust in recognizing proper names, as well as not being capable of determining types of named entities.

Experiments with gazetteer lookup + part-of-speech tagging/lemmatizing in No. 6, or gazetteer lookup + stemming in No. 7, yielded even better results compared with the results when they were used separately (as in No. 2, No. 3, No. 4). Despite the result in No. 6 exceeded No. 7 by 0.0033 in micro-average F-score, the difference was proved to be statistically significant.

More interestingly, the results also support our second hypothesis: grammatical tools (part-of-speech tagger/lemmatizer and stemmer) can be replaced with affix information. The same effect can be achieved by automatically slicing n characters from the beginning and the end of the token as it is done with *Prefix*-3-5(t) and *Suffix*-3-5(t). Experiments with *Prefix*-3-5(t) and *Suffix*-3-5(t) in No. 5 outperformed No. 4 (with stemming) by 0.0221 in micro-average F-score (the difference was proved to be statistically significant to a very high degree for all measures). No. 5 yielded similar results as No. 3 (with part-of-speech taggering/lemmatization): despite the increment in No. 5 was by 0.0102 in micro-average F-score, but the difference was proved to be statistically significant in terms of micro-precision and macro-recall only and not statistically significant for all the other measures.

Experiments with gazetteer lookup + affixes as it is in No. 8 yielded even better results compared with the results obtained separately (as in No. 2, No. 5) (all differences were proved to be statistically significant to a very high degree), besides No. 8 outperformed gazetteer lookup + stemming in No. 7 (the differences were proved to be statistically significant) and No. 8 yielded the same micro-average F-score as with gazetteer lookup + part-of-speech tagging/lemmatization in No. 6 (the differences were proved to be statistically significant for all measures, except for micro-recall). The best results were obtained using all available features in No. 9. Despite that the difference between sets of features No. 8 and No. 9 was proved to be statistically significant, the increment is only by 0.0021 in micro-averaged F-score.

The observations obtained from the experiments allow us to conclude that simple automatic prefix and suffix information capture enough of the Lithuanian language inflection information; therefore it can replace features generated by part-of-speech taggers, lemmatizers, and stemmers. It is indeed very good news, because the Lithuanian part-of-speech tagger/lemmatizer has limited availability, is not very convenient and slow to use; the Lithuanian stemmer is low in accuracy.

If we take a close look at the confusion matrix (see TABLE 4) obtained with feature set No. 9 and window $[t_{x-2}; t_{x+1}]$, we would notice the main errors made by named entity classifier. Below we discuss main named entity classification error types (summarized by Nadeu & Sekine, 2007).

		Predicted class						
		B-PER	*I-PER*	*B-LOC*	*I-LOC*	*B-ORG*	*I-ORG*	*O*
Actual class	*B-PER*	*8,719*	155	789	4	25	7	1,203
	I-PER	63	*13,354*	14	15	17	25	373
	B-LOC	263	169	*10,192*	23	234	36	1,235
	I-LOC	8	138	24	*939*	17	97	99
	B-ORG	82	31	557	6	*3,762*	157	1,342
	I-ORG	29	171	33	48	54	*6,674*	3,473
	O	449	709	547	47	475	1,551	*57,3993*

TABLE 4 – Confusion matrix obtained with the feature set No. 9 and window $[t_{x-2}; t_{x+1}]$.

The amount of correct predictions (see TABLE 4) is presented in diagonal where the actual class label is equal to predicted, thus from 632,427 instances, only 14,794 were predicted incorrectly: 3,788 times the classifier hypothesized as named entities where there was none; 7,725 times a named entity was completely missed by the classifier; 2,444 times classifier correctly recognized the boundary of named entity, but got the wrong type; 476 times the classifier recognized the type of named entity, but got its boundary wrong; 371 times the classifier recognized that it is a named entity, but got wrong type and boundary.

The major problem is the 25.54% of all errors where the classifier determined named entity where there was none and 52.22% of all errors where named entity was completely missed. These problems arose because of different ambiguities in Lithuanian texts between proper and common words: i.e. a lot of person and location names are ambiguous with common words (especially at the beginning of the sentence), but the major problem is ambiguity between organization names and common words (typically only the first word in an organization name is capitalized and all other words are written in lower-case), because in our experiments we could not use a gazetteer for organization names, because such gazetteer is not yet available.

The experiments with different windows revealed, that the best results for Lithuanian were obtained using a rather small window $[t_{x-2};\ t_{x+1}]$ (compared with the results obtained e.g. for Polish $[t_{x-2},\ t_{x+2}]$ (Marcinczuk & Janicki, 2012) or Turkish $-\ [t_{x-3},\ t_{x+3}]$ (Gokhan & Gulsen, 2012)): i.e. two instances before and one after the current. Thus, we can conclude, that even if the word order in the sentence in Lithuanian is free, the nearest information is more useful in NER process.

7 Conclusion and Outlook

In this paper we were solving NER task for Lithuanian language using supervised machine learning approach: i.e. we explored different sets of features in terms of orthographic and grammatical information, different windows, etc.

We have formulated and experimentally confirmed two hypotheses:

- The language dependent features (based on dictionaries, part-of-speech tagger, lemmatizer, and stemmer) increase the NER results, especially due to the importance of inflection information in Lithuanian language.
- The features based on external grammatical tools (part-of-speech tagger, lemmatizer, and stemmer) can be replaced with affixes that can capture relevant patterns intrinsically.

The best results were obtained using all available features and the window $[t_{x-2};\ t_{x+1}]$. The decrease of micro-average F-score was only 0.0021 when features generated by the grammatical tools were eliminated. This result should be promising for other resource-scarce languages with similar properties as Lithuanian.

In future research, it would be interesting to experiment with different named entity types and classification methods.

Acknowledgments

This research was funded by European Union Structural Funds project "Postdoctoral Fellowship Implementation in Lithuania" (No. VP1-3.1-ŠMM-01) and initiated when the first author was visiting the Department of Linguistics and Nordic Studies at the University of Oslo, Norway.

References

Al-Rfou', R. and Skiena, S. (2012). SpeedRead: A Fast Named Entity Recognition Pipeline. In *Proceedings of the 24th International Conference on Computational Linguistics* (*COLING 2012*), pages 51–66.

Daudaravičius, V., Rimkutė, E. and Utka, A. (2007). Morphological annotation of the Lithuanian corpus. In *Proceedings of the Workshop on Balto-Slavonic Natural Language Processing: Information Extraction and Enabling Technologies* (ACL'07), pages 94–99.

Desmet, B. and Hoste, V. (2010). Dutch named entity recognition using ensemble classifiers. In *Computational Linguistics in the Netherlands 2010: selected papers from the twentieth CLIN meeting* (*CLIN* 2010), pages 29–41.

Elsebai, A., Meziane, F. and Belkredim, F. Z. (2009). A Rule Based Persons Names Arabic Extraction System. In *Proceedings of the 11th International Conference on Innovation and Business Management* (*IBIMA*), pages 53–59.

Georgiev, G., Nakov, P., Ganchev, K., Osenova, P. and Simov, K. (2009). Feature-Rich Named Entity Recognition for Bulgarian Using Conditional Random Fields. In *Proceedings of the International Conference on Recent Advances in Natural Language Processing* (*RANLP-2009*), pages 113–117.

Gokhan, A. S. and Gulsen, E. (2012). Initial Explorations on using CRFs for Turkish Named Entity Recognition. In *Proceedings of the 24th International Conference on Computational Linguistics* (*COLING* 2012), pages 2459–2474.

Haaland, Å. (2008). *A Maximum Entropy Approach to Proper Name Classification for Norwegian.* PhD thesis, University of Oslo.

Hasan, K. S., Rahman, A., and Ng, V. (2009). Learning-based named entity recognition for morphologically-rich, resource-scarce languages. In *Proceedings of the 12th Conference of the European Chapter of the Association for Computational Linguistics*, pages 354–262.

Johannessen, J. B., Hagen, K., Haaland, Å., Nøklestad, A., Jónsdottir, A. B., Kokkinakis, D., Meurer, P., Bick, E. and Haltrup, D. (2005). Named Entity Recognition for the Mainland Scandinavian Languages. *Literary & Linguistic Computing*, 20(1): 91–102.

Kapočiūtė, J. and Raškinis, G. (2005). Rule-based annotation of Lithuanian text corpora. *Information technology and control*, Kaunas, Technologija, 34 (3): 290–296.

Kitoogo F. E., Baryamureeba, V, and De Pauw, G. (2008). Towards Domain Independent Named Entity Recognition. *International Journal of Computing and ICT Research*, 2 (2): 84–95.

Krilavičius, T. and Medelis, Ž. Lithuanian stemmer. (2010). May, 2012. <https://github.com/tokenmill/ltlangpack/tree/master/snowball/>.

Lafferty, J. D., McCallum, A. and Pereira, F. (2001). Conditional Random Fields: Probabilistic Models for Segmenting and Labeling Sequence Data. In *Proceedings of the Eighteenth International Conference on Machine Learning* (*ICML'01*), pages 282–289.

Mai, M. O. and Khaled, S. (2012). A Pipeline Arabic Named Entity Recognition Using a Hybrid

Approach. In *Proceedings of the 24th International Conference on Computational Linguistics (COLING* 2012), pages 2159–2176.

Marcinczuk, M. and Janicki, M. (2012). Optimizing CRF-Based Model for Proper Name Recognition in Polish Texts. In *Proceedings of the 13th international conference on Computational Linguistics and Intelligent Text Processing (CICLing*'12), (1): 258–269.

Marcinczuk, M., Stanek, M., Piasecki, M. and Musial, A. (2011). Rich Set of Features for Proper Name Recognition in Polish Texts. *SIIS,* Lecture Notes in Computer Science, 7053: 332–344.

Marcinkevičienė, R. (2000). Tekstynų lingvistika (teorija ir paktika) [Corpus linguistics (theory and practice)]. *Darbai ir dienos,* 24: 7–63. (in Lithuanian).

Nadeau, D. and Sekine, S. (2007). A survey of named entity recognition and classification. *Linguisticae Investigationes,* 30 (1): 3–26.

Nøklestad A. (2009). *A Machine Learning Approach to Anaphora Resolution Including Named Entity Recognition, PP Attachment Disambiguation, and Animacy Detection.* PhD Thesis, University of Oslo.

Pinnis, M. (2012). Latvian and Lithuanian Named Entity Recognition with TildeNER. In *Proceedings of the Eight International Conference on Language Resources and Evaluation (LREC*'12), pages 1258–1265.

Popov, B., Kirilov, A., Maynard, D. and Manov, D. (2004). Creation of Reusable Components and Language Resources for Named Entity Recognition in Russian. In *Proceedings of the 4th International Conference on Language Resources and Evaluation (LREC* 2004), pages 309–312.

Savickienė, I., Kempe, V. and Brooks, P. J. (2009). Acquisition of gender agreement in Lithuanian: exploring the effect of diminutive usage in an elicited production task. *Journal of Child Language,* 36: 477–494.

Singh, U., Goyal, V. and Lehal, G. S. (2012). Named Entity Recognition System for Urdu. In *Proceedings of the 24th International Conference on Computational Linguistics (COLING* 2012), pages 2507–2518.

Sundheim, B. (1995). Overview of results of the muc-6 evaluation. In *Proceedings of the 6th Conference on Message Understanding (MUC*-6), pages 13–31.

Willett, P. (2006). The Porter stemming algorithm: then and now. *Program: electronic library and information systems,* 40 (3): 219–223.

Yeh, A. (2000). More Accurate Tests for the Statistical Significance of Result Differences. In *Proceedings of the 18th International Conference on Computational Linguistics (COLING*'00), 2, pages 947–953.

Zinkevičius, V. (2000). Lemuoklis – morfologinei analizei [Morphological analysis with Lemuoklis]. In: Gudaitis, L. (ed.) *Darbai ir Dienos,* 24: 246–273. (in Lithuanian).

Zinkevičius, V., Daudaravičius, V. and Rimkutė, E. (2005). The Morphologically annotated Lithuanian Corpus. In *Proceedings of the Second Baltic Conference on Human Language Technologies,* pages 365–370.

Tagging the Past: Experiments using the Saga Corpus

Hrafn Loftsson

School of Computer Science, Reykjavik University, Iceland

`hrafn@ru.is`

ABSTRACT

There is an increasing interest in the NLP community in developing tools for annotating historical data, for example, to facilitate research in the field of corpus linguistics. In this work, we experiment with several PoS taggers using a sub-corpus of the Icelandic Saga Corpus. This is carried out in three main steps. First, we evaluate taggers, which were trained on Modern Icelandic, when tagging Old Icelandic. Second, we semi-automatically correct errors in the training corpus using a bootstrapping method. Finally, we evaluate the taggers on the corrected training corpus. The best performing single tagger is Stagger, a tagger based on the averaged perceptron algorithm, obtaining an accuracy of 91.76%. By combining the output of three taggers, using a simple voting scheme, the accuracy increases to 92.32%.

KEYWORDS: Historical Data, Icelandic Saga Corpus, Part-of-Speech Tagging.

1 Introduction

Most Natural Language Processing (NLP) tools, for various languages, have been developed for processing and analyzing modern texts, as opposed to historical (cultural heritage) texts. This is due to the abundance of modern texts in digital form, and, often, the lack of availability of historical texts. Another reason is that when the first NLP tools are developed for a given language, the emphasis is usually on producing tools for processing and analyzing the modern language.

More and more historical texts are now gradually becoming available in digital form. Consequently, there is an increasing interest in the NLP community in developing annotated historical resources, and tools for analyzing historical texts.

Examples of recent annotated resources are: Penn Parsed Corpora of Historical English (Kroch and Taylor, 2000), Icelandic Parsed Historical Corpus (Wallenberg et al., 2011), and Corpus of Early Modern German (Scheible et al., 2011a). These three example resources are all tagged with Part-of-Speech (PoS), while the first two are also syntactically annotated.

Examples of recent experiments with NLP tools for historical texts are: an identification of verb constructions in Swedish (Pettersson et al., 2012), a study of the performance of basic NLP tools for Italian (Pennacchiotti and Zanzotto, 2008), an adaptation of existing NLP tools for Spanish (Sánchez-Marco et al., 2011), and an evaluation of an "off-the-shelf" PoS tagger for German (Scheible et al., 2011b).

Recently, Rögnvaldsson and Helgadóttir (2011) developed the first tagger for Old Icelandic. They bootstrapped a Hidden Markov Model (HMM) tagger by creating a tagged sub-corpus (95,000 tokens) from the Saga Corpus (Old Icelandic Sagas).[1] Hereafter, we refer to the tagged sub-corpus as *Saga-Gold*.

The aim of our work is to complement the work of Rögnvaldsson and Helgadóttir (2011). The overall goal is similar, i.e. developing a high accuracy tagger for Old Icelandic texts. We carry this out in the following three main steps. First, we evaluate several PoS taggers, which were trained on Modern Icelandic, on Saga-Gold produced by Rögnvaldsson and Helgadóttir (2011). Second, we semi-automatically correct tagging errors in Saga-Gold, with a bootstrapping method using the same taggers.[2] Finally, we perform 10-fold cross-validation on the corrected corpus, again using the same taggers and a combination method. All the PoS taggers and corpora used in our work are freely available and open-source.

The best performing single tagger is Stagger (Östling, 2012), a tagger based on the averaged perceptron algorithm, obtaining an accuracy of 91.76%. By combining the output of three taggers using a simple voting scheme, the accuracy increases to 92.32%. We intend to use our combination method to annotate the whole of the Saga Corpus.

The problem of domain adaptation has received increasing attention in recent years. The problem arises in a variety of NLP applications where the distribution of the training data differs in some way from that of the test data. Our work, as well as, for example, (Rögnvaldsson and Helgadóttir, 2011; Sánchez-Marco et al., 2011), essentially deals with the issue of adapting a PoS tagging model based on a modern language to a different domain, an older language.

---

[1]Available for download at `http://www.malfong.is`

[2]Although Saga-Gold is a gold corpus, we found that it contained many errors that needed to be corrected. The corrected training corpus will be made available at `http://www.malfong.is`

Several other experiments with domain adaptation within the field of PoS tagging have been described in the literature, e.g. adapting a model based on finanical data to biomedical data (Blitzer et al., 2006) and to dialogues (Kübler and Baucom, 2011), respectively.

This paper is structured as follows. In Section 2, we describe the individual PoS taggers used in our experiments. We discuss previous work in tagging both Modern and Old Icelandic in Section 3. Our development and evaluation work is described in Section 4. Error analysis is performed in Section 5, and, finally, we draw conclusions and propose future work in Section 6.

2 PoS Taggers Used

We use four different PoS taggers for tagging Old Icelandic texts in Section 4: Stagger, TriTagger, IceTagger and HMM+Ice+HMM. These taggers are freely available, open-source, and, importantly, fast during training and testing.[3]

Stagger (Östling, 2012) is an implementation of the averaged perceptron algorithm by Collins (2002). Stagger uses feature-vector representations commonly used in maximum entropy taggers (Ratnaparkhi, 1996; Toutanova et al., 2003). The feature vectors represent "histories", the context in which a tagging decision is made. For every feature, the perceptron algorithm calculates integer weight coefficients, which are updated for every training sentence. After the final update, these coefficients are stored with the corresponding features. When tagging new texts, the perceptron algorithm sums up all the coefficients of the features in a given context and returns the highest scoring sequence of tags for an input sentence.

TriTagger is a HMM tagger, a re-implementation of the well-known TnT tagger (Brants, 2000). TriTagger uses a trigram model to find the sequence of tags for words in a sentence, which maximizes:

$$P(t_1)P(t_2|t_1)\prod_{i=3}^{n} P(t_i|t_{i-2}, t_{i-1})\prod_{i=1}^{n} P(w_i|t_i) \tag{1}$$

In equation 1, w_i denotes word i in a sentence of length n $(1 \leq i \leq n)$ and t_i denotes the tag for w_i. The probabilities are derived using maximum likelihood estimation based on the frequencies of tags found during training.

IceTagger (Loftsson, 2008) is a linguistic rule-based tagger. It is reductionistic in nature, i.e. it removes inappropriate tags from the set of possible tags for a specific word in a given context. IceTagger first applies local rules for initial disambiguation and then uses a set of heuristics for further disambiguation. If a word is still ambiguous after the application of the heuristics, the default heuristic is simply to choose the most frequent tag for the given word.

HMM+Ice+HMM (Loftsson et al., 2009) is a hybrid tagger, comprising both IceTagger and TriTagger. It works as follows. First, TriTagger (the HMM) performs initial disambiguation only with regard to the word class. Then, the rules of IceTagger are run. Finally, the HMM disambiguates words that IceTagger is not able to fully disambiguate.

In addition to these four taggers, we use CombiTagger[4] (Henrich et al., 2009), a system for developing combined taggers. Tagger combination methods are a means of correcting for the biases of individual taggers, and they are especially suitable when tagging a corpus, i.e.

---

[3]TriTagger, IceTagger and HMM+Ice+HMM are all part of the IceNLP toolkit, available for download at `http://icenlp.sourceforge.net`. Stagger is available for download at `http://www.ling.su.se/stagger`

[4]CombiTagger is open-source – available for download at `http://combitagger.sourceforge.net`

when effectiveness (accuracy) is more important than efficiency (running time). It has been shown that combining taggers will often result in a higher tagging accuracy than is achieved by individual taggers (Brill and Wu, 1998; van Halteren et al., 2001; Loftsson, 2006). The reason is that different taggers tend to produce different errors, and the differences can often be exploited to yield better results.

3   Previous Work on Tagging Icelandic

The Icelandic language is one of the Nordic languages which comprise the North-Germanic branch (Danish, Swedish, Norwegian, Icelandic, Faroese) of the Germanic language tree. Linguistically, Icelandic is most closely related to Faroese and the dialects of Western Norway.

The Icelandic language is morphologically rich, mainly due to inflectional complexity. From a syntactic point of view, Icelandic has a basic subject-verb-object (SVO) word order, but, in fact, the word order is relatively flexible, because morphological endings carry a substantial amount of syntactic information.

The main change in Modern Icelandic since Old Icelandic is in the phonological system.

> On the other hand, the inflectional system and the morphology has in all relevant respects remained unchanged from the earliest texts up to the present, although a number of nouns have shifted inflectional class, a few strong verbs have become weak, one inflectional class of nouns has been lost, and the dual in personal and possessive pronoun has disappeared. The syntax is also basically the same, although a number of changes have occurred. The changes mainly involve word order, especially within the verb phrase, and the development of new modal constructions. (Rögnvaldsson et al., 2012)

In this section, we describe previous work on tagging Iceland texts – first Modern Icelandic, and then Old Icelandic.

3.1   Tagging Modern Icelandic

A few years ago, no PoS tagger existed for tagging Modern Icelandic. Now, however, various PoS taggers have been developed, i.e. data-driven taggers (Helgadóttir, 2005; Dredze and Wallenberg, 2008; Loftsson et al., 2009) and a rule-based tagger (Loftsson, 2008). All these taggers have been trained and developed using the Icelandic Frequency Dictionary[5] (IFD) (Pind et al., 1991), a corpus of about 590,000 tokens of Modern Icelandic. The tagset used in the compilation of the IFD has become the standard tagset for tagging Icelandic. It contains about 700 possible tags, of which 639 appear in the IFD. Thus, the tagset mirrors the morphological complexity of the language.

The PoS tags in the IFD are character strings where each character has a particular function. The first character denotes the *word class*. For each word class there is a predefined number of additional characters (at most six), which describe morphological features, like *gender*, *number* and *case* for nouns; *degree* and *declension* for adjectives; *voice*, *mood* and *tense* for verbs, etc. To illustrate, consider the word form "markari" 'tagger'. The corresponding tag is *nken*, denoting noun (*n*), masculine (*k*), singular (*e*), and nominative (*n*) case.

---

[5]Available for download at `http://www.malfong.is`

Tagger	Unknown	Known	All
TriTagger	72.98	92.18	**90.86**
Stagger	63.77	93.02	**91.04**
IceTagger	77.02	93.07	**91.98**
HMM+Ice+HMM	77.47	93.84	**92.73**

Table 1: Average tagging accuracy (%) of four taggers when tagging the IFD corpus (Modern Icelandic) using 10-fold cross-validation. Average unknown word rate (UWR) in testing is 6.8%.

In recent work on tagging Icelandic, the tagset has been reduced, by removing named-entity classification for proper nouns and labeling all number constants with a single tag – resulting in 565 tags appearing in the changed version of the IFD (Loftsson et al., 2011). Nevertheless, the PoS (morphosyntactic) tagging of modern Icelandic texts is a challenging task. The reason is, for example, that the tagset is large in relation to the size of the available training corpus, and the tagset makes very fine distinctions.

Table 1 shows the accuracy of the four taggers, described in Section 2, when tagging the IFD corpus (565 tags) using 10-fold cross-validation. The accuracy figures for TriTagger, IceTagger, and HMM+Ice+HMM are copied from (Loftsson et al., 2011), whereas we trained and tested Stagger ourselves.[6] All the four taggers were run using default options. A PoS tag predicted by a tagger is correct only if it agrees in the whole tag string with the gold (correct) tag.

It is noteworthy that Stagger's accuracy for known words is significantly higher than the corresponding figure for the other purely data-driven tagger, i.e. TriTagger. This may be explained by the fact that the HMM model used by TriTagger only conditions on the (already assigned) tags to the left of the current word w when predicting the tag for w, whereas a model based on the averaged perceptron algorithm (Stagger) can, in addition to the left hand tag features, use word features to the right of w.

Note, however, that the accuracy of Stagger for unknown words is much lower than for the other taggers. TriTagger's handling of unknown words is based on an effective suffix analysis algorithm proposed by Brants (2000). IceTagger (and thus HMM+Ice+HMM) uses a morphologically-based guesser, IceMorphy (Loftsson, 2008), for providing the set of possible tags for an unknown word.[7]

3.2 Tagging Old Icelandic

The Saga Corpus contains old Icelandic narrative texts in modern Icelandic spelling, assumed to be written in the 13th and 14th centuries. It contains text from four different categories of stories: "Íslendingasögur" (Family Sagas), "Sturlunga" (Sturlunga Saga), "Heimskringla" (Sagas of the Kings of Norway), and "Landnámabók" (The Book of Settlement). In total, the Saga Corpus contains about 1,650,000 tokens.

Using the TnT tagger, Rögnvaldsson and Helgadóttir (2011) have semi-automatically annotated a third (about 95,000 tokens) of the 283,000 tokens from Sturlunga Saga. This annotated

---

[6]When training Stagger on the IFD, we used 12 iterations.

[7]The newest experiments using Stagger for tagging Modern Icelandic show that Stagger indeed obtains state-of-the-art tagging accuracy when enriched with language-dependent linguistic features and given access to IceMorphy (Loftsson and Östling, 2013).

sub-corpus is referred to as Saga-Gold and was used by Rögnvaldsson and Helgadóttir (2011) as a training corpus for developing a tagger for Old Icelandic. For testing, they used 1,000 tokens from each of the four different texts in the Saga Corpus, i.e. 4,000 tokens in total.

Three tagging experiments using TnT were performed by Rögnvaldsson and Helgadóttir (2011). First, training the tagger on the IFD, i.e. on modern texts only, resulted in an accuracy of 88.0%. Second, training on Saga-Gold, i.e. on old texts only, resulted in an accuracy of 91.7%. Finally, by training on the union of the IFD and Saga-Gold, the accuracy increased to 92.7%.

Note that the tagging accuracy increases substantially when training on Saga-Gold, a small training corpus, compared to when only training on the IFD, a corpus whose size is more than 6 times larger. There are two reasons for this, as explained by Rögnvaldsson and Helgadóttir (2011). First, many of the tagging errors made in the first experiment are due to constructions found only in Old Icelandic, and by training on Saga-Gold the tagger learns the correct tagging of these constructions. Second, the unknown word rate (UWR) was much lower in the second experiment (9,6%) than in the first experiment (14.6%), reflecting the fact that many words in Old Icelandic do not appear in Modern Icelandic.

The accuracy of 92.7%, obtained by training TnT on the union of the IFD and Saga-Gold, is high compared with the accuracy of 90.4% obtained by the same tagger when tested on Modern Icelandic only (Helgadóttir, 2005). Texts from the Saga Corpus are much less diversified and simpler than the texts in the IFD corpus, and therefore, in principle, one should be able to achieve higher accuracy on Old Icelandic texts compared to Modern Icelandic. It has to be noted, however, that the test data of only 4,000 tokens, used for evaluating TnT on Old Icelandic, may be too small for obtaining reliable tagging figures. In our experiments, we more than double the size of the test data (see Section 4.4).

4 Development and Evaluation

Our main goal was to the develop a high accuracy tagger for Old Icelandic. We carried this out in the following three main steps. First, we evaluated four PoS taggers trained on Modern Icelandic on Saga-Gold (see Section 4.2). Second, we semi-automatically corrected tagging errors in Saga-Gold, with a bootstrapping method using the same four taggers (see Section 4.3). Finally, we performed 10-fold cross-validation on the corrected corpus, again using the same taggers and a combination method (see Section 4.4).

Our work complements the work of Rögnvaldsson and Helgadóttir (2011), described in Section 3.2. Our work is different from (or extends) the previous work in that i) we correct errors in the Saga-Gold corpus; ii) we evaluate many taggers, as opposed to a single one; iii) we perform testing using cross-validation, as opposed to testing on a single (small) file; and iv) we present results of error analysis.

4.1 The training corpora

We used two training corpora: the IFD corpus, described in Section 3.1, and the Saga-Gold corpus, described in Section 3.2. For both corpora, we used a version in which the tagset has been reduced as explained in Section 3.1. The number of unique tags appearing in Saga-Gold is 459, whereas 565 unique tags appear in the IFD.

In the IFD corpus, the first letter of the first word in each sentence is a lower case letter, except for proper nouns. This is not the case in Saga-Gold. For the sake of consistency, we changed the first letter of the first word in each sentence to an upper case letter in the IFD corpus. Henceforth, when referring to the IFD corpus, we mean this changed version.

4.2   Evaluation of taggers trained on Modern Icelandic

We started our evaluation work by testing PoS taggers, that had been trained or developed for tagging Modern Icelandic (see Section 3.1), on Old Icelandic (Saga-Gold). We trained TriTagger and Stagger on the IFD. IceTagger comes "off-the-shelf" with dictionaries derived from the IFD, and thus does not need training. The HMM+Ice+HMM tagger uses the trained model generated by TriTagger.

The results of the evaluation are shown in columns 2-4 in Table 2. The tagging accuracy is much lower than shown in Table 1. The ordering of the taggers, from lowest accuracy to highest, is also different. When tagging Modern Icelandic, TriTagger obtained the lowest accuracy of the four taggers. In contrast, when tagging the Saga-Gold corpus, it obtains the highest accuracy for all words. Nevertheless, its accuracy drops by 4.17 percentage points.

Tagger	Original Saga-Gold			Corrected Saga-Gold			Increase
	Unknown	Known	All	Unknown	Known	All	
IceTagger	63.99	85.88	**83.55**	65.47	87.03	**84.74**	1.19
Stagger	56.58	87.44	**84.15**	57.02	88.27	**84.94**	0.79
HMM+Ice+HMM	63.71	88.07	**85.48**	65.20	89.17	**86.62**	1.14
TriTagger	65.56	89.29	**86.69**	65.11	89.55	**86.87**	0.18

Table 2: Average tagging accuracy (%) of four taggers, trained on the IFD corpus (Modern Icelandic), when tagging the original Saga-Gold corpus (Old Icelandic) and the corrected version. Average UWR in testing is 10.7%.

IceTagger, which obtained the second highest accuracy for Modern Icelandic, performs badly when tagging Saga-Gold. Its accuracy drops by 8.43 percentage points. This was to be expected, because the hand-crafted rules of IceTagger have been developed to tag modern texts. This poor performance of a rule-based tagger, developed for contemporary texts, when tagging historical text is consistent with the results of (Pennacchiotti and Zanzotto, 2008) when tagging Italian historical texts.

The HMM+Ice+HMM tagger benefits from using the HMM generated by TriTagger and therefore performs much better than IceTagger alone. Stagger performs significantly worse than TriTagger, partly due to much lower accuracy for unknown words.

The results of this experiment show that using taggers trained on Modern Icelandic is hardly a viable option when tagging the whole of the Saga Corpus – the accuracy is simply not high enough. The drop in accuracy is in line with results from related work on tagging historical data with taggers trained on modern texts, e.g. (Rögnvaldsson and Helgadóttir, 2011; Pennacchiotti and Zanzotto, 2008; Scheible et al., 2011b).

On the other hand, these results are better (i.e. not as bad) than found by Scheible et al. (2011b) for German. When they used a tagger trained on Modern German to tag texts (58,000 tokens) with normalized modern spelling from the period 1650-1800, the accuracy dropped from about 97%, for the modern texts, to 79.7% for the older texts. This may partly be explained by the fact that the German experiment used a variety of genres for testing, while we use texts from one genre, Sturlunga Saga. However, the main reason is probably the fact that "[...] Icelandic is often claimed to have undergone relatively small changes from the oldest written sources up to the present", and "[the changes] have not affected the inflectional system, which has not changed in any relevant respects" (Rögnvaldsson and Helgadóttir, 2011). Therefore, we do not witness such a dramatic drop in tagging accuracy as found in the German experiment.

4.3   Correcting tagging errors

When we looked at the errors made by the taggers when tagging the Saga-Gold corpus, we noticed that the gold tags in Saga-Gold were incorrect in many cases. In order to obtain more reliable evaluation results, we thus corrected some of the errors in Saga-Gold. Instead of inspecting each and every word-tag pair in the corpus (about 95,000 pairs), we only looked at those pairs for which a tagger predicts a different tag compared to the gold. We inspected these mismatches (error candidates) and manually corrected the true positives.

Correcting errors in corpora is a time consuming task, and therefore it is important to apply methods that can speed up the process. We carried out the error correction based on a general bootstrapping method, i.e. i) manually annotate/correct a small part of a corpus C; ii) train a tagger T using the annotated/corrected training corpus; iii) use the resulting tagging model to tag more (unannotated or uncorrected) data from C; iv) hand-correct the tagging of the new data and add it to the training set; iv) repeat steps ii)-iv), until all the data of C has been tagged by T and corrected (cf. (Zavrel and Daelemans, 2000; Forsbom, 2009)).

Step/Tagger	Trained on	Tokens tagged in Saga-Gold
1. HMM+Ice+HMM	IFD	1-30,000 = A
2. TriTagger	IFD $\cup$ A	30,000-50,000 = B
3. Stagger	IFD $\cup$ A $\cup$ B	50,000-70,000 = C
4. CombiTagger	IFD $\cup$ A $\cup$ B $\cup$ C	70,000-95,000 = D

Table 3: The error correction bootstrapping method.

We devised an error correction bootstrapping method using several taggers. We define an error candidate, produced by a tagger T, as a word-tag pair (w, t), such that T predicts the tag t, which is different from the corresponding gold tag in the corpus.

Table 3 shows which taggers were used during each phase of the error correction, which part of the corpus they were trained on, and the part they tagged.[8] In step 1, we used the HMM+Ice+HMM tagger, trained on the IFD corpus, to tag the first 30,000 tokens in Saga-Gold, and then we inspected/corrected the error candidates generated by the tagger for these tokens. In step 2, we used TriTagger, trained on the union of the IFD corpus and the first 30,000 corrected tokens from Saga-Gold, to tag tokens 30,000-50,000 in the corpus. Then we inspected/corrected the error candidates generated by the tagger for these 20,000 tokens. In step 3, we used Stagger, trained on the union of the IFD corpus and the first 50,000 corrected tokens in Saga-Gold (corrected in steps 1 and 2), to tag tokens 50,000-70,000 in the corpus. Then we inspected/corrected the error candidates generated by Stagger for these 20,000 tokens.

---

[8]The error correction phase took 40-50 hours.

In the last step, we trained TriTagger, Stagger and HMM+Ice+HMM on the union of the IFD corpus and the first 70,000 corrected tokens in Saga-Gold (corrected in steps 1-3). Using the resulting models, we tagged the last 25,000 tokens in Saga-Gold. Then, we applied CombiTagger on the output of the three taggers in a simple voting scheme. If at least two taggers out of three agree on a tag then the corresponding tag is selected. If all taggers disagree, then the tag of the best performing tagger is selected. Finally, we inspected/corrected the error candidates generated by the combined tagger, for the last 25,000 of the 95,000 tokens in Saga-Gold.

In total, we corrected the tags for 2,144 tokens in Saga-Gold, i.e. 2.3% of the total number of tokens. Note that we used different taggers at different stages to point to error candidates. If we had used a single tagger T, then the accuracy of T might have been overestimated when testing on the corrected corpus. The reason is that we only look at those instances where T predicts a tag which is different from the gold tag. This means that we miss those cases where T agrees with the gold tag, but the gold tag is indeed incorrect!

Columns 5-7 in Table 2 show the accuracy of the four taggers when tested against the corrected version of Saga-Gold. We can see that all the taggers obtain higher accuracy on all words when tagging the corrected corpus.

The four taggers benefit differently from the error correction. Considering all words, the tagging accuracy of IceTagger, HMM+Ice+HMM, Stagger and TriTagger increases by 1.19, 1.14, 0.79, and 0.18 percentage points, respectively. The reason why IceTagger and HMM+Ice+HMM benefit the most is probably that in many cases the rules of IceTagger had indeed predicted a correct tag, but the taggers were "penalized" because of incorrect annotation in Saga-Gold (i.e. before the correction was carried out).

4.4   Cross-validation using Saga-Gold

The previous section showed that using taggers trained on Modern Icelandic to tag Old Icelandic resulted in accuracies below 87%. In the next experiment, we trained and tested the taggers on the corrected Saga-Gold corpus only, using 10-fold cross-validation.[9] We split Saga-Gold into 10 folds, such that the 1st sentence of Saga-Gold was put into the 1st fold, the 2nd sentence into the 2nd fold, ..., the 11th sentence into the 1st fold, the 12th sentence into the 2nd fold, etc. The resulting test files have 9,520 tokens, on average. We only evaluated TriTagger and Stagger in this experiment, since the dictionaries of IceTagger (and thus also of HMM+Ice+HMM) are derived from the IFD corpus.

Tagger	Unknown	Known	All
TriTagger	61.07	90.96	**89.26**
Stagger	52.67	92.53	**90.29**

Table 4: Average tagging accuracy (%) of two taggers when tagging the corrected Saga-Gold using 10-fold cross-validation. Average UWR in testing is 5.7%.

In Table 4, we can see that TriTagger obtains 89.26% accuracy for all words, and that Stagger performs better, i.e. it obtains an accuracy of 90.29%. The accuracies for both taggers increases substantially compared to when trained on Modern Icelandic. Note also that the UWR in Table

---

[9]When training Stagger on Saga-Gold, we used 8 iterations.

4 is 5.7%, only about half of the UWR in Table 2. We had indeed expected that Stagger would out-perform TriTagger, since this is what we found when the taggers were trained and tested using modern texts only (see Table 1).

The accuracy of 90.29% obtained by Stagger is less than 1 percentage points lower than the accuracy of the same tagger when trained and tested on Modern Icelandic (see Table 1), despite a large difference in the size of the training material available in the two corpora, Saga-Gold and the IFD. Note, however, that Saga-Gold only contains one genre, whereas the IFD contains several genres. The tagging of the former corpus is thus, presumably, easier than the tagging of the latter, given the same amount of training data.

In order to reduce the UWR of 5.7%, and to increase the training material, we, next, added data from the IFD. We thus trained the three taggers, TriTagger, Stagger and HMM+Ice+HMM, on the union of Saga-Gold and the IFD, i.e. we added the whole of the IFD corpus to each fold from Saga-Gold. Furthermore, we used CombiTagger in a simple voting scheme on the output of the three taggers.

The results are shown in Table 5. The UWR drops down to 3.6% by adding data from the IFD. Stagger is the best performing single tagger, obtaining an accuracy of 91.76% for all words. By combining the output of three taggers, the accuracy increases to 92.32% for all words.

Tagger	Unknown	Known	All
TriTagger	71.50	90.96	**90.26**
HMM+Ice+HMM	70.91	91.29	**90.58**
Stagger	64.01	92.77	**91.76**
CombiTagger	72.38	93.09	**92.32**

Table 5: Average tagging accuracy (%) of three taggers, and a combination method, when tagging the corrected Saga-Gold using 10-fold cross-validation. The IFD corpus is added to each training fold. Average UWR in testing is 3.6%.

Even though the accuracy of 92.32% can likely be improved (see Section 5), we believe that it is high enough for applying the combination method for tagging the whole of the Saga Corpus. Recall from our discussion in Section 3.1, that the tagset is large and makes fine distinctions. However, this level of detail in the tags might not be necessary for all research in corpus linguistics.

In two additional experiments, we relaxed the condition that the whole tag string needs to be correct. First, we allowed the gold tag and the tag of the combined tagger to differ in only one of the morphological features, given that the word class was correct. This results in an accuracy of 96.63%. Second, when only demanding that the word class is correct (thus ignoring all morphological features), the accuracy increases to 97.55%.

5 Discussion and Error Analysis

Since research on tagging Old Icelandic is currently in its starting phase, the accuracy can most likely be improved in future work. For the reason mentioned at the end of Section 3.2, one should be able to achieve higher accuracy on Old Icelandic texts compared to Modern Icelandic. Furthermore, since a tagger for Old Icelandic does not (necessarily) need to be able to handle modern texts, it should not need to be trained on large amount of the IFD corpus. In future work, we would thus like to experiment with using only a part of the IFD for training our tagger.

In the remainder of this section, we discuss some of the most frequent tagging errors. We performed error analysis on the output of Stagger, when trained on the union of Saga-Gold and the IFD. We combined the tagging errors from the test sets of all of the 10 folds.

We define an error type as a pair (x, y), where x is the predicted tag and y is the gold tag. Stagger makes 1876 different error types. 1121 of those, or 59.8%, appear only once. The 10 most frequent errors account for 18.5% of the total errors, as shown in Table 6.

Error type	Rate	Cumulative rate
(c,aa)	2.80	2.80
(aþ,ao)	2.70	5.50
(sfg3en,ct)	2.49	7.99
(ct,c)	1.81	9.80
(ao,aþ)	1.66	11.46
(c,ct)	1.49	12.95
(aa,aþ)	1.49	14.44
(sfg3en,c)	1.48	15.92
(nken-s,nkeo-s)	1.31	17.23
(aa,ao)	1.30	18.53

Table 6: The 10 most frequent error types and their rate of occurrence in % in the output of Stagger. An error type is a pair (x, y): x is the predicted tag and y is the gold tag. aa=adverb; ao/aþ=preposition governing accusative/dative case; c=conjunction; ct=relative particle; nken-s/nkeo-s=noun, masculine, singular, nominative/accusative, proper noun; sfg3en=verb, indicative mood, active voice, third person, singular, present tense.

The rate of the most frequent error type, (c,aa), is 2.80%. This error occurs when Stagger predicts a conjunction (c), while an adverb (aa) is correct. The word "og" is to blame for this error type. In Modern Icelandic it usually denotes the coordinating conjunction 'and', while in Old Icelandic it often denotes the adverb 'also'. Below, one such tagging error made by Stagger is shown, when tagging the sentence "Þar var og Eyvindur prestur Þórarinsson" 'There was also Eiríkur priest Þórarinsson':

```
Word              Stagger      Gold tag
--------------------------------------------
Þar               aa           aa
var               sfg3eþ       sfg3eþ
og                c            aa
Eyvindur          nken-s       nken-s
prestur           nken         nken
Þórarinsson       nken-s       nken-s
```

The rate of the third most frequent error type, (sfg3en,ct), is 2.49%. The *sfg3en* tag denotes: verb (*s*), indicative mood (*f*), active voice (*g*), third person (*3*), singular (*e*), and present tense (*n*). The *ct* tag denotes a relative particle. This particular error type occurs with the word "er". In Modern Icelandic this word most often means 'is, am', while in Old Icelandic it is most often used as a temporal conjunction ('when') (tag *c*) or a relative particle ('that, which, who') (tag *ct*) (Rögnvaldsson and Helgadóttir, 2011).

Below, one such tagging error made by Stagger is demonstrated, when tagging the sentence part "Maður hét Haukur er kallaður var Víga-Haukur" 'Man named Haukur who called was Víga-Haukur':

```
Word            Stagger     Gold tag
---------------------------------
Maður           nken        nken
hét             sfg3eþ      sfg3eþ
Haukur          nken-s      nken-s
er              sfg3en      ct
kallaður        sþgken      sþgken
var             sfg3eþ      sfg3eþ
Víga-Haukur     nken-s      nken-s
```

When Stagger was trained on the IFD only and tagged Saga-Gold (see Section 4.2), the aggregate rate of the error types (sfg3en,ct) and (sfg3en,c) was 5.67%. In contrast, when Stagger is trained on the union of Saga-Gold and the IFD, the rate of the same two error types is 2.49% + 1.48% = 3.97% (see Table 6). Thus, by adding training data from Saga-Gold, the tagger learns to tag these constructions correctly in some instances, but still tags many of them incorrectly, due to the large amount of training data coming from the IFD. In contrast, when Stagger is trained on Saga-Gold only (no data from IFD), the rate of the same error types is only 0.2%.

Finally, in Table 6, the following four error types appear: *(aþ,ao)*, *(ao,aþ)*, *(aa,aþ)*, and *(aa,ao)*. The first two differentiate between a preposition governing the accusative (*ao*) or dative case (*aþ*). The latter two differentiate between an adverb (*aa*) and a prepositions (*ao/aþ*). The underlying constructions, from which these four error types originate, are difficult to annotate correctly, even for humans.

6   Conclusion

In this paper, we first evaluated taggers, which were trained on Modern Icelandic, when tagging Saga-Gold, a sub-corpus of the Icelandic Saga Corpus. Second, we described a bootstrapping method used to correct 2.3% of the tokens in Saga-Gold. Third, we performed experiments in using several taggers to tag the corrected corpus. Finally, we discussed the results of error analysis.

Stagger is the best performing single tagger, obtaining an accuracy of 91.76% when trained on the union of Saga-Gold and the IFD corpus. By combining the output of three different taggers using a simple voting scheme, the accuracy increases to 92.32%.

In future work, we intend to: i) experiment with increasing the accuracy of Stagger for unknown words; ii) find ways to tackle the most frequent error types; and iii) experiment with using only a part of the IFD corpus as training material.

We would also like to find and correct more errors in Saga-Gold, using our combined tagger to point to error candidates. We intend to use the combined tagger to tag the whole of the Saga Corpus and make the results public – to facilitate corpus linguistics research on Old Icelandic.

Acknowledgments

We thank Sigrún Helgadóttir and Eiríkur Rögnvaldsson for making the training corpus, Saga-Gold, available to us. We are also grateful to Robert Östling for his willingness in improving Stagger's functionality based on our suggestions.

References

Blitzer, J., McDonald, R., and Pereira, F. (2006). Domain adaptation with structural correspondence learning. In *Proceedings of the Conference on Empirical Methods in Natural Language Processing*, EMNLP, Sydney, Australia.

Brants, T. (2000). TnT: A statistical part-of-speech tagger. In *Proceedings of the 6th Conference on Applied Natural Language Processing*, Seattle, WA, USA.

Brill, E. and Wu, J. (1998). Classifier Combination for Improved Lexical Disambiguation. In *Proceedings of the 36th Annual Meeting of the Association for Computational Linguistics and 17th International Conference on Computational Linguistics*, COLING-ACL, Montreal, Quebec, Canada.

Collins, M. (2002). Discriminative Training Methods for Hidden Markov Models: Theory and Experiments with Perceptron Algorithms. In *Proceedings of the ACL-02 Conference on Empirical methods in Natural Language Processing*, Philadelphia, PA, USA.

Dredze, M. and Wallenberg, J. (2008). Icelandic Data Driven Part of Speech Tagging. In *Proceedings of the 46th Annual Meeting of the Association for Computational Linguistics: Human Language Technologies*, ACL-HLT, Columbus, OH, USA.

Forsbom, E. (2009). Extending the View: Explorations in Bootstrapping a Swedish PoS Tagger. In *Proceedings of the 17th Nordic Conference of Computational Linguistics*, NoDaLiDa, Odense, Denmark.

van Halteren, H., Zavrel, J., and Daelemans, W. (2001). Improving Accuracy in Wordclass Tagging through Combination of Machine Learning Systems. *Computational Linguistics*, 27(2):199–230.

Helgadóttir, S. (2005). Testing Data-Driven Learning Algorithms for PoS Tagging of Icelandic. In Holmboe, H., editor, *Nordisk Sprogteknologi 2004*. Museum Tusculanums Forlag, Copenhagen.

Henrich, V., Reuter, T., and Loftsson, H. (2009). CombiTagger: A System for Developing Combined Taggers. In *Proceedings of the 22nd International FLAIRS Conference, Special Track: Applied Natural Language Processing*, Sanibel Island, Florida, USA.

Kroch, A. and Taylor, A. (2000). The Penn-Helsinki Parsed Corpus of Middle English (PPCME2). Department of Linguistics, University of Pennsylvania. CD-ROM, second edition.

Kübler, S. and Baucom, E. (2011). Fast Domain Adaptation for Part of Speech Tagging for Dialogues. In *Proceedings of Recent Advances in Natural Language Processing*, RANLP, Hissar, Bulgaria.

Loftsson, H. (2006). Tagging Icelandic text: An experiment with integrations and combinations of taggers. *Language Resources and Evaluation*, 40(2):175–181.

Loftsson, H. (2008). Tagging Icelandic text: A linguistic rule-based approach. *Nordic Journal of Linguistics*, 31(1):47–72.

Loftsson, H., Helgadóttir, S., and Rögnvaldsson, E. (2011). Using a morphological database to increase the accuracy in PoS tagging. In *Proceedings of Recent Advances in Natural Language Processing*, RANLP, Hissar, Bulgaria.

Loftsson, H., Kramarczyk, I., Helgadóttir, S., and Rögnvaldsson, E. (2009). Improving the PoS tagging accuracy of Icelandic text. In *Proceedings of the 17th Nordic Conference of Computational Linguistics*, NoDaLiDa, Odense, Denmark.

Loftsson, H. and Östling, R. (2013). Tagging a Morphologically Complex Language Using an Averaged Perceptron Tagger: The Case of Icelandic. In *Proceedings of the 19th Nordic Conference of Computational Linguistics*, NoDaLiDa, Oslo, Norway.

Pennacchiotti, M. and Zanzotto, F. M. (2008). Natural Language Processing across time: an empirical investigation on Italian. In Nordström, B. and Ranta, A., editors, *Advances in Natural Language Processing, 6th International Conference on NLP, GoTAL 2008, Proceedings*. Springer, Berlin.

Pettersson, E., Megyesi, B., and Nivre, J. (2012). Parsing the past – identification of verb constructions in historical text. In *EACL 2012 workshop on: Language Technology for Cultural Heritage, Social Sciences, and Humanities*, Avignon, France.

Pind, J., Magnússon, F., and Briem, S. (1991). *Íslensk orðtíðnibók [The Icelandic Frequency Dictionary]*. The Institute of Lexicography, University of Iceland, Reykjavik, Iceland.

Ratnaparkhi, A. (1996). A Maximum Entropy Model for Part-Of-Speech Tagging. In *Proceedings of the Conference on Empirical Methods in Natural Language Processing*, Philadelphia, PA, USA.

Rögnvaldsson, E. and Helgadóttir, S. (2011). Morphosyntactic Tagging of Old Icelandic Texts and Its Use in Studying Syntactic Variation and Change. In Sporleder, C., van den Bosch, A., and Zervanou, K., editors, *Language Technology for Cultural Heritage: Selected Papers from the LaTeCH Workshop Series*. Springer, Berlin.

Rögnvaldsson, E., Ingason, A. K., Sigurðsson, E. F., and Wallenberg, J. (2012). The Icelandic Parsed Historical Corpus (IcePaHC). In *Proceedings of the 8th International Conference on Language Resources and Evaluation, LREC 2012*, Istanbul, Turkey.

Sánchez-Marco, C., Boleda, G., and Padró, L. (2011). Extending the tool, or how to annotate historical language varieties. In *Proceedings of the 5th ACL-HLT Workshop on Language Technology for Cultural Heritage, Social Sciences, and Humanities*, Portland, OR, USA.

Scheible, S., Whitt, R. J., Durrell, M., and Bennett, P. (2011a). A Gold Standard Corpus of Early Modern German. In *Proceedings of the ACL-HLT 2011 Linguistic Annotation Workshop (LAW V)*, Portland, OR, USA.

Scheible, S., Whitt, R. J., Durrell, M., and Bennett, P. (2011b). Evaluating an 'off-the-shelf' POS-tagger on Early Modern German text. In *Proceedings of the 5th ACL-HLT Workshop on Language Technology for Cultural Heritage, Social Sciences, and Humanities*, Portland, OR, USA.

Toutanova, K., Klein, D., Manning, C. D., and Singer, Y. (2003). Feature-rich part-of-speech tagging with a cyclic dependency network. In *Proceedings of the 2003 Conference of the North American Chapter of the Association for Computational Linguistics on Human Language Technology*, NAACL.

Wallenberg, J. C., Ingason, A. K., Sigurðsson, E. F., and Rögnvaldsson, E. (2011). Icelandic Parsed Historical Corpus (IcePaHC). Version 0.9.

Zavrel, J. and Daelemans, W. (2000). Bootstrapping a Tagged Corpus through Combination of Existing Heterogeneous Taggers. In *Proceedings of the 2nd International Conference on Language Resources and Evaluation*, LREC, Athens, Greece.

Östling, R. (2012). Stagger: A modern POS tagger for Swedish. In *Proceedings of the 4th Swedish Language Technology Conference*, SLTC, Lund, Sweden.

Tagging a Morphologically Complex Language Using an Averaged Perceptron Tagger: The Case of Icelandic

Hrafn Loftsson[1], Robert Östling[2]

(1) School of Computer Science, Reykjavik University, Iceland
(2) Department of Linguistics, Stockholm University, Sweden

`hrafn@ru.is, robert@ling.su.se`

ABSTRACT

In this paper, we experiment with using Stagger, an open-source implementation of an Averaged Perceptron tagger, to tag Icelandic, a morphologically complex language. By adding language-specific linguistic features and using IceMorphy, an unknown word guesser, we obtain state-of-the-art tagging accuracy of 92.82%. Furthermore, by adding data from a morphological database, and word embeddings induced from an unannotated corpus, the accuracy increases to 93.84%. This is equivalent to an error reduction of 5.5%, compared to the previously best tagger for Icelandic, consisting of linguistic rules and a Hidden Markov Model.

KEYWORDS: Averaged Perceptron, Part-of-Speech Tagging, Morphological Database, Linguistic Features, Word Embeddings.

1 Introduction

Part-of-Speech (PoS) tagging is the task of assigning labels, denoting word classes and morphosyntactic features, to words in running text.

The state-of-the-art tagging accuracy for English, using supervised methods, is above 97%, e.g. (Collins, 2002; Toutanova et al., 2003; Giménez and Màrquez, 2004; Shen et al., 2007), and newest results using semi-supervised methods are close to 97.5% (Spoustová et al., 2009; Søgaard, 2011).

English is a morphologically simple language and most work on tagging English has used the 48 tags in the Penn TreeBank tagset (Marcus et al., 1993). Many morphologically complex languages use much larger tagsets, which encode detailed morphosyntactic features, in addition to the basic PoS categories. For example, 1100 tags appear in the Prague Dependency Treebank 2.0 (Spoustová et al., 2009), over 1000 tags appear in a Polish tagset (Radiszewski, 2013), a tagset for Bulgarian contains 680 tags (Georgiev et al., 2012), and a reduced version of an Icelandic tagset contains 565 tags (Loftsson et al., 2011).

The state-of-the-art for many morphologically complex languages is well below the 97+% figures for English (Spoustová et al., 2009; Loftsson et al., 2011; Radiszewski, 2013). A notable exception is the work of Georgiev et al. (2012) for Bulgarian, in which about 98% accuracy was achieved, using bidirectional sequence classification (Shen et al., 2007), in combination with linguistic rules and a morphological lexicon (which included *all* the words in the test set, resulting in 0% unknown word rate).

In this paper, we experiment with using Stagger (Östling, 2012), an open-source implementation of the Averaged Perceptron tagger by Collins (2002), to tag Icelandic. Our motivation for applying Stagger to Icelandic is threefold. First, the training time in Stagger is relatively short compared to other data-driven methods like (Lafferty et al., 2001; Giménez and Màrquez, 2004; Shen et al., 2007), when using a large tagset. Second, Stagger has been shown to obtain state-of-the-art results for Swedish (Östling, 2012), a closely related language to Icelandic. Third, Stagger is implemented in Java and thus allows easy integration to components in the Java-based IceNLP toolkit (Loftsson and Rögnvaldsson, 2007).

By training and testing on the Icelandic Frequency Dictionary (IFD) corpus (Pind et al., 1991), using a tagset of 565 tags, we obtain state-of-the-art tagging accuracy for Icelandic: *i)* 92.82% by adding language-specific linguistic features to the base feature set of Stagger, and using IceMorphy (Loftsson, 2008) as an unknown word guesser; and *ii)* 93.84%, by adding data from a full form database of Icelandic inflections (Bjarnadóttir, 2012), and word embeddings generated with a neural network language model (Collobert and Weston, 2008).

It is notable that our best tagging results using Stagger (93.84%) beat the previous best results for Icelandic (93.48%), obtained by using a hybrid tagger based on a linguistic rule-based method and a Hidden Markov Model (Loftsson et al., 2011). The increase in accuracy is equivalent to an error reduction of 5.5%.

This paper is structured as follows. In Section 2, we describe Stagger. We discuss previous work in tagging Icelandic in Section 3. Our development and evaluation work is described in Section 4. Error analysis is carried out in Section 5, and we conclude in Section 6.

2 Stagger

Stagger was originally developed for Swedish, where it achieves the state-of-the-art accuracy of 96.57%, using a tagset of size 150 (Östling, 2012). In this section, we give an overview of Stagger, i.e. the underlying Averaged Perceptron algorithm, the base feature set, PoS filters, and word embeddings.

2.1 Averaged Perceptron

The Averaged Perceptron algorithm of Collins (2002) uses a discriminative, feature-rich model that can be trained efficiently. Recent research also shows that the algorithm, given a good search method, can be used for PoS tagging with state-of-the-art accuracy (Shen et al., 2007; Tsuruoka et al., 2011).

Features are modeled using *feature functions* of the form $\phi(h_i, t_i)$ for a history h_i and a tag t_i, in the way pioneered by Maximum Entropy models (Berger et al., 1996; Ratnaparkhi, 1996). The history h_i is a complex object modeling different aspects of the sequence being tagged. It may contain previously assigned tags in the sequence to be annotated, as well as other contextual features such as the form of the current word, or whether the current sentence ends with a question mark. Intuitively, the job of the training algorithm is to find out which feature functions are good indicators that a certain tag t_i is associated with a certain history h_i.

A model consists of feature functions ϕ_s, each paired with a *feature weight* α_s which is to be estimated during training. The scoring function is defined over entire sequences, which in a PoS tagging task typically means sentences. For a sequence of words w of length n in a model with d feature functions, the scoring function is defined as:

$$score(w, t) = \sum_{i=1}^{n} \sum_{s=1}^{d} \alpha_s \phi_s(h_i, t_i)$$

The highest scoring sequence of tags:

$$\bar{t} = \arg\max_t score(w, t)$$

can be computed, for example, using the Viterbi algorithm or (as in in our case) a beam search of width 8.

Training the model is done in an error-driven fashion: tagging each sequence in the training data with the current model, and adding to the feature weights the difference between the corresponding feature function for the correct tagging, and the model's tagging.

Algorithm 1 shows one iteration of the perceptron training algorithm over the training set T of sequences. The model is initialized to $\alpha_s = 0$ for all s. Collins (2002) shows that rather than using the estimated model parameters α_s directly when tagging data outside the training set, both tagging accuracy and the speed of convergence can be improved by using values of α_s averaged during the training process. In our case, we average the weights after every 4096 training instances (sentences), which seems to strike a good balance between efficiency and accuracy.

Algorithm 1 Perceptron training iteration.

---

for all $\tilde{h}, \tilde{t} \in T$ **do**
    $\bar{t} \leftarrow \arg\max_t score(w, t)$
    for $i \leftarrow 1..n$ **do**
        for $s \leftarrow 1..d$ **do**
            $\alpha_s \leftarrow \alpha_s + \phi_s(\tilde{h}_i, \tilde{t}_i) - \phi_s(\bar{h}_i, \bar{t}_i)$
        end for
    end for
end for

2.2 Features

Stagger uses a basic feature set similar to that of Ratnaparkhi (1996). All of the basic features are binary, i.e. with the value 0 or 1.

Table 1 shows the templates on which the basic features used in Stagger are based. One instance of the first template may be:

$$\phi_s(h, t) = \begin{cases} 1 & \text{if } t = \mathrm{c} \wedge w_i = \mathrm{og} \wedge i \neq n \\ 0 & \text{otherwise} \end{cases}$$

or in other words, 1 if the current tag is "c" (conjunction), the current word (w_i) is "og" 'and', and the current word is not the last in the sentence.

History-independent features
$t_i = x, w_i = y, i = n$
$t_i = x, w_i = y, i = 1, c(i)$
$t_i = x, w_{i-1} = y, w_i = z$
$t_i = x, w_i = y, w_{i+1} = z$
$t_i = x, w_{i-1} = y, w_i = z, w_{i+1} = u$
$t_i = x, w_{i-2} = y, w_{i-1} = z, w_i = u$
$t_i = x, w_i = y, w_{i+1} = z, w_{i+2} = u$
$t_i = x, w_{i+\{-2,-1,1,2\}} = y$
$t_i = x, prefix_{\{1,2,3,4\}}(w_i) = y, i = 1, c(i)$
$t_i = x, suffix_{\{1,2,3,4,5\}}(w_i) = y, i = 1, c(i)$
$t_i = x, k(i), \text{"-"} \in w_i$
$t_i = x, k(i), k(i+1)$
History-dependent features
$t_i = x, t_{i-1} = y$
$t_{i-2} = x, t_{i-1} = y, t_i = z$
$t_i = x, t_{i-1} = y, w_i = z$
$t_i = x, t_{i-1} = y, w_i = z, w_{i+1} = u$

Table 1: Templates for the basic features of Stagger. t_i is the tag at position i in the sequence (of length n). w_i is the lower-cased word at position i. $k(i)$ is the type of token i (e.g. digits, Latin letters, symbol). $c(i)$ is the capitalization of token i (upper, lower, N/A). $prefix/suffix_k(w_i)$ is the k-letter prefix/suffix of word w_i. x, y, z, u are constants, which in any given feature function has a fixed value.

The features can be divided into two categories: those who describe previously assigned tags in the sequence (history-dependent features), and those who do not. Making this distinction can lead to a large speed increase, since the history-independent feature functions only have to be evaluated once for each tag and word sequence, while the history-dependent ones must also be evaluated for every history.

In addition to the basic feature set detailed above, we also performed an experiment adding Collobert and Weston (2008) embeddings through feature functions of the following form:

$$\phi_{x,j}(h_i, t_i) = \begin{cases} \text{CW}(w_i)_j & \text{if } t_i = x \\ 0 & \text{if } t_i \neq x \end{cases}$$

where $\text{CW}(w_i)_j$ is the j:th dimension of word w_i's Collobert and Weston embedding. The embeddings are described in Section 2.4.

2.3   PoS filter

Ratnaparkhi (1996) observed that both accuracy and speed can be improved by not considering *all* tags for every word. We use the following basic method for determining which tags to consider for a given word. If the word w is known, i.e. occurs in the training data, only the tags found during training for w are considered (we refer to this set of possible tags as the tag profile for w). Other words are limited to manually created tags from the set of open word classes.

There is, however, one complication: during training, all words are known. Using the tag filtering approach exactly as described above during training would give unrealistically good accuracy on the training data, but since the perceptron algorithm learns from its errors, this tends to lead to *decreased* accuracy on other data. To prevent this, words occurring between 1 and 3 times in the training data may be assigned tags from the union of the set of tags they occur with in the training data, and the set of open word class tags.

In Section 4.3.1, we show how the PoS filter can be further improved using a morphological analyzer, and in Section 4.3.2 using a lexicon.

2.4   Collobert and Weston embeddings

Neural network language models have been used to create word embeddings, vectors in $\mathbb{R}^d$ that represent syntactic and semantic properties of words based on their distributional properties (Collobert and Weston, 2008; Collobert et al., 2011). Collobert and Weston (C&W) embeddings have been shown to improve accuracy when used as features in named entity recognition and shallow parsing (Turian et al., 2010) as well as PoS tagging (Östling, 2012). This amounts to a type of semi-supervised learning, since properties of words learned from an unannotated text corpus are used to benefit a supervised learning task. In the case of PoS tagging, C&W embeddings are useful because words of the same word class tend to receive similar embeddings due to the similar syntactic contexts in which they occur.

Stagger can optionally be provided with word embeddings, for use during training.

3   Icelandic and Previous Tagging Work

The Icelandic language is morphologically rich, mainly due to inflectional complexity. Nouns can appear in 16 inflectional forms, depending on number, case and the presence or absence of a suffixed definite article. Adjectives can have as many as 120 inflectional forms, depending on gender, number, case, strong or weak declension, and degree. Verbs conjugate in person, number, tense, mood and voice, and can have as many as 107 inflectional forms (Bjarnadóttir, 2012).

From a syntactic point of view, Icelandic has a basic subject-verb-object (SVO) word order, but, in fact, the word order is fairly flexible, because morphological endings carry a substantial amount of syntactic information. However, the word order in Icelandic is not as flexible as is allowed in some Slavic languages. As pointed out by Dredze and Wallenberg (2008a), this combination of morphological complexity and syntactic constraints makes Icelandic a good test case for data-driven tagging methods.

3.1   Resources

All PoS taggers for Icelandic (see Section 3.2) have been trained/developed and tested using the 10 pairs of training and test sets of the Icelandic Frequency Dictionary (IFD)[1] (Pind et al., 1991), a balanced corpus of about 590,000 tokens. All 100 text fragments in the IFD were published for the first time in 1980–1989. The corpus comprises five categories of texts, i.e. Icelandic fiction, translated fiction, biographies and memoirs, non-fiction and books for children and youngsters. The tagset used in the compilation of the IFD has become the standard tagset for tagging Icelandic. It contains about 700 possible tags, of which 639 appear in the IFD. Thus, the tagset mirrors the morphological complexity of the language.

The PoS tags are character strings, in which each character has a particular function. The first character denotes the *word class*. For each word class there is a predefined number of additional characters (at most six), which describe morphological features. To illustrate, consider the word form "fiskur" 'fish'. The corresponding tag is *nken*, denoting noun (*n*), masculine (*k*), singular (*e*), and nominative (*n*) case. Table 2 shows an example of the declension for the lemma "fiskur" 'fish', in singular and plural (without the definite article) and the corresponding PoS tags.

	Singular		Plural	
Case	Form	Tag	Form	Tag
Nominative	fiskur	nken	fiskar	nkfn
Accusative	fisk	nkeo	fiska	nkfo
Dative	fiski	nkeþ	fiskum	nkfþ
Genitive	fisks	nkee	fiska	nkfe

Table 2: The declension for the noun lemma "fiskur" 'fish'.

The other main resource used in the development of Icelandic taggers is the Database of Icelandic Inflection[1] (Bjarnadóttir, 2012). Its Icelandic abbreviation is *BÍN* and henceforth we use that term. BÍN contains about 270,000 paradigms, with about 5.8 million inflectional forms.

3.2   Previous tagging work

A few years ago, no PoS tagger existed for tagging Icelandic. Now, however, various PoS taggers have been developed, in particular data-driven taggers (Helgadóttir, 2005; Dredze and Wallenberg, 2008b; Rögnvaldsson and Helgadóttir, 2011), a rule-based tagger (Loftsson, 2008), and a hybrid tagger (Loftsson et al., 2009).

---

[1]Available at `http://www.malfong.is`

In recent work on tagging Icelandic, the tagset has been reduced, by removing named-entity classification for proper nouns and labeling all number constants with a single tag – resulting in 565 tags appearing in the changed version of the IFD. Moreover, the newest evaluation has been carried out on a corrected version of the IFD corpus (Loftsson et al., 2011). Nevertheless, the PoS (morphosyntactic) tagging of Icelandic texts has turned out to be a challenging task. The reason is, for example, that the tagset is large in relation to the size of the available training corpus, and the tagset makes very fine distinctions.

Table 3 shows the accuracy of three taggers, TriTagger, IceTagger, and HMM+Ice+HMM[2], used by Loftsson et al. (2011), when tagging the (corrected version of the) IFD corpus (565 tags) using 10-fold cross-validation. Tagging accuracy is shown both with and without using data from BÍN. Loftsson et al. (2011) used the 10th fold of the IFD for development, and the figures are thus based on the average of the first nine folds. Data from BÍN was used to extend the dictionaries used by the taggers, thereby reducing the unknown word rate (UWR) from 6.8% (when not using data from BÍN) down to 1.1%. According to Loftsson et al. (2011), when adding data from BÍN, only "hard" unknown words remain – mostly proper nouns and foreign words.

Without data from BÍN			
Tagger	Unknown	Known	All
TriTagger	72.98	92.18	90.86
IceTagger	77.02	93.07	91.98
HMM+Ice+HMM	77.47	93.84	**92.73**
With data from BÍN			
Tagger	Unknown	Known	All
TriTagger	65.84	92.22	91.93
IceTagger	63.47	93.11	92.78
HMM+Ice+HMM	60.50	93.85	**93.48**

Table 3: Average tagging accuracy (%) of three taggers when tagging the IFD corpus using 10-fold cross-validation. Average unknown word rate (UWR) in testing is 6.8% when not using data from BÍN, compared to 1.1% when using data from BÍN.

Below, we briefly describe the three taggers used by Loftsson et al. (2011). The first tagger, TriTagger, is a Hidden Markov Model (HMM) tagger, a re-implementation of the well-known TnT tagger (Brants, 2000).

The second tagger, IceTagger (Loftsson, 2008), is a linguistic rule-based tagger, but it derives its dictionaries from a training corpus. It is reductionistic in nature, i.e. it removes inappropriate tags from the tag profile for a specific word in a given context. An important part of IceTagger is its unknown word guesser, IceMorphy. It guesses the tag profile for unknown words by applying morphological analysis and ending analysis. In addition, IceMorphy can fill in the *tag profile gaps*[3] in the dictionary for words belonging to certain morphological classes (Loftsson, 2008).

The third tagger, HMM+Ice+HMM (Loftsson et al., 2009), is a hybrid tagger, comprising both IceTagger and TriTagger. It works as follows. First, TriTaggger (the HMM) performs initial

---

[2]These taggers are part of the open-source IceNLP toolkit, available at `http://icenlp.sourceforge.net`

[3]A tag profile gap for a word occurs when a tag is missing from the tag profile. This occurs, for example, if not all possible tags for a given word are encountered during training.

disambiguation only with regard to the word class. Then, the rules of IceTagger are run. Finally, the HMM disambiguates words that IceTagger is not able to fully disambiguate.

Before the work described in this paper (see Section 4), the HMM+Ice+HMM tagger was the state-of-the-art tagger for Icelandic, obtaining an overall accuracy of 93.48% and 92.73%, with and without using data from BÍN, respectively (see Table 3).

One additional tagger, Bidir (Dredze and Wallenberg, 2008b,a), is relevant to our work. It is based on the bidirectional sequence classification method by Shen et al. (2007). In Bidir, the learning phase is divided into separate learning problems. First, a word class (WC) tagger classifies a word according to the word class. Then the tagger only considers and evaluates tags that are consistent with the predicted word class. Secondly, a case tagger (CT) retags the case of nouns, adjectives and pronouns, given the predicted tags from the WC tagger. This combination resulted in an accuracy of 92.06%, when using the uncorrected version of the IFD corpus and the full 639 tags. For comparison, the HMM+Ice+HMM tagger obtains an accuracy of 92.31% when tagging the IFD corpus under these same settings (Loftsson et al., 2009).

4 Development and Evaluation

In this section, we describe various experiments carried out with the goal of obtaining state-of-the-art tagging accuracy for Icelandic using Stagger.[4] Following previous work, in all the experiments we trained and tested on folds 1-9 of the IFD, whereas fold 10 was used for development. Furthermore, following Loftsson et al. (2011), we used the corrected version of the IFD corpus and the reduced tagset of 565 tags appearing in the IFD (see Section 3.2). During training, we used 12 iterations.[5]

4.1 Generic Stagger

In the first experiment, we evaluated the generic version of Stagger, with only the addition of a list of open word class tags from the IFD tagset.

When comparing the results of experiment no. 1, shown in Table 4, to the results without BÍN data in Table 3, we can see that Stagger performs better than a pure HMM model (TriTagger). Stagger obtains an accuracy of 91.29% for all words, whereas TriTagger obtains 90.86%.

On the other hand, Stagger's accuracy is lower than both IceTagger (91.98%) and HMM+Ice+HMM (92.73%). It is notable, however, that Stagger's accuracy for known words (93.11%) is higher than the corresponding accuracy in both TriTagger (92.18%) and IceTagger (93.07%). This is already a promising result, given the fact that IceTagger is developed using linguistic knowledge.

In contrast, Stagger's accuracy for unknown words (66.29%) is much lower compared to the other three taggers. In Section 4.3, we experiment with increasing the accuracy of unknown words, and with reducing the UWR.

4.2 Adding linguistic features

The base features of Stagger are language-independent. In the second experiment, we added language-specific linguistic features (LF), that use particular properties of Icelandic.

---

[4]The additions we made to the generic version of Stagger are available at http://www.ling.su.se/stagger

[5]For each fold of about 530,000 tokens, training time on an Intel i5, 2.50GHz system, with 8G RAM, is 45-90 minutes, depending on the type of experiment carried out in the subsections below.

Exp.	Tagger	Unknown words	Known words	All words	Error Δ^a	Error Δ^b
1	Stagger	66.29	93.11	91.29		
2	Stagger+LF	66.06	93.26	91.42	1.5	1.5
3	Stagger+LF+IceMorphy	77.03	93.97	**92.82**	16.3	17.7
4	Stagger+LF+IceMorphy+BÍN	61.45	94.02	**93.70**	12.3	27.7
5	Stagger+LF+IceMorphy+BÍN+WE	61.99	94.15	**93.84**	2.2	29.3

[a]Error reduction with regard to the previous experiment.
[b]Error reduction with regard to the 1st experiment.

Table 4: Average tagging accuracy (%) of Stagger, for different experiments, when tagging the IFD corpus using 10-fold cross-validation. Error reduction is shown for all words. State-of-the-art results are shown in bold font. Average UWR in testing is 6.8% without using data from BÍN, compared to 1.0% when using BÍN. LF=Linguistic features; WE=Word embeddings. Differences in all-word accuracy are significant at $p < 0.001$, using McNemar's test.

Previous research on tagging Icelandic has revealed that many tagging errors are due to case confusion for nominals (Helgadóttir, 2005; Dredze and Wallenberg, 2008a; Loftsson et al., 2009). In order to more accurately select the case of nominals, Dredze and Wallenberg (2008a), in their Bidir tagger (see Section 3.2), use a separate case tagger which is essentially a second-pass PoS tagger that is only permitted to change the case and gender selections of the first-pass tagger, whose output the case tagger has access to.

We first implemented a separate case tagger following Dredze and Wallenberg (2008a), although using only their *Feature Group 1* (which they reported to be by far the most useful one), and could confirm their finding that the overall tagging accuracy is improved by the case tagger.

However, since their Feature Group 1 only uses previously assigned tags to the left of the current tag, and we use a left-to-right beam search, we were able to add the case tagger features to the PoS tagger and perform the tagging in only one pass. This led to a small improvement in accuracy over the separate case tagger, but, perhaps more importantly, eliminated much of the overhead in performance and code complexity caused by re-tagging all sentences with the case tagger.

The result of this experiment no. 2, with Stagger+LF, is shown in Table 4. We obtain an accuracy of 91.42% for all words, which corresponds to a 1.5% error reduction compared to the basic feature set. Dredze and Wallenberg (2008a) obtained an error reduction of 4.6% when adding their case tagger to their base tagger. It is not clear to us why we do not achieve similar gains, even though we use very similar features.

4.3   Handling unknown words

As mentioned in Section 4.1, Stagger's accuracy for unknown words (66.06% in experiment no. 2) is significantly lower than the corresponding accuracy of the three taggers shown in Table 3 (e.g. 77.47% by the HMM+Ice+HMM tagger). The competition in this category is indeed tough. First, TriTagger uses an effective suffix algorithm, based on probability distributions for suffixes of various lengths (Brants, 2000), which has worked well for various languages. Second, both IceTagger and HMM+Ice+HMM use IceMorphy for guessing the tag profile for unknown words.

Nevertheless, Stagger's accuracy for unknown words is higher than the corresponding accuracy in various other data-driven taggers tested by Helgadóttir (2005).

The next logical step was thus trying to increase the accuracy for unknown words and minimizing the UWR. We carried this out in two ways. First, in Section 4.3.1, by integrating IceMorphy with Stagger, and, second, in Section 4.3.2, by providing Stagger with data from BÍN.

Note that unknown word guessers (like IceMorphy) exist for various languages (Mikheev, 1997; Nakov et al., 2003; Nakagawa and Yuji, 2006), whereas large comprehensive inflectional databases like BÍN are rare.

4.3.1   Stagger with IceMorphy

As mentioned in Section 3.2, IceMorphy is an unknown word guesser and a "filler" for tag profile gaps for known words. Since both IceMorphy and Stagger are open-source, and implemented in Java, we could easily integrate the two components.

We did so, in the following manner. During testing, we look up a word w in the dictionary derived by Stagger during training. If w is known, then the tag gap filling method of IceMorphy is used to guess missing tags in the profile for w.[6] If w is unknown, then IceMorphy is used to guess the whole tag profile for w. The dictionaries used by IceMorphy are generated from the IFD corpus (Loftsson, 2008). When we evaluate each test fold F, using the integration of Stagger and IceMorphy, we thus only make IceMorphy have access to the dictionaries generated from fold F.

The results for this tagger, Stagger+LF+IceMorphy (generic Stagger, in addition to linguistic features and IceMorphy), are shown as experiment no. 3 in Table 4. We obtain a large increase in tagging accuracy for all words, from 91.42% to 92.82%, which is equivalent to an error reduction of 16.3%. By integrating IceMorphy with Stagger, accuracy for unknown words increases from 66.06% to 77.03% (error reduction of 32.3%), and for known words from 93.26% to 93.97% (error reduction of 10.5%).

4.3.2   Adding data from BÍN

As discussed in Section 3.1, BÍN is a large morphological database. It has been used by Loftsson et al. (2011) to extend the dictionaries of PoS taggers, thereby minimizing the UWR.

In our fourth experiment, we added data from BÍN to Stagger, which during training can be provided with an optional lexicon. We used exactly the same data as used by Loftsson et al. (2011), i.e. a file of about 5.3 million entries from BÍN, in which the PoS tags used in BÍN have been mapped to the IFD tags (see Loftsson et al. (2011) for details on how the file is generated). From this file, we generated the entries for the optional lexicon, i.e. a 4-tuple: <word, lemma, tag, frequency>. The first three elements of this tuple come from BÍN, whereas the last element is 0, in our case. During training, the provided lexicon is automatically extended by the training set.

Since BÍN contains a very large amount of word forms, there is no need to use IceMorphy to fill in tag profile gaps – adding the data from BÍN indeed means that most such gaps disappear. Hence, in this experiment, we tested only using IceMorphy to guess the tag profile for unknown words.

---

[6]We do not use tag profile gap filling for verbs, because IceMorphy overgenerates (recall is higher than precision (Loftsson, 2008)) and testing on the development set resulted in higher accuracy by excluding the verbs.

The result of this experiment no. 4 is shown as the tagger Stagger+LF+IceMorphy+BÍN in Table 4. For all words, we obtain a state-of-the-art accuracy of 93.70%, which is equivalent to 3.4% error reduction compared to the previously best result of 93.48%, obtained by the HMM+Ice+HMM tagger (see Table 3). Stagger's accuracy for known words (94.02%) is somewhat higher than the corresponding accuracy of the HMM+Ice+HMM tagger (93.85%), and for unknown words Stagger's accuracy (61.45%) also surpasses that of HMM+Ice+HMM (60.50%).

4.4   Adding word embeddings

In our final experiment, no. 5, we added C&W word embeddings (WE), discussed in Section 2.4, as features during training. We induced 48-dimensional C&W embeddings using the tool of Robert Östling[7] and 10 million sentences (ca. 170 million words) of Icelandic web texts from the Wortschatz project.[8] We limited the vocabulary to words occurring at least 100 times in the data, in total 65 426 words. The embeddings were trained for 25 billion updates, or about 150 iterations through the entire corpus, which took about ten days on a 2.66 GHz Intel Core2 system.

As shown in Table 4, we obtain an overall accuracy of 93.84% for the Stagger+LF+IceMorphy+BÍN+WE tagger, which is equivalent to 29.3% error reduction compared to the first experiment (see Table 4), and 5.5% error reduction compared to the previous best results.

5   Error analysis

We performed preliminary error analysis on the output of the Stagger+LF+IceMorphy+BÍN+WE tagger. We combined the tagging errors made on the test sets of the first nine folds.

We define an error type as a pair (x, y), where x is the predicted tag and y is the gold tag. Stagger makes 4,108 different error types. 1,796 of those, or 43.72%, appear only once. The 10 most frequent errors account for 14.60% of the total errors, as shown in Table 5. It is notable that 6 of the 10 most frequent errors are due to mistakes in case assignments (errors no. 1-4 and 9-10 in Table 5).

The two most frequent error types (aþ,ao) and (ao,aþ) differentiate between a preposition governing the accusative (*ao*) or dative case (*aþ*). The case marking in these tags "[...] do not reflect any morphological distinctions in the words they are attached to, but only indicate the effect (case government) that these words have on their complements" (Loftsson et al., 2009).

For example, for the prepositional phrase "með bók" 'with book', tagged as "ao nveo", the fourth letter (o) in the tag for the noun "bók" denotes accusative case and the corresponding case marking on the preposition "með" is really redundant. In a way, a tagger is penalized twice for such case tagging errors, because of the wrong case in the preposition in addition to the error in the complement. If we do not make a distinction between the tags "ao" and "aþ", the tagging accuracy of the Stagger+LF+IceMorphy+BÍN+WE tagger increases from 93.84% to 94.17%.

6   Conclusion

We have applied Stagger, an open-source implementation of an Averaged Perceptron tagger, to the morphologically complex Icelandic language, obtaining state-of-the-art tagging accuracy

---

[7]http://www.ling.su.se/english/nlp/tools/svek
[8]http://corpora.uni-leipzig.de/

No.	Error type	Rate	Cumulative rate
1	(aþ,ao)	2.97	2.97
2	(ao,aþ)	2.35	5.32
3	(nveþ,nveo)	1.49	6.81
4	(nveo,nveþ)	1.33	8.14
5	(sng,sfg3fn)	1.24	9.37
6	(ao,aa)	1.21	10.58
7	(sfg3eþ,sfg1eþ)	1.18	11.76
8	(aa,ao)	1.01	12.77
9	(nheo,nhen)	0.93	13.70
10	(nhen,nheo)	0.90	14.60

Table 5: The 10 most frequent error types and their rate of occurrence in % in the output of the Stagger+LF+IceMorphy+BÍN+WE tagger. An error type is a pair (x, y): x is the predicted tag and y is the gold tag.

when using a version of the IFD corpus in which 565 different tags appear. Our best result, the accuracy of 93.84%, is equivalent to 5.5% error reduction compared to the previous best results on the same data.

Our largest gain in accuracy was obtained by integrating Stagger with IceMorphy, an open-source unknown word guesser for Icelandic, for the purpose of guessing the tag profile for unknown words, and to fill in gaps in the tag profile for known words. Nearly as much was gained when we used data from a large morphological database to reduce the UWR. Small increases in accuracy were obtained by adding some language-specific features, and by using word embeddings induced from a large unannotated corpus.

For a morphologically complex language, where unknown word forms are particularly frequent, we conclude that simple suffix features (as used in the generic version of Stagger) can not compare to a good morphological analyzer (unknown word guesser) or a large morphological database, and that the analyzer probably represents the best time investment when improving a PoS tagger.

In future work, we would like to experiment further with semi-supervised training, and apply the lessons learned from the Icelandic case to other morphologically complex languages. For Icelandic in particular, we want to explore ways to reduce the most frequent errors based on incorrect case assignments.

References

Berger, A. L., Pietra, V. J. D., and Pietra, S. A. D. (1996). A Maximum Entropy Approach to Natural Language Processing. *Computational Linguistics*, 22:39–71.

Bjarnadóttir, K. (2012). The Database of Modern Icelandic Inflection. In *Proceedings of the workshop "Language Technology for Normalization of Less-Resourced Languages", SaLTMiL 8 – AfLaT*, LREC, Istanbul, Turkey.

Brants, T. (2000). TnT: A statistical part-of-speech tagger. In *Proceedings of the 6th Conference on Applied Natural Language Processing*, Seattle, WA, USA.

Collins, M. (2002). Discriminative training methods for hidden markov models: Theory and experiments with perceptron algorithms. In *Proceedings of the ACL-02 Conference on Empirical Methods in Natural Language Processing*, Philadelphia, PA, USA.

Collobert, R. and Weston, J. (2008). A Unified Architecture for Natural Language Processing: Deep Neural Networks with Multitask learning. In *Proceedings of the 25th International Conference on Machine learning*, ICML, Helsinki, Finland.

Collobert, R., Weston, J., Bottou, L., Karlen, M., Kavukcuoglu, K., and Kuksa, P. (2011). Natural Language Processing (Almost) from Scratch. *Journal of Machine Learning Research*, 12:2493–2537.

Dredze, M. and Wallenberg, J. (2008a). Further Results and Analysis of Icelandic Part of Speech Tagging. Technical report, Department of Computer and Information Science, University of Pennsylvania.

Dredze, M. and Wallenberg, J. (2008b). Icelandic Data Driven Part of Speech Tagging. In *Proceedings of the 46th Annual Meeting of the Association for Computational Linguistics: Human Language Technologies*, ACL-HLT, Columbus, OH, USA.

Georgiev, G., Zhikov, V., Simov, K., Osenova, P., and Nakov, P. (2012). Feature-Rich Part-of-speech Tagging for Morphologically Complex Languages: Application to Bulgarian. In *Proceedings of the 13th Conference of the European Chapter of the Association for Computational Linguistics*, EACL, Avignon, France.

Giménez, J. and Màrquez, L. (2004). SVMTool: A general POS tagger generator based on Support Vector Machines. In *Proceedings of the 4th International Conference on Language Resources and Evaluation*, LREC, Lisbon, Portugal.

Helgadóttir, S. (2005). Testing Data-Driven Learning Algorithms for PoS Tagging of Icelandic. In Holmboe, H., editor, *Nordisk Sprogteknologi 2004*. Museum Tusculanums Forlag, Copenhagen.

Lafferty, J., McCallum, A., and Pereira, F. (2001). Conditional Random Fields: Probabilistic Models for Segmenting and Labeling Sequence Data. In *Proceedings of the 18th International Conference on Machine Learning*, ICML, Williamstown, MA, USA.

Loftsson, H. (2008). Tagging Icelandic text: A linguistic rule-based approach. *Nordic Journal of Linguistics*, 31(1):47–72.

Loftsson, H., Helgadóttir, S., and Rögnvaldsson, E. (2011). Using a morphological database to increase the accuracy in PoS tagging. In *Proceedings of Recent Advances in Natural Language Processing*, RANLP, Hissar, Bulgaria.

Loftsson, H., Kramarczyk, I., Helgadóttir, S., and Rögnvaldsson, E. (2009). Improving the PoS tagging accuracy of Icelandic text. In *Proceedings of the 17th Nordic Conference of Computational Linguistics*, NoDaLiDa, Odense, Denmark.

Loftsson, H. and Rögnvaldsson, E. (2007). IceNLP: A Natural Language Processing Toolkit for Icelandic. In *Proceedings of Interspeech 2007, Special Session: "Speech and language technology for less-resourced languages"*, Interspeech, Antwerp, Belgium.

Marcus, M. P., Santorini, B., and Marcinkiewicz, M. A. (1993). Building a Large Annotated Corpus of English: The Penn Treebank. *Computational Linguistics*, 19(20):313–330.

Mikheev, A. (1997). Automatic Rule Induction for Unknown Word Guessing. *Computational Linguistics*, 21(4):543–565.

Nakagawa, T. and Yuji, M. (2006). Guessing parts-of-speech of unknown words using global information. In *Proceedings of the 21st International Conference on Computational Linguistics and the 44th Annual meeting of the Association for Computational Linguistics*, Sydney, Australia.

Nakov, P., Bonev, Y., Angelova, G., Cius, E., and Hahn, W. v. (2003). Guessing Morphological Classes of Unknown German Nouns. In *Proceedings of Recent Advances in Natural Language Processing*, RANLP, Borovets, Bulgaria.

Pind, J., Magnússon, F., and Briem, S. (1991). *Íslensk orðtíðnibók [The Icelandic Frequency Dictionary]*. The Institute of Lexicography, University of Iceland, Reykjavik, Iceland.

Radziszewski, A. (2013). A tiered CRF tagger for Polish. In Bembenik, R., Skonieczny, Ł., Rybiński, H., Kryszkiewicz, M., and Niezgódka, M., editors, *Intelligent Tools for Building a Scientific Information Platform: Advanced Architectures and Solutions*. Springer Verlag.

Ratnaparkhi, A. (1996). A Maximum Entropy Model for Part-Of-Speech Tagging. In *Proceedings of the Empirical Methods in Natural Language Processing Conference*, Philadelphia, PA, USA.

Rögnvaldsson, E. and Helgadóttir, S. (2011). Morphosyntactic Tagging of Old Icelandic Texts and Its Use in Studying Syntactic Variation and Change. In Sporleder, C., van den Bosch, A., and Zervanou, K., editors, *Language Technology for Cultural Heritage: Selected Papers from the LaTeCH Workshop Series*. Springer, Berlin.

Shen, L., Satta, G., and Joshi, A. (2007). Guided Learning for Bidirectional Sequence Classification. In *Proceedings of the 45th Annual Meeting of the Association of Computational Linguistics*, ACL, Prague, Czech Republic.

Søgaard, A. (2011). Semi-supervised condensed nearest neighbor for part-of-speech tagging. In *Proceedings of the 49th Annual Meeting of the Association for Computational Linguistics: Human Language Technologies*, ACL-HLT, Portland, Oregon.

Spoustová, D. j., Hajič, J., Raab, J., and Spousta, M. (2009). Semi-supervised Training for the Averaged Perceptron POS Tagger. In *Proceedings of the 12th Conference of the European Chapter of the Association for Computational Linguistics*, EACL, Athens, Greece.

Toutanova, K., Klein, D., Manning, C. D., and Singer, Y. (2003). Feature-rich part-of-speech tagging with a cyclic dependency network. In *Proceedings of the 2003 Conference of the North American Chapter of the Association for Computational Linguistics on Human Language Technology*, NAACL, Edmonton, Canada.

Tsuruoka, Y., Miyao, Y., and Kazama, J. (2011). Learning with Lookahead: Can History-Based Models Rival Globally Optimized Models? In *Proceedings of the Fifteenth Conference on Computational Natural Language Learning*, CoNLL, Portland, Oregon, USA.

Turian, J., Ratinov, L., and Bengio, Y. (2010). Word representations: a simple and general method for semi-supervised learning. In *Proceedings of the 48th Annual Meeting of the Association for Computational Linguistics*, ACL, Uppsala, Sweden.

Östling, R. (2012). Stagger: A modern POS tagger for Swedish. In *Proceedings of the Swedish Language Technology Conference*, SLTC, Lund, Sweden.

IPhraxtor - A linguistically informed system for extraction of term candidates

Magnus Merkel, Jody Foo, Lars Ahrenberg

Department of Computer and Information Science, Linköping University

magnus.merkel@liu.se, jody.foo@liu.se lars.ahrenberg.liu.se

ABSTRACT

In this paper a method and a flexible tool for performing monolingual term extraction is presented, based on the use of syntactic analysis where information on parts-of-speech, syntactic functions and surface syntax tags can be utilised. The standard approaches to evaluating term extraction, namely by manual evaluation of the top *n* term candidates or by comparing to a gold standard consisting of a list of terms from a specific domain can have its advantages, but in this paper we try to realise a proposal by Bernier-Colborne (2012) where extracted terms are compared to a gold standard consisting of a test corpus where terms have been annotated in context. Apart from applying this evaluation to different configurations of the tool, practical experiences from using the tool for real world situations are described.

KEYWORDS: computational terminology, term extraction, evaluation, terminological work.

1   Introduction

The task of creating domain-specific terminologies can be approached with different strategies. The traditional terminological approach within terminology work, performed by terminologists, often consisted of more or less manual term extractions from texts, in combination with concept-oriented analysis of the domain. Today, much of the tedious term extraction can be replaced by automatic approaches where a computer tool can harvest term candidates from large document collections without human intervention for later processing. The results from the term candidate extraction phase is then the starting point for further selection, filtering, categorizations before the terms can be put into a term database and used by other applications, such as writing support tools, translation tools, search engines, linguistic quality assurance systems, etc.

In this paper a background to the field of automatic term extraction is presented. The background is followed by a presentation of a flexible tool for performing monolingual term extraction, based on the use of syntactic analysis where information on syntactic function and surface syntax tags can be utilised. The results from this tool can then be used in subsequent manual or automatic phases, e.g. when building a terminology or an ontology. Standard approaches to evaluating term extraction are then described and the setup for the evaluation method used in this work is described. This section is followed by a description of the corpus used in the evaluation as well as different configurations that were tested. Results for precision and recall are presented and discussed. The final section before the conclusions contains a description of how the extraction tool has been used in real world situations in the initial stages of creating term banks for Swedish government agencies. The paper ends with conclusions and a discussion of the results.

1.1   Background

Automatic term extraction is a field within language technology that deals with "extraction of technical terms from domain-specific language corpora" (Zhang et al., 2008). All approaches within automatic term extraction involve some kind of text analysis, some method of selecting and filtering term candidates. Typically the text analysis stages requires some kind of parts-of-speech analysis and lemmatization of inflected word forms, but it could also involve more complex analysis like dependency relations between tokens in the input text.

Term exctraction may have different applications in areas such as construction of ontologies, document indexing, validation of translation memories, and even classical terminology work. All the different applications share the constructive nature of the activity, and the need to distinguish terms from non-terms, or, if we prefer domain-specific terms from general vocabulary (Justeson & Katz, 1995).

The automatic term extraction process will usually be followed by a manual, sometimes computer-aided, process of *validation*. For this reason, the outputs of a term extraction process are better referred to as *term candidates* of which some, after the validation process, may be elevated to term status.

Early work on term extraction focused on linguistic analysis and POS patterns (e.g. Bourigault, 1992; Ananiadou 1994) for identifying term patterns. Later, these methods have been complemented by using more statistical measures, especially for ranking and filtering of the results (e.g. Zhang 2008; Merkel & Foo 2007).

2   The term extraction tool (IPhraxtor)

The tool presented here is in a way a standard term extraction tool relying mainly on the linguistic data. In this experiment the Connexor Machinese Syntax software (Tapanainen & Järvinen, 1997) has been used, but in principle any linguistic analyzer for any language could be used as long as the analysed texts conform to the xml dtd used. When texts are analyzed using the Connexor Machinese Syntax framework, information on various levels are produced such as base form, morpho-syntactic description (number, definiteness, case, etc.), syntactic function and dependency relation. The output data from the text analysis could look something like the following for the sentence "8. Increasing or decreasing the viscosity of the cement slurry.":

```
Input sentence: 8. Increasing or decreasing the viscosity of the cement slurry.

XML representation after text analysis:
<s id="s25628":C04B|FILE_OR_GROUP:88303835.en.lwa|ID:38">
<w id="w637528" base="8" pos="NUM" msd="CARD" func="main" stag="NH"  >8</w>
<w id="w637529" base="." pos="INTERP" msd="Period" func="" stag="INTERP" >.</w>
<w id="w637530" base="increase" pos="V" msd="" func="" stag="VA" >Increasing</w>
<w id="w637531" base="or" pos="CC" msd="" func="cc" fa="3" stag="CC" >or</w>
<w id="w637532" base="decrease" pos="V" msd="" func="cc" fa="3" stag="VA" >decreasing</w>
<w id="w637533" base="the" pos="DET" msd="" func="attr" fa="7" stag="&gt;N" >the</w>
<w id="w637534" base="viscosity" pos="N" msd="NOM-SG" func="obj" fa="5" stag="NH" >viscosity</w>
<w id="w637535" base="of" pos="PREP" msd="" func="mod" fa="7" stag="N&lt;" >of</w>
<w id="w637536" base="the" pos="DET" msd="" func="attr" fa="10" stag="&gt;N" >the</w>
<w id="w637537" base="cement" pos="N" msd="NOM-SG" func="attr" fa="11" stag="&gt;N" >cement</w>
<w id="w637538" base="slurry" pos="N" msd="NOM-SG" func="pcomp" fa="8" stag="NH" >slurry</w>
<w id="w637539" base="." pos="INTERP" msd="Period" func="" stag="INTERP" sem="" >.</w>
</s>
```

TABLE 1. Output from the text analysis.

The information from Machinese Syntax includes the base form of each text word ("base"), morpho-syntactic features ("msd") like number and case, dependency relations/syntactic function ("func"), syntactic surface "stag", which can be utilised by the term extraction tool in the next step.

The analysed text is stored in xml format following the illustration in Table 1. The xml files are then loaded into the term extraction tool, called IPhraxtor. IPhraxtor is implemented in java with a graphical interface that can be used to test different strategies sentence by sentence from the input. On the Rules tab in IPhraxtor (see Figure 1), the user can specify different configurations that will govern the term extraction.

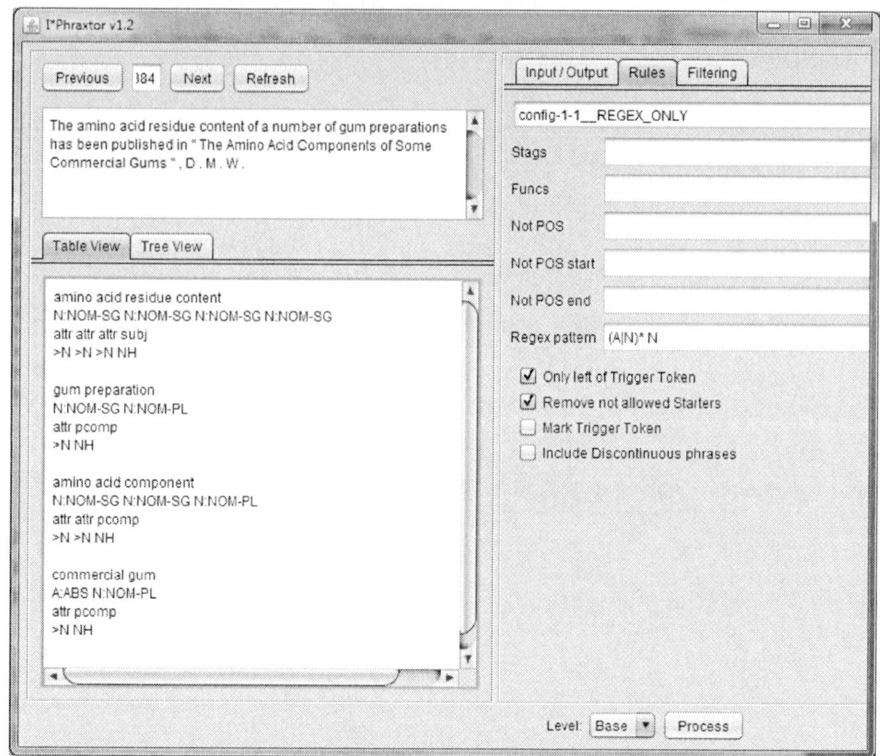

Figure 1. The Rules tab in IPhraxtor where configurations of
patterns and tags used can be tested.

By using the Rules tab, the user can test different regular expressions (on the POS level). In Figure 1, only the simple pattern "(A|N)* N" is used for extraction. The active sentence of the input text is shown in top left panel and below this panel the extracted term candidates, used by only using the given regular expression pattern are shown. In this case the extracted term candidates for the input sentence are "amino acid residue content", "gum preparation" "amino acid component" and "commercial gum".

The other fields that could be used to restrict and change the way term candidates are extracted are:

- Stags: Surface syntactic tags

- Funcs: Syntactic functions/dependency relations, such as subject, object, prepositional complement, etc.

- Not POS: POS tags that should never occur inside a term candidate

- No POS start: POS tags that are ignored at the start of term candidates

- No POS end: POS tags that are ignored at the end of term candidates

- Regex pattern: regular expression containing POS tags

Apart from giving values to these fields in order to tune the term candidate extraction process, it is also possible to specify files with stop words that will be used to trim the term candidates. The stop word lists are of two types: 1) stop words that are used at the beginning of term candidates (initial_stop_words); and 2) stopwords used at the end of term candidates (trailing_stop_words). The reason for separating the stop word lists in this fashion is that there could be cases where it is necessary to treat them differently, for example if a noun can be included in term candidate as a nominal modifier, but not as a head word. In that case, the noun in question would only be listed in the trailing stop word file, but not in the initial stop word file.

Term candidates can be exported to a database including all available information such as base forms, inflected forms, part-of-speech, frequency, and with the surrounding contexts, for later use in the terminology validation process.

The hypothesis behind extending the extraction patterns to more than just POS patterns was that some terms could actually be captured by syntactic functions (for example subjects and objects). If we use the simple regular expression used in Figure 1, term candidates like "the Save As command" will not be detected, but the candidate is indeed found if it was used as a syntactic functional subject, object or prepositional complement, and *SUBJ|OBJ|PCOMP* was specified as values in *Funcs* field.

2.1   Evaluation of terminology extraction and evaluation setup

Evaluation of term extraction systems can be done in different ways. One often used strategy is to let the system rank the output of term candidates as n-best lists where the highest ranking term candidates are at the top of the list. Then a human evaluator evaluates the top 100, 500 or 1000 term candidates with regards to whether term candidates are likely terms in the given domain. This evaluation technique has its advantages, but it also fails to capture how good the system is to capture the proportion of available terms (recall). The n-best evaluation strategy gives a good picture of how well the ranking of term candidates are and an estimate of the precision of the system, but does not provide any information on the recall of the system.

An alternative approach is to have a gold standard list of terms for a specific domain and let the output from term extraction tools be evaluated against that gold standard. This strategy was for example used in the CESART evaluation project (Mustafa el Hadi et al., 2006). In the Quæro evaluation initiative (Mondary et al., 2012), the approach of using a domain-specific terminological gold standard was further developed using the terminological precision, recall and F-measure metrics first proposed by Nazarenko et al. (2009). In principle, the output of the term extraction system is evaluated against the gold standard, thereby making it possible to compare different systems and different versions of systems applied on a specific domain. Such a gold standard should be based on the whole corpus from which terms are to be extracted. Having a gold standard also means, in essence that we already have all terms contained in a specific corpus. For practical applications, this kind of evaluation is impossible as extracting terminology from a corpus is the actual goal.

A recent proposal by Bernier-Colborne (2012) is to annotate a corpus with information on where terminological units occur in the text, "accounting for the wide variety of realizations of terms in context". Using an annotated corpus rather than a term list has several advantages. A term list will measure precision and recall on the type level, and a gold standard consisting of an annotated corpus can measure precision and recall on the token level. This is important for two reasons: (1) a terminological unit can be composed of different linguistic objects (e.g. different parts-of-speech) depending on context; and (2) linguistic tagging tools (e.g. POS taggers) are not 100 per cent accurate which can result in a decrease in either precision or recall. Having a handle on all the term candidate instances in the gold standard, makes it possible to perform error analysis and locate where the actual errors occur. Furthermore, with the right support tools, creating an annotated gold standard from a sample from the target corpus is relatively feasible for practical applications.

From a practical point of view, the Bernier-Colborne proposal, with the modification that the gold standard is created on a subset of the full corpus, is a reasonable method in order to measure the quality of a term candidate extraction system. In other words, a gold standard has to be created where terms are marked up in the subset of the actual text collection and the performance of the term candidate extraction system has to be evaluated against that gold standard. In this way, measures like precision and recall can be used in exactly the same way as they are done in for example the named entity extraction field.

The evaluation of how well different extraction strategies would work was set up in the following way:

- Creating a corpus of patent texts from five different subject areas

- Separating the corpus into a training set and a test set

- The training sets for all different texts were used to find out general strategies, using the interactive Rules tab in IPhraxtor (see Figure 1).

- Each test set consisted of 100 sentences which were marked up manually with instances of term candidates in each sentence. The aim was to only extract term candidates that were considered to be noun phrases, no attempts at catching verbs or independent adjectives were made for the evaluation. Two independent evaluators were given instructions to create the gold standards as uniformly as possible.

- Scripts for measuring precision and recall for each run against the gold standard was created.

- In the first stage ten different strategies were tested, and in the second stage, three strategies were evaluated in more detail.

The creation of the gold standard was made in a special environment where the annotator reviewed the test section of the corpus and highlighted each term candidate in the 100 sentences:

FIGURE 2. Simple annotation of instances of terms in the gold standard. Five terms are marked up as being terms.

The corpus used for the tests consisted of five patent application domains:

Corpus	Name	#words: en
Edible oils or fats	A23D	705,764
Cocoa	A23G	610,893
Hats: head coverings	A42B	73,991
Non-metallic elements	C01B	1,847,571
Lime, Magnesia, Slag, Cements	C04B	2,075,622

TABLE 2. Corpus description of the five different patent domains.

Initially 10 configurations were tested ranging from using one simple regular only to various setups where the use of combinations of stop words, no_start_POS, no_end_POS, Funcs, STAG was evaluated, as well as using more complex regular expressions. After this stage, it was clear that the regular expressions had contributed substantially to the overall result. Extending the simplest regular expression to other NP regular expressions only had minor effects. However, there was a clear improvement for the end result if we combined the use of stop word lists, filters for start and end POS tags, as well as functional and syntactic surface tags with the regular expression.

So if we compare the A, B and C strategies below (A using only a simple regular expression of POS tags, B using stop word lists, syntactic functional and surface tags but no regular expressions; and C using regular expression plus stopword lists)

A. Regex: (A|N)* N

B. No Regex
    Func: SUBJ|OBJ|PCOMP
    No_Start_POS: DET|NUM|CC|CS|PRON|PREP|ADV|INTERP
    No_End_POS: DET|NUM|CC|CS|PRON|PREP|ADV|INTERP|V|A
    Func: SUBJ|OBJ|PCOMP
    Stag: NH|>N|N<
    Stopword lists: Yes

C. Regex: "(A|N)* N"
    Stopword lists: Yes

we get the following precision and recall figures for the different subcorpora[1]:

Corpus	A23D		A23G		A42B		C01B		C014B	
	P	R	P	R	P	R	P	R	P	R
RegExp (A)	0.52	0.80	0.64	0.81	0.62	0.8	0.57	0,74	0,60	0,81
Synt. Tags (no RegExp (B)	0.36	0.78	0.4	**0.91**	0.44	0.69	0.35	0.74	0.37	0.77
RegExp + stop word lists (C)	**0.63**	**0.84**	**0.72**	0.84	**0.68**	**0.82**	**0.6**	0,76	**0,67**	**0,82**

TABLE 3. Precision (P) and recall (R) figures for the different strategies and subcorpora.

In all cases we get clear increases in both recall and precision when the C strategy is used, except in A23G, where recall is actually higher for strategy B, but then with a substantially lower precision score.

---

[1] The scores are calculated as an average score for the two annotators of the gold standard.

We also tested several more elaborate regular expressions for catching more complex noun phrases, including coordinated noun phrases, but this did not result in better scores. Recall was slightly increased but always at the cost of lower precision. The one single factor that contributes most is whether stop words are used or not. The use of syntactic functions and syntactic surface tags does indeed lower recall in all except one of the corpora (A23G) and syntactic functions result in lower precision. Parts-of-speech tagging is usually of a very high quality in syntactic analyzers, and it could be expected that text analysers do not perform on the same level as POS tagging when it comes to detecting dependency relations and syntactic functions. This could be a factor that contributes to the poor precision rates of the B strategy, but we have no in-depth analysis to support such a claim.

3   Practical use

The term candidate extraction tool presented above has also been applied in more real life situations for making an inventory of terminology used at government agencies in Sweden. As a starting point for creating a terminology bank for Försäkringskassan (The Swedish Social Security Agency), IPhraxtor was used to explore what terminology was actually used on their external web site[2]. The idea was to assist government agency in getting a picture of what their terminology usage and combine this with a comparison of the existing term lists and other resources available on the internet, such as the Swedish National Termbank, Rikstermbanken, created by Terminologicentrum (2012).

All documents from the website was processed into text format and analyzed by the Machinese Syntax tool described earlier. Then various tests were performed using the IPhraxtor tool for extracting terminology. Because all the texts were in Swedish and the expected terminology should cover verb and adjective constructions as well as noun phrases, modifications to the strategies described above were made. The terminology that existed in old term lists from the agency gave indications on what type of constructions they already used. This led to the decision that we had to prioritize recall over precision, in order to be sure that no important term candidates were missed. In Swedish it seems to be more common than in English to have prepositional complements inside noun phrase terms, for example the term "barn med funktionsnedsättning" (eng. children with disabilities). This meant that the use of the syntactic tags inside IPhraxtor could be used better as all instances of terms of this form that functioned as subjects and objects could be located, for example. The chosen strategy led to a loss of precision, as expected, but by using different ways of filtering term candidates during the validation phase, it did not cause extensive extra hours of manual work.

All in all, around 55,000 unique term candidates were extracted with the aid of IPhraxtor from the 8 million words that formed the input data from the external web site. These term candidates were then processed with a mixture of automatic, interactive and manual techniques into a remaining set of around 17.000 term candidates. The filtering process removed misspellings, term candidates in other languages than Swedish, non-words due to poor processing of PDF files as well as term candidates that simply should not be considered to be terms later on (general words that had not been filtered out by stop word lists, words that had been tagged incorrectly by the tagger, etc.). After that the 17.000 term candidates were processed in order to see if they occurred in the Swedish National Termbank (Rikstermbanken) or in any other term resource that

---

[2] http://www.forsakringskassan.se

already existed at the agency (e.g. Swedish English word lists). The output from this stage was handed over to Terminologicentrum and the agency as an Excel file with the intention to further categorize the term candidates into different categories and decide which term candidates that should be evaluated to "real terms" in the domain.

Examples of the resulting term candidates are shown in Figure 2:

	C KonceptID	D POS	E Term	G Frek	RTB	FKEN	FKBK .	Varianter	Exempel
227	#00097&	verb	anslå	29				anslagit anslagits anslogs anslå anslår anslås	Riksdagen har **anslagit** särskilda r Försäkringskassan måste ha fått d De medel som **anslogs** till--och--m Försäkringskassan räknar heller in Sedan det nuvarande statliga tandv Besluten **anslås** på Försäkringska
228	#00097&	verb	kungöra	5				kungjorts kungöras kungörs	Märkningen ska vidare göras inom Försäkringskassan anser att det är ha Beslutet **kungörs** i Post-och
229	#00098&	subst	efterlevandestöd	563		survivor's support; surviving children's allowance	efterlevan destöd (Status: Preliminä r i väntan på PMU)	efterlevandestöd Efterlevandestöd EFTERLEVANDESTÖD efterlevandestödet Efterlevandestödet	2007 : 03 -Ankomstdatum för ansö **Efterlevandestöd** räknas som en 22 12345678901 19150909TF01 aa Skulle det finnas motsvarande förm **Efterlevandestödet** fyller upp--till
230	#00098&	subst	EL-stöd	8				EL-stöd EL-stödet	63 = Restbelopp Övr 64 = Restbel Om ÄP-GARP , **EL-stödet** eller ga
231	#00099&	subst	folkmängd	39				folkmängd Folkmängd folkmängden Folkmängden	250 miljoner kronor fördelas som fa SCB (1996) **Folkmängd** efter åld Om inte alla landsting gör sådana l **Folkmängden** i Haninge har ökat
232	#00099&	subst	invånarantal	8				invånarantal Invånarantal invånarantalet Invånarantalet	Det ekonomiska utvärderingsresult Kommuntyp **Invånarantal** , Minst antal besök gjordes på Gotla **Invånarantalet** har successivt mir
233	#00099&	subst	population	208	population (Status: Tillrådd)			population Population populationen Populationen Populationens populationer populationerna populations Populations	Det gäller till--exempel Ageing pop Publicerad : Journal of **Population** Att ökningen av hushåll med sökar Andelen av olika åldersklasser son **Populationens** utseende och bevi Två olika **populationer** ingick i und En jämförelse mellan Tabell 1 och Prison **populations** as political co Populations " (2001 Populatio

TermKoncept / Delsträngar

Ready — 100%

FIGURE 3. Term candidates from extraction using IPhraxtor with conceptual groupings as well as information on use of term in other resources, inflectional variants and contexts where the term candidate is used.

The term candidates shown in Figure 3 are grouped as possible synonyms using the same concept ID (KonceptID), which is indicated by the fact that the term candidates "efterlevandestöd" and "EL-stöd" share the concept ID. There are also information about whether the term candidate occurs in any other resource ("efterlevandestöd" has the English translations "survivor's support" and "surviving children's allowance" in column FKEN (Försäkringskassan's English term list). Also the term candidate "population" has also been located somewhere in the Swedish national term bank (Rikstermbanken) in column H, RTB.

Another place where IPhraxtor has been used is at the Swedish Unemployment Insurance Board (Inspektionen för arbetslöshetsförsäkringen – IAF). In the same way as with Försäkringskassan, the external web site was used as input for the term extraction process. Due to a smaller volume of text, the extraction stage resulted in around 12,000 term candidates which were reduced to around 3,500 term candidates during the validation stage.

The top forty "surviving" term candidates for IAF were the following:

Term candidate	Freq.
arbetslöshetskassa	5338
IAF	4178
arbetsförmedling	2354
arbete	1740
ärende	1526
arbetslöshetsförsäkring	1403
underrättelse	1323
ersättning	1264
sökande	1100
arbetslöshetsersättning	1086
genomströmningstid	1050
uppgift	901
arbetssökande	839
beslut	805
uppdrag	760
myndighet	668
verksamhet	625
åtgärd	542
lag	508
söka	451
kassa	440
medlem	431
intyg	414
ALF	412
förordning	411
regelverk	405
arbetslös	399
arbetsförmedlare	387
arbetsgivare	383
handläggning	381
föreskrift	370
Inspektionen för arbetslöshetsförsäkringen	369
ersättningstagare	367
utbetalning	366
medarbetare	353
aktör	352
uppföljning	344
rutin	319
arbetsgivarintyg	318
arbeta	309

TABLE 4. The top 40 term candidates from IAF

The term candidates extracted for both the government agencies have turned out to be a vital step towards creating standardized term banks. Not only did the extraction provide an insight to how terminology actually is used on their web site, it also highlighted problems regarding inconsistent usage of synonyms and acronyms as well as sets of spelling variants of terms. It was also a showcase for claiming that IPhraxtor also works for Swedish.

4   Summary and conclusion

In this paper we have presented a tool for extracting term candidates based on linguistically analyzed data, including POS, syntactic function, and surface syntax tags. The tool provides an interactive environment where combinations of regular expressions for POS sequences and the use of various linguistic tags and stop lists can be expressed and tested in a very flexible manner. We have also investigated the use of an evaluation method where a test corpus is annotated with instances of term candidates, i.e., terms in real context. This is an alternative to using terminological gold standards consisting of lists of terms for a specific domain, and, we argue that the presented approach gives another view of the quality of term extraction tools. Measuring recall for term extraction has always been a bit complicated. Even when system results are compared to a gold standard comprising of a list of validated terms for a specific domain, the results are not taking into account the specific features of how terms are distributed in the tested corpus. If the output of the system is designed to actually pinpoint each instance of a possible term in the test corpus, then it is straightforward to measure precision and recall in the same way as in, for example, named entity recognition. It could be argued that 100 sentences per subcorpora is too small a size for making this kind of evaluation; the actual number of term instances per gold standard varied between 300 and 500, but more elaborate testing would need to be performed in order to establish what size the gold standard need to be.

The evaluation from running the extraction tool on five different corpora from the patent text domain showed that the best strategy with the current tool is to use regular expressions of POS tags and stop word lists. Adding information from syntactic tags for grammatical functions like subject and object did lower the precision substantially. The most likely reason for this is that the automatic linguistic analysis did not provide complete information. However, in certain situations where more complex terms need to be captured, one might have to live with lower precision to actually bring all relevant term candidates into the validation stage. Another obstacle might be the quality of syntactic tags for grammatical functions; if linguistic analysers can provide data for grammatical functions that are as good as for parts-of-speech, then the results may be improved.

In experiences from practical applications of extracting terminology from web sites of Swedish government agencies, the tool was shown to work for Swedish and proved to be very flexible in that it provided a solid basis for further work on filtering, validating and standardizing terminology, i.e. moving from term candidates to validated terms.

Acknowledgements

This work has been funded by the Swedish Research Council (Vetenskapsrådet). Many thanks also go to Michael Petterstedt and Mikael Andersson for their help with work on software and scripting.

References

Ananiadou, S. 1994. A methodology for automatic term recognition. In Proceedings of the 15th conference on Computational linguistics, pages 1034–1038, Morristown, NJ, USA. Association for Computational Linguistics.

Bernier-Colborne, G. (2012). Defining a Gold Standard for the evaluation of Term Extractors. In: Proceedings of the colabTKR workshop Teminology and Knowledge Representation, Istanbul, Turkey.

Justeson, J.S. & Katz S.M. 1995. Technical terminology: some linguistic properties and an algorithm for identification in text. *Natural Language Engineering* 1:9-27. Bourigault, 1992;

Merkel, Foo. 2007. Terminology extraction and term ranking for standardizing term banks. In Proceedings of NODALIDA'07, Tartu, Estonia.

Mustafa El Hadi, W., Timimi, I.. Dabadie, M., Choukri, K., Hamon, O., Chiao, Y.-C. (2006). Terminological resources acquisition tools: Toward a user-oriented evaluation model. In Proceedings of LREC'06, pp. 945-958, Genova, Italy.

Nazarenko, A. & Zargayouna, H. (2009). Evaluating term extraction. In: Proceedings of the International Conference RANLO 2009, pp. 299-304, Borovets, Bulgaria.

Terminologicentrum (2012). Rikstermbanken. http:www.rikstermbanken.se. Terminologicentrum, Stockholm.

Tapanainen, P., & Järvinen, T. (1997). A non-projective dependency parser. In Proceedings of the fifth conference on Applied Natural Language Processing (pp. 64-71). Washington, DC, USA. Stroudsburg, PA, USA: Association for Computational Linguistics.

Zhang, Z., Iria, J., Brewster, C. & Ciravegna, F. (2008). A comparative evaluation of term recognition algorithms. In: *Proceedings of LREC'08*, pp. 2108-2113, Marrakech, Morocco.

Classifying Multimodal Turn Management in Danish Dyadic First Encounters

Costanza Navarretta[1] Patrizia Paggio[1,2]

(1) University of Copenhagen, Njalsgade 140 Buil. 25,4. Copenhagen Denmark
(2) University of Malta, Valletta Malta

`costanza@hum.ku.dk, paggio@hum.ku.dk`

ABSTRACT

This paper deals with multimodal turn management in an annotated Danish corpus of video recorded dyadic conversations between young people who meet for the first time. Conversation participants indicate whether they wish to give, take or keep the turn through speech as well as body behaviours. In this study we present an analysis of turn management body behaviours as well as classification experiments run on the annotated data in order to investigate how far it is possible to distinguish between the different types of turn management expressed by body behaviours using their shape and the co-occurring speech expressions. Our study comprises body behaviours which have not been previously investigated with respect to turn management, so that it not only confirms preceding studies on turn management in English but also provides new insight on how speech and body behaviours are used together in communication. The classification experiments indicate that the shape annotations of all kinds of body behaviour together with information about the gesturer's co-occurring speech are useful to classify turn management types, and that the various behaviours contribute to the expression of turn features in different ways. Thus, knowledge of the different cues used by speakers in face-to-face communication to signal different types of turn shift provides the basis for modelling turn management, which is in turn key to implement natural conversation flow in multimodal dialogue systems.

KEYWORDS: Multimodal Communication, Turn Management, Multimodal Corpora, Machine Learning.

1   Introduction

This article deals with turn management in the Danish NOMCO first encounters corpus. Turn management concerns the regulation of the conversation flow (Allwood et al., 2007) and is achieved through verbal and non verbal behaviours. Determining these cues is important for implementing conversational systems which can interact with users in a natural way.

Since conversations are social activities, they are influenced by many factors including the communicative situation, the cultural, physical and social setting, the number and role of the participants, their age, gender, and relation. These factors also play a role in the conversation flow, which turn management is an important part of (Du-Babcock, 2003; Allwood et al., 2007; Tanaka, 2008).

According to the Conversation Analysis (CA) tradition, starting with (Sacks et al., 1974), the conversation flow is regulated according to a set of so-called turn-taking rules consisting of a turn-construction and a turn-allocation component. According to these rules, the conversation participants alternate their speech smoothly. The turn-taking system has been criticised because it presupposes that the interaction flow is determined by pre-defined rules, thus it does not account for the fact that turn management as conversations also depend on social and cultural factors, inter alia (O'Connell et al., 1990; Cowley, 1998). Furthermore, more analyses of conversations indicate that the ideal smooth turn-taking system described by (Sacks et al., 1974) does not occur: in conversations participants often speak at the same time. Also long pauses occur and are acceptable in many conversations (O'Connell et al., 1990; Cowley, 1998; Campbell, 2008, 2009a). Recognising that many speech overlaps can occur in conversations, (Schegloff, 2000) defines rules describing how overlaps are managed. Furthermore, he distinguishes between non problematic and problematic overlap cases. Only in the latter, overlap management is needed. Differing from this CA-related view, other researchers suggest that co-occurring speech, and co-occurring body behaviours, are a natural aspect of conversations, signalling that people communicate in synchrony (Campbell, 2009b).

Independently of the research tradition, however, most studies point out that the interaction, flow, comprising both sequential and overlapping behaviours, is regulated by multimodal cues, thus involving both speech and non-verbal behaviours, inter alia (Kendon, 1967; Yngve, 1970; Ford and Thompson, 1996; Duncan, 1972; Allwood et al., 2007; Hadar et al., 1984b).

In this paper we present an analysis of how head movements, hand movements, facial expressions and body postures relate to turn management in a corpus of dyadic Danish first encounter conversations, and we compare these findings to results from preceding studies of the same topic.

Furthermore, we investigate the relation between body behaviours and turn management types by applying supervised machine learning to the annotated corpus data to test how far the shape of the body behaviours and the co-occurring speech can be used to carry out automatic classification of the turn management type of the behaviours. The focus in the paper is on the investigation of the contribution of each type of behaviour to turn management, thus both in the analysis and classification each behaviour type is considered separately. Although the expression of a turn management behaviour is probably a combination of speech and different gestural cues, at this stage of our research we wanted to find out to what degree and in what way each channel (head, face, body) contributed to the phenomenon of turn management. For each channel, however, we consider the whole range of movement types available in the corpus. The rest of the paper is organised as follows. In section 2 we discuss relevant background literature while in section 3 we describe our data. Section 4 contains the analysis of turn management in the data and in section 5 we describe and discuss the classification experiments conducted on the corpus annotations. Finally, we conclude and present future work in section 6.

2   Background Literature

Many researchers (Kendon, 1967; Argyle and Cook, 1976; Duncan and Fiske, 1977; Goodwin, 1981) recognise the importance of body behaviours, especially gaze, head movements and hand gestures in turn management. (Kendon, 1967) and (Argyle and Cook, 1976) focus on the role of gaze direction and of mutual gaze, respectively, while turn management multimodal cues comprising intonation, syntax and hand gesture are described in (Duncan, 1972). In (Duncan and Fiske, 1977), also the behaviours of the listener are analysed, and backchannelling signals by the listeners are distinguished from regular turns. (Hadar et al., 1984b) find that linear movements of the head ("postural shifts") tended to occur after "grammatical" pauses (between clauses or sentences) and towards the initiation of speech, both between speaking turns and between syntactic boundaries inside speaking turns. Their analysis is based on the automatically collected head movements of four subjects engaged in conversations. The authors conclude that head movements are involved in regulating turn taking and marking syntactic boundaries inside speaking turns. Smaller and quicker movements tended to occur after dysfluencies inside grammatical boundaries, especially after short pauses (Hadar et al., 1984a).

(Gravano and Hirschberg, 2009) examine the relation between particular acoustic and prosodic turn-yielding cues and turn taking in a large corpus of task-oriented dialogues.

Machine learning has been applied to annotated multimodal data in numerous studies. For example, feedback nods and shakes are successfully predicted from speech, prosody and eye gaze in a multimodal corpus of conversations (Morency et al., 2005, 2007, 2009), while (Jokinen and Ragni, 2007) train machine learning algorithms on manually annotated multimodal data in order to recognise some of the communicative functions of head movements and facial expressions. They achieve promising results although their data is small.

In the rest of the paper, we discuss to what extent body behavioural cues are also present in our data in connection to turn management and, in line with preceding machine learning experiments we train classifiers on speech and body behaviours to predict the communicative function of these behaviours, in this case their turn management function.

3   The Corpus

The corpus which we have used in our analysis is a Danish corpus of first encounter conversations which is freely available for research. The corpus was collected and annotated during the NOrdic Multimodal Corpora (NOMCO) project, and it is part of a Nordic corpus of comparable recorded conversations in Danish, Finnish and Swedish (Paggio et al., 2010; Navarretta et al., 2011, 2012). The Danish first encounter dialogues comprise 12 five-minutes conversations between two young people who did not know each other in advance. The participants are 6 female and 6 male university students or university educated young people, aged 19-36 years. They were instructed to talk in order to get acquainted, as if they met at a party. The interactions were recorded by three cameras in a studio at the University of Copenhagen. Each person participated in two conversations, one with a female and one with a male. The two conversations were recorded on two different days (Paggio and Navarretta, 2011). In Figure 1 and 2 snapshots from one of the recordings are given.

Figure 1: Snapshot from the corpus: frontal camera views

Figure 2: Snapshot from the corpus: side camera view

3.1   The Annotations

The corpus is orthographically transcribed with time stamps at the word level, and the body behaviours are annotated with pre-defined shape and function features according to the MUMIN annotation scheme (Allwood et al., 2007). Body behaviours can be assigned more functions at the same time, and they can be linked to speech segments produced by the gesturer or the interlocutor if the coders judge that they are semantically related.

The data were annotated by a coder and than corrected by a second coder. Disagreement cases were resolved by a third coder. An agreed upon version of the data was created. The coders were instructed to take into account the whole context when annotating. This comprises the multimodal behaviours of both speakers. With respect to turn management, the coders were instructed to annotate signals of turn management by the participants. Note that an actual turn change is not considered a necessary prerequisite for the assignment of a turn management feature. For instance, a turn elicit or a turn take signal can be coded independently of its success. Likewise, a turn hold signal can be coded if the speaker is attempting to keep the turn even though the interlocutor may take it from them.

Inter-coder agreement tests on the annotations of facial expressions and head movements resulted in kappa scores (Cohen, 1960) between 0.6-0.9 depending on the categories. The scores comprise segmentation and classification. The lowest scores were due to differences in the segmentation of facial expressions. The highest scores were achieved in the annotation of head movements. Agreement on the classification of functional categories was 0.82. More details about the corpus annotation and inter-coder agreement experiments are given in (Paggio and Navarretta, 2011; Navarretta et al., 2011). In this study, we used the annotations of head movements, facial expressions and body postures related to turn management. The shape features describing these behaviours are in Table 1. Head movements are

Shape attribute	Shape values
HeadMovement	Nod, Jerk, HeadForward, HeadBackward,Tilt, SideTurn, Shake, Waggle, HeadOther
HeadRepetition	Single, Repeated
General face	Smile, Laugh, Scowl, FaceOther
Eyebrows	Frown, Raise, BrowsOther
BodyDirection	BodyForward,BodyBackward, BodyUp, BodyDown, BodySide, BodyTurn, BodyDirectionOther
BodyInterlocutor	BodyToInterlocutor, BodyAwayFromInterlocutor
Shoulders	Shrug, ShouldersOther

Table 1: Shape attributes and values

annotated with features describing the form of the movement and an indication of whether the movement is performed once or more times. A general face attribute is used to annotate facial expressions together with the form of the eyebrows. Finally, body postures are annotated with information on direction, whether the body is facing the interlocutor, and what the movement of the shoulders is.

We distinguish six types of turn related behaviours:

- TurnTake: the speaker signals that she wants to take a turn that wasn't offered, possibly by interrupting;
- TurnHold: the speaker signals that she wishes to keep the turn;
- TurnAccept: the speaker signals that she is accepting a turn that is being offered;
- TurnYield: the speaker signals that she is releasing the turn under pressure;
- TurnElicit: the speaker signals that she is offering the turn to the interlocutor;
- TurnComplete: the speakers signals that she has completed the turn.

In the ANVIL tool, each modality is coded in a so called track, while links joining an annotation from a track to the other indicate that the two annotations are semantically related.

4   The Analysis

The corpus consists of 18000 speech tokens, 3117 head movements, 1448 facial expressions and 982 body postures. Out of these, 738 head movements, 247 facial expressions and 223 body postures have been labelled with a turn management function. Thus, 24% of the head movements, 17% of the facial expressions and 23% of the body postures have a turn

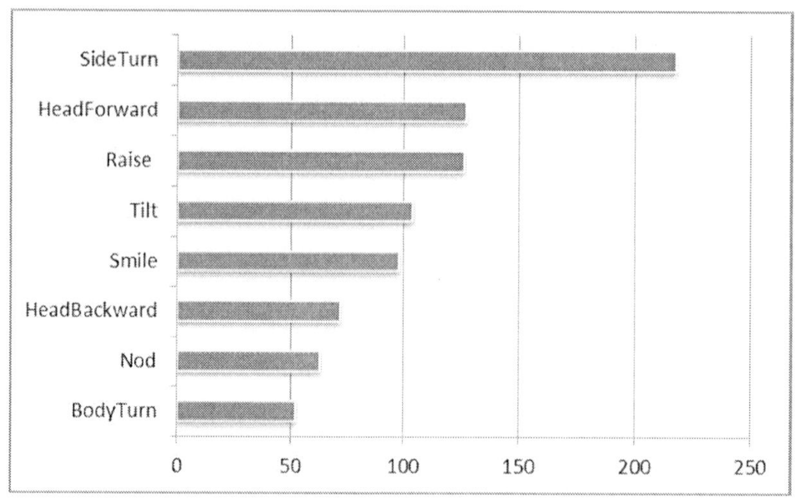

Figure 3: Most frequently occurring turn management behaviours

management function in the corpus. Table 2 shows, conversely, how the turn management associated with body behaviours is distributed across the three different types.

Body behaviour	%
Head movements	61
Facial expressions	20.5
Body postures	18.5

Table 2:   Turn management distribution across body behaviours

Figure 3 shows the body behaviours which are most frequently related to a turn management function in this corpus. It is interesting to notice that all three body parts are related to turn management, and not only head movements, hand gestures and gaze which have been studied in preceding studies. Furthermore, more types of head movement than those indicated in the literature are relevant to turn management.

The most frequently assigned turn management categories are TurnHold, TurnAccept and TurnElicit, while TurnYield is rare in the corpus. This is not surprising given the type of social activity and the setting: people who meet for the first time and have to get acquainted are in general both friendly and polite, and they avoid interrupting their interlocutor. Figure 4 shows the turn management categories which are assigned more frequently to the three main types of body behaviour in the first encounter conversations.

The most common turn management functions of head movements are TurnHold, TurnAccept and TurnElicit, while TurnElicit, TurnAccept and TurnTake are the most frequent turn management functions of the facial expressions. Finally, TurnAccept, TurnElicit and TurnHold are the functions must frequently assigned to body postures. It must be noted that here we report each body part independently, but in conversations often several body behaviours co-occur.

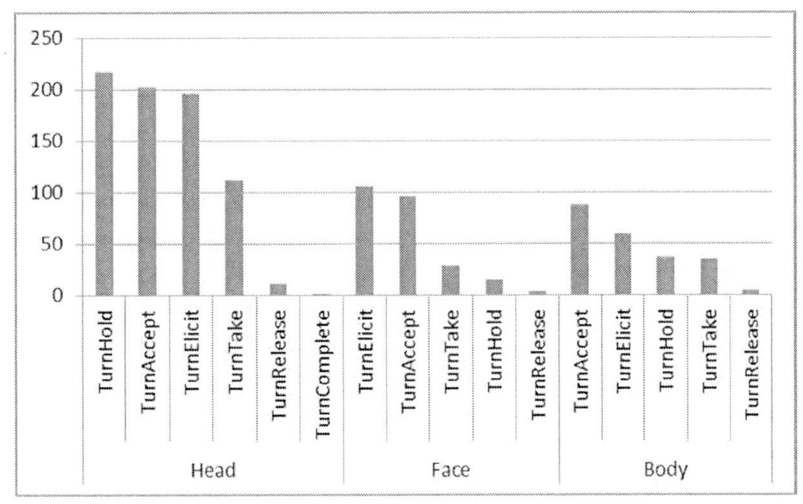

Figure 4: Turn management related types and body behaviours

4.1 Discussion

Our study of body behaviours and turn management indicates that not only head movements, but also facial expressions and body postures are often used in turn management in the Danish first encounter dialogues. The data show that the proportion of different turn management features varies depending on the body part involved. Especially the proportion of TurnHold changes a lot from being rather large in connection with head movements to being low for face and body, whereas TurnElicit is the feature that has the largest proportion only in connection with facial expressions. In the corpus, behaviours related to the three body parts are not explicitly linked to each other. Therefore, in the present stage of our research, we do not yet know whether the relations we see between body behaviours and turn management are additive, as could be expected for features associated with all three body parts, e.g. TurnAccept, or whether different body parts are associated with different turn behaviours.

Another observation relates to the fact that various types of head movements are involved in turn management. This finding is in line with other studies of Danish conversations which have shown that the participants not only use nods and shakes to give or elicit feedback, but also tilts, side movements and forward and backward movements (Paggio and Navarretta, 2011; Navarretta, 2011).

Approximately 20% of the communicative head movements, facial expressions and body postures have a turn management function in the conversations. The frequency of the turn management values assigned in the corpus, in particular the fact that very few occurrences of turn release under pressure are found, reflect the type of social interaction. The participants meet for the first time, thus they are kind and avoid interrupting each other.

5 Classification of Turn Management Types

In this section we describe classification experiments on the annotated corpus. We investigate to which extent it is possible to carry out automatic classification of the turn management types expressed by body behaviours on the basis of their shape, together with the co-occurring words. In these experiments we again consider each body part independently, thus the features modelling the shape of each body behaviour and the words they are semantically connected with were extracted and used as different datasets.

More specifically, we trained classifiers on datasets containing descriptions of the shape of each body behaviour and its turn management function. Then we run the classifiers on data where only shape values were considered, in order to predict the turn management function of the behaviours. In succeeding experiments we also included the gesturer's or interlocutor's words linked to each body behaviour with the purpose of investigating whether the speech-related information improved the classification.

All experiments were run in WEKA (Witten and Frank, 2005). As baseline in each experiment, we use the results from WEKA's ZeroR algorithm which always chooses the most frequently occurring nominal class in the dataset. The most frequently occurring nominal class is a reasonable baseline for this data, given the fact that there are no other studies of multimodal turn management involving the same types of behaviour which we could compare our results with. An alternative possibility one could consider is taking actual turn change as a baseline measure. However, since the assignment of turn management features, as was explained earlier, does not necessarily imply a change of turn (or keeping the turn in the case of a TurnHold feature), such a baseline would make little sense. The classifier run in all experiments is WEKA's SMO algorithm, which implements John Platt's sequential minimal optimization algorithm for training a support vector classifier. SMO was chosen because it is the best performing algorithm on this type of data (Navarretta and Paggio, 2010)[1]. We report the results of classification in term of Precision (**P**), Recall (**R**) and F-measure (**F**) figures. The results were evaluated using ten-fold cross-validation.

Table 3 shows the results obtained for head movements, while Table 4 and Table 5 contain the results for facial expressions and body postures, respectively. In all cases, the classifiers are first trained on shape features for each body behaviours, then on shape features and the related gesturer's words (*gest-words* in the tables), on shape features and the related interlocutor's words (*interl-words*) and, finally, on shape features and gesturer's or interlocutor's words (*all-words*).

Algorithm	Dataset	P	R	F
ZeroR		0.09	0.29	0.13
SMO	shape	0.36	0.43	0.39
SMO	shape+gest-words	**0.47**	**0.5**	**0.48**
SMO	shape+interl-words	0.36	0.43	0.39
SMO	shape+all-words	0.46	0.5	0.46

Table 3: Identification and classification of turn management from head movements and related speech

The shape features of the head movements, and especially shape information enriched with the co-occurring gesturer's words, considerably improve the identification of the relevant turn management types of the head with respect to the baseline. In this case the improvement in terms of F-score with respect to the baseline is of 0.35%.

---

[1] The performance of various algorithms on the data was tested according to the strategy proposed in (Daelemans et al., 2003) and previously tested in (Navarretta, 2009). The other classifiers tested on these data are Naive Bayes, KStar and BFTree.

```
  a    b    c    d    e    f    <-- classified as
123   74    7   13    0    0  |   a = TurnHold
 41  137    2   16    0    0  |   b = TurnElicit
 40   53    2   17    0    0  |   c = TurnTake
 45   49    5  103    0    0  |   d = TurnAccept
  4    6    0    0    0    0  |   e = TurnYield
  0    1    0    0    0    0  |   f = TurnComplete
```

Figure 5: Confusion matrix for head movement

As can be seen in the confusion matrix relevant to the third dataset, and shown in (Fig. 5), the best results are obtained by the classifier on the three features TurnHold, TurnElicit and TurnAccept, which are also the most represented in the data. Performance drops dramatically with TurnTake, which is the fourth most represented category with 202 tokens. TurnYield and TurnComplete are almost not represented, so the results for these two features are not interesting.

Algorithm	Dataset	P	R	F
ZeroR		0.18	0.43	0.25
SMO	shape	0.41	0.51	0.45
SMO	shape+gest-words	**0.42**	**0.51**	**0.46**
SMO	shape+interl-words	0.41	0.51	0.45
SMO	shape+all-words	0.42	0.50	0.45

Table 4:   Identification and classification of turn management from face and related speech

Turning now to facial expressions, we see again an improvement with respect to the baseline, this time of 0.21%. However, it makes very little difference whether words are added to the training. As it was to be expected given the distribution of the classes shown earlier in Figure 4, the classifier does best at identifying TurnElicit and TurnAccept, whilst it cannot recognise the other three turn behaviours.

Algorithm	Dataset	P	R	F
ZeroR		0.16	0.4	0.22
SMO	shape	0.42	0.4	0.35
SMO	shape+gest-words	0.42	0.44	0.39
SMO	shape+interl-words	0.38	0.41	0.35
SMO	shape+all-words	**0.43**	**0.45**	**0.4**

Table 5:   Identification and classification of turn management from body postures and related speech

Finally, for body postures, using shape information and all words (both the gesturer's and the interlocutor's) gives the best classification results (F-measure improves with 18% with respect to the baseline), although the contribution of words is not as important as it is for head movements. Once again, TurnElicit and TurnAccept are the features that the classifier identifies with the highest accuracy (both are classified correctly 63% of the time).

5.1 Discussion of experimental results

All our classification experiments show that the shape of body behaviours can be used for the classification of the turn management type associated with the behaviours obtaining an F-score of around 0.4. The best results are obtained for head movements and body postures if also the gesturer's co-occurring words are considered. The words of the interlocutor, on the other hand, do not improve the results, but it must be noted that body behaviours related to turn management are related to the gesturer's own words more often than to the interlocutor's. As far as facial expressions are concerned, on the other hand, considering the words that co-occur with the expression makes little difference to the results. This is probably due to the fact that facial expressions are often quite long and may co-occur with long stretches of speech, so that the word tokens provide rather diverse and therefore potentially confusing information.

The best classification results are obtained using head movements. This is not uprising since head movements provide for the largest number of body behaviours in the data. However, not all classes are identified with the same accuracy. Whilst TurnHold, TurnElicit and TurnAccept are classified with an accuracy in the 0.5-0.6 range, TurnTake, TakeYield and TurnComplete seem very difficult to identify. It is somewhat puzzling that TurnTake should perform so poorly, given its frequency. It remains to be seen whether turn taking behaviour can be classified by means of different features, e.g. prosody patterns, or whether more data are necessary to achieve higher accuracy.

Turning now to the results achieved with facial expressions and body posture, it is again not surprising that TurnElicit and TurnAccept, the most frequent classes in this case, are those for which the classification achieves reasonable accuracy. However, it is interesting to note that TurnElicit performs a little better than TurnAccept in both sets of experiments, even though it is less frequently represented in conjunction with body postures. Presumably, the words associated with TurnElicit help optimise the classification.

In general, the results of these experiments are promising given the restricted size of the corpus. However, the F-score we obtain is not really high enough to allow for automatic annotation of the turn management of body behaviours. However, we believe there is scope for improvement in that co-occurring body behaviours, as was explained earlier, were not considered together in this study. Furthermore, additional cues, such as prosody patterns or actual turn change, could be added to the datasets to improve classification accuracy especially for the TurnTake class, which the classifiers we have trained in this study cannot identify on the basis of body features and associated words.

6 Conclusions and Future Work

In this paper we have presented an analysis of turn management behaviours in the Danish NOMCO first encounters corpus. Our study both confirms preceding studies on turn management, and provides new insights. In particular, we found that all kinds of head movement, facial expression and body posture are involved in turn management. Furthermore, the turn management types frequently occurring in this corpus depend on the type of social activity in which the participants are involved. Since a number of studies of multimodal conversations have found that there is a relation between factors such as social activity, cultural environment, number of participants and communicative body behaviours (Lu et al., 2011; Maynard, 1987; Navarretta et al., 2012), we also plan to compare turn management behaviours in this corpus with corresponding behaviours in other types of corpora.

Acknowledgements

The collection and annotation of the NOMCO corpus was funded by the NORDCORP program under the Nordic Research Councils for the Humanities and the Social Sciences (NOS-HS) and by the Danish Research Council for the Humanities (FKK). We would like to thank Anette Luff Studsgård, Sara Andersen, Bjørn Wessel-Tolvig and Magdalena Lis for their codings. Special thanks also go to the NOMCO project's partners, Elisabeth Ahlsén, Jens Allwood and Kristiina Jokinen.

References

Allwood, J., Cerrato, L., Jokinen, K., Navarretta, C., and Paggio, P. (2007). The mumin coding scheme for the annotation of feedback, turn management and sequencing. *Multimodal Corpora for Modelling Human Multimodal Behaviour. Special Issue of the International Journal of Language Resources and Evaluation*, 41(3–4):273–287.

Argyle, M. and Cook, M. (1976). *Gaze and mutual gaze*. Cambridge University Press, Cambridge, UK.

Campbell, N. (2008). Multimodal processing of discourse information; the effect of synchrony. In *Second International Symposium on Universal Communication*, pages 12–14.

Campbell, N. (2009a). An audio-visual approach to measuring discourse synchrony in m ultimodal conversation data. In *Proceedings of Interspeech 2009*, pages 12–14.

Campbell, N. (2009b). Multimodal Processing of Discourse Information; The Effect of Synchrony. In *ISUC - Second International Symposium on Universal Communication*, pages 12–15, Osaka.

Cohen, J. (1960). A coefficient of agreement for nominal scales. *Educational and Psychological Measurement*, 20(1):37–46.

Cowley, S. J. (1998). Of Timing, Turn-Taking, and Conversations. *Journal of Psycholinguistic Research*, 27(5):541–571.

Daelemans, W., Hoste, V., Meulder, F. D., and Naudts, B. (2003). Combined Optimization of Feature Selection and Algorithm Parameter Interaction in Machine Learning of Language. In *Proceedings of the 14th European Conference on Machine Learning (ECML-2003)*, pages 84–95, Cavtat-Dubrovnik, Croatia.

Du-Babcock, B. (2003). A comparative analysis of individual communication processes in small group behavior between homogeneous and heterogeneous groups. In *Proceedings of the 68th Association of Business Communication Convention*, pages 1–16, Albuquerque, New Mexico, USA.

Duncan, S. Junior (1972). Some Signals and Rules for Taking Speaking Turns in Conversations. *Journal of Personality and Social Psychology*, 23(2):283–292.

Duncan, S. Junior. and Fiske, D. (1977). *Face-to-face interaction*. Erlbaum, Hillsdale, NJ.

Ford, C. and Thompson, S. (1996). Interactional Units in Conversation: Syntactic, Intonational, and Pragmatic Resources for the Management of Turns. In Ochs, E., Schegloff, E., and Thompson, S., editors, *Interaction and Grammar*, pages 134–184. Cambridge University Press, Cambridge.

Goodwin, C. (1981). *Conversational organization: Interaction between speakers and hearers*. Academic Press, New York.

Gravano, A. and Hirschberg, J. (2009). Turn-yielding cues in task-oriented dialogue. In *Proceedings of SIGDIAL 2009: the 10th Annual Meeting of the Special Interest Group in Discourse and Dialogue, September 2009*, pages 253–261, Queen Mary University of London.

Hadar, U., Steiner, T., and Rose, F. C. (1984a). The Relationship Between Head Movements and Speech Dysfluencies. *Language and Speech*, 27(4):333–342.

Hadar, U., Steiner, T., and Rose, F. C. (1984b). The timing of shifts of head postures during conversation. *Human Movement Science*, 3(3):237–245.

Jokinen, K. and Ragni, A. (2007). Clustering experiments on the communicative properties of gaze and gestures. In *Proceeding of the 3rd. Baltic Conference on Human Language Technologies*, Kaunas, Lithuania.

Kendon, A. (1967). Some functions of gaze-direction in social interaction. *Acta Psychologica*, 26:22–63.

Lu, J., Allwood, J., and Ahlsén, E. (2011). A study on cultural variations of smile based on empirical recordings of Chinese and Swedish first encounters. In Heylen, D., Kipp, M., and Paggio, P., editors, *Proceedings of the workshop on Multimodal Corpora at ICMI-MLMI 2011*, Alicante, Spain.

Maynard, S. (1987). Interactional functions of a nonverbal sign: Head movement in Japanese dyadic casual conversation. *Journal of Pragmatics*, 11:589–606.

Morency, L.-P., de Kok, I., and Gratch, J. (2009). A probabilistic multimodal approach for predicting listener backchannels. *Autonomous Agents and Multi-Agent Systems*, 20:70–84.

Morency, L.-P., Sidner, C., Lee, C., and Darrell, T. (2005). Contextual recognition of head gestures. In *Proceedings of the International Conference on Multi-modal Interfaces*.

Morency, L.-P., Sidner, C., Lee, C., and Darrell, T. (2007). Head gestures for perceptual interfaces: The role of context in improving recognition. *Artificial Intelligence*, 171(8–9):568–585.

Navarretta, C. (2009). Automatic recognition of the function of third-person singular pronouns in texts and spoken data. In S. Lalitha Devi, A. B. and Mitkov, R., editors, *Anaphora Processing and Applications. 7th Discourse Anaphora and Anaphor Resolution Colloquium - DAARC 2009, Goa, India Proceedings*, volume 5847 of *LNAI*, pages 15–28. Springer Verlag., Berlin/Heidelberg.

Navarretta, C. (2011). Annotating non-verbal behaviours in informal interactions. In Esposito, A., Vinciarelli, A., Vicsi, K., Pelachaud, C., and Nijholt, A., editors, *Analysis of Verbal and Nonverbal Communication and Enactment: The Processing Issues*, volume 6800 of *LNCS*, pages 317–324. Springer Verlag.

Navarretta, C., Ahlsén, E., Allwood, J., Jokinen, K., and Paggio, P. (2011). Creating Comparable Multimodal Corpora for Nordic Languages. In *Proceedings of the 18th Conference Nordic Conference of Computational Linguistics*, pages 153–160, Riga, Latvia.

Navarretta, C., Ahlsén, E., Allwood, J., Jokinen, K., and Paggio, P. (2012). Feedback in nordic first-encounters: a comparative study. In *Proceedings of LREC 2012*, pages 2494–2499, Istanbul Turkey.

Navarretta, C. and Paggio, P. (2010). Classification of feedback expressions in multimodal data. In *Proceedings of the 48th Annual Meeting of the Association for Computational Linguistics (ACL 2010)*, pages 318–324, Upssala, Sweden.

O'Connell, D., Kowal, S., and Kaltenbacher, E. (1990). Turn-Taking: A Critical Analysis of the Research Tradition. *Journal of Psycholinguistic Research*, 19(6):345–373.

Paggio, P., Ahlsén, E., Allwood, J., Jokinen, K., and Navarretta, C. (2010). The NOMCO multimodal Nordic resource - goals and characteristics. In *Proceedings of LREC 2010*, pages 2968–2973, Malta.

Paggio, P. and Navarretta, C. (2011). Head movements, facial expressions and feedback in Danish first encounters interactions: a culture-specific analysis. In Stephanidis, C., editor, *Universal Access in Human-Computer Interaction. Users Diversity. Proceedings of 6th International Conference, UAHCI 2011, Held as Part of HCI International 2011*, pages 583–590, Orlando, FL, USA. Springer.

Sacks, H., Schegloff, E., and Jefferson, G. (1974). A simplest systematics for the organization of turn-taking for conversation. *Language*, 50(4):696–735.

Schegloff, E. A. (2000). Overlapping talk and the organization of turn-taking for conversation. *Language in Society*, 29:1–63.

Tanaka, H. (2008). Communication strategies and cultural assumptions: An analysis of French-Japanese business meetings. In Tietze, S., editor, *International Management and Language*, pages 154–170. Routledge, New York, NY.

Witten, I. and Frank, E. (2005). *Data Mining: Practical machine learning tools and techniques*. Morgan Kaufmann, San Francisco, second edition.

Yngve, V. (1970). On getting a word in edgewise. In *Papers from the sixth regional meeting of the Chicago Linguistic Society*, pages 567–578.

Nordic and Baltic wordnets aligned and compared through "WordTies"

Bolette S. Pedersen[1], Lars Borin[2], Markus Forsberg[2], Neeme Kahusk[3]

Krister Lindén[4], Jyrki Niemi[4] Niklas Nisbeth[1], Lars Nygaard[5]

Heili Orav[3], Eirikur Rögnvaldsson[6], Mitchel Seaton[1] Kadri Vider[3], Kaarlo Voionmaa[2]

(1) University of Copenhagen, Njalsgade 140 2300 Copenhagen S
(2) University of Gothenburg, Box 200, 405 30 Gothenburg, Sweden (3)
University of Tartu, Ülikooli 18, 50090 Tartu, ESTONIA (4) University of Helsinki, P.O. Box 33
(Yliopistonkatu 4) (5) Kaldera Language Technology, Oslo, Norway

`bspedersen@hum.ku.dk`, `lars.borin@svenska.gu.se`, `markus.forsberg@gu.se`,
`neeme.kahusk@ut.ee`, `krister.linden@helsinki.fi`, `Jyrki.Niemi@helsinki.fi`,
`niklas@nisbeth.dk`, `larsnyga@gmail.com`, `heili.orav@ut.ee`, `eirikur@hi.is`,
`seaton@hum.ku.dk`, `kadri.vider@ut.ee`

ABSTRACT

During the last few years, extensive wordnets have been built locally for the Nordic and Baltic languages applying very different compilation strategies. The aim of the present investigation is to consolidate and examine these wordnets through an alignment via Princeton Core WordNet and thereby compare them along the measures of taxonomical structure, synonym structure, and assigned relations to approximate to a best practice. A common web interface and visualizer "WordTies" is developed to facilitate this purpose. Four bilingual wordnets are automatically processed and evaluated exposing interesting differences between the wordnets. Even if the alignments are judged to be of a good quality, the precision of the translations vary due to considerable differences in hyponymy depth and interpretation of the synset. All seven monolingual and four bilingual wordnets as well as WordTies have been made available via META-SHARE through the META-NORD project.

KEYWORDS: wordnets, multilingual links, wordnet web interface, Nordic and Baltic languages, META-NORD.

1   Wordnets as a multilingual action in the Nordic and Baltic countries

Wordnets (cf. Fellbaum 1998, Vossen 1998) have emerged as one of the basic standard lexical resources in the language technology (LT) field. They encode fundamental semantic relations among words, relations that further in many cases have counterparts in relations among concepts in formal ontologies. According to the BLARK (Basic Language Resource Kit) scheme, wordnets along with treebanks, are central resources when building language enabled applications. The semantic proximity metrics among words and concepts defined by a wordnet are considered useful in applications such as information access systems and authoring tools because in addition to identical words, the occurrence of words with similar (more general or more specific) meanings contribute to measuring of the similarity of content or context or recognizing the meaning. Based on this impact, there is a crucial need for continuously comparing and improving such lexical semantic resources in order to approximate to a best practice. This is particularly relevant if we foresee an integration of them in cross-lingual LT.

For the Nordic and Baltic languages, an extensive development of wordnets has taken place during the last five years, excluding here the Estonian wordnet, which has existed for more than a decade as part of the EuroWordNet project. During the META-NORD project (2011–2013) these wordnets have been further consolidated via extensions, validations and documentation. Thus, the relevance of cross-lingual alignment and comparison of wordnets in this region has emerged only recently. Wordnets or wordnet-like resources of a considerable size exist now for the Finnish, Danish, Estonian, Swedish, Icelandic and the Norwegian languages. They have not, like several previous wordnet projects such as EuroWordNet, BalkaNet, Asian Wordnet, and IndoWordNet (cf. Section 2) been built as part of collaborative projects, but have rather emerged locally through national projects and initiatives. The META-NORD project thus poses a unique opportunity for actually coordinating a Nordic-Baltic action on wordnets and investigating the results of the very different compilation strategies that have been applied.

The aim of this investigation can be expressed as threefold:

- To facilitate browsing, alignment and comparison of the Nordic and Baltic wordnets through the development of an intuitive and easy-to-extend web interface.
- To estimate the perspective of alignment via Princeton Core WordNet by generating four bilingual wordnets and evaluating them.
- Via this alignment to perform a comparison of the involved wordnets along the measures of taxonomical structure, synset structure, and relational structure.

The web interface, WordTies, is documented in Section 4. Four pilot bilingual wordnets have been produced semi-automatically via established links to Princeton Core Wordnet: Danish-Swedish, Danish-Finnish, Estonian-Finnish, Finnish-Swedish. An evaluation of these linked resources is included in Section 5 and a further comparison of a selected set of the wordnets is given in Section 6. All seven monolingual and four bilingual wordnets as well as WordTies have been made available via META-SHARE: www.meta-share.org under a variety of open source licenses.

Broadly speaking, wordnets can be compiled applying two different approaches: the merge vs. the expand method (cf. Rigau & Agirre 2002). By an expand method is meant that translations are made from Princeton WordNet and further customised to the target language, by a merge approach is meant that the wordnet is built monlingually and then (eventually) merged with Princeton WordNet.

The EuroWordNet project, which was concerned with the compilation of wordnets for a series of European languages (Vossen 1998), launched the idea of compiling and expanding wordnets via a so-called Inter Lingual Index (ILI) constituted by Princeton WordNet 1.5, cf. Peters et al. 1998. A successor of EuroWordNet was the BalkaNet project, where several wordnets were built in the Balkan area and aligned simultaneously. These projects all provide valuable reference points for a best practice within the expand approach, for example, BalkaNet uses a validation system based on word sense disambiguation for pinpointing wrong interlingual alignments, incomplete or missing synsets in one or another of the wordnets (Tufis, Ion & Ide 2004). Other works included mapping algorithms for aligning, tuning and validating wordnets as presented in Daudé, Padró & Rigau 1999, & Daudé, Padró & Rigau 2003 and several others. More recent collaborative wordnet projects include MultiWordNet (http://multiwordnet.itc.it) which relates Italian and Princeton wordnets, Asian WordNet which also applies the expand method for several Asian languages through a common management interface (Robkop et al. 2010), and IndoWordNet which include a series of Indian languages (Bhattacharyya 2010). Last but not least should be mentioned a recent initiative, Open Multilingual WordNet http://casta-net.jp/~kuribayashi/multi/ which aligns wordnets available through the Global WordNet Association's WordNet Grid (http://www.globalwordnet.org/gwa/gwa_grid.html).

In contrast, several recent European wordnets that have typically been compiled on a more local basis apply the merge technique (cf. Derwojedowa 2008, Borin & Forsberg 2010, Pedersen et al. 2009) applying monolingual language resources such as existing dictionaries and corpora as the initial source.

There are obvious risks related to both approaches. An expand approach based on Princeton WordNet runs the high risk of being biased towards the conceptual structure of the English language. However, with thorough customizations to the target language these risks can be reduced. A merge approach may reflect the target language better since it is based on more linguistic grounds (corpora and existing lexica) for that particular language. On the other hand, such wordnets typically differ so much from Princeton WordNet in structure that a merge becomes indeed very hard and extremely complex. These differences originate partly from different language cultures, partly from different levels of specialization depending on the source material used. For instance, a typical feature of wordnets based on monolingual lexica is that they adopt a perspective which is more geared towards the layman and therefore typically not so deep in taxonomical structure (cf. Pedersen et al. 2010).

3 Status of wordnets in the Nordic and Baltic countries

3.1 About META-NORD

During the last decade, linguistic resources have grown rapidly for all EU languages, including lesser-resourced languages such as the Nordic and Baltic ones. However they have typically been located in different places, have developed in different standards and in many cases were not well documented. The META-NORD project has aimed to establish an open linguistic infrastructure in the Baltic and Nordic countries to serve the needs of the industry and research communities. The project, which was completed in January 2013, has focused on 8 European languages – Danish, Estonian, Finnish, Icelandic, Latvian, Lithuanian, Norwegian and Swedish – each with less than 10 million speakers. The project has provided descriptions of the national landscapes in these countries via the META-NET White Paper Series "Europe's Languages in the Digital Age" and has assembled, linked across languages, and made widely available close to 500 language resources and tools of different types via the common network META-SHARE http://www.meta-share.org/. META-SHARE is a network of repositories of language data, tools and related web services documented with metadata, aggregated in central inventories allowing for uniform search and access to resources. The horizontal action on wordnets constitutes one of several cross-language initiatives in the project. In the following a brief status of each of the involved wordnets is given.

3.2 Estonian wordnet

The Estonian wordnet was built as part of the EuroWordNet project and thus used the expand method as a starting point. Base concepts from English were translated into Estonian as a first basis for a monolingual extension. The extensions have been compiled manually from Estonian monolingual dictionaries and other monolingual resources. In this sense, EstWN applies a hybrid method including both expand and monolingual techniques. EstWN includes nouns, verbs, adjectives and adverbs; as well as a set of multiword units, cf Kahusk et al. 2012. The database currently (Jan 2013) contains approx. 59 000 concepts are interlinked by175,000 relations and work is still in progress. The database is available under a CC-NY-NC license. The database can be accessed partly via WordTies, partly at http://www.cl.ut.ee/teksaurus and www.keeleveeb.ee.

3.3 Finnish wordnet

FinnWordNet is compiled using the expand method and supplemented with monolingual localisations (see http://www.ling.helsinki.fi/cgi-bin/fiwn/search). FinnWordNet contains nouns, verbs, adjectives and adverbs grouped by meaning into synonym sets representing concepts. Version 1.0 of FinnWordNet was created by translating the word senses in the Princeton WordNet 3.0 (Lindén & Carlson 2010). To ensure quality, the word senses were translated by professional translators. This approach allowed a very rapid and cost-efficient creation of an extensive Finnish wordnet directly aligned with the Princeton WordNet providing a translation relation between English and Finnish.

It is often claimed that translating a wordnet from English is somehow problematic, so to dispel such doubts several rounds of evaluations were performed, only to discover very few translation or concept problems (cf. Lindén et al. 2012). During the evaluation some missing common Finnish words and concepts were added to FinnWordNet from a large corpus of Finnish as well as from Wiktionary and Wikipedia. The resulting FinnWordNet 2.0 has 120,449 concepts containing 208,645 word senses and linked to each other with 265,690 relations. It thus surpasses Princeton WordNet in the number of concepts and word senses. FinnWordNet is licensed under the Creative Commons Attribution (CC-BY) 3.0 licence. As a derivative of the Princeton WordNet, FinnWordNet is also subject to the Princeton WordNet licence.

3.4   Danish Wordnet

DanNet has been constructed using the merge approach where the wordnet is built on monolingual grounds and thereafter merged with Princeton WordNet. It currently contains 66,308 concepts which are interlinked by 326,564 relations (see also Pedersen et al. 2009). The wordnet has been compiled as a collaboration between the University of Copenhagen and the Danish Society for Language and Literature and is based on *Den Danske Ordbog* (Hjorth & Kristensen 2003). Furthermore, the Danish version of the SIMPLE lexicons (cf. Lenci et al. 2001) has influenced the construction of DanNet in the sense that it includes also qualia information such as the telic and the agentive role (purpose and origin). Qualia roles are encoded in DanNet in terms of relations such as used_for and made_by as well as by means of features such as SEX and CONNOTATION. DanNet is licensed under the Princeton WordNet licence.

3.5   Swedish wordnet (Swesaurus)

Swesaurus (Borin & Forsberg 2010, Borin & Forsberg 2011) is a Swedish wordnet developed at Språkbanken, University of Gothenburg. It is being built by reusing lexical-semantic relations collected from a number of pre-existing, freely available lexical resources: SALDO (Borin & Forsberg 2009), SDB (Järborg 2001), Synlex (Kann & Rosell 2006), and Swedish Wiktionary. A novel feature of Swesaurus is its fuzzy synsets derived from the graded synonymy relations of Synlex. Swesaurus and several other lexical resources are available for download and inspection at http://spraakbanken.gu.se/karp. Swesaurus is an integral part of a large and diverse lexical macroresource compiled in the Swedish FrameNet++ project (Borin et al. 2010). It includes 13,724 senses and is licensed under a CC-BY license. Due to its slightly different structure, Swesaurus is currently only partly visible through WordTies.

3.6   Norwegian Wordnet

A Norwegian Wordnet (NWN) has been developed as a part of The Norwegian Language Bank (*Språkbanken*). It consists of around 50,000 synsets, for both Norwegian Nynorsk and Norwegian Bokmål and covers more than 90 per cent of the senses of open word classes in running newspaper text. Both wordnets are available via META-SHARE (http://www.nb.no/clarin/repository/search/?q=ordnett) under the Princeton WordNet License. The compilation is based on the Danish wordnet (DanNet), and thus NWN contains the same lexical relations and much of the same semantic analysis as DanNet. The data format and licence are also identical.

Semantically, Danish and Norwegian are very closely related, and word senses are mostly equivalent (though the frequency with which the senses are used often varies). Some synsets are dropped: some are only relevant for Danish society, and do not have natural equivalent in Norwegian. These synsets are almost exclusively infrequent and "peripheral" in the DanNet (i.e. they are leaf nodes in the synset graph). A partial semantic annotation of a Norwegian corpus has been developed to ensure that the most frequent senses for Norwegian text are covered. Using this method, it has been possible to create a very extensive wordnet for a fraction of the cost for development from scratch, and without the quality problems associated with translation from for example English.

3.7   Icelandic wordnet (MerkOr)

The semantic database MerkOr, which constitutes the Icelandic wordnet, has been developed using a monolingual approach with automatic methods for the extraction of semantic information from texts. Both pattern-based and statistical methods are used, as well as a hybrid methodology.

The structure of the database is not based on hierarchies, like the Princeton WordNet, but rather on clusters of strongly related words and semantic relations often describing common sense knowledge and associations. The database contains about 110,000 words, primarily nouns, but also a number of verbs and adjectives. About 2.93 million relations between these words are listed in the database which also contains 305 semantic clusters – lists of words that belong to the same semantic field. The database is distributed under the GNU Lesser General Public License and can be queried online at http://merkor.skerpa.com. This wordnet is not yet made available via WordTies.

4   WordTies: A common web interface for viewing aligned wordnets

WordTies (wordties.cst.dk) is a web interface developed to visualize monolingual wordnets as well as their alignments with the other wordnets, cf. Figure 1. In this browser the user can chose either of the (currently four) relevant wordnets as a source language and see how a concept is linked to its sister wordnets.

Figure 1: Introductory screen of WordTies

WordTies builds on a monolingual browser, AndreOrd, which was built to browse DanNet, cf. Johannsen & Pedersen (2011). In this browser, the semantic relations are made available in a more graphical fashion compared to what is found in most other wordnet browsers which tend to focus primarily on visualizing the *hyponymy* structure of the wordnet. The particular choice of graph very compactly encodes large numbers of relations – each represented by its own colour – and thus gives a good overview of the general structure of the wordnet. In order to make room for all relations in the graph – also the inherited ones –, only one representative sense is visualized per synset. However, all senses are presented below the graph. By clicking on a related synset in the graph the user can dynamically move around in the wordnet. For illustration, see Figure 2 where Danish has been chosen as the source and the Danish concept *håb* ('hope') has been looked up and aligned with Estonian, Swedish and Finnish wordnets.

A click on either of these links will bring the users into these particular wordnets and enable them to browse the wordnet and view the established relations as well as its taxonomical structure, as seen in Figure 3 where we see that the Finnish wordnet has a much deeper taxonomical structure (expert perspective) than the Danish (layman perspective) of the concept *tree*. In this way, the web interface eases comparison and evaluation of the wordnets.

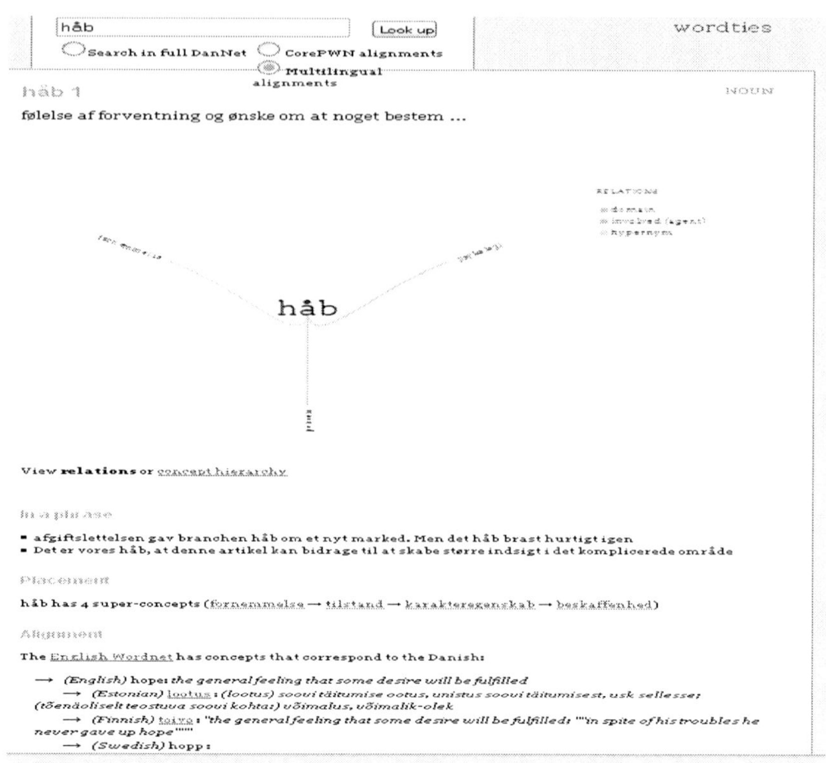

Figure 2: A Danish synset look-up (*håb* (hope)) with multilingual alignments to English, Finnish, Estonian and Swedish wordnets.

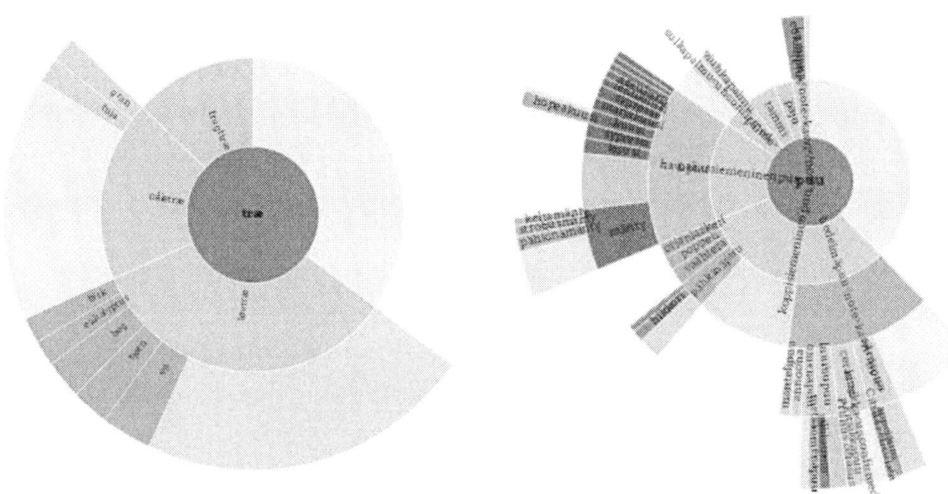

Figure 3: Graphical views of the taxonomical differences of the concept *tree* in the Danish and Finnish wordnets, respectively. DanNet includes three major (layman) subtypes of trees: deciduous trees, coniferous trees, and fruit trees, whereas the Finnish wordnet includes further subtypes based on a specialist, botanical structuring.

Major changes to the AndreOrd source-code were model changes including the addition of instance, source model classes and modification to alignment and its relations. These three model classes handle the relational structure and data used to enable the multilingual relations (connections), facilitating a link between application instances via a wordnet's imported Princeton Core WordNet relations.

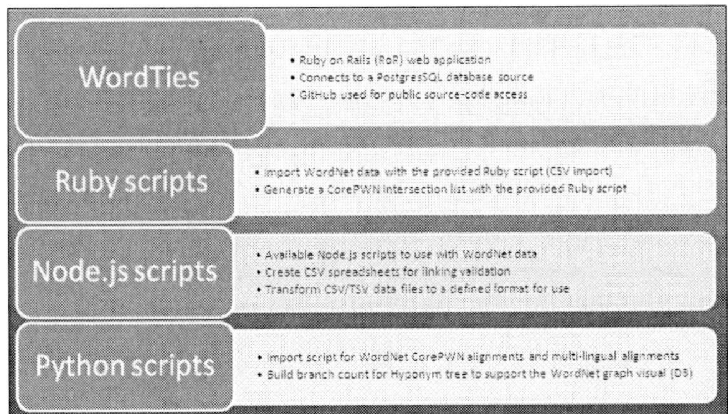

Figure 4: Overview and scripts used in WordTies.

WordTies can be dynamically extended to include more wordnets. There are two compulsory steps for import, firstly to calculate and update the hyponym count for each synset record, and secondly to import alignments to Princeton Core WordNet. Optionally, the import alignments script can be used to import multilingual alignments, alignments to other wordnet synsets via Princeton Core WordNet.

The application is able to have a customised locale, and language files. Currently, Danish and English are supported languages with the application. An index page is customisable based on the locale, and new language support can be easily added with valid translation of labels. Currently multi-locale support is not included with the application, a single locale is set for the application instance to operate in. Other customisations available, include filter values and path names (routes), and custom colour mappings for the relations graph.

5   Alignment and evaluation of bilingual wordnets

Four bilingual wordnets have been automatically processed on the basis of each wordnet's links to Princeton WordNet. In other words, English has functioned as an interlingua in a triangulation method, and a central aim has been to examine to which extent this strategy influenced the quality of the bilingual translations.

However, since the Nordic and Baltic wordnets were built locally using both the expand and merge techniques as we have seen, they differ in the extent to which they were bilingually linked before the META-NORD project was initiated. Therefore, a first task was to ensure a common linked coverage of all the involved wordnets. To this end, all wordnets were manually linked to Princeton Core WordNet containing 5,000 core synsets.[1] Princeton Core WordNet is a recent, semi-automatically compiled list of 5,000

---

[1] http://wordnetcode.princeton.edu/standoff-files/core-wordnet.txt

"core" word senses in WordNet corresponding approximately to the 5,000 most frequently used word senses, followed by some manual filtering and adjustment. This set of basic concepts is considered to be deduced on better statistical grounds than the previously applied "base concepts" used in the EuroWordNet and SIMPLE projects. Further, Princeton Core WordNet is characterized by being relatively coarse-grained compared to the full Princeton WordNet and thus much better suited for alignment tasks.

For the evaluation, a top 1000 set of this 5,000 synset intersection with a POS ratio of 6:2:2 for nouns, verbs, and adjectives, respectively was generated. The extract was also based on provided frequency data from Swedish and Finnish. Even if one-to-one synset alignments are by far the most frequent ones, one-to-many and many-to-one synset alignments occur as well. Valid relations to Princeton Core WordNet include eq_synonym, which are by the most frequent one, eq_has_hyponym, as well as eq_has_hyperonym, allowing thus in some cases for alignments to more or less specific synsets. All in all, four linked wordnets were processed and evaluated. Table 1 sums up the evaluation results.

	Slight mismatches	Linking errors
Danish-Swedish	2.3	2.4
Finnish-Swedish	2.6	1.1
Finnish-Danish	0.7	0
Estonian-Finnish	22.6	5.3

Table 1: Percentage of errors and mismatches in bilingual wordnets

As can be read, the semi-automatic alignments are judged to be of a relatively good quality even if translations are in several cases not 100% precise. An average of 2.2% errors and 7.0% slight mismatches is reported on. However, there are some clear divergences to be commented on in Table 1: the evaluation of Estonian-Finnish reports on 53 errors and 226 slight mismatches whereas no errors and only 7 mismatches are reported on for Finnish-Danish. Since the evaluations are made by different partners with the necessary bilingual language skills, part of this divergence is due to somewhat different interpretations of the concepts 'slight mismatches'. Furthermore, the different nature of the wordnets seems to have influenced the evaluations to a certain extent. Thus, some evaluators have focused on a good definition-to-definition match between two synsets, whereas others have applied a somewhat stricter criterion by evaluating the exact sense-to-sense correspondence.

WN synset	ET	FI	WN gloss	Comment
album%1:06: 00::	Album_2	albumi; valokuva-albumi	a book of blank pages with pockets or envelopes; for organizing photographs or stamp collections etc	FinnWN synset member 'valokuva-albumi' is more specific (eq_has_hyponym)
apparatus%1: 06:00::	aparaat_1, seadis_1	aparaatti; koneisto; laite; laitteisto; väline	equipment designed to serve a specific function	EstWN synset members are in singular, as one particular piece of equipment
gun%1:06:00 ::	tulirelv_1	kivääri; pistooli; pyssy; tykki	a weapon that discharges a missile at high velocity (especially from a metal tube or barrel)	FinnWN synset have more specific members

Table 2: Estonian-Finnish translations that are considered to be slight mismatches.

For instance, the Estonian-Finnish evaluator has registered differences in synonyms or differences in specificity as slight mismatches, influenced by the fact that not *all* senses in two aligned synset represent fully precise translations of each other. See Table 2 for comments on particular alignments between Estonian and Finnish.

An additional explanation to the divergences is that since the Finnish and Estonian languages are very close, the Estonian evaluator expected to see exact matches sense-to-sense in the translations between Finnish and Estonian, irrespective of the fact that the wordnets were built from more or less different starting points. The phenomenon with very close words (and mismatching translations) could presumably also have been observed between other close language pairs such as Swedish and Danish, but since these two wordnet are characterized by having less senses per synset, synonym mismatch is not observed to the same extent. The evaluator of the two "extremes" with respect to senses per synset, Danish and Finnish wordnets, reports on few mismatches, influenced by the fact that focus has here been more directed towards the definition-to-definition alignment.

Not surprisingly, wordnets that have been compiled via translations from Princeton WordNet have many senses per synsets (just as Princeton WordNet), whereas wordnets that are monolingually compiled and rather based on synonymy registrations in conventional dictionaries, have much less; (see also Section 5). As can be seen, it has proven difficult to 'neutralize' such differences initial to the evaluations.

With regards to alignment *errors*, there does not appear to be a systematic bias, some are due to false friends, others however, seem to be just random errors introduced during the linking to Princeton Core WordNet, as in the following, where the English synset has been linked to a too specific sense of 'waste' in DanNet than what was actually indicated by the English gloss, cf. Table 3.

WN synset	DA	SV	WN gloss	Comment
waste%1:27:00::	{spildprodukt_0}	avfall..1	any materials unused and rejected as worthless or unwanted	refers to byproducts of uction; should be the more ral 'affald'.

Table 3: Example of Danish-Swedish link which is considered an error

6   Further comparison of selected wordnets

Via the evaluations presented in Section 5 and by browsing the wordnets in WordTies, further insights have been achieved wrt. the very diverse characteristics of the selected wordnets in terms of taxonomical differences, different understandings of the synset, and differences in compiling semantic relations.

First of all, we can observe some differences in average hyponym depth, number of senses per synset and average number of relations connected to a synset as shown in Table 4.

	DanNet	FinnWordNet	EstWN
Hyponym depth/SynSet	4.38	7.49	5.93
Word Senses/SynSet	1.09	1.74	1.65
Relations/SynSet	4.97	2.21	2.91

Table 4: Hypnonym depth, word sense per synset and relations per synset for Danish, Finnish and Estonian wordnets

FinnWordNet has the highest average of hyponymy depth, relating well to our intuition of this wordnet being more expert oriented at least in the fields of botany and zoology (see also Figure 3). In contrast, EstWN and DanNet which rely more on monolingual dictionaries and the genus proximums given in the definitions of these, have less depth. This fact can also be illustrated by extracting the path to the top from a botanical concept like *tree* in Danish and Finnish, respectively:

træ (tree) has 4 super-concepts (plante → organisme →fysisk genstand→entitet) (plant → organism → physical entity→entity)

puu (tree) has 9 super-concepts (puumainen kasvi → putkilokasvi → kasvi → eliö → elävä olio → kokonaisuus → esine → fyysinen entiteetti → entiteetti) (woody plant → vascular plant → plant → organism → animate thing →whole → object → physical entity → entity)

Figure 5: Differences in number of relations in Finnish and Danish, respectively, attached to the concept candle (*kynttilä, stearinlys*). For example, Danish includes relations such as used_for=light and is_made_of=stearin whereas the Finnish wordnet includes only hyponyms, parts and hyperonym.

The number and selection of relations in the wordnets also differ; some have included only Princeton relations, others include EuroWordNet relations (i.e. Estonian, Danish, Norwegian) and others again have adapted qualia-inspired (Pustejovsky 1995) relations also from the SIMPLE project (Lenci et al. 2001), such as the used_for and made_by relations in the Danish and Norwegian wordnets. This extension of the relation set to include also purpose and origin is again influenced by sense definitions in conventional dictionaries where it is typically expressed for which purpose a given artifact is made and eventually how it is made (i.e. baked, grown, cooked, produced), see Figure 5 for such differences in number of relations between Danish and Finnish wordnets.

7 Conclusion and further steps

Apart from consolidating, extending and providing richer documentation for the Nordic and Baltic wordnets, the META-NORD multilingual wordnet initiative has ensured an alignment and comparison of the most mature of these wordnets and have made them all easily accessible through META-SHARE. Central aims have been to understand better the different nature of the lexical-semantic resources in order to approximate to a best practice, to test the perspective of linking them and to make them visible in an intuitive way in a common web interface. Four core bilingual wordnets have been compiled, made visible and evaluated with diverging, but still promising, results. The evaluations and comparisons have exposed a considerable variety of the wordnets wrt. taxonomical structure, structure of the synset (many or few senses per synset) and number of relations attached to each synset, a variety which proves to originate from the different compilation strategies used for the different Nordic and Baltic languages. As we have shown, the two compilation strategies (expand versus merge) have considerable impact on how the lexical-semantic information is represented and on the depth of the lexical hierarchies. In spite of these differences, an alignment through Princeton Core WordNet has proven feasible.

Three wordnets were not fully mature when the META-NORD project started and have therefore not yet been aligned or made visible in WordTies, namely the Icelandic and Norwegian wordnets; the plan is to include them during 2013.

References

Rigau, G. and Agirre, E. (2002). Semi-automatic Methods for WordNet Construction. Tutorial at 2002 International WordNet Conference, Mysore, India.

Bhattacharyya, P. (2010) IndoWordNet. Proceedings of LREC 2010. Valletta: ELRA.

Borin, L., Danélls, D., Forsberg, M., Kokkinakis, D. and Gronostaj, M.T. (2010). The past meets the present in Swedish FrameNet++. In Proceedings of the 14th EURALEX International Congress, pp. 269–281. Leeuwarden: EURALEX.

Borin, L. and Forsberg, M. (2009). All in the family: A comparison of SALDO and WordNet. In Proceedings of the Nodalida 2009 Workshop on WordNets and other Lexical Semantic Resources – between Lexical Semantics, Lexicography, Terminology and Formal Ontologies, pp. 7–12. Odense: NEALT.

Borin, L. and Forsberg, M. (2010). Beyond the synset: Swesaurus – a fuzzy Swedish wordnet. In Workshop on Re-thinking synonymy: Semantic sameness and similarity in languages and their description. Helsinki.

Borin, L. and Forsberg, M. (2011). Swesaurus – ett svenskt ordnät med fria tyglar. LexicoNordica vol. 18, pp. 17–39.

Borin, L., Forsberg, M. and Lönngren, L. (2008). The hunting of the BLARK – SALDO, a freely available lexical database for Swedish language technology. Joakim Nivre, Mats Dahllöf and Beáta Megyesi (eds.), Resourceful language technology. Festschrift in honor of Anna Sågvall Hein, pp. 21–32. Acta Universitatis Upsaliensis: Studia Linguistica Upsaliensia 7. Uppsala: Uppsala University.

Derwojedowa, M., Piasecki, M., Szpakowicz, S., Zawislawska, M. and Broda, B. (2008). Words, concepts and relations in the construction of the polish WordNet. In Global WordNet Conference 2008, pp. 162–177. Szeged, Hungary.

Daudé J., Padró L. and Rigau G. (2003). Validation and Tuning of Wordnet Mapping Techniques. Proceedings of the International Conference on Recent Advances on Natural Language Processing (RANLP'03). Borovets, Bulgaria.

Daudé J., Padró L. and Rigau G. (1999). Mapping Multilingual Hierarchies Using Relaxation Labeling. Joint SIGDAT Conference on Empirical Methods in Natural Language Processing and Very Large Corpora (EMNLP/VLC'99). Maryland, US.

Fellbaum, C. (ed) (1998). WordNet – An Electronic Lexical Database. Cambridge, Massachusetts: The MIT Press.

Hjorth, E. and Kristensen, K. (2003). Den Danske Ordbog. Gyldendal, Denmark.

Järborg, J. (2001). Roller i Semantisk databas. Research Reports from the Department of Swedish, No. GU-ISS-01-3. University of Gothenburg: Dept. of Swedish.

Johannsen, A. and Pedersen, B.S. (2011). "Andre ord" – a wordnet browser for the Danish wordnet, DanNet. In Proceedings from 18th Nordic Conference of Computational Linguistics, NODALIDA 2011, Riga, Latvia. Nothern Association for Language Technology, Vol. 11 pp. 295–298, University of Tartu.

Kann, V. and Rosell, M. (2006). Free construction of a free Swedish dictionary of synonyms In Proceedings of the 15th NODALIDA conference, pp. 105–110. Joensuu: University of Eastern Finland.

Martola, N. (2011). FinnWordNet och det finska samhället. In: Symposium om onomasiologiske ordbøker i Norden. Schæffergården, Copenhagen.

Kahusk, N., Orav, H. and Vare, K. (2012). Cross-linking Experience of Estonian WordNet. In: Human Language Technologies – The Baltic Perspective: The Fifth International Conference on Human Language Technologies – The Baltic perspective. Tartu, Estonia, October 4-5, 2012. (Ed. Arvi, Tavast; Kadri Muischnek; Mare, Koit). IOS Press, pp. 96–102. Online access: doi:10.3233/978-1-61499-133-5-96

Lenci, A., Bel, N., Busa, F., Calzolari, N., Gola, E., Monachini, M., Ogonowski, A., Peters, I., Peters, W., Ruimy, N., Villegas, M. and Zampolli, A. (2000). SIMPLE: A general framework for the development of multilingual lexicons. International Journal of Lexicography, vol. 13, pp. 249–263

Lindén, K. and Carlson, L. (2010). FinnWordNet – WordNet på finska via översättning. LexicoNordica – Nordic Journal of Lexicography, vol. 17, pp. 119–140

Lindén, K., Niemi, J. and Hyvärinen, M. (2012) Extending and Updating the Finnish Wordnet. In Diana Santos, Krister Lindén and Wanjiku Ng'ang'a (eds.), Shall We Play the Festschrift Game? Essays on the Occasion of Lauri Carlson's 60th Birthday, pp. 67–98. Springer: Berlin, Heidelberg. ISBN 978-3-642-30773-7.

Pedersen, B.S, Nimb, S., Asmussen, J., Sørensen, N., Trap-Jensen, L. and Lorentzen, H. (2009). DanNet – the challenge of compiling a WordNet for Danish by reusing a monolingual dictionary. Language Resources and Evaluation, Computational Linguistics Series, pp. 269–299.

Pedersen, B.S., Nimb, S. and Braasch, A. (2010). Merging specialist taxonomies and folk taxonomies in wordnets. - a case study of plants, animals and foods in the Danish wordnet In: Proceedings from the Seventh International Conference on Language Resources and Evaluation, pp. 3181–3186. Malta.

Peters, W., Vossen, P., Díes-Orzas, P. and Adriaens, G. (1998). Cross-lingual Alignment of Wordnets with an Inter-Lingual-Index. In: EuroWordNet – A Multilingual Database with Lexical Semantic Networks, pp. 149–179. Kluwer Academic Publishers.

Pustejovsky, J. (1995). The Generative Lexicon. Cambridge, Massachusetts: MIT Press.

Robkop, K., Thoongsup, S., Charoenpron, T., Sornlertlamvanich, V. and Isahara, H.. (2010). WNMS: Connecting Distributed Wordnet in the Case of Asian WordNet. In: Proceedings of the 5th International Conference of the Global WordNet Association (GWC 2010), Mumbai, India.

Tufiş, D., Ion, R. and Ide, N. (2004). Word Sense Disambiguation as a Wordnets Validation Method in BalkaNet. In Proceedings of the 4th International Conference on Language Resources and Evaluation (LREC 2004), pp. 1071–1074. Lisbon: ELRA

Vossen, P. (ed.) (1998). EuroWordNet: A Multilingual Database with Lexical Semantic Networks. Dordrecht: Kluwer Academic Publishers.

Normalisation of Historical Text Using Context-Sensitive Weighted Levenshtein Distance and Compound Splitting

Eva Pettersson[1,2]*, Beáta Megyesi*[1] *and Joakim Nivre*[1]

(1) Department of Linguistics and Philology, Uppsala University
(2) Swedish National Graduate School of Language Technology

`firstname.lastname@lingfil.uu.se`

ABSTRACT

Natural language processing for historical text imposes a variety of challenges, such as to deal with a high degree of spelling variation. Furthermore, there is often not enough linguistically annotated data available for training part-of-speech taggers and other tools aimed at handling this specific kind of text. In this paper we present a Levenshtein-based approach to normalisation of historical text to a modern spelling. This enables us to apply standard NLP tools trained on contemporary corpora on the normalised version of the historical input text. In its basic version, no annotated historical data is needed, since the only data used for the Levenshtein comparisons are a contemporary dictionary or corpus. In addition, a (small) corpus of manually normalised historical text can optionally be included to learn normalisation for frequent words and weights for edit operations in a supervised fashion, which improves precision. We show that this method is successful both in terms of normalisation accuracy, and by the performance of a standard modern tagger applied to the historical text. We also compare our method to a previously implemented approach using a set of hand-written normalisation rules, and we see that the Levenshtein-based approach clearly outperforms the hand-crafted rules. Furthermore, the experiments were carried out on Swedish data with promising results and we believe that our method could be successfully applicable to analyse historical text for other languages, including those with less resources.

KEYWORDS: Digital Humanities, Natural Language Processing, Historical Text, Normalisation, Levenshtein Edit Distance, Compound Splitting, Part-of-Speech Tagging, Underresourced Languages, Less-Resource Languages.

1 Introduction

When working with natural language processing (NLP) for historical text, one problem is that there are often not large enough amounts of annotated corpus data available for training NLP tools specifically aimed at handling historical text. Nevertheless, using existing NLP tools as they are is rarely an option, since these generally rely on dictionaries and/or statistics based on certain word forms observed in the training data. Spelling in historical texts however differs from contemporary spelling, and due to the lack of spelling conventions, spelling may also vary between different authors, genres and time periods, and even within the same text written by the same author.

Even though there are differences between old and modern text, there are also similarities, and a native speaker of the language is often able to understand all or part of a historical text in spite of the odd spelling. Bearing this in mind, one way to get around the lack of NLP tools for historical text is to first normalise the input text to a more modern spelling, before applying existing NLP tools trained on contemporary corpora. In this context, the normalisation process may be viewed as a kind of spelling correction, where the historical word form is treated as a misspelling, that should be corrected to the most probable modern spelling.

In this paper we describe an approach to normalisation of historical text based on Levenshtein edit distance, where certain edits can be weighted to reflect common (and thus more likely) spelling variation in texts from this time period. Apart from handling single edit operations, we also include operations involving multiple characters. Another innovative feature of our approach is the use of a compound splitter for normalising parts of a compound word individually. Finally, we explore the effect of using manually annotated historical data to learn the normalisation of frequent words in a supervised fashion. We evaluate our results on historical Swedish data, both regarding normalisation accuracy, and by running a modern tagger on the historical text, before and after normalisation.

The outline of this paper is as follows. Section 2 describes related work on normalisation of historical text. In Section 3, we present the data used in our experimental setup, whereas our approach is described in detail in Section 4. In Section 5, we present the results. Finally, conclusions and future work are discussed in Section 6.

2 Related Work

The use of NLP tools for analysing historical text is still largely unexplored, even though there is a rapidly growing interest in this field. The idea of implementing spelling correction techniques for normalising the input text to a more modern spelling before applying existing NLP tools is a popular approach, and may be performed using rule-based or data-driven methods, or a combination of both.

Rayson et al. (2005) tried a rule-based approach based on dictionary lookup. A large mapping scheme from historical to modern spelling for 16th to 19th century English texts was manually created. The resulting VARD tool (VARiant Detector) comprises 45,805 entries, and also includes fuzzy matching techniques and context rules for normalisation of ambiguous words. The performance of the normalisation tool was evaluated on a set of 17th century texts, and compared to the performance of modern spell checkers (MS-Word and Aspell) on the same text. The results showed that between a third and a half of all tokens (depending on which test text was used) were correctly normalised by both VARD and MS Word, whereas approximately one third of the tokens were correctly normalised only when using VARD. The comparison between VARD and Aspell showed similar results. VARD was later further developed into VARD2, combining the original word list with data-driven techniques in the form of phonetic matching against a modern dictionary, and letter replacement rules based on common spelling variation patterns (Baron and Rayson, 2008).

Another rule-based method, based on pattern matching, was developed by Pettersson et al. (2012). In this experiment, a relatively small set of 29 hand-crafted normalisation rules for handling spelling variation in Early Modern Swedish texts (1550–1800) was produced, based on a subset of a 17th century court records text. The resulting rule set was applied to a gold standard corpus of 600 sentences (33,544 tokens) extracted from 15 documents within two separate genres (court records and church documents), varying in time from 1527 to 1812. Even though the rule set had been developed on a single 17th century court records text, normalisation had a positive effect on texts from all centuries and for both genres within the scope of the study. In fact, the largest error reduction was achieved for a 16th century church document. On average, an error reduction of 22% was achieved, meaning that approximately 73% of the tokens were correctly normalised.

A third rule-based technique, referred to as conflation by phonetic form, was explored by Jurish (2008) for normalisation of historical German text. In this approach, the similarity between phonetic forms is computed, rather than comparing orthographic forms. The general assumption is that since there were no orthographic conventions for writers of historical text, spelling generally reflects the phonetic form of the word. Furthermore, it is assumed that phonetic properties are less resistant to diachronic change than orthography. For the grapheme-to-phoneme transition, they used the conversion module of the IMS German Festival text-to-speech system (Black and Taylor, 1997), with a rule-set adapted to historical word forms. The method was evaluated on a corpus of historical German verse quotations extracted from *Deutsches Wörterbuch*, containing 5,491,982 tokens (318,383 types). Without normalisation, approximately 84% of the tokens were known to their morphological analyser. After conflation by phonetic form, coverage was extended to 92% of the tokens. When adding lemma-based heuristics to this method, coverage increased further to 94% of the tokens.

As an extension to the work on conflation by phonetic form, Jurish (2010) further explored the impact of taking the sentential context into consideration in the normalisation process. For this purpose, a Hidden Markov Model (HMM) was developed for contextual disambiguation of a set of normalisation candidates that were originally extracted on a token level using four different normalisation techniques: string identity, transliteration, phonetization and rewrite transduction. The resulting HMM produced precision scores of 99.7% and recall scores of 99.1% on a test corpus of 152,776 tokens from the time period 1780–1880, extracted from the *Deutsches Textarchiv*.

A data-driven approach based on Levenshtein similarity was presented by Bollmann et al. (2011) for normalisation of Early New High German (14th to 16th century). Normalisation rules were automatically derived by means of the Levenshtein edit distance, based on a word-aligned parallel corpus consisting of the Martin Luther bible in its 1545 edition and its 1892 version, respectively. Since bible text is rather conservative in spelling and terminology, approximately 65% of the words in the old bible version already had an identical spelling to the one occurring in the more modern version. For non-identical word forms, only word forms that could be found in the modern version of the bible were accepted. Other word forms produced by the Levenshtein-based rules were discarded, leaving the old spelling preserved. Using this method, the proportion of words with an identical spelling in the normalised text as compared to the "modern" text increased from 65% to 91%. Bollmann (2012) also tried a combination of dictionary lookup and different modifications to the original Levenshtein distance measure, improving normalisation accuracy further to 92.6% for the same training and test corpora.

3 Data

In this study, we make use of a 787,122 token corpus consisting of 15 Swedish texts, from the genres of court records and church documents, ranging from 1527 to 1812. The texts have been automatically digitized, and only parts of the corpus have been manually reviewed and corrected with regard to OCR errors. For evaluation we use the same subset of this corpus as was used for evaluation by Pettersson et al. (2012), i.e. 600 sentences extracted by randomly selecting 40 sentences from each text in the entire data set. For training, i.e. for estimating different parameters of our model, we extracted another 600 sentences out of the remaining sentences in the corpus (40 randomly selected sentences from each text). The resulting token distribution for training and evaluation is given in Table 1.

Court Records				
Name	**Year**	**Total**	**Training**	**Evaluation**
Östra Härad	1602–1605	38,477	1,980	2,069
Vendel	1615–1645	64,977	1,583	2,509
Per Larsson	1638	12,864	2,848	2,987
Hammerdal	1649–1686	75,143	1,508	1,859
Revsund	1649–1689	113,395	2,275	2,328
Stora Malm	1728–1741	458,548	1,627	1,895
Vendel	1736–1737	61,664	3,032	3,450
Stora Malm	1742–1760	74,487	2,034	2,336
Stora Malm	1761–1783	66,236	1,905	1,825
Stora Malm	1784–1795	58,738	2,036	1,378
Stora Malm	1796–1812	47,671	2,345	1,683
Church Documents				
Name	**Year**	**Total**	**Training**	**Evaluation**
Västerås	1527	14,149	2,831	3,709
Kyrkoordning	1571	60,354	2,093	2,246
Uppsala Möte	1593	34,877	1,070	1,184
Kyrkolag	1686	35,201	1,660	2,086
Total	1527–1812	787,122	30,827	33,544

Table 1: Corpus distribution, given in number of tokens in the documents. Total = Number of tokens in the whole corpus. Training = Number of tokens in the training sample of the corpus. Evaluation = Number of tokens in the evaluation sample of the corpus.

4 Method

This paper explores an approach to normalisation of historical text using the Levenshtein edit distance measure for comparing the original word form to word forms listed in an electronically available dictionary or corpus of contemporary language. Our approach is similar to the one presented by Bollmann et al. (2011) in that Levenshtein similarity is used in the normalisation process. In the Bollmann approach, however, the Levenshtein weights are calculated on the basis of aligned parallel data, consisting of the same text in an old spelling version and a modern spelling version, respectively. Our approach does not presuppose access to such a corpus, since the Levenshtein distance is solely computed by comparing the historical word forms to tokens present in a contemporary dictionary or corpus.

Two steps are included in the normalisation process: *generation of normalisation candidates* and *candidate selection*. As stated above, the generation of normalisation candidates is performed by comparing the historical word form to the tokens present in a contemporary language resource. In our experiments we use the SALDO dictionary (version 2.0) for this purpose. SALDO is an electronically available lexical resource developed for present-day written Swedish, comprising approximately 100,000 lexical entries (Borin et al., 2008). The dictionary entry/entries with the smallest edit distance as compared to the original word form are stored as possible normalisation candidates, given that certain requirements are met concerning string length and edit distance, as further discussed in Section 4.1.

The generation of candidates may optionally be refined, to improve precision further. For example, if there is a set of manually normalised historical tokens available, this corpus could be included as a *validated cache*, mapping historical word forms to a manually validated modern spelling. The validated cache is consulted before possible normalisation candidates are generated based on Levenshtein distance. If the token is present in the validated cache, the normalised form found in the cache is chosen, and no Levenshtein-based candidates are generated.[1] Such a corpus could also be used for optimisation of the Levenshtein calculations, as described further in Section 4.1. Another optional refinement that we have experimented with is the addition of a *compound splitter* (Stymne, 2008). In this case, the token is first matched against the contemporary language resource as usual. If no normalisation candidates are found by the Levenshtein comparisons, the word is split into its compound parts (provided that the splitter regards the token as a compound) and each compound part is matched separately against the contemporary language resource by means of Levenshtein calculations. Finally, the resulting normalised parts are merged into a compound normalisation candidate.

When possible normalisation candidates have been extracted, one candidate is to be selected as the final choice. In the default setting, a final candidate is randomly chosen from the list of highest-ranked candidates. The candidate selection step can however be further refined, if there is a corpus of modern language available. In this case, the candidate with the highest frequency in the corpus is chosen. Only if none of the highest-ranked normalisation candidates are present in the corpus, or if there are several candidates with the same frequency distribution, a final candidate is randomly chosen. In our experiments, we use the Stockholm-Umeå corpus (SUC) (Ejerhed and Källgren, 1997) for frequency calculations. SUC is a balanced corpus consisting of approximately one million tokens extracted from a number of different text types representative of the Swedish language in the 1990s.

The whole normalisation process, as described above, is illustrated in Figure 1, where optional resources are marked by dotted lines and arrows.

---

[1] We also include *unvalidated* items in the cache, solely for reasons of efficiency. This means that normalisations previously performed by the algorithm, as well as tokens present in the modern dictionary, are stored in the cache and consulted as a first step in the normalisation process.

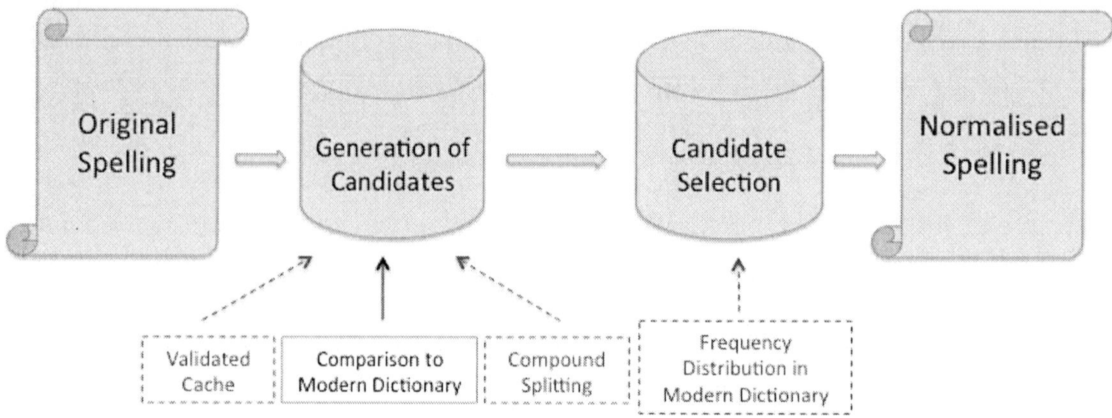

Figure 1: Overview of the normalisation workflow. Optional resources are dotted.

4.1 Parameter Optimisation

The Levenshtein distance gives an indication of the similarity between two strings (Levenshtein, 1966). Still, in the context of normalisation, it is not a trivial decision what string similarity to regard as close enough for considering a normalisation candidate as valid. In a traditional spelling correction context, it has been shown that for the majority of the human-generated spelling errors, the misspelled word form is within one letter in length of the intended word form, and that most errors constitute single instances of insertion, deletion, substitution or transposition (Kukich, 1992). If no empirical data on the correlation between historical and modern spelling is available, one could thus assume that a valid normalisation candidate should be maximally one character shorter or longer than the original word form, with a maximum Levenshtein distance of 1. In the following we explore the characteristics of our manually normalised training data as regards edit distances and differences in string length between the original word forms and their normalised counterparts. The aim is to find out whether the traditional spelling correction assumptions hold also in the context of normalisation, or (if not) what the optimal configuration would be. We also explore the inclusion of context-sensitive, weighted edit operations, compound handling and supervised learning by means of manually validated normalisations.

4.1.1 Observed String Length Differences

To decide what string length differences to consider in the normalisation process, we investigated the differences in string length between the original word forms and their normalised counterparts in the training corpus. As previously stated, the training corpus comprises in total 30,827 tokens (see further Section 3). Approximately 35% of these tokens (10,735) differ from the manually normalised spelling. As shown in Table 2, the assumption that most errors do not influence string length by more than one character may still be regarded as appropriate even in the context of normalisation. However, the proportion of tokens meeting this requirement is limited to approximately 86.9%. Instead, if we consider all cases where the normalised word form is at most one character longer down to four characters shorter than the original word form, approximately 99.5% of the tokens observed in the training corpus will be covered. We will therefore focus on varying the valid difference in string length within this interval.

Length Difference	Frequency	Example	Translation
−7	1	*besluthninger/beslut*	'decisions'
−6	3	*fadherbrodher/farbror*	'uncle'
−5	7	*noghsambligha/nogsamma*	'careful'
−4	127	*närvarellse/närvaro*	'presence'
−3	308	*slechttenn/släkten*	'the relatives'
−2	918	*kyrckian/kyrkan*	'the church'
−1	4804	*aff/av*	'of/off'
0	3326	*wara/vara*	'be'
+1	1201	*til/till*	'to'
+2	35	*sokn/socken*	'parish'
+3	2	*tilbragte/tillbringade*	'spent'
+5	3	*församhs/församlingens*	'the congregation's'

Table 2: Observed differences in string length between the historical word form and the manually normalised version in the training corpus. Grey rows illustrate string length differences with a special focus in our experimental setup.

4.1.2 Observed Edit Distances

As illustrated in Table 3, we see that if we consider only normalisation candidates with a maximum Levenshtein distance of 1 as compared to the original word form, we merely cover approximately 55.8% of the tokens in the training corpus. Furthermore, we see that all edit distances up to and including 4 have a high frequency in the training corpus. If we consider an edit distance span where 4 is the maximum value, we cover 98.8% of the observed entities in the training corpus. Hence, to broaden normalisation coverage, we will focus our experiments on considering edit distances up to and including 4.

Edit Distance	Frequency	Example	Translation
1	5986	*sigh/sig*	'oneself/himself/herself/itself'
2	3008	*dher/där*	'there'
3	1161	*blefwe/blev*	'became'
4	455	*afwachta/avvakta*	'await'
5	86	*öfwertalter/övertalad*	'persuaded'
6	28	*söllfuermynthe/silvermynt*	'silver coin'
7	10	*sielffuer/själv*	'himself/herself/itself'
8	1	*öffuergiffua/överge*	'abandon'

Table 3: Observed edit distance between the historical word form and the manually normalised version in the training corpus. Grey rows illustrate edit distances with a special focus in our experimental setup.

4.1.3 Weighted Edit Operations

When computing a traditional Levenshtein distance, all edit operations have a cost of one. However, in the context of normalisation of historical text, some edits seem more likely than others. For example, as historical texts to some degree are written in a spoken-language fashion, substituting the letter *c* for a *k* is more likely than substituting for example a *c* for an *r*. For this reason, we have experimented on assigning weights lower than 1 for frequently occurring edits in the training corpus.

Out of the 8,881 edits observed in the training corpus, we have assigned special weights to edits occurring at least 50 times. The weights have been calculated by comparing the frequency of each edit occurring in the training corpus to the frequency with which the specific source characters are left unchanged, in accordance with the formula below:

$$1 - \frac{\text{FrequencyOfEdit}}{\text{FrequencyOfEdit} + \text{FrequencyOfSourceCharacterLeftUnchanged}}$$

which could be further simplified into:

$$\frac{\text{FrequencyOfSourceCharacterLeftUnchanged}}{\text{FrequencyOfEdit} + \text{FrequencyOfSourceCharacterLeftUnchanged}}$$

To illustrate, the deletion of the letter h happens in 2,382 cases in the training corpus, when comparing the historical spelling to the modernised spelling. In the rest of the 3,912 cases where the letter h occurs, it is preserved in the modernised spelling. Thus, the weight for the deletion of the letter h is calculated as: $\frac{3912}{2382+3912} \approx 0.6215$.

In some cases, the observed edits involve more than one character, for example when comparing the historical spelling *oförsichtigt* to the modernised version *oförsiktigt* ("carelessly"). This would intuitively be regarded as a substitution of *ch* for *k*, rather than first substituting the *c* for a *k*, and then deleting the *h*. To deal with cases like this, we therefore included the following context-sensitive edit operations, in addition to the standard single-character operations:

- double deletion
  example: -fv, *gifvvett* → *givet*
- double insertion
  example: +es, *orklöse* → *orkeslöse*
- single-to-double substitution
  example: l/ll, *tilbytt* → *tillbytt*
- double-to-single substitution
  example: ss/s, *frälsse* → *frälse*

For all strings in the training corpus that are not identical in the historical and the modern spelling, all possible single-character edits as well as multi-character edits are counted. Hence, the token pair *oförsichtigt-oförsiktigt* will yield weights for (i) single deletion of *c*, single substitution of $h{\to}k$; (ii) single deletion of *h*, single substitution of $c{\to}k$; and (iii) double-to-single substitution of $ch{\to}k$.

4.1.4 Compound Handling

The Levenshtein method described in this paper is based on comparison of a historical word form to similar word forms found in a modern dictionary. Since the Swedish language has a high degree of compounds, some of the intended words will inevitably not be found in the dictionary, even if the word could perfectly well be used in contemporary Swedish. Stymne and Holmqvist (2008) showed that in their Swedish evaluation corpus, approximately 37% of all the words with a length of 12 characters or longer were compounds (and approximately 5% of the shorter words). This was calculated on modern Swedish European Parliament text, but might still be indicative of the frequencies in historical Swedish texts as well. To deal with the compounding issue, we included a compound splitter developed by Stymne (2008). When the compound splitter is included, any word form for which no appropriate normalisation candidate is found by the ordinary Levenshtein calculations, is run through the compound splitter. If the splitter is able to split the word into compound parts, each part is processed separately by the normalisation program, and the resulting normalisation candidates are merged into a final normalisation candidate. For example a word like *krigztienst* will be split into *krigz* (normalised as *krigs* "war") and *tienst* (normalised as *tjänst* "duty"). The two normalised versions *krigs* and *tjänst* will then be merged into the final normalisation candidate *krigstjänst*.

4.1.5 Manually Validated Normalisations

Even though historical texts present a high degree of spelling variation, some word forms are frequently occurring in many of these texts. Incorrect normalisation of a few frequently occurring word forms might result in poor NLP performance, even when a high proportion of the remaining word forms has been normalised correctly. Therefore we will explore the effect of adding a set of manually validated normalisation candidates for the most frequently occurring word forms in the training corpus. When such a word form is encountered in a text, only the manually validated set of normalisation candidates will be considered, and no Levenshtein distance is computed for finding alternative candidates.

Since each token in the training corpus has been manually assigned its normalised counterpart, we use this annotation for providing a cache with information on what manual normalisation(s) that have been assigned for the word form in question. In order to avoid incorrect attempts at normalisation, the caching procedure also involves word forms where the original spelling has been preserved in the manual validation, as illustrated by the first entry in Table 4, where the historical word form *och* is mapped to its identical modern spelling *och* ("and"). Furthermore, if one word form has been manually normalised in several ways in the training corpus, all candidates are stored in the cache, as illustrated by the second entry, where the historical word form *i* is mapped both to the modern spelling *i* ("in") and to *ni* ("you"). A sample from the manually validated normalisations is given in Table 4. In order to explore the impact of caching manually validated normalisations, we will consider different frequency thresholds in our experimental setup.

Frequency	Original form	Normalised Form(s)	Translation(s)
1,144	*och*	*och*	'and'
634	*i*	*i* or *ni*	'in' or 'you'
242	*at*	*att*	'to/that'
229	*på*	*på*	'on'
219	*af*	*av*	'of'
121	*effter*	*efter*	'after'
109	*thet*	*det*	'it'
92	*ther*	*där*	'there'
45	*j*	*i*	'in'
35	*meth*	*med*	'with'

Table 4: A sample from the manually validated normalisations observed in the training corpus.

5 Results

Evaluation of our proposed Levenshtein-based normalisation algorithm has been performed on the basis of the evaluation corpus (see further Section 3). The results are presented below, both in terms of actual normalisation accuracy and by measuring the performance of a modern tagger on the historical text, before and after normalisation.

5.1 Normalisation

Normalisation results are evaluated using two different measures: *normalisation accuracy* and *error reduction*. By normalisation accuracy we mean the percentage of tokens in the normalised version of the text that are identical to the manually reviewed tokens in the gold standard, whereas error reduction refers to the percentage of correctly normalised tokens that were not originally identical to the gold standard spelling. Error reduction has been calculated by the following formula:

$$\frac{CorrectAfterNormalisation - CorrectBeforeNormalisation}{IncorrectBeforeNormalisation}$$

where *CorrectAfterNormalisation* is the percentage of tokens with an identical spelling to the gold standard version *after* normalisation, *CorrectBeforeNormalisation* is the percentage of tokens with an identical spelling to the gold standard version *before* normalisation, and *IncorrectBeforeNormalisation* is the percentage of tokens differing in spelling from the gold standard version before normalisation.

Furthermore, we have experimented on different restrictions for the algorithm, regarding 1) valid string length difference between the original word form and its normalisation candidate (as described in Section 4.1.1), 2) valid edit distance between the original word form and its normalisation candidate (as described in Section 4.1.2), 3) special weights for frequently occurring edits (as described in Section 4.1.3), compound handling (see further Section 4.1.4, and 4) a frequency threshold for inclusion of manually validated normalisation candidates in a cache (as described in Section 4.1.5).

It could also be noted that in the following, normalisation accuracy and error reduction are calculated on the evaluation corpus as a whole, without taking differences between genres and age of the subtexts into account. For an investigation of the impact of age and genre on normalisation performance, see further Pettersson et al. (2012).

5.1.1 String Length Restrictions

Table 5 shows the normalisation results when varying the threshold for valid difference in string length between the original word form and its normalisation candidate. As shown in Section 4.1.1, 99.5% of the manually normalised word forms in the training corpus are within the range of one character longer to four characters shorter compared to the original historical word form. We experimented with different settings within this range. No manually validated cache entries nor compound handling or weighted edits are included at this stage, and the accepted edit distance for a normalisation candidate to be regarded as valid is set to 4, i.e. the value needed to capture the majority of the instances in the training corpus.[2] The results are also compared to the baseline, i.e. the unnormalised version of the evaluation corpus, and to

---

[2]It would of course have been preferable to have no limit on the accepted edit distance in these experiments. However, due to computational complexity, a threshold had to be included.

the approach of Pettersson et al. (2012) using hand-crafted rules. We see that approximately 64.6% of the original tokens already have a spelling identical to the manually normalised gold standard spelling. The hand-written rules have a positive impact, improving accuracy to 72.7%. This is however outperformed by the Levenshtein approach, for which accuracy is higher in all settings. Furthermore, we see that the general spelling correction assumption that the original string should not differ in length with more than one character from the intended word form does not hold in this context, since we get better results if we increase the valid difference in string length so that the normalised word form may be two or three characters shorter than the original form. Increasing this range to four characters however does not have a noticeable effect on the results. In the following we will therefore regard the $+1$ to -3 setting as the setting to be used as a basis for further experiments.

Approach	Accuracy	Error Reduction
Baseline	64.6%	n/a
Hand-written	72.7%	22.9%
Levenshtein stringdiff $+1$ to -1	76.2%	32.7%
Levenshtein stringdiff $+1$ to -2	76.9%	34.9%
Levenshtein stringdiff $+1$ to -3	77.0%	35.0%
Levenshtein stringdiff $+1$ to -4	77.0%	35.0%

Table 5: Normalisation accuracy and error reduction for different normalisation settings. Baseline = Unnormalised version of the evaluation corpus. Hand-written = Normalisation using a set of hand-crafted rules, as presented by Pettersson et al. (2012). Levenshtein = The normalisation approach described in this paper. Stringdiff = Valid difference in string length between the original word form and its normalisation candidate(s).

5.1.2 Edit Distance Restrictions

As presented in the previous section, normalisation results are influenced by what string length differences we accept for a normalisation candidate to be considered valid. Another important factor to take into consideration is the maximum edit distance allowed. We have experimented on varying the accepted edit distance between 1 and 4. However, if we statically accept an edit distance of for example 3, a three-letter word that is to be normalised may be transformed into a completely different word, where each character in the original word has been substituted by another character. To avoid such cases, we also experimented on a stringlength-based measure for deciding the maximum edit distance allowed for a certain source word. First, we calculated the average number of edits per character for all historical words in the training corpus that were not identical to the modern spelling. This showed an average edit distance of 0.27/character. With a standard deviation of approximately 0.18, the valid edit distance is then calculated as follows (where 1.96 times the standard deviation is added to cover 95% of the cases):

$$\text{distance} \leq 1 \text{ OR distance} \leq ((0.27 * \text{wordlength}) + (1.96 * 0.18))$$

The first condition is included to assure that one edit is always allowed, also in short words consisting of only one or two characters. The above formula could be further simplified into:

$$\text{distance} \leq \max(1, ((0.27 * \text{wordlength}) + (1.96 * 0.18)))$$

Table 6 presents our findings on varying the accepted edit distance between 1 and 4, as well as including the stringlength-based method. For all settings in this experiment, the string length restrictions are set to the best-performing settings as presented in the previous section, i.e. letting the normalisation candidates differ in string length from the original word form by at most $+1$ to -3 characters. Again, the results show that we may not rely on findings from general spelling correction observations, stating that edit distance should not exceed a value of 1. In our data, we get better results when increasing this threshold to 2, 3 or 4. We can also see that the stringlength-based method is slightly less successful than the approach where we always allow for an edit distance of 3 or 4. In the following we will therefore regard a Levenshtein distance threshold of 4 as the setting to be used for further experiments.

A closer look at the results of the stringlength-based method as compared to the static Levenshtein method, shows that the stringlength-based method has a higher precision, but a lower recall. The cases where a word form has been normalised in an incorrect way is substantially lower in the stringlength-based method, whereas the proportion of word forms that have incorrectly been left unnormalised is higher. This is particularly striking for words consisting of 4–9 characters. Both shorter and longer words are more or less equally well handled by both methods. Thus, in cases where precision is considerably more important than recall, the stringlength-based method could be preferred.

Approach	Accuracy	Error Reduction
Baseline	64.6%	n/a
Hand-written	72.7%	22.9%
Levenshtein max distance 1	74.7%	28.5%
Levenshtein max distance 2	76.7%	34.1%
Levenshtein max distance 3	77.0%	34.9%
Levenshtein max distance 4	77.0%	35.0%
Levenshtein stringlength-based	76.2%	32.9%

Table 6: Normalisation accuracy and error reduction for different normalisation settings. Baseline = Unnormalised version of the evaluation corpus. Hand-written = Normalisation using a set of hand-crafted rules, as presented by Pettersson et al. (2012). Levenshtein = The normalisation approach described in this paper. Max distance = Maximum valid edit distance between the original word form and its normalisation candidate(s).

5.1.3 Introducing Lower Weights for Frequently Occurring Edits

As stated in Section 4.1.3, some edits are more likely to occur than others. Table 7 presents the results of adding weights lower than 1 to frequently occurring differences when comparing the spelling of the original historical word form to the spelling of the corresponding manually normalised form in the training corpus. For this experiment, the string length and edit distance restrictions are set to the best-performing settings as presented in the previous sections, i.e. letting the normalisation candidates differ in string length from the original word form by at most $+1$ to -3 characters, with an allowed edit distance of maximally 4.

As seen from the results, the inclusion of context-free weights lower than 1 means that normalisation accuracy increases from 77.0% to 78.7% as compared to normalisation without special weights. Including context-sensitive weights as well, the normalisation accuracy increases further to 79.1%. The training corpus used in this experiment is however rather small (10,735 tokens with a spelling that is different from the manually normalised spelling). It is likely that the inclusion of weights would have a larger impact on normalisation accuracy if more training data was available.

Approach	Accuracy	Error Reduction
Baseline	64.6%	n/a
Hand-written	72.7%	22.9%
Levenshtein no weights	77.0%	35.0%
Levenshtein context-free weights	78.7%	39.9%
Levenshtein context-sensitive weights	79.1%	40.9%

Table 7: Normalisation accuracy and error reduction for different normalisation settings. Baseline = Unnormalised version of the evaluation corpus. Hand-written = Normalisation using a set of hand-crafted rules, as presented by Pettersson et al. (2012). Levenshtein no weights = The normalisation approach described in this paper, with no special weights included. Levenshtein weights = The normalisation approach described in this paper, with weights lower than 1 for frequently occurring edits.

5.1.4 Compound Handling

For compound handling, we experimented on adding a compound splitter to the normalisation process. In this setting, words that are not found in the modern dictionary by the ordinary normalisation approach, are split into their compound parts, and Levenshtein distance is calculated for each compound part separately. This feature has a small but positive effect on the normalisation process. The normalisation accuracy is still 79.1%, as for the best Levenshtein setting presented in the previous section. At a token level however, 26,997 tokens in the normalised text are identical to the manually modernised spelling when no compound handling is performed, as compared to 27,013 identically spelled tokens in the compound setting.

5.1.5 Varying the Threshold for Manually Validated Normalisations

As argued in Section 4.1.5, a small number of frequently occurring incorrectly normalised word forms may have a large negative impact on the result of contemporary NLP tools when applied to the normalised text. To avoid this, we created a cache function for manually validated normalisations observed in the training corpus. As could be expected, the manually validated cache boosts normalisation performance further. Table 8 summarises the results of varying the frequency threshold for what words to include in the cache. In this table, cache100 means that only word forms that occur 100 times or more in the training corpus are included in the cache. Based on our training corpus, this means that the cache of manually validated word forms holds 28 entries. In this setting, accuracy improves from 79.1% to 80.9%, increasing error reduction from 40.9% to 46.0%. If the word forms in the training corpus are sorted by frequency before manual normalisation is performed, this improvement is achieved by a rather modest manual annotation effort, since only 28 word forms need to be normalised. Including less frequent words in the cache improves accuracy as well as error reduction in all cases. When including all tokens in the validated corpus, regardless of frequency, an overall accuracy of 86.9% is achieved, corresponding to an error reduction of 63.0%.

Approach	Cache Entries	Accuracy	Error Reduction
Baseline	n/a	64.6%	n/a
Hand-written	n/a	72.7%	22.9%
Levenshtein, no cache	n/a	79.1%	40.9%
Levenshtein, cache100	28	80.9%	46.0%
Levenshtein, cache50	51	81.5%	47.7%
Levenshtein, cache40	71	81.8%	48.6%
Levenshtein, cache30	107	82.1%	49.4%
Levenshtein, cache20	156	82.5%	50.6%
Levenshtein, cache10	319	83.5%	53.4%
Levenshtein, cache1	8272	86.9%	63.0%

Table 8: Normalisation accuracy and error reduction for different normalisation settings. Baseline = Unnormalised version of the evaluation corpus. Hand-written = Normalisation using a set of hand-crafted rules, as presented by Pettersson et al. (2012). Levenshtein = The normalisation approach described in this paper. Cache Entries = Number of entries in the manually validated cache.

5.2 Tagging

The ultimate goal of the normalisation process is to improve the performance of contemporary NLP tools when applied to historical texts. In the scope of this study, we do not have access to a fully linguistically annotated data set for assessing for example tagger performance before and after normalisation. However, the corpus used in our experiments has been created within the Gender and Work project (Ågren et al., 2011), where there is a specific interest in the verbs included in the text. Therefore, all verbs in the evaluation corpus have been manually annotated as verbs, and we may indirectly evaluate the performance of the tagger based on precision and recall measures regarding verb identification. In these experiments, part-of-speech tagging is performed using HunPOS (Halácsy et al., 2007), a free and open source reimplementation of the HMM-based TnT-tagger by Brants (2000). The tagger is used with a pre-trained language model based on the Stockholm-Umeå Corpus (SUC).

Table 9 presents precision and recall measures for verb extraction, based on the best settings for our Levenshtein approach as regards normalisation accuracy, i.e. 1) allowing for the normalisation candidates to differ in string length from the original word form by at most +1 to −3 characters, 2) with a valid edit distance of maximally 4, 3) with weights lower than 1 for frequently occurring edits, 4) with compound handling, and 5) with a threshold of 1 for manually validated normalisations in the cache. The results are also compared to verb extraction from unnormalised text, as well as verb extraction based on normalisation using manually written rules. The hand-crafted normalisation rules have a positive impact on the results, increasing recall from 64.2% for unnormalised text to 78.0%. With the Levenshtein approach this figure is increased further to 86.2%. At the same time, precision increases from 77.9% to 80.0% with the rule-based approach, and increases further to 83.3% using the Levenshtein method. To get an idea of the optimal performance on historical text, we also tried verb extraction based on the manually normalised gold standard version of the test text. This resulted in a precision of 90.1% and a recall of 92.3%. This could be compared to the evaluation scores achieved for verb extraction for contemporary text, in this case the SUC corpus, with a 99.1% precision and recall. This indicates that even with perfect spelling normalisation, some differences in language such as vocabulary, morphology and syntax, still need to be handled to achieve the same results as for modern language.

Approach	Precision	Recall	F-score
Baseline	77.9%	64.2%	70.4%
Hand-written	80.0%	78.0%	79.0%
Levenshtein	83.3%	86.2%	84.7%
Gold Standard Normalisation	90.1%	92.3%	91.2%
Contemporary text (SUC)	99.1%	99.1%	99.1%

Table 9: Precision and recall measures for verb identification based on the approach of hand-written rules (Pettersson et al., 2012) versus Levenshtein distance calculations. Baseline = Verb identification results when no normalisation is performed.

6   Conclusion

In this paper, we have proposed an approach to normalisation of historical text based on string similarity, using context-sensitive, weighted Levenshtein edit distance combined with compound splitting. We have evaluated our method both with respect to normalisation accuracy and regarding verb identification performance using a contemporary part-of-speech tagger on the normalised version of the input text.

With the presented approach, the proportion of tokens with an identical spelling to the gold standard spelling increased from a baseline of 64.6% (for unnormalised text) to 77.0%, using no manually annotated data for training. When including Levenshtein weights and a validated cache created on the basis of a small, manually normalised historical training corpus, normalisation accuracy increased further to 86.9% in the best setting. Furthermore, it is encouraging that both precision and recall increase for verb identification based on tagging, since the ultimate goal of the normalisation procedure is to enable the use of contemporary NLP tools for analysing historical data. The results are indeed promising, since our approach requires little or no manually annotated historical data, and is generalisable to similar (or somewhat distant) normalisation tasks for historical or other low density languages.

Future work includes refinement of the Levenshtein approach to normalisation, as well as exploring alternative techniques. One refinement could be to make the choice of normalisation candidates context-sensitive. Currently, the final normalisation candidate is solely chosen on a word-by-word basis, meaning that the same candidate will be chosen regardless of context. As for alternative techniques, it would be interesting to experiment with a phonetically based similarity measure for generating normalisation candidates. This seems reasonable since the lack of spelling conventions probably made the texts more alike spoken language than today.

Finally, it would also be interesting to try our normalisation approach in a different setting, such as other time periods and languages. This is enabled by the modularity and generalisability of the appoach, only requiring access to an electronically available dictionary of contemporary language. Modules such as the cache of manually validated normalisations could then be discarded in case of limited resources.

References

Ågren, M., Fiebranz, R., Lindberg, E., and Lindström, J. (2011). Making verbs count. The research project 'Gender and Work' and its methodology. *Scandinavian Economic History Review*, 59(3):271–291. Forthcoming.

Baron, A. and Rayson, P. (2008). Vard2: A tool for dealing with spelling variation in historical corpora. In *Postgraduate Conference in Corpus Linguistics*, Aston University, Birmingham.

Black, A. W. and Taylor, P. (1997). Festival speech synthesis system: system documentation. Technical report, University of Edinburgh, Centre for Speech Technology Research.

Bollmann, M. (2012). (semi-)Automatic Normalization of Historical Texts using Distance Measures and the norma tool. In *Proceedings of the Second Workshop on Annotation of Corpora for Research in the Humanitites (ACRH-2)*.

Bollmann, M., Petran, F., and Dipper, S. (2011). Rule-based normalization of historical texts. In *Proceedings of the Workshop on Language Technologies for Digital Humanities and Cultural Heritage*, pages 34–42, Hissar, Bulgaria.

Borin, L., Forsberg, M., and Lönngren, L. (2008). Saldo 1.0 (svenskt associationslexikon version 2). Språkbanken, University of Gothenburg.

Brants, T. (2000). TnT - a statistical part-of-speech tagger. In *Proceedings of the 6th Applied Natural Language Processing Conference (ANLP)*, Seattle, Washington, USA.

Ejerhed, E. and Källgren, G. (1997). Stockholm Umeå Corpus. Version 1.0. Produced by Department of Linguistics, Umeå University and Department of Linguistics, Stockholm University. ISBN 91-7191-348-3.

Halácsy, P., Kornai, A., and Oravecz, C. (2007). HunPos - an open source trigram tagger. In *Proceedings of the 45th Annual Meeting of the Association for Computational Linguistics*, pages 209–212, Prague, Czech Republic.

Jurish, B. (2008). Finding canonical forms for historical German text. In Storrer, A., Geyken, A., Siebert, A., and Würzner, K.-M., editors, *Text Resources and Lexical Knowledge: Selected Papers from the 9th Conference on Natural Language Processing* (KONVENS 2008), pages 27–37. Mouton de Gruyter, Berlin.

Jurish, B. (2010). More Than Words: Using Token Context to Improve Canonicalization of Historical German. *Journal for Language Technology and Computational Linguistics*, 25(1):23–39.

Kukich, K. (1992). Techniques for automatically correcting words in text. *ACM Computing Surveys (CSUR)*, 24(4):377–439.

Levenshtein, V. (1966). Binary Codes Capable of Correcting Deletions, Insertions and Reversals. *Soviet Physics Doklady*, 10(8):707–710.

Pettersson, E., Megyesi, B., and Nivre, J. (2012). Rule-based normalisation of historical text - a diachronic study. In *Proceedings of the First International Workshop on Language Technology for Historical Text(s)*, Vienna, Austria.

Rayson, P., Archer, D., and Nicholas, S. (2005). VARD versus Word – A comparison of the UCREL variant detector and modern spell checkers on English historical corpora. In *Proceedings from the Corpus Linguistics Conference Series on-line e-journal*, volume 1, Birmingham, UK.

Stymne, S. (2008). German compounds in factored statistical machine translation. In Ranta, A. and Nordström, B., editors, *Proceedings of GoTAL, 6th International Conference on Natural Language Processing*, volume 5221, pages 464–475, Gothenburg, Sweden. Springer LNCS/LNAI.

Stymne, S. and Holmqvist, M. (2008). Processing of Swedish Compounds for Phrase-Based Statistical Machine Translation. In *Proceedings of the 12th EAMT conference*, Hamburg, Germany.

Modeling OOV Words With Letter N-Grams in Statistical Taggers: Preliminary Work in Biomedical Entity Recognition

Teemu Ruokolainen[1] Miikka Silfverberg[2]

(1) Aalto University, Helsinki, Finland
(2) University of Helsinki, Helsinki, Finland

`teemu.ruokolainen@aalto.fi`, `miikka.silfverberg@helsinki.fi`

We discuss sequential tagging problems in natural language processing using statistical methodology. We propose an automatic and domain-independent approach to modeling out-of-vocabulary (OOV) words, that is words that do not occur in training data. Our method is based on using probabilistic letter n-gram models to model orthography of different tags. We show how to combine the approach with two widely used statistical models Hidden Markov Models and Conditional Random Fields. Instead of taking the common approach of directly using sub-strings as features resulting in an explosion in the number of model parameters, we compress orthographic information into a small number of parameters. Experiments in biomedical entity recognition on the Genia corpus show that the approach can alleviate the OOV problem resulting in improvement in overall model performance.

KEYWORDS: Biomedical Entity Recognition, CRF, HMM, Letter N-Grams, OOV, Tagging.

1 Introduction

We discuss sequential tagging problems in natural language processing (NLP) including tasks such as part-of-speech (POS) tagging (Brants, 2000), shallow parsing (Tjong Kim Sang and Buchholz, 2000), and named entity recognition (NER) (Tjong Kim Sang and De Meulder, 2003). Modern NLP approaches rely on data-driven statistical models trained using manually tagged training corpora. Commonly applied models include Hidden Markov Models (HMMs) (Brants, 2000), Maximum Entropy Markov Models (MEMMs) (McCallum et al., 2000), and Conditional Random Fields (CRFs) (Lafferty et al., 2001). In this work, we present preliminary work on an automatic, domain-independent approach for extracting orthographic features useful for modeling rare words and out-of-vocabulary words, that is words which were not observed in the training data.

All existing supervised statistical models utilize some form of feature functions, which extract relevant information from training sentences. In sequential word tagging problems, the word forms themselves and the words surrounding them are by default the most useful features. Consider for example POS tagging given a relatively large training corpus. For words that are frequently observed during training, it is reasonable to assume that all of the possible tags of the words are present in the training data. For these words, tagging is thus reduced to *disambiguation* between a limited set of known tags based on neighboring words and their tags.

Unfortunately, the word form itself is not a useful feature for out-of-vocabulary (OOV) words. For OOV words essentially all tags are possible, which makes disambiguation based on word and tag context more difficult. The OOV problem is typically most severe when only a small amount of data is available for model training, and when dealing with languages with rich morphology. The OOV problem is important, because manually tagging large amounts of training data is resource intensive. In order to alleviate the OOV problem, it is beneficial to enrich the model with *sub-word features* which model *word orthography and morphology*.

In some modeling problems, designing the sub-word features requires little knowledge about the domain of the problem. For example in POS tagging, simple features describing capitalized letters, presence of digits and suffixes of varying lengths, are sufficient for many languages (Brants, 2000). However, for morphologically complex languages and tasks such as NER this approach is inadequate. Instead, domain-specific knowledge is required for manually writing a set of regular expressions, which are then used in feature extraction. An alternative domain independent and automatic approach is to utilize sub-strings as features. In this work, we discuss a modification of this approach. In contrast to using a large amount of sub-string features, out approach is based on a small number of features utilizing *letter n-gram models*, which are easy to employ using existing efficient toolkits. We describe how to incorporate the features with HMM and CRF models.

In order to evaluate our method, we present experiments in biomedical entity recognition, a special case of NER, on the Genia corpus (Kim et al., 2004). Our results show, that the letter n-gram features can improve the model performance with small training sets. The improvements are more notable with CRFs, which as a discriminative log-linear model can naturally incorporate complex, non-independent features. Although the present work focuses on biomedical entity extraction, we believe that the approach could be beneficial in other domains as well.

The rest of the paper is as follows. In Section 2, we briefly discuss previous, related research. In Section 3, we describe the letter n-gram models and how to use them to extract orthographic features for the HMM and CRF models. Experiments conducted in biomedical entity recognition are described In Section 4 along with a discussion. We provide conclusions in Section 5.

2   Related Work

In the experimental section of this work, we provide results on the Genia corpus, the data set used in the shared task of biomedical entity recognition in the joint workshop of BioNLP/NLPBA 2004 (Kim et al., 2004). Among the participants of this task, the most commonly adopted approach to modeling OOV words was to use manually constructed regular expressions and affixes combined with gazetteers and POS features. This was the approach taken by the best performing system described by (Zhou and Su, 2004). We compare our n-gram-based feature extraction approach with the regular expression set used in their system, originally described by (Shen et al., 2003), and show that our method performs better[1].

The idea of constructing a domain-independent set of orthographic features utilizing letter n-grams is not new. Probabilistic letter n-gram models have been used in term recognition. For example (Vasserman, 2004) employed them as classifiers in chemical name recognition in a similar manner they have been utilized in language identification (Vatanen et al., 2010). Our use of the n-gram models to capture word orthography closely resembles theirs. However, we investigate incorporating letter n-gram models as *feature extractors* in statistical taggers. Also, plain letter n-grams (raw sub-strings of words) have been used extensively as features in taggers, see for example (Rössler, 2004). However, this approach results in an explosion in the number of model parameters, which could be avoided by using the feature extraction approach presented in this work.

Automatic and domain-independent orthographic feature extraction was recently discussed by (Fujii and Sakurai, 2012). The central idea in their work was to employ combined tag level and character level language models based on a hierarchical Bayesian approach. They also described experiments on the Genia corpus. However, our CRF model appears to outperforms their model. Additionally, although orthographic features are used to combat the OOV problem and have little effect on recognition of frequent words, the discussion provided by (Fujii and Sakurai, 2012) lacks this aspect completely.

To our knowledge, the highest performance on the Genia corpus has been reported by (Vishwanathan et al., 2006). Our work is similar to theirs in that we use a CRF model. The key differences are that their results were obtained using an extensive regular expression set and manually prepared features. Unfortunately, the description of the features in the work was severely underspecified and we could not reproduce their results. This made it impossible to compare the system to our system. Additionally, their evaluation is non-standard in that they fitted model parameters directly to the test set instead of using a development set. This results in overly optimistic performance. The reason for the non-standard evaluation in their work was that they focused on comparing time complexities of model optimization algorithms instead of model performances.

3   Methods

In this section, we describe the methods. We first describe the letter n-gram models. Then, we go on to describe how to utilize the n-grams in the lexical model of an HMM and for feature extraction in CRFs.

---

[1]Note, however, that their system incorporates a wide variety of other contextual features thus achieving higher overall performance.

3.1 Obtaining Tag-Specific Word Likelihoods Using Letter N-Grams

Letter-based language models are used to assign a probability for a word represented as a sequence of letters $(w_1, w_2, \ldots, w_{m-1}, w_m)$. Given the sequential nature, a suitable approach to obtaining the probability is to use a factorization

$$p(word) = \prod_{i=1}^{m} p(w_i \mid w_1, \ldots, w_{i-1}), \tag{1}$$

where $p(w_i \mid w_1, \ldots, w_{i-1})$ denotes the probability of letter w_i given the context $(w_1, \ldots, w_{i-1})$. Due to sparsity, the context is usually approximated utilizing only the $n-1$ previous letters (Markov assumption) yielding the approximation

$$p_{ng}(word) \approx \prod_{i=1}^{m} p_{ng}(w_i \mid w_{i-n+1}, \ldots, w_{i-1}), \tag{2}$$

where the distribution $p_{ng}(w_i \mid w_{i-n+1}, \ldots, w_{i-1})$ is referred to as the *letter n-gram model*. The individual probabilities $p_{ng}(w_i \mid w_1, \ldots, w_{i-1})$ can be obtained using smoothed maximum likelihood estimates (Chen and Goodman, 1999) or the maximum entropy model (Chen and Rosenfeld, 2000).

The key idea of our approach for is to learn a separate letter n-gram model for each tag in the tag set. This can be achieved by dividing the words observed in the training corpus into L sets, where L is the number of tags, so that each set contains words that have been tagged at least once with the corresponding tag. Then, a tag-specific n-gram model

$$p_{ng}(w_i \mid w_1, \ldots, w_{i-1}, tag)$$

can be trained on each of the words sets. Hence, the likelihood of a word being generated by a n-gram model corresponding to a particular tag can then be written as

$$p_{ng}(word \mid tag) = \prod_{i=1}^{m} p_{ng}(w_i \mid w_{i-n+1}, \ldots, w_{i-1}, tag). \tag{3}$$

3.2 Hidden Markov Models

Model. Hidden Markov Models (HMMs) are a well known generative statistical model suitable for tagging and segmentation tasks (Brants, 2000). In this work, we employ a second degree HMM. In a second degree HMM for sentence tagging, the estimate of the probability of a sequence of tags $y = (y_1, \ldots, y_t, \ldots, y_T)$ given an input sentence $x = (x_1, \ldots, x_t, \ldots, x_T)$ is

$$p(y \mid x) = \prod_{t=1}^{T} p(x_t \mid y_t) p(y_t \mid y_{t-1}, y_{t-2}). \tag{4}$$

The estimates $p(y_t \mid y_{t-1}, y_{t-2})$ are called *transition probabilities* and can be readily computed from a training corpus. To deal with data sparseness, some form of smoothing is usually necessary. We use deleted interpolation following (Brants, 2000).

Two extra tags y_0 and y_{-1} are needed in formula (4) for the trigram estimates $p(y_2 \mid y_1, y_0)$ and $p(y_1 \mid y_0, y_{-1})$. These are so called buffer tags #, which are appended to tag sequence boundaries.

Lexical modeling utilizing letter n-grams.   The conditional probabilities $p(x_t \mid y_t)$ are called *lexical emission probabilities*. They are determined by a *lexical model*. Our HMM implementation uses a lexical model, which estimates $p(x_t \mid y_t)$ for known words based on smoothed ML estimates computed from training data. It estimates the conditional probability $p(x_t \mid y_t)$ for an OOV word x_t and a tag y_t as the probability $p_{ng}(x_t \mid y_t)$ given by the letter n-gram model for tag y_t. The lexical emission probability is thus

$$p(x_t \mid y_t) = \begin{cases} (C(x_t, y_t) + \alpha)/(C(x_t) + N\alpha) & \text{if } x_t \text{ is known.} \\ p_{ng}(x_t \mid y_t) & \text{if } x_t \text{ is OOV.} \end{cases} \tag{5}$$

The term N in formula 5 denotes the number of unique word forms in the training data and its smoothing coefficient α is determined by minimizing the tagging error on a development data set.

3.3   Linear-chain Conditional Random Fields

Model.   Linear-chain Conditional Random Fields (CRFs) are a discriminative, log-linear model for tagging and segmentation presented originally by Lafferty et al. (2001). The central idea of the linear-chain CRF is to exploit the dependencies between the output variables using a chain structured undirected graph, also referred to as a Markov random field.

Formally, the model for input x (words in sentence) and output y (tags) is written as

$$p(y \mid x; w) \propto \prod_{t=1}^{T} \exp\left(w^{\top} f(y_t, x, t)\right) \prod_{t=2}^{T} \exp\left(w^{\top} f(y_{t-1}, y_t, x, t)\right), \tag{6}$$

where t indexes the characters, T denotes sentence length, w the model parameter vector, f the vector-valued feature extraction function, and $w^{\top} f$ dot product between w and f. The purpose of f is to capture the co-occurrence behavior of the output configurations (y_t) and (y_{t-1}, y_t) and a set of features describing the input x at word position t.

As a discriminative log-linear model, the CRFs can naturally incorporate arbitrary, overlapping features which might be useful for the prediction. The downside of this freedom in feature design is the larger computational cost of model training compared to the HMM models.

Enriching Orthographic Feature Extraction With Letter N-Grams.   The performance of the CRF model depends heavily on the quality of the features included in the feature vector. As our default feature set, we use binary-valued features describing the input x at position t with *word identities* in position $t - 2, \ldots, t + 2$. This feature set performs well if there exists ample training data, or generally, if the number of OOV words is small.

In order to alleviate the OOV problem, we propose modeling word orthography utilizing tag-specific letter n-gram models, $p_{ng}(word|tag)$, presented in section 3.1. They key idea is to to represent any arbitrary word using L features, where L is the number of tags in tag set. The value of each of these features is the *posterior probability* of the corresponding tag given the word, $p_{ng}(tag|word)$. Therefore, instead of using the *likelihoods*, the CRFs exploit the posterior probabilities which directly hold the relevant information when choosing best tags for words. The features are combined with different tag configurations in a standard manner. The aim of these features is simply to associate a high tag posterior value to a high probability of assigning the word with that particular tag.

Formally, the posterior probability of a word given a tag is given by the standard Bayes' rule as

$$p_{ng}(tag|word) = \frac{p_{ng}(word|tag)p(tag)}{\sum_{tag'} p_{ng}(word|tag')p(tag')} \tag{7}$$

where the likelihoods $p_{ng}(word|tag)$ are obtained as presented in Section 3.1. The tag priors $p(tag)$ are simply the counts of tags in the training data normalized to sum up to one.

Parameter estimation.   In general, the CRF model parameters w are estimated using a training set of annotated text using, for example, the maximum likelihood criterion as in (Lafferty et al., 2001). In this work, we estimate the parameters using the averaged structured perceptron algorithm presented by Collins (2002). The perceptron algorithm proceeds one training instance at a time by performing maximum a posteriori (MAP) inference, that is prediction of most likely output configuration over the graph, using the standard Viterbi search, and by updating the model parameters using a simple additive rule if an erroneous prediction occurs. Subsequent to training, test instances are tagged again using the Viterbi search. The structured perceptron has a single hyper-parameter, namely the number of passes over training data, which is optimized using a separate development set.

4   Experiments

We present experiments conducted in biomedical entity recognition on the extended GENIA (version 3) corpus (Kim et al., 2004). We compare three feature sets, namely word identities for baseline, word identities combined with a set of regular expressions adapted from the ones used by (Shen et al., 2003), and word identities combined with letter n-gram based features using HMM and CRF models as described in Section 3. Appendix A contains the complete set of regular expressions that we used.

4.1   Setup

Task and data.   Bio-entity recognition is the task of finding and classifying biological entities such as the protein *CD28 surface receptor* in the sentence fragment "Activation of the CD28 surface receptor provides...". The task is viewed as tagging the words in a sentence using three basic tag types: *beginning of an entity (B)* , *inside an entity (I)* and *outside an entity (O)* as illustrated in Figure 1.

```
MTIIa    mRNA    level    increased    significantly    .
B-RNA    I-RNA   I-RNA    O            O                O
```

Figure 1: Biological entities X are chains B-X I-X ...

The GENIA corpus (Kim et al., 2004) consists of biomedical abstracts with a manually prepared named entity annotation. Each word token in the corpus is annotated with a bio-entity tag or an O tag if the word does not belong to a bio-entity. The tag set consists of 11 entity tags: the O tag and $\{B, I\}$ tags for five entity classes corresponding to DNA, RNA, protein, cell line and cell type respectively. Additionally, we assume sentence start and end tags and markers.

Data Set	Sentences	Words
Train.	114	2798
Train.	229	5865
Train.	459	11667
Train.	918	23675
Train.	1836	48291
Train.	3672	97290
Train.	7345	194637
Train.	14690	390058
Devel.	3856	102493
Test	3856	101039

Table 1: Number of sentences and word tokens in training, development and test data sets.

By default, the corpus is divided into training (18,546 sentences, 492,551 tokens) and test (3,856 sentences, 101,039 tokens) sets. We form a separate development set by extracting the last 3,856 sentences (102,493 tokens) from the training set. In order to observe the effect of training data set size on model performances, we form eight training sets by taking first n sentences from the total 14,690 training instances for various values of n, see Table 1.

Model evaluation.   The model performances are evaluated using the *f-score*. The f-score is the geometric mean of micro-averaged *precision* (the percentage of correctly assigned entities with respect to all assigned entities) and *recall* (the percentage of correctly assigned entities with respect to the gold standard entities).

Feature extraction.   We compare three different feature sets. The first set is the WORD set, which includes only the current word to be tagged for HMMs and a five word window around the current word for CRFs as described in Sections 3.2 and 3.3, respectively. The second set is the REGEXP set, which additionally contains the regular expressions originally presented by (Shen et al., 2003) (see Appendix A). The third set is the N-GRAM set, which consists of the WORD features combined with letter n-gram features as described in Sections 3.2 and 3.3, respectively.

N-gram model, CRF and HMM training.   We trained the tag-specific letter n-gram models on training sets of various sizes described in Table 1. We used the SRILM toolkit (Stolcke et al., 2011) to implement the n-gram models. More specifically, we used n-grams of length 9 with Witten-Bell smoothing, which appeared to work sufficiently well in preliminary experiments on the development data set. The HMM and CRF models were trained on the training data sets using three feature sets (WORD, REGEXP, N-GRAM) as described in Sections 3.2 and 3.3. As to CRF model training, the perceptron algorithm is terminated when development set performance has not improved during the last five passes over the training set.

Software.   We used our own implementations of the CRF and HMM models. For training the letter n-gram models, we used SRILM as described above.

Train.	OOV	WORD			REGEXP			N-GRAM		
114	35.8	34.1	22.7	27.3	33.2	26.8	29.7	29.4	37.5	**33.0**
229	28.3	41.5	28.2	33.5	40.4	33.2	36.4	33.1	46.1	**38.5**
459	22.1	48.8	35.5	41.1	48.0	40.1	43.7	41.2	47.8	**44.2**
918	17.4	52.8	41.0	46.1	52.3	40.1	48.7	46.0	53.0	**49.3**
1836	13.5	56.7	44.3	49.8	56.8	49.2	52.7	52.4	56.8	**54.5**
3672	10.0	61.1	51.2	55.7	59.8	54.8	57.2	57.0	61.7	**59.3**
7345	7.2	64.2	58.7	61.3	63.6	61.0	62.2	61.9	65.4	**63.6**
14690	5.2	67.5	64.2	66.5	65.8	65.5	66.0	65.5	69.4	**67.4**

Table 2: Results for the CRF model using varying training data set sizes (in sentences) and feature sets. For each feature set, the figures are recall, precision and f-score.

Train.	OOV	WORD			REGEXP			N-GRAM		
114	35.8	22.0	35.6	**27.2**	20.5	34.5	25.7	16.5	7.7	10.5
229	28.3	27.2	37.0	**31.4**	26.3	35.7	30.3	27.1	15.1	19.4
459	22.1	33.4	42.3	**37.3**	32.5	40.8	36.2	34.6	32.4	33.5
918	17.4	37.0	44.8	40.6	39.1	44.7	**41.7**	41.5	40.3	40.0
1836	13.5	40.5	47.7	43.8	42.8	47.8	45.1	47.1	45.9	**46.5**
3672	10.0	46.7	51.0	48.7	49.0	50.5	49.7	53.4	50.9	**52.1**
7345	7.2	52.0	53.8	52.9	53.5	53.0	53.3	57.1	55.1	**56.1**
14690	5.2	56.5	56.6	56.6	57.8	56.3	57.0	60.4	57.4	**58.9**

Table 3: Results for HMMs using varying training data set sizes (in sentences) and feature sets. For each feature set, the figures are recall, precision and f-score.

4.2   Results

The results for varying training data set sizes are presented in Tables 2 and 3 for the CRF and HMM models, respectively. The columns titled *OOV* correspond to the percentages of OOV word tokens in the test set. The performance values obtained using different feature sets are in order recall, precision, and f-score.

Using the CRF model, the regular expression feature set provided modest, yet consistent, improvement over the word identity context baseline. Utilizing the letter n-gram features yielded performance gains compared to both the word identity context baseline and the regular expression feature set. This improvement took place when small training sets were used.

The results for the HMM models using the different feature sets differ somewhat from the results of the CRF models. Both the REGEXP and N-GRAM features initially perform worse than the WORD features. Roughly the same performance for all features is achieved when there are 918 sentences of training data and in the next training set of 1836 sentences the N-GRAM features outperform the other feature sets. The result for the complete training set of 14690 sentences shows that the N-GRAM feature set is the best one achieving f-score 58.9 versus 57.0 for the REGEXP features and 56.6 for the WORD features. Overall, the HMMs consistently resulted in considerably worse performance compared to the CRF models for all training sets and features. The improvement given by the N-GRAM features is comparable to the improvements for the CRF model.

4.3 Discussion

For the complete data set, the letter n-gram features give the best results for both the HMM and the CRF. However, the CRF model clearly outperforms the HMM for all training data set sizes and all feature sets. The improvements given by the letter n-gram features are similar for the CRF and HMM models. However the CRF model with letter n-gram features consistently outperform the models with other feature sets for all training data set sizes. In contrast, the HMM with letter n-gram features performs worse than the models with word and regex features when the training set is smaller than 918 sentences.

Unfortunately, our baseline models are too weak to allow for a conclusive assessment of the impact of our approach. A model trained on suffixes and prefixes or all sub-strings of words should have been included in the evaluation. Such an approach could give higher performance, but would also result in a substantially higher number of features implying a longer training time and greater memory footprint.

The performance of the letter n-gram feature HMM clearly shows that the letter n-grams are not very reliable on small training sets. Nevertheless the letter n-gram model of the CRF model achieves improvements even for the smallest training set of 114 sentences. This is most likely a direct result of the discriminative training of CRF models, which can successfully integrate the uncertain information given by the letter n-grams.

The poor performance of the HMM compared to the CRF may partly be explained by the fact that there are two useful information sources which the HMM cannot use, but the CRF can utilize. Neighboring words cannot be used in the lexical model of the HMM. Our attempts to do this in the development phase were unsuccessful.

Finally, direct comparison of our models with the hierarchical Bayesian approach reported by (Fujii and Sakurai, 2012) is difficult because their model was trained using a *semi-supervised* approach. In other words, when using small data set sizes, their model exploited the remainder of the training corpus without the tagging information. Effectively, this means that compared to our approaches, their model utilized more data in training. However, a fair comparison can be made when all the models used the complete training data set of 18,546 sentences for training and model development. Using this full data, our CRF model outperformed their model regardless of the feature set. Additionally, the CRF model utilizing the letter n-gram features appeared to yield at least comparable if not improved performance compared to their model on smaller data sets.

5 Conclusions

We discussed biomedical entity recognition using statistical methodology. We proposed an automatic and domain-independent approach to modeling OOV words utilizing probabilistic letter n-gram models. We described how to combine the approach with Hidden Markov Models and Conditional Random Fields. The motivation behind our approach was to compress orthographic information captured by sub-strings in a small set of features. Experiments in biomedical entity recognition showed that the approach did alleviate the OOV problem resulting in improved overall model performance. Unfortunately, the true impact of the discussed approach is left unclear due to the lack of strong baselines in this preliminary work.

In future work, we aim to extend the experimental results provided in this paper with additional data sets, improved baseline models, and closer error analysis on OOV words.

Acknowledgments

This work was financially supported by the Academy of Finland under the grant no 251170 (Finnish Centre of Excellence Program (2012-2017)) and Langnet (Finnish doctoral programme in language studies).

References

Brants, T. (2000). Tnt - a statistical part-of-speech tagger. In *Proceedings of the Sixth Applied Natural Language Processing (ANLP-2000)*, Seattle, WA.

Chen, S. and Goodman, J. (1999). An empirical study of smoothing techniques for language modeling. *Computer Speech & Language*, 13(4):359–393.

Chen, S. and Rosenfeld, R. (2000). A survey of smoothing techniques for me models. *Speech and Audio Processing, IEEE Transactions on*, 8(1):37–50.

Collins, M. (2002). Discriminative training methods for hidden markov models: Theory and experiments with perceptron algorithms. In *Proceedings of the ACL-02 conference on Empirical methods in natural language processing*, volume 10, pages 1–8. Association for Computational Linguistics.

Fujii, R. and Sakurai, A. (2012). Technical term recognition with semi-supervised learning using hierarchical bayesian language models. *Natural Language Processing and Information Systems*, pages 327–332.

Kim, J.-D., Ohta, T., Tsuruoka, Y., Tateisi, Y., and Collier, N. (2004). Introduction to the bio-entity recognition task at jnlpba. In *Proceedings of the International Joint Workshop on Natural Language Processing in Biomedicine and its Applications*, JNLPBA '04, pages 70–75, Stroudsburg, PA, USA. Association for Computational Linguistics.

Lafferty, J. D., McCallum, A., and Pereira, F. C. N. (2001). Conditional random fields: Probabilistic models for segmenting and labeling sequence data. In *Proceedings of the Eighteenth International Conference on Machine Learning*, ICML '01, pages 282–289, San Francisco, CA, USA. Morgan Kaufmann Publishers Inc.

McCallum, A., Freitag, D., and Pereira, F. (2000). Maximum entropy markov models for information extraction and segmentation. In *Proceedings of the Seventeenth International Conference on Machine Learning*, volume 951, pages 591–598.

Rössler, M. (2004). Adapting an ner-system for german to the biomedical domain. In *Proceedings of the International Joint Workshop on Natural Language Processing in Biomedicine and its Applications*, JNLPBA '04, pages 92–95, Stroudsburg, PA, USA. Association for Computational Linguistics.

Shen, D., Zhang, J., Zhou, G., Su, J., and Tan, C. (2003). Effective adaptation of a hidden markov model-based named entity recognizer for biomedical domain. In *Proceedings of the ACL 2003 workshop on Natural language processing in biomedicine-Volume 13*, pages 49–56. Association for Computational Linguistics.

Stolcke, A., Zheng, J., Wang, W., and Abrash, V. (2011). Srilm at sixteen: Update and outlook. In *Proceedings of IEEE Automatic Speech Recognition and Understanding Workshop*.

Tjong Kim Sang, E. F. and Buchholz, S. (2000). Introduction to the conll-2000 shared task: chunking. In *Proceedings of the 2nd workshop on Learning language in logic and the 4th conference on Computational natural language learning - Volume 7*, ConLL '00, pages 127–132, Stroudsburg, PA, USA. Association for Computational Linguistics.

Tjong Kim Sang, E. F. and De Meulder, F. (2003). Introduction to the conll-2003 shared task: language-independent named entity recognition. In *Proceedings of the seventh conference on Natural language learning at HLT-NAACL 2003 - Volume 4*, CONLL '03, pages 142–147, Stroudsburg, PA, USA. Association for Computational Linguistics.

Vasserman, A. (2004). Identifying chemical names in biomedical text: an investigation of the substring co-occurrence based approaches. In *Proceedings of the Student Research Workshop at HLT-NAACL 2004*, HLT-SRWS '04, pages 7–12, Stroudsburg, PA, USA. Association for Computational Linguistics.

Vatanen, T., Väyrynen, J. J., and Virpioja, S. (2010). Language identification of short text segments with n-gram models. In Chair), N. C. C., Choukri, K., Maegaard, B., Mariani, J., Odjik, J., Piperidis, S., Rosner, M., and Tapias, D., editors, *Proceedings of the Seventh conference on International Language Resources and Evaluation (LREC'10)*, Valletta, Malta. European Language Resources Association (ELRA).

Vishwanathan, S. V. N., Schraudolph, N. N., Schmidt, M. W., and Murphy, K. P. (2006). Accelerated training of conditional random fields with stochastic gradient methods. In *Proceedings of the 23rd international conference on Machine learning*, ICML '06, pages 969–976, New York, NY, USA. ACM.

Zhou, G. and Su, J. (2004). Exploring deep knowledge resources in biomedical name recognition. In *Proceedings of the International Joint Workshop on Natural Language Processing in Biomedicine and its Applications*, JNLPBA '04, pages 96–99, Stroudsburg, PA, USA. Association for Computational Linguistics.

A   Regular expression features

The regular expression features in Python Re-syntax adapted from (Shen et al., 2003).

Feature name	Regular expression
Comma	`^[,]$`
Dot	`^[.]$`
Left Paren.	`^[(]$`
Right Paren.	`^[)]$`
Left Square Bracket	`^[\[]$`
Right Square Bracket	`^[\]]$`
Roman Numeral	`^[IVXCM]+$`
Greek Letter	`^(Alpha| ... |Omega|alpha| ... |omega)$`
Stop Word	`^(a|about|...)$`
ATCG Sequence	`^[ATCG]+$`
Digit	`^[0-9]$`
All Digits	`^[0-9]+$`
Digit Comma Digit	`^[0-9]+[,][0-9]+$`
Digit Dot Digit	`^[0-9]+[.][0-9]+$`
Capital	`^[A-Z]$`
All Capitals	`^[A-Z]+$`
Capital Low Alpha	`^[A-Z][a-z]+$`
Capital Mix Alpha	`^[A-Z]([A-Za-z]*[a-z][A-Za-z]*[A-Z][A-Za-z]*|$` `[A-Za-z]*[A-Z][A-Za-z]*[a-z][A-Za-z]*)$`
Low Mix Alpha	`^[a-z]([A-Za-z]*[a-z][A-Za-z]*[A-Z][A-Za-z]*|$` `[A-Za-z]*[A-Z][A-Za-z]*[a-z][A-Za-z]*)$`
Alpha Digit Alpha	`^[A-Za-z][0-9]+[A-Za-z]$`
Alpha Digit	`^[A-Za-z][0-9]+$`
Digit Alpha Digit	`^[0-9]+[A-Za-z][0-9]+$`
Digit Alpha	`^[0-9]+[A-Za-z]$`

Baltic and Nordic Parts of the European Linguistic Infrastructure

Inguna Skadiņa[1], Andrejs Vasiļjevs[1], Lars Borin[2],
Krister Lindén[3], Gyri Losnegaard[4], Sussi Olsen[5], Bolette S. Pedersen[5],
Roberts Rozis[1], Koenraad De Smedt[4]

(1) Tilde, Vienibas gatve 75a, Riga, Latvia
(2) University or Gothenburg, Box 100, 405 30 Gothenburg, Sweden
(3) University of Helsinki, Unioninkatu 40, Helsinki, Finland
(4) University of Bergen, Postboks 7800, 5020 Bergen, Norway
(5) University of Copenhagen, CST, Njalsgade 140, 2300 Copenhagen S

`metanord@tilde.lv`

ABSTRACT

This paper describes scientific, technical, and legal work done on the creation of the linguistic infrastructure for the Nordic and Baltic countries. The paper describes the research on assessment of language technology support for the languages of the Baltic and Nordic countries, work on establishing a language resource sharing infrastructure, and collection and description of linguistic resources. We present improvements necessary to ensure usability and interoperability of language resources, discuss issues related to intellectual property rights for complex resources, and describe extension of infrastructure through integration of language-resource specific repositories. Work on treebanks, wordnets, terminology resources, and finite-state technology is described in more detail. Finally, our approach on ensuring the sustainability of infrastructure is discussed.

KEYWORDS: language resources and tools, linguistic infrastructure, under-resourced languages, multilinguality, treebanks, wordnets, terminology banks.

1   Introduction

The previous decades of research in language technologies (LT) have produced numerous language resources and tools for languages of the Nordic and Baltic countries. At the same time, not only are there major gaps in availability of the key resources, but the existing ones are often hard to find and difficult to use. Resources are dispersed among different institutions and local repositories, and they are often coded in proprietary formats lacking interoperability and uniformity. There are also restricted or unclear intellectual property rights. These factors are major stumbling blocks for the development and research of language technology.

To overcome these difficulties, the Nordic and Baltic countries play a leading role in pan-European activities regarding the creation of the European open linguistic infrastructure. Major progress is achieved by the CLARIN [1] (Váradi et al., 2008) initiative creating a language resource infrastructure for research in humanities. Another complementary infrastructure is under development by the META-NET network[2] focusing on the practical needs of developers, users, and researchers of multilingual resources.

The Baltic and Nordic countries are active participants in both — CLARIN and META-NET — networks. Official languages of these countries (Danish, Estonian, Finnish, Icelandic, Latvian, Lithuanian, Norwegian, and Swedish), as well as other languages spoken in these countries, are under-resourced in respect to availability of at least some of the key language technologies or resources. Thus, such initiatives as CLARIN and META-NET are essential for identification, documentation, and making widely available the language resources for these languages, and these initiatives provide significant support in filling essential gaps in resources and technologies.

In the META-NET network, work on the creation of an open European linguistic infrastructure and making language resources widely available was performed through four projects supported by the European Commission: CESAR (Central and Eastern European countries), METANET4U (Southern European countries and the United Kingdom), META-NORD (Baltic and Nordic countries), and T4ME (initiator and coordinator of META-NET network). In this paper, we describe our experience and work done on building the Baltic and Nordic parts of the European linguistic infrastructure in the META-NORD project (Vasiļjevs et al., 2011; Skadiņa et al., 2011), which included the following major tasks:

- Research on the language technology landscape in the Nordic and Baltic countries in terms of language use, language technology and resources, and main actors.
- Work on identification and collection of language resources in the Baltic and Nordic countries and documenting, processing, linking, and upgrading them to agreed standards and guidelines.
- Research and practical work on consistent approaches, practices, and standards that ensure wider accessibility, easier access, and reuse of quality language resources.
- Research and development work done on linking and validating the Nordic and Baltic wordnets, harmonisation of multilingual Nordic and Baltic treebanks, consolidation of multilingual terminology resources across European countries, and development of mature and language independent tools.
- Issues related to intellectual property rights (IPR) for the sharing of language resources.

---

[1] Common Language Resources and Technology Infrastructure, http://www.clarin.eu
[2] http://www.meta-net.eu

- Work on building and operating broad, non-commercial, community-driven, inter-connected repositories, exchanges, and facilities that can be used by different categories of user communities.

2   Language technology landscape

Important steps towards the creation of a linguistic infrastructure are an assessment of the state of the art of the language technology field, identification of existing language resources, assessment of resources, and understanding the needs of potential users. Reports on the national language technology landscape[3] for each official language spoken in the Nordic and Baltic geographical area (Danish, Estonian, Finnish, Icelandic, Latvian, Lithuanian, both Norwegian varieties Nynorsk and Bokmål, and Swedish) describe and analyse the situation of the language community and the position of the language service and language technology industry. These reports also contain general facts about the language (number of speakers, official status, dialects, etc.), particularities of the language, recent developments in the language, language cultivation, language in education, international aspects, as well as the role of the language on the Internet.

The reports also present assessment of language technology support and the core application areas of language and speech technology (e.g., language checking, web search, speech interaction, machine translation, etc.), and describe the situation with respect to these application areas. For each language, language resources and tools (LRT) are assessed based on the following criteria: quantity, availability, quality, coverage, maturity, sustainability, and adaptability. The results indicate that only with respect to the most basic tools and resources, such as tokenisers, PoS taggers, morphological analysers/generators, reference corpora, and lexicons/terminologies, the status is reasonably positive for all languages. However, tools for information extraction, machine translation, and speech recognition, as well as resources such as parallel corpora, speech corpora, and grammar, are rather simple and have limited functionality for some of the languages. For the most advanced tools and resources, such as discourse processing, dialogue management, semantics and discourse corpora, and ontological resources, most of the languages either have nothing of the kind, or their tools and resources have a quite limited scope.

This assessment of language technology support clearly demonstrates that for languages of the Baltic and Nordic countries, where the community of language resource creators and users is small, even a modest increase in the availability and quality of language resources is appreciable for technology developers, researchers, and end users.

In addition, detailed analysis and comparison of language technologies and resources across 30 European languages was carried out within the framework of META-NET. The comparison presents the situation for four key areas: machine translation, speech processing, text analysis, and resources. This study puts three small languages of the Nordic and Baltic region – Icelandic, Latvian, and Lithuanian – in the last cluster, defined as having major gaps for all of the four key areas (see Table 1). The relative ranking of the remaining five languages is slightly higher, although none of them comes close to the "larger" languages (English, French, Spanish, and German). "Moderate" support is provided only for Finnish in speech technologies and for Swedish with respect to language resources.

Besides objective limitations in the size of the LRT creator and user community, there are other obstacles which put some languages in the "upper" cluster, while others remain in the "bottom".

---

[3] These reports, also called Language White Papers, are available at http://www.meta-net.eu/whitepapers.

Among them is a lack of continuity in research and development funding. For instance, due to limited funding, Latvian language technology support does not reach the quality and coverage not only of that for English, but also for many under-resourced languages of the Baltic and Nordic region with a smaller number of speakers. In many cases, targeted national research and development activities are urgently needed to fill LRT gaps.

Speech processing				
Excellent	**Good**	**Moderate**	**Fragmentary**	**Weak/None**
	English	Czech, Dutch, **Finnish,** French, German, Italian, Portuguese, Spanish	Basque, Bulgarian, Catalan, **Danish, Estonian,** Galician, Greek, Hungarian, Irish, **Norwegian,** Polish, Serbian, Slovak, Slovene, **Swedish**	Croatian, **Icelandic, Latvian, Lithuanian,** Maltese, Romanian

Machine Translation				
Excellent	**Good**	**Moderate**	**Fragmentary**	**Weak/None**
	English	French, Spanish	Catalan, Dutch, German, Hungarian, Italian, Polish, Romanian	Basque, Bulgarian, Croatian., Czech, **Danish, Estonian, Finnish,** Galician, **Icelandic,** Irish, **Latvian, Lithuanian,** Maltese, **Norwegian,** Portuguese, Serbian, Slovak, Slovene, **Swedish**

Text Analysis				
Excellent	**Good**	**Moderate**	**Fragmentary**	**Weak/None**
	English	Dutch, French, German, Italian, Spanish	Basque, Bulgarian, Catalan, Czech, **Danish, Finnish,** Galician, Greek, Hungarian, **Norwegian,** Polish, Portuguese, Romanian, Slovak, Slovene, **Swedish**	Croatian, **Estonian, Icelandic,** Irish, **Latvian, Lithuanian,** Maltese, Serbian

Resources				
Excellent	**Good**	**Moderate**	**Fragmentary**	**Weak/None**
	English	Czech, Dutch, French, German, Hungarian, Italian, Polish, Spanish, **Swedish**	Basque, Bulgarian, Catalan, Croatian, **Danish, Estonian, Finnish,** Galician, Greek, **Norwegian,** Portuguese, Romanian, Serbian, Slovak, Slovene	**Icelandic,** Irish, **Latvian, Lithuanian,** Maltese

TABLE 1: Availability of LRT for languages of the Baltic and Nordic countries[4].

The need for large amounts of data and the complexity of language technology systems make it vital to develop both an open infrastructure and a more coherent research cooperation in order to spur greater sharing and reuse of language resources.

---

[4] The table is also available at http://www.meta-net.eu/whitepapers/key-results-and-cross-language-comparison

3   META-SHARE infrastructure in the Baltic and Nordic countries

For distribution and sharing of language resources, the distributed online platform META-SHARE (Piperidis, 2012) is used. It consists of independent META-SHARE nodes set up in different countries and interlinked into a federated repository. This freely accessible distributed online infrastructure provides facilities for describing, storing, preserving of language resources, and making them publicly available. Among various language data that can be considered useful for different purposes, META-SHARE places a strong focus on language data that are important in language technology development for building applications that are useful to EU citizens, primarily in their everyday communication and information search needs. META-SHARE is intended for providers and users of language resources and technologies such as LT developers, researchers, students, translators, technical writers and others.

Currently, META-SHARE nodes are set at the following organisations in the Baltic and Nordic countries: Tilde[5] (Latvia), University of Gothenburg[6] (Sweden), University of Helsinki[7] (Finland), Institute of Lithuanian Language[8] (Lithuania), University of Copenhagen[9] (Denmark), Norwegian National Library[10] (Norway), and University of Tartu[11] (Estonia). According to the architecture of META-SHARE, these nodes are networked, and the content of the individual LR repository is harvested into the managing META-SHARE node, which for the META-NORD consortium is set at Tilde. In a managing node, information about catalogued language resources is collected and synchronised with other managing nodes across Europe, thus providing access to the full catalogue of the pan-European infrastructure[12].

Besides META-SHARE repositories, we have a natural interest to integrate into our infrastructure several existing collections and databases of specific linguistic resources, such as term banks and treebanks. These repositories are collections of language resources, where each individual resource is a candidate to be listed in the META-SHARE catalogue. This could be done manually by entering all resource descriptions in the META-SHARE editor or by exporting the metadata from the respective repository, converting it into META-SHARE compliant schema (Gavrilidou et al., 2012), and importing into META-SHARE node. However, such approaches are time-consuming and need regular manual updates.

Our proposed and implemented solution for this infrastructure is to integrate complex linguistic resources or repositories of resources by adapting them to relevant data access and sharing specifications and interlinking them with META-SHARE. This means that a language resource-specific repository could seamlessly become a part of the META-SHARE network by enabling the harvesting of metadata through the META-SHARE communication protocol and ensuring the mapping of the respective data categories.

For this approach to work the metadata model of the language resource-specific node must include all the data categories that are mandatory in the META-SHARE repository, as well as include additional attributes required for the synchronization, such as unique ID, creation and modification date and revision number.

---

[5] http://metashare.tilde.com/
[6] http://spraakbanken.gu.se/metashare/
[7] http://metashare.csc.fi/
[8] http://meta-share.lki.lt/
[9] http://metashare.cst.dk/
[10] http://metashare.nb.no/
[11] http://metashare.ut.ee/
[12] META-SHARE described in details in Piperidis (2012).

The integration of a language resource-specific node with META-SHARE is implemented via proxy: it connects to a META-SHARE managing node just like any other META-SHARE node – the LR metadata provider is proxied to the rest of the META-SHARE network. Integration of a language resource-specific node with META-SHARE allows users to access a specific resource located on a remote repository directly via a link supplied to META-SHARE.

META-NORD project piloted extension of the META-SHARE infrastructure with resource-specific nodes by integrating distributed terminology database EuroTermBank as described in the Section 5.3.

4   Identification, collection, and description of language resources in META-SHARE

During the last two years, more than 500 resources and tools have been identified and made available by the META-NORD consortium. These include a broad range of different resources for different languages and language pairs that are suitable for a range of different LT purposes. Statistical breakdown of the language resources for META-NORD languages available from META-SHARE platform is summarized in Table 2.

Danish	Estonian	Finnish	Icelandic	Latvian	Lithuanian	Norwegian	Swedish
68	67	86	70	69	38	47	151

TABLE 2: Language resources and tools for META-NORD languages documented in META-SHARE platform.

The criteria for the selection of resources included: availability, popularity, suitability of resources for technology and product/application development, fitness for multilingual purposes, longevity, quality, and extensibility.

Initially, the main focus has been on written resources, however, recently there has been an increased effort to also include a certain number of audio/video resources and tools. Table 3 shows the distribution of tools and resources available through META-SHARE for the Baltic and Nordic languages.

Lexical resources (excl. wordnets & speech)	211
Corpora (excl. treebanks & speech)	182
Tools (excl. speech)	43
Language description (grammars)	2
Treebanks	31
Resources for speech	28
WordNets	12
Total	**509**

Table 3: META-NORD tools and resources identified and made available through META-SHARE.

Considerable work documenting, processing, linking, and upgrading these resources to agreed standards and guidelines has been performed as described in sections 4.1 and 4.2 below.

Activities dealing with multilingual wordnets, treebanks, and terminology (cf. Sections 5.1–5.3) provide examples of how these goals of interoperability in content have actually been achieved for several of the provided resources.

4.1   Metadata model for the description of language resources

Bird and Simons (2003) have proposed a very useful taxonomy for discussing language documentation and description. Although originally framed in the context of linguistic description, their 'seven dimensions of portability' are quite useful also when discussing language resource interoperability for language technology purposes. Here, language resource metadata and widely accessible metadata repositories are absolutely essential, addressing – directly or indirectly – four of their seven dimensions, namely *discovery*, *access*, *citation*, and *rights*.

All of the contributed language resources are consistently identified and described using a metadata standard developed as a part of the META-SHARE initiative (Gavrilidou et al. 2011, 2012; Desipri et al. 2012). The standard, which draws heavily on experiences from previous efforts – such as the OLAC (Bird and Simons 2001) and CLARIN CMDI (Broeder et al. 2010) metadata schemas – defines a minimal set of descriptors which must be specified for any resource, but also allows for supplying much richer information if desired, including free-form narrative descriptions. It is published in the form of an XML schema. Using the META-SHARE metadata editor makes it easy to describe resources using the META-SHARE metadata schema, since the editor, for example, provides listings of the controlled vocabularies of the metadata schema.

Uploading a large number of diverse language resources and tools and the concomitant creation or conversion of the associated metadata by several large European projects have constituted a kind of empirical acid test of the appropriateness and usefulness of the META-SHARE schema. We are happy to report that it has passed this test successfully. For the 'baseline' cases, metadata creation has on the whole been straightforward and unproblematic, and the META-SHARE community online support[13] has generally been able to help in many of the more non-obvious cases.

Of course, it has inevitably turned out that the schema does not cover everything. For instance, it was discovered that it caters less well for complex multilingual resources, such as the mixed-language variety text corpora collected in Norway (with articles written in the two official written Norwegian varieties, Bokmål and Nynorsk, in the same newspaper), as well as for the multilingual treebanks and linked wordnets (see section 5). This issue, in fact, touches on several design decisions made for the META-SHARE metadata schema at the very beginning, having to do, for example, with how language information is encoded and with the structuring of the metadata records themselves. Because of the work in CESAR, METANET4U, META-NORD, and T4ME projects, the issues arising in connection with the description of complex language resources have been brought to the forefront and will be addressed in future releases of the META-SHARE metadata schema.

4.2   Improving usability and interoperability of language resources

An important focus of our work has been on enhancing the interoperability of language resources and tools by upgrading selected resources to agreed standards. The upgrading activities have included the following:

---

[13] http://www.meta-share.org/portal/ (Note that for some reason all issues listed there are labelled "unanswered", although most of them actually have answers which can be seen if you click on the heading of an issue to open the discussion thread for that issue.)

Improvement of resource documentation, both formally structured (as META-SHARE metadata) and narrative documentation. For many resources, the narrative documentation has been much improved; the partners have in several cases spent a considerable amount of time writing and improving resource documentation, as well as – in practice, very important for wider interoperability – on producing documentation in English. Also, for increased user-friendliness, an XSL stylesheet (developed in the CESAR sister project) is routinely used to automatically convert META-SHARE metadata into a more human-readable form - from XML into a more human-readable textual rendering (which however does not add any information to that already present in the XML metadata).

Technical format conversion, e.g., a proprietary corpus format into TEI (Text Encoding Initiative[14]) or an idiosyncratic lexicon format into LMF[15] (Lexical Markup Framework; ISO 24613:2008; Francopoulo et al. 2006). Several partners have converted their lexical resources into LMF, e.g., the STO Danish dictionary lexical database, the SweFN++ Swedish lexical macro resource, the Norwegian SCARRIE lexicon, and the Lithuanian Standard language lexical database. Terminology resources, such as the Icelandic Term Bank and UHR's Termbase for Norwegian higher education institutions, have been converted into TBX[16] format (Term Base eXchange; ISO 30042:2008; Melby 2012).

Most of the corpus resources uploaded are now available in TEI-compatible formats. A specific example of how this format harmonisation has enhanced interoperability is the relative ease[17] with which the open-source Korp corpus processing and presentation platform, developed in Sweden at the University of Gothenburg (Borin et al. 2012)[18], has been deployed in Finland by the University of Helsinki for their Finnish corpora[19].

Content model conversion/mapping/linking, e.g., harmonising POS tagsets among corpora, or linking word senses among lexical resources with different sense granularities. The Danish STO lexicon, the Swedish lexicons developed at Språkbanken, University of Gothenburg, and Swedish corpus annotations have been partly linked to the ISOCAT DCR (Data Category Registry; ISO 12620:2009; Windhouwer and Wright 2012), although no explicit attempt has been made to use the same categories across the languages, except in the specific cases discussed below in sections 5.1–5.3. Several partners (e.g., the Icelandic and Swedish partners) have taken advantage of their work on harmonising content and upgraded their corpus resources, adding consistent linguistic annotations to corpora that previously were either unannotated or used several different annotation schemes.

Ensuring that language resources and tools adhere to standard formats is a necessary prerequisite for resource interoperability. As always, the proof of the pudding is in the eating, and the outcomes of investing a limited, quite reasonable amount of time on horizontal action lines (see section 5 below) – where selected resources have been interlinked between languages of the Nordic and Baltic countries – demonstrate clearly that the upgrading activities have successfully achieved their objectives.

---

[14] http://www.tei-c.org

[15] http://www.lexicalmarkupframework.org/

[16] http://www.ttt.org/oscarStandards/tbx/

[17] The characterisation "relative ease" is impressionistic, based on a comparison with practical experience from earlier attempts to deploy another piece of corpus software both at Gothenburg and Helsinki, for which obviously much less effort had been spent on issues of interoperability and modularity during its development.

[18] http://spraakbanken.gu.se/korp/#lang=eng

[19] http://korp.csc.fi/#lang=en

As a means to upgrade existing resources in the META-NORD consortium to agreed standards, various lexical resources have been upgraded to the Lexical Markup Framework (LMF). One example is University of Gothenburg's 21 lexical resources which have all been upgraded to LMF. As reported in Borin et al. 2012, this lexical infrastructure has one primary lexical resource SALDO as a pivot to which all other resources are linked.

Upgrading some of the more semantically orientated resources to LMF turned out to be quite complicated. The main obstacle being that, even though the framework contains mechanisms for specifying semantic information, the model is based upon the assumption that lexical entries are formal entities expressing one or more senses, not semantic entities having one or more formal realisations. For example, the Swedish Framenet has the semantic frame as the natural conceptual unit, but to be able to fit the information into LMF, the frame had to be split into several entries. Searching these resources can be done from the web page http://spraakbanken.gu.se/karp, and all of the resources can be downloaded from http://spraakbanken.gu.se/eng/resources/lexicon.

Another example is the multilingual dictionary ISLEX[20] with modern Icelandic as the source language and Danish, Norwegian, and Swedish as target languages. ISLEX has been upgraded to LMF in the META-NORD project by the Icelandic partner, University of Iceland (cf. Helgadóttir & Rögnvaldsson forthcoming). When converting multilingual dictionaries into LMF format, a special record would usually be made for each sense of every word in all the languages of the dictionary. A so-called "Sense Axis" would then be used to link closely related senses in different languages. For ISLEX, however, another course was taken: special records were made for each sense of the words in the source language, Icelandic, which in turn had translations for that sense in each of the target languages.

Finally, it should be mentioned that the upgrade of the Danish lexical database STO[21] (built on PAROLE[22]) has been completed by the University of Copenhagen. This database provides an 'intensional' morphological description meaning that each word form is not explicitly listed anywhere but the lexical entry is associated with a morphological pattern. In other words, the word forms are created on demand. Even if an intensional morphological description is possible in LMF, an extensional description of the morphology, where all word forms are created when dumping data from database to LMF, was chosen as the most user-friendly approach. In some aspects, the predefined LMF schemata did not correspond with the structure of the linguistic information in the STO, and various kinds of generalisation or nested information had to be expressed in new ways by means of features which have made it easier to get an overview of the lexical entries. Furthermore, the LMF nomenclature is much closer to general linguistic terminology. In LMF for example, STO data categories such as 'description' and 'construction' are called 'subcategorisation frame' and 'syntactic argument' respectively, concepts much easier for a user to comprehend.

4.3   Approach to intellectual property rights

Collecting Intellectual Property Rights (IPR) for a corpus often requires that permissions are acquired from multiple parties in order to make copies of the copyrighted parts of the corpus. Copies for personal use are often readily available from many sources but the right to distribute

---

20 The ISLEX dictionary can both be searched and downloaded from http://www.malfong.is/index.php?pg=islex&lang=en.
21 A Danish lexical database developed by the University of Copenhagen, Centre for language technology (Braasch et al. 2004). Samples and documentation of the STO-LMF lexicon can be found at http://cst.ku.dk/english/sto_ordbase/.
22 PAROLE was an EU project running from 1996-1998 with the aim of creating large, generic, and re-usable Written Language Resources for all EU Languages.

such copies is not (see, e.g., Oksanen and Lindén (2012)). In this section, we look at a practical solution for multilingual treebanks in META-SHARE created within the project.

The right to distribute linked multilingual treebanks requires a right to copy and distribute a collective work, so the most practical solution is that one party collects the rights to copy and distribute all parts of the work, after which that party can sign for all the others. This is not that much different from collecting a corpus of several books and their annotations. In our case, the multilingual corpora were open-source or the rights already allowed distribution via META-SHARE, so the only work that needed to be given an explicit right to be copied and distributed were the hand-made annotations and cross-lingual links. Since the cross-lingual linking of the multilingual treebanks was done during the project, the ownership of the links belonged to the project parties. Only the annotations that had been done before the project or with separate funding needed to be provided with an explicit license for META-SHARE to distribute them. For the treebanks, we chose CC-BY as the common license.

5 Horizontal action lines

Besides identification and description of linguistic resources in the Baltic and Nordic countries, a particular focus in our work was on the following linguistic resources and tools: treebanks, wordnets, terminology, and finite-state techniques. We call this work 'horizontal action lines', as these activities focus on a particular resource type and aim to harmonise, link across languages, and make these resources available through a common interface.

5.1 Treebanks

The horizontal action on treebanking has been aimed at improving the accessibility of treebanks and harmonising and linking treebanks across languages. Special regard was taken to the Nordic and Baltic languages which are under-resourced in this respect, but the action was also a truly open initiative inclusive of other languages and addressing needs of other META-NET members.

Efforts were focused on the annotation, harmonisation, curation, documentation, and licensing of treebanks. To reach these goals, we collaborated extensively with the INESS project,[23] which provided state-of-the-art tools based on an advanced server-based solution and a user-friendly web interface for browsing, search, visualisation, and download. The resources which were made available by the action include a number of monolingual treebanks and two parallel treebanks based on multiple alignments of monolingual treebanks.

One notable outcome was the Sofie Parallel Treebank, based on the Norwegian novel Sofies verden (Gaarder 1991), which is linguistically rich and professionally translated in many languages. Some monolingual treebanks previously existed for text selections from this material, but not all were accessible. Annotations developed by the Nordic Treebank Network (NTN) were obtained from Tekstlaboratoriet (University of Oslo), and those that were deemed suitable were integrated in INESS. An additional new treebank was constructed for Norwegian. Annotations for the bigger European languages — German and English (the latter from SMULTRON24) were included for completeness, as well as a Georgian annotation by Paul Meurer. Intellectual property rights were cleared for both source texts and annotations, but for Finnish no permission has been obtained. Although the amount of annotated material varies between languages and is somewhat limited (52

---

[23] http://iness.uib.no
[24] http://www.cl.uzh.ch/research/paralleltreebanks/smultron_en.html

to 1052 sentences), the number of pairwise alignments is high. The Sofie Parallel Treebank currently consists of 26 aligned language pairs and is open to new languages.

A small parallel treebank was also constructed from a single document selected from the JRC Acquis Multilingual Parallel Corpus of EU/EEA law texts,25 which provides materials from a different genre in both the official EU languages and some non-official European languages. The Acquis Parallel Treebank is also rather small (73 to 122 sentences depending on the language), but it currently consists of 21 aligned language pairs. Even if the Sofie and Acquis treebanks are based on relatively small texts, they demonstrate the potential of aligning treebanks across many languages. These parallel treebanks are documented in META-SHARE and are available for download on the INESS website.

Besides the monolingual treebanks which form the basis of the two parallel treebanks, the INESS infrastructure provides access to other treebanks in several languages. Among treebanks in the linguistic area of the Baltic and Nordic countries, we mention the Icelandic Parsed Historical Corpus (73,014 sentences), FinnTreebank3 (170,000 tokens), Turku Dependency Treebank (88,418 tokens), the Faroese Parsed Historical Corpus (3,713 sentences), and the INESS Norwegian treebank (about 5000 analysed sentences and still expanding). Treebanks for other languages outside this linguistic area include Abkhazian, Bulgarian, Georgian, Hungarian, Northern Sami, Polish, Tamil, Turkish, Urdu, Wolof, and the classical languages (Ancient Greek, Church Slavic, Classical Armenian, Latin, and Gothic).

The different types of treebanks (Lexical-Functional Grammar, Dependency Grammar, Constituency Annotation) are accommodated in standard formats (TigerXML, CoNLL-X, CG3-dependency, Penn Treebank II bracketing, and XLE prolog). Treebanks can be explored (searched, browsed, and viewed), aligned with other treebanks, and downloaded, all from a uniform web interface. A screenshot is presented in Figure 1.

Drawing on the obtained experience, INESS will sustain the treebanking action and continue to pursue good practices for documentation and IPR clearance. We encourage treebank developers to clear rights with rights holders of source texts prior to annotation and promote the use of explicit licenses wherever possible.

The metadata description of treebanks remains problematic, in particular for parallel treebanks which are complex resources, since META-SHARE does not provide for adequate description of such resources. A more appropriate treatment of complex resources will need attention in future work.

The mechanisms for linking external resource portals with META-SHARE (described in Section 3) make it possible to dynamically list each specific resource in META-SHARE and can be applied to other language resource-specific portals such as INESS.

---

25 http://ipsc.jrc.ec.europa.eu/index.php?id=198

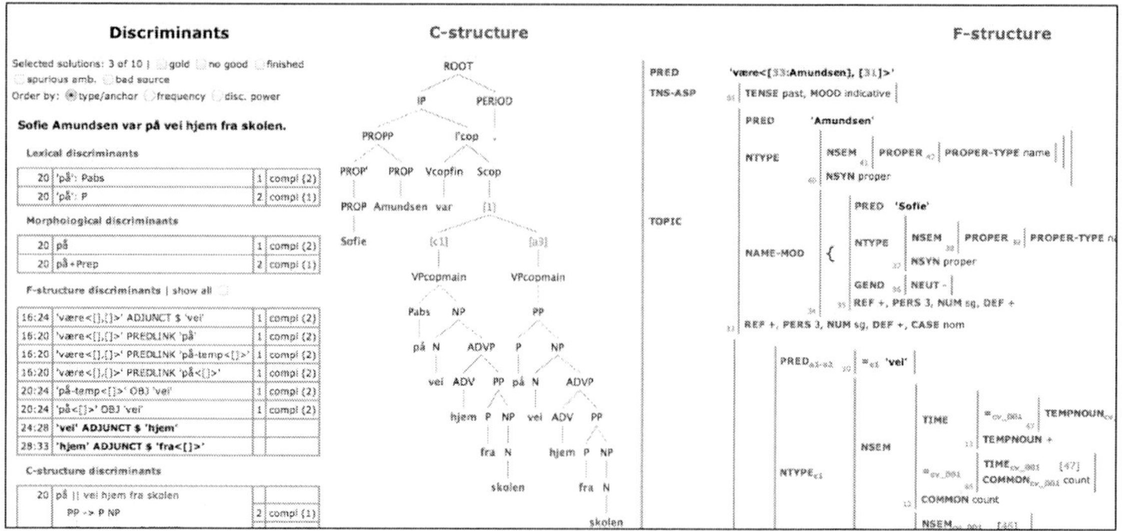

Figure 1: INESS web interface for treebanking, shown with the first sentence of the Norwegian Sofie treebank annotated in LFG.

5.2   Wordnets

The multilingual wordnet initiative has dealt with the pilot linking and validation of wordnets between the Nordic and Baltic languages. One central aim has been to perform a tentative comparison and validation of the linked wordnets, a related aim being to make the mono- and multilingual wordnets visible for further validation and comparison via a common web interface.

To this end, four pilot bilingual wordnets, each of 1,000 synsets, have been compiled using Princeton Core WordNet[26] as an Interlingua: Danish-Swedish, Danish-Finnish, Estonian-Finnish, and Finnish-Swedish.

In general, the semi-automatically linked wordnets are judged to be of a rather good quality, even if translations are not always 100% precise. An average of 2.2% errors and 7.0% slight mismatches have been reported from the individual validations. There does not appear to be a systematic bias to the errors. Though of course, some errors are systematically biased due to false friends, however, others seem to be just random errors. Most of the slight mismatches derive from diverging opinions on the understanding of *what a synset should contain*. Not surprisingly, wordnets that have been compiled via translations from Princeton WordNet have many senses per synset (just as Princeton WordNet), whereas wordnets that are monolingually compiled and based rather on synonymy registrations in conventional dictionaries have much less. A majority of the reported mismatches in the links are derived from exactly this discrepancy, since translations seem to be become more imprecise when a synset contains many word senses (Pedersen et al., 2013).

Apart from compiling the bilingual wordnets, all of the involved wordnets have undergone extensions and upgrades, including the Icelandic WordNet and the Norwegian WordNet, of which the latter has been developed from scratch during the project period (based on the Danish wordnet

---

[26] http://wordnetcode.princeton.edu/standoff-files/core-wordnet.txt

DanNet). All six monolingual wordnets and the four bilingual ones have been made available via META-SHARE[27], and the linked wordnets are viewable from the *WordTies*[28] web interface.

Future work includes an extension of the web interface to include more wordnets, as well as the generation of a broader comparison and validation of the wordnets included, i.e, broader than the ones provided via the 1,000 common links. We plan to include multilingual links for the full Core WordNet (5,000 synsets) for browsing and validation.

A broader comparison and validation of the wordnets would furthermore be fruitful and should be made feasible when the web interface is extended to include multilingual links for the full Princeton Core WordNet. Several discrepancies have been registered during the linking – other than the aforementioned different approach to the interpretation of the *synset* – such as discrepancies in taxonomical structure. Some have used an expert perspective, for example on animals, and thereby compiled a relatively deep taxonomy (i.e., the Finnish WordNet), whereas others have used a layman perspective adapted from a dictionary which is much more flat (i.e., the Danish wordnet). The number and selection of relations in the wordnets also differ; some have included only Princeton relations, others include EuroWordNet (Vossen, 1998) relations (i.e., Estonian and Danish), and others have adapted relations from other lexical projects, including qualia relations such as *used_for* and *made_by* relations (Danish and Norwegian WordNet).

5.3   Terminology resources

This task addressed a growing demand to consolidate distributed terminology resources across languages and domains and thus, has extended an open linguistic infrastructure with multilingual terminology resources.

Major progress in consolidating distributed terminology resources was accomplished by the EuroTermBank platform (Vasiļjevs and Schmitz, 2006). Our intention was not to duplicate resources stored on EuroTermBank, but to interconnect this content-specific Language Resource repository with META-SHARE. Using the approach described in the Section 3, we enabled harvesting of EuroTermBank metadata and integrated EuroTermBank within the META-SHARE infrastructure. This interlinking yielded 99 additional terminology resources now listed in META-SHARE. These resources themselves are available in EuroTermBank for online search.

As EuroTermBank provides specific facilities for searching, representing, and using terminology data, we use this platform for depositing new resources identified and collected in our work. As a result, EuroTermBank was extended from 2.3 to 2.8 million terms internally by adding 43 terminology collections to EuroTermBank – LKI (Lithuanian) terminology, EASTIN terminology of Assistive Technology, and 41 collection from Icelandic Termbank. Three other terminology collections remain in the negotiation stage. One external term base (BFT) was connected to EuroTermBank during this activity, two other (STRUNA — Croatian term bank, PIRARC – Multilingual database of Road Terms) remain in the negotiation stage. BFT is the Bank of Finnish Terminology in Arts and Sciences provided to META-SHARE by the University of Helsinki. This resource has been integrated for one-stop terminology search with EuroTermBank and, through interconnection of EuroTermBank with META-SHARE, is also listed in the META-SHARE catalogue.

The most outstanding result was achieved by Icelandic partners who succeeded at negotiating with 41 author whose work is contained in the Icelandic terminology bank. The rights to share for

---

[27] Note, however, that Norwegian WordNet actually includes two wordnets, one for Bokmål and one for Nynorsk.
[28] http://wordties.cst.dk

download were negotiated through a long and exhaustive process of negotiations. The resulting content was converted to the industry standard TBX format of terminology interchange, and both were uploaded to the META-SHARE network, as well as imported for centralised online lookup by users of the EuroTermBank terminology portal.

5.4 Finite-state techniques

To promote the development of language-independent natural language processing software, HFST–Helsinki Finite-State Technology[29] is included in CLARIN and META-NET. HFST is a framework for compiling and applying linguistic descriptions with finite-state methods. HFST currently collects some of the most important finite-state tools for creating morphologies and spellcheckers into one open-source platform and supports extending and improving the descriptions with weights to accommodate the modelling of statistical information. HFST offers a path from language descriptions to efficient language applications. Here, we have focused on making the HFST library available to the developers of new tools, new features in existing tools, or new language applications.

HFST is primarily designed for creating and compiling morphologies, which have been documented, for example, in Lindén et al. (2009; 2011; 2012). HFST contains open-source replicas of *xfst, lexc,* and *twolc*, which are well-known and well-researched tools for morphology building (see Beesley and Karttunen, 2003). The tools support both parallel and cascaded application of transducers.

There are a number of tools for describing morphologies. Many of them start with the item-and-arrangement approach in which an arrangement of sublexicons contains lists of items that may continue in other sublexicons. A formula for compiling such lexical descriptions was documented in Lindén et al. (2009). To realise the morphological processes, rules may be applied to the finite-state lexicon. In addition, HFST also offers the capability to train and apply part-of-speech taggers on top of the morphologies using parallel weighted finite-state transducers on text corpora (Lindén et al., 2012).

Using compiled morphologies, a number of applications have been created, e.g., spellcheckers for nearly 100 languages and hyphenators for approximately 40 different languages. The spellcheckers were derived from open-source dictionaries and integrated with OpenOffice and LibreOffice, e.g., a full-fledged Greenlandic spellchecker, which is a polyagglutinative language, is currently available for OpenOffice via HFST. By adding the tagger capability, we have also created an improved spelling suggestion mechanism for words in context (Lindén et al., 2012).

Some additional applications, such as synonym and translation dictionaries as well as a framework for recognising multi-word expressions for information extraction using HFST, have also been developed.

6 Conclusions and continuing activities

As described in this paper, a fully functional LR infrastructure is established in the Nordic and Baltic countries as a part of the pan-European META-NET network. This infrastructure will greatly support researchers, developers, and users providing information and access to variety of monolingual and multilingual resources for the languages of the Nordic and Baltic countries.

---

[29] http://hfst.sf.net

The cornerstone of the long-time viability of the developed infrastructure is the involvement of the following main national and/or regional actors:

- Producers, i.e., 'competence centres', typically public research centres, language institutes and academies, as well as private content owners like media companies and publishing houses.
- Aggregators, i.e., 'data centres' (repositories), usually supported by national and/or regional authorities.
- Sponsors, i.e., public authorities, research agencies, language councils, companies with language resource needs.
- Individual and institutional users from the research and industry sectors.

The META-SHARE infrastructure relies on the operation of interlinked META-SHARE nodes that are distributed and autonomously maintained by the participating institutions. As META-SHARE is a distributed platform, its sustainability depends on the willingness and ability of participating institutions to run META-SHARE nodes and to provide related services.

By signing letters of intent (indicating commitment, but not legally binding), we have committed to sustain the infrastructure by hosting and making available the META-SHARE repository of LRs through the META-SHARE network and providing technical and/or user support services for a period of at least 2 years.

In addition, the clearinghouse concept (a service centre for collection, classification and distribution of language resources) is considered for cooperation on long-term storage of resources with other similar service centres in other European countries, using cost-sharing principles. Inclusion of new actors and countries in the business model will be further elaborated in cooperation with the best practices of other META-SHARE centres. In most of the Baltic and Nordic countries, national centres promoting LR availability have already been established.

Specific plans for the curation of META-SHARE nodes and specific types of LRs are provided:

- Treebank resources are maintained and disseminated through the INESS project coordinated by the University of Bergen.
- Terminology resources are taken care of by EuroTermBank, which is maintained and supported by Tilde.
- The interlinked wordnet resources are maintained and disseminated nationally under coordination of the University of Copenhagen.
- In Norway, the National Library has set up a META-SHARE node and will continue to run it as a part of its efforts in CLARINO (the Norwegian CLARIN project).
- The University of Iceland is working on the formation of a national consortium, consisting of the University of Iceland, the Árni Magnússon Institute, the Reykjavik University, the National and University Library, and a few others, to maintain an Icelandic national repository of language resources.

Acknowledgements

The META-NORD project has received funding from the European Commission through the ICT PSP Programme, grant agreement no. 270899. Many thanks to colleagues in META-NORD partner organizations: Jolanta Zabarskaitė from the Lithuanian language institute, Eiríkur Rögnvaldsson and Sigrún Helgadóttir from the University of Iceland and Kadri Vider from the University of Tartu.

References

Beesley, K. and Karttunen, K. (2003). Finite State Morphology, CSLI publications.

Bird, S. and Simons, G. (2001). The OLAC metadata set and controlled vocabularies. In *Proceedings of the ACL Workshop on Sharing Tools and Resources for Research and Education*, pages 7–18.

Bird, S. and Simons, G. (2003). Seven dimensions of portability for language documentation and description. *Language* 79(3), pages 557–582.

Borin, L., Forsberg, M., Roxendal, J. (2012). Korp – the corpus infrastructure of Språkbanken. In *Proceedings of LREC 2012*, pages 474–478.

Borin, L., Forsberg, M., Olsson. L., Uppström, J. (2012). The open lexical infrastructure of Språkbanken. *Proceedings of LREC 2012*, pages 3598-3602.

Braasch, A. and Olsen, S. (2004). STO: A Danish Lexicon Resource - Ready for Applications. In *Fourth International Conference on Language Resources and Evaluation*, Proceedings, Vol. IV. Lisbon, pages 1079-1082.

Broeder, D., Kemps-Snijders, M., Van Uytvanck, D., Windhouwer, M., Withers, P., Wittenburg, P., Zinn, C. (2010). A data category registry- and component-based metadata framework. In *Proceedings of LREC 2010*, pages 43–47.

Desipri, E., Gavrilidou, M., Labropoulou, P., Piperidis, S., Frontini, F., Monachini, M., Arranz, V., Mapelli, V., Francopoulo, G., Declerck, T. (2012). Documentation and user manual of the META-SHARE metadata model. http://www.meta-net.eu/meta-share/META-SHARE%20%20documentationUserManual.pdf.

Francopoulo, G., George, M., Calzolari, N., Monachini, M., Bel, N., Pet, M., Soria, C. (2006). Lexical Markup Framework (LMF). *Proceedings of LREC 2006*, pages 233–236.

Gavrilidou, M., Labropoulou, P., Piperidis, S., Speranza, M., Monachini, M., Arranz, V., Francopoulo, G. (2011). Specification of metadata-based descriptions for language resources and technologies. T4ME deliverable D7.2.1. http://www.meta-net.eu/public_documents/t4me/META-NET-D7.2.1-Final.pdf .

Gavrilidou, M., Labropoulou, P., Desipri, E., Piperidis, S., Papageorgiou, H., Monachini, M., Frontini, F., Declerck, T., Francopoulo, G., Arranz, V., Mapelli, V. (2012). The META-SHARE metadata schema for the description of language resources. *Proceedings of LREC 2012*, pages 1090–1097.

Helgadóttir, S., Rögnvaldsson, E. (forthcoming). Language Resources for Icelandic, *Workshop on Nordic Language Research Infrastructure*, NODALIDA 2013, Oslo.

Lindén, K., Silfverberg, M., Pirinen, T. (2009). HFST tool for morphology: An efficient open-source package for construction of morphological analyzers. In *State of the Art in Computational Morphology*, Mahlow, C. and Piotrowski, M. (eds.). Berlin, Heidelberg: Springer Berlin Heidelberg, pages 28-47.

Lindén, K., Silfverberg, M., Axelson, E., Hardwick, S., Pirinen, T. (2011). HFST—Framework for Compiling and Applying Morphologies. In *Systems and Frameworks for Computational Morphology*. Mahlow, C. & Piotrowski, M. (eds.). Springer, Vol. 100, pages 67-85.

Lindén, K., Axelson, E., Drobac, S., Hardwick, S., Silfverberg, M., Pirinen, T. A. (2012). Using HFST for Creating Computational Linguistic Applications. In *Computational Linguistics Applications*, Piasecki, M., and Przepiórkowski, A., Springer-Verlag.

Melby, A.K. (2012). Terminology in the age of multilingual corpora. *Journal of Specialized Translation* 18, pages 7–29.

Oksanen, V. and Lindén, K. (2012). Building shared language research environments inside the European Union: How to optimize the system based on experiences from real life. In *First Thematic Conference on the Knowledge Commons*. Louvain-la-Neuve, Belgium.

Pedersen, B. S., Borin, L., Forsberg, M., Kahusk, N., Lindén, K., Niemi, J., Nisbeth, N., Nygaard, L., Orav, H., Rögnvaldsson, E., Seaton, M., Vider, K., Kaarlo, V. (2013) Nordic and Baltic wordnets aligned and compared through "WordTies". In *Proceedings of Nodalida 2013* (in press).

Piperidis, S. (2012). The META-SHARE Language Resources Sharing Infrastructure: Principles, Challenges, Solutions. In *Proceedings of the Eight International Conference on Language Resources and Evaluation (LREC'12)*, Istanbul, Turkey, pages 36-42.

Skadiņa, I., Vasiljevs, A., Borin, L., de Smedt, K., Linden, K., Rognvaldsson, E. (2011). META-NORD: Towards Sharing of Language Resources in Nordic and Baltic Countries. In *Proceedings of Workshop on Language Resources, Technology and Services in the Sharing Paradigm (LRTS)*, Chiang Mai, Thailand, pages 107-114.

Váradi, T., Krauwer, S., Wittenburg P., Wynne, M., Koskenniemi, K. (2008). CLARIN: common language resources and technology infrastructure. In *Proceedings of the Sixth International Language Resources and Evaluation Conference.*

Vasiljevs, A., Pedersen, B.S., de Smedt, K., Borin, L., Skadiņa, I. (2011). META-NORD: Baltic and Nordic Branch of the European Open Linguistic Infrastructure. In *NODALIDA 2011 workshop Visibility and Availability of LT Resources, NEALT Proceedings Series,* Vol.13, pages 18-22.

Vasiljevs, A. and Schmitz, K.D. (2006). Collection, harmonization and dissemination of dispersed multilingual terminology resources in an online terminology databank. In *Proceedings of TSTT 2006, Third International Conference on Terminology, Standardization and Technology Transfer*, pages 265-272.

Vossen, P. (ed.) (1998). *EuroWordNet: A Multilingual Database with Lexical Semantic Networks.* Dordrecht: Kluwer Academic Publishers.

Windhouwer, M.A. and Wright, S.E. (2012). Linking to linguistic data categories in ISOcat. In Chiarcos, C., Nordhoff, S., Hellmann, S. (eds), *Linked Data in Linguistics*, pages 99–107. Berlin: Springer.

The IPP effect in Afrikaans: a corpus analysis

Liesbeth Augustinus[1], Peter Dirix[1,2]

(1) Centre for Computational Linguistics, University of Leuven
(2) Nuance Communications, Inc.

`{liesbeth,peter}@ccl.kuleuven.be`

ABSTRACT

Compared to well-resourced languages such as English and Dutch, NLP tools for linguistic analysis in Afrikaans are still not abundant. In order to facilitate corpus-based linguistic research for Afrikaans, we are creating a treebank based on the *Taalkommissie* corpus. We adapted a tokenizer and a shallow parser, while using a TnT tagger to do part-of-speech annotation. A first linguistic phenomenon we are investigating is the occurrence of *infinitivus pro participio* (IPP) in Afrikaans. IPP refers to constructions with a perfect auxiliary, in which an infinitive appears instead of the expected past participle. The phenomenon has been studied extensively in Dutch and German, but studies on Afrikaans IPP triggers are sparse. In contrast to the former two languages, it is often mentioned in the literature that in Afrikaans, IPP occurs optionally. We want to check this statement doing a corpus analysis.

KEYWORDS: Afrikaans, tokenizer, parser, chunker, corpus search tool, IPP.

1 Introduction

Afrikaans is a West Germanic language spoken as a first language by about 7 million people in South Africa and Namibia and by many millions more as a second language. It can be considered a daughter language of Dutch, as it originates in 17th-century Dutch dialects, brought to southern Africa by settlers from the Netherlands. Although there are some influences from Malay, Portuguese, Bantu, and Khoisan languages, Dutch and Afrikaans are still more or less mutually comprehensible. One of the main features of Afrikaans is a simplification of Dutch morphology, e.g. dropping the nominal gender distinction and only keeping two verb forms for all but the most common verbs (present/infinitive and past participle).

In recent years, several NLP tools were created for Afrikaans, cf. Grover et al. (2011) for an overview of the available tools. Compared to well-resourced languages such as English and Dutch, however, it seems that the tools which are available for Afrikaans are less well-performing.

The purpose of our research is twofold. As a starting point, we describe the NLP tools that were used to process and query the data, as well as the first step towards the creation of a treebank based on an Afrikaans text corpus (the *Taalkommissie* corpus[1]) (cf. section 2).

In the second part of this paper we investigate whether and how the tools and resources that are currently available can be used as a means for descriptive linguistics. As a case study, we will look for the occurrence of *infinitivus pro participio*, a.k.a. the IPP effect, in the *Taalkommissie* corpus. In this linguistic study we compare the IPP phenomenon as it is described in the literature (cf. section 3) to its occurrence in the data (cf. section 4 and 5).

Besides improving the performance of the existing annotation tools, we intend to include the parsed corpus into a user-friendly query engine in order to facilitate corpus-based linguistic research for Afrikaans (cf. section 6).

2 Tools

In order to investigate the linguistic case study described in sections 3 to 5, we automatically annotated the *Taalkommissie* corpus. This section describes the tools used to annotate and query the corpus. We adapted a tokenizer and a shallow parser, while using a TnT tagger (Brants, 2000) trained on Afrikaans to do part-of-speech (PoS) annotation. We furthermore added a search engine to facilitate corpus exploitation.

2.1 Tokenizer

The Dutch tokenizer (Dirix et al., 2005) used in the METIS-II project is rule-based, using regular expressions which model the finite-state characteristics of tokenization and gives only one tokenization per sentence, so the output does not contain any ambiguities. The tokenizer basically splits on white space and detaches punctuation marks from the adjacent words. We adapted the Dutch rules to Afrikaans in order to deal with abbrevations that include a period and the ones to deal with words containing apostrophes (e.g. the indefinite article 'n).

---

[1]Taalkommissie van die Suid-Afrikaanse Akademie vir Wetenskap en Kuns (2011).

2.2   Tagger and tag set

We used the TnT Tagger (Brants, 2000), a Hidden Markov Model based *n*-gram tagger, which was trained by CTexT[2] to tag the corpus (further referred to as the *CTexT tagger*). The tag set consists of 139 different tags, based mainly on morphosyntactic features (Pilon, 2005).

In the case of verbs, which is the most relevant PoS for our research (cf. sections 3 and 5), a distinction is made between transitive and intransitive verbs, between separable and inseparable verbs, and also between main verbs, modal verbs, temporal auxiliaries and passivizing auxiliaries. Marked forms (*ge*-marking or simple past in the case of a few auxiliaries) and unmarked forms are also distinguished. Altogether, there are 17 verbal tags, as shown in Table 1.

Tag	Value
VTHOG	inseparable transitive main verb, unmarked
VVHOG	inseparable transitive main verb, marked
VTHOO	inseparable intransitive main verb, unmarked
VVHOO	inseparable intransitive main verb, marked
VTHOV	inseparable intransitive main verb requiring preposition, unmarked
VVHOK	inseparable intransitive main verb requiring preposition, marked
VTHOK	copula, unmarked
VVHOK	copula, marked
VTHSG	separable transitive main verb, unmarked, marked
VTHSO	separable intransitive main verb, unmarked
VTUOM	modal auxiliary, present
VVUOM	modal auxiliary, past
VTUOA	aspectual auxiliary, present
VVUOA	aspectual auxiliary, past
VTUOP	passive auxiliary, present
VVUOA	passive auxiliary, past
VUOT	temporal auxiliary

Table 1: Verbal tags in the CTexT tagger.

The author of the tagger claims an accuracy of 85.87% on a small data set, which is rather low compared to state-of-the-art PoS taggers for well-resourced languages.[3] Although there are some other taggers trained for Afrikaans, they did not seem to meet our research goals. For example, Schlünz (2010) reports an accuracy of 94.64%, but with a tag set reduced to only 17 different tags. The TiMBL-based tagger for Afrikaans (Puttkammer, 2006) is not usable for our purpose, because it mainly identifies different categories of named entities instead of the regular PoS tags.

2.3   Parser

We aim to create a treebank for Afrikaans. As a starting point for syntactic annotations, we used ShaRPa, a shallow rule-based parser (Vandeghinste, 2008) coming with grammars for English and Dutch. In order to parse the *Taalkommissie* corpus, we created an Afrikaans grammar. The different steps can either be defined as context-free grammars, using the PoS tags as preterminals or as Perl subroutines, defined in a Perl module. Note that the grammars are not automatically processed in a recursive mode. The module allows the application of rules which cannot be formulated in the context-free grammar formalism. An

---

[2]Centre for Text Technology, North-West University, Potchefstroom, South Africa.
[3]The low accuracy is probably due to the fact that the tagger is trained on only 20,000 tokens.

option file defines the application order of the different grammars and subroutines. Both grammars and subroutines can be applied more than once.

Since this is a shallow parser, there is not much depth in the resulting parse tree. It uses the tagged corpus as input, and returns the parsed structure, with marked NPs, PPs, verb groups (VG), and some APs and VPs. The head of a phrase is also marked (/M). Each phrase is presented on one line. Each line is divided into three columns: the phrase tokens, the phrase name (assigned by ShaRPa), and the phrase structure, representing the parse building history (containing the PoS tags assigned by the tagger).

An example parse for the sentence *Dis haar handpalms wat begin sweet het, besef sy.* (It is the palms of her hands that had started to sweat, she noticed.):

```
<s>
dis                    NP    NP[NSEO[NSE]]
haar handpalms         NP    NP[POOB[PDVEB] NSEO[NSE]/M]
wat                    PB    PB
begin sweet het VG     VG[VP[VTHOO] VP[VVHOO] VUOT/M]
,                      ZM    ZM
besef                  NP    NP[NA]
sy                     POOB  POOB[PDHEB]
.                      ZE    ZE
</s>
```

Note that *dis*, a shortened form of *dit is* (it is), is mistagged as the far more infrequent homograph noun (a formal word for 'table') and that *besef*, which can be both a verb (to notice) and a noun (notion), is mistagged as noun.

The verb groups, however, do not give more information than the sequence of tags. As our shallow parser currently does not identify discontinuous verb groups, we will need to introduce a full parse in order to be able to use this information. The quality of the tagging also influences the quality of the parse, so we need to improve the tagger results in order to achieve better results.

2.4   Corpus search tool

In order to look for linguistic constructions in the *Taalkommissie* corpus, we have created a corpus search tool.

The preprocessing consisted of tokenizing and tagging the corpus with the tokenizer and PoS tagger described in section 2.1 and 2.2 respectively. Next, we assigned a unique identifier to each sentence. Then we stored the complete corpus into a PostgreSQL database.[4] For each sentence, we included the following information in the database:

```
ID | sentence | PoS string | token-PoS string
```

Since the *Taalkommissie* corpus is rather large, we used the (built-in) B-tree indexing aiming to speed up corpus search.

In order to facilitate querying the corpus, we added a search interface on top of the database. The interface is a combination of PHP scripts and HTML, resulting in a web-based search

---

[4]http://www.postgresql.org

tool which allows users to query the corpus without any local installation of corpora and/or software.

As input, the user provides a query which could be a string of tokens, e.g. `het kom kuier` (lit. 'have come visit'), a string of PoS tags, e.g. `[VUOT] [VTUOA] [VTHOG]` (base form of temporal auxiliary, aspectual verb, main verb), or a combination of both tokens and tags, e.g. `het[VUOT] kom[VTUOA] kuier[VTHOG]`. Note that PoS tags should be put between square brackets. It is furthermore possible to use a wildcard for the PoS tags. For example, if one wants to look for any verb form, `[V*]` can be used; if one want to differentiate between base forms and inflected verb forms, `[VT*]` and `[VV*]` can be used respectively.

Furthermore, there is an option to include some context before and after the matching sentences. This might be useful to disambiguate homonyms in the case of short sentences, or if one is interested in discourse phenomena.

After querying the corpus, the results are presented to the user (see screenshot in Figure 1). At the top of the page, the search instruction is repeated. Below the query, a list of matching sentences is displayed. The constructions matching the query are highlighted in each sentence. It is also possible to view/save the results as plain text format (with and without PoS tags).

Query: het[VUOT] kom[VTUOA] [V*] [CI]

MATCHES

You can view/download the results as .txt format, as a printer friendly version, or as a printer friendly version with POS tags.

a24-48742	die vorige paar dae het almal hand bygesit toe Koos Petroos die huis binne en buite uitgeverf het. Die manne **het kom help** om die leë blikke en sinke en goed wat die agterwerf vol gestaan het , weg te valt. Die vroue het vir Drienie Petroos die huis van hoek tot kant kom help skoonmaak
a24-58395	hulle **het kom baklei** , vir meneer kom vra om sy neus uit hul sake te hou , en te kom sê dat indien hy dink dat hulle enigsins van plan is om selfs een sent uit te gee , hy maar weer kan dink .
a24-58457	dis Gerit. " Ek **het kom hoor** of ek nie kan help nie , " sê hy toe hy nog 'n paar tree van haar af is
a24-77099	" ek **het kom vra** of oom nie miskien hierdie sal kan koop nie .
a24-89769	Magties , Iris , Hendrik , ek's bly julie **het kom inloer**
a24-93076	wat maak jy hier " " Ek **het kom kyk** hoe dit gaan
a24-118812	tot sy op 'n dag haar navorsing geformuleer het , haar tas gepak het , en die oorlewingstrategieë van 'n motsoort hier kom ondersoek het. Sy **het kom kyk** hoe die mot onder moeilike eksterne omstandighede oorleef .

Figure 1: Corpus search tool interface

At the bottom of the page, a grid with the corpus results is printed. It indicates how many hits in how many matching sentences were found. Furthermore, the ratio (matching sentences/sentences in the corpus) is given.

At the moment, it is not possible to query the corpus partially. It might be interesting to look into specific parts of the corpus (e.g. newspaper texts only), but unfortunately the corpus lay-out did not allow us to divide the corpus along those lines.

3 Infinitivus pro participio

3.1 IPP in double infinitive constructions

Infinitivus pro participio (IPP) or *Ersatzinfinitiv* is a linguistic phenomenon occurring in a subset of the West Germanic languages, such as Dutch, German, and Afrikaans. IPP refers to constructions with a perfect auxiliary, in which an infinitive appears instead of the expected past participle. In Afrikaans, one expects the temporal auxiliary for the perfect tense to select a past participle, marked in various ways, most generally by a prefix *ge-* and sometimes an ending (usually either *-d/-t* or *-en*), cf. *gebly* in example (1a).[5] However, when a verb occurring in the perfect tense selects another verb, it commonly occurs as an infinitive, cf. *bly* in example (1b), instead of the expected past participle, as illustrated in example (1c).[6]

(1) (a) *Hy   het   stil   **gebly***.
         he   have:PRES   silent   stay:PP

         'He remained silent.'

     (b) *Hy   het   **bly**   praat*.
         he   have:PRES   stay:INF   talk:INF

         'He kept on talking.'

     (c) *Hy   het   **gebly**   praat*.
         he   have:PRES   stay:PP   talk:INF

         'He kept on talking.'

While Dutch and German grammars mention general types of verbs (e.g. modal verbs) for which IPP is either required or optional, none of our Afrikaans sources do. Nevertheless, Ponelis (1979), Zwart (2007), and De Vos (2001) report that the IPP effect appears optionally in Afrikaans. This contrasts with Dutch and German, as in those languages the IPP phenomenon is obligatory for certain verbs, see amongst others Haeseryn et al. (1997), and Dudenredaktion (2006). Donaldson (1993) mentions however that IPP is triggered in most cases, such as in example (1b). Constructions with a past participle such as (1c) do occur, but Donaldson considers them non-standard Afrikaans. A similar construction as (1c) in Dutch is not possible, as the cognate verb *blijven* (stay) always triggers IPP.

De Vos (2001) also reports that some of the IPP triggers, esp. *laat* (let), tend to passivize fairly productively (2). This phenomenon is ungrammatical in Dutch and German.

(2) *Hierdie   huis   is   deur   my   oom   (ge)laat   bou.*
     This   house   be:PRES   by   my   uncle   let:PRES/PP   build:PRES

     'My uncle had this house built.'

3.2   IPP in progressive constructions

Apart from *double infinitive* constructions, there is a second construction in which IPP can be triggered. Afrikaans has a serialization pattern using the conjunction *en* (and) in order to express the continuous or progressive aspect of the verb, as in example (3a). Such constructions also exist in English (e.g. *He sits and reads*), but not in Dutch nor German. In the perfect of this construction, the first main verb has optional *ge*-marking, so it optionally triggers IPP, while the second main verb always occurs in the infinitive, as shown for the verb *staan* (stand) in examples (3b-c). Both forms are considered standard Afrikaans by Ponelis (1979), Zwart (2007), Donaldson (1993), and Verdoolaege and Van Keymeulen (2010).

---

[5] Some verbs have no *ge*-prefix though, so the past participle might actually be the same as the infinitive, e.g. *bestuur* (drive), *begin* (start, begin).

[6] Note that both examples (1b) and (1c) are grammatical in Afrikaans.

(3) (a) *Ons   staan   stil   en   luister.*
        we   stand:PRES still and   listen:PRES

        'We are standing and listening.'

     (b) *Ons   het   stil   **staan**   en   luister.*
        we   have:PRES   still stand:INF   and   listen:INF

        'We were standing and listening.'

     (c) *Ons   het   stil   **gestaan** en   luister.*
        he   have:PRES   still stand:PP   and   listen:INF

        'We were standing and listening.'

De Vos (2001) reports that, although speaker judgments might vary, it is generally difficult to passivize indirect linking verbs (4), while Breed (2012) considers them grammatical.

(4) *Die   appel   word   deur hom   gesit   en   eet.*
     The   apple   become:PRES   by   him   sit:PP and   eat:PRES

     'The apple was being eaten by him.'

This construction is also impossible in both Dutch and German.

4 Hypothesis, data, and methodology

Based on the literature, the hypothesis is that, in contrast to Dutch and German, IPP occurs optionally in Afrikaans. We will test the hypothesis through a corpus-based study, using a PoS-tagged version of the *Taalkommissie* corpus.[7] The corpus, which is compiled by the Afrikaans language committee of the South African Academy for Science and Arts, contains about 58 million words of formal, written Afrikaans. It comprises many different text types, including newspaper articles, magazines, Bible texts, scientific articles, and study guides.

In order to query the corpus, we have created a corpus search tool (cf. section 2.4), which enables us to look for IPP constructions and their counterexamples with a past participle. We aim to find out whether IPP is actually optional or required in both double infinitive constructions and progressive constructions. Furthermore, we will investigate which verbs occur as IPP triggers in Afrikaans. The results of the corpus study are presented in section 5.

5 Results and discussion

5.1 IPP in double infinitive constructions

In order to retrieve IPP in double infinitive constructions and counterexamples with past participles in the *Taalkommissie* corpus, we extracted all combinations in which the verb form *het* (have) was followed or preceded by two verbs.[8] In addition, we also look at the sequence where there is one other word between *het* and the two other verbs. Although it is possible that more than one word occurs between *het* and the verbal group, we limited our research to constructions with zero or one word between *het* and the two verb forms.[9] This

---

[7] Taalkommissie van die Suid-Afrikaanse Akademie vir Wetenskap en Kuns (2011).

[8] We used the query `het[VUOT] [VT*] [VT*]` to retrieve double infinitive constructions. Discontinuous constructions as well as counterexamples were found using variations of this query.

[9] Since we only have a 'flat' corpus, it is hard to retrieve discontinuous structures. Using a treebank should solve this problem.

results in 9,880 hits, which were manually checked and categorized. We threw out the false positives due to wrong tagging and cases that did not involve main verbs that are triggering an infinitive. We also ignored the modal verbs *kan* (can), *mag* (could) and *moet* (must), as in those cases it is often hard to distinguish the matrix verb from the embedded verb.

We retained 5,679 matches for the infinitive selecting verbs, of which 5,616 occur as IPP triggers (98.89% of the constructions under consideration). The results are shown in Table 2.

Verb	IPP	No IPP	Two PPs	Total	% IPP	Translation
aanhou	45	6	0	51	88.24	keep on
begin	1,454	1	0	1,455	99.93	begin
bly	270	0	1	271	99.63	stay
doen	1	0	0	1	100.00	do, make
durf	35	1	0	36	97.22	dare
gaan	853	0	0	853	100.00	go
help	110	8	0	118	93.22	help
hoor	4	0	0	4	100.00	hear
kom	645	5	12	662	97.43	come
laat	1,458	2	0	1,460	99.86	let
leer	26	7	0	33	78.79	learn/teach
loop	0	1	0	1	0.00	walk, run
maak	1	5	0	6	16.67	make, do
ophou	16	6	0	22	72.73	stop, end
probeer	564	1	0	565	99.82	try
sien	130	5	2	137	94.89	see
wil	4	0	0	4	100.00	want
TOTAL	**5,616**	**48**	**15**	**5,679**	**98.89**	

Table 2: IPP in double infinitive constructions.

Although some verbs are used rather infrequently in this construction, it is clear that in most of the cases, IPP is actually applied. Only for *maak* and the separable verbs *aanhou* and *ophou*, we see a slightly higher percentage of cases that do not have IPP. Verbs like *begin*, *bly*, *durf*, *gaan*, *help*, *hoor*, *kom*, *laat*, *probeer*, and *sien* seem to require IPP, cf. examples (5) and (7a), while we could consider it optional at least for *leer*, cf. example (6). We also see a few cases, esp. for *kom*, in which both the main verb and the verb triggered by it appear as past participles, cf. example (7b). This is not allowed by any of the Afrikaans grammars we consulted (cf. section 3.1). In general, we can conclude that there is a clear tendency for infinitive-selecting verbs to trigger IPP. We have only found 63 sentences in which the selecting verb receives *ge*-marking, which might explain why Donaldson considers such constructions substandard. De Vos (2001) links the optionality to the level of formality.

(5)   *My maag het* **begin** *draai.*
     my stomach have:PRES begin:INF turn:INF

     'My stomach has started to turn. [TKK, a00-2487]'

(6)   (a) *Hoe ek* **leer** *lees het,* *weet ek nie.*
       how I learn:INF read:INF have:PRES know I not

       'I do not know how I have learned to read.' [TKK, a21-26482]

(b) *Dink   terug   hoe   jy   **geleer**   bestuur   het   (...)*
   think   back   how   you   learned:PP   drive:INF   have:PRES

'Think about the time you learned to drive (...)' [TKK, a16-20128]

(7) (a) *(...)   Ons   het   **kom**   kuier.*
          we   have:PRES   come:INF   visit:INF

'(...) We came to visit.' [TKK, a26-9964]

(b) *'n Vragmotor   wat   in   die   teenoorgestelde   rigting   aangery*
    a lorry   which   in   the   opposite   direction   drive-towards:PP
gekom   *het*   *(...)*
come:PP   have:PRES

'A lorry which came from the opposite direction (...)' [TKK, a44-12672]

As De Vos (2001) claimed, we found some passivized constructions with these selecting verbs (see Table 3), but they are far less frequent than the active variant. We investigated both the present form with *word* and the perfect form with *is*. Of the selecting verbs used in the passive, *laat* is by far the most frequent. There is only one counterexample using a past participle instead of the IPP construction.

Verb	IPP present	No IPP present	IPP perfect	No IPP perfect	Total	% IPP	Translation
begin	2	0	5	0	7	100.00	begin
help	0	0	1	0	1	100.00	help
laat	11	1	43	0	55	98.18	let
probeer	8	0	3	0	11	100.00	try
TOTAL	21	1	52	0	74	98.65	

Table 3: IPP in passive double infinitive constructions.

5.2 IPP in progressive constructions

In a second test, we looked at IPP triggers in the serialized form of progressive constructions.[10] We again selected cases with *het*, but now with the conjunction *en* (and) between the two content verbs. This resulted in 1,743 hits, which were again categorized manually. We only retained 244 positive examples, of which 50.82% appeared as IPP triggers. The results are shown in Table 4.

It is clear that the construction as such is only frequent using *lê*, *sit* and *staan* as IPP triggers. IPP occurs in slightly less than half of the cases for *sit* and *staan*, so we can agree with the grammars that IPP is optionally triggered in progressive constructions, cf. example (8). For *lê* however, there seems to be a clear preference for the IPP construction. The progressive also occurs a few times with *loop*, but in that case the past participle seems to be preferred. We encounter again a few cases of two past participles, cf. example (9b). Similar to the constructions with double participles in section 5.1, such constructions seem less preferred. If we compare the results with the frequencies of a verb being the trigger for the progressive construction in this corpus (Breed, 2012), we see that verbs using the progressive frequently

---

[10]We used the query `het[VUOT] [VT*] en[KN] [VT*]` to retrieve double infinitive constructions. Discontinuous constructions as well as counterexamples were found using variations of this query.

(*sit*, *staan*, and *lê*) are more likely to apply IPP then *loop*, which is less likely to occur in this construction.

Verb	IPP	No IPP	Two PPs	Total	% IPP	Translation
bly	0	0	1	1	0.00	stay, remain
bystaan	0	1	0	1	0.00	stand near
kom	0	0	1	1	0.00	come
lê	30	5	0	35	85.71	lie
loop	1	4	1	6	16.67	walk, run
rondstaan	0	1	0	1	0.00	stand around
sit	48	58	1	107	44.86	sit
staan	45	47	0	92	48.91	stand
TOTAL	**124**	**116**	**4**	**244**	**50.82**	

Table 4: IPP in progressive/continuous constructions.

Note that most of the verbs that use this construction do not occur in the double infinitive construction (cf. Table 2), while their Dutch cognates do (e.g. Afrikaans *lê* vs. Dutch *liggen* (to lie)). We can conclude that both constructions are in general mutually exclusive.

(8) (a) *(...) waar hy die spul onder 'n soetdoring* **sit** *en dophou*
where he the stuf under a sweet thorn tree sit:INF and watch:INF

het *(...)*
have:PRES

' (...) where he was watching the stuff under a sweet thorn tree (...)' [TKK, a25-14908]

(b) *Ek het daar* **gesit** *en wag op Brett (...)*
I have:PRES there sit:PP and wait:INF for Brett

'I was waiting there for Brett (...)' [TKK, a34-8014]

(9) (a) *Hy vertel hoe hy (...) vir die hysbak* **staan** *en wag*
he tell:PRES how he for the lift stand:INF and wait:INF

het *(...)*
have:PRES

'He tells how he (...) waited in front of the lift (...)' [TKK, a34-1063]

(b) *(...) 'n paar meter van waar ek nog so rustig* **gestaan** *en gesels*
a couple metre from where I still so quiet stand:PP and chat:INF

het.
have:PRES

'(...) a couple of metres from where I was chatting (...)' [TKK, a34-1086]

According to Breed (2012) passive constructions with indirect linking verbs are possible, but she was, like us, not able to find any examples in the *Taalkommissie* corpus.

6   Conclusions and future work

The case study on IPP triggers in Afrikaans shows that a corpus-based study can shed a new light on the descriptive research of a linguistic phenomenon. Based on the literature, we assumed that IPP is optionally triggered in Afrikaans (both in double infinitive constructions and in progressive constructions). The corpus results, however, reveal that infinitive-selecting verbs in double infinitive constructions trigger IPP in almost 99% of the constructions under investigation. The results of the progressive constructions are more consistent with the current literature, since the IPP phenomenon optionally occurs in such constructions (i.e. in ca. 50% of the cases). Moreover, we can conclude that verbs that occur as IPP triggers in the double infinitive construction, do not occur as IPP triggers in the progressive construction and vice versa.

Although we obtained some nice results from the present study, we had to do a lot of (semi-)manual filtering of the results. In order to reduce such tasks, as well as to improve the quality of the annotated data, we will improve the output of the annotation tools in future research. As the CTexT tagger still contains a lot of errors which could be corrected by a simple rule-based extension, we will create a rule-based tag corrector based on the Brill tagger (Brill, 1992).

We also want to extend the parser in order to have different options from the current shallow parsing (including updating and improving the current grammars) to a full parse tree. The parser will then be used to find constructions with more tokens intervening between the relevant items (i.e. between the auxiliary *het* and the infinitives and past participles in our case study). We will need to adapt the search tool to be able to search for chunks as well. Of course, this includes dealing with issues like efficient querying, indexing, and the representation of the trees in the tool. Besides improving existing tools, we will run a lemmatizer on the data, in order to include lemmas in the search tool as well.

Finally, all of this will be integrated in an Afrikaans equivalent of GrETEL (Augustinus et al., 2012), a query engine in which linguists can use a natural language example as a starting point for searching a treebank with limited knowledge about tree representations and formal query languages.

Using all these tools, we want to further investigate the IPP effect in Afrikaans. For example, it would be interesting to investigate whether the number of tokens occurring between the auxiliary and the other verb(s) have an influence on the construction used. Those results can also be useful for a cross-linguistic comparison with similar work in Dutch and German.

Acknowledgments

We wish to thank the people of the Taalkommissie and CTexT for providing us with the *Taalkommissie* corpus and the PoS tagger.

References

Augustinus, L., Vandeghinste, V., and Van Eynde, F. (2012). Example-Based Treebank Querying. In *Proceedings of the 8th International Conference on Language Resources and Evaluation (LREC 2012)*, Istanbul.

Brants, T. (2000). TnT – A Statistical Part-of-Speech Tagger. In *Proceedings of the Sixth Applied Natural Language Processing Conference (ANLP-2000)*, pages 224–231, Seattle.

Breed, A. (2012). *Die grammatikalisering van aspek in Afrikaans: semantiese studie van perifrastiese progressiewe konstruksies*. PhD thesis, North-West University, Potchefstroom.

Brill, E. (1992). A simple rule-based part of speech tagger. In *Proceedings of the third conference on Applied natural language processing (ANLC 42)*, pages 152–155, Stroudburg, PA.

De Vos, M. (2001). Afrikaans Verb Clusters: A Functional-Head Analysis. Master's thesis, University of Tromsø, Tromsø.

Dirix, P., Vandeghinste, V., and Schuurman, I. (2005). METIS-II: Example-based machine translation using monolingual corpora – System description. In *Proceedings of MT Summit X, Workshop on Example-Based Machine Translation*, pages 43–50, Phuket.

Donaldson, B. C. (1993). *A Grammar of Afrikaans*. Mouton de Gruyter, Berlin/New York.

Dudenredaktion (2006). *DUDEN. Die Grammatik. Unentbehrlich für richtiges Deutsch.* Dudenverlag, Mannheim/Leipzig/Vienna/Zürich.

Grover, A. S., van Huyssteen, G. B., and Pretorius, M. W. (2011). A Technology Audit: The State of Human Language Technologies (HLT) R&D in South Africa. In *Proceedings of PICMET'11: Technology Management In The Energy-Smart World (PICMET)*, pages 1693–1706.

Haeseryn, W., , Romijn, K., Geerts, G., de Rooij, J., and van den Toorn, M. (1997). *Algemene Nederlandse Spraakkunst*. Martinus Nijhoff/Wolters Plantyn, Groningen/Deurne, second edition.

Pilon, S. (2005). Outomatiese Afrikaanse woordsoortetikettering. Master's thesis, North-West University, Potchefstroom.

Ponelis, F. A. (1979). *Afrikaanse Sintaksis*. J.L. van Schaik, Pretoria.

Puttkammer, M. J. (2006). Outomatiese Afrikaanse tekseenheididentifisering. Master's thesis, North-West University, Potchefstroom.

Schlünz, G. I. (2010). The effects of part-of-speech tagging on text-to-speech synthesis for resource-scarce languages. Master's thesis, North-West University, Potchefstroom.

Taalkommissie van die Suid-Afrikaanse Akademie vir Wetenskap en Kuns (2011). Taalkommissiekorpus 1.1., CTexT, North West University, Potchefstroom.

Vandeghinste, V. (2008). *A Hybrid Modular Machine Translation System*. PhD thesis, University of Leuven.

Verdoolaege, A. and Van Keymeulen, J. (2010). *Grammatica van het Afrikaans*. Academia Press, Ghent.

Zwart, J.-W. (2007). Some notes on the origin and distribution of the IPP-effect. *Groninger Arbeiten zur Germanistischen Linguistik*, 45:77–99.

Using Factual Density to Measure Informativeness of Web Documents

Christopher Horn[*], *Alisa Zhila*[†], *Alexander Gelbukh*[†], *Roman Kern*[*], *Elisabeth Lex*[*]

[*]Know-Center GmbH, Graz, Austria
{chorn,elex,rkern}@know-center.at

[†]Centro de Investigación en Computación, Instituto Politécnico Nacional, Mexico City, Mexico
alisa.zhila@gmail.com, gelbukh@gelbukh.com

ABSTRACT

The information obtained from the Web is increasingly important for decision making and for our everyday tasks. Due to the growth of uncertified sources, blogosphere, comments in the social media and automatically generated texts, the need to measure the quality of text information found on the Internet is becoming of crucial importance. It has been suggested that factual density can be used to measure the informativeness of text documents. However, this was only shown on very specific texts such as Wikipedia articles. In this work we move to the sphere of the arbitrary Internet texts and show that factual density is applicable to measure the informativeness of textual contents of arbitrary Web documents. For this, we compiled a human-annotated reference corpus to be used as ground truth data to measure the adequacy of automatic prediction of informativeness of documents. Our corpus consists of 50 documents randomly selected from the Web, which were ranked by 13 human annotators using the MaxDiff technique. Then we ranked the same documents automatically using ExtrHech, an open information extraction system. The two rankings correlate, with Spearman's coefficient $\rho = 0.41$ at significance level of 99.64%.

KEYWORDS: quality of texts, Web, fact extraction, open information extraction, informativeness, natural language processing.

1　Introduction

Assessment of information quality becomes increasingly important because nowadays decision making is based on information from various sources that are sometimes unknown or of questionable reliability. Besides, a large part of the information found in the Internet has low quality: the Internet is flooded with meaningless blog comments, computer-generated spam, and documents created by copy-and-paste that convey no useful information.

As one might assume, talking about the quality of the Internet content on the whole is too general and practically impossible, because the content on the Web is of an extremely versatile form and serves to very different needs. It is unreasonable to compare the quality of an online encyclopedia to the quality of a photo storing resource because the assessment of the quality of any object depends on the purpose to which the object serves. Hence, we restrict ourselves to the scope of text documents and assume that the general purpose of a text document is to inform a reader about something. Therefore, the quality of a text document can be related to its *informativeness*, i.e. the amount of useful information contained in a document. (Lex et al., 2012) suggest that informativeness of a document can be measured through factual density of a document, i.e. the number of facts contained in a document, normalized by its length.

Due to the lack of a standard corpus, previous works on the estimation of Web quality concidered only Wikipedia articles, in fact assessing their informativeness. No special studies were performed about human judgement on text informativeness. Therefore, (Lex et al., 2012; Blumenstock, 2008; Lex et al., 2010; Lipka and Stein, 2010) considered Wikipedia editors' choice of *featured* and *good* articles as a reasonable extrapolation of high judgement on their informativeness. (Lex et al., 2012) showed the feasibility of factual density application as measurement of informativeness on the base of automatic prediction of the featured/good Wikipedia articles.

In this work we have conducted experiments to estimate the adequacy of application of factual density to informativeness evaluation in the "real" Internet, i.e. not limited to particular web-sites with a particular form of content but rather covering a wide variety of web-sources, which a user could browse through while looking for information. For this purpose we created a dataset of 50 randomly selected documents in Spanish language from CommonCrawl corpus (Kirkpatrick, 2011), which is a large extraction of texts from the Internet. We assessed factual density automatically using an open information extraction system for Spanish language, ExtrHech (Zhila and Gelbukh, 2013), which is adequate for Web-scale applications. Further, 13 human annotators ranked 50 documents according to their informativeness using the MaxDiff (Louviere and Woodworth, 1991) technique. The automatic ranking produced by ExtrHech system correlates with the ground truth ranking by human annotators with Spearman's ρ coefficient of 0.41 (coinciding rankings would have 1, and the random baseline is 0.018).

The paper is organized as follows. In section 2 we review the related work on the Web text quality evaluation as well as the open information extraction as a method for factual density estimation. Section 3 describes the dataset created in this work and the human annotation procedure. The method for automatic factual density estimation and a brief description of the architecture of ExtrHech system is given in section 4. The experiment and its results are presented in section 5. In section 6 we give a brief discussion of a possible expansion of our text quality measuring method to other languages. Section 7 concludes this paper with an overview of the presented work and proposals for future work.

2   Related work

Evaluation of the quality of Web text content has been mainly performed with metrics capturing content quality aspects like objectivity (Lex et al., 2010), content maturity, and readability (Weber et al., 2009). These methods are based on selection of appropriate features for document presentation. For example, in (Lex et al., 2010) stylometric features were used to assess the content quality. Character trigram distributions were exploited in (Lipka and Stein, 2010) to identify high quality *featured/good* articles in Wikipedia. (Blumenstock, 2008) considered simple word count as an indicator for the quality of Wikipedia articles. (Lex et al., 2012) proposed factual density as a measure of document informativeness and showed that it gives better results for Wikipedia articles than other methods. Wikipedia articles were taken into consideration mainly due to the lack of a standard corpus in this field of work. For evaluation purposes, those Wikipedia articles that have the featured article or good article template in the wikitext were considered to be of a high quality or more informative. No specially designed human annotation or evaluation was involved, and no scale or ranking of informativeness was introduced.

To asses factual density of a text document, (Lex et al., 2012) apply the open information extraction (Open IE) methods. Open IE is the task of extracting relational tuples representing facts from text without requiring a pre-specified vocabulary or manually tagged training corpora. A relational tuple in most current Open IE systems is a triplet consisting of two arguments in the form of noun phrases and a relational phrase expressed as a verb phrase. Consequently, a fact is presented as a triplet like $f = $ *(Mozart, was born in, Salzburg)*. The abscence of a pre-specified vocabulary or a list of predetermined relations makes such systems scalable to a broader set of relations and to a far larger corpora as the Web (Etzioni et al., 2008).

Nevertheless, the output of the Open IE systems contains a large portion of uninformative and incoherent extractions that can lead to overestimating of the factual density in a document. (Fader et al., 2011) show that a part-of-speech based system like ReVerb with simple syntactic and lexical constraints increases the precision of the output and needs no annotating or training effort for its implementation compared to other Open IE systems like TextRunner (Banko et al., 2007), WOE[pos], and WOE[parse] (Wu and Weld, 2010), which all include a relation learning step.

3   Building the Ground Truth Dataset

Since no special corpus for informativeness evaluation previously existed, we aimed at creation of such a corpus of texts extracted from the Internet broader than Wikipedia.

3.1   The dataset

For the purpose of evaluation of the factual density as a measure of informativeness, we needed to create a dataset that would be a reasonable projection of texts on the Web and small enough to be able to conduct the experiment with available resources. To create our dataset we performed the following steps:

- We used a 1 billion page subset from the CommonCrawl corpus (Kirkpatrick, 2011) from 2012, which is a corpus of the web crawl data composed of over 5 billion web

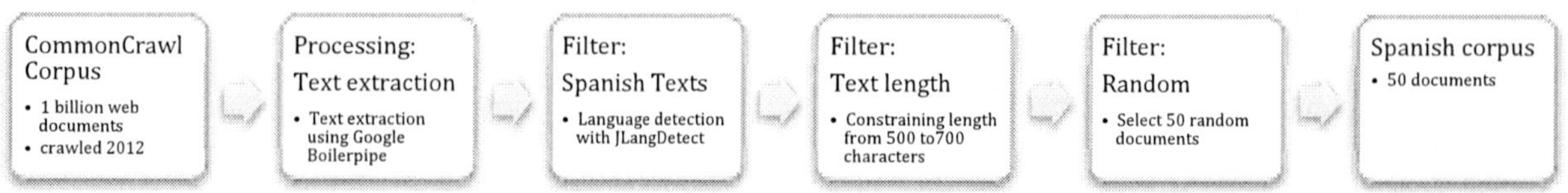

Figure 1: Process of corpus generation

pages, as an initial source of Web texts. From that corpus, we extracted textual content of websites using Google's Boilerpipe framework (Kohlschütter et al., 2010).

- For each article, the language was detected using JLangDetect (Nakatani, 2011).

- From this dataset, we randomly selected 50 documents in Spanish. In order to avoid the length-based bias on the human annotation stage described in the next subsection (e.g. users might tend to rate longer texts as more informative than shorter ones), we constrained the text length to range from 500 to 700 characters.

In the end, we formed a corpus of 50 text documents in Spanish of similar length that represent a random sample of the textual content from the Web. Figure 1 shows the process.

We would like to emphasize that not all textual content presented on the Web is coherent text. The texts encountered on the Internet can consist of pure sequences of keywords, or be elements of web-page menus, for example, " *For more options click here Leave your comment CAPTCHA*". Lists and instructions are another common form of texts, characterized by incomplete sentences normally starting with a verb in the infinitive or imperative form, e.g. *"To open a file: – click the Microsoft Office button; – select Open"*. Texts can be sets of short comments or tweets that also tend to be incomplete sentences often lacking grammatical correctness. Commercials and announcements also typically consist of incomplete sentences, e.g. *"Information about the courses, dates, and prices"*, numbers, e.g. *"$65 $75 $95 All prices in US dollars"*, and telephone numbers and addresses. We manually performed a rough classification of the texts from our dataset shown in Table 1. Since we used only short documents for the experiment, each document mainly corresponded to only one text type.

In the current work we did not do any additional pre-processing for text type detection. This was not done for several reasons. First, we want to keep the system as simple and fast as possible for the purpose of scalability to large amounts of text. Next, we believe that the factual density approach presented in the paper will be appropriate for automatic detection of incoherent and uninformative texts. Consequently, there will be no need for additional filtering.

3.2   Ground Truth Ranking by Human Annotators

To overcome the lack of a standard corpus in the field of web text informativeness assessment, we formed a ground truth ranking of the documents based on inquiry of 13 human annotators. All human annotators are natively Spanish speaking people with graduate level of education. For the questionnaire, we opted for the MaxDiff (Maximum Difference Scaling) technique (Louviere and Woodworth, 1991). According to MaxDiff technique, instead of ranking all items at once, a participant is asked to choose the best and the worst item from a subset of items at a time. This procedure is repeated until all items are covered.

Type of text	# of docs	Characteristics
keywords	2	sequence of nouns with no verbs
web page menu	1	short phrases, verbs
commercials, announcements	18	addresses, phone numbers, prices, imperatives
coherent narrative: descriptions, news	13	full sentences with subjects, verbs, and objects
comments, tweets	6	short sentences, lacking grammatical correctness
instructions, lists	9	phrases starting with infinitives or no verbs
incorrectly detected language	1	impossible to POS-tag for the system and to read for human annotators

Table 1: Classification of the documents in the dataset by the types of text content

MaxDiff is considered to be a strong alternative to standard rating scales (Almquist and Lee, 2009). The advantage of the MaxDiff technique is that it is easier for a human to select the extremes of a scale rather than to produce a whole range of scaling. Consequently, MaxDiff avoids the problems with scale biases and is more efficient for data gathering than the simple pairwise comparison.

For this purpose, we created a set S of MaxDiff questions. Each question, which will subsequently be called Q, contained 4 different documents d. Four items is few enough for a participant to be able to concentrate and to make a decision, and large enough to be able to cover all 50 documents in a reasonable number of questions.

The set S was created as follows:

- First, we calculated all possible combinations of how 4 documents can be chosen from 50 documents. This resulted in 230,300 possible combinations.

- Then, in a loop, we picked up one random question Q from the set of combinations and added it to the resulting set S, until every document d was included three times in the set S. This ensures that every document is compared at least three times with other documents. Once finished, the resulting set S contained 103 questions Q, which we used for the MaxDiff inquiry.

Further, we created a MaxDiff questionnaire system that displayed one question Q' (= 4 documents d') at a time to a participant. A participant was asked to select the most informative document and the least informative document from the set of 4 documents. The interface of the questionnaire system is shown in Figure 2. In the experiment, the instructions and the documents were given to the annotators in Spanish language. In Figure 2 they are translated into English for convenience of the reader of this article. The selection of the most and the least informative documents was based on the intuitive understanding of the notion of "informativeness" by the participants. Each of the participants rated 25 questions on average. The system ensured that each question Q is (i) rated three times in total and

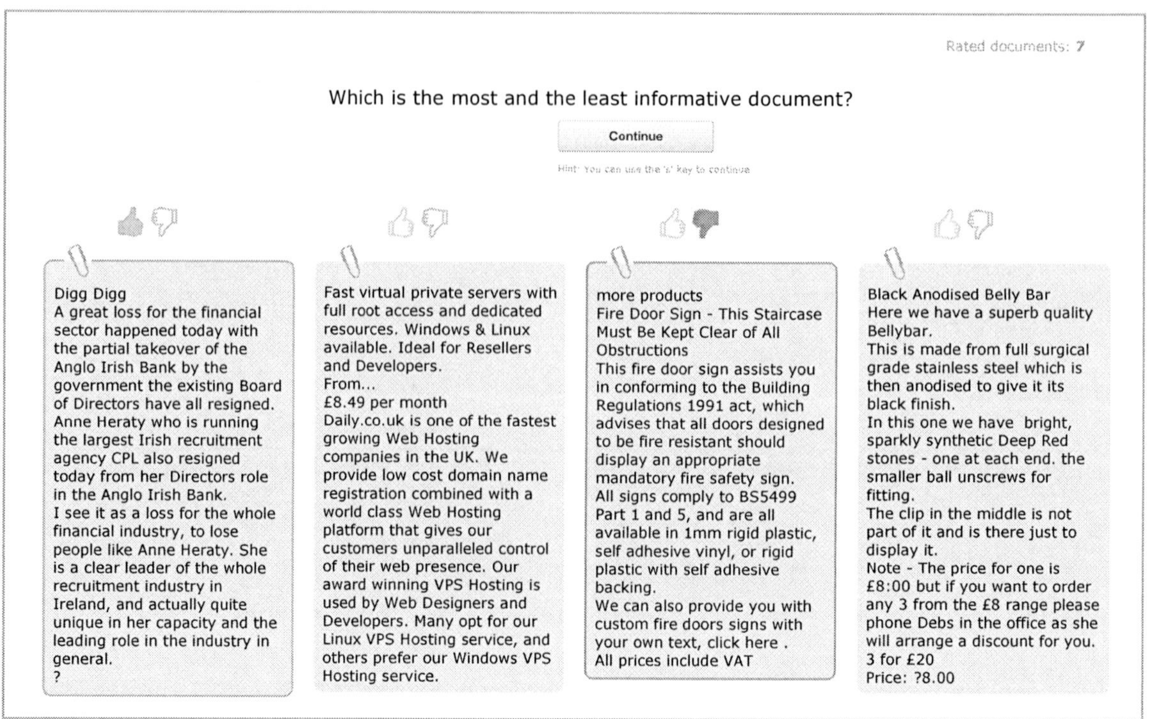

Figure 2: Screenshot of the MaxDiff questionnaire tool

(ii) rated by different users. This resulted in 309 ratings, with each question being answered 3 times.

We applied the MaxDiff technique to the answeres obtained from the user-study. The rank for each document d was calculated proportionally to its MaxDiff scoring $\text{Score}_{\text{maxdiff}}(d)$, which was calculated using the following formula:

$$\text{Score}_{\text{maxdiff}}(d) = R_{\text{pos}}(d) - R_{\text{neg}}(d), \tag{1}$$

where $R_{\text{pos}}(d)$ is the number of positive answers and $R_{\text{neg}}(d)$ is the number of negative answers for the same document d.

After calculating the score for each document d, we formed a ground truth ranking of the 50 documents in our dataset.

4 Automatic Ranking

The aim of this work is to study the feasibility of automatic factual density estimation for informativeness measurement for text documents on the Web. This section describes the procedure for the automatic ranking.

4.1 Factual Density

In the factual density approach to web informativeness assessment, each text document is characterized by the factual density feature. To calculate the value of factual density, first, the simple fact count is determined for each document d using the Open IE method. That means that only direct information on the number of facts, i.e. fact count $fc(d)$, obtained from a text resource d is taken into account. It is obvious that the fact count in a document is correlated with its length, i.e. longer documents would tend to have more facts than shorter ones. To overcome this dependency, factual density $fd(d)$ is calculated as a fact count in a document $fc(d)$ divided by the document size $size(d)$: $fd(d) = \frac{fc(d)}{size(d)}$.

In this work we used the Open IE system for Spanish ExtrHech, which is described in the next subsection, to determine the fact count in a document. The length of a document was calculated as a number of characters including white spaces.

4.2 Fact Extraction

ExtrHech is a POS-tag based Open IE system for Spanish with simple syntactic and lexical constraints (Zhila and Gelbukh, 2013). The system takes a POS-tagged text as an input. For POS-tagging we used Freeling-2.2 (Padró et al., 2010). Then, it imposes syntactic constraints in the form of regular expressions to each sentence. Since in our framework a fact is a triplet of two arguments and a relation between them, the system requires a relation to be a verb phrase that appears between two arguments expressed as noun phrases. Appropriate syntactic constrains detect adequate verb phrases, resolve coordinating conjunctions for relations and noun phrase arguments, correctly treat participle and relative clauses. In the current version of ExtrHech system, lexical constraints limit the length of relational phrases to prevent overspecifying of a relation. Specifically for Spanish language, the current version is adjusted to EAGLES POS-tag set and properly treats reflexive pronouns for verb phrases.

At the current stage, ExtrHech system has various limitations. It does not resolve anaphora, zero subject construction, and free word order that occur in Spanish. Yet despite of these limitations, its precision and recall is comparable to that of ReVerb system for English language, which was used in previous work on the text quality assessment for Wikipedia articles (Lex et al., 2012).

It is also shown in (Fader et al., 2011) that, although deeper syntactic analysis would increase the precision of syntactic and lexical constraint based Open IE systems, it would inevitably slow down execution time that highly affects the overall time of processing for a Web-scale corpus.

5 Experiment and Results

In this work we conducted an experiment to study the appropriateness of factual density measure for assessment of web text informativeness. In order to prove the hypothesis, we compared the ranking based on automatic factual density scoring to the ground truth ranking based on the MaxDiff inquiry of human annotators.

To form the factual density based ranking, 50 documents were fed into a pipeline: Freeling-2.2 POS-tagger, ExtrHech Open IE system, and a script for factual density calculation shown in Figure 3.

Then, each document d was ranked according to its factual density scoring $\text{Score}_{\text{factdens}}(d)$:

$$\text{Score}_{\text{factdens}}(d) = fc(d)/size(d), \tag{2}$$

where $fc(d)$ is the fact count for a document d, and $size(d)$ is its length in characters including white spaces.

Figure 3: Diagram of the factual density estimation

Human annotator ranking was formed as described in Section 3.2. The rankings are shown in Table 2, where HA rank is the human annotator ranking and FD rank is the factual density ranking.

Doc ID	HA rank	FD rank	Doc ID	HA rank	FD rank
1	1	3	26	24.5	40
2	2.5	11	27	27	14
3	2.5	29.5	28	29.5	15
4	4.5	2	29	29.5	22
5	4.5	7	30	29.5	32
6	6	6	31	29.5	16
7	7	12	32	33	24
8	8.5	33	33	33	9
9	8.5	1	34	33	43
10	10	5	35	37	47
11	11.5	27	36	37	47
12	11.5	8	37	37	35
13	14.5	42	38	37	34
14	14.5	39	39	37	10
15	14.5	19.5	40	40	17
16	14.5	41	41	41.5	47
17	19	21	42	41.5	47
18	19	4	43	44	18
19	19	29.5	44	44	47
20	19	36	45	44	37
21	19	38	46	46	26
22	22	23	47	47	19.5
23	24.5	13	48	48	25
24	24.5	47	49	49	31
25	24.5	47	50	50	28

Table 2: Human annotator ranking and factual density ranking

Once the rankings were scored, we applied various statistical measures to calculate the correlation between them. Table 3 shows the results of the statistical evaluation using Spearman's ρ coefficient, Pearson product-moment correlation r, and Kendall's rank correlation τ with the corresponding levels of significance. All these correlation coefficients may vary between 1 for coinciding rankings and -1 for completely opposite rankings. Random baseline for Spearman's ρ is 0.018. The coefficients should be significantly positive for the rankings to be considered correlated.

In our work we obtained Spearman's ρ as high as 0.41, Pearson's r of 0.38, and Kendall's τ of 0.29. Since all measures give significantly positive correlations with the significance level equal to or higher than 99.49%, we can conclude that medium correlation significantly exists between the two rankings. Consequently, the obtained result show that the factual density measure proves to be feasible as a measure of informativeness for text content on the Web.

Method	Value	P-Value	Significance Level
Spearman's ρ	0.404	0.00365	99.636%
Pearson's r	0.390	0.00514	99.486%
Kendall's τ	0.293	0.00347	99.653%

Table 3: Result of correlation tests between factual density algorithm ranking and human annotator ranking for 50 document dataset

6 Discussion: Applicability to Other Languages

In the current work we studied the adequacy of the factual density estimation as a quality measure for arbitrary Web texts on the material of Spanish language. As mentioned in Section 2, the text quality measuring through factual density estimation with an Open IE system for English was shown to be adequate for English language Wikipedia articles (Lex et al., 2012). Our future goal is to show the adequacy of the method for arbitrary English texts as well, especially social media texts.

Moreover, the approach outlined in Sections 3 and 4 can be applied to texts in any languages, to which the fact extraction paradigm described in Section 4.2 is applicable. To the best of our knowledge, so far such Open IE methods have been elaborated and corresponding fact extraction systems have been implemented only for English (Fader et al., 2011) and Spanish (Zhila and Gelbukh, 2013). Generally, this approach to fact extraction requires a POS-tagger and relies on the assumption of a single prevailing word order. Therefore, this fact extraction technique can be similarly implemented for languages with a fixed or dominating word order and for which reliable POS-taggers exist. This is the case for most European languages, e.g. $97 - 98\%$ POS-tagging accuracy for the languages supported by Freeling-3.0 package (Padró and Stanilovsky, 2012). However, currently POS-tagging in other languages performs with lower accuracy, e.g. ~88% for Bengali (Dandapat et al., 2007) or 94.33% for Chinese (Ma et al., 2012). The issue of how POS-tagging accuracy affects performance of a fact extraction system and, consequently, what effect it has on the text quality measuring is out of the scope of the paper and is an interesting direction for future work.

Next, the sensitivity of the fact extraction method to the word order questions the feasibility of text quality measuring using similar approach for languages with flexible word order, e.g. Chinese. We believe that further research in this area will answer these questions.

7 Conclusions and Future Work

In this work we moved the research on informativeness of the Web from Wikipedia articles to the arbitrary Web texts. We formed a dataset of 50 Spanish documents extracted from the Web. Then, we presented a MaxDiff questionnaire to 13 human annotators to be able to form a ground truth ranking of informativeness of Web text documents based on the human judgements. Further, with the use of the open information extraction system ExtrHech, we calculated the factual density of the documents and estimated the corresponding ranking. In the end, we showed that significant positive correlation exists between the automatically generated ranking based on factual density and the ranking based on human judgements (Spearman's rank correlation of 0.404 at a significance level of 99.636%, n=50). Consequently, we conclude that the factual density measure can be applied for adequate assessment of the informativeness of textual content on the Web.

In future work, we plan to conduct similar experiments for other languages to analyze how language affects factual density estimation. Next, we are going to analyze how a text form of a document, i.e. lists, instructions, announcements, comments, news, etc., is related to its informativeness. We also want to consider how a topic of a text document and human annotator's personal interests might change his or her judgements about the informativeness of a document. For example, whether a person interested in sports would always choose sport-related articles as more informative. Another branch of our research is dedicated to the improvement of the fact extraction method and increase of the precision of the factual density estimation.

Acknowledgements

This work has been funded by the European Commission as part of the WIQ-EI project (project no. 269180) within the FP7 People Programme and Instituto Politécnico Nacional grant SIP 20131702 .

References

Almquist, E. and Lee, J. (2009). What do customers really want? `http://hbr.org/2009/04/what-do-customers-really-want/ar/1`. [last visited on 09/04/2013].

Banko, M., Cafarella, M. J., Soderland, S., Broadhead, M., and Etzioni, O. (2007). Open information extraction from the web. In *IN IJCAI*, pages 2670–2676.

Blumenstock, J. E. (2008). Size matters: word count as a measure of quality on wikipedia. In *Proceedings of the 17th international conference on World Wide Web*, WWW '08, pages 1095–1096, New York, NY, USA. ACM.

Dandapat, S., Sarkar, S., and Basu, A. (2007). Automatic part-of-speech tagging for bengali: an approach for morphologically rich languages in a poor resource scenario. In *Proceedings of the 45th Annual Meeting of the ACL on Interactive Poster and Demonstration Sessions*, ACL '07, pages 221–224, Stroudsburg, PA, USA. Association for Computational Linguistics.

Etzioni, O., Banko, M., Soderland, S., and Weld, D. S. (2008). Open information extraction from the web. *Commun. ACM*, 51(12):68–74.

Fader, A., Soderland, S., and Etzioni, O. (2011). Identifying relations for open information extraction. In *Proceedings of the Conference on Empirical Methods in Natural Language Processing*, EMNLP '11, pages 1535–1545, Stroudsburg, PA, USA. Association for Computational Linguistics.

Kirkpatrick, M. (2011). New 5 billion page web index with page rank now available for free from common crawl foundation. `http://readwrite.com/2011/11/07/common_crawl_foundation_announces_5_billion_page_w`. [last visited on 25/01/2013].

Kohlschütter, C., Fankhauser, P., and Nejdl, W. (2010). Boilerplate detection using shallow text features. In *Proceedings of the third ACM international conference on Web search and data mining*, WSDM '10, pages 441–450, New York, NY, USA. ACM.

Lex, E., Juffinger, A., and Granitzer, M. (2010). Objectivity classification in online media. In *Proceedings of the 21st ACM conference on Hypertext and hypermedia*, HT '10, pages 293–294, New York, NY, USA. ACM.

Lex, E., Voelske, M., Errecalde, M., Ferretti, E., Cagnina, L., Horn, C., Stein, B., and Granitzer, M. (2012). Measuring the quality of web content using factual information. In *Proceedings of the 2nd Joint WICOW/AIRWeb Workshop on Web Quality*, WebQuality '12, pages 7–10, New York, NY, USA. ACM.

Lipka, N. and Stein, B. (2010). Identifying featured articles in wikipedia: writing style matters. In *Proceedings of the 19th international conference on World wide web*, WWW '10, pages 1147–1148, New York, NY, USA. ACM.

Louviere, J. J. and Woodworth, G. (1991). Best-worst scaling: A model for the largest difference judgments. Technical report, University of Alberta.

Ma, J., Xiao, T., Zhu, J. B., and Ren, F. L. (2012). Easy-first chinese pos tagging and dependency parsing. In *COLING 2012, 24th International Conference on Computational Linguistics, Proceedings of the Conference: Technical Papers*, pages 1731–1746. Indian Institute of Technology Bombay.

Nakatani, S. (2011). Language detection library for java. `http://code.google.com/p/language-detection/`. [last visited on 25/01/2013].

Padró, L., Reese, S., Agirre, E., and Soroa, A. (2010). Semantic services in freeling 2.1: Wordnet and ukb. In Bhattacharyya, P., Fellbaum, C., and Vossen, P., editors, *Principles, Construction, and Application of Multilingual Wordnets*, pages 99–105, Mumbai, India. Global Wordnet Conference 2010, Narosa Publishing House.

Padró, L. and Stanilovsky, E. (2012). Freeling 3.0: Towards wider multilinguality. In Chair), N. C. C., Choukri, K., Declerck, T., Doğan, M. U., Maegaard, B., Mariani, J., Odijk, J., and Piperidis, S., editors, *Proceedings of the Eight International Conference on Language Resources and Evaluation (LREC'12)*, Istanbul, Turkey. European Language Resources Association (ELRA).

Weber, N., Schoefegger, K., Bimrose, J., Ley, T., Lindstaedt, S., Brown, A., and Barnes, S.-A. (2009). Knowledge maturing in the semantic mediawiki: A design study in career guidance. In *Proceedings of the 4th European Conference on Technology Enhanced Learning: Learning in the Synergy of Multiple Disciplines*, EC-TEL '09, pages 700–705, Berlin, Heidelberg. Springer-Verlag.

Wu, F. and Weld, D. S. (2010). Open information extraction using wikipedia. In *Proceedings of the 48th Annual Meeting of the Association for Computational Linguistics*, ACL '10, pages 118–127, Stroudsburg, PA, USA. Association for Computational Linguistics.

Zhila, A. and Gelbukh, A. (2013). Comparison of open information extraction for english and spanish. In *Accepted for Proceedings of the 19th International Computational Linguistics Conference Dialogue*, Dialogue 2013.

Using Topic Models in Content-Based News Recommender Systems

Tapio Luostarinen[1], Oskar Kohonen[2]

(1) Comtra Oy, Savonlinna, Finland
(2) Aalto University School of Science
Department of Information and Computer Science, Finland

`tapio.luostarinen@comtra.fi, oskar.kohonen@aalto.fi`

ABSTRACT

We study content-based recommendation of Finnish news in a system with a very small group of users. We compare three standard methods, Naïve Bayes (NB), K-Nearest Neighbor (kNN) Regression and Regulairized Linear Regression in a novel online simulation setting and in a cold-start simulation. We also apply Latent Dirichlet Allocation (LDA) on the large corpus of news and compare the learned features to those found by Singular Value Decomposition (SVD). Our results indicate that Naïve Bayes is the worst of the three models. K-Nearest Neighbor performs consistently well across input features. Regularized Linear Regression performs generally worse than kNN, but reaches similar performance as kNN with some features. Regularized Linear Regression gains statistically significant improvements over the word-features with LDA both on the full data set and in the cold-start simulation. In the cold-start simulation we find that LDA gives statistically significant improvements for all the methods.

KEYWORDS: Recommender Systems, Content-Based Recommendation, Topic Models, Latent Dirichlet Allocation, Cold-start.

1   Introduction

With online news it is possible to read a large amount of different news sources on a large array of topics, but since there are more articles available, finding interesting ones becomes more difficult, as reading even just every headline becomes cumbersome. Consequently automatic filtering with recommender systems, becomes attractive. We consider the specific problem of how to build a news recommender system to find interesting news within a specific language group, Finnish. We use content-based recommender systems, which is the less studied of the two main paradigms of recommender systems (Adomavicius and Tuzhilin, 2005). The main benefit of this content-based recommendation is that it allows others than large user communities and their parent companies to build recommender systems for any material they want to, also any niche content, be it by language, topic or anything else. By contrast, collaborative filtering requires a large user community, since it bases its recommendation on how similar users have rated the items. Another problem for news recommendation and collaborative filtering is that, even if there is a sufficient number of similar users, the items need to have been rated by at least some of these users, and in the case of news recommendation, it is the new items which are most interesting, and these are the ones least likely to have been rated. Because of this, news recommendation systems usually include content-based recommendation, where items are recommended to users based on a profile of what kind of content the user has liked in the past (Lang, 1995; Billsus and Pazzani, 2000).

Because our collected data is from a small community of users, we concentrate purely on content-based recommendation. We consider the case where users provide explicit ratings of how well they liked the content, rather than using the implicit feedback based on their reading behavior. We compare three standard methods, Naïve Bayes (NB), K-Nearest Neighbor Regression (kNN) and Regularized Linear Regression (Lin), which have all been suggested earlier in the literature, but no comparison seems to be available.

Since we have comparatively few ratings, but a large corpus of news, a natural extension is to apply unsupervised learning to the unrated news and discover features that reflect the statistical structure of news items. These discovered features can then be used to improve performance of the supervised recommender system. While this is a common approach in machine learning, it has not been applied to content-based recommender systems. We apply Latent Dirichlet Allocation (LDA) (Blei et al., 2003) and compare the learned features to those found by Latent Semantic Indexing (Deerwester, 1988).

To motivate a user to keep using a recommender system, it needs to provide recommendations already with very few rated items. This is known as the cold-start problem (see e.g. (Schein et al., 2002; Rashid et al., 2008)), and we study how the amount of ratings affects recommendation performance.

2   Related Work

Content-based news recommendation has been addressed in the literature by several authors. Lang (1995) describes a method combining nearest neighbors and linear regression, using a combination of TF-IDF features and features selected with Minimum Description Length (MDL). Billsus and Pazzani (2000) used a combination of Nearest Neighbor Classification and Naïve Bayes classification for explicit feedback in an interesting/not interesting classification. In contrast to this work, we use the methods as straightforward predictors, rather than in combinations, and we use a rating on the scale 1-5. Naïve Bayes has also been applied to content-based book recommendation (Mooney and Roy, 2000).

Topic models have not been used directly in content-based recommendation with explicit feedback, but with implicit feedback, a method similar to probabilistic Latent Semantic Indexing (Hofmann, 1999) has been applied by (Cleger-Tamayo et al., 2012). The topic model used is adapted to user behavior. We don't consider topic model adaptation, but rather use Latent Dirichlet Allocation (Blei et al., 2003) as an unsupervised feature extraction procedure. We argue, that while adaptation is likely to be useful for users with many rated items, lower dimensional features from topic models are most interesting in the cold-start situation when it is difficult for the methods to fit to a high-dimensional content vector.

Rashid et al. (2008) derive information theoretic strategies for how the first recommendations for a new users should be made. In our work, we will merely measure the cold-start performance of the methods, to assess how different methods work with very few rated items.

Recommender systems are increasingly seen as ranking problems, since we are trying to suggest the most relevant items to the user (see e.g. (Takács and Tikk, 2012)). However, the methods that we consider, reduce the recommendation problem to predicting the user ratings, since this allows simpler methods. We do agree that ranking performance is more important than prediction performance, and therefore we evaluate also ranking accuracy.

3 Methods

We implement the recommender systems separately for each user. For each user we have a training set of documents $d_i \in \mathcal{D}$ that the user has assigned ratings $r(d_i) \in \{1, 2, 3, 4, 5\}$. The documents are represented by feature vectors, where the feature set is denoted $\mathcal{V}$. We implement the recommender methods in two ways. Firstly, as a five class classification task, where the classes correspond to the ratings 1-5 or, secondly, as a regression task, where the rating is seen as a continuous value to be predicted. The former is used in combination with Naïve Bayes, and the latter with K-Nearest Neighbors and Regularized Linear Regression. The latter approach suffers from the problem that the method may assign scores outside the scale 1-5. This is however irrelevant when ranking documents.

3.1 Naïve Bayes classification

We implement the Naïve Bayes classifier following (McCallum and Nigam, 1998), where documents are modeled as sequences of samples drawn from a multinomial distribution of words, with as many independent draws as the number of words in the document, each class having its own multinomial distribution. Here, as the class represents the rating, we denote it r_j, where $j \in C = \{1, 2, 3, 4, 5\}$. The word probability parameters can then be calculated from the labeled data:

$$P(d_{i,k}|r_j; \hat{\theta}) = \frac{\sum_{i=1}^{|\mathcal{D}|} d_{i,k} P(r_j|d_i)}{\sum_{s=1}^{|\mathcal{V}|} \sum_{i=1}^{|\mathcal{D}|} d_{i,s} P(r_j|d_i)} \tag{1}$$

Here $d_{i,k}$ are the word counts in document d_i and $P(r_j|d_i)$ are known for the training data. While doing classification, we assign the rating to a new document d_{new} by finding find the most likely mixture component that could have generated the document, i.e. to find the mixture component r' that has the maximum a posteriori probability, which can be done by applying

Bayes' rule.

$$\hat{r}_{NB}(d_{new}) = \arg\max_{r' \in C} P(r_j|d) = \arg\max_{r_j \in C} \frac{P(r_j)P(d|r_j)}{P(d)} = \arg\max_{r_j \in C} P(r_j)P(d|r_j) \qquad (2)$$

3.2   Nearest Neighbor Regression

Nearest neighbor methods are very simple to implement and they can be used for both classification and regression. They simply store in memory all the training samples and the outcome for a new sample is based solely on the *nearest neighbor* or k nearest neighbors in the training set. The nearest neighbor is selected as the most similar sample:

$$d' = \arg\max_{d_i \in \mathscr{D}} sim(d_i, d_{new}) \qquad (3)$$

where $sim(d_i, d_j)$ is the similarity measure being used. The performance of the nearest neighbor methods depends significantly on the similarity measure. We used *cosine similarity* as the measure and it is defined as (Salton, 1989):

$$sim(d_i, d_j) = \cos(\alpha) = \frac{\sum_{k=1}^{|\mathscr{V}|}(d_{i,k}d_{j,k})}{\sqrt{\sum_{k=1}^{|\mathscr{V}|} d_{i,k}^2} \sqrt{\sum_{k=1}^{|\mathscr{V}|} d_{j,k}^2}} \qquad (4)$$

Let $d_j, j = 1, ..., k$ be the set of k nearest neighbors for the item d_{new}. We calculate the value for a new item as a weighted average of the k nearest neighbors (Billsus and Pazzani, 2000):

$$\hat{r}_{kNN}(d_{new}) = \frac{\sum_{j=1}^{k} r(d_j) \times sim(d_{new}, d_j)}{\sum_{j=1}^{k} sim(d_{new}, d_j)} \qquad (5)$$

3.3   Regularized Linear Regression

The basic idea of linear models is to find in some sense optimal coefficients β_k for each variable $d_{i,k}$ in the linear equations:

$$\hat{r}_{Lin}(d_i) = \beta_0 + \sum_{k=1}^{|\mathscr{V}|} \beta_k d_{i,k} \qquad (6)$$

The recommender system we are building should be able to present some recommendations even with just a few rated items, so we used a regularized least squares formulation, which can be applied with only a few samples. We used *elastic net*, a combination of *lasso* and *ridge* regressions. This model still minimizes the squared errors, but the coefficients are regularized by both L_1-norm and L_2-norm. The regularization part of the expression can be stated with a scale parameter λ and a linear weight parameter $\alpha \in [0,1]$ to select between L_1-norm and L_2-norm (Friedman et al., 2010):

$$\hat{\beta}^{elastic} = \arg\min \sum_{i=1}^{|\mathcal{D}|} \left[r(d_i) - (\beta_0 + \sum_{k=1}^{|\mathcal{V}|} \beta_k d_{i,k}) \right]^2 \tag{7}$$
$$+ \lambda \sum_{i=1}^{|\mathcal{D}|} \left[\frac{1}{2}(1-\alpha)\beta_k^2 + \alpha|\beta_k| \right]$$

Zou et al. (Zou and Hastie, 2005) have also shown that elastic net, in case of highly correlated variables, tends to select all of them at once or leave them all out at once. Studies have shown that this kind of grouping effect clearly improves the prediction accuracy of linear models compared to lasso when there are correlated variables.

3.4 Topic models

Latent Dirichlet Allocation (LDA) is a fully generative probabilistic topic model initially introduced by Blei et al. (Blei et al., 2003). It has been a widely applied method during the last few years and there are several implemented variants of it. LDA assumes that the documents are generated through the following process (Griffiths and Steyvers, 2004):

1. Generate topics by randomly choosing a word distribution $\phi_k \sim Dir(\beta)$ for each K topics

2. Choose a number of words for the document: $N \sim Poisson(\xi)$

3. Randomly choose a distribution of topics for the document $\theta \sim Dir(\alpha)$

4. For each N words in the document:

    (a) Randomly choose a topic index $z_n \sim Multinomial(\theta)$ to indicate from which topic the word w_n will be sampled

    (b) Randomly choose a word w_n by sampling a conditioned multinomial probability $P(w_n|z_n, \phi_{z_n})$

The distributions for the model parameters are very hard to compute directly, but different approximate inference algorithms, such as *variational inference* (Blei et al., 2003) or *Gibbs sampling* (Griffiths and Steyvers, 2004), solve the problem efficiently.

4 Experiments

The data we used in our experiments were gathered with a news aggregator during a 10 month period and during which, end users could read and rate the news on their own. The experiments were then conducted offline without user iteraction.

4.1 Data Set

The news content we used was gathered by the news aggregator by automatically reading RSS-feeds from Finnish online newspapers. The data from the feeds contains at least timestamp, link and title fields, but these were extended by parsing out the news content from the linked web pages using a java version of *Readability* [1]. If Readability failed to find the content, the text from the RSS-feed was used instead. In topic modeling we used all the pieces of news from the time span of stored ratings yielding a set of 592 886 news articles.

The aggregator made it possible for the registered users to assign ratings for the news articles on a scale from 1 to 5, where 5 means the user found it the most interesting. These ratings were used in the experiment to express user preferences. The aggregator has only a few active users and we selected from the database all users having more than 100 assigned ratings. There were 10 such users with a total of 10 401 ratings. The distribution of labels are shown in table 1.

4.2 Pre-processing

The preprocessing is illustrated in figure 1. The pieces of news were first concatenated into a single string with the title joined to the content, and then tokenized into words. Then morphological analysis was performed, using *OmorFi*[2], a morphological analyzer for Finnish (Lindén et al., 2011). If there were many possible lemmas, we used a simple heuristic to select one, by preferring part of speech in the following order: numeral, adjective, verb, noun, pronoun, adverb, conjunction, particle. When Omorfi recognized a word as a compound word, we used as features both the whole compound and the separate components, to reduce the sparsity of the data. This means, for example, that a compound word consisting of two components will be used as three features: the first component, the second component and their compound. After morphological analysis, we used a stop word list to remove the 100 most common words from the documents and also words occurring in only one document. This process left us 395 343 distinctive words. Then the documents were transformed into vectors of lemma counts. As Naïve Bayes requires this representation, these vectors were stored, but also their TF-IDF transformation was calculated.

4.3 Experiment Setup

We created a novel way of simulating the normal recommender system usage by predicting the ratings for previously unseen items in a stream fashion. First we took 20 articles from the beginning of a chronologically ordered list of ratings and used them as training samples for the model. After the training, the methods predict ratings for the next 20 items. After this, the reference ratings were then added to the training set for predicting the next batch of 20 ratings. This process was repeated separately for each user and until the end of the list was reached. This produced lists of predictions where each prediction was made using only ratings given before the one being predicted.

We could have used the simple division into training and evaluation sets, but that would not mimic the real situation as well. When a recommender system is implemented online, it faces a situation similar to the one described above. This is a way of simulating online evaluation in an offline environment.

---

[1] http://www.readability.com/
[2] http://www.ling.helsinki.fi/kieliteknologia/tutkimus/omor/ newest Java version as of 23 May 2011

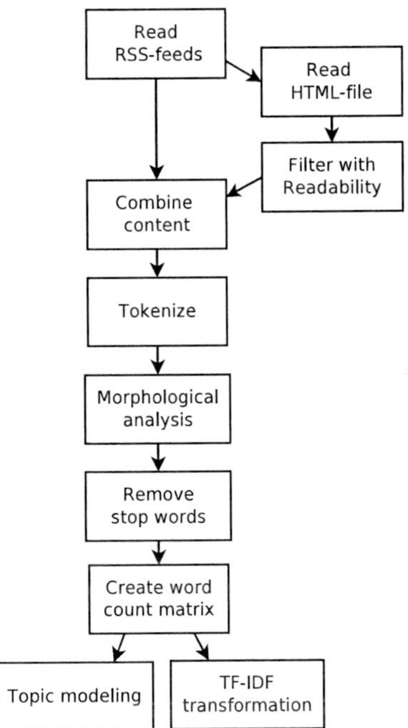

Figure 1: The data collection and preprocessing

User	Rating					Total
	1	2	3	4	5	
1	629	393	783	912	1174	3891
2	297	310	487	823	960	2877
3	521	638	322	519	187	2187
4	100	197	259	341	204	1101
5	54	84	107	162	147	554
6	33	69	81	100	44	327
7	16	8	90	82	77	273
8	30	20	37	18	41	146
9	3	13	35	48	20	119
10	1	3	27	29	45	105

Table 1: The rating distributions from each user.

We additionally simulated a simple cold-start situation where a new user starts to use the system. We reserved the first 150 rated samples from each user to be used in the training phase and the samples from indices 151 to 300 were used in the evaluation set. We evaluated the models with different sizes of training sets by using only part of the training set at each iteration. In other words, the evaluation set was kept fixed while the size of the training set was increased in steps of 5. Since only users 1,2,3,4,5 and 6 had enough rated samples, the rest of the users were excluded from this test.

The algorithms were trained on each training batch as explained above. For Naïve Bayes we used Laplace smoothing. Hyperparameters for K-Nearest Neighbors and Regularized Linear Regression were found by splitting each training batch in half into a training and test set. A grid search was then performed, and best parameters were, for K-Nearest Neighbors $k = 25$, and Regularized Linear Regression $\alpha = 0.2$ and $\lambda = 0.001$. The parameters were then reestimated for the full training batches with the selected hyperparameters. We also considered a random baseline recommender that assigns the mean of the ratings from the training set for all the evaluation items.

We computed four different topic models with LDA using *Matlab Topic Modeling Toolbox* (Griffiths and Steyvers, 2004) and standard parameters recommended in the toolbox documentation: $\alpha = 50/K, \beta = 200/|V|$. The models had 50, 100, 300 and 500 topics. When used as input data for recommender models, the distributions $\theta = P(z|d)$ were used as features. To assess how much the performance is affected by feature extraction and how much is due to lower input dimension, we also tested the recommendation methods using SVD as a dimensionality reduction method. Here the SVD is, in practice, the same as LSI (Deerwester, 1988). We projected the TF-IDF news data into three subspaces with 50, 100 and 300 dimensions or features. The subspace with 500 dimensions was left out, because of its computational requirements. Because the SVD produces continuous values in the subspace, we did not find any straightforward way to use them with the naïve Bayes method, and hence it was left out from the comparison.

We evaluated the recommender system by using two different evaluation metrics. As a prediction accuracy metric we used the *root mean squared error* (RMSE):

$$RMSE = \sqrt{\frac{1}{|\mathcal{D}|} \sum_{i \in \mathcal{D}} (r(d_i) - \hat{r}(d_i))^2} \tag{8}$$

In many cases it is not important to predict the actual ratings accurately, but rather ordering the items correctly. Also, some learning methods are not bound to give values in the same interval as the given ratings or do not necessarily use the interval efficiently, but they can still order the items accurately. To measure ranking performance we used the *normalized distance-based performance measure* (NDPM) (Yao, 1995). NDPM is suitable for measuring two weakly ordered rankings, because it will not penalize the system for placing two items in different order when the given ratings for these items are equal. It is calculated as a pairwise comparison of ratings and the value is the ratio of incorrectly ranked pairs and pairs that have a defined order. NDPM is defined as follows:

$$NDPM = \frac{2C^- + C^u}{2C} \tag{9}$$

Here C is the maximum distance of two rankings, that is to say the total number of pairs where the reference ranking defines an order. C^- is the number of incorrectly ordered pairs in system rankings and C^u is the number of pairs where the reference ranking defines an order but the system does not. The NDPM is bounded between 0 and 1, where 0 means the list is ordered perfectly and 1 means the list is ordered perfectly in reverse. When the ordering is completely wrong, the NDPM is about 0.5.

We performed the experiments with all the three methods described above and with word data and topic data. We ran the same test separately with each of the four topic models and compared the results with our baseline settings, which was with the same methods, but with word-based data.

The statistical significance of the results were estimated by using Wilcoxon signed-rank test (Wilcoxon, 1945). The results from each user were considered as samples and we used the significance level of 0.05. In the cold-start tests the significances were estimated when all the 150 training samples were used in training.

5   Results

The results for the full set are shown in Table 2. For the random baseline method, we can see average NDPM value very close to 0.5, the expected value for a random ranking. It can be seen that Naïve Bayes performs worse than the two other methods. Its RMSE is worse than the random baseline, but the NDPM is better, which implies that Naïve Bayes is performing very badly as a prediction algorithm, but is still ordering the items better than chance levels. We verified that Naïve Bayes assigns the majority rating to most items. For K-Nearest

Model	Features	Accuracy			Ranking		
		RMSE	*p-value*	*num*	*NDPM*	*p-value*	*num*
RANDOM	-	1.255			0.507		
NB	Words	1.430			0.413		
	LDA (50)	1.332	0.625	5/10	0.328	**0.006**	9/10
	LDA (100)	1.347	0.557	6/10	0.327	**0.004**	9/10
	LDA (300)	1.398	0.922	5/10	0.329	**0.002**	10/10
	LDA (500)	1.447	1.000	5/10	0.340	**0.027**	9/10
kNN 25	Words	1.087			0.307		
	LDA (50)	1.058	0.160	7/10	0.308	0.695	6/10
	LDA (100)	1.058	0.131	7/10	0.308	0.922	5/10
	LDA (300)	1.057	0.084	8/10	0.303	0.557	6/10
	LDA (500)	1.077	0.625	5/10	0.314	0.846	6/10
	SVD (50)	1.068	0.193	8/10	0.315	0.322	3/10
	SVD (100)	1.059	0.084	8/10	0.310	0.695	4/10
	SVD (300)	1.053	**0.006**	9/10	0.304	0.131	8/10
Lin	Words	1.160			0.360		
	LDA (50)	1.067	**0.037**	8/10	0.311	**0.014**	8/10
	LDA (100)	1.072	**0.048**	7/10	0.316	**0.006**	9/10
	LDA (300)	1.096	**0.006**	9/10	0.333	0.065	9/10
	LDA (500)	1.118	**0.027**	8/10	0.344	0.084	6/10
	SVD (50)	1.161	0.922	4/10	0.323	**0.037**	9/10
	SVD (100)	1.107	0.322	5/10	0.316	**0.027**	9/10
	SVD (300)	1.065	**0.006**	9/10	0.305	**0.002**	10/10

Table 2: Full data set performance results with random ordering (RANDOM), Naïve Bayes (NB), K-Nearest Neighbor with $k = 25$ (kNN 25) and Regularized Linear regression (Lin). The p-value column shows the result of a Wilcoxon signed-rank test compared to the *words* model and statistically significant results at 0.05 are emphasized, and the *num* column indicates for how many users the performance improved with a topic model

Neighbors we can see consistently good performance, which is not affected by topic-modeling or dimensionality reduction, as the small differences are not statistically significant. Regularized Linear Regression generally performs worse than kNN, except with LDA 50 and SVD 300, in which cases the results are very close to kNN. Surprisingly, for all algorithms, performance drops for LDA of higher dimension, sometimes starting at 100, sometimes at 500 features, while performance using SVD improves with higher dimension.

Figure 2 shows the cold-start performance for the different methods when increasing the amount of labeled data, and Table 3 shows the performance with 150 rated items. At this small amount of labeled data we can see that LDA50 gives statistically significant improvements for all methods and measures except Naïve Bayes and RMSE. We can see from figure 2, that LDA50 improves results already at much fewer than 150 ratings. At 10-20 ratings performance is better than the word-based model, being similar before that. For SVD and K-Nearest Neighbors we get improvements, but they are significant only at 300 features. In contrast, with Regularized Linear Regression SVD gives either statistically significant *reductions* in performance, or statistically insignificant improvements.

6   Discussion

The bad performance of Naïve Bayes may be partly due to our using the 1-5 rating as 5 separate classes, which leads to a higher number of parameters to estimate than for the other methods. Better performance may be achieved if the ratings were converted into a two-class interesting-uninteresting distinction, but doing so is not straightforward. The worse

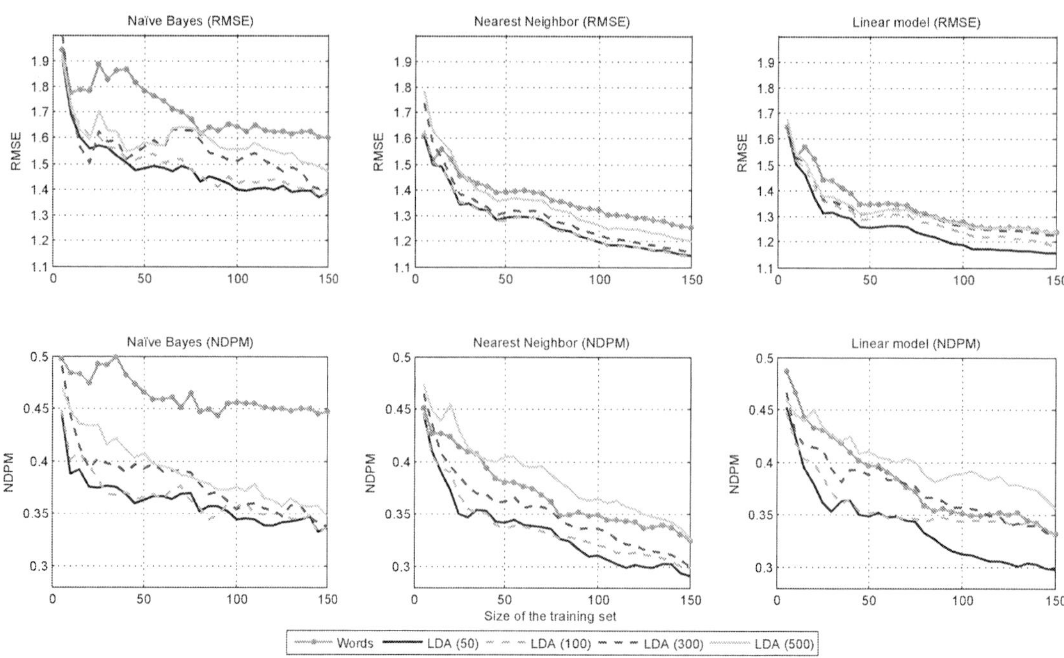

Figure 2: Performances of different methods in a simple cold-start situation. On each figure the results with LDA-models along with the results with word data are shown. The upper row shows the results with RMSE and the lower row with NDPM.

Model	Features	Accuracy			Ranking		
		RMSE	*p-value*	*num*	*NDPM*	*p-value*	*num*
NB	Words	1.602			0.448		
	LDA (50)	1.386	0.438	4/6	0.337	**0.031**	6/6
	LDA (100)	1.384	0.563	3/6	0.338	0.063	5/6
	LDA (300)	1.389	0.438	4/6	0.338	**0.031**	6/6
	LDA (500)	1.470	1.000	2/6	0.348	0.063	5/6
kNN 25	Words	1.257			0.325		
	LDA (50)	1.146	**0.031**	6/6	0.292	**0.031**	6/6
	LDA (100)	1.143	**0.031**	6/6	0.299	0.094	5/6
	LDA (300)	1.159	**0.031**	6/6	0.300	**0.031**	6/6
	LDA (500)	1.199	0.156	4/6	0.326	1.000	3/6
	SVD (50)	1.139	**0.031**	6/6	0.300	0.313	4/6
	SVD (100)	1.147	**0.031**	6/6	0.302	0.094	5/6
	SVD (300)	1.162	**0.031**	6/6	0.293	**0.031**	6/6
Lin	Words	1.239			0.332		
	LDA (50)	1.165	**0.031**	6/6	0.307	**0.031**	6/6
	LDA (100)	1.186	0.438	4/6	0.332	0.688	2/6
	LDA (300)	1.229	0.313	4/6	0.328	0.688	4/6
	LDA (500)	1.241	1.000	3/6	0.356	**0.031**	0/6
	SVD (50)	1.248	1.000	3/6	0.339	0.563	3/6
	SVD (100)	1.367	0.313	2/6	0.367	**0.031**	0/6
	SVD (300)	1.158	**0.031**	6/6	0.302	0.094	5/6

Table 3: Cold-start data set performance results for, Naïve Bayes (NB), K-Nearest Neighbor with $k = 25$ (kNN 25) and Regularizes Linear Regression (Lin). The p-value column shows the result of a Wilcoxon signed-rank test compared to the *words* model and statistically significant results at 0.05 are emphasized, and the *num* column indicates for how many users the performance improved with a topic model

performance of Regularized Linear Regression in the cold-start setting, may be because we adjust the hyperparameters for the full set. However, this can be seen as a weakness in the method, since it is very computationally demanding to optimize the hyperparameters for each data size (and user) separately. The Linear Regressor is very fast at recommendation time, requiring only one dot-product per user for each new item. The Nearest Neighbor method, in comparison, requires one dot-product calculation for each item the user has rated. However, when the number of ratings is small this is not a serious downside.

7   Conclusions

We evaluated three standard content-based recommender algorithms for a task of Finnish news recommendation. We used word counts, TF-IDF weighted word features both directly and after dimensionality reduction with SVD, and topics learned with Latent Dirichlet Allocation. We evaluated both a full data set where 10 users had 105–3891 labels each, and a cold-start data set where 6 users had 5–150 rated news items. We found that Naïve Bayes was the worst of the tested models, sometimes performing worse than a random baseline. Nearest Neighbors worked consistently well regardless of input features. Regularized Linear Regression performed well with some features, reaching similar performance as Nearest Neighbors on these features.

On the full data set LDA50 and SVD300 yielded statistically significant improvements over the word features for Regularized Linear Regression, but for the other methods the improvements were not statistically significant for both measures. In the cold start simulation, we found that LDA50 yielded statistically significant improvements over the word-features for all methods. The LDA models with more than 50 topics seem to perform increasingly worse with growing amounts of topics. In contrast SVD performance improves with growing dimension, but SVD50 is worse than LDA50. These results suggest that LDA can find good features with a smaller dimension than what SVD requires, however LDA performance seems to decrease with additional topics, which can be problematic. With the amount of rated samples we have in our experiments, applying Nearest Neighbor regression is preferrable over applying Regularized Linear regression for content-based recommendation, since Nearest Neighbors is more robust, and adjusting its hyperparameter k is easier than adjusting the regularization parameters of Regularized Linear Regression.

Acknowledgments

This paper is based on the Master's Thesis work of the first author. The second author was funded by the Academy of Finland project *Multimodally grounded language technology*. We are grateful to Erkki Oja for valuable comments during the work.

References

Adomavicius, G. and Tuzhilin, A. (2005). Toward the next generation of recommender systems: A survey of the state-of-the-art and possible extensions. *IEEE Transactions on Knowledge and Data Engineering*, 17(6):734–749.

Billsus, D. and Pazzani, M. J. (2000). User modeling for adaptive news access. *User Modeling and User-Adapted Interaction*, 10:147–180.

Blei, D. M., Ng, A. Y., and Jordan, M. I. (2003). Latent Dirichlet Allocation. *Journal of Machine Learning Research*, 3:993–1022.

Cleger-Tamayo, S., Fernández-Luna, J. M., and Huete, J. F. (2012). Top-n news recommendations in digital newspapers. *Knowledge-Based Systems*, 27(0):180 – 189.

Deerwester, S. (1988). Improving Information Retrieval with Latent Semantic Indexing. In Borgman, C. L. and Pai, E. Y. H., editors, *Proceedings of the 51st ASIS Annual Meeting (ASIS '88)*, volume 25, Atlanta, Georgia. American Society for Information Science.

Friedman, J. H., Hastie, T., and Tibshirani, R. (2010). Regularization paths for generalized linear models via coordinate descent. *Journal of Statistical Software*, 33(1):1–22.

Griffiths, T. L. and Steyvers, M. (2004). Finding scientific topics. *Proceedings of the National Academy of Sciences of the United States of America*, 101(Suppl 1):5228–5235.

Hoerl, A. E. and Kennard, R. W. (1970). Ridge Regression: Biased Estimation for Nonorthogonal Problems. *Technometrics*, 12(1):55–67.

Hofmann, T. (1999). Probabilistic latent semantic indexing. In *Proceedings of the 22nd annual international ACM SIGIR conference on Research and development in information retrieval*, SIGIR '99, pages 50–57, New York, NY, USA. ACM.

Lang, K. (1995). Newsweeder: Learning to filter netnews. In *Proceedings of the 12th International Machine Learning Conference (ML95*.

Lindén, K., Silfverberg, M., Axelson, E., Hardwick, S., and Pirinen, T. A. (2011). Hfst-framework for compiling and applying morphologies. In *Communications in Computer and Information Science*, volume 100 of *Systems and Frameworks for Computational Morphology*, pages 67–85. Springer.

McCallum, A. and Nigam, K. (1998). A comparison of event models for naive bayes text classification. In *AAAI-98 Workshop on Learning for Text Categorization*, pages 41–48. AAAI Press.

Mooney, R. J. and Roy, L. (2000). Content-based book recommending using learning for text categorization. In *Proceedings of the Fifth ACM Conference on Digital Libraries*, pages 195–204. ACM Press.

Rashid, A. M., Karypis, G., and Riedl, J. (2008). Learning preferences of new users in recommender systems: an information theoretic approach. *SIGKDD Explor. Newsl.*, 10(2):90–100.

Salton, G. (1989). *Automatic text processing: the transformation, analysis, and retrieval of information by computer*. Addison-Wesley Longman Publishing Co., Inc., Boston, MA, USA.

Schein, A. I., Popescul, A., Ungar, L. H., and Pennock, D. M. (2002). Methods and metrics for cold-start recommendations. In *Proceedings of the 25th annual international ACM SIGIR conference on Research and development in information retrieval*, SIGIR '02, pages 253–260, New York, NY, USA. ACM.

Takács, G. and Tikk, D. (2012). Alternating least squares for personalized ranking. In *Proceedings of the sixth ACM conference on Recommender systems*, RecSys '12, pages 83–90, New York, NY, USA. ACM.

Wilcoxon, F. (1945). Individual Comparisons by Ranking Methods. *Biometrics Bulletin*, 1(6):80–83.

Yao, Y. Y. (1995). Measuring retrieval effectiveness based on user preference of documents. *J. Am. Soc. Inf. Sci.*, 46(2):133–145.

Zou, H. and Hastie, T. (2005). Regularization and variable selection via the Elastic Net. *Journal of the Royal Statistical Society B*, 67:301–320.

Bootstrapping an Unsupervised Approach for Classifying Agreement and Disagreement

Bernd Opitz, Cäcilia Zirn

University of Mannheim

`jopitz@mail.uni-mannheim.de`, `caecilia@informatik.uni-mannheim.de`

ABSTRACT

People tend to have various opinions about topics. In discussions, they can either agree or disagree with another person. The recognition of agreement and disagreement is a useful prerequisite for many applications. It could be used by political scientists to measure how controversial political issues are, or help a company to analyze how well people like their new products. In this work, we develop an approach for recognizing agreement and disagreement. However, this is a challenging task. While keyword-based approaches are only able to cover a limited set of phrases, machine learning approaches require a large amount of training data. We therefore combine advantages of both methods by using a bootstrapping approach. With our completely unsupervised technique, we achieve an accuracy of 72.85%. Besides, we investigate the limitations of a keyword based approach and a machine learning approach in addition to comparing various sets of features.

KEYWORDS: Text Classification, Agreement, Disagreement, Opinion Mining.

1 Introduction

It is commonly known that humans do not always agree with each other. Where people disagree, discussions emerge. Discussions are an important manner of communication. For many purposes such as analyses in political sciences, it is relevant to have knowledge about agreement and disagreement. For instance, by measuring the degree of disagreement in ongoing discussions it can be compared how controversial different political issues are. To give another example, detecting heated discussions in online conversations could signal the need for a moderator or mediator to get involved. Knowledge about agreement and disagreement might further be useful for identifying groups that support or oppose a given opinion. In the context of business meetings, it might help to identify decisions and controversy. Furthermore, detecting agreement and disagreement helps understanding social dynamics (Hillard et al., 2003) and can generally aid summarizing conversations or discussions (Janin et al., 2003).

We intend to develop a method to recognize agreement and disagreement (referred to as A/D from now on) automatically, which turns out to be a challenging task. The most intuitive approach might be to watch out for indicating phrases like "I disagree" or "that's wrong". We compiled lists of expressions for both agreement and disagreement based on existing research and classified text snippets based on their occurrences. While this simple approach achieves a high precision, it is not able to make informed choices on how to classify instances that either do not contain any key phrase or even contain indicators for both classes. Another straightforward approach is using machine learning. While this works quite well, the drawback of this approach is that it requires a large amount of manually annotated training data. In order to work around these problems we developed a bootstrapping approach combining the advantages of both previous approaches, which is the main contribution of this paper. In the bootstrapping approach, we first classify a part of the data set by using keywords only. We then take these classified instances as the training data for machine learning and classify the remaining instances with the resulting classifier. For comparison, we describe and evaluate keyword based and machine learning approaches as well.

2 Related Work

Detection of A/D is quite a new research field and as such there is only limited work about it. However, the interest seems to increase, as most of the publications we are aware of were published in 2012.

The research of (Galley et al., 2004) is very close to our work. They applied machine learning techniques, more precisely Bayesian Networks, to the ICSI Meeting corpus (Janin et al., 2003), a collection of human-to-human multi-party conversations, with the preliminary goal of identifying A/D. To do so they used a wide-ranging set of global contextual features as well as local features consisting of structural, durational and lexical features. Among the lexical features, they used positive and negative polarity adjectives as known from sentiment analysis. Their approach achieved an accuracy of 86.9%. Adjectives expressing polarity are commonly used for sentiment analysis, as in the research of (Fahrni and Klenner, 2008) and (Moghaddam and Popowich, 2010). Moghaddam et al. made use of adjective polarity to classify the opinion expressed in a product review as positive, negative or neutral. Their approach reached an accuracy of 73% and thus outperforms Naïve Bayes classifiers which usually achieve accuracies of 58-64% in the same area.

Consistent with the insights outlined in the papers listed above, (Hillard et al., 2003) and (Galley et al., 2004) state that "lexical information make the most helpful local features", so these were also applied in analyses for our work. A wide range of the features we used, especially discourse markers and repeated punctuation, were chosen based on the findings in (Abbott et al., 2011). In their work they made use of word-based features, among others, to analyze online dialogic discussions concerning subjects such as politics, society or religion in an attempt to recognize A/D. Their approach was carried out using two different Machine Learning algorithms, namely the NaiveBayes and JRip implementations in the Weka toolkit. The success of their approach was an accuracy of 68% which is 5% higher than a simple unigram baseline.

(Yin et al., 2012) analyze online discussions for agreement and disagreement using machine learning methods, among them SVMs which perform quite well. The features they use are similar to our, in so far that they too use e.g. sentiment, emotional and durational features. These features include keywords such as discourse markers as well as occurrences of special characters such as question or exclamation marks, the sentiment polarity of posts, the length of a post and foul words. They developed a multistage process for agreement and disagreement detection, which first decides whether two posts in a discussion agree or disagree with each other. In the second step, these results are aggregated and then in the third step the position towards the initial post in the discussion is determined as the "global" position. The experiments were carried out on two corpora and in the best case achieved an accuracy of 64% and an F-measure of 77%.

(Mukherjee and Liu, 2012) analyze product reviews and comments on them. Agreement and disagreement detection plays a role in their analyses because reviews that people agree with may be more useful than those that a lot of people disagree with. One reason for that is that fake reviews may receive a lot of disagreeing responses as fake reviews are often authored by people who are not users of the product which commenters (as actual users) can usually detect.

Besides approaches to automatically identify agreement and disagreement, new corpora with manual agreement/disagreement annotations were released. (Walker et al., 2012) extracted discussions from 4forums.com and annotate the topic of the discussion as well as agreement of the posts including additional information about the type of agreement (e.g. sarcasm) and its degree. (Andreas et al., 2012) contains data of livejournal blogs and Wikipedia discussion forums. Maintaining the discussion thread structure, they annotate agreement and disagreement and the mode, i.e. either a direct/indirect response or a direct/indirect paraphrase.

3   Agreement and Disagreement

Agreement and disagreement as commonly understood can occur in various forms. Generally, agreement is defined as "harmony of opinion, action, or character" (Merriam-Webster.com, 2012a) whereas disagreement is defined as "the state of being at variance" (Merriam-Webster.com, 2012b). In a wider sense, agreement or disagreement are also present if a person positively respectively negatively refers to another person's statement. Beyond that, agreement and disagreement can either be direct or indirect. Direct agreement or disagreement is present if a speaker explicitly aligns with one or more other speakers (see Example 1 and Example 2).

Example 1: Example of explicit and direct positive alignment.
"I agree.", "Great idea", "As you mentioned earlier"

Indirect alignment, such as a shared or contradictory opinion between two speakers can be

Example 2: Example of explicit and direct negative alignment.
"That's wrong.", "That's questionable." , "That's a terrible idea."

seen in Example 3 and Example 4.

Example 3: Example of indirect alignment move: shared opinion.
Speaker1: *I think we should elect John Kerry.*
Speaker2: *John Kerry should be elected as President of the United States.*

*Example 4: Example of indirect alignment move: Contradicting opinion (disagreement that should
not be coded).*
Speaker1: *So you don't think we should use the [. . .] Iraqi government casualty number in this
section?*
Speaker2: *The number doesn't come from the Iraqi government, it comes from the LA Times.*

In this work, we restrict our experiments to recognizing direct and explicit A/D only, as the corpus we are using is limited to these annotations.

3.1   Classifying Agreement and Disagreement

Our goal was to come up with an approach for identifying A/D that is independent of manually annotated training data, yet able to identify sentences that do not contain an explicit, predefined keyword. We hypothesized that classification based on keywords only would yield a high precision but low recall, i.e. that it would be able to correctly classify instances containing keywords, but failing to classify any of the others. We will show later that this intuition turned out to be true (see subsection 4.4). A machine learning approach, on the other hand, requires a large amount of training data, which is time and labor intensive to create. We therefore developed a bootstrapping approach combining the keyword approach with machine learning. In brief, the idea is the following: First, we pick those sentences from a corpus that contain predefined key expressions that indicate either agreement or disagreement and classify them accordingly. We then use the result as training data for a machine learning approach.

For the first part of the bootstrapping approach, the keyword based labeling process, we begin by collecting keywords that indicate utterances of agreement and disagreement. In the following, by keyword we refer to single terms as well as expressions or phrases consisting of more than one word,, e.g. "conversely" and "on the contrary". We then check the instances within the data set for the occurrence of those keywords. The range of an instance, i.e. the unit that is classified, depends on the data set, it could be defined as a sentence or a coherent sequence of sentences that comprise a complete utterance of a speaker. In our case, an instance consists of a speaker's turn, which will be described in detail in subsection 4.1. If the instance contains more keywords for agreement, we label it as agreement; in case we find more keywords for disagreement, we label it as disagreement. For a more precise classification, we also consider negations. A negation is an expression that negates the meaning of a phrase. We consider keywords directly following a negation as an indicator for the opposite label. If an instance contains an even number of cues for agreement and disagreement or if it does not contain any keywords at all, it is not labeled in this step. It is important to point out that neither the handling of negations nor the classification based on the key expressions for the instances are necessarily correct.

However, as we will show later in Table 1, the precision of this simple classifier achieves over 61% for Agreement and over 90% for Disagreement.

The resulting annotations derived by this keyword based approach will be used as training data for machine learning. The remaining part of the corpus that could not be classified in the first step - either because it did not contain any keywords or because it contained an equal number of agreeing and disagreeing keywords - will then be classified by trained the machine learning classifier. The features we used for machine learning are described below in 4.2.

After these two steps, all instances are classified as either Agreement or Disagreement. The salient advantage of this approach is that it does not require any manual annotations and thus represents an unsupervised approach. To evaluate the potential of this approach while discovering its limitations, we compared it to two different baselines. On the one hand, we will evaluate the results of using the keyword-based approach only. On the other hand, we explore the performance of a standard machine learning scenario training on manually annotated labels. Furthermore, we will experiment with different combination of features to find out how helpful they are for the classification task of distinguishing between agreement and disagreement.

4   Evaluation

In the following, we will explain how we evaluate the different approaches for classifying agreement and disagreement and which features we use. Furthermore, we describe the data in more detail.

4.1   Corpus

For the experiments in this work we used the Authority and Alignment in Wikipedia Discussions (AAWD) corpus by (Bender et al., 2011), which is a set of 365 discussions taken from 47 Wikipedia talk pages. The corpus contains annotations for alignment and authority claims by three independent annotators and is available in multiple versions and languages. Experiments are solely based on the merged alignment annotations – i.e. the combination of the three annotators – from the English version. From this corpus, we take 3390 turns from 211 discussions that are annotated for alignment moves. Out of these 3390 instances, we take all the sentences that have been annotated for either agreement or disagreement but not both. This leaves us with 2302 sentences out of which 478 (roughly 21%) are annotated for agreement, the remaining 1824 sentences are labeled as disagreement. All data files of the corpus are supplied in extended tab-delimited format (xtdf).

4.2   Features

To distinguish between agreement and disagreement, we use various features that we selected based on findings in existing research. All features' values were calculated at the level of turns, where a turn is defined as a "contiguous body of text on the [. . .] page that was modified as part of a single revision" (Bender et al., 2011).

1. *Keywords:* Based on the findings of related work(Schourup, 1999; Anand et al., 2011)), we made use of specific keywords to identify A/D. They serve as well for the keyword based approach as for the machine learning. We compiled separate keyword lists for different types of keywords. The keywords were collected by introspection and looking at related work as well as the annotation guidelines of the corpus. It must be noted that

expressions taken from the corpus itself would weaken the generality of our approach. For that reason, we included only few expression from the annotation guidelines of the corpus and only those, which we considered sufficiently generic.

As an indicator for agreement, we created distinctive lists:

- positive adjectives, such as "excellent" or "perfect"
- positive alignment cues, such as "i agree" or "that's right" (Ali, 2011)
- positive discourse markers, such as "I think" or "I know" (Abbott et al., 2011)
- various additional agreement keywords, such as "agreement"

For disagreement, we compiled the following lists:

- negative adjectives, such as "questionable" or "unsatisfactory"
- negative alignment cues, such as "i doubt that" or "that's irrelevant" (Ali, 2011)
- negative discourse markers, such as "actually" or "but" (Abbott et al., 2011)
- insults/swear words, such as "idiot" or "narrow-minded"
- various additional disagreement keywords, such as "disagreement"

For the machine learning approaches, we consider each of these lists as one separate feature. If a term of the particular list is located in the text, the value of the feature is increased by one. Please note that regarding the machine learning, we do not explicitly connote the lists with agreement or disagreement, but the algorithm is supposed to learn from the training data which label is indicated by a particular list. In subsection 4.3, we will give more details about how we use the lists for the keyword based approach.

2. *Unigrams:* Most common in text analysis, the unigrams of the text - i.e. its words - are used as features modeling a bag of words approach.

3. *Word count:* For this feature, the total amount of words in a turn is counted. According to (Cohen, 2002), disagreeing statements are usually longer than agreeing statements.

4. *Pronouns:* The hypothesis is that there is a difference in the amount of usage in agreement and disagreement. This is supported by (Anand et al., 2011) , who found that pronouns such as you occurred more frequently in rebuttals. We treat them as distinct features.

5. *Negations:* In general, negations describe the concept of reversing the value of a statement. For instance, "This is not true" obviously is the opposite of "This is true". As for disagreement, people tend to negate the utterances of the previous speaker, we expect them to contain a higher amount of negations. For the experiments, we collect various keywords for negations and use the sum of their negations as one feature.

6. *Special characters:* We counted special characters such as ? ! , . ; - _ each individually, resulting in 7 distinct features.

7. *Repeated punctuation:* Repeated punctuation such as !! has a different meaning than simple punctuation (Abbott et al., 2011). For example, if a person questions the utterance of a previous speaker, he might indicate this by using "?!" marking a rhetorical question. We implement the repeated punctuation feature by counting occurrences of more than one question or exclamation mark in a row, i.e. any combination of question and exclamation marks.

8. *Formatting:* Participants of written discussions tend to highlight certain points, such as the strong points of their argument, using markup text to draw special attention to it. It can be compared to raising the voice or emphasizing something using intonation in spoken language. We capture this by counting the number of formatting instructions for **bold** and *italic* markup each as an individual feature.

4.3   Experiments

As mentioned before, we compare our bootstrapping approach to straightforward baseline approaches. In each case, the entities that we classify - thus the instances - consist of a speaker's turn as described in subsection 4.1. More precisely, we compare the following approaches:

1. Keywords baseline:
   Keyword-based classification for a single instance works as follows: We first initialize a score with 0. For each occurrence of a keyword indicating agreement, we add 1. For each occurrence of a keyword for disagreement, we subtract 1. For a more precise classification, we also consider negations, utilizing the same list we described in subsection 4.2: If a negation, i.e. a keyword from the list of negations directly precedes an agreement keyword, instead of adding 1 to the score, 1 is subtracted. The same applies analogously for negated keywords for disagreement. If the final score is greater than 0, the instance is considered to be agreement, if it is less than 0 it is considered to be disagreement. A score of 0 indicates that this instance cannot be classified which may have two reasons: either no keyword at all occurred in the instance or the amount of keywords for agreement and disagreement was even. Therefore, we calculate the performance of the keyword baseline in two ways:

   - *Containing keywords:* We regard those instances only that could be classified and calculate precision and recall relative to this number.
   - *Whole dataset:* We calculate precision and recall for the whole dataset. Instances that have a score of 0 are regarded as misclassified for agreement as well as for disagreement.

2. Machine learning baseline
   For the machine learning, we extract all features described in subsection 4.2 for each instance. We compare different combinations of those features.

   - *Unigrams:* To explore how efficient this task can be solved using a bag-of-words approach, we consider unigrams only.
   - *Others:* In this scenario, all features except for unigrams are used.
   - *Unigrams + others:* Finally, all features are used. We want to point out that there might be an overlap between some of the features, concerning unigrams, keywords, pronouns and the number of negations.

   Please note: For machine learning we only use the number of negation keywords and do not consider their effect on any other features.

3. Bootstrapping:
   The bootstrapping approach is implemented as described in 3.1. We first apply the

keyword approach to the data. In a second step, we train an SVM on the data that could be classified, and use the trained SVM to classify the data that had not been assigned a class by the keyword approach. As for the machine learning baseline, we compare the three combination of features:

- *Unigrams*

- *Others*

- *Unigrams + others*

For each of these three configurations, we separately calculate the performance for the instances that were classified in the second step, i.e. by the SVM. In contrast to the baseline, we do not apply cross-validation in the Bootstrapping approaches. The reason for that is this is that the number of seeds is already quite low and cross-validating would provide an even lower number of training instances for each run.

4. Bootstrapping upper bound:
   For better comparison of the bootstrapping approach, we evaluate its upper bound: If the label assigned by the keyword approach is wrong, we correct it for those instances. In this way, we can evaluate how the performance of the bootstrapping approach is influenced by the mistakes of the keyword approach.

All machine learning experiments were conducted using the tool Weka[1]. We used the SMO implementation of a Support Vector Machine (SVM) which is available in Weka and evaluated its performance using 10-fold cross-validation with stratified sampling.

4.4   Results

Table 1 shows the results for the keyword baseline. Out of 2302 instances, only 954 could be classified (41% of the data). However, 80.29% of these classifications were correct. As can be seen in the first line of the table ("containing keywords"), the approach achieves good results for both classes with an F-measure of 68.49% for agreement and 85.67% for disagreement. It even achieves a precision of 90.50% for disagreement. Due to the fact that more than half of the data was not classified at all, however, the performance for the whole corpus is rather low, with an F-measure of 20.99% and 42.26% respectively. As the input data was unbalanced, the following tables always show measures for two cases: the Agreement part shows the measures under the assumption that agreement was considered the positive class and disagreement was considered the negative class, analogously for the Disagreement part.

Keyword baseline						
	Agreement			Disagreement		
	P	**R**	**F$_1$**	**P**	**R**	**F$_1$**
containing keywords	61.26	77.57	**68.46**	**90.50**	81.33	**85.67**
whole dataset	13.92	42.68	20.99	67.22	30.81	42.26

Table 1: **Precision**, **Recall** and **F**-Measure for the keyword based approach.

---

[1]`http://www.cs.waikato.ac.nz/ml/weka/`

Machine learning baseline						
	Agreement			Disagreement		
	P	**R**	**F$_1$**	**P**	**R**	**F$_1$**
unigrams	64.19	52.51	57.77	88.12	92.32	90.17
others	74.16	32.43	45.12	84.57	97.04	90.38
unigrams + others	66.92	56.28	**61.14**	89.00	92.71	**90.82**

Table 2: **Precision**, **Recall** and **F**-Measure for the machine learning approach.

The machine learning baseline surprised with comparably high results (table 2). Among the three combinations of features, the best result was achieved using all features (unigrams + others). Especially for the classification of disagreement, it shows excellent results with precision, recall and F-measure around 90%. For agreement, due to a low recall of 56.28%, it results in an F-measure of 61.14%, which is still significantly better than the keyword baseline on the complete data set. We assume that the reason for the higher results in the class of disagreement is caused by the imbalanced data set of which about 80% of the instances are labeled as disagreement. Comparing the three feature combinations, it is interesting to see that for disagreement, both the unigrams and the other features alone achieve good results. For agreement, which seems to be more difficult to classify, they supplement each other and their combination boosts the results.

Bootstrapping						
	Agreement			Disagreement		
	P	**R**	**F$_1$**	**P**	**R**	**F$_1$**
whole dataset	43.40	52.30	**47.44**	86.79	82.13	**84.39**
(2. step)	18.93	21.40	20.09	84.76	82.61	83.65
Bootstrapping - upper bound						
(2. step)	37.84	19.53	**25.77**	86.01	93.91	**89.79**

Table 3: Precision, Recall and **F**-Measure for the bootstrapping approach using all features. (2. step) gives the results for the subset of the data that was labeled in the second step, i.e. by the SVM trained on the data labeled by keywords.

The bootstrapping approach was performed using the same sets of features for the machine learning part as for the machine learning baseline. Again the combination of all features showed better results than using unigrams and the other features separately, we therefore omit the latter ones in the table for better readability. The results are shown in table 3. For the whole data set, the bootstrapping approach yielded in an accuracy of 72.85% with an F-measure of 47.44% for agreement and 84.39% for disagreement. As expected, the results are not as high as the machine learning baseline, but one has to keep in mind the fact that this approach is completely unsupervised and does not require any labeled data. To explore whether the correct classifications are mainly due to the labeling process in the first step, namely the keyword based approach, and to get a better insight in the performance of the classifier that was trained on the automatically acquired training data, we separately measure the correctness of the instances labeled in the second step. We find that the results for disagreement are quite high (precision and recall both above 80%), but very low for agreement (precision and recall around 20%).

This might be partly caused by the fact that the data set that is labeled in the second step contains only 215 instances of agreement in contrast to 1133 instances of disagreement.

Given that the machine learning approach itself does not seem to be inefficient, as demonstrated by the baseline, we further investigated whether the performance of the trained classifier in the bootstrapping approach suffers from the misclassifications of the keyword based approach in the first step, or whether some of the agreement instances are just very difficult to be classified at all. This gives us an upper bound for the bootstrapping approach on the data set. For this experiment, we correct all misclassifications produced by the keyword approach in the first step and train the classifier on the true labels. The results are displayed in the last row of table 3. Although the performance is increased, it still achieves an F-measure of 25.77% only for classifying agreement.

4.5 Error Analysis

We analyze some of the misclassified instances to figure out the problems of the particular approaches. The following list shows some examples of misclassified instances. We come up with explanations for the errors, though it cannot always be determined with certainty.

- *Keyword*: Good luck putting your pov [point of view] in the article.
  This instance is misinterpreted as Agreement due to the occurrence of the word "good". The obvious deficiency of the keyword approach is its inability to detect irony.

- *Bootstrapping(others)*:

    - It's obvious and disgusting POV. → 6 words, 1 period

    - I actually agree to an extent, in that at an article addressing past powerful Hurricanes that have struck the U.S. could be relevant for perspective. → 26 words, 1 negative discourse marker, 1 other positive keyword, 3 periods, 1 comma, 1 "I"

  The first instance is misclassified as agreement which seems to be due to a lack of useful information. Note that this instance also shows that the lists of adjectives used are far from complete. The second instance is misclassified as disagreement which may be due to the negative discourse marker, word count and punctuation, which the model may have trained to be connected with disagreement.

- *Bootstrapping(unigrams + others)*: Your edit is cool with me., 6 words, 1 period
  This instance is misclassified as disagreement. The same instance is also misclassified by the bootstrapping approach using unigrams. What is surprising, is that bootstrapping using all features except for unigrams would label this instance as agreement (since its non-unigram properties are: 6 words, 1 period).

These examples show that the combination of all features fixes some misclassifications but also introduces errors. Thus, finding the right feature set is a balancing act.

5 Conclusion and Future Work

In a supervised scenario, we were able to achieve F-measures of 61.14% for classifying agreement and 84.39% for disagreement. Combining a keyword based approach with machine learning, we implemented a completely unsupervised approach that is able to classify agreement and disagreement with an accuracy of 72.85%, achieving an F-measure of 47.44% and 84.39% for the particular classes. In all experiments, we merely used local features, i.e. only features that were extracted from the particular text unit that is assigned a label. Our experiments show that while unigrams alone already seem to be able to distinguish between agreement and disagreement statements, features like the length of an utterance, punctuation or information about negations add to their performance. We see types of additional information that might further improve the classification of agreement and disagreement. As shown in (Galley et al., 2004), knowledge about the context could be included by extracting information about surrounding pieces of the discussion, especially the utterances of previous speakers. On the other hand, external sources could be used to derive knowledge about opposing opinions for a topic. Furthermore, we assume that methods for detecting sarcasm and irony would increase the performance of this task. Up to this point, we only considered explicit agreement and disagreement. In the future, we also plan to investigate the limitations of recognizing implicit agreement and disagreement. Another point for potential improvement is the way the Bootstrapping approach was applied. In our experiments we did not modify the classifier once it was trained. One could carry out classification iteratively, i.e. carry out classify instances based on previous classifications.

References

(2011). Alignment annotation guidelines (version 14). [Online; accessed 05 March 2012].

Abbott, R., Walker, M., Anand, P., Fox Tree, J. E., Bowmani, R., and King, J. (2011). How can you say such things?!?: Recognizing disagreement in informal political argument. In *Proceedings of the Workshop on Language in Social Media (LSM 2011)*, pages 2–11, Portland, Oregon. Association for Computational Linguistics.

Anand, P., Walker, M., Abbott, R., Fox Tree, J. E., Bowmani, R., and Minor, M. (2011). Cats rule and dogs drool!: Classifying stance in online debate. In *Proceedings of the 2nd Workshop on Computational Approaches to Subjectivity and Sentiment Analysis (WASSA 2.011)*, pages 1–9, Portland, Oregon. Association for Computational Linguistics.

Andreas, J., Rosenthal, S., and McKeown, K. (2012). Annotating agreement and disagreement in threaded discussion. In *Proceedings of the 8th International Conference on Language Resources and Computation (LREC), Istanbul, Turkey, May*.

Bender, E. M., Morgan, J. T., Oxley, M., Zachry, M., Hutchinson, B., Marin, A., Zhang, B., and Ostendorf, M. (2011). Annotating social acts: Authority claims and alignment moves in wikipedia talk pages. In *Proceedings of the Workshop on Language in Social Media (LSM 2011)*, pages 48–57, Portland, Oregon. Association for Computational Linguistics.

Cohen, S. (2002). A computerized scale for monitoring levels of agreement during a conversation. In *Proc. of the 26th Penn Linguistics Colloquium*.

Fahrni, A. and Klenner, M. (2008). Old wine or warm beer: Target-specific sentiment analysis of adjectives. In *Proc. of the Symposium on Affective Language in Human and Machine, AISB*, pages 60–63.

Galley, M., McKeown, K., Hirschberg, J., and Shriberg, E. (2004). Identifying agreement and disagreement in conversational speech: use of bayesian networks to model pragmatic dependencies. In *Proceedings of the 42nd Annual Meeting on Association for Computational Linguistics*, ACL '04, Stroudsburg, PA, USA. Association for Computational Linguistics.

Hillard, D., Ostendorf, M., and Shriberg, E. (2003). Detection of agreement vs. disagreement in meetings: training with unlabeled data. In *Proceedings of the 2003 Conference of the North American Chapter of the Association for Computational Linguistics on Human Language Technology: companion volume of the Proceedings of HLT-NAACL 2003–short papers - Volume 2*, NAACL-Short '03, pages 34–36, Stroudsburg, PA, USA. Association for Computational Linguistics.

Janin, A., Baron, D., Edwards, J., Ellis, D., Gelbart, D., Morgan, N., Peskin, B., Pfau, T., Shriberg, E., Stolcke, A., et al. (2003). The icsi meeting corpus. In *Acoustics, Speech, and Signal Processing, 2003. Proceedings.(ICASSP'03). 2003 IEEE International Conference on*, volume 1, pages I–364. IEEE.

Merriam-Webster.com (2012a). "agreement". [Online; accessed 6 April 2012].

Merriam-Webster.com (2012b). "disagreement". [Online; accessed 6 April 2012].

Moghaddam, S. and Popowich, F. (2010). Opinion polarity identification through adjectives. *CoRR*, abs/1011.4623.

Mukherjee, A. and Liu, B. (2012). Modeling review comments. In *Proceedings of the 50th Annual Meeting of the Association for Computational Linguistics: Long Papers - Volume 1*, ACL '12, pages 320–329, Stroudsburg, PA, USA. Association for Computational Linguistics.

Schourup, L. (1999). Discourse markers. *Lingua*, 107(3-4):227 – 265.

Walker, M., Anand, P., Tree, J. F., Abbott, R., and King, J. (2012). A corpus for research on deliberation and debate. In *Proceedings of the Eighth International Conference on Language Resources and Evaluation, LREC*, pages 23–25.

Yin, J., Thomas, P., Narang, N., and Paris, C. (2012). Unifying local and global agreement and disagreement classification in online debates. In *Proceedings of the 3rd Workshop in Computational Approaches to Subjectivity and Sentiment Analysis*, WASSA '12, pages 61–69, Stroudsburg, PA, USA. Association for Computational Linguistics.

Morphological analysis with limited resources:
Latvian example

Pēteris PAIKENS, Laura RITUMA, Lauma PRETKALNIŅA
University of Latvia, Institute of Mathematics and Computer Science
`peteris@ailab.lv, laura@ailab.lv, lauma@ailab.lv`

ABSTRACT

We describe an approach for morphological analysis combining a rule-based word level morphological analyzer with statistical tagging, detailing its application to Latvian language. Latvian is a highly inflective Indo-European language with a rich morphology.

The tools described here include an implementation of Latvian inflectional paradigms, a morphological analysis tool with a guessing module for out-of-vocabulary words, and a statistical POS/morphology tagger for disambiguation of multiple analysis possibilities. Currently achieved accuracy with a training set of only ~40 000 words is 97.9% for part of speech tagging and 93.6% for the full morphological feature tag set, which is better than any previously publicly available taggers for Latvian.

We also describe the construction and methodology of the necessary linguistic resources – a morphological dictionary and an annotated morphological corpus, and evaluate the effect of resource size on analysis accuracy, showing what results can be achieved with limited linguistic resources.

KEYWORDS : morphology, inflective language, POS tagging, Latvian language, morphological corpus.

1 Introduction

For inflective languages, where a large part of grammatical meaning is expressed by the morphological features of words, a wide variety of computational tasks require a way to perform automated part of speech tagging and morphological analysis. It is needed both in specialized use cases such as linguistic research, and also in end-user tasks such as searching within documents or automated spelling correction.

Smaller languages usually have a limited amount of resources and effort available for developing linguistic resources such as annotated corpora or dictionaries, so it is useful to explore analysis methods that would work with smaller amount of resources and allow reusing software tools developed for other, larger languages.

In this paper we describe the construction process of such a toolkit for Latvian language, integrating word-level morphological analysis based on a formalization of Latvian inflection paradigms with a statistical tagger to exploit sentence context. We also provide an evaluation for the effect of resource (annotated corpora and lexicon) size on analysis accuracy.

2 Latvian Morphology

Latvian is an Indo-European language with around 1.5 million native speakers. It is a synthetic inflected language with rich morphology somewhat similar to the commonly analyzed Czech morphology (Hajič, 2000).

Latvian nouns and pronouns have 6 cases in singular and plural in traditional grammar. Nouns are traditionally divided in 6 declensions with different inflectional paradigms. Adjectives, numerals and some participles have 6 cases in singular and plural, 2 genders (masculine and feminine) and separate definite and indefinite forms. In verb conjugation system are 2 numbers (singular and plural), 3 persons, 3 tenses (present, future and past, both simple and compound) and 5 moods, as well as multiple types of participles. Qualitative adjectives and adverbs formed from these adjectives have also degrees of comparison noted in their word form.

The morphology creates more than 200 verb and participle forms derived from each verb lexeme, and more than 100 forms for each adjective. Many of the endings are overlapping, creating homoforms – for example, singular accusative and plural genitive forms are identical for many words.

2.1 Related Work on Latvian Morphological Analysis

The earliest experiments with automated Latvian morphological analysis have been performed in 1970s (Drīzule, 1978), implementing noun and adjective analysis. In 1990s, with the advent of personal computers, there have been multiple attempts to create analysis systems for all parts of speech (Greitāne, 1994; Levāne & Spektors, 2000; Sarkans, 1996, Vasiļjevs, Ķikāne & Skadiņš, 2004) based on linguistic rules for word endings and morphemes.

Systems currently being used in practice for Latvian morphology include lexicon based analysis systems (Paikens, 2007; Skadiņa, 2004) – while requiring more computational and dictionary resources, such systems provide better accuracy than earlier research.

Morphological analysis of Latvian is rather ambiguous – about half of words have multiple valid interpretations if viewed without context, so disambiguation as analyzed in this paper is an important open problem. There exists a recently developed morphological tagger based on Maximum Entropy Model (Pinnis and Goba, 2011), but it is not available to public[1].

3   Development of a Morphologically Annotated Corpus

A morphologically annotated corpus is a key resource for all further work – even for methods that do not require input from a large corpus, it is crucial to have at least a small set of verified data that can be used for testing and evaluation.

3.1   Morphological Annotation Standard

The morphological feature annotation standard used for Latvian corpora was initially (Levāne, 2000) derived from the annotation principles used for other languages in the MULTEXT-East project (Erjavec, 2004). It is a way to represent word annotation with a short tag, each character position representing a separate, independent feature. The meaning of each character position depends on the part of speech (marked in the first character) in order to keep the tag length short enough for human reading.

For an example, Figure 1 illustrates the morphological feature tag for noun *draugam*, the singular dative form of *draugs* (a friend).

Tagset for noun	part of speech	type	gender	number	case	declension
	n	**c**	**m**	**s**	**d**	**1**
	noun	common	masculine	singular	dative	first

FIGURE 1 – Example of a morphological tag for noun *draugam* ('friend') **ncmsd1**

It should be noted that in addition to purely morphological features, the annotation includes also lexical properties (such as type and declension in Figure 1) necessary for other research uses of the annotated corpora. The tag element names and values are matched to the ISOcat standard as recommended by CLARIN project[2].

The annotation process starts with generating the possible readings with an automatic analyzer described in the next section, and then a manual review and entry of missing

---

[1] The tagger is used in company Tilde proprietary tools - the training data and tagger are not available for other research purposes.

[2] http://www.clarin.eu

features. The speed of annotation is around 300 words per hour for a skilled operator with appropriate software tools.

3.2 Annotated Corpora

There have been multiple efforts on building morphologically annotated corpora of Latvian. Currently publicly available corpora are shown in Table 1. As noted earlier, the corpora were developed for projects of varying goals, and there are some differences between exact annotation standards used.

Corpus	Text source / domain	Tokens	Sentences
Balanced	Latvian Balanced Corpus[3]	50 795	3 940
Legal	EU documents[4]	23 359	1 038
Plāns Ledus	A fiction book	16 708	1 314
Latvijas Vēstnesis	A newspaper	28 956	2 035

TABLE 1 – Morphologically annotated Latvian corpora.

These corpora have been reviewed by a single annotator only. To ensure adequate data quality we performed a second annotator review and correction of the balanced corpus annotation to reduce the number of annotation errors, and serve as a valid 'gold standard' data for analyzer training and evaluation in this paper.

4   Automated Morphological Analysis

Our basic morphological analysis – generation of all possible morphological interpretations of a word form – is based on an earlier publicly available lexicon-based morphological analyzer (Paikens, 2007), extending it with additional lexical data. It is based on matching possible word form endings and the inflectional changes to stems as described in classical linguistic research, and verifies the stem candidates against a lexicon marked with declensions and conjugations of common nouns and verbs.

The currently used morphological lexicon has been assembled from multiple sources, including an electronic version of an inverse dictionary (Soida, 1970), manual review of the closed word classes and words with irregular inflection, scientific terminology data, and updates based on . It is not properly balanced – the contents reflect what resources were available, so coverage may vary depending on the text domain. The lexicon contains 47 000 lexemes.

Even with such lexicon size, 5-6% of test data is still out of vocabulary. Most of these words are formed according to Latvian grammatical rules, so it is still reasonable to deduce morphological properties based on the word ending, and for these cases, a 'guessing' system is implemented that generates a large number of possible analysis

---

[3] http://www.korpuss.lv

[4] White Paper. Preparation of the Associated Countries of Central and Eastern Europe for Inte-gration into the Internal Market of the Union.

options. This includes the correct reading for all except some 0.5-1% foreign words or brand names that are used literally as inflexive nouns, but happen to have an ending that matches a Latvian flexive form.

5   Statistical Disambiguation Methods

For many languages, pure morphological analysis will have a significant amount of ambiguity. For Latvian, our current analyzer gives multiple interpretations for 50-55% of words, with an average of 3.5-3.8 options for ambiguous words, depending on text domain, and similar amount of ambiguity has been observed in other morphologically rich languages (Yuret & Türe, 2006). The above ambiguity measurement includes morphological features – part of speech, case, number, gender, etc., and also lemmas in case of inflectional homonymity.

We examine two main use cases for disambiguation – choosing the most likely option for a single token, or selecting the most likely morphological tags for a whole sentence, looking at words in context. Single token analysis has less data for accurate disambiguation, but can be used in analysis of incomplete text fragments such as search queries, and is simpler to implement.

5.1   Baseline - Single Token Disambiguation

If there are multiple valid interpretations, clearly some of them are more frequent than others – we can intuitively note that some inflective forms may be more commonly used; or that one of theoretically possible lemmas is a rare, archaic word.

For this scenario, we can count the frequencies in a morphologically disambiguated corpus for two main features – the inflectional paradigm that generated the option, and the lexicon entry (if any) of the source lemma. This allows a quick estimation of the likelihoods, choosing the analysis option with the most likely paradigm and lexeme. While this method is naturally limited, it provides reasonable results with very tiny resources, providing us with a baseline to evaluate more complex options described later.

This is similar to the first stage of a Brill tagger if the surface form was seen in training corpus, but this heuristic generalizes well also to cases where the exact form was not seen before.

5.2   Morphological Tagging Within a Sentence

There are two main directions to use sentence context in disambiguation of homoforms in order to appy the appropriate morphological tags. One approach would be to invoke syntax rules, such as general syntactic analyzers (e.g. Bārzdiņš, Grūzītis, Nešpore & Saulīte, 2007 or Deksne & Skadiņš, 2011) that could also be adapted for morphological disambiguation. On the other hand, it is also possible to obtain these rules directly from an annotated corpus with machine learning algorithms. Our initial experiments with available Latvian syntactic analysers gave poor results due to limited syntactic coverage, driving us to the machine learning direction – although other research (Hajic,

Krbec, Kveton, Oliva & Petkevic, 2001; Hulden & Francom, 2012) suggests that a hybrid approach may bring further improvements.

Further in description we use our currently best performing solution, a conditional Markov model (CMM) based morphological tagging module. We have also trained various other systems, including hidden Markov model (HMM) and conditional random field (CRF) based classifiers, but we achieved better results with CMM.

The CMM module software is a modified version of the Stanford NLP[5] system CMM classifier implementation (Toutanova, Klein, Manning & Singer, 2003). A major difference between our solution and the original Stanford POS-tagger is the integration of the classifier with a rule based morphological analyzer supplying multiple possible analysis options to the classifier for disambiguation.

The standard approach for other languages (Hulden & Francom, 2012; Toutanova, Klein, Manning & Singer, 2003; Gahbiche-Braham, Bonneau-Maynard, Lavergne & Yvon, 2012) is to train a classifier on features directly derived from the word form string, such as letter n-grams, capitalization features, etc. While this may be effective for languages with a smaller range of word forms, this is not optimal for morphologically rich languages, as suggested by research in other languages (Youret & Türe, 2006). Word form specific features would greatly suffer from feature sparsity, as even in a huge training corpus many rarer word forms would not be seen at all; and a large part of word ending inflection rules cannot be adequately captured by letter n-gram features.

However, this morphological knowledge can be exploited by adding as training features the results from rule based morphological analysis described in section 4. That gives a reasonably accurate (contains correct form in 98% cases) list of what tags seem possible for each word. So in addition to the used classifier training features commonly used for other languages, we also supply a list of possible part-of-speech and tag options for the selected word and its closest neighbours. We also provide a 'recommended' POS and tag, calculated as described in section 5.1, which gives ~1% additional boost in accuracy. This change augments the machine learning of ending (letter n-gram) relations with morphological features with the linguistic rules in analyser, and allows to achieve good results with rather small training corpora.

6   Evaluation

6.1   Methodology

We used a morphologically annotated balanced corpus of 50 795 words, using 46 306 of it as training data (5 344 of it for tuning and developing the systems), and a separate set of 4 489 words for evaluation in this paper. Text content is taken as-is from the corpus, leaving intact any spelling issues or insertions of foreign words.

Lexical features such as declension, verb modality, semantic grouping, etc. are discarded for both training and evaluation data, as they can be retrieved afterwards from

---

[5] http://nlp.stanford.edu/software/tagger.shtml

the lexicon when the lemma is determined. The following morphological features are used for evaluation: part of speech, gender, number, case, person, verb mood, and definiteness for adjectives and participles.

6.2   Rule-based analyzer module evaluation

On our test corpus, the rule-based morphological analysis module includes a correct analysis option for 98.2% words, incorrect analysis for 1.3% words, and no analysis for 0.5% words (mostly insertions from other languages). Rule-based analysis results are unambiguous for 46.6% words, and the ambiguous words have on average 3.8 options each.

6.3   Statistical disambiguation methods

Comparing the results of automatic morphological disambiguation on the evaluation data set shows a tag accuracy level of 87.0% for baseline single token analysis and 93.6% for the best performing CMM model.

Both methods are suitable for analysis of large text corpora, with single token analysis being able to analyze approx. 100 000 words per second per core on a 2.8Ghz processor, and the CMM tagger around 3 000 words per second.

Reviewing the distribution of disambiguation errors by feature category (break-down shown in Table 2) indicates that the most common error is a combination of number and case mismatch, confusing singular accusative and plural genitive forms of nouns or whole noun phrases. These are homoforms for a large portion of Latvian nouns and adjectives, and both accusative and dative may be syntactically reasonable after a verb, indicating respectively the object or recipient of the action. We plan to reduce this class of errors by integration of morphological disambiguation with deeper syntactic analysis (statistical dependency parsers) that should be able to better resolve such ambiguities.

Part of speech	2.1 %
Gender	3.2 %
Number	4.5 %
Case	7.0 %
Verb mood	1.8 %
Person	0.8 %
Definiteness	1.4 %

TABLE 2 – CMM tagger error rates within feature categories.

6.4   Training data size effect on accuracy

Experiments on running the same disambiguation methods with limited training data, illustrated in Figure 2, show that the naive single token disambiguation quickly reaches its limit at around 10 000 words already. The CMM based model would likely provide better accuracy with additional training data, which is also supported by experiments of Pinnis and Goba (2011) performed on a training set of 117 000 words, but it already provides an improvement above the single-token baseline with even very small training corpus such as 5 000 words.

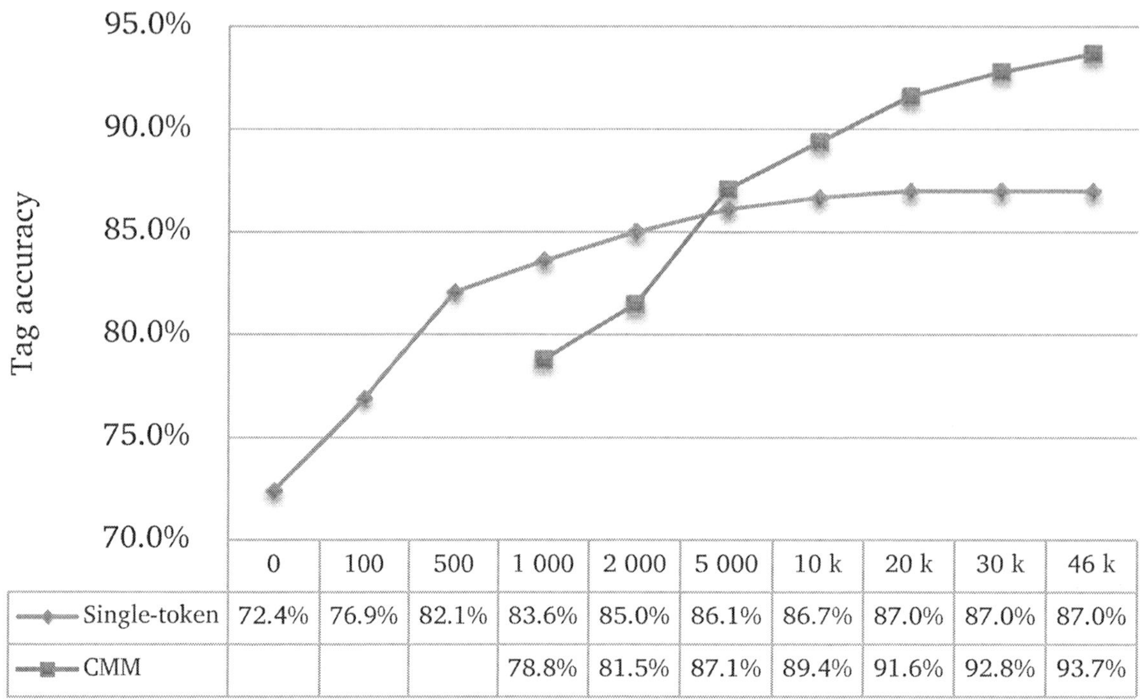

	0	100	500	1 000	2 000	5 000	10 k	20 k	30 k	46 k
Single-token	72.4%	76.9%	82.1%	83.6%	85.0%	86.1%	86.7%	87.0%	87.0%	87.0%
CMM				78.8%	81.5%	87.1%	89.4%	91.6%	92.8%	93.7%

FIGURE 2 – Effect of corpus size on CMM disambiguation accuracy compared to single-token baseline

6.5   Effect of Lexicon Size on Accuracy

To evaluate the necessity of a morphological lexicon (a dictionary annotated with declensions or inflectional paradigms), we performed a series of tests, training and running the CMM classifier with an artificially reduced lexicon. The minimal dictionary contains 5 000 lexemes for the closed word classes – pronouns, conjunctions, prepositions, and irregular verbs, with further experiments measured by randomly adding nouns and verbs from the full dictionary up to the indicated limit.

The evaluation results shown in Figure 3 indicate that a proper lexicon has a strong impact in reducing error rate, however, when considering languages or dialects where large dictionaries are unavailable (such as the Latgalian language closely related to Latvian), it is not strictly necessary since our experiments show a practically usable accuracy of 90.6% even with the minimal lexicon.

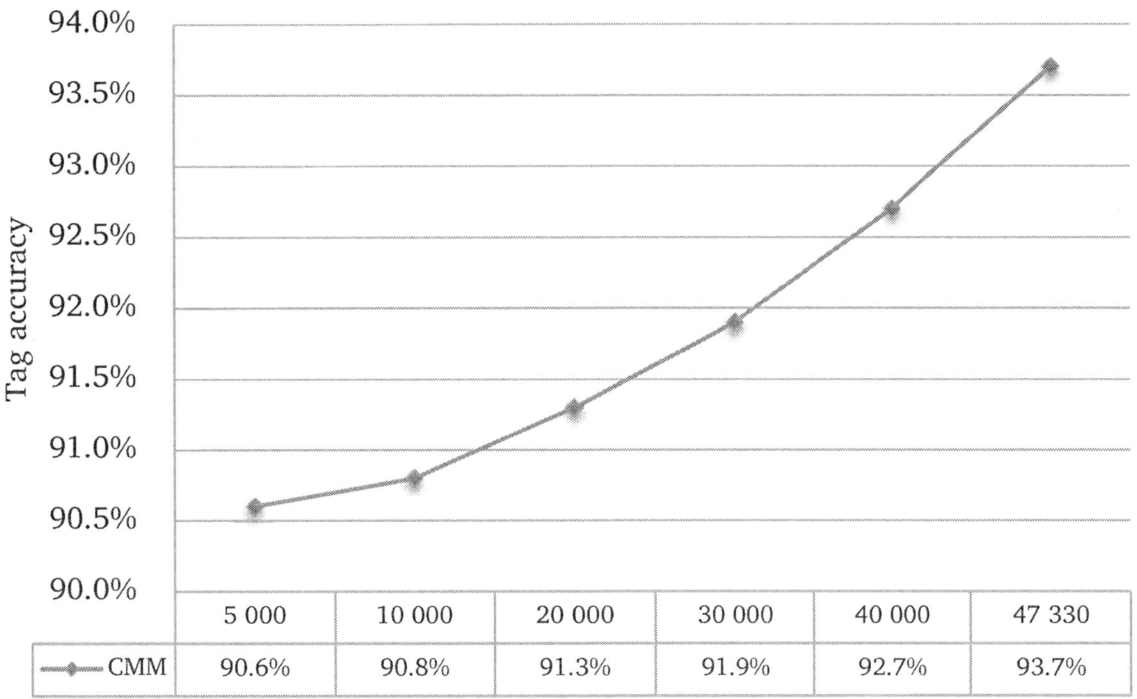

	5 000	10 000	20 000	30 000	40 000	47 330
CMM	90.6%	90.8%	91.3%	91.9%	92.7%	93.7%

FIGURE 3 – Effect of corpus size on CMM disambiguation accuracy compared to single-token baseline

7   Conclusion and Outlook

We have developed a freely available morphological analysis and disambiguation solution for Latvian language. The tools, resources and corpora are publicly available under an open source licence.

We demonstrate that morphological analysis and disambiguation for languages with rich morphology can be performed with small amounts of language-specific resources. In particular, if the inflection rules can be formally defined, then a morphological tagging module with a useful accuracy of 90% can be trained even with a small annotated corpus of 10-20 thousand words and a limited dictionary.

We expect to further improve accuracy of the morphological tagger by extending the training data up to 100 000 words and exploring options for integration with syntactic parsers.

A future goal is to attempt to apply this methodology for Latgalian language – a regional language with approx. 165 000 native speakers and very limited digital resources. We also hope that this experience can inspire linguistic tool development for other languages with limited size of corpora, noting that a practically useful accuracy can be obtained with very limited language data.

Acknowledgments

We thank the University of Latvia for the financial support in preparing and presenting this paper, and the anonymous reviewers for their improvement recommendations.

References

Bārzdiņš G., Grūzītis N., Nešpore G. and Saulīte B. (2007). Dependency-Based Hybrid Model of Syntactic Analysis for the Languages with a Rather Free Word Order. In *Proceedings of the 16th Nordic Conference of Computational Linguistics*, pages 13–20, Tartu.

Erjavec, T. (2004). MULTEXT-East Version 3: Multilingual Morphosyntactic Specifications, Lexicons and Corpora. In *Proceedings of the Fourth International Conference on Language Resources and Evaluation (LREC'2004)*, pages 1535–1538, Paris.

Deksne, D. and Skadiņš, R. (2011). CFG Based Grammar Checker for Latvian. In *Proceedings of the 18th Nordic Conference of Computational Linguistics NODALIDA 2011*, Riga, Latvia.

Drīzule, V. (1978). Об автоматическом распознавании омонимии флексий латышского языка [On automated recognition of flexive homonymy in Latvian language]. In *LZA Vēstis 1978*, 10, pages 79–87, Rīga, LZA.

Gahbiche-Braham, S., Bonneau-Maynard, H., Lavergne, T. and Yvon, F. (2012). Joint Segmentation and POS Tagging for Arabic Using a CRF-based Classifier. In *Proceedings of the Eight International Conference on Language Resources and Evaluation (LREC'12)*, Istanbul, Turkey.

Greitāne I. (1994). Latviešu valodas lokāmo vārdšķiru locīšanas algoritmi. (Algorithms for Latvian Form Generation) In *LZA Vēstis 1994*, 1, pages 32–39, Rīga, LZA.

Hajic, J., Krbec, P., Kveton, P., Oliva, K. and Petkevic, V. (2001). Serial combination of rules and statistics: A case study in Czech tagging. In *Proceedings of the 39th Annual Meeting on Association for Computational Linguistics*, pages 268–275.

Hajič, J. (2000). Morphological Tagging: Data vs. Dictionaries. In: *Proceedings of the 6th Applied Natural Language Processing and the 1st NAACL Conference*, pages 94-101, Seatle, Washington, U.S.A.

Hulden, M. and Francom, J. (2012). Boosting statistical tagger accuracy with simple rule-based grammars. In *Proceedings of the Eight International Conference on Language Resources and Evaluation (LREC'12)*, Istanbul, Turkey.

Levāne, K. and Spektors A. (2000). Morphemic Analysis and Morphological Tagging of Latvian Corpus. In *Proceedings of the Second International Conference on Language Resources and Evaluation*, vol. 2, pages 1095–1098.

Levāne-Petrova K. (2011). Morfoloģiski marķēta valodas korpusa izmantošana valodas izpētē. In *"Vārds un tā pētīšanas aspekti": Rakstu krājums 15(1)*, pages 187–193, Liepāja, LiePA.

Paikens, P. (2007). Lexicon-based morphological analysis of Latvian language. In *Proceedings of 3rd Baltic Conference on Human Language Technologies (HLT 2007)*, pages 235-240, Kaunas.

Pinnis, M. and Goba, K. (2011). Maximum Entropy Model for Disambiguation of Rich Morphological Tags. In *Systems and Frameworks for Computational Morphology,*

Communications in Computer and Information Science, 1, Volume 100, The 2nd Workshop on Systems and Frameworks for Computational Morphology (SFCM2011), pages 14-22, Heidelberg, Springer.

Sarkans U. (1996). Morphemic and Morphological Analysis of the Latvian Language. In *Proceedings of the Forth conference on Computational Lexicography and Text Research*, pages 219–225, Budapest

Skadiņa I. (2004). Latviešu valodas morfoloģiskās analīzes sistēma – tās nozīme teikuma pareizrakstības pārbaudē. In *Vārds un tā pētīšanas aspekti 8*, pages 282–290, Liepāja.

Soida, E. and Kļaviņa, S. (1970). *Latviešu valodas inversā vārdnīca*, Rīga, LVU.

Toutanova K., Klein D., Manning C.D. and Singer Y. (2003). Feature-Rich Part-of-Speech Tagging with a Cyclic Dependency Network. In *Proceedings of HLT-NAACL 2003*, pages 252–259.

Vasiļjevs, A., Ķikāne, J. and Skadiņš, R. (2004). Development of HLT for Baltic languages in widely used applications. In *Proceedings of First Baltic Conference „Human Language Technologies – the Baltic Perspective"*, pages 198-202, Riga.

Yuret, D. and Türe F. (2006). Learning morphological disambiguation rules for Turkish. In *Proceedings of the main conference on Human Language Technology Conference of the North American Chapter of the Association of Computational Linguistics (HLT-NAACL '06)*, pages 328-334, Association for Computational Linguistics, Stroudsburg, PA, USA.

Statistical syntactic parsing for Latvian

Lauma Pretkalniņa, Laura Rituma

Institute of Mathematics and Computer Science, University of Latvia
Raiņa 29, Rīga, LV–1459, Latvia

lauma@ailab.lv, laura@ailab.lv

ABSTRACT

Syntactic parsing is an important technique in the natural language processing, yet Latvian is still lacking an efficient general coverage syntax parser. This paper reports on the first experiments on statistical syntactic parsing for Latvian — a highly inflective Indo-European language with a relatively free word order. We have induced a statistical parser from a small, non-balanced Latvian Treebank using the MaltParser toolkit and measured the unlabeled attachment score (UAS). As MaltParser is based on the dependency grammar approach, we have also developed a convertor from the hybrid dependency-based annotation model used in the Latvian Treebank to the pure dependency annotation model. We have obtained a promising 74.63% UAS in 10-fold cross-validation using only ~2500 sentences. The results revealed that best results can be achieved using non-projective stack parsing algorithm with lazy arc adding strategy, but comparably good results can be achieved using projective parsing algorithms combined with appropriate projectiviziation preprocessing.

KEYWORDS: Latvian, treebank, dependency parsing, statistical parsing, MaltParser.

1   Introduction and related work

Latvian is a highly inflective Indo-European language with a relatively free word order. Even though several experiments on automatic syntax parsing for Latvian have been carried out, it is still an open problem as no efficient general coverage parser is currently available. The closest one is an experimental rule-based partial parser based on a hybrid grammar model (Bārzdiņš, et al., 2007), however it uses hand-crafted rules that cover only simple extended sentences and is already highly ambiguous. Others address specific use-cases e.g. grammar checking (Deksne and Skadiņš, 2011) or the development of multilingual controlled languages (Paikens and Grūzītis, 2011). The aim of our research is to produce a general coverage statistical parser induced from currently available syntactically annotated data.

We use the Latvian Treebank (Pretkalniņa et al., 2011b) as the data source. The treebank is under active development, and it is still relatively small (approx. 2500 sentences) and by no means balanced, therefore acquiring good results for a language with a free word order is rather challenging. For current experiments we have chosen MaltParser as the parser induction framework mainly for two reasons. First, we consider that the hybrid grammar used in the Latvian Treebank is more in lines with the dependency formalism than with the phrase structure approach. Second, MaltParser is distributed in a handy, well documented implementation and can be trained in reasonable time. We plan to continue our experiments, comparing these results with what can be obtained with other data-driven approaches, e.g. (Koo and Collins, 2010).

The paper first gives an overview of the Latvian Treebank annotation model and transformations to make the data compliant with MaltParser (Chapter 2). In Chapter 3 we describe our experimental setup for MaltParser. In Chapter 4 we evaluate the results in terms of unlabeled attachment score.

2   Latvian Treebank

The Latvian Treebank is being developed since 2010 (Pretkalniņa et al., 2011a). It features multilayer annotations, containing both syntactical and morphological information. The approach used in the Latvian Treebank is similar to Prague Dependency Treebank's (Hajič et al., 2000) multilayered approach. The main difference is that Latvian Treebank has no tectogrammatical annotation layer yet, but some features of it are treated in the syntax layer. TrEd toolkit (Hajič et al., 2001) is used for annotating the Latvian Treebank. The annotation process is mainly done manually, and all the treebank data is human-verified. The analytical or syntactic layer is annotated using the SemTi-Kamols grammar model (Nešpore et al, 2010), further described in Chapter 2.1. The morphological layer is annotated by adding a positional tag to every token. Apart from morphological features, these tags represent also some lexical features like declension group. The tagset is derived from the annotation principles used for other languages in the MULTEXT-East project (Erjavec, 2010). Currently the Treebank contains 2519 sentences representing various genres (e.g. news and fiction), however, the genres are by no means balanced. There is an ongoing work on the corpus expansion and genre diversification. Up to our knowledge, it is the biggest syntactically annotated corpus for Latvian.

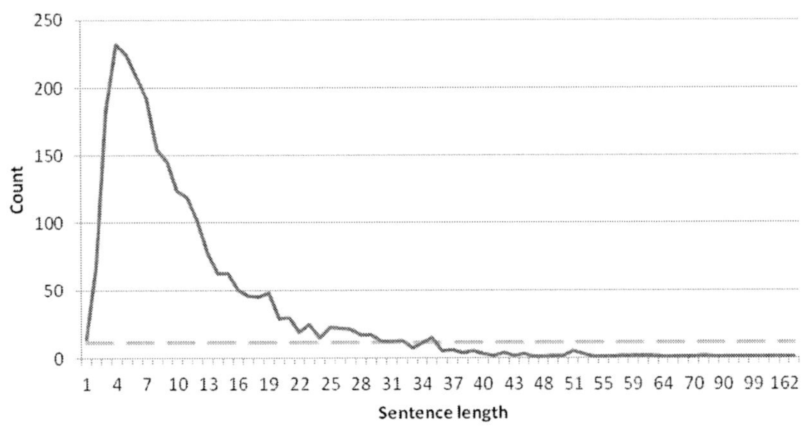

FIGURE 1: Latvian Treebank centence counts per length; average length shown dashed

Latvian Treebank contains 29 398 tokens. Sentence length varies from 1 to 200 tokens with average length on 11.67 tokens. 13.29% of all sentences are non-projective (measurement done after converting Treebank to pure dependency annotation, see section 2.2). For sentence length distribution see Figure 1.

2.1 Annotation model

The Latvian Treebank uses the hybrid dependency-based SemTi-Kamols annotation model (Pretkalniņa et al., 2011b). In essence, SemTi-Kamols annotations can be described as dependency trees that are augmented with phrase structure nodes (an example is given in Figure 2). Each phrase node can act as a dependency head or as a dependant. Each constituent in a phrase node can also act as a dependency head, but not as a dependant. Each constituent in a phrase node can be either a word or a phrase node.

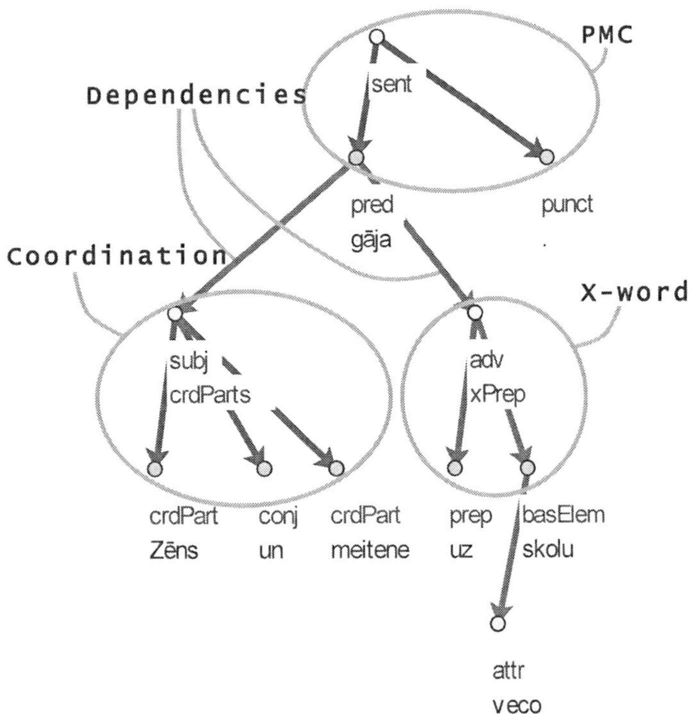

FIGURE 2: Latvian Treebank annotation example — *Zēns un meitene gāja uz veco skolu.* 'A boy and a girl went to the old school.'

281

Dependency links are used to depict subordination relations in a sentence. Apart from dependency relations, the Latvian Treebank has three types of phrase nodes: coordination, punctuation mark constructs (PMC), and the so-called x-words. Coordination nodes consist of coordinated parts of sentences, conjunctions, and punctuation marks that are used to bind together coordinated parts of sentences. Coordinated clauses are annotated in the same way. PMCs are introduced to annotate how punctuation marks in Latvian are used to show the syntactical structure. A PMC consists of one base element, a word or a phrase, and the punctuation marks whose usage are invoked by the base element, e.g. participle clauses and subordinated clauses. The x-words are the closest units to the classical understanding of phrases in the phrase structure grammars: they consist of several ordered words and are used to annotate constructions where the word order is important, e.g. analytical verb forms, multi-word numerals, named entities etc. For each type of a phrase node, several subtypes are distinguished depending on different features that the particular type of syntactic construction can represent. E.g. x-words are further divided in prepositional constructions, complex predicates, etc., but coordination is further divided in coordinated parts of sentence and coordinated clauses.

2.2 Transformation to pure dependency trees

In order to use the Latvian Treebank data for parser induction with MaltParser, we had to develop procedures for converting the hybrid SemTi-Kamols annotations to pure dependency annotations. Consulting with linguists, we have developed precise rules detailing how each type and subtype of phrase nodes is converted to a fragment of a dependency tree. Linking between constituents of phrase node is based on linguistic considerations taking into account the intention to develop these rules so that the obtained labelled dependency tree would contain as much from original information as possible, and that the trees eventually returned by the parser could be converted back as close to original model as possible. Currently, the SemTi-Kamols annotation scheme allows vast amount of all kinds of nested phrase structures, e.g. coordination of coordination (of coordination, etc.). As SemTi-Kamols also makes distinction between dependents of phrase (as whole) and dependents of its constituents, it is more expressive than the pure dependency model. In future we plan to use this information as additional features for parser training and to explore other parsing algorithms to obtain parser for full annotation model. These rules are implemented in a treebank conversion script.

According to the conversion rules (a transformation example is given in Figure 3), each phrase is converted to a dependency tree fragment which is a valid dependency tree itself. The constituents of a phrase structure node are each transformed to a single dependency tree node, and all dependents of these constituents (in the original tree) remain as dependents of the corresponding nodes in the dependency tree. Nodes connected to a phrase node as a whole become connected to the root node[1] of the subtree representing the phrase node after the transformation. The constituent that becomes the root node of the subtree is determined by the type, subtype and structure of the phrase. Whenever it is possible, we choose a constituent that cannot have dependents itself, so that dependents of a phrase node as a whole and dependents of the head constituent would not mix. In a coordination phrase, the root node is a conjunction (or punctuation, if there is no

---

[1] The head of the phrase structure.

conjunction). In punctuation mark constructs, the root node is a punctuation mark (the first, if multiple occurs in the phrase). For x-words the root node differs depending on the subtype of the x-word, e.g. the preposition in a prepositional construction, the last numeral in a multi-word numeral, etc. All other constituents are either directly linked to the chosen root, or chained in the order they occur in the sentence, and then linked to the chosen root. The way in which other constituents are added to the root depends on the phrase type, e.g. multi-word numerals are chained, but PMC constituents are linked directly to the root. If no other considerations are available, all other constituents are added as dependents of the last constituent.

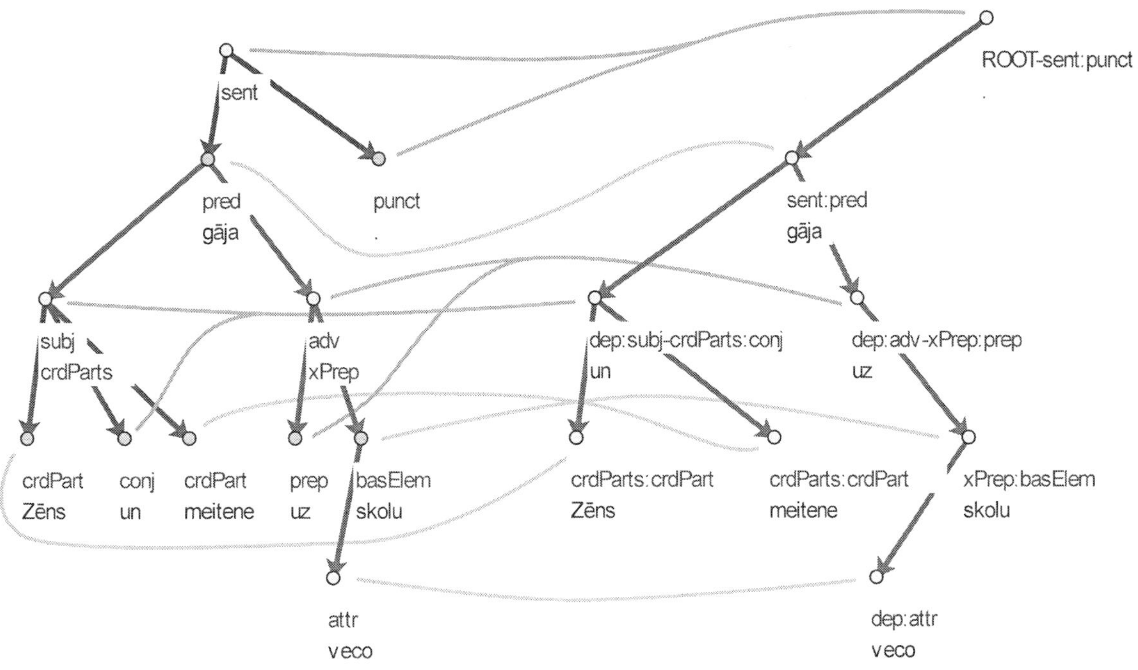

FIGURE 3: Example of transforming a hybrid tree (on the left) to a pure dependency tree (on the right). Corresponding showed with gray lines.

During the transformation, the syntactic roles of the obtained dependency tree can be augmented to reveal the full information needed to convert the trees back to the hybrid grammar representation, but this can lead to potentially infinite set of roles: when the chosen root element for some phrase is a phrase itself, we need to add additional information to the role labels, and, theoretically, phrases can stack infinitely. In practice, at least three levels deep stacking has been observed in the treebank. Thus, we still need to explore the linguistic background and the actual data to find the best way to define the set of syntactic roles for the obtained dependency trees. As the original treebank data contain annotations with sentence-scope ellipsis, appropriate roles for displaying this information in dependency trees are also needed.

3   Experimental setup

Currently, state of the art parsers (Bohnet and Nivre, 2012) achieve up to 93% unlabeled attachment score for English — a highly analytic language — and up to 88.8% for Czech which is grammatically more similar to Latvian. Acquiring comparably good parsing results for Latvian is highly challenging due to the very limited size of the available data set and due to the rich annotation model used in the treebank. The data set consists of 2519 manually annotated sentences (29496 tokens). To obtain a better understanding of what parsing accuracy limitations are imposed by such corpus size, we use the treebank's original morphological tagging (manually verified) for accuracy testing. However, to get small insight about errors caused by possible mistakes in statistical morphological tagging we perform single experiment with POS tagged data, using statistical tagger, described by Paikens et al. (2013).

For parser induction we use MaltParser, version 1.7.1[2]. Following the advice given by Nivre and Hall (2010) we use LIBSVM (Chang and Lin, 2011) as the learning agent to avoid necessity of manual feature combination and cross-validation to evaluate our parsers, again — due to the limited size of the data set. We use 10-fold cross-validation in terms of sentence count and report the minimal, maximal and average score for each parsing experiment. To obtain a more even distribution, we form the validation sets by selecting approx. 10% of sentences of each document in treebank.

We have performed several experiments with various parsing algorithms and various representations of morphological features. As the Latvian Treebank contains non-projective annotations (e.g. parenthesis, direct speech), for the baseline we have performed a series of experiments with the non-projective stack algorithm (Nivre, 2009; Nivre et al. 2009) with MaltParser's default feature configuration (tags and wordforms). First, we trained a parser with the full morphological tag. To reduce the sparseness of the morphological tags (the full tagset has approx. 500 different tags), we continued with an experiment with a dataset where the lexical features are removed from the tags. Finally, we split the positional tags into sets of multiple features representing each morphological feature separately to increase the parser's ability to learn regularities like "an adjective depending on a noun has to agree on the number, case and gender".

In the next step, we performed a series of experiments using various parsing algorithms provided by the MaltParser toolkit and combining their settings to see how the algorithm choice influences the parsing accuracy. We used the non-projective stack algorithm, both eager and lazy versions, and several projective algorithms combined with different pseudo-projective tree processing. We run both experiment series with no pseudo-projective transformations and series where we used arc-eager, arc-standard (Nivre, 2003; Nivre, 2004) and the stack projective algorithms (Nivre, 2009; Nivre et al., 2009). We used head, path and head+path marking strategies for pseudo-projective transformations (Nivre and Nilsson, 2005). We also performed experiments with planar and 2-planar algorithms (Gómez-Rodríguez and Nivre, 2010).

In the last step, we added additional features containing lemmas to the dataset and then run best-performing algorithms from the previous experiment sessions.

For evaluating the parser performance, we used the unlabeled attachment score (UAS), calculating it using the script provided in the CoNLL-07 shared task toolbox[3].

---

[2] Available at http://www.maltparser.org/ [last visited on 26/01/2013]
[3] Available at http://nextens.uvt.nl/depparse-wiki/SoftwarePage [last visited on 26/01/2013]

4   Evaluation

The first series of experiments — with the non-projective stack parser using forms and morphological tags as features — gave the following results: with no additional features, the data set with smaller tag sparseness performs better. By adding additional features — decoding each morphological tag into separate positions, the results get better, and the difference between full or pruned tags usage becomes insignificant as LIBSVM does feature combination itself. On these data, the stack-lazy algorithm tends to achieve slightly better results. During these experiments we have achieved 74% UAS. The full results of the first experiment series are shown in Table 1. Thus, the further experiments were done with a dataset containing full morphological tags and decoded features.

Algorithm	Stack eager				Stack lazy			
Feature decoding	No		Yes		No		Yes	
Tag type	Full	Short	Full	Short	Full	Short	Full	Short
AVG %	69.24	71.95	73.78	73.47	69.77	72.55	**74.15**	**74.04**
MIN %	65.59	69.75	71.51	71.02	67.22	69.57	71.41	71.17
MAX %	72.53	73.79	77.72	77.9	73.79	75.91	77.77	78.68

TABLE 1: Non-projective stack parser training: 10-fold cross-validation results.

Algorithm	Nivre's arc-eager				Nivre's arc-standard				Stack projective			
Projecti-vization	No	Head	Path	Head, path	No	Head	Path	Head, path	No	Head	Path	Head, path
AVG %	71.96	73.66	73.78	73.78	70.77	73.71	73.47	73.47	71.89	**74.03**	73.74	73.74
MIN %	69.36	71.2	70.8	70.8	68.54	70.5	70.6	70.6	69.47	71.97	70.86	70.86
MAX %	76.34	77.38	77.85	77.85	75.56	77.12	76.86	76.86	76.3	76.38	76.95	76.95

TABLE 2: Pseudo-projective parser training: 10-fold cross-validation results. Full morphological tags are used.

The next series of experiments compare different projective algorithms and different pseudo-projective transformations. These results show that the pseudo-projective approach gives equivalently good results compared to the non-projective stack algorithm. The chosen algorithm and projectivization strategy does not matter much — less than 0.5% points. Using the projectivization improves the UAS for 1–2% points over not using the projectivization at all. The full results are shown in Table 2.

Algorithm	Planar	2-planar	Stack lazy	Stack projective with head coding
AVG %	72.38	71.96	**74.15**	**74.03**
MIN %	69.57	70.26	71.41	71.97
MAX %	76.9	76.25	77.77	76.38

TABLE 3: Summary on parser training algorithms: 10-fold cross-validation results.

In the last step, to compare the different parsing algorithms, we have used the planar and 2-planar algorithms on the same data, but they fail to repeat success of the stack parsing algorithm. The comparison between these two algorithms, the best performing projective algorithm and the best performing non-projective stack algorithm is given in Table 3.

Algorithm	Stack eager	Stack lazy	Stack projective with head coding	Nivre's arc-eager with path encoding	Nivre's arc-standard with head encoding
AVG %	74.21	**74.63**	74.57	74.47	74.49
MIN %	71.22	71.51	71.86	71.44	72.16
MAX %	78.63	79.24	77.98	79.11	77.9

TABLE 4: Summary on the parser training with lemmas: 10-fold cross-validation results.

Finally, we have retrained five best performing parsers on data augmented with lemmas. This gives UAS increase of approx. 1.5% point using stack-lazy algorithm, thus, giving the best UAS achieved — 74.63%. This is achieved by non-projective stack algorithm with the lazy swap strategy. The full results are shown in Table 4.

Algorithm	Stack lazy on morpho-tagged data
AVG %	72.2
MIN %	69.39
MAX %	76.95

TABLE 5: Parser training with on automatically tagged data: 10-fold cross-validation results.

To get some insight about impact of the morphological tagger inaccuracies to the parsing accuracy we redo experiment with best performing parser configuration (stack-lazy algorithm, lemmas) with Treebank retagged with statistical morphological tagger (Paikens et al., 2013). Morphological tagger also adds some lexical features not available in manual tagging, e.g. source lemma for verbs derived with prefixes and deverbal nouns. Result is given in Table 3. This gives UAS decrease by approx. 2.4%, but this should be viewed as rather preliminary result.

5   Conclusion and future tasks

We have presented first general coverage statistical (data-driven) parser for Latvian. The parser is induced from a small Latvian Treebank with the help of the MaltParser toolkit. The parser achieves 74.63% unlabeled attachment score with gold standard morphological tags and 72.2% UAS — with automatically tagged morphology, which we consider a good result taking into account, that only 2500 annotated sentences were available for the parser development and that Latvian has rich morphology and, thus, a relatively free word order. We have also briefly described the current state of the Latvian Treebank and have laid out our methodology for transforming the treebank from a hybrid annotation model to the pure dependency trees.

Our experiments show that the best results can be obtained using the non-projective stack algorithm with the lazy arc adding strategy. Almost as good results can be achieved combining the projective stack algorithm with the head marking strategy for the projectivization transformation, or Nivre's arc-eager algorithm with path marking, or Nivre's arc-standard algorithm with head marking. By decoding morphological tags into separate features and providing lemmas as additional features, it gave us significant increase of UAS — 2% points total.

Our future work will include the use of dependency labels adapted to allow the transformationing back to original hybrid annotation format and to do labelled parsing experiments. We also plan to compare the current results with what can be achieved with a parser proposed by Koo and Collins (2010). The further work will include the estimation of accuracy decrease when a statistical morphological tagger is used instead of human-verified tags. We also plan to compare these results with the approach proposed by Bohnet and Nivre (2012) to find out if it can improve the accuracy when a comparatively smaller treebank is available. In the future we hope to expand our research beyond the pure dependency parsers to use to the full extent the hybrid annotations that the Latvian Treebank has. We also plan to work with lexicalization of our parsers, but this will require more work on resource development.

6   Acknowledgements

This work is supported by ERDF project „Informācijas un komunikāciju tehnoloģiju kompetences centrs" nr. KC/2.1.2.1.1/10/01/001, agreement L-KC-11-0003 research 2.7 "Teksta automātiskas datorlingvistikas analīzes pētījums jauna informācijas arhīva produkta izstrādē". We thank the University of Latvia for the financial support in preparing and presenting this paper and the anonymous reviewers for their improvement recommendations.

References

Bārzdiņš, G., Grūzītis, N., Nešpore, G. and Saulīte, B. (2007). Dependency-Based Hybrid Model of Syntactic Analysis for the Languages with a Rather Free Word Order. In: *Proceedings of the 16th Nordic Conference of Computational Linguistics*, pages 13–20, Tartu.

Bohnet, B. and Nivre, J. (2012) A Transition-Based System for Joint Part-of-Speech Tagging and Labeled Non-Projective Dependency Parsing. In *Proceedings of the 2012 Joint Conference on Empirical Methods in Natural Language Processing and Computational Natural Language Learning*, pages 1455–1465.

Chang, C.-C. and Lin, C.-J. (2011). LIBSVM : a library for support vector machines. In *ACM Transactions on Intelligent Systems and Technology*, 27(2), pages 1–27.

Deksne, D. and Skadiņš, R. (2011). CFG Based Grammar Checker for Latvian. In *Proceedings of the 18th Nordic Conference of Computational Linguistics*, pages 275–278 Riga.

Erjavec, T. (2010). MULTEXT-East Version 4: Multilingual Morphosyntactic Specifications, Lexicons and Corpora. In *Proceedings of the International Conference on Language Resources and Evaluation (LREC'2010)*, pages 19–21, Malta.

Gómez-Rodríguez, C. and Nivre, J. (2010). A Transition-Based Parser for 2-Planar Dependency Structures. In *Proceedings of the 48th Annual Meeting of the Association for Computational Linguistics*, pages 1492–1501

Hajič, J., Böhmová, A., Hajičová, E. and Vidová Hladká, B. (2000). The Prague Dependency Treebank: A Three-Level Annotation Scenario. A. Abeillé (ed.): *Treebanks: Building and Using Parsed Corpora*, pages 103–127, Amsterdam, Kluwer.

Hajič, J., Vidová Hladká, B. and Pajas, P. (2001). The Prague Dependency Treebank: Annotation Structure and Support. In *Proceedings of the IRCS Workshop on Linguistic Databases*, pages 105–114, Philadelphia.

Koo, T. and Collins, M. (2010). Efficient Third-order Dependency Parsers. In *Proceedings of the 48th Annual Meeting of the Association for Computational Linguistics*, pages 1–11, Association for Computational Linguistics.

Nešpore G., Saulīte B., Bārzdiņš G. and Grūzītis N. (2010). Comparison of the SemTi-Kamols and Tesnière's Dependency Grammars. In *Proceedings of the 4th International Conference on Human Language Technologies — the Baltic Perspective*. Frontiers in Artificial Intelligence and Applications, Vol. 219, pages. 233–240, IOS Press.

Nivre, J. (2003). An Efficient Algorithm for Projective Dependency Parsing. In *Proceedings of the 8th International Workshop on Parsing Technologies (IWPT 03)*, pages 149–160, Nancy.

Nivre, J. (2004). Incrementality in Deterministic Dependency Parsing. In *Incremental Parsing: Bringing Engineering and Cognition Together. Workshop at ACL-2004*, Barcelona.

Nivre, J. (2009). Non-Projective Dependency Parsing in Expected Linear Time. In *Proceedings of the Joint Conference of the 47th Annual Meeting of the ACL and the 4th*

International Joint Conference on Natural Language Processing of the AFNLP, pages 351–359.

Nivre, J. and Nilsson, J. (2005). Pseudo-Projective Dependency Parsing. In *Proceedings of the 43rd Annual Meeting of the Association for Computational Linguistics (ACL)*, pages 99–106.

Nivre, J., Kuhlmann, M. and Hall, J. (2009). An Improved Oracle for Dependency Parsing with Online Reordering. In *Proceedings of the 11th International Conference on Parsing Technologies (IWPT'09), pages 73–76.*

Nivre J. and Hall J. (2010). A Quick Guide to MaltParser Optimization. http://maltparser.org/guides/opt/quick-opt.pdf [last visited on 16/01/2013].

Paikens P., Grūzītis N. (2012). An implementation of a Latvian resource grammar in Grammatical Framework. In *Proceedings of the 8th International Conference on Language Resources and Evaluation (LREC)*, pages 1680–1685, Istanbul.

Paikens P., Rituma L., and Pretkalniņa L. (2013). Morphological analysis with limited resources: Latvian example. In *Proceedings of 19th Nordic Conference of Computational Linguistics*, to be published, Oslo.

Pretkalniņa L., Nešpore G., Levāne-Petrova K., and Saulīte B. (2011a). A Prague Markup Language Profile for the SemTi-Kamols Grammar Model. In *Proceedings of the 18th Nordic Conference of Computational Linguistics*, pages 303–306, Riga.

Pretkalniņa L., Nešpore G., Levāne-Petrova K., and Saulīte B. (2011b). Towards a Latvian Treebank. In *Actas del 3 Congreso Internacional de Lingüística de Corpus. Tecnologias de la Información y las Comunicaciones: Presente y Futuro en el Análisis de Corpus*, pages 119–127, Valence.

Building a Large Automatically Parsed Corpus of Finnish

Filip Ginter[1]*, Jenna Nyblom*[1]*, Veronika Laippala*[2]*, Samuel Kohonen*[1]*,*
Katri Haverinen[1,3]*, Simo Vihjanen*[4] *and Tapio Salakoski*[1,3]

(1) Department of IT, University of Turku, Finland
(2) Department of Languages and Translation Studies, University of Turku, Finland
(3) Turku Centre for Computer Science (TUCS), Turku, Finland
(4) Lingsoft, Inc., Turku, Finland

`figint,jmnybl,mavela,sskoho,kahave,tapio.salakoski@utu.fi,`

`simo.vihjanen@lingsoft.fi`

ABSTRACT

We describe the methods and resources used to build FinnTreeBank-3, a 76.4 million token corpus of Finnish with automatically produced morphological and dependency syntax analyses. Starting from a definition of the target dependency scheme, we show how existing resources are transformed to conform to this definition and subsequently used to develop a parsing pipeline capable of processing a large-scale corpus. An independent formal evaluation demonstrates high accuracy of both morphological and syntactic annotation layers. The parsed corpus is freely available within the FIN-CLARIN infrastructure project.

KEYWORDS: dependency parsing, Finnish, CLARIN, parsebank, treebank.

1 Introduction

In this paper, we describe the methods and resources used to build the *FinnTreeBank-3* (FTB-3) parsebank, a 76.4 million token corpus of Finnish with automatically produced morphological and dependency syntax analyses. The corpus is a resource developed within the FIN-CLARIN consortium, the Finnish member of the CLARIN infrastructure project[1] and aims at supporting research and language technology development requiring large-scale parsed corpora. Further, as the underlying texts consist of the multilingual parallel corpora EuroParl (Koehn, 2005) and JRC-Acquis (Steinberger et al., 2006), corresponding parsebanks can be constructed for a number of other languages into which these two corpora have been translated as well. The larger context of the FTB-3 parsebank is described by Voutilainen et al. (2012b); our involvement in its development was through a public request for quotation issued by FIN-CLARIN, seeking the development of a sufficiently accurate Finnish syntactic parser and its application to the EuroParl and JRC-Acquis corpora. Our starting point for the development was thus untypical as the corpus text, morphological tagset, as well as the dependency scheme were all defined by FIN-CLARIN and not negotiable. Our sole task was to develop a parsing pipeline with sufficient accuracy and produce the actual parsebank data, in a contract research setting. Therefore, rather than being used as-is, all tools and resources at our disposal had to be adjusted so as to conform to the specifications of the project.

In the following sections, we will summarize the tools and resources used when developing FTB-3 as well as their adaptation to the target scheme and text corpus. Then, we will present the parsing pipeline and the evaluation of the resulting parsebank.

2 Available tools and resources

The parsing process consists of two major steps: morphological tagging and dependency parsing. Morphological tagging is carried out using an adapted version of *FinCG*, a commercial morphological tagger by Lingsoft, Inc.[2] The adaptations of FinCG specific to FTB-3 development are described in Section 4.1. Unlike for tagging, no pre-existing tools were at our disposal for dependency parsing. It was thus necessary to train a statistical dependency parser which, in turn, requires a suitable treebank that is annotated in the target dependency scheme.

For Finnish, there are two manually annotated treebanks available: the *Turku Dependency Treebank (TDT)* (Haverinen et al., 2010, 2011) and *FinnTreeBank (FTB)*, in its first version *FTB-1* (Voutilainen et al., 2011) when this work was carried out. The treebanks are developed for different purposes and are in many respects complementary. TDT has been specifically developed to support statistical parser training and consists of texts from various genres and text sources, aiming to serve as a representative selection of general Finnish. FTB-1, on the other hand, was developed within FIN-CLARIN as a grammar definition treebank. Its underlying corpus comprises all grammar examples from the Finnish grammar reference book of Hakulinen et al. (2004), in total 162,312 tokens in 19,140 examples. Together with its accompanying annotation manual (Voutilainen et al., 2012a), FTB-1 serves as the definition of the target dependency scheme for FTB-3. While, by its nature, it exhibits a wide variety of grammatical phenomena, this corpus of carefully selected grammar examples is not intended for statistical parser training as it does not have the same distributional properties as general Finnish text.

We based the statistical parser used in this work on TDT, as the treebank is more suitable

---

Dependency type	Description
main	main predicate of the sentence
aux	auxiliary
subj	subject
obj	object
scomp	predicative
advl	adverbial
attr	attribute
phrm	phrase marker (conjunctions, adpositions etc.)
modal	the nominal part of a verb chain
phrv	phrasal verb
comp	comparison structure
idiom	idiom
conjunct	conjunct, coordination
voc	vocative
mod	post-modifier

Table 1: Dependency types of the FTB scheme.

for statistical parser training. To further improve the applicability of the treebank to the development of FTB-3, we manually annotated additional data from the EuroParl (19,964 tokens in 1,082 sentences) and JRC Acquis (24,909 tokens in 1,141 sentences) corpora, resulting in the final training data size of 190,271 tokens in 13,997 sentences.

3 Dependency scheme transformation

TDT is annotated in a slightly modified version of the widely used *Stanford Dependencies (SD)* scheme (de Marneffe and Manning, 2008b,a; Haverinen, 2012) which differs notably from the target scheme of FTB-3. The annotation of the treebank thus needs to be transformed to conform to the target scheme.

The two schemes differ both in the dependency types they define, as well as in the structure of the dependency trees for a number of important phenomena. While the SD scheme, as used in TDT, defines a total of 46 dependency types, the FTB scheme defines a considerably smaller set of 15 types, listed in Table 1. The tree structures notably differ as well, with 19.8% of the tokens in the target (FTB) trees being governed by a different token than in the source (SD) trees. The transformation therefore involves both dependency type mapping and modification of the governor–dependent relation. The transformation is carried out using a hybrid system consisting of hand-written rules, followed by a machine learning component that finalizes the trees by connecting islands resulting from incomplete rule coverage.

3.1 Transformation rules

Each transformation rule matches an arbitrarily complex pattern in the source tree and produces a single dependency in the target tree. The rule definition syntax allows restrictions on token text, lemmas and morphological tags, as well as dependency types and directions. Further, any restriction can also be negated, requiring that it must not be met for the pattern to match.

A typical rule transforms one SD dependency into the FTB scheme. Multiple additional constraints limiting the rule application to the correct context are typical as the two schemes treat differently several important structures. For instance, while in the SD scheme the subject in a

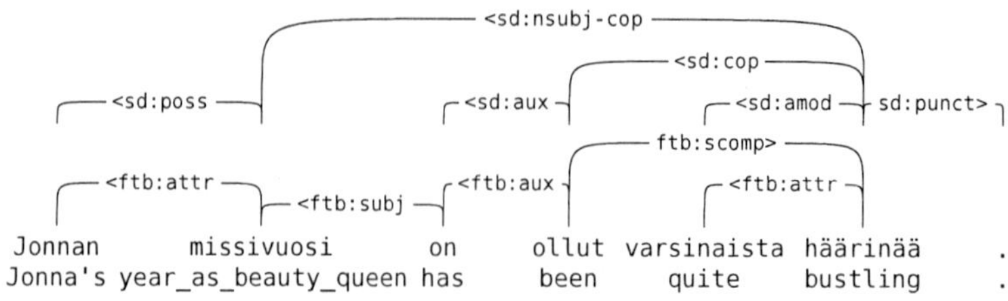

Figure 1: Example trees in the SD and FTB scheme for copula constructs.

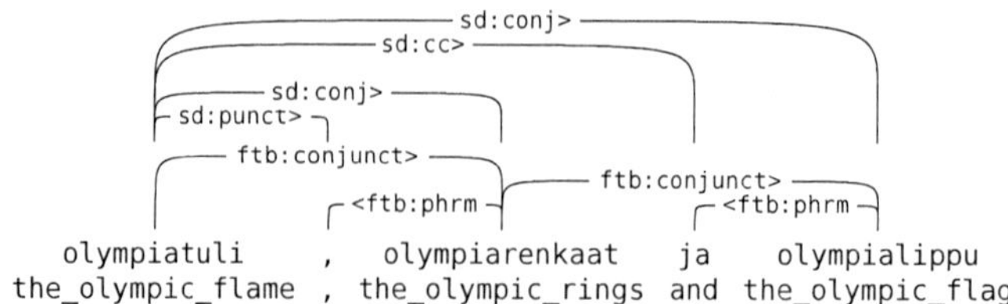

Figure 2: Example trees in the SD and FTB scheme for coordination.

copula construct is governed by the predicative, in the FTB scheme the subject is governed by the copular verb or, if present, the auxiliary (see Figure 1). Similarly, if a noun is preceded by several modifiers, the SD scheme attaches them all to the noun whereas the FTB chains them and only attaches the closest modifier to the noun. In addition, as the schemes often differ in parts of speech assignment in borderline cases, every rule possibly concerning for instance auxiliaries or adpositions must take into account the differences between the definitions of these groups of words.

As an example, the rule

$$\text{dep}(amod, T_1, T_2) \text{ and not } \text{dep}(amod \mid poss \mid num, T_1, T_x) \rightarrow \text{dep}(attr, T_1, T_2)$$

describes the transformation of an adjectival modifier dependency (*amod*) to an attribute dependency (*attr*), with the token T_1 governing the token T_2. The negated restriction indicates that the rule should not be applied if T_1 also has another dependent with the dependency type *amod*, *poss* or *num*. This is because in such a case, the FTB scheme chains the modifiers and only attaches the closest one to the noun.

As a second example, the rule

$$\text{dep}(xcomp, T_1, T_2) \text{ and is-ftb-aux}(T_2) \text{ and not } \text{dep}(cop, T_1, T_x) \rightarrow \text{dep}(aux, T_2, T_1)$$

describes the transformation of a clausal complement dependency *xcomp* between T_1 and T_2 to an *aux* dependency between T_2 and T_1, for a verb that is defined as an auxiliary in the FTB scheme. For this, the rule is delimited to apply only when the T_2 token belongs to a group of lemmas including all the auxiliaries in the FTB scheme. The negation declares that the rule should not be applied if T_1 governs a *cop* dependency, meaning that it actually is a predicative. In this case the FTB scheme assigns the copular verb as the head (see Figure 1).

A specific challenge is posed by the transformation of coordination structures, shown in Figure 2, which can consist of arbitrarily many coordinated elements and are thus not easily addressed by the rules. Coordination structures are therefore transformed separately, by a dedicated program. A second case transformed by a dedicated program rather than by the rules are the *null tokens* which in TDT represent the missing head token in gapping structures and fragments. The target FTB scheme, on the other hand, does not allow null tokens. As the last step of the transformation, we thus remove these tokens from TDT, selecting one of their dependents to act as the new governor using a priority list of dependency types and re-attaching all other dependents to the new governor.

3.2   Development of the transformation rules

To facilitate the development of the transformation rules, we have manually annotated the SD scheme trees for 17,061 tokens (1,992 sentences) from FinnTreeBank-1. These nearly 2,000 sentences thus have their syntax available in both schemes and can serve as test data in rule development.

The rules were developed iteratively in a GUI application designed for the purpose. The application presents the source and target trees, using color-coding to distinguish correct, missing, and extraneous dependencies in the transformation output. Further, the application allows to search among all sentences for arbitrary patterns, with the same expressive power as the rule pattern matching, both on the source and target side.

In total, the transformation ruleset consists of 305 rules. The rules are applied independently of each other, that is, all rules are tested and applied to all matching positions in the tree. Out of all trees, 83.3% are transformed in their entirety, resulting in a tree in the target scheme. Further 10.0% are transformed partially, resulting in several disconnected islands which are themselves trees. Such partial transformation results from the inevitable incomplete coverage of the transformation rules. Finally, the transformation output for the remaining 6.8% of trees contains a structure violating treeness: either a token with two governors or a cycle. These erroneous structures can be attributed to rule conflicts. We therefore post-process the transformation output using a machine learning component which connects the islands into complete trees as well as corrects erroneous structures by removing extra dependencies. This component is described in the following section.

3.3   Transformation post-processing using machine learning

The post-processing involves two distinct operations: removal of extraneous dependencies and insertion of new dependencies so as to connect islands in the analysis. We approach both of these subtasks using a classifier which, given any two tokens T_1 and T_2, returns the score of the most likely dependency type for the hypothetical $T_1 \rightarrow T_2$ dependency, and the score of there being no dependency with T_1 governing T_2. As the underlying machine learning algorithm for the classifier, we apply the regularized least squares ranker implemented in the RLScore package of Pahikkala et al. (2007).

We use several distinct types of features in the classification. *Token features* are generated separately for T_1 and T_2 and include the token itself, its lemma, and a binary feature for each of its morphological tags. *Target tree features* are extracted separately for T_1 and T_2 from the target, i.e. transformed, tree and consist of the governor type and all dependent types of the token in question. If there is no governor, or there are no dependents, a binary feature encoding this information is issued instead. Further, a binary feature encodes whether the token in question is a left or right dependent in the linear order of the sentence. A final group of features are the *source tree features* which capture the syntactic relationship between the two tokens in the source (SD) tree. If there is a source-tree dependency between T_1 and T_2, concatenation of its type and direction (i.e. whether the dependency is $T_1 \rightarrow T_2$ or $T_2 \rightarrow T_1$ regardless of the linear order of the tokens in the sentence) are given as a feature. If there is no such direct dependency, a "middle man" token T_x is searched such that it links T_1 and T_2, regardless of dependency directions. If found, features encoding the type and direction of the connection between T_x and T_1 and T_x and T_2 are generated, as well as a feature encoding the entire path from T_1 to T_2 via T_x. If no such interconnecting token is found, a feature is generated encoding this fact.

The classifier is trained on the treebank transformed using the 305 rules described previously. A positive example is generated from every dependency in the target tree. We cannot, however, assume that any dependency not present in the target tree constitutes a valid negative example. First, these include dependencies that should have been generated by the rules and the ranker thus should specifically not be given these cases among the negative examples. Second, producing a negative example from any pair of tokens unconnected in the target tree would result in a large number of irrelevant negative examples of tokens that are in no way related to each other. Therefore, for every dependency $T_1 \rightarrow T_2$ in the tree, we produce a negative example from $g(T_1) \rightarrow T_2$ and every $d(T_1) \rightarrow T_2$ where $g(T_1)$ and $d(T_1)$ refer to the governor and dependents of T_1. In this way, more plausible negative examples are generated, between tokens that are more closely, even though not directly, related.

The first step in the post-processing is the removal of extraneous dependencies. Whenever a token has several governors, only the dependency with the highest score as given by the classifier is preserved, all others are removed. Directed cycles are broken by removing the dependency with the lowest score in the cycle.

In the second step, we connect islands in the analysis using a simple greedy algorithm. Note that the first post-processing step guarantees that each of the islands is itself a tree. First, we generate the set of all token pairs (T_1, T_2) such that T_1 and T_2 belong to different islands and T_2 is the root of the island to which it belongs. These pairs represent all hypothetical dependencies $T_1 \rightarrow T_2$ that can be, individually, inserted into the analysis without violating its treeness. Then we use the classifier to obtain the most likely dependency type and its score for each of these token pairs, even in cases where the prediction of there being no dependency had a higher score. Finally, progressing through the list of candidate dependencies ranked by their score, we insert each dependency if and only if it would not violate the treeness constraints, taking into account also the dependencies inserted so far.

This completes the description of the transformation of TDT into the target FTB dependency scheme. We now turn to describe the dependency parsing pipeline, trained on the transformed treebank.

4 Parsing pipeline

The dependency parsing pipeline comprises of a sentence splitter, tokenizer, morphological tagger, and statistical dependency parser.

4.1 Morphological tagging

Tokenization, sentence splitting, and morphological tagging were carried out using the commercial *FinCG* tagger and associated tools developed by Lingsoft, Inc.[3] The target morphological tagset was given as part of the FTB-3 specification, however, unlike for dependency syntax

---

no specification was given regarding the preferred analysis of borderline wordforms which can be analyzed in several equally plausible ways (Voutilainen et al., 2012b). Therefore, adapting FinCG to the target scheme could be implemented via a mapping table from FinCG's morphological tagset to the target tagset and did not require adjustments to the lexicon.

The underlying text of the FTB-3 corpus is comprised of European Union legal and parliamentary texts, and contains a number of domain-specific words not included in the general-purpose FinCG lexicon. Such unrecognized words are not given any lexical analysis by FinCG and their proportion in text must be kept to a minimum. The general-purpose FinCG lexicon was therefore augmented with Lingsoft's proprietary EU style checker lexicon and with a special domain lexicon for commercial vocabulary. The lexicon was thereafter further extended with a number of additional frequent unrecognized words found in the FTB-3 corpus. We also created heuristic components to handle unrecognized proper names and abbreviations together with their inflected forms, giving them an appropriate morphological analysis. Finally, a transformation component was implemented to expand common contracted forms such as *jollei* (*if_not*). An illustrative English example of this component would be the expansion of *don't* to *do not*. After the application of these techniques, only 2.2% of all tokens were left without a morphological analysis.

4.2   Dependency parsing

Dependency parsing of the morphologically tagged input is carried out using the *Mate-Tools*[4] parser of Bohnet (2010), a state-of-the-art graph-based statistical dependency parser. The parser is trained on the entire Turku Dependency Treebank transformed to the FTB scheme, as described in Section 3. The Mate-Tools parser was selected after a careful parsing accuracy comparison with the transition-based MaltParser of Nivre et al. (2007).

An issue particularly apparent in the legal text of the JRC-Acquis corpus is the $O(n^2)$ complexity of the dependency parser which makes parsing of long sentences exceeding 100 tokens impractical. In a large parsebank even a small proportion of such sentences becomes an issue as, ultimately, every parallel parsing process will be stuck parsing a long sentence, impairing the whole pipeline. Adopting a practical solution to the problem, we automatically split each sentence longer than 120 tokens to approximately evenly sized sections of roughly 100 tokens or less, and parse these sections separately. Candidate points to split the sentence are, in order of preference, after a semicolon, between items of numbered lists and, finally, after a comma or a colon. To reconstruct a full parse tree from the sections, we connect them using the classifier discussed in Section 3.3, only this time for performance reasons we connect the islands sequentially from left to right and only insert dependencies between the roots of the islands. This step affects 0.37% of all sentences in the parsebank. The possibility of parsing the long sentences with a transition-based parser was considered, however, we decided on the abovementioned procedure as it allows the re-use of the classifier as well as simplifies the software distribution of the final parsing pipeline.

Upon initial feedback from the FIN-CLARIN representatives, we have also implemented a separate post-processing step to address the cases where the parser produces two subject dependents of a verb (5.0% of all subjects). This is not a syntactically possible structure, however the purely statistical parser has no hard constraint preventing its generation. Further, double subject is an easily noticeable parsing error which we thus were specifically required to

---

[4]`http://code.google.com/p/mate-tools/`

address. Again relying on the classifier, in all multiple subject cases we preserve the subject with the highest score and replace all other subject dependencies with the highest-scoring non-subject dependency type.

4.3   Corpus text and parsing speed

The corpus to be parsed consists of 44.1M tokens from the JRC-Acquis corpus and 32.2M tokens from the EuroParl corpus. Parsing the total 76.4M tokens in 4.37M sentences (for an average sentence length of over 17 tokens) required approximately 900 CPU hours, using 4-core CPUs. This corresponds to processing speed of roughly 0.7 seconds per sentence, or, 24 tokens per second. The processing was split to 850 batches and parallelized on a cluster computer, resulting in actual parsing time of approximately 10 hours.

5   Evaluation

Since the parsebank was developed in a contract research setting, a formal evaluation, fully independent of us, was carried out by FIN-CLARIN and compared against pre-agreed acceptance thresholds. We did not carry out a separate evaluation ourselves since we do not have at our disposal the necessary gold-standard reference trees in the FTB scheme, and since there was no need for such an evaluation, the FIN-CLARIN results being the sole acceptance criterion of the output. The results of the evaluation are reported by Voutilainen et al. (2012b) and summarized here in Table 2. The accuracy of morphological information is in the 97-98% range while the dependency type accuracy (proportion of tokens whose dependency type is correct) and dependency relation accuracy (proportion of tokens whose governor is correct, usually referred to as *unlabeled attachment score*) are both in the 88-90% range. The commonly used *labeled attachment score* (i.e. the proportion of tokens which have both their governor and dependency type correctly assigned) is, unfortunately, not reported by Voutilainen et al. Overall, we can conclude that the accuracy of the parsebank is high, and above the acceptance threshold which was set to 95% for morphology accuracy, 85% for dependency type accuracy, and 87% for dependency relation accuracy.

Metric	Accuracy
Lemma	98%
Morphological analysis	97%
Dependency type	89–90%
Dependency relation	88–89%

Table 2: Official external evaluation results of the parsebank. The dependency type and dependency relation accuracies are reported as two values by Voutilainen et al. (2012b), the first value is obtained by directly inspecting the parsebank, while the second is obtained by comparison with an independently annotated gold standard.

The accuracy of the dependency scheme transformation procedure can be estimated directly on the 1,992 grammar examples from FTB-1 which we have annotated in the SD scheme and used when developing the transformation rules. The first, rule-based step of the transformation results in incomplete trees which we evaluate in terms of precision and recall of individual dependencies. The post-processed transformation forms complete trees, and is thus evaluated in terms of dependency type accuracy, dependency relation accuracy, and labeled attachment score. The first step results in precision of 83.4% and recall of 80.7%. The final transformed output after the machine learning based postprocessing, and after removing the null tokens, has dependency type accuracy of 91.1%, dependency relation accuracy of 90.1%, and labeled attachment score of 88.2%.

The FTB-1 grammar examples is the only data at our disposal which allows a direct evaluation of the transformation. However, the grammar examples considerably differ in style from the target legal and parliamentary domain and are not fully representative of the transformation of the whole treebank. As a further, indirect evaluation we thus compare the FTB scheme parsing results reported in Table 2 with parsing results in the SD scheme on the JRC-Acquis and EuroParl sentences which we have annotated as in-domain data, as described in Section 2. Taking a weighted average in the proportions of JRC-Acquis and EuroParl texts in FTB-3, the dependency type and dependency relation accuracies for a parser trained on the SD scheme can be estimated as 92.3% and 89.1%. These figures are closely comparable with the figures achieved after transformation, as reported in Table 2. This suggests a successful transformation as the overall performance of the parser has not deteriorated compared to that prior to transformation.

6   Conclusions

In this paper, we have introduced the methods and resources used to build a large-scale Finnish dependency parsebank. Having started from an external, non-negotiable specification of the text to parse and the target scheme, we have developed a parsing pipeline capable of processing the 76.4 million token corpus, resulting in a parsebank with highly accurate morphological and syntactic annotation. The accuracy of the morphological information in the parsebank is in the 97-98% range whereas the accuracy of the dependency types and relations is in the 88-90% range, both figures being the result of an independent evaluation carried out by FIN-CLARIN.

We have applied several techniques to modify the existing resources to conform to the specification of the parsebank. In particular, we have introduced a dependency scheme transformation procedure with hand-written rules followed by a machine-learning based post-processing component. This procedure was used to transform the Turku Dependency Treebank into the target dependency scheme, enabling us to train a statistical dependency parser on this treebank.

The resulting parsebank is made freely available by FIN-CLARIN at
`http://www.ling.helsinki.fi/kieliteknologia/tutkimus/treebank/`.

Acknowledgments

Computational resources for the dependency parsing step of the pipeline were provided by CSC — IT Center for Science, Espoo, Finland.

References

Bohnet, B. (2010). Top accuracy and fast dependency parsing is not a contradiction. In *Proceedings of COLING'10*, pages 89–97.

de Marneffe, M.-C. and Manning, C. (2008a). Stanford typed dependencies manual. Technical report, Stanford University. Revised for Stanford Parser v. 2.0.4 in November 2012.

de Marneffe, M.-C. and Manning, C. (2008b). Stanford typed dependencies representation. In *Proceedings of COLING'08, Workshop on Cross-Framework and Cross-Domain Parser Evaluation*, pages 1–8.

Hakulinen, A., Vilkuna, M., Korhonen, R., Koivisto, V., Heinonen, T.-R., and Alho, I. (2004). *Iso suomen kielioppi / Grammar of Finnish*. Suomalaisen kirjallisuuden seura.

Haverinen, K. (2012). Syntax annotation guidelines for the Turku Dependency Treebank. Technical Report 1034, Turku Centre for Computer Science.

Haverinen, K., Ginter, F., Laippala, V., Kohonen, S., Viljanen, T., Nyblom, J., and Salakoski, T. (2011). A dependency-based analysis of treebank annotation errors. In *Proceedings of Depling'11*, pages 115–124.

Haverinen, K., Viljanen, T., Laippala, V., Kohonen, S., Ginter, F., and Salakoski, T. (2010). Treebanking Finnish. In *Proceedings of TLT9*, pages 79–90.

Koehn, P. (2005). Europarl: a parallel corpus for statistical machine translation. In *Proceedings of MT Summit X*, pages 79–86.

Nivre, J., Hall, J., Nilsson, J., Chanev, A., Eryiğit, G., Kübler, S., Marinov, S., and Marsi, E. (2007). MaltParser: A language-independent system for data-driven dependency parsing. *Natural Language Engineering*, 13(2):95–135.

Pahikkala, T., Tsivtsivadze, E., Airola, A., Boberg, J., and Salakoski, T. (2007). Learning to rank with pairwise regularized least-squares. In Joachims, T., Li, H., Liu, T.-Y., and Zhai, C., editors, *SIGIR 2007 Workshop on Learning to Rank for Information Retrieval*, pages 27–33.

Steinberger, R., Pouliquen, B., Widiger, A., Ignat, C., Erjavec, T., Tufiş, D., and Varga, D. (2006). The JRC-Acquis: A multilingual aligned parallel corpus with 20+ languages. In *Proceedings of LREC'06*, pages 2142–2147.

Voutilainen, A., Lindén, K., and Purtonen, T. (2011). Designing a dependency representation and grammar definition corpus for Finnish. In *Las tecnologías de la información y las comunicaciones: Presente y future en el análisis de córpora. Actas del III Congreso Internacional de Lingüística de Corpus*, pages 151–158.

Voutilainen, A., Purtonen, T., and Muhonen, K. (2012a). FinnTreeBank2 manual. Technical report, University of Helsinki, Department of Modern Languages.

Voutilainen, A., Purtonen, T., and Muhonen, K. (2012b). Outsourcing parsebanking: The FinnTreeBank project. In *Shall We Play the Festschrift Game?*, pages 117–132. Springer.

Constructing a Multilingual Database of Verb Valence

Lars Hellan[1], Tore Bruland[2]

(1) Department of Language and Communication Studies, NTNU, N-7491 Trondheim
(2) Department of Informatics, NTNU, N-7491 Trondheim

lars.hellan@ntnu.no, torebrul@idi.ntnu.no

ABSTRACT

We show the initial stage of an incremental on-line multilingual valence pattern demo, presently populated with two languages, Norwegian and Ga. The procedure for establishing the Norwegian part of the valence database resides in reusing material available in the computational HPSG-grammar Norsource, which has a rich array of lexical information, in part developed from earlier existing lexical resources for Norwegian. The procedure used for Ga is based on a Toolbox lexicon for Ga, with a first stage of processing enabling its data to join the conversion strategy used for Norwegian. A common template is used for the valence information display, although neither source fills in the template completely, reflecting their original differences in content. Essential among these is the availability of example sentences illustrating each valence option for each verb – this is available for Ga, but not for Norwegian. The results are implemented but not yet widely published, serving at the moment partly for self-improvement through exhibiting weaknesses in the resources from which they were derived, and partly for development of the multilingual design.

KEYWORDS: Valence, Syntactic Argument Structure, Computational Grammar, Norwegian, Ga, LKB, HPSG, Toolbox.

1   Introduction

We present the initial version of an on-line multilingual database, so far with two languages represented – Norwegian and Ga (spoken in the Accra area of Ghana). Such a database is of potential value for machine-aided translation, and for language comparison from both practical and theoretical perspectives. No multilingual valence database exists yet, to our knowledge, thus neither standards nor 'good examples' are available for reference for the present enterprise. Monolingual valence databases do exist, including, for instance, the Erlangen Valence Patternbank, [1] VerbNet, [2] and E-VALBU, [3] and standards set by those could be carried over to the information provided by the partaking languages of a multilingual database. A requirement of a multilingual database, though, is that the encoding of information must be uniform across the languages involved, which means that (i) a 'mechanical' combination of existing monolingual bases would not suffice; and (ii) the design of a common categorization and classification will be a crucial challenge. Still, since assembling lexical material for a language, making a classification system, and making consistent use of it in the construction of the database for the language, are major tasks, the more one can make use of existing resources, the better.

In the present demonstration, we make use of two pre-existing lexical resources: the verb-lexicon of the Norwegian HPSG grammar *Norsource*, [4] based on the LKB platform, [5] and a Toolbox lexicon of Ga[6]. The former consists of about 10,000 entries (for verbs), the latter nearly 2000 (for verbs), both on what we may call a 'full-frame' basis, namely a design where alternative valence frames for a given lemma are represented by different entries.[7]

2   The Norwegian valence lexicon

The Norsource lexicon has adopted and adapted resources from the TROLL project[8] and the NorKompLex project, conducted previously at NTNU. The format of an LKB type entry is exemplified in (1) below from the Norwegian lexicon, with the lexical entry for regne 'rain', as in det regner 'it rains'; the lexical type of the entry - here *v-intrImpers* [9] - carries all aspects of syntactic and semantic information reflected in the grammar: [10]

(1)   regne_impers := v-intrImpers &
          [INFLECTION nonfinstr,
          STEM < "regne" >,
          PRED "_regne_v_rel"].

---

[1] http://www.patternbank.uni-erlangen.de/cgi-bin/patternbank.cgi?do=introtxt
[2] http://verbs.colorado.edu/~mpalmer/projects/verbnet.html
[3] http://hypermedia2.ids-mannheim.de/evalbu/
[4] http://typecraft.org/tc2wiki/Norwegian_HPSG_grammar_NorSource ; on HPSG, cf. Pollard and Sag 1994.
[5] Cf. (Copestake 2002).
[6] See Dakubu 2009, 2010
[7] This in contrast to approaches like (Levin 1993), and VerbNet, which rather identify as the main unit a verb together with its cluster of possible frames (belonging to what is called a 'verb class').
[8] Cf. (Hellan et al. 1989).
[9] For the system of type labels used, cf. (Hellan and Dakubu 2009, 2010).
[10] The expression in (1) reads : 'regne-impers' is a subtype of the type 'v-intrImpers', with the specifications for inflection class, stem and predicate values indicated, following the tdl code used in LKB grammars.

A conversion list with members like (i), (ii) and (iii) in TABLE 1 below is then used to populate the database; to the left of the arrow is the lexical type name, and the lines to the right provide 'expansions' of this type name, in the format chosen for the database:

(i)   v-intrImpers   =>   SAS: "EXPL"
                                                          SFP: impersonal-weatherProcess
                                                          Example of type: "det regner"

(ii)   v-intrImpersPrtcl   =>   SAS: "EXPL+adpos"
                                                          SFP: impersonal-weatherProcess
                                                          Example of type: "det klarner opp"

...

(iii)   v-ditr   =>   SAS: "NP+NP+NP"
                                                          SFP: ternaryRel

...

TABLE 1: Sample from the conversion of valence-types to specifications used in the database view.

'SAS' stands for 'syntactic argument structure'. For Norwegian, the set of possible SAS specifications is currently 158, which is close to being exhaustive at this level of specification, based on so-called 'formal' categories – (2) is a snippet of the list:

(2)   ....
        NP+INF
        NP+INF:equiSBJ
        NP+INF:raisingSBJ
        NP+NP
        NP+NP+APpred
        ...

'SFP' stands for 'semantic and functional properties', and is so far a more tentative and restricted assembly of categories, but an area of further development. The total number of conversion rules including those in TABLE 1 is currently 350.

Every entry of the grammar's lexicon (i.e., entries like (1) above) is run through the conversion list, and the expansions for each verb populate the database. In the user interface, the search for any specific verb lemma can be combined with a menu of lexical types, and with a SAS or SFP specification; see below.

3   Expansion to a bi- and multi-lingual valence lexicon

For the multilingual demo, the material also for Ga comes from verb lexicon files available in the form of a TDL-formalism lexicon, based on a separate conversion from the Toolbox format to the

LKB lexicon format. [11] In the TDL-entries, exemplified in (3), each attribute corresponds to a 'field' in the Toolbox file:

A conversion list as exemplified in TABLE 1 will convert the lexical types used in the Ga file into the same general array of SAS and SFP labels as for Norwegian (with some labels specific to Norwegian, and some to Ga, reflecting typological differences). The database for Ga will have specification slots corresponding to all of the attributesexemplified in (3), along with those induced by the conversion rules, just as the Norwegian database will have specifications for the relevant parameters in (1) along with those induced by the conversion rules. Thus, the database is created on a 'pot-luck' basis, each language contributing its own resources, on a common form.

Multilanguage Valency Patterns

Version 1.0

Languages:
☑Norwegian ☑Ga

Search fields:

V-key	Syntactic Arguments	Semantic and Functional Properties	Type
b	NP+NP+NP		

[Search] [Count] [Clear] [Download]

Search Result

ga [show] ba_14
ga [show] ba_8
no [show] bake_ditr
ga [show] baŋ_28
no [show] belære_ditr
no [show] benevne_ditr
no [show] berøve_ditr
no [show] beskjære_ditr
no [show] beta_ditr
no [show] betale_ditr
no [show] betro_ditr
no [show] bevilge_ditr
ga [show] bi_52
no [show] bibringe_ditr
no [show] booke_ditr
no [show] bringe_ditr
ga [show] bu_90
no [show] by_ditr
ga [show] bɔ_74
ga [show] bɔ_76
ga [show] bɔle_85
ga [show] bɔɔs_88

FIGURE 1: Search result for ditransitive frame.

With these prerequisites, a search in the combined database will be able to define its targets by SAS, or SFP, or Lexical Type, or any combination of these - see FIGURE 1 above and FIGURE 2 below for screen-shot examples of the two types of views available. [12] The view in FIGURE 1

---

[11] See (Hirzel 2006, 2012) for earlier explorations of such conversions.

[12] The demo website is http://regdili.idi.ntnu.no:8080/multilanguage_valence_demo/multivalence.

brings out, for the language(s) selected, the set of entry-IDs of verbs satisfying the criteria indicated, viz. here the SAS frame "NP+NP+NP" (the formal pattern of a d-transitive or double-object construction).

Each verb-ID in the list in FIGURE 1 is provided with a button 'Show', and FIGURE 2 is an instance of what can be called up with this button, a view for the second lowest verb on the list in FIGURE 1, stating all of the information directly or indirectly encoded in the entry in (3). This information thus includes the attribute 'Verb Type', with a value *v-ditr* being the expression explicitly entered behind the symbol ':=', and a value for 'Semantic and Functional Properties', which is not explicitly entered in (3), but induced from the Verb Type *v-ditr* in the conversion list illustrated in TABLE 1, here the by item (iii) in that list.

Multilanguage Valency Patterns

Version 1.0

Languages:
[✓] Norwegian [✓] Ga

Search fields:

V-key	Syntactic Arguments	Semantic and Functional Properties	Type
b	NP+NP+NP ⌄	⌄	⌄

[Search] [Count] [Clear] [Download]

Lexicon Instance

Language	ga
Verb Id	bɔle_85
Syntactic Arguments	NP+NP+NP
Semantic and Functional Properties	ternaryRel
Verb Type	v-ditr
Example of type	
Orthography	<"bɔle">
Phon	<"bɔlè">
Engl-gloss	<"expect">
Example	Wɔ-bɔle-ee bo nakai
Gloss	1P.AOR-go.around-NEG.IMPERF 2S that
Free-transl	we didn't expect it of you, that you would behave in that manner.

FIGURE 2: Result for 'Show' for a verb displayed on the search result in FIGURE 1.

Having mentioned machine translation as a possible application of such a database, it is clear that valence information by itself is not a carrier of translation, but together with information about semantic equivalence of putative verb pairs in two languages, valence equivalence or similarity will serve as an additional parameter to induce quality of translation. For the marking of semantic equivalence there will be in principle two routes – 'bridging' through the availability of shared English (or other language) glosses, and sameness of semantic representation in some formalism rich and tractable enough to be readily searchable. Per this day, no system of the latter kind is available, [13] and the information located in the present slot 'semantic and functional properties' is too general to induce translation. For the option of going via English glosses, the Ga database has the necessary information, but the Norwegian database not, hence the database at present could not contribute substantively towards translation by itself, only offer valence information supplementing translation hypotheses generated elsewhere.

4   Logistic perspectives

The database architecture is open for the addition of further languages. The database and its interface are independent of the data provenance – the data, when already acquired and systematized, could come from lexically based grammars (of which HPSG grammars are only one type), or from digital lexical resources generally. The classification systems can vary, as long as correspondence rules like those suggested in TABLE 1 can map them to the system of SAS and SFP here adopted. The conversion pipeline can be of any form whatsoever - in the present case, they come for both languages from LKB files, but this is because one of the provenance sources actually is formalized in LKB, and for Ga, there is indeed an LKB grammar also for this language, [14] where the lexicon file is also used.

The scalability of the approach nevertheless will depend on for how many languages a process as here suggested can be fairly directly replicated. Since there are many languages for which LKB grammars have been defined, the present process can in principle be used for many of these languages; [15] the same holds for other frameworks of 'deep grammars'. Replicability of the process from Toolbox projects is likewise conceivable, but since these are developed in much less mutual concordance than the grammar types mentioned, they have to be considered more on a one-by-one basis.

Another issue is that of incremental improvement of the database – what we have so far described is a 'once-and-for-all' line of action, which is obviously insufficient for tasks of such complexity as a valence database. LKB grammars, among others, typically lack specifications like the lower lines in (3), and a question will be how to add such specifications, i.e., example sentences with instructive glossing. Incremental improvement of any aspect of the database can in general be done through the grammar/lexical resource, with uploading of the system to the database from time to time; acquisition of examples from corpora, or by individual contribution, will constitute a different path. Conceivably there could be a direct contribution interface to the database for relevant examples; or one could use corpus and annotation tools to feed the relevant information into the 'source' grammars, [16] from which the information could be further propagated to the database using the established pipeline. This issue will be in focus in further design developments, with Norwegian being first in line for testing.

---

[13]   Initiatives   that   may   lead   towards   such   formats   include   FrameNet   ((cf. https://framenet.icsi.berkeley.edu/fndrupal/), and the Leipzig Valency Classes Project (http://www.eva.mpg.de/lingua/valency/index.php ; cf. Comrie and Malchukov, to appear).

[14] Cf. Dakubu et al. 2007.

[15] Aside from a conversion strategy from verb types as here illustrated, one can also induce SAS information from the actual feature structure of the lexical entries, when run through the grammar unification mechanism; this has been done for Norsource, but is not included in the current system.

[16] For instance using TypeCraft (http://typecraft.org – cf. (Beermann and Mihaylov 2011)), as described in (Hellan and Beermann 2011),

5   Linguistic perspectives

There is general consensus that parameters like the following ought to be represented in an account of valence types:[17]

(4)   a. syntactic argument structure, i.e., whether there is a subject, an object, a second/indirect object, etc., referred to as grammatical functions, and the formal categories carrying them;

b. semantic argument structure, that is, how many participants are present in the situation depicted, and which roles they play (such as 'agent', 'patient', etc.);

c. linkage between syntactic and semantic argument structure, i.e., which grammatical functions express which roles; - identity relations, part-whole relations, etc., between arguments;

d. aspect and Aktionsart, that is, properties of a situation expressed by a sentence with the valence in question in terms of whether it is dynamic/stative, continuous/instantaneous, completed/ongoing, etc.;

e. type of the situation expressed, in terms of some classificatory system.

The slot 'SAS' used presently may be said to represent the formal part of (4a), while the functional part of (4a), the '–arity' part of (4b), (4d), and to a small extent (4e), are included under the current slot 'semantic and functional properties', a slot which may well become split up according to these parameters in the future. 'Type' in the current demo represents the lexical type label used in the input grammar; the array of such types relevant for Norwegian is described in (Hellan 2008), and the general system of type labels in question is described in (Hellan and Dakubu 2009, 2010). Other grammars or sources providing valence data may well use other type or type label inventories, and we leave open at this point whether each provenance system should be introduced as it is under 'Type', or some approach of standardization be attempted – counting against the latter are the circumstances that the other slots will be fully standardized anyhow, and that the 'pot luck' approach to acquisition will be easier the less conversion operations are called for. What one may still strive for is that similar ranges of discriminants are included in the classification systems used - thus, the type labels used presently cover the parameters already mentioned, whereas inclusion of participant roles, for instance, or more fine-grained situation type specifications, would increase the number of types considerably.

In general, it is given that valence frames will differ across languages and across language typologies, Norwegian and Ga illustrating both. We may refer to a language's valence type inventory as its *v(alence)-profile*, and it will be a natural desideratum that a valence demo as here constructed should display not only valence information for particular verbs of each language involved, but also its v-profile generally. For the purpose of exposing such profiles, the online database has a 'select' functionality whereby for a specific language chosen, its v-profile is shown through the circumstance that only the Types and SAS options of relevance for the language are displayed on the roll-down menu. The task of establishing v-profiles, on the other hand, is a purely linguistic enterprise, aided through general descriptive work, corpus acquisition, or any combination of strategies. As an instance of decisions to be made in the linguistic

---

[17] See, for instance (Fillmore 2007), and other articles in (Herbst et al. 2007).

classification, a point brought out in the representation of the present pair of languages is that Ga, as a typical Kwa language making extensive use of verb serialization, encodes through serial verb constructions many of the contents for which Norwegian uses extended valence frames like those involving secondary predicates[18] and other complex relations.[19] The question then arises whether v-profiles should include constellations based on two verbs or more, or one should create a related notion of *c(onstruction)-profile* where also constructs like the relevant serial verb constructions are included. In the Ga lexical database, we have chosen the latter option, thereby including labels like 'ev-' for 'extended verb construction', visible in the Ga Type inventory, and 'pv-' for 'preverb', and 'SVC' (as a placeholder for possible more detailed specifications) for 'serial verb construction', in the Ga SAS inventory.[20]

Both the Norwegian and the Ga underlying resources are in active development. In the case of Ga, the Toolbox version indeed has a layer of fine-grained semantic information added to the discriminants shown currently in the Type inventory of Ga, not included in the current LKB file but included in another file not used yet. The inclusion of this information will be done at a later point, and the SFP list for Ga will then be considerably richer than it is currently. For Norsource there is also a background inventory of not-yet-employed semantic notions. In addition, some valence frame specifications are employed on a try-out basis for a few verbs, which means that in the Type inventory, whereas types like 'v-intr' and 'v-tr' have a large number of entries (2195 and 4668, respectively), some types have just 2 or 3 members. As the current import to the valence database is based on the actual state of the lexicon, some instances of mal-proportions thereby ensue, which might be eliminated at later points; on the other hand, the views offered by the current demo are instructive to the grammar developers in these respects, and so are being maintained for the present.

In general, the linguistic notions encoded in such a database have to be generally understood, sufficiently that contributors can agree in the ways notions apply or correspond across frameworks, and so that users can understand them fairly directly. When a large range of such notions are put together in a comprehensive database, and with an in principle unlimited span of typological linguistic variation, the enterprise of course faces profound challenges relating both to the analytic understanding of phenomena and the terminologies and analytic systems applied to them. Rather than perceiving such a situation as just a 'challenge', however, one could, from a linguistic point of view, appreciate it for providing a space of investigation which is central to the concerns of linguistics, namely arriving at cross-typological, cross-framework understanding of phenomena and their analyses.

6 Concluding remarks

The architecture of a valence demo here described is fairly straightforward, computationally speaking; the basic work sits in the previous development of resources like the underlying grammar or lexicon, and in maintaining theoretical command of the linguistic issues involved. The latter task has been facilitated through the prior close linguistic cooperation behind the

---

[18] In the v-profile encoded in Norsource, no less than 40 valence frames include a secondary predicate ('small clause predicate').

[19] We here have in mind constructions referred to as 'integrated' serial verb constructions, as opposed to 'chaining' constructions, i.e., those linking together indefinite sequences of consecutive events.

[20] For explanation of these notions, see (Hellan and Dakubu 2010), and (Dakubu et al. 2007).

contributing resources; bringing together resources with less of such a background is likely to be more challenging, linguistically as well as computationally.

We hope to have identified an interesting avenue for re-utilization of linguistically rich resources, to be confirmed through further developments of the current design, including the population of it with more languages, and through further developments of the demo, both in its monolingual and its bi-lingual capacities.

References

Beermann, D. and Mihaylov, P. (2011). e-Research for Linguists. *Proceedings of the 5th ACL-HLT Workshop on Language Technology for Cultural Heritage, Social Sciences, and Humanities*

Comrie, B. and Malchukov, A. (eds) (to appear) *Handbook of Valency classes.*

Copestake, A. (2002). *Implementing Typed Feature Structure Grammars.* CSLI.

Dakubu, M.E.K. (2009). *Ga-English Dictionary with English-Ga Index.* Accra: Black Mask Publishers.

Dakubu, M.E.K. (2010) Toolbox project Ga, University of Ghana.

Dakubu, M.E.K., L. Hellan., and D. Beermann. (2007). Verb Sequencing Constraints in Ga: Serial Verb Constructions and the Extended Verb Complex. In St. Müller (ed) *Proceedings of the 14th International Conference on Head-Driven Phrase Structure Grammar.* CSLI Publications, Stanford. (/http://csli-publications.stanford.edu/)

Fillmore, C. (2007): Valency issues in FrameNet. In: Herbst and Götz-Votteler (eds.).

Hellan, L. 2008. Enumerating Verb Constructions Cross-linguistically. COLING Workshop on Grammar Engineering Across frameworks. Manchester. http://www.aclweb.org/anthology-new/W/W08/#1700

Hellan, L., Johnsen, L. and A. Pitz. (1989) The TROLL Project. Ms., NTNU.

Hellan, L. and M.E.K. Dakubu. 2009. A methodology for enhancing argument structure specification. *Proceedings from the 4th Language Technology Conference (LTC 2009),* Poznan.

Hellan, L. and Dakubu, M.E.K. (2010) *Identifying Verb Constructions Cross-linguistically.* SLAVOB series 6.3, Univ. of Ghana.

Herbst, T and K. Götz-Votteler (eds.) (2007): *Valency: Theoretical, Descriptive and Cognitive Issues,* Berlin/New York: Mouton de Gruyter.

Hirzel, H.. 2006. Deriving LKB lexicons from Toolbox. Talk given at Workshop on Grammar Engineering, NTNU, June 2006.

Hirzel, H. 2012. Converting a Toolbox lexical database to LKB format. http://typecraft.org/tc2wiki/Converting_a_Toolbox_lexical_database_to_LKB_format.

Levin, B. (1993) *English Verb Classes and Alternations.* Univ. of Chicago Press, Chicago, IL.

Pollard, C. and Sag, I. (1994). *Head-Driven Phrase Structure Grammar.* Univ. of Chicago Press, Chicago, IL.

New Measures to Investigate Term Typology by Distributional Data

Jussi Karlgren

from
Kungliga Tekniska Högskolan
and
Gavagai, Stockholm

`jussi@kth.se`

ABSTRACT

This report describes a series of exploratory experiments to establish whether terms of different semantic type can be distinguished in useful ways in a semantic space constructed from distributional data. The hypotheses explored in this paper are that some words are more variant in their distribution than others; that the varying semantic character of words will be reflected in their distribution; and this distributional difference is encoded in current distributional models, but that the information is not accessible through the methods typically used in application of them. This paper proposes some new measures to explore variation encoded in distributional models but not usually put to use in understanding the character of words represented in them. These exploratory findings show that some proposed measures show a wide range of variation across words of various types.

KEYWORDS: Term typology, distributional semantics.

1   Words and terms in use — general requirements for a language model

For text analysis tasks such as information retrieval, terminology mining, or conceptual modelling, words and terms naturally lend themselves as surrogates for documents or representations of concepts. A necessary component in any system for text analysis is a representation, explicit or implicit in the text analysis process, for the concepts expressed in text by computation over the terms that express them. Since the lexical variation is great, such a representation must select or weight or consider the words, terms, and constructions judiciously, typically based on observable characteristics of the items in the text collection under consideration, sometimes consulting language resources compiled elsewhere such as lexica or ontologies.

Target notions for the usefulness of a word or term for some typical text analysis tasks are e.g. *representativeness* for some topic, *specificity* in discriminating between documents of different topics, and *topicality* in general, meaning how likely its appearance in a text is evidence of it being a carrier of text topic. (Spärck Jones, 1972; Hisamitsu et al., 2000; Katz, 1996) A representation or language model, whether probabilistic, geometric, or symbolic, should obviously be designed to capture the target notions most relevant for the task at hand. The three characteristics given above are not immediately observable in themselves — they are derived from observed distributional behaviour of words and terms in text and discourse and from an understanding of what topic is, extratextually.

But, aside from a word's potential usefulness for a task, it will have semantic characteristics which usually are acknowledged by the community of language users: terminological *vagueness*, *abstraction*, *indefiniteness*, and *change* over time are obvious, ubiquitous, and salient characteristics of words and terms in human language, but seldom afforded any place in computation. Any language model, whether it addresses hands-on tasks in information access application, machine translation, dialogue systems or other application area for human alnguage processing or if it built to elucidate the workings of human communicative behaviour in the abstract should be expected to address those semantic characteristics which are most obvious to human users of language.

What character can words and terms then have, observably? An observable difference between words and terms is their distribution over semantic neighbourhoods. Some words and terms are focussed and specific; others are inspecific and spread over several usage patterns. In this initial paper we propose some measures to explore this distributional variation.

2   Experiments on word distributions

These first experiments concern the behaviour of *words*. Terms are frequently composed of several words in conventional fixed configurations (Smadja, 1993; Justeson and Katz, 1995) and the arguments and experiments given here can be generalised to multi-word terms and even constructions, but for practical reasons these initial experiments are performed on single-token words. The distribution of words is here studied in two text collections — a collection of newprint from Reuters comprising 200 million words in short news telegrams, and one month of collected English-language blog text comprising 189 million words in short blog posts.

Our hypotheses are (1) that some words are more variant in their distribution than others — an assumption that is not difficult to defend; (2) that the varying semantic character of words will be reflected in their distribution; and (3) this distributional difference is encoded in current distributional models, but that the information is not accessible through the methods typically used in application of them.

abstract terms

ability adventure amazed anger anxious awe bad beauty belief brave brutal calm chaos charity childhood clarity comfort communication compassion confidence content courage crime curious customer death deceit dedication defeat delight democracy despair determined dictatorship disappointment disbelief disquiet disturbance education ego elegance energy enhancement enthusiasm envy evil excited failure faith faithful fascination fear forgive fragile frail free freedom friend friendship generous glitter good grace gracious grief happiness happy hate hatred hearsay helpful helpless home honest hope hurt idea imagination impression improvement infatuation inflation insanity intelligence jealousy joy justice kindness knowledge laughter law liberty life loss love loyal loyalty luck lucky luxury mature maturity memory mercy moral motivation move movement music need opinion opportunity pain patience peace peculiar peculiarity pleasure poor poverty power pride principle real reality refreshment relief restoration rich rumour sacrifice sad sadness sanity satisfaction self-control sensitive service shock silly skill sparkle speculation speed strength stupid success surprise sympathy talent thrill tired tolerance trust unemployment upset warm weak weakness wealth wisdom worth

Swadesh terms

i you we this that who what not all many one two big long small woman man person fish bird dog louse tree seed leaf root bark skin flesh blood bone grease egg horn tail feather hair head ear eye nose mouth tooth tongue nail foot knee hand belly neck breast heart liver drink eat bite see hear know sleep die kill swim fly walk come lie sit stand give say sun moon star water rain stone sand soil cloud smoke fire ashes burn path mountain red green yellow white black night hot cold full new good round dry name

Figure 1: Abstract and Swadesh terms used in the experiment

To test the hypotheses under consideration we established two word lists to provide a basis for differentiating behaviour of different types of word. We initially took the 100 word list by Swadesh with cross-linguistically translatable words as an example of concrete and fairly invariant concept references. (Swadesh, 1971) We added a list of some 160 abstract terms taken from various author guides.[1] The terms used are given in Figure 1.

2.1 Simple distributional measures

For practical semantic tasks such as search engines, topic modelling, or text categorisation, term usage is computed from their occurrence statistics. The typical search engine categorises terms according to their potential information content inasmuch can be determined from its distribution over a document collection, the target task being to separate documents from each other using search terms as a criterion. This sort of computation serves well to distinguish topical from non-topical words. Table 2.1 shows how the Okapi BM25 formula (Robertson and Zaragoza, 2009), the base for many, or even most, practical search engines today weights terms differentially depending on their topical qualities based on a combination of term frequency within documents, the number of documents the term appears in often with a document length factor added in to compensate for the effect of long documents on term frequency counts.

In general, formulæ such as BM25 do a good job of taking out words with a broad and uninteresting distribution, as well as infrequent words. Words with a low BM25 tend to be function words, misspellings, and unusual compounds. Words with a high BM25 score will be trade marks, names, and technical terms. This serves the needs of a topical search engine well.

A more principled approach to modelling word distribution is the three-parameter burstiness model formulated by Slava Katz (Katz, 1996). His model uses occurrence statistics to estimate α, the likelihood of encountering a term, γ the likelihood of its being topical if encountered, and B, the burstiness of the term, if established as topical. These estimates are handily calculated with α being the observed relative frequency of the term, γ the observed number of documents where the term occurs more than once, and B the average frequency of a term in those documents

---

[1] Author guidelines tend to issue blanket warnings to aspiring writers, discouraging abstract and vague vocabulary, irrespective of if it would be warranted or not.

	Newsprint		
	average tf	idf	$BM25$
and	4.29	2.92e-7	3.20
it	2.74	6.45e-7	5.61
	...		
food	1.72	2.09e-5	13.2
hunger	1.50	0.000453	14.8
eat	1.21	0.000653	12.3
beef	2.40	8.50e-5	10.56
seafood	1.43	0.00239	10.56
barbecue	1.19	0.0149	2.97
jerky	1.00	0.0454	0.841

Table 1: Search engine measures for some sample words for news text.

	Newsprint		
	α	γ	B
	$\hat{p}(occurrence)$	$\hat{p}(topicality)$	$\hat{p}(burstiness)$
and	0.270	0.819	6.20
it	0.177	0.589	3.52
	...		
food	0.0123	0.347	3.09
hunger	0.000616	0.319	2.59
eat	0.0000545	0.159	2.3
beef	0.00236	0.613	3.29
seafood	0.000131	0.242	2.79
barbecue	0.0000239	0.121	2.57
jerky	0.00000907	0	0

Table 2: Katz measures for some sample words for news text.

where its frequency is over 1. Katz' α is high for frequent and low for infrequent words; Katz' γ is high for words that are likely to be repeated and thus likely to be topical in the contexts where it is used; for Katz' burstiness we find very high scores for function words, high scores indicative of technical terms and trade marks and low burstiness scores for hapax legomena and misspellings, as exemplifed in Table 2.1. A word such as *music* will has in our present data set an observed likelihood of 0.38 of being repeated once seen in text, and thus, following Katz' estimate, a relatively high probability of being a topical term in discourse; a word such as *stupid* an observed repeat likelihood of 0.09 and a lower attendant estimated probability of being topical.

2.2 Variation in local context size

As a first test we collected the variation in the immediate neighbourhood of the words under consideration. For each word, we tabulated its occurrences and its immediately adjacent words

| | #different words/#observations ||
	blog text	newsprint
eat	0.09	0.35
sun	0.18	0.58
		...
talent	0.91	0.95
gossip	1.10	1.56

Table 3: Number of neighbours in local context

in a window of two words to the left and to the right. We find that function words such as *and it*, vague terms such as *good*, and very general verbs such *see* have a more wide range of neighbours than do more referentially specific terms such as *frail soil* or *defeat*.

Table 3 gives some examples of terms ranging from 0.09 to 1.56. The theoretical maximum of this score is 4 for a completely dispersed neighbourhood: with two words collected to the left and two to the right, if every observation has all those four words different the score will be 4. The table of results is sorted by score, and subsequent rank sum tests show significant differences between the Swadesh terms and the abstract and vague term list, with the former having a more focussed and presumably semantically more constrained neighbourhood. (Mann Whitney U, p > 0.95) This gives us reason to experiment further, to see how their neighbourhood evaloves, related to the two different types of word and to their respective occurrence statistics over a growing number of observations.

2.3   Variation in a semantic space

In the following experiments a distributional semantic space representation is used. Distributional semantic models are based on the assumption that similarity in meaning between entails similarity in usage and thus in the distribution of the words under consideration over a text collection. This assumption holds, as shown in numerous word semantic evaluation experiments. The model in these experiments is built from the two data sets given above using a standard implementation of the random indexing framework (Kanerva et al., 2000) using 1000-dimensional ternary vectors of density 3. Each word encountered in the text is at time of first observation accorded one randomly generated index vector. The distributional context of a word is then represented with another 1000-dimensional *context vector*, into which, for each occurrence of the word, are added the index vectors of adjacent words in the immediate left and right contexts (Sahlgren et al., 2008). This context vector will over time, after a number of observations, capture the close distributional neighbourhood of the word in all occurrences encountered thus far. Words with similar contextual distributions will converge towards similar context vectors. The context in these experiments are modelled by a $2 + 2$ window which has been shown by previous work to best capture tight semantic relations such as synonymy (Sahlgren, 2006). This setting is naturally an obvious one to vary in future experiments — is the semantic variation more noticeable in the tight semantic relations or in the broader more associative relations given by a broad window.

This context vector constitutes the basic data on which the following experiments are performed. This model is a fairly general distributional model and is used not for its specific characteristics but for processing convenience. It is reasonable to assume that most results would in the main

honest	25
person	74
education	85
law	96

Table 4: Number of second-order neighbours for some selected words

translate to any more sophisticated semantic space or probabilistic language model.

2.3.1 Semantic tightness: Overlap

In a semantic space, the meaning of a word is determined by its neighbours. This first measure computes the number of second order-neighbours by taking the ten nearest neigbours to a word and then the ten nearest neighbours for each of those neighbours. If the ten closest neighbours of the ten closest neighbours overlap well, the neighbourhood is semantically well connected. If they do not, the neighbourhood is semantically diverse. The minimum score is 10, the maximum is 110, if all terms have ten different nearest neighbours. A graph of how the number of neighbours evolves as text is being processed is shown in Figure 2 and some example words are given in Table 4. The range of variation for words with a score starting to flatten out is between about 20 and 90 and do so at about a hundred occurrences. Rank sum tests show significant differences between the Swadesh terms and the abstract and vague term list, with the former having a larger average number of second-order neighbours, in partial contradiction to the above result of local neighbourhood size given in Table 3. (Mann Whitney U, p > 0.95) Presumably this shows that the while the immediate distributional neighbourhood of the concrete Swadesh words is close, the words used with it are of a general character.

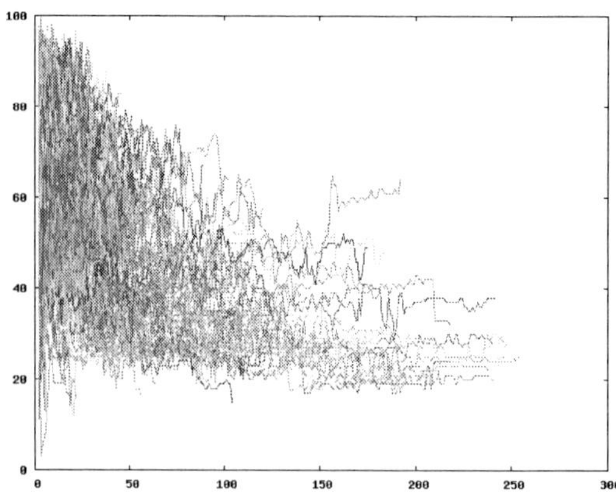

Figure 2: Semantic tightness measured by the number of second order neighbours among the ten nearest neighbours.

2.3.2 Semantic tightness: Angle-at-10

This measure is computed by taking cosine between the target word and its tenth nearest neighbour in the word space. If the word has few semantically similar words, this measure should remain close to 0; if this measure is closer to one, there is a tighter semantic context around this word. A graph of how this measure evolves as text is processed is shown in Figure 3 and some example words are given in Table 5. The range of variation for words with a score

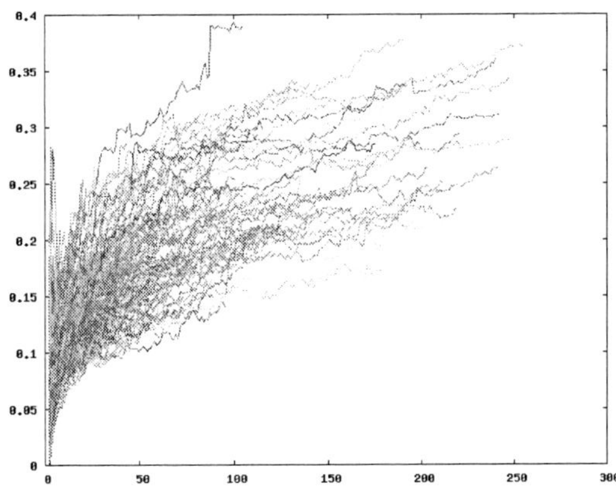

Figure 3: Semantic tightness measured by the cosine to the tenth neighbour.

$know \rightarrow feel$	0.37
$bad \rightarrow substandard$	0.24
$peace \rightarrow harmony$	0.20

Table 5: Cosine to the tenth neighbour for some selected words

starting to flatten out is between about 0.15 and 0.5 — the latter is already a noteworthy score of closeness in this type of model. Rank sum tests show significant differences between the Swadesh terms and the abstract and vague term list, with the former having a lower cosine score to the tenth neighbour, again in partial contradiction to the above result of local neighbourhood size given in Table 3. (Mann Whitney U, $p > 0.95$) Presumably this shows that the constrained neighbourhood may not extend to as many as ten neighbouring words.

2.3.3 Semantic wobble

The third measure we propose is how much the position of the word changes with additional information as new observations of the word are encountered. This measure is computed by taking the cosine between the position of the word in word space before and after each observation. This measure thus captures the semantic impact of the latest observation. A graph of how this measure evolves as text is processed is shown in Figure 4. The great majority of words converge relatively rapidly towards values of over 0.9, indicating that their meaning remains stable in this implementation. Some vary more: *group, position,* and *break* with rather less specific semantics have lower scores than words such as *election* and *university*.

2.3.4 Converging to known synonym

For words with very obviously identifiable synonyms — a small minority of terms in human language — a measure of *convergence* can be used to test the quality of the implementation at hand. Semantically very similar words should be assumed to relatively rapidly converge towards each other — meaning that their representations in this implementation should find each other after not too many occurrences. As an example, words such as *he* and *she* as well as *man* and *woman* should be expected to end up with similar representations. This assumption is borne out by data from this experiment as shown in Table 6 with the notable exception of the delay for *man* to match with *woman* as its closest synonym in blog text, where various names

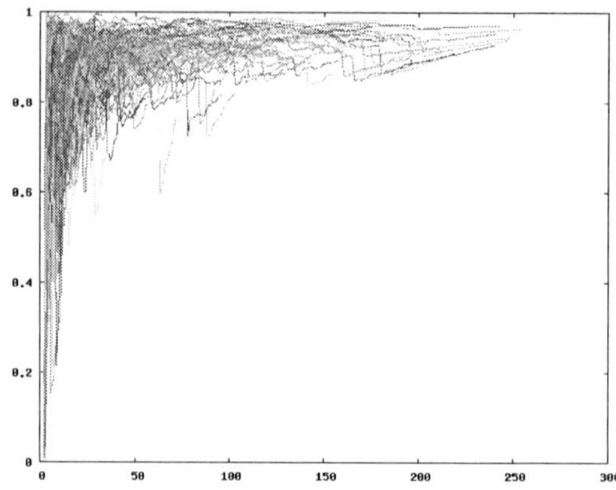

Figure 4: Semantic wobble measured by divergence from centroid.

	blog text		newsprint	
	first occurrence	stable occurrence	first occurrence	stable occurrence
$he \rightarrow she$	12	37	216	384
$she \rightarrow he$	21	34	4	5
$woman \rightarrow man$	214	284	4	4
$man \rightarrow woman$	228	562	40	74

Table 6: Number of occurrences until most reasonable synonym is established

and synonyms such as *guy* confound the process.

3 Conclusion

This first — quite explorative — study is intended to provide a first basis for measures beyond first-order term and document frequency as a measurement of terminological specificity. Some of the proposed measures appear to give purchases to separate terminology quite broadly: the range of variation shows promise for semantically useful distinctions to be made. A notable observation is that by most measures, words appear to find their semantic position in but a few mentions. Most words are fairly consistent in their meaning, even in the more fluid material given by blog authors.

Acknowledgements

This work is supported by Vetenskapsrådet, the Swedish Research Council through a grant for the project "Distributionally derived grammatical analysis models".

References

Hisamitsu, T., Niwa, Y., and Tsujii, J.-i. (2000). A method of measuring term representativeness: baseline method using co-occurrence distribution. In *Proceedings of the 18th conference on Computational linguistics*, pages 320–326, Morristown, NJ, USA. Association for Computational Linguistics.

Justeson, J. S. and Katz, S. M. (1995). Technical terminology: some linguistic properties and an algorithm for identification in text. *Natural Language Engineering*, 1:9–27.

Kanerva, P., Kristofersson, J., and Holst, A. (2000). Random indexing of text samples for latent semantic analysis. In *Proceedings of the 22nd Annual Conference of the Cognitive Science Society, CogSci'00*, page 1036. Erlbaum.

Katz, S. (1996). Distribution of content words and phrases in text and language modelling. *Natural Language Engineering*, 2(1):15–60.

Robertson, S. and Zaragoza, H. (2009). The probabilistic relevance framework: BM25 and beyond. *Foundations and Trends in Information Retrieval*, 3:333–389.

Sahlgren, M. (2006). *The Word-Space Model: Using distributional analysis to represent syntagmatic and paradigmatic relations between words in high-dimensional vector spaces*. PhD Dissertation, Department of Linguistics, Stockholm University.

Sahlgren, M., Holst, A., and Kanerva, P. (2008). Permutations as a means to encode order in word space. In *Proceedings of the 30th Annual Conference of the Cognitive Science Society, CogSci'08*, pages 1300–1305, Washington D.C., USA.

Smadja, F. (1993). Retrieving collocations from text: Xtract. *Computational Linguistics*, 19:143–177.

Spärck Jones, K. (1972). A statistical interpretation of term specificity and its application in retrieval. *Journal of Documentation*, 28:11–21.

Swadesh, M. (1971). *The origin and diversification of language*. Aldine, Chicago. Edited by Joel Sherzer post mortem.

Analysis of phonetic transcriptions for Danish automatic speech recognition

Andreas Søeborg Kirkedal

Department of International Business Communication, CBS
Dalgas Have 15, DK-2000 Frederiksberg
Denmark

`ask.ibc@cbs.dk`

ABSTRACT

Automatic speech recognition (ASR) relies on three resources: audio, orthographic transcriptions and a pronunciation dictionary. The dictionary or lexicon maps orthographic words to sequences of phones or phonemes that represent the pronunciation of the corresponding word. The quality of a speech recognition system depends heavily on the dictionary and the transcriptions therein. This paper presents an analysis of phonetic/phonemic features that are salient for current Danish ASR systems. This preliminary study consists of a series of experiments using an ASR system trained on the DK-PAROLE corpus. The analysis indicates that transcribing e.g. stress or vowel duration has a negative impact on performance. The best performance is obtained with coarse phonetic annotation and improves performance 1% word error rate and 3.8% sentence error rate.

KEYWORDS: Automatic speech recognition, phonetics, phonology, speech, phonetic transcription.

1 Introduction

Automatic speech recognition systems are seeing wider commercial use now more than ever before. No longer are ASR systems restricted to rerouting scenarios in call centres with a small and domain-specific vocabulary. The largest commercial experiment in Europe to date has taken place in the Danish public sector in Odense municipality and entailed more than 500 case workers dictating reports rather than typing them.

To be a practical alternative to manual transcriptions or typing in general, the recognition rate must be high. Otherwise, the potential gain will be spent correcting the recognised output. Many approaches to optimisation of ASR have been investigated including multiple pronunciation variants, direct modelling of acoustic features and domain-specific language modelling. One thing that seems to be missing is an investigation of what features of pronunciation are salient for the ASR system. This is likely a result of the complexity of ASR systems, meaning that ASR research is usually conducted by computer scientists or engineers, who can better understand the intricacies of acoustic models, language models, acoustic feature extraction etc.

1.1 Related work

From a phonetic point of view, research into the importance of the transcription chosen for the pronunciation dictionary and the phonetic features in the alphabet has not been carried out extensively. The phonetic transcriptions available in corpora are usually not created for computational modelling. In many cases, the description *itself* is the goal rather than what the description can be used *for*. Therefore, the transcription contains symbols for phonetics and prosody.

One related study investigates the effect of rate of speech (ROS) on Danish ASR (Brøndsted and Madsen, 1997). The article shows that low and high ROS have a negative impact on recognition accuracy and that e.g. long and short vowels should be modelled separately because long vowels are more sensitive to ROS than short vowels are.

Modelling long and short vowels separately supports the observation that all vowels in Danish have a short and a long version and this a distinctive lexical feature (Grønnum, 2005).

(Ljolje, 1994) introduced the use of Gaussian Mixture Models (GMMs) and probabilistic duration modelling to distinguish between long and short vowels. Using duration modelling and GMMs the word error rate (WER) on a 25000 word task was reduced by 10% and GMMs have been part of standard ASR systems ever since.

Schwa assimilation in Danish has been investigated in (Schachtenhaufen, 2010, In Danish). From a linguistic point of view the article describes a set of rules for schwa assimilation, schwa elision and distinct schwa pronunciation based in part on sonority principles and on syllable and word boundaries. This is further condensed into a single rule for the manifestation of schwa assimilation. The linguistic investigation is conducted on the DanPASS corpus and is mainly a qualitative study.

2 Speech recognition overview

An ASR system consists of an acoustic model, a language model and a pronunciation dictionary. The acoustic model is a phone classifier. The input for an acoustic model is a vector of acoustic parameters such as Mel Feature Cepstral Coefficients (MFCC). The feature vector is extracted from 10-20 ms windows of the speech input. Each of the MFCC vectors are then classified as

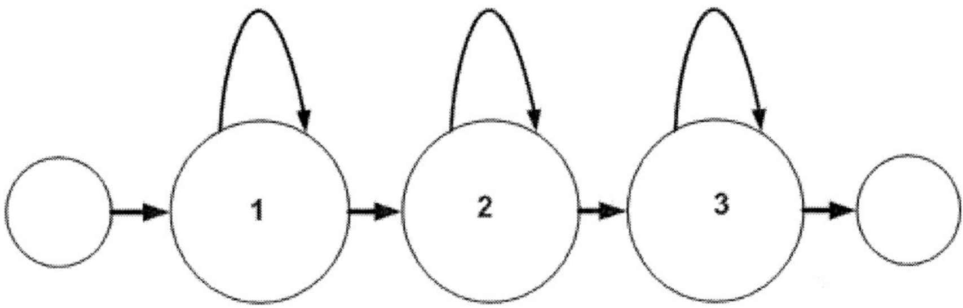

Figure 1: A triphone model.

a set of phones with an associated probability. Usually, there is a n-to-1 relationship between MFCC vectors and phonetic symbols, because the phone duration will be longer than the window a vector is derived from.

To take coarticulation effects into account and make the phone classification more context-dependent, each phone is subdivided into three subphones: *start*, *middle* and *end* as shown in Figure 1. The *start* state is the transition into the current phone and is dependent on the previous phone, the *middle* state is the current phone, which is most context-independent and the *end* state is the transition out of this phone, which is sensitive to the next phone and affects the *start* of the next phone. These groups of subphones are called *triphones*. An n-to-1 relationship holds between MFCC vectors and subphones as well and is handled in a triphone model by allowing transitions from a state back to the same state.

Sequences of triphones are compared to the pronunciation dictionary and a set of possible orthographic sentences or phrases are created from the triphone sequences. They are then weighted by the language model and ranked according to the acoustic model score and the language model score. The highest scoring sentence is found using e.g. the Viterbi algorithm and output by the decoder as the result. A toy example of the decoding process can be seen in Figure 2.

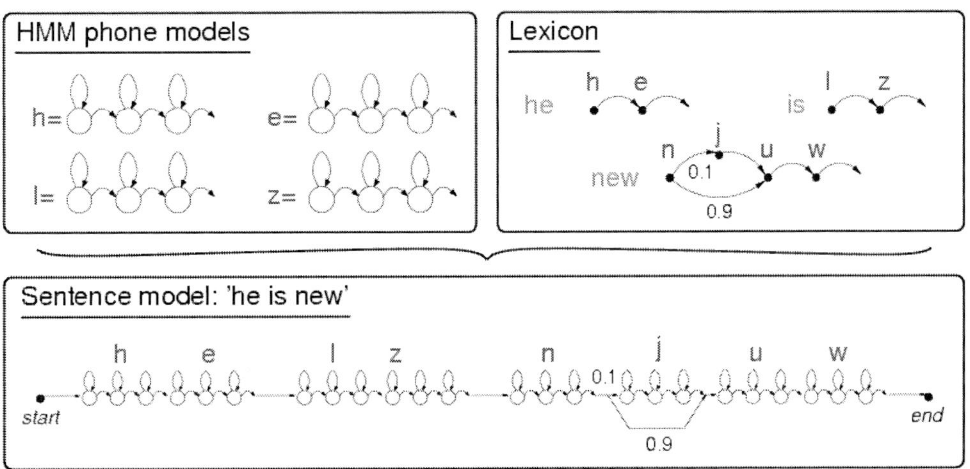

Figure 2: A toy decoding example. Notice that in this example, a pronunciation variant of *new* is allowed.

2.1 Training

ASR is data-driven and needs large amounts of data to train acoustic and language models. The type of data is important for the performance of the ASR system and features such as voice, domain, noise, volume and variation in the training data has an impact on the performance of an ASR system. Recordings must be transcribed and a phonetic dictionary with a transcription for each word must be created or acquired. The audio files and the transcriptions are fundamental to train an ASR system. The audio files must be recorded in such a way that they are suitable for training an ASR system. The audio files should preferably be in uncompressed format such as MSWAV, a sampling rate of 16kHz, 16 bit and use only a single channel, i.e. mono, not stereo. To train a recogniser for telephone speech, the sampling rate must be 8kHz. If you have audio files, which have a higher sampling rate and/or is in stereo, it is possible to downsample and convert into mono, but it is not possible to upsample your data.

3 Phonetic transcription

Several alphabets are used to create phonetic or phonemic transcriptions. They have been used by researchers for decades and can be seen in almost any dictionary entry. Depending on the researcher or the purpose of a transcription, the full expressive power of an alphabet can be used or a subset thereof. Common for all the alphabets mentioned below are that they can also express suprasegmentals such as stress or Danish *stød*.

3.1 International Phonetic Alphabet

Most known is IPA (International Phonetic Association, 1999), which is used extensively around the world by researchers in and teachers of phonetics and phonology. The IPA alphabet contains symbols for the pronunciation of vowels and consonants as well as symbols or diacritics for different positions of speech organs, duration and prosodic features such as stress and tones.

3.2 Speech Assesment Methods Phonetic Alphabet

Speech Assesment Methods Phonetic Alphabet (Wells et al., 1997) (SAMPA) is a machine-readable language specific phonetic alfabet. It is developed as a collaborative effort between native speakers and phoneticians of all the languages it can be applied to. An extension - X-SAMPA - is a recoding of IPA symbols in ASCII symbols to make the symbols machine-readable.

4 Experiment

The goal is to study the impact of transcription granularity and different phone sets on word error rate (WER). To be able to conduct these experiments, a corpus or corpora suitable for training an ASR system that contains high quality transcription is needed. In addition, a strategy for converting phonetic/phonemic transcriptions to a machine-readable format and for filtering the transcriptions must be chosen and finally, a toolkit for training the ASR systems must be chosen.

4.1 Corpora

There are several Danish spoken language corpora. Some suitable corpora are listed here:

- LANCHART
- DanPASS

- DK-Parole

LANCHART (Gregersen, 2007) contains more than 1000 hours of spontaneous speech. The corpus is automatically transcribed, which means the transcription is generated from orthographic transcription, and all annotations are encoded in PRAAT textgrids (Boersma, 2002). The corpus is designed to monitor language change over time and is representative with respect to regional dialects, age, gender, educational background etc. However, due to the highly overlapping nature of the interviews, the recordings are not suitable for training ASR systems. It is likely that a subcorpus would be suitable, but this kind of filtering is beyond the scope of the project due to the size of the original corpus.

DanPASS (Grønnum, 2006) is a highly accurate, manually annotated speech corpus with time-coded phonetic and phonemic transcriptions, POS, lemmata etc. It consists of two subcorpora containing monologues and dialogues. The dialogues corpus contains recordings of experiments with two participants. Each participant has a map and one participant must guide the other to follow a route on the map. However, the two maps are not identical. When the participants must explain to each other the differences in the maps, semi-spontaneous speech occurs during the unscripted negotiation of the different maps. The monologues corpus contains recordings where one participant is asked to describe a network of coloured geometric networks. Even though the corpus contains dialogues, there are no overlapping speech. Speakers of different age, gender and different dialects are represented. The annotation in the corpus is the most fine-grained in all the corpora using most of the expressive power of IPA. DanPASS also uses textgrids to encode annotations and transcriptions.

DK-Parole (Henrichsen, 2007) contain recordings of read-aloud speech of one speaker. The annotation is not as fine-grained as DanPASS, but uses the same alphabet as LANCHART, is manually annotated and easier to use for training data. In addition, the SAMPA alphabet is created to be machine-readable and therefore does not require any conversion of the transcriptions to be usable for training an ASR system.

4.2 Phonetic character conversion

Character encoding conversion is possible with existing methods. In the case of IPA symbols, the character encoding must be changed to ASCII from Unicode and the best resource is conversion with X-SAMPA[1]. In addition, ASR toolkits have reserved symbols such as underscore ("_") because they are used for e.g. segmentation during computation that also must be filtered in a way that does not introduce unintended ambiguity. The symbols will be usable for the machine learning algorithms, but may become unintelligible to linguists, which constitutes a problem for debugging.

4.3 Transcription filtering

The phonetic and/or phonemic transcriptions in all the corpora from Section 4.1 contain symbols and diacritics for segments and suprasegments. The classical phonological definition of segments is the smallest discrete unit of speech that you can find (Grønnum, 2005). All the phones in Figure 2 are segments. Suprasegments are phenomena in speech that cover a larger time domain than segments. In general, suprasegmental features such as tone, stress, stød and duration are related to prosody, which is related to syllables, words and phrases.

---

[1]See http://www.phon.ucl.ac.uk/home/sampa/x-sampa.htm.

Suprasegmental features are annotated with diacritics[2].

In current ASR systems, there are no concepts of syllables, stress groups or prosody in general. Due to transcription conventions, suprasegmental features are affixed to segments in phonetic transcription and often used in the training procedure without criticism. This can lead to data sparsity when training triphone models. The ASR system inventories the number of phones/phonemes in the training data to determine the number of triphone models that should be estimated. Supposing that a given phone can have up to 5 separate diacritics affixed, this results in an upper bound of 120 different phone models for a single segment depending on the occurrences in the training data. In DanPASS, the fine-grained transcription results in a phone inventory of at least 400 distinct phones, which are different realisations of the segments. If the difference between two models is very small, the system will not be able to discriminate between the two realisations. Intuitively it seems an ASR systems would become more robust if a model trained for a segment encompassed all the different realisations of that segment rather than 120 models that describe the different realisations of one segment.

Transcription conventions for annotation of stress are also problematic in an ASR context. Stress is annotated with a diacritic that is affixed to a syllable, i.e. a series of segments. In IPA, the convention is to annotate stress as a prefix ('s i r k a) and in the Danish SAMPA alphabet, e.g. in DK-PAROLE, the convention is to annotate stress as a suffix (s i r!   g a). For an ASR system, this will be interpreted as another phone symbol and result in different phone sets.

Duration and syllabification are two features of interest. Syllabification in Danish usually occurs when a schwa is assimilated and a sonorant becomes syllabic. In Danish, syllabification most often occur as the result of schwa-assimilation (SA) and happens when the sonorant is not part of the onset (Schachtenhaufen, 2010). It is interesting to see what happens if the symbol is treated as a segment. It is easier to annotate and altering this transcription convention will decrease annotation time considerably. Schwa is the fourth most common segment in DanPASS and the combination of sonorant+schwa in the coda is quite common because of the Danish definite article suffix *-en* where assimilation is almost obligatory (Schachtenhaufen, 2010). An example of syllabification with SA can be seen in Table 1 as well as the dictionary entry used for the experiments.

No assimilation	l ɛ n g d ə n
Syllabification (SA)	l ɛ n g d n̩
Dictionary entry	l E N d – n

Table 1: Different phonetic transcriptions of the Danish word *længden* (the length).

Duration is of interest because, while it may or may not have prosodic information, it is affixed and related to a single segment. However, this annotation overlaps with the functionality of the transitions in Figure 1 which return to the same state and model the n-to-1 relationship between vectors and phone symbols. Since duration is implicitly modelled, it is interesting to see if filtering away duration can improve the WER and not introduce too much ambiguity. Omitting annotation for duration will also decrease annotation time.

5   Results

For this setup, CMU Sphinx (Placeway et al., 1997) is used to train an ASR system with SphinxIII as the decoder. SphinxIII is a C++ implementation and the main Large Vocabulary Continuous

---

[2]Note that not all diacritics are suprasegmental features, but all suprasegmental features are diacritics.

Speech Recognition (LVCSR) version. To ease reproducibility, the standard configuration of SphinxIII is used in all experiments together with a trigram language model trained on the orthographic material in DK-PAROLE. 3574 recordings or 80% of the corpus was used as training data and the remaining 20% as test set. The experiments were setup with a set of scripts from Henrichsen and Kirkedal (2011). Slight alterations were necessary to make the scripts handle IPA characters and the different tier names in the textgrids. The changes will be added to the github repository[3] when ready. DK-Parole has been used for preliminary studies due to the easy conversion from PRAAT textgrids to the sphinx training database layout, which did not entail any phonetic character conversion, only filtering. Also, the audio was recorded between 2006 and 2008 and the corpus contains the most recent speech recordings of standard Danish available at the time.

Evaluation Metrics:	WER	Words (3574)	Sentence Error	Sentences (894)
No diacritics	5.7%	691	34.3%	307
SA	5.6%	678	34.5%	308
Stød	5.9%	720	36.4%	325
+SA	5.7%	693	34.3%	307
Duration	5.9%	714	35.9%	321
+SA	5.8%	707	36.8%	329
Stress	6.0%	722	36.0%	322
+SA	5.9%	711	36.1%	323
Duration and stress	6.5%	791	38.0%	340
+SA	6.0%	734	36.7%	328
Stress and stød	6.5%	791	38.4%	343
+SA	6.3%	769	37.4%	334
Duration and stød	5.9%	719	36.4%	325
+SA	5.9%	720	36.4%	325
Duration, stress and stød	6.7%	808	38.0%	340
+SA	6.4%	775	38.1%	341

Table 2: Error rates for the DK-Parole ASR experiments. SA is short for schwa-assimmilation.

The WER and sentence error rates of 16 experiments were calculated using SClite (Fiscus, 1998) and are reported in Table 2. WER is the number of substitutions, deletions and insertions normalised by the number of words in the reference:

$$WER = \frac{Substitutions + deletions + insertions}{\# words} \tag{1}$$

Sentence error rate is also reported. In a post-editing scenario, it is relevant to know how many sentences needs to be edited. If a user of an ASR system needs to edit every sentence, the potential gains in efficiency will not be realised, but editing many mistakes in few sentences are not as time-consuming.

The experiments are grouped in pairs where the only difference in the paired experiments are the annotation of SA. In the sets of paired experiments, the transcription in the dictionary was

---

[3]https://github.com/dresen/sphinx_setup

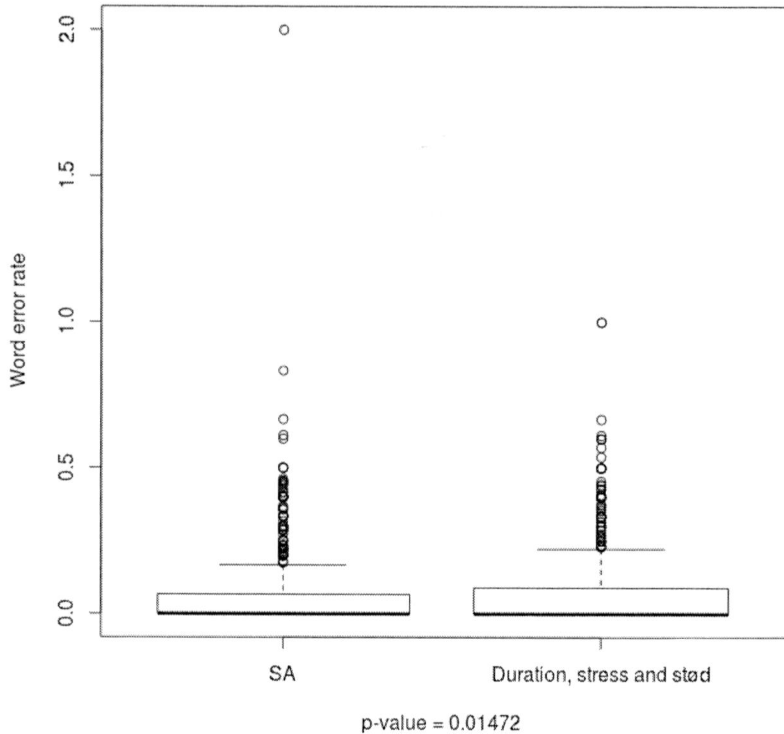

Figure 3: WER significance tests.

changed so all combinations of annotations for stress, duration, stød and SA have been carried out.

6 Discussion

Table 2 shows that including annotation for stress, stød, and duration increases the error rate. In each set of experiments, adding SA annotation has either no impact or decreases the reported error rates.

These preliminary results should be interpreted with caution. The training data is based on recordings of a single speaker reading text aloud. It is possible that this configuration of the pronunciation dictionary is only an improvement on this data set and does not generalise to other speakers.

Treating SA as a segment decreases the WER in the ASR experiments. This is so far the only case where the change from a diacritical to a segmental representation (from [n-] to [-] [n]) has improved the recognition rate. Adding a SA symbol and therefore an SA triphone model, seems to make the systems more robust. This is clear when comparing the WER of experiments including annotation for duration and stress with and without annotation for SA. Adding SA increases the recognition rate in seven out of nine comparisons.

Filtering out duration annotation improves the recognition rate by up to 0.5% WER. This indicates that the implicit modelling of time in triphone models are sufficient to model duration and the lack of this annotation does not introduce unresolvable ambiguity. The amount of ambiguity introduced and whether the ambiguity is resolved by the language model or elsewhere has not been determined. This is interesting because vowel duration is a distinctive lexical feature in Danish and all vowels in Danish exist in a long and short form (Grønnum, 2005). It also conflicts with the conclusions of Brøndsted and Madsen (1997) and indicates that long and

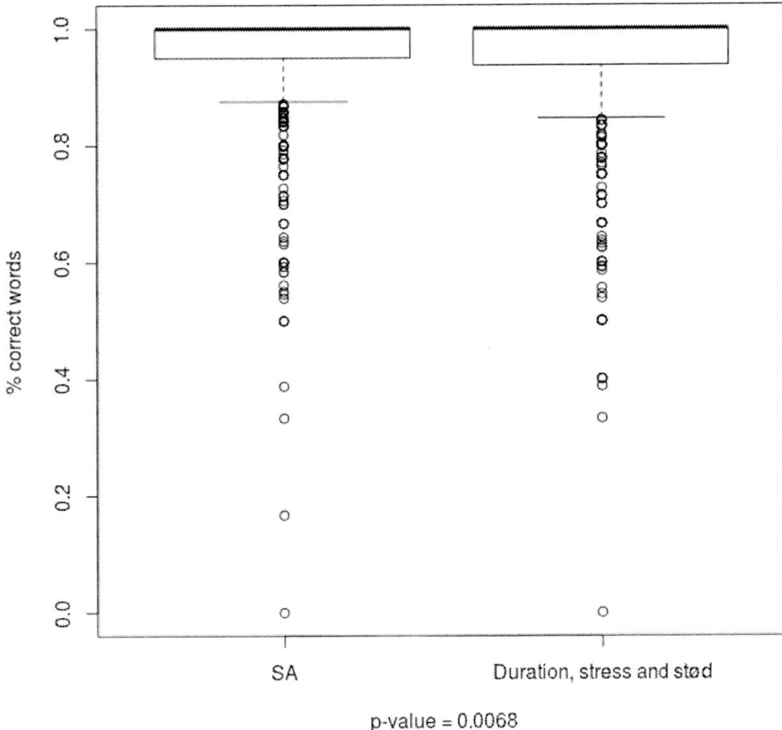

Figure 4: Number of correct words significance tests.

short versions of the same vowel symbol should be used to train a single model.

The changes in transcription give in small improvements. The combined improvement from the worst performing system to the best is statistically significant in terms of correctly recognised words and WER. The p-value and WER significance test can be seen in Figure 3.

A significance test for the number of correctly recognised words have been carried out as well. The results and p-value can be seen in Figure 4.

Some of the most difficult perceptual features to annotate are not salient for ASR systems. This conflicts with transcription conventions from the Danish phonetic community where these suprasegmental features are considered salient for human listeners. This could indicate that transcription can be handled by non-experts, e.g. via Amazon's Mechanical Turk to either create training data or acquire human evaluations (Novotney and Callison-Burch, 2010).

7   Conclusion and Outlook

Conventional speech transcription seems to be more fine-grained than necessary and annotation of suprasegmental features and duration in pronunciation dictionaries for state-of-the-art ASR systems did not improve the recognition rates. Currently, adding annotation for suprasegmental features are counter-productive. These features are important for human listeners, but the HMM and triphone structure of current ASR systems cannot take advantage of this information.

To verify these findings, it is important to repeat the experiments with a different corpus. With the very fine-grained transcription, multiple speakers and semi-spontaneous speech, DanPASS will make a good next step. The transcriptions in DanPASS will also make it possible to experiment with additional annotation.

References

Boersma, P. (2002). Praat, a system for doing phonetics by computer. *Glot international*, 5(9/10):341–345.

Brøndsted, T. and Madsen, J. (1997). Fonemteori og talegenkendelse. *Sprog og multimedier. Aalborg Universitetsforlag.*

Fiscus, J. (1998). Sclite scoring package version 1.5. *US National Institute of Standard Technology (NIST), URL http://www. itl. nist. gov/iaui/894.01/tools.*

Gregersen, F. (2007). The lanchart corpus of spoken danish, report from a corpus in progress. *Current Trends in Research on Spoken Language in the Nordic Countries*, 2:130–143.

Grønnum, N. (2005). Fonetik og fonologi, 3. udg. *Akademisk Forlag, København.*

Grønnum, N. (2006). Danpass-a danish phonetically annotated spontaneous speech corpus. In *Proceedings of the 5th International Conference on Language Resources and Evaluation (LREC), Genova, Italy, May.*

Henrichsen, P. (2007). The danish parole corpus-a merge of speech and writing. *Current Trends in Research on Spoken Language in the Nordic Countries*, 2:84–93.

Henrichsen, P. and Kirkedal, A. (2011). Founding a large-vocabulary speech recognizer for danish. In *Speech in Action,* pages 175–193.

International Phonetic Association (1999). *Handbook of the International Phonetic Association: A guide to the use of the International Phonetic Alphabet.* Cambridge University Press.

Ljolje, A. (1994). High accuracy phone recognition using context clustering and quasi-triphonic models. *Computer Speech & Language*, 8:129–151.

Novotney, S. and Callison-Burch, C. (2010). Cheap, fast and good enough: Automatic speech recognition with non-expert transcription. In *Human Language Technologies: The 2010 Annual Conference of the North American Chapter of the Association for Computational Linguistics*, pages 207–215. Association for Computational Linguistics.

Placeway, P., Chen, S., Eskenazi, M., Jain, U., Parikh, V., Raj, B., Ravishankar, M., Rosenfeld, R., Seymore, K., Siegler, M., et al. (1997). The 1996 hub-4 sphinx-3 system. In *Proc. DARPA Speech recognition workshop*, pages 85–89. Citeseer.

Schachtenhaufen, R. (2010). Schwa-assimilation og stavelsesgrænser. *NyS*, (39):64–92.

Wells, J. et al. (1997). Sampa computer readable phonetic alphabet. *Handbook of standards and resources for spoken language systems*, 4.

Combining Statistical Machine Translation
and Translation Memories with Domain Adaptation

Samuel Läubli[1], Mark Fishel[1], Martin Volk[1], Manuela Weibel[2]

(1) Institute of Computational Linguistics, University of Zurich, Binzmühlestrasse 14, CH-8050 Zürich
(2) SemioticTransfer AG, Bruggerstrasse 37, CH-5400 Baden

`{laeubli,fishel,volk}@cl.uzh.ch`   `manuela.weibel@semiotictransfer.ch`

ABSTRACT

Since the emergence of translation memory software, translation companies and freelance translators have been accumulating translated text for various languages and domains. This data has the potential of being used for training domain-specific machine translation systems for corporate or even personal use. But while the resulting systems usually perform well in translating domain-specific language, their out-of-domain vocabulary coverage is often insufficient due to the limited size of the translation memories. In this paper, we demonstrate that small in-domain translation memories can be successfully complemented with freely available general-domain parallel corpora such that (a) the number of out-of-vocabulary words (OOV) is reduced while (b) the in-domain terminology is preserved. In our experiments, a German–French and a German–Italian statistical machine translation system geared to marketing texts of the automobile industry has been significantly improved using Europarl and OpenSubtitles data, both in terms of automatic evaluation metrics and human judgement.

KEYWORDS: Machine Translation, Translation Memory, Domain Adaptation, Perplexity Minimization.

1   Introduction

Technological advances in the field of automated translation have increased economic pressure on translation companies and freelance translators. According to a recent study published by the European Union (Pym et al., 2012), there is evidence that the per-word rate for professional translations has decreased significantly in some western European countries.

On the other hand, computer-assisted translation tools such as translation memory (TM) systems—allowing translators to store their translations in a personal or corporate database and reuse them on future occasions—have become an integral part of state-of-the-art translation workflows, even for freelancers.

More recently, there have been efforts to combine machine translation systems with translation memories (Kanavos and Kartsaklis, 2010; Koehn and Senellart, 2010). As a result, major commercial systems such as SDL TradosStudio[1], Across LanguageServer[2], and even open source alternatives such as OmegaT[3] now offer machine translation interfaces, allowing translators to have segments automatically (pre-)translated in case there is no corresponding translation available in their translation memory.

In a joint project between the UZH Institute of Computational Linguistics and SemioticTransfer AG, we currently explore the potential of using domain-specific statistical machine translation (SMT) systems in human-based translation workflows. We hypothesize that SMT systems trained on SemioticTransfer's translation memory data will enable their translators to work more efficiently while preserving translation quality.

In our present paper, we report on training and evaluating statistical machine translation systems for two language pairs on a relatively small amount of marketing texts related to the automobile industry. In Section 2, we outline the foreseen translation scenario and introduce means of compensating for the limited size of our in-domain training material. In Section 3, we present SMT systems that are based on a combination of in-domain and out-of-domain data. The combined systems are compared against an in-domain-only baseline. We discuss our findings in Section 4, and lastly, we conclude and outline the further course of our project in Section 5.

2   Background

In this section, we first describe the translation scenario that our domain-specific SMT systems should be applied in. Second, we detail techniques for combining limited amounts of in-domain with out-of-domain translation data.

2.1   Translation Scenario

In SemioticTransfer's current translation workflow, new language material to be translated is imported into a corporate translation memory system by specially trained staff termed translation managers. Subsequently, the manager prepares one or several work packages, each of which consists of a number of documents in the source language with an accompanying empty document in the target language. Next, each source language segment is automatically looked up in the translation memory, and exact matches are directly inserted into the target

---

[1]http://www.sdl.com/products/sdl-trados-studio/index-tab3.html
[2]http://www.across.net/en/across-machine-translation-integration.aspx
[3]http://www.omegat.org/en/howtos/google_translate.html

language document. A specialist translator then translates all remaining segments one-by-one. This process is again supported by the translation memory system: For each segment, the translator is shown similar segments that are already stored in the TM—it is her or his decision whether to take an existing segment and adapt it or translate the segment from scratch instead.

There are many ways to integrate machine translation in such a workflow. Kanavos and Kartsaklis (2010) propose a pragmatic approach that uses a simple SMT model trained on all available translation memory data. This model is used to translate segments for which no fuzzy match with more than 80% similarity is available in the TM, which are subsequently post-edited by specialist translators. The automatic translation is either invoked in an "on-demand" (the translator requests an SMT hypothesis for a segment he is currently translating) or a "one time" mode. We focus on the latter which automatically inserts SMT translations for segments with fuzzy matches below 80% into the target language document before it is handed to the translator, i.e., we produce a pre-translation which is then completed and post-edited inside the translation memory system.

2.2 Domain Adaptation

Unlike Kanavos and Kartsaklis (2010), we focus on a specific text genre: marketing texts of the automobile industry. For this reason, we cannot use large general-domain parallel corpora for training our translation models as (a) many domain-specific terms are not contained in such resources and (b) domain-specific terms would be prone to mistranslation because of domain mismatches. For example, the German word *Arten* could be translated as *espèces* (species) in a general-domain DE–FR translation system. While this translation could be used, for example, in biological texts, it is not adequate in the automobile domain as cars are of certain *types* (types) rather than species.

To counteract these problems, Koehn and Senellart (2010) have proposed to retrieve a fuzzy match in the TM for each source segment to be translated, identify the mismatched parts, and replace these parts by an SMT translation. Their approach relies on automatic word alignment to find the target words that are affected by the mismatch.

In contrast to Koehn and Senellart (2010) we approach combining parallel texts from domain-specific translation memories and general-domain corpora as a domain adaptation problem. We use the approach of mixture-modeling, commonly used for language model adaptation and extended to translation models by Foster and Kuhn (2007). The main distinctive feature of this approach for both language and translation models is that instead of separating the data and models into in-domain/out-of-domain in a binary setting, different domains are assigned real-valued weights, reflecting their similarity to in-domain text material. Using these weights the single domain models $\mathbf{p} = \{p_i\}_{i=1...N}$ are combined into a single adapted model:

$$p(\mathbf{x}) = \mathbf{w}\mathbf{p}(\mathbf{x}) = \sum_{i=1}^{N} w_i p_i(\mathbf{x}).$$

The weights $\mathbf{w}$ are selected to optimize the performance of the adapted model on an in-domain development set. Language model performance is estimated with its entropy on the said set. Unlike Foster and Kuhn (2007) who use a monolingual performance measure for translation models we follow Sennrich (2012) and use the cross-entropy of the adapted translation model on the development set, a bilingual performance measure:

$$\hat{p}(\mathbf{x}) = \arg\min_{\mathbf{w}} H(p), \text{ where } H(p) = -\sum_{\mathbf{x} \in \mathbf{X}^{(d)}} \tilde{p}(\mathbf{x}) \log_2 p(\mathbf{x})$$

Here $H(p)$ is the cross-entropy of the adapted language or translation model p and $\mathbf{X}^{(d)}$ is the development set. The empirical probability distribution $\tilde{p}$ is based on the development set. The nature of $\mathbf{x} \in \mathbf{X}^{(d)}$ depends on which models are handled: in case of language models, it represents a single sentence; in case of translation models it stands for a $\langle source, translation \rangle$ tuple. For more details see (Sennrich, 2012; Chen and Goodman, 1998).

3 Combining In-Domain with Out-of-Domain Data

In this section, we describe the statistical machine translation systems we have trained for our experiments. We briefly describe the training data (Section 3.1) and the system setups (Section 3.2), which we have evaluated by automatic means (Section 3.3.1) as well as with a human evaluator (Section 3.3.2).

3.1 Training Data

3.1.1 In-Domain

The in-domain data has been extracted from SemioticTransfer's translation memories for German–French (DE–FR) and German–Italian (DE–IT). All texts are related to the automobile industry; the translated segments stem from brochures, websites, and price lists. For this reason, a segment may refer to a whole sentence, but also to smaller units such as short phrases or even single words of table entries. After cleaning the memories, we were able to extract 166'957 segments for DE–FR and 112'166 segments for DE–IT, which corresponds to ~2.0 and ~1.5 million tokens, respectively. Please note that all segments are unique. Unlike text from a corpus of running words, each segment from a translation memory occurs only once. The exact numbers are shown in Table 1.

3.1.2 Out-of-Domain

As for out-of-domain data, we have chosen two freely available parallel corpora: Europarl v7 (EP7) (Koehn, 2005) and OpenSubtitles 2011 (OS11) (Tiedemann, 2009). We extracted the DE–FR and DE–IT translations from each of them, resulting in ~48.5 (EP7) and~16.0 (OS11) million tokens per language pair. See Table 1. We point out that these parallel corpora are not thematically related to our in-domain data. Rather than that, they are much more extensive and thus cover a broader vocabulary, which is missing in our in-domain data due to its limited size.

	In-Domain		Europarl		OpenSubtitles	
	DE–FR	DE–IT	DE–FR	DE–IT	DE–FR	DE–IT
Segments	166'957	112'166	1'903'628	1'805'792	2'852'474	2'131'004
Tokens F	2'011'872	1'413'452	48'405'406	48'419'389	16'858'070	15'642'379
Tokens E	2'632'256	1'731'219	56'372'702	50'689'987	16'370'845	15'458'666
Tokens/Segment F	12.05	12.60	25.43	26.81	5.91	7.34
Tokens/Segment E	15.77	15.43	29.61	28.07	5.74	7.25

Table 1: In-Domain and Out-of-Domain Training Data

3.2   Domain-Specific SMT Systems

We have trained an in-domain-only baseline and three systems that combine in-domain and out-of-domain data (see Section 3.1) in different weighting modes for each language pair.

3.2.1   Baseline Systems

Using only the in-domain data, we trained a standard phrase-based statistical machine translation system for DE–FR and DE–IT. 5-gram language models were trained using the IRST Language Modeling Toolkit (Federico and Cettolo, 2007). Otherwise, we relied on the Moses decoder (Koehn et al., 2007) and its dedicated scripts for training, tokenization, and truecasing.

3.2.2   Combined Systems

Additionally, we trained separate translation and language models using our out-of-domain corpora. Apart from the training data, the setup was the same as for our baseline systems. This left us with three phrase tables and language models per language pair: in-domain, EP7, and OS11. All combined systems presented in this section comprise all of these models, but they are differently weighted. The weighting modes are defined as follows.

Unweighted Combination (*unweighted*)

In the *unweighted* mode, we simply concatenated the in-domain, EP7, and OS11 language material. On this basis, we trained a combined translation and language model for each language pair.

Weighted Language Model (*weighted LM*)

In the *weighted LM* mode, we used an interpolated language model alongside an *unweighted* translation model for each language pair. We employed `interpolate-lm` of the IRST Language Modeling Toolkit (Federico and Cettolo, 2007) to estimate interpolation weights for the in-domain, EP7, and OS 11 language models by minimizing their perplexity on a development set of 2'000 in-domain segments (see section 2.2).

| | DE–FR | | DE–IT | |
Corpus	TM	LM	TM	LM
In-Domain	-	91.9	-	92.9
EP7	-	5.8	-	5.0
OS11	-	2.3	-	2.1

Interpolation weights for translation (TM) and language (LM) models in %, *weighted LM* mode.

Weighted Translation Model (*weighted TM*)

| | DE–FR | | DE–IT | |
Corpus	TM	LM	TM	LM
In-Domain	92.3	-	93.7	-
EP7	6.2	-	5.1	-
OS11	1.5	-	1.2	-

Interpolation weights for translation (TM) and language (LM) models in %, *weighted TM* mode.

In the *weighted TM* mode, we combined an interpolated translation model with an *unweighted* language model for each language pair. We applied Sennrich's approach (Sennrich, 2012) for estimating interpolation weights for the in-domain, EP7, and OS11 translation models, again using a development set of 2'000 in-domain segments (see section 2.2).

Weighted Language and Translation Model (*weighted LM+TM*)

In the *weighted LM+TM* mode, we used *both* interpolated language and translation models, i.e., we combined the interpolated language models of the *weighted LM* mode with the interpolated translation models of the *weighted TM* mode for each language pair.

	DE–FR		DE–IT	
Corpus	TM	LM	TM	LM
In-Domain	92.3	91.9	93.7	92.9
EP7	6.2	5.8	5.1	5.0
OS11	1.5	2.3	1.2	2.1

Interpolation weights for translation (TM) and language (LM) models in %, *weighted LM+TM* mode.

3.3 Evaluation

3.3.1 Automatic Evaluation

For evaluating the systems described in Section 3.2, we compiled a test set of 500 segments for both language pairs. The segments were taken from a recent contract of SemioticTransfer: the translation of an automobile company's website from German to French and Italian. The translation was carried out by two professional translators using SemioticTransfer's translation memories.

We used `multeval` (Clark et al., 2011) for evaluating our systems. As there is no full METEOR support for Italian (Denkowski and Lavie, 2011), this score is only available for the DE–FR system. Table 2 gives an overview on all metrics and the performance of the systems; a discussion of these and other results is given in Section 4.

		DE–FR				DE–IT			
Metric	Mode	Avg	$\bar{s}_{sel}$	s_{Test}	*p*-value	Avg	$\bar{s}_{sel}$	s_{Test}	*p*-value
	baseline	32.2	1.3	0.1	-	31.3	1.4	0.3	-
	unweighted	31.3	1.3	0.1	0.00	30.8	1.4	0.2	0.12
BLEU ↑	weighted LM	31.8	1.3	0.2	0.15	32.9	1.5	0.3	0.00
	weighted TM	32.8	1.3	0.3	0.00	31.9	1.4	0.0	0.02
	weighted LM+TM	33.0	1.3	0.2	0.00	31.9	1.4	0.1	0.00
	baseline	51.7	1.2	0.3	-	55.9	1.4	0.6	-
	unweighted	52.9	1.2	0.1	0.00	54.3	1.3	0.5	0.00
TER ↓	weighted LM	51.7	1.2	0.4	0.99	51.9	1.3	0.6	0.00
	weighted TM	50.9	1.2	0.6	0.00	54.7	1.4	0.0	0.00
	weighted LM+TM	50.6	1.2	0.6	0.00	53.3	1.3	0.5	0.00
	baseline	50.5	1.1	0.1	-				
	unweighted	50.1	1.1	0.2	0.12				
METEOR ↑	weighted LM	50.8	1.1	0.2	0.10				
	weighted TM	51.6	1.1	0.3	0.00				
	weighted LM+TM	51.7	1.1	0.3	0.00				

Table 2: Automatic Evaluation. Baseline and Combined Systems. *p*-values are relative to baseline and indicate whether a difference of this magnitude (between the baseline and the system on that line) is likely to be generated again by some random process (a randomized optimizer). Metric scores are averages over 5 MERT runs (Och, 2003; Bertoldi et al., 2009). s_{sel} indicates the variance due to test set selection and has nothing to do with optimizer instability.

Mode	DE–FR			DE–IT		
	baseline	eq.	weighted TM	baseline	eq.	weighted TM
general	15.3	48.7	36.0	15.3	30.7	54.0
terminology	14.7	48.7	36.7	15.3	30.7	54.0

Table 3: Human Evaluation. Subjective preference for 150 Segments translated by the *baseline* and *weighted TM* systems in terms of general and terminological accuracy in %. "eq." indicates that both translation hypotheses were considered equally well.

3.3.2   Human Evaluation

In order to reinforce our automatic evaluation, we conducted a further experiment with a human evaluator who is familiar with SemioticTransfer's automobile domain terminology. We wanted to assess whether and to which extent the difference between the baseline's and a combined system's scores was perceptible for an actual human translator. We chose the *weighted TM* systems for the comparison as preliminary results suggested negligible differences between *weighted TM* and *weighted LM+TM* scores. At the time, we concluded that weighting the language model in addition to the translation model is not worth the additional effort.

We provided our subject with a source segment (DE) alongside a reference translation (FR/IT) and two translation hypotheses for 150 randomly selected segments. One hypothesis was produced by the *baseline*, the other by the *weighted TM* system. The subject's task was to rate which hypothesis was better, (a) in general and (b) with regard to domain technology, with ties allowed. This evaluation setup, known as pairwise system comparison, has lately been favored by the MT community for it is simpler and better reproducible than, e.g., fluency/adequacy judgements on a five-point scale (Callison-Burch et al., 2012). Furthermore, genuine differences between two systems can easily be quantified using the Sign Test for paired observations.

The results, shown in Table 3, reveal the evaluator's clear preference towards the *weighted TM* system's translations. This holds especially for DE–IT. Statistically, the *weighted TM* systems outperform the *baseline* in all regards at $p \leq 0.001$, except for the adequacy of domain terminology in the DE–FR systems ($p \leq 0.01$).

4   Discusson

Our evaluation (see Section 3.3) shows that adding large amounts of out-of-domain data without adequate weights is no suitable means of improving our in-domain-only baseline systems (see Table 2, *unweighted* mode). An unweighted combination with the out-of-domain models lowers the scores for DE–FR compared to the baseline. The difference is statistically significant for BLEU ($p \leq 0.01$) and TER ($p \leq 0.01$), but not for METEOR. For DE–IT, TER improves ($p \leq 0.01$), but at the same time, BLEU decreases slightly (though not significantly). Insights into corresponding translations reveal that the added material reduces the number of out-of-vocabulary (OOV) words, but this effect is by far outclassed by the number of domain-specific terms and phrases that get translated in an inadequate way in the *unweighted* mode (see Table 5).

The *weighted LM* mode has opposing effects on the two language pairs. On one hand, the language model adaptation highly affects DE–IT. *Weighted LM* performs best out of all modes for this language pair and outperforms the baseline significantly, both in terms of BLEU ($p \leq 0.01$) and TER ($p \leq 0.01$). This improvement is in line with the finding of Foster and Kuhn (2007) that language model adaptation works well. Conversely, an interpolated language model has no positive effect on the DE–FR language pair.

Set	Feature	DE–FR		DE–IT	
		$H_{unweighted}$	$H_{weighted}$	$H_{unweighted}$	$H_{weighted}$
DEV	inverse phrase translation probability	2.21	2.18	1.90	1.88
	inverse lexical weighting	6.91	5.85 –	7.19	5.75 – –
	direct phrase translation probability	2.64	2.59	2.14	2.06
	direct lexical weighting	7.35	6.13 –	7.66	5.92 – –
TEST	inverse phrase translation probability	2.91	3.32 +	3.39	3.78 +
	inverse lexical weighting	5.24	5.22	5.53	5.55
	direct phrase translation probability	3.63	3.88	3.37	3.77 +
	direct lexical weighting	6.38	5.81	5.82	5.49

Table 4: Cross entropies H between the DEV and TEST sets and the *unweighted* and *weighted* phrase tables. Plus and minus signs denote changes of $\geq$10% (+/−) and $\geq$20% (+ +/− −).

In contrast, weighting the translation models (*weighted TM* mode) leads to a significant improvement of *all* scores in *both* language pairs (all at $p \leq 0.01$, except $p \leq 0.05$ for BLEU in DE–IT). Here, it turns out that using Sennrich's approach (Sennrich, 2012) to estimate weights for in-domain and out-of-domain translation models is a promising way for improving our systems. The high weights given to the in-domain models ensure that translations in the domain-specific phrase tables are normally preferred over identical source segments with different translations in the out-of-domain data (see Table 5). At the same time, the added out-of-domain translations lower the OOV rate in the *weighted TM* systems, no matter how small their translation probabilities become due to the weighted combination. In our DE–FR test set, this corresponds to a reduction from 194 to 124 OOV types (-36.1%) .

Using both a weighted language and translation model results in no further improvement. For DE–FR, there is a small increase in BLEU and TER, as well as a slight decrease in METEOR, but neither of these changes is significant. For DE–IT however, adding the weighted translation models on top of the weighted language models significantly decreases BLEU and TER (both at $p \leq 0.01$). This can only happen if the development set is too far apart from the test set – in other words, the development set is a poor generalization over the in-domain material, as a result of which the weighting overfits to it. Comparison of the unoptimized and optimized cross-entropies (presented in Table 4) confirms this conclusion: the cross-entropies naturally decrease on the development set both in case of DE–FR and DE–IT as the result of optimization; however, optimization also leads to increased cross-entropy of the combined model on the DE–IT test set.

Further experiments are needed to clarify the influence of interpolated language and translation models, as well as their interplay, on translation quality. Our evaluation of the combined DE–FR systems stands in contrast to the claim by Foster and Kuhn (2007) that "LM adaptation works well, and adding an adapted TM yields no improvement"—rather than that, TM combination works well, and adding an adapted LM yields no significant improvement in our case. However, we cannot generalize this finding to the combined DE–IT systems.

Apart from that, it is remarkable that the estimated interpolation weights of all in-domain models clearly exceed 90%, both in the DE–FR and DE–IT systems (see Section 3.2.2). The high percentages confirm that the marketing texts we look at are very different from our out-of-domain language material, which justifies the development of domain-specific SMT models instead of using out-of-the-box systems that are mostly trained on general-domain resources.

f	$\arg\max\limits_{e} \varphi(e|f)_{unweighted}$	$\arg\max\limits_{e} \varphi(e|f)_{weighted}$
Abgasemissionen	émissions de gaz	émissions de gaz d'échappement
Arten	espèces	types
Decke	couverture	plafond
Kiste	boîte	caisse
Klappe	ferme	clapet
Linksverkehr	conduite	conduite à gauche
PKW	voitures	voiture particulière
Tempo	rythme	vitesse
Unterbodenverkleidung	caisse	garnitures du dessous de caisse
Werke	œuvres	usines
Zulassungen	autorisations	immatriculations
Zünder	détonateur	amorce

Table 5: French terms *e* that maximize the translation probabilities in the unweighted (*unweighted* mode) and weighted (*weighted TM* and *weighted LM+TM* modes) translation models of the DE–FR systems, given a selection of German terms *f*.

5   Conclusion and Future Work

In our present study on using domain-specific translation memories for training machine translation systems, we have shown that very limited amounts of in-domain data can be successfully complemented with general-domain parallel corpora for improving translation performance. Our experiments demonstrate that assigning adequate weights to the in-domain and out-of-domain language and translation models is crucial for successful combinations. Our evaluations confirm that while the number of OOV types decreases through adding large amounts of out-of-domain data, the in-domain terminology prevails over alternative translations due to the weighting. In our German–French and German–Italian systems, using both an interpolated language and translation model has resulted in significant BLEU, METEOR and TER increases. These performance gains have been confirmed by a human evaluator who is familiar with the domain terminology.

In the further course of our project, we would like to give particular attention to German compounds, which constitute approximately 65% of the remaining OOV words in our combined systems, depending on test set and target language. We would like to assess in a systematic way which of the numerous approaches to decompounding such as (Koehn and Knight, 2003; Dyer, 2009; Stymne, 2009; Hardmeier et al., 2010) is suitable for our data and translation scenario. Ultimately, we plan to conduct targeted *in-situ* experiments in order to measure the impact of using our domain-adapted SMT systems in their designated human-based translation workflows.

Acknowledgements

We would like to thank Rico Sennrich as well as our anonymous reviewers for their valuable feedback and support. This work was supported by Grant No. 11926.2 PFES-ES from the Swiss Federal Commission for Technology and Innovation CTI.

References

Bertoldi, N., Haddow, B., and Fouet, J.-B. (2009). Improved minimum error rate training in moses. *The Prague Bulletin of Mathematical Linguistics*, 91(1):7–16.

Callison-Burch, C., Koehn, P., Monz, C., Post, M., Soricut, R., and Specia, L. (2012). Findings of the 2012 workshop on statistical machine translation. In *Proceedings of the Seventh Workshop on Statistical Machine Translation*, pages 10–51, Montréal, Canada. Association for Computational Linguistics.

Chen, S. F. and Goodman, J. (1998). An empirical study of smoothing techniques for language modeling. *omputer Speech & Language*, 13:359–393.

Clark, J. H., Dyer, C., Lavie, A., and Smith, N. A. (2011). Better hypothesis testing for statistical machine translation: Controlling for optimizer instability. In *Proceedings of the 49th Annual Meeting of the Association for Computational Linguistics: Human Language Technologies: short papers - Volume 2*, HLT '11, pages 176–181, Stroudsburg, PA, USA. Association for Computational Linguistics.

Denkowski, M. and Lavie, A. (2011). Meteor 1.3: automatic metric for reliable optimization and evaluation of machine translation systems. In *Proceedings of the Sixth Workshop on Statistical Machine Translation*, WMT '11, pages 85–91, Stroudsburg, PA, USA. Association for Computational Linguistics.

Dyer, C. (2009). Using a maximum entropy model to build segmentation lattices for MT. In *Proceedings of Human Language Technologies: The 2009 Annual Conference of the North American Chapter of the Association for Computational Linguistics*, NAACL '09, pages 406–414, Stroudsburg, PA, USA. Association for Computational Linguistics.

Federico, M. and Cettolo, M. (2007). Efficient handling of n-gram language models for statistical machine translation. In *Proceedings of the Second Workshop on Statistical Machine Translation*, StatMT '07, pages 88–95, Stroudsburg, PA, USA. Association for Computational Linguistics.

Foster, G. and Kuhn, R. (2007). Mixture-model adaptation for SMT. In *Proceedings of the Second Workshop on Statistical Machine Translation*, StatMT '07, pages 128–135, Stroudsburg, PA, USA. Association for Computational Linguistics.

Hardmeier, C., Bisazza, A., and Federico, M. (2010). FBK at WMT 2010: word lattices for morphological reduction and chunk-based reordering. In *Proceedings of the Joint Fifth Workshop on Statistical Machine Translation and MetricsMATR*, WMT '10, pages 88–92, Stroudsburg, PA, USA. Association for Computational Linguistics.

Kanavos, P. and Kartsaklis, D. (2010). Integrating machine translation with translation memory: A practical approach. In *JEC 2010: Second joint EM+/CNGL Workshop "Bringing MT to the user: research on integrating MT in the translation industry"*, pages 11–20.

Koehn, P. (2005). Europarl: A Parallel Corpus for Statistical Machine Translation. In *Machine Translation Summit X*, pages 79–86, Phuket, Thailand.

Koehn, P., Hoang, H., Birch, A., Callison-Burch, C., Federico, M., Bertoldi, N., Cowan, B., Shen, W., Moran, C., Zens, R., Dyer, C., Bojar, O., Constantin, A., and Herbst, E. (2007). Moses: open source toolkit for statistical machine translation. In *Proceedings of the 45th Annual Meeting of the ACL on Interactive Poster and Demonstration Sessions*, ACL '07, pages 177–180, Stroudsburg, PA, USA. Association for Computational Linguistics.

Koehn, P. and Knight, K. (2003). Empirical methods for compound splitting. In *Proceedings of the tenth conference on European chapter of the Association for Computational Linguistics - Volume 1*, EACL '03, pages 187–193, Stroudsburg, PA, USA. Association for Computational Linguistics.

Koehn, P. and Senellart, J. (2010). Convergence of translation memory and statistical machine translation. In *JEC 2010: Second joint EM+/CNGL Workshop "Bringing MT to the user: research on integrating MT in the translation industry"*, pages 21–31.

Och, F. J. (2003). Minimum error rate training in statistical machine translation. In *Proceedings of the 41st Annual Meeting on Association for Computational Linguistics - Volume 1*, ACL '03, pages 160–167, Stroudsburg, PA, USA. Association for Computational Linguistics.

Pym, A., Grin, F., Sfreddo, C., and Chan, A. L. J. (2012). *The Status of the Translation Profession in the European Union*, volume 7/2012 of *Studies on translation and multilingualism*. Publications Office of the European Union.

Sennrich, R. (2012). Perplexity Minimization for Translation Model Domain Adaptation in Statistical Machine Translation. In *Proceedings of the 13th Conference of the European Chapter of the Association for Computational Linguistics*, EACL '12, pages 539–549, Stroudsburg, PA, USA. Association for Computational Linguistics.

Stymne, S. (2009). Compound processing for phrase-based statistical machine translation. Master's thesis, Linköping University, Sweden.

Tiedemann, J. (2009). News from OPUS - A Collection of Multilingual Parallel Corpora with Tools and Interfaces. In Nicolov, N., Bontcheva, K., Angelova, G., and Mitkov, R., editors, *Recent Advances in Natural Language Processing*, volume V, pages 237–248, Borovets, Bulgaria. John Benjamins, Amsterdam/Philadelphia.

Building an open-source development infrastructure for language technology projects

Sjur N. Moshagen[1], Tommi A Pirinen[2], Trond Trosterud[1]

(1) University of Tromsø, Norway
(2) Helsinki university, Finland

sjur.n.moshagen@uit.no, tommi.pirinen@helsinki.fi, trond.trosterud@uit.no

ABSTRACT

The article presents the Giellatekno & Divvun language technology resources, more specifically the effort to utilise open-source tools to improve the build infrastructure, and the solutions to help adapt to best practices for software development. The article especially discusses how the infrastructure has been remade to cope with an increasing number of languages without incurring extra overhead for the maintainers, and at the same time let the linguists concentrate on the linguistic work. Finally, the article discusses how a uniform infrastructure like the one presented can be used to easily compare languages in terms of morphological or computational complexity, coverage or for cross-lingual applications.

KEYWORDS: NoDaLiDa 2013, Infrastructure, Computational linguistics, Finite-state transducers, Language resources, Multilinguality.

1 Introduction

There are about 7000 languages in the world, according to Ethnologue. According to the same source, about 2200 of them have a standardised orthography[1]. Of these, roughly 100-150 have keyboard layouts preinstalled on major operating systems (Trosterud, 2012), and only ~50 are available as a user interface language. The languages with good, continuous speech recognition can be counted on one hand (domain-specific speech recognition on a couple of hands).

The infrastructure described in this article is targeted at languages with limited textual resources: a small literary body, often no PC keyboard layout standard (and thus not delivered as part of any OS), quite often a limited grammatical description. The goal of the work done for these languages is to develop a grammatical description in the form of a morphological grammar and lexicon, and use the lexicon and morphology as the basis for NLP tools and end user tools such as proofing tools and electronic dictionaries. Most of the targeted languages worked on so far are morphologically rich, and the chosen technology is well suited for this type of languages.

Language technology infrastructure is a fairly broad concept, and is covered in many papers and on-going projects (see a.o. (Broda et al., 2010), (Loper and Bird, 2002)).

Many projects could be seen as *resource infrastructure* projects making resources and tools *available* to developers (e.g. META-SHARE (Federmann et al., 2012), CLARIN (Váradi et al., 2008)), our work could instead be characterised as a *development environment* infrastructure project, where the goal is to improve the language processing. This is close to the objectives of environments such as GATE ((Cunningham et al., 1997), (Cunningham et al., 2011)), NLTK[2] and UIMA/OpenNLP[3]. These are language-independent statistically based toolkits, where the linguistic analysis is left to the annotator. Such tools are less feasible for languages with rich morphology and little text, and they are also not able to do language generation. Another type of language processing tools is HPSG[4] and LFG XLE[5]. These tools are also grammar-based, but their focus is on syntactic analysis and not on end-user applications.

The technology presented here has been developed for morphology-rich languages. It offers a framework for building language-specific analysers, and directly turn them into a wide range of useful programs. It shares

2 Infrastructure requirements

The infrastructure presented here meets the following requirements: it separates between language-independent and language-specific data and constructs; it works the same for all languages, thereby letting the linguists focus on the actual linguistics, and ease comparison and cooperation across languages; it uses standard and widely available tools as far as possible; it uses and depends on open-source LT tools, either exclusively or as an alternative; it is platform neutral (but requires un*x for compilation); it supports building a large number of scientific and end-user tools, both normative and descriptive; it supports dialect variation in a standardised way; it integrates with or exports end-user tools for different platforms (e.g. spellers, hyphenators, grammar checkers, for both open-source and closed-source host systems and applications); and finally: it supports reuse of code as much as possible.

---

[1] `http://www.ethnologue.com/statistics/status` - the sum of languages with an EGIDS value 0-5: 2216.
[2] `http://nltk.org/`
[3] `http://opennlp.apache.org/`
[4] `http://moin.delph-in.net/`
[5] `http://www2.parc.com/isl/groups/nltt/xle/`

This is a tall order. While everything is not yet implemented, most of the items on the list are already in place and working well.

3 Technical details

In this section we will present the strategy employed to handle a large number of languages in a consistent way, while at the same time allowing language-specific flexibility — and all of it hopefully without increasing the maintenance burden regarding the infrastructure.

Although many of the points mentioned below are standard good practice of software development, it bears repeating. And to our knowledge nothing like this has been done for morphology-rich minority languages before, targeting both the scientific community and the language communities to the extend and breadth done here. The importance of good software design and an infrastructure supporting code reuse is crucial for language communities with limited resources which can not afford to support several different language technology projects and competing technologies. The choices are made on the ground that it gives double return of the investments: both grammars and tools for linguistic analysis, and software products for the end user community.

3.1 Layout and design

The basic model for the build and configuration infrastructure consists of two parts:

- a central core, containing resources shared by all languages
- a templating system, by which new functionality and new resources are propagated to all languages

The template contains both build files (automake files) and language resource template files. The language resources are copied once, either when a new language is initialised, or the first time a new language resource is made available in the template. The build files, on the other hand, are merged from the template whenever requested. A schematic view of the infrastructure can be seen in figure 1.

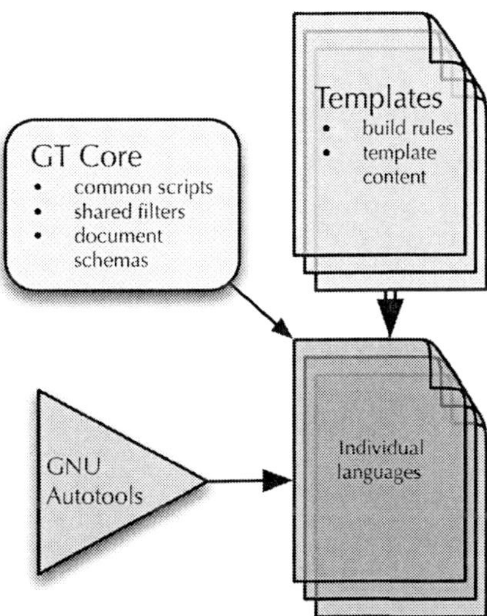

Figure 1: A schematic view of the new Giellatekno/Divvun infrastructure.

3.2 Software

The software used in the infrastructure can also be grouped in two. The first category contains the build tools — the tools used to configure, test, enable and create the build environment. The second category covers the language technology tools — the tools used to build analysers, proofing tools and more, using the linguistic resources and source code.

3.2.1 Build software

One goal with the infrastructure is to use a standard set of build tools combined with established practises for source code layout and organisation. This gives several benefits. It makes it easy for any other open-source project to include our resources, since the build system follows a known pattern. It makes it easier for newcomers, even those who have never seen a software project before - the source code is clearly organised in logical units, and the commands to build and test the tools are few, and the same for all languages.

We base the infrastructure build system on the GNU Autotools[6]: *automake* and *autoconf* and their supporting tools. The tool set is well established in the open-source community, has broad support and handles most cross-platform issues quite well.

3.2.2 Language-technology software

From the very beginning most of the work has been done on languages with rich morphology, and it has been important that the linguistic resources should be usable for as many purposes as possible. Another aspect has been that all the initial languages were minority languages with very little available corpus data. All this is to say that statistical methods and tools have *not* been seen as alternatives. Instead morphological analysis and disambiguation, as well as syntactic analysis, has been rule-based. The basic observation is that there is little corpus data, but as long as there are speakers there is also a grammar and a lexicon — and that is (almost) all that is needed for a rule-based approach.

Initially all work on morphological analysis were done using Xerox' finite state transducer tools, and still today they dominate our daily work. But the Xerox FST tools are closed source, fixing bugs depends on others, the licensing terms have changed and might change again, and who knows what may happen in the future.

During the last years there has been a continuous effort at the Helsinki university to develop a source-code compatible, open-source alternative to the Xerox tools, the HFST tools (Lindén et al., 2011)[7]. These tools are now quite stable and well suited as an alternative, and at the same time they provide more features than the Xerox tools, most notably weighted transducers.

The infrastructure uses the Xerox tools as the default tool set, but has a parallel build system made for hfst. Turning *off* Xerox and *on* HFST is just two options away at configuration time. It is even possible to have both tool sets enabled at the same time - this will cause the build system to produce double sets of transducers, one set for each technology. This gives the added benefit of double error checking of the source code — and it also makes it possible to compare the two tool sets side by side (more on this further down).

For morphological disambiguation and higher level analysis we use Constraint Grammar

---

((Karlsson, 1990) as implemented by the VislCG3 project[8]). VislCG3 is open source as well, and together with HFST this gives a complete open-source tool chain from source code to high-quality analysers including dependency analysis.

3.3 Support for best practices: in-source documentation and unit testing

One of the problems with large software projects (which the development of a complete morphological and syntactic description and a large-scale lexicon is) is that the system becomes so complex that no-one can overview it in full and with all details. This is true both for the linguistic source code and for the infrastructure.

The infrastructure supports a simple system for writing documenting comments as part of the source code. The system is inspired by numerous systems for other programming languages, many of which goes back to (Knuth, 1984). The generated documentation is converted to html, and viewable online.

In addition to in-source documentation, the infrastructure also supports specifying test data as part of the source code. This becomes essentially a unit-test-like setup (Huizinga and Kolawa, 2007): when you write a new inflectional lexicon for a new inflectional class, you can start by spelling out the wanted behaviour in the form of test cases. This also helps with refactoring the code.

The morphological testing is done using a tool developed as part of the Apertium[9] Quality Assurance project[10], but further developed to fit the needs of this infrastructure. The test tool supports bidirectional testing of the morphologies (both generation and analysis), and is thus well suited to test for overgeneration and errors in the morphology and morphophonology. The test tool is integrated with the generic testing facilities in Autotools.

3.4 Availability and sustainability

Going open-source is not only a generally good principle, it is a prerequisite for long-term sustainability and control over the language technology resources developed for minority and lesser resourced languages. To that end, all the required tools for the infrastructure are open source — or an open-source alternative is available via a configuration option — and all the linguistic resources themselves are of course open source[11]. Each language can set its own licence policy, but we encourage everybody involved to choose as open a license as possible.

As far as possible, we also try to support and develop end-user tools for open-source applications and solutions. While established tool sets that are taken for granted, like spellers, can be integrated system-wide on most platforms, newer or more advanced language technology solutions like speech recognition or grammar checkers are blocked[12].

The target audience for the infrastructure is first and foremost linguists and computation linguists. The tools are accessed and used from a Unix command line, and basic familiarity with

---

[8]`http://beta.visl.sdu.dk/cg3.html`

[9]`http://www.apertium.org`

[10]`http://wiki.apertium.eu/index.php?title=Session_7:_Data_consistency_and_quality&oldid=2173`

[11]`http://divvun.no/doc/infra/GettingStarted.html`

[12]On some new platforms it isn't even possible to install keyboards for your own language, if you want to follow the license of the platform.

Development status keyword	Explanation
started	some initial work has been done, but the lexical content is very limited
developed	the morphological description is well on its way, the lexicon is substantial
large	the morphological description is more or less done, the lexicon is big
production	good coverage, complete grammatical description, used for end user tools

Table 1: Brief explanation of the development status categorisation.

unix systems is assumed. Furthermore, as has probably become clear, the main focus is on text processing applications, although new applications and data types will certainly be added in the future.

4 Language coverage

Here we list the languages presently in our infrastructure, along with their development status. (briefly described in table 1).

Production: Finnish, Lule Sami, Northern Sámi, Kalaallisut, Southern Sami,
Large: Erzya, Faroese, Norwegian Bokmål
Developed: Cornish, Eastern Mari, Komi-Zyrian, Kven Finnish, Iñupiaq, Old Norse, Somali
Started: Amharic, Buriat, Guaraní, Inari Sami, Ingrian, Inuktitut, Karelian, Kildin Sami, Kinyarwanda, Komi-Permyak, Livonian, Livvi, Moksha, Nenets, Ojibwe, Pite Sami, Romanian, Skolt Sami, Tagalog, Tigrinya, Udmurt, Ume Sami, Veps, Võro, Western Mari

5 The tools produced by the infrastructure

The infrastructure will build a number of tools for all the covered languages (the quality of the tools varies a lot depending on the development stage of each language).

The most important compiled resources are **morphological analysers and generators**, both normative and descriptive ones. In addition to being at the core of the textual analysis pipeline, these are also used as parts of electronic dictionaries, language learning tools, online services such as paradigm and word-form generation, and as important blocks in machine translation.

The infrastructure will compile any CG3 rules file into **syntactic analysers**, possibly with **dependency analysis** if the source file exists (for many of the languages covered, it is quite possible to reuse the dependency analysis (Antonsen et al., 2010)).

A classic application (Oflazer, 1996)) of transducers is as **proofing tools** - spellers and hyphenators. At the time of writing, spellers based on a combination of HFST and Voikko[13] are produced by the infrastructure. For most of the languages listed in table 3 this is a first, and the value for the user community is very real and direct.

The proofing tool example also illustrates the double benefit of working rule-based: grammatical models are developed, which often means new insight into the language, or that knowledge that earlier was only indirectly described needs to be made explicit. That is, the grammatical description of the language often becomes better and more explicit, one gets a large lexicon usable as a starting point for many different projects and research efforts, and at the same time — literally — one can give back to the language community in the form of usable and valuable tools. This is a great inspiration for the work described in this paper.

---

[13]`http://voikko.sf.net/`

System: Language	HFST	Xerox
Greenlandic	1 h 11 min	37 min 12 s
Faroese	6 min 25 s	3 min 55 s
Lule Sámi	2 min 44 s	30.9 s
South Sámi	2 min 4 s	11.1 s
Finnish	18.7 s	16.4 s
Komi-Zyrian	59.3 s	4.6 s
Moksha	39.9 s	2.7 s
Eastern Mari	36.8 s	2.7 s
Western Mari	36.7 s	2.7 s
Udmurt	29.3 s	0.9 s
Erzya	26.7 s	2.1 s
Skolt Sámi	26.2 s	3.0 s
Voru	22.7 s	1.5 s
Ingrian	21,6 s	1.5 s
Livvi	21.1 s	1.6 s
Inari Sámi	18.8 s	1.3 s
Pite Sámi	16.0 s	3.6 s
Kildin Sámi	8.1 s	1.4 s
Kven	7,8 s	1,1 s
Livonian	4.6 s	0.8 s
Veps	4.3 s	0.9 s
Nenets	4.3 s	0.9 s
Khanty	3.7 s	0.9 s
Nganasan	3.4 s	0.8 s

Table 2: The compilation speed of the languages in the system (times given in seconds unless otherwise noted)

6 Some interesting figures for comparative computational linguistics

One of the interesting features we gain from a uniform, standardised suite for building and using computational linguistic descriptions is easy access to comparable evaluations of the implementations. We can measure the quality of the analysers by coverage, by the ambiguity potential of the languages, we can compare features like morphological complexity of the languages by measuring the morpheme to word ratios. We can measure the computational complexity of languages in terms of used processing power, the physical sizes of the models built and so forth. In the following we lay out and present a few of such measurements that can be attained by very simple testing leveraging the strength of the standard build suites we have created.

The computational complexity of the models can be measured using two very practical figures: build time of the language models and the physical size. In figure 2 we show the build times of the systems in our repository, both using commercial tools and open source ones. In that table, the horizontal lines separate the systems on basis of completeness: the first set of languages is considered stable and widely usable, and the second set work in progress. Other than that, the languages are in alphabetical order of ISO 639-3 language codes.

These need to be contrasted with the initial, linguistic sizes of the models from table 3. In this table we show how big the dictionaries are in terms of words in the dictionary and in terms of approximate[14] suffix morphemes. In table 3 we show the actual sizes of the language models as resulting computational objects, measured both in bytes and in components of the data structure holding the data.

One rough figure to measure readiness of a linguistic description is *coverage*, which tells how much of a given text would be recognised as something using the given language model, without taking correctness into consideration. Formally it is given as $\mathrm{Cov} = \frac{\text{Analysed}}{\text{tokens}}$. In table 3 we measure each language's coverage against up to the first 10,000,000 tokens in the native language Wikipedia, where one exists.

---

[14]The actual number is not apparent from the count of morpheme-like elements as the formalism may require to treat combinatorical branching as zero-morpheme

Units Language	Roots	Affixes	States	Edges	On-Disk Size	Corpus	Missing	Coverage
Greenlandic			398,622	13,018,901	170 MiB	27674	7650	72.4 %
South Sámi	88,239	3,090	92,191	215,501	6 MiB			
Faroese	87,567	1,460	80,969	1,282,798	32 MiB			81.5 %
Lule Sámi	73,101	2,943	103,504	260,401	7 MiB			
Finnish	71,761	55,895	179,891	403,944	9.6 MiB			85.1 %
Erzya	106,550	2,860	65,571	174,427	5.8 MiB	63028	10379	83.5 %
Komi-Zyrian	88,734	1,336	56,146	147,618	4.4 MiB	98573	17286	82.5 %
Moksha	59,377	311	35,013	86,086	2.9 MiB	52803	28883	45.3 %
Eastern Mari	56,684	180	35,139	87,578	2.8 MiB	212393	59371	72.0 %
Western Mari	53,236	180	28,734	70,890	2.2 MiB	219337	105857	51.7 %
Udmurt	37,101	84	35,986	65,296	1.8 MiB	107453	63096	41.3 %
Livvi	10,936	173	9,476	19,476	533 KiB			
Voru	15,799	56	10,204	23,855	642 KiB			
Inari Sámi	3,560	280	7,930	12,595	349 KiB			
Ingrian	2,032	1,641	7,922	16,349	377 KiB			
Kildin Sámi	1,840	139	2,951	5,089	157 KiB			
Pite Sámi	1,470	318	3,184	6,281	174 KiB			
Kven	662	131						
Skolt Sámi	583	426	2,761	4,718	120 KiB			

Table 3: Three aspects of the automata: number of relevant morphs and affixes, graph properties, and corpus coverage measured on a Wikipedia corpus, where available

6.1 Platform for linguistically oriented comparisons

One of the potential use cases for a standardised repository of closely related languages would be for diachronic and comparative linguistics. It would not be difficult to formulate finite-state models to verify theories and similarities of related languages, e.g. in style of (Wettig et al., 2011).

Another immediate advance for a standardised structure like this is that we can build rule-based machine-translation systems easier. In shallow-transfer systems like Apertium (Forcada et al., 2011), when building closely related languages like in the Uralic family, we may get quite far by only writing transfer code between lemmas, with no other rules, or very minimal case mappings.

7 Conclusion

In this article we have presented our work with the Divvun and Giellatekno new infrastructure. It is in daily use for roughly half the languages being worked on, and for many of the production languages. Both our experience and the feedback from linguists and other users have shown that it is a definite improvement over the old one. It is based on open-source tools, and contain almost only open-source resources. We welcome many more languages, and we are confident we can handle them.

Acknowledgments

Thanks to our colleagues, especially Jack Rueter, for very valuable feedback and comments.

References

Antonsen, L., Trosterud, T., and Wiechetek, L. (2010). Reusing Grammatical Resources for New Languages. In Calzolari, N., Choukri, K., Maegaard, B., Mariani, J., Odijk, J., Piperidis, S., Rosner, M., and Tapias, D., editors, *Proceedings of the Seventh International Conference on Language Resources and Evaluation (LREC'10)*, Valletta, Malta. European Language Resources Association (ELRA).

Broda, B., Marcińczuk, M., and Piasecki, M. (2010). Building a Node of the Accessible Language Technology Infrastructure. In *Proceedings of the Seventh conference on International Language Resources and Evaluation (LREC'10)*.

Cunningham, H., Humphreys, K., Gaizauskas, R., and Wilks, Y. (1997). Software infrastructure for natural language processing. In *Proceedings of the fifth conference on Applied natural language processing*, ANLC '97, pages 237–244, Stroudsburg, PA, USA. Association for Computational Linguistics.

Cunningham, H., Maynard, D., Bontcheva, K., Tablan, V., Aswani, N., Roberts, I., Gorrell, G., Funk, A., Roberts, A., Damljanovic, D., Heitz, T., Greenwood, M. A., Saggion, H., Petrak, J., Li, Y., and Peters, W. (2011). *Text Processing with GATE (Version 6)*. Gate.

Federmann, C., Giannopoulou, I., Girardi, C., Hamon, O., Mavroeidis, D., Minutoli, S., and Schröder, M. (2012). META-SHARE v2: An Open Network of Repositories for Language Resources including Data and Tools. In Calzolari, N., Choukri, K., Declerck, T., Doğan, M. U., Maegaard, B., Mariani, J., Odijk, J., and Piperidis, S., editors, *Proceedings of the Eight International Conference on Language Resources and Evaluation (LREC'12)*, Istanbul, Turkey. European Language Resources Association (ELRA).

Forcada, M. L., Ginestí-Rosell, M., Nordfalk, J., O'Regan, J., Ortiz-Rojas, S., Pérez-Ortiz, J. A., Sánchez-Martínez, F., Ramírez-Sánchez, G., and Tyers, F. M. (2011). Apertium: a free/open-source platform for rule-based machine translation. *Machine Translation*.

Huizinga, D. and Kolawa, A. (2007). *Automated Defect Prevention: Best Practices in Software Management*. Wiley.

Karlsson, F. (1990). Constraint Grammar As A Framework For Parsing Running Text. *Proceedings of the 13th International Conference on Computational Linguistics*, pages 168–173.

Knuth, D. E. (1984). Literate Programming. *The Computer Journal*, 27(2):97–111.

Lindén, K., Axelson, E., Hardwick, S., Pirinen, T., and Silfverberg, M. (2011). Hfst—framework for compiling and applying morphologies. *Systems and Frameworks for Computational Morphology*, pages 67–85.

Loper, E. and Bird, S. (2002). NLTK: the Natural Language Toolkit. In *Proceedings of the ACL-02 Workshop on Effective tools and methodologies for teaching natural language processing and computational linguistics - Volume 1*, ETMTNLP '02, pages 63–70, Stroudsburg, PA, USA. Association for Computational Linguistics.

Oflazer, K. (1996). Error-tolerant finite state recognition with applications to morphological analysis and spelling correction. *COMPUTATIONAL LINGUISTICS*, 22:73–89.

Trosterud, T. (2012). A restricted freedom of choice: Linguistic diversity in the digital landscape. *Nordlyd*, 39(2):89–104.

Váradi, T., Krauwer, S., Wittenburg, P., Wynne, M., and Koskenniemi, K. (2008). CLARIN: Common Language Resources and Technology Infrastructure. In Calzolari, N., Choukri, K., Maegaard, B., Mariani, J., Odijk, J., Piperidis, S., and Tapias, D., editors, *Proceedings of the Sixth International Conference on Language Resources and Evaluation (LREC'08)*, Marrakech, Morocco. European Language Resources Association (ELRA). http://www.lrec-conf.org/proceedings/lrec2008/.

Wettig, H., Hiltunen, S., and Yangarber, R. (2011). MDL-based Models for Alignment of Etymological Data. In *Proceedings of RANLP: the 8th Conference on Recent Advances in Natural Language Processing, Hissar, Bulgaria.*

From speech corpus to intonation corpus: clustering phrase pitch contours of Lithuanian

Gailius Raškinis, Asta Kazlauskienė

Vytautas Magnus University, K. Donelaičio g. 58, 44248, Kaunas, Lithuania

`g.raskinis@if.vdu.lt, a.kazlauskiene@hmf.vdu.lt`

ABSTRACT

This paper presents our research in preparation to compile a Lithuanian intonation corpus. The main objective of this research was to discover characteristic patterns of Lithuanian intonation through clustering of pitch contours of intermediate intonation phrases. The paper covers the set of procedures that were used to extend an ordinary speech corpus to make it suitable for intonation analysis. The process of intonation analysis included pitch extraction, pitch normalization, estimation of the representative frequency of a syllable, measurement of an inter-phrase similarity, k-means phrase clustering, and visualisation of clustering results. These computational procedures were applied to 23 hours of read speech containing 41417 phrases. The clustering results revealed some interesting intonation patterns of Lithuanian that could be related to the well known linguistic-prosodic phenomena. Language-independence is an important feature of computational procedures covered by this paper. If speech waveforms and the knowledge of phone and phrase boundaries are given, these procedures can be used for the analysis of intonation of other languages.

KEYWORDS: corpus, prosody, intonation, pitch, syllable, dynamic time warping, k-means clustering, Lithuanian.

1   Introduction

Intonation corpus can be thought of as a speech corpus that has its orthographic / phonetic annotations complemented with prosodic labels. Prosodic labels may characterize both prosodic phenomena themselves (e.g. pitch accents and boundary tones) and features that affect prosody (e.g. logical stress). Some prosodic labels may be associated to a precise timing in speech.

Fuelled by the needs of the text-to-speech synthesis, corpus-based intonation research has been an active research field for more than two decades. Automatic prosodic labelling is among its main topics of interest. Prosodic labels such as word boundary strength (Wightman and Ostendorf, 1994; Vereecken et al., 1998, Heggtveit and Natvig, 2004), stress (Heggtveit and Natvig, 2004), syllable prominence (Wightman and Ostendorf, 1994), word prominence (Vereecken et al., 1998), and pitch accent type (Levow, 2008; Escudero-Mancebo et al, 2012) have been predicted using a variety of supervised machine learning techniques. These techniques included decision trees (Wightman and Ostendorf, 1994), artificial neural nets (Vereecken et al., 1998), classification and regression trees (Heggtveit and Natvig, 2004) sometimes coupled with probabilistic sequential smoothing methods such as Markov models (Wightman and Ostendorf, 1994) and Conditional Random Fields (Levow, 2008).

Supervised machine learning techniques must be trained on a carefully hand-labelled intonation corpora. Manual labelling is usually done by domain experts and represents a tedious and time consuming task. It comes as no surprise that Lithuanian has not any intonation corpus available.

Consequently, corpus-based research of Lithuanian intonation has not received much attention. It has been suggested that Lithuanian is characterized by 7 distinct intonation patterns (Kundrotas, 2008), this suggestion being based on the hypothesis-driven investigative approach inspired by the Lithuanian-Russian intonation parallels (Kundrotas, 2009). Those few audio recordings that have been made during these investigations represent cases illustrating the preliminary set of hypotheses.

Our ultimate research objective is to compile a Lithuanian intonation corpus which could be further explored via supervised machine learning techniques. The main objective of this research is limited in scope and aims to discover characteristic patterns of Lithuanian intonation. In contrast to the abovementioned investigation, we follow a data-driven approach. It assumes that reliable discoveries about intonation patterns of a given language can be made through the computer-aided analysis of a real world intonation phenomena. It would be of a great help to a human expert if similar intonation patterns are collected together and presented to him/her in a user-friendly way. Then, he/she could assign these collections to particular intonation categories, construct "an inventory" of intonation patterns, easily detect and eliminate "false" members out of these collections, mark pitch accents and boundary tones in a more uniform way.

This paper describes computational procedures that allow to find clusters of pitch[1] contours of spoken phrases[2] in a speech corpus consisting of audio records and their orthographic transcriptions. The whole process consists of the following steps:

- manually complementing speech corpus with the word "break indices" that show the strength of the boundary between two orthographic words.
- automatic alignment of speech waveforms and phonetic symbols (phone level) resulting in the knowledge of both phone boundaries and phrase boundaries.
- estimation of pitch contours of speech waveforms.
- chunking pitch contours to segments corresponding to phrases, and estimating a "representative" pitch for every syllable nucleus of a phrase.
- estimating distances between all possible phrase pairs (on the basis of a pitch).
- grouping phrases by their distances using the k-means clustering technique.
- concatenating clustered data into one audio and one annotation file per cluster.

The steps above are described in more detail in the following sections.

2   Extending speech corpus

We started from the speech corpus that had been used for speech recognition research of Lithuanian (Vaičiūnas, 2006). This corpus consists of audio recordings produced by 50 speakers (25 males, 25 females), each of them speaking for 1 hour. The speech is stored as a collection of 2 min. audio files. The orthographic word-level transcriptions had been prepared to describe the content of audio recordings as accurately as possible.

2.1   Extending speech corpus with word "break indices"

Word "break indices", representing the strength of the boundary between two orthographic words, were assigned to each pair of contiguous words and were inserted at the "orthographic" level of a text (see fig 1) by a human expert. Our set of indices followed the standard of the ToBI transcription framework (Beckman et. al., 2005).

```
<file name="SIR_A001"> devyni4 kieti4 / plieni4niai skam3balo smū3giai /
paža3dino liu4dą vasa3rį iš_mie3go // krū9ptelėjęs jis_atme9rkė aki4s /
ir_valandė3lę negalė9jo susivo9kti kame4 / <accent correct="e3sąs">esą3s</accent>
// bu4vo ly9giai penkta4 valanda4 ša9lto ruden3s ry9to </file>
```

FIGURE 1: An excerpt of the "extended" orthographic transcription associated to an audio file. Both "ortographic" and "break index" levels of the ToBI framework are mixed together. The symbols / and // indicate an intermediate and a full intonation phrase boundary respectively. The symbol _ indicates the absence of a word boundary (with evidence of cliticisation).

---

[1] Though the term "pitch" is a perceptual characteristics, we use it in the sense of fundamental frequency.

[2] We use the short term "phrase" to denote the speech segment within intermediate phrase boundaries.

2.2 Automatic alignment of speech waveforms and phonetic symbols

The process of automatic alignment of speech waveforms and phonetic symbols (phone level) had the objective of identifying timings of phone and phrase boundaries within speech waveforms. The extended orthographic transcription was submitted to the Lithuanian grapheme-to-phoneme converter (Norkevičius et al, 2005) which output the corresponding sequence of phones. Within this sequence, full intonation phrase boundaries were replaced by the "silence" phone, and the optional "short pause" phone was allowed between words.

Given speech waveforms and their corresponding phone sequences the stochastic alignment approach was used. First, speaker-specific (trained on 1 hour of speech) acoustic models were constructed closely following the sequence of processing steps suggested by the HTK book (Young et al., 2000). Thereafter automatic alignment of speech waveforms and phonetic symbols was realized by the Viterbi algorithm which makes part of the same HTK toolkit. Phone and phrase boundaries were identified with the time resolution of 5 ms.

The results of automatic alignment were inspected manually and were found to be satisfactory. Phone boundaries resulting from an automatic alignment procedure are illustrated in fig. 4 (top tier out of three tiers)

3 Intonation analysis and clustering

3.1 Pitch extraction

The following processing steps were used for pitch extraction out of speech waveforms:

- low-pass filtering speech files at cut-off frequency of 1837.5 Hz and downsampling them to 3675 Hz[3].
- estimating the average pitch period *avgp* per speech file on the basis of the downsampled speech in order to define the pitch analysis range of 3 octaves from $1/(4*avgp)$ to $2/avgp$
- low-pass filtering the original speech waveform at a cut-off frequency of $2/avgp + 200$ Hz.
- finding pitch period candidates in this filtered waveform using a cross-correlation technique and time resolution of 2.5 ms (400 Hz sampling rate).
- smoothing pitch contour (selecting one candidate per frame) using the "islands of confidence" approach (Raškinis, 2000)

3.2 Grouping phrases into similarity clusters

3.2.1 Estimating the representative pitch of a syllable

In order to minimize the inter-talker variability (males, females), pitch contours were converted to logarithmic scale (semitones) and zero-centred by subtracting the pitch average of an entire audio file.

---

[3] The frequency of 3675 Hz was selected for its integer ratios with the common sampling frequencies of 11025Hz, 22050Hz and 44100Hz.

In order to make the intonation description of a phrase more compact the pitch contour of a phrase (sampled at 400 Hz) was replaced by the sequence of syllable pitches of that phrase. The pitch of a syllable varies over time. Thus, every syllable was assigned a "representative" pitch on the basis of the pitch contour over a syllable nucleus (vowel/diphthong). Because of the assumption that the pitch target is best approximated in the later portion of the syllable (Xu, 2004), the representative pitch was calculated by linearly weighting pitch contour values. Pitch contour values at the beginning and the end of a syllable nucleus were de-emphasized and emphasized respectively. Let $f_0[i]$ denote the normalized pitch value of the ith frame, and let $[t_{beg}\ t_{end}]$ be the boundaries of a syllable nucleus, then the frequency representative sf of the syllable was estimated as follows:

$$sf = \frac{\displaystyle\sum_{i=t_{beg}}^{t_{end}} \left(f_0[i] \cdot \frac{i - t_{beg}}{t_{end} - t_{beg}}\right)}{\displaystyle\sum_{i=t_{beg}}^{t_{end}} \frac{i - t_{beg}}{t_{end} - t_{beg}}}$$

Unvoiced frames (undefined $f_0[i]$ values) were skipped when iterating through pitch contour values. Unvoiced syllables, i.e. syllables for which the pitch detection failed for every frame, were omitted from further consideration.

3.2.2 Defining distance between two phrases

One of the main problems in estimating the similarity of intonation between two phrases was the large variation in their syllable numbers (see fig. 2). Let $F_1 = \{sf_{1,1}, sf_{1,2}, ..., sf_{1,n1}\}$ and $F_2 = \{sf_{2,1}, sf_{2,2}, ..., sf_{2,n2}\}$ be two phrases consisting of sequences of representative syllable pitches, where n_1 and n_2 denote the number of syllables in the phrases F_1 and F_2 respectively. Let $d(i, j)$ denote the distance between truncated sequences $\{sf_{1,1}, sf_{1,2}, ..., sf_{1,i}\}$ and $\{sf_{2,1}, sf_{2,2}, ..., sf_{2,j}\}$ both corresponding to initial segments of F_1 and F_2 respectively. Then the similarity between F_1 and F_2 $d(F_1, F_2) = d(n_1, n_2)$ was defined by the recursive formula below:

$$d(i,j) = \min \begin{cases} d(i-1, j-1) + |sf_{1,i} - sf_{2,j}| \\[2mm] d(i-1, j-2) + \dfrac{3}{4} \cdot (|sf_{1,i} - sf_{2,j-1}| + |sf_{1,i} - sf_{2,j}|) \\[2mm] d(i-1, j-3) + \dfrac{2}{3} \cdot (|sf_{1,i} - sf_{2,j-2}| + |sf_{1,i} - sf_{2,j-1}| + |sf_{1,i} - sf_{2,j}|) \\[2mm] d(i-2, j-1) + \dfrac{3}{4} \cdot (|sf_{1,i-1} - sf_{2,j}| + |sf_{1,i} - sf_{2,j}|) \\[2mm] d(i-3_i, j-1) + \dfrac{2}{3} \cdot (|sf_{1,i-2} - sf_{2,j}| + |sf_{1,i-1} - sf_{2,j}| + |sf_{1,i} - sf_{2,j}|) \end{cases}$$

This formula means that the sequences F_1 and F_2 can be matched by "warping" them non-linearly in the time dimension. One syllable from the first sequence can be matched up to three syllables from the second sequence and vice versa.

Distances between all possible pairs of phrases in the corpus need to be calculated using this formula. For this purpose an efficient dynamic time warping procedure (Vintsyuk, 1968) was implemented that estimates phrase-to-phrase distances in polynomial time $O(n_1{*}n_2)$

3.2.3 K-means based clustering

Having obtained distances among all possible pairs of phrases, k-means clustering can be applied to them. The clustering consists of iterating through every phrase, removing it from its current cluster and placing it into the nearest cluster (it may also be the same cluster). The distance between the phrase F and the cluster C is estimated by:

$$d(F,C) = \frac{1}{|C|}\sum_{F_i \in C} d(F,F_i)$$

The initial assignment of phrases to clusters is randomized. However the assignment process forbids placing or later moving a phrase into a cluster if there exists at least one other phrase in that cluster that is incompatible with the phrase under scrutiny (the distance between the two might not be calculated due to the required extension/ contraction exceeding the factor of 3). This prevents the formation of mutually incompatible sub-clusters within a single cluster. The k-means algorithm stops when either there's no phrase changing its cluster through the entire iteration or the maximum number of allowed iterations is reached.

4 Experimental evaluation

Human experts have selected 14 male and 9 female speakers (23 hours of speech) out of our 50 hour speech corpus. They selected speakers whose reading intonation was as expressive as possible as well as the accuracy of time aligned transcriptions. There were 41417 spoken phrases in the selected part of the corpus. Spoken phrases had a wide variety of durations.

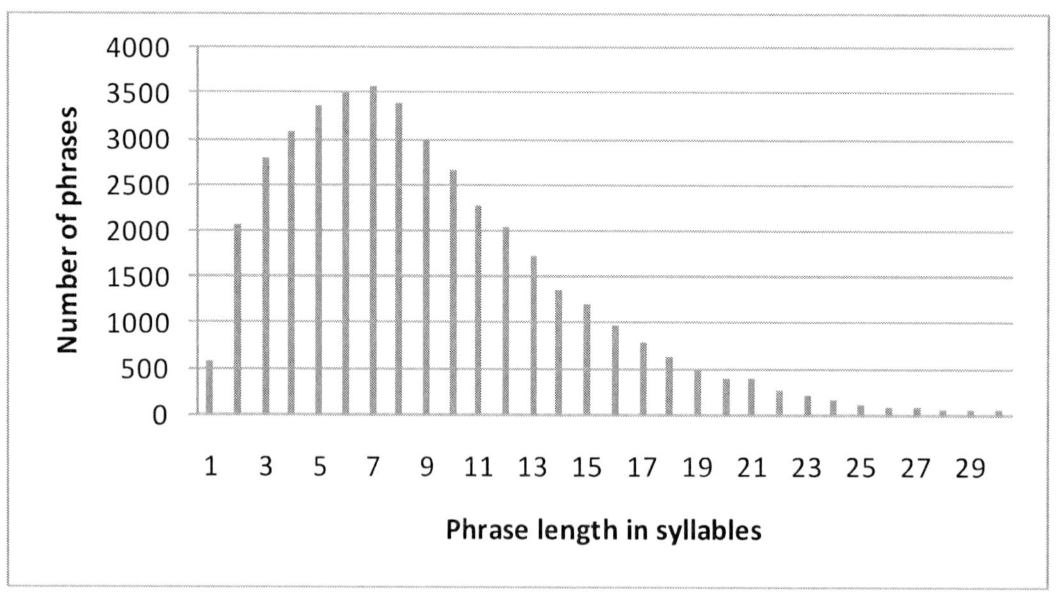

FIGURE 2: The histogram of phrase durations in syllables.

The set of 41417 phrases was divided into two subsets of "short" (15417 items) and "long" (26000 items) phrases[4]. A phrase was considered to be short if it had 6 syllables or less. Otherwise it was considered to be long. The number of clusters k was set to 40 and 80 for the sets of short and long phrases respectively. The clustering algorithm was run for a maximum of 100 iterations, though 10 iterations were generally enough for the convergence (see fig. 3).

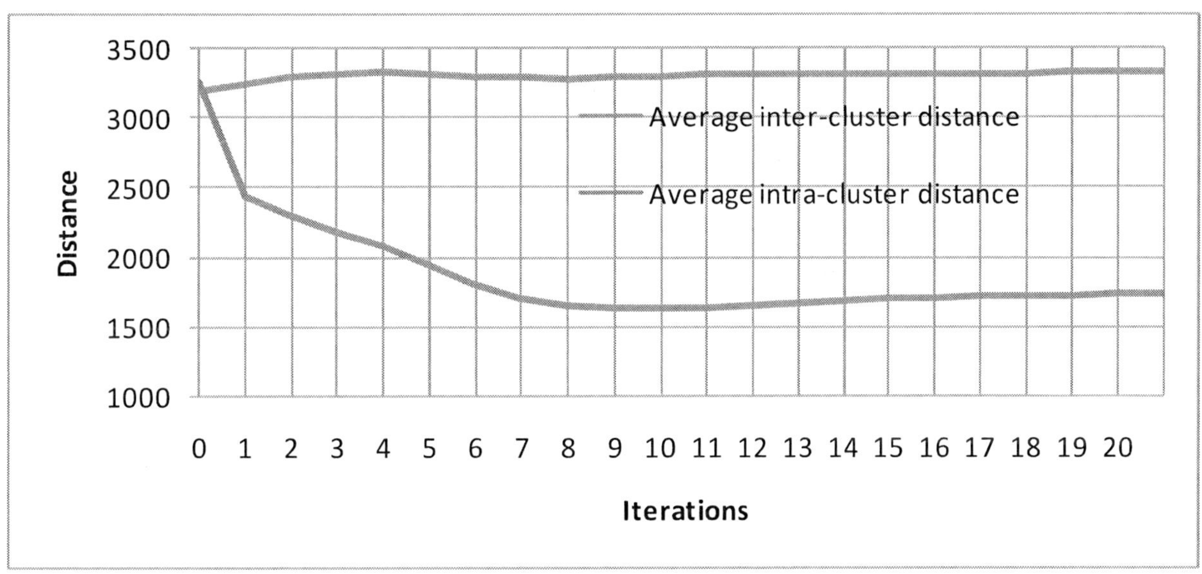

FIGURE 3: The convergence of the k-means clustering algoritm while processing the long phrase set.

Once the clustering process was finished the clustered data was concatenated into one audio and one annotation file per cluster, so that clusters could be visualised (see fig. 4) by Praat software (Boersma and Weenink, 2006).

Human experts complained about clusters being denoted by integer numbers, so we had to look for a more comprehensive naming approach. The decision was taken to find the most "central" phrase of a cluster, i.e. the phrase which has the least average distance to every other phrase in that same cluster, and to use it as the basis for naming the cluster. Every syllable of such "central" phrase was assigned an integer number denoting its pitch in semitones either below (L) or above (H) the normalized pitch average. For instance, the cluster name H5_L5_H1 signifies that the "central" phrase of this cluster is characterized by pitch movements of the high-low-high type that are 5 semitones above, 5 semitones below, and 1 semitone above the normalized pitch average respectively.

---

[4] This division was due to the limitations in computer memory. It would have been necessary to store 857 mln. distances between all possible pairs of 41417 phrases. We assume that this division is not significant because many phrases from the "short" set and from the "long" set cannot belong to the same cluster simultaneously due to the maximum allowed warping factor of 3.

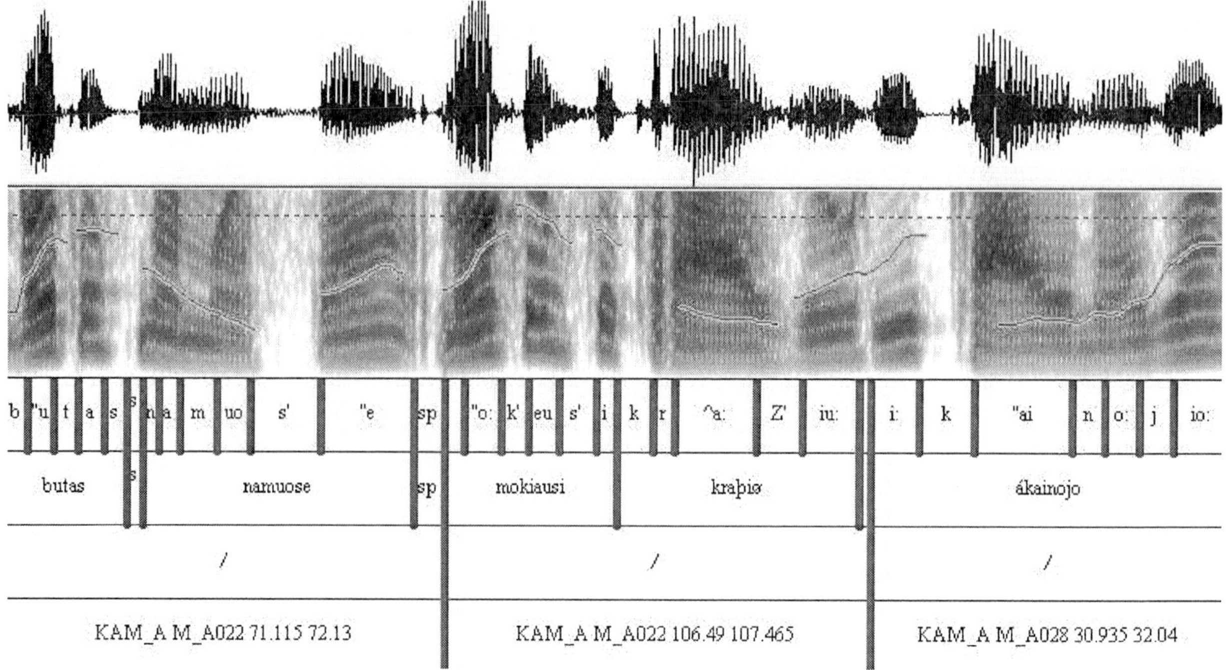

FIGURE 4: An excerpt of the clustering results (cluster H5_L5_H1) visualised by Praat software. Concatenated speech waveform is shown on the top, pitch contours are shown in the middle, and concatenated annotations (phone, word, phrase levels) are at the bottom.

Clustering results are presently being examined by professional phoneticians. Though the evaluation is still in progress, the following remarks can already be made:

- Clustering procedure is efficient in revealing annotation errors (misplaced phrase boundaries). Such phrases tend to form their own clusters.
- Some clusters are dominated by phrases of a few particular speakers. This observation needs further investigation as it may indicate that either pitch normalization is still imperfect or speaker-specific intonation patterns are discovered (e.g. dialect).
- Some clusters contain phrases that should be placed to different clusters from the perceptual point of view. This is mainly due to the emphasis put on different words. This suggests reviewing our present inter-phrase distance metrics and probably including other physical characteristics of speech such as intensity and duration.
- Some clusters appear to be related to certain phenomena of spoken language. There are clusters characterized by the imitation of emotions (not natural for read speech) by the enumerative intonation, by ellipses indicating an unfinished thought at the end of a phrase, etc.

5   Discussion and future work

Language-independence is an important feature of our computational approach. Though computation steps covered by the section 2 are language-specific, all computation steps covered by the section 3 (intonation analysis and clustering) are language-independent.

If speech waveforms and the knowledge of phone and phrase boundaries is available for some language, the set of abovementioned computation steps could be applied.

Computations have been implemented in C++ and optimized for speed. The most costly computational procedure is the step of inter-phrase distance estimation. It has the worst case complexity of $O(N^2{*}n^2)$, where N denotes the number of phrases in the corpus and n denotes the average phrase length in syllables.

Processing	N	n	Computation time, hours
Short phrases	15417	4.11	1.68
Long phrases	26000	11.87	12.74

TABLE 1: Computation time on a computer with Intel® Core™ 2 Duo T7300 2.00 GHz processor and 3 GB of memory.

The table 1 shows that despite speed optimizations scaling this procedure to larger intonation corpora may be problematic. However, we believe that the discovery of intonation patterns proper to a given language could be made within smaller but more carefully selected intonation corpora.

Our future research will be mostly driven by the feedback received from human experts. In addition to those few research issues that have been mentioned in the section 4.2, our future research may focus on the optimization of the number of clusters, on different methods of estimating the representative frequency of a syllable, on the normalization of this frequency with respect to the intrinsic vowel pitch.

Acknowledgements

This research has been supported by a grant from the Research Council of Lithuania under the National Lithuanian studies development programme for 2009-2015. through the project A unified approach to Lithuanian prosody: the intonation, rhythm, and stress (reg. no. LIT-12020).

References

Beckman, M. E., Hirschberg, J., and Shattuck-Hufnagel, S. (2005). The original ToBI system and the evolution of the ToBI framework. In S.-A. Jun (ed.) *Prosodic Typology -- The Phonology of Intonation and Phrasing.*

Boersma, P., and Weenink, D. (2006). Praat: doing phonetics by computer [Computer program]. Version 4.4.26, retrieved 24 July 2006 from http://www.praat.org/

Hartigan, J. A.; Wong, M. A. (1979). Algorithm AS 136: A K-Means Clustering Algorithm. *Journal of the Royal Statistical Society,* Series C (Applied Statistics) 28(1):100–108.

Kundrotas, G. (2008). Lietuvių kalbos intonacinių kontūrų fonetiniai požymiai (Phonetic features of Lithuanian intonation contours). *Žmogus ir žodis. Didaktinė lingvistika.* Mokslo darbai, Vilnius, 10(1): 43-55.

Kundrotas, G. (2009). *Lyginamoji lietuvių ir rusų kalbų intonacinių sistemų analizė* (A comparative analysis of intonation systems of Lithuanian and Russian), Vilnius Pedagogical University.

Levow, G.-A. (2008). Automatic Prosodic Labeling with Conditional Random Fields and Rich Acoustic Features. In *Proceedings of International Joint Conference on Natural Language Processing (IJCNLP),* pages. 217-224.

Heggtveit, P. O., Natvig, J. E. (2004). Automatic prosody labelling of read Norwegian. In *Proceedings of the International Conference on Spoken Language Processing (ICSLP),* vol. 4, pages 2741-2744.

Escudero-Mancebo, D., Vizcaíno-Ortega, F., González-Ferreras, C., Vivaracho-Pascual, C., Cabrera-Abreu, M., Estebas-Vilaplana, E., and Valenítn Cardeñoso-Payo, V. (2012). Multiclass Pitch Accent Classification for Assisting Manual Prosodic Labeling. In *Proceedings of IberSPEECH 2012,* pages 73-82.

Norkevičius, G., Raškinis, G., and Kazlauskienė, A. (2005). Knowledge-based grapheme-to-phoneme conversion of Lithuanian words. In *Proceedings of the 10th International Conference on Speech and Computer – Specom,* Patras, Greece. pages 235–238.

Raškinis, G. (2000). Lietuvių liaudies dainų užrašymas muzikos simbolių sekomis (Automatic transcription of Lithuanian folk songs), Phd Thesis, Vytautas Magnus University.

Vaičiūnas, A. (2006). Lietuvių kalbos statistinių modelių ir jų taikymo šnekos atpažinimui tyrimas, kai naudojami labai dideli žodynai (Investigation of Lithuanian statistic language models and of their application to speech recognition in case of very large vocabularies), Phd Thesis, Vytautas Magnus University.

Vereecken, H., Martens, J.-P., Grover, C., Fackrell, J., and Van Coile, B. (1998). Automatic prosodic labeling of 6 languages. In *Proceedings of the 5th International Conference on Spoken Language Processing,* Sidney Australia.

Vintsyuk, T. K. (1968). Speech discrimination by dynamic programming. *Kibernetika*, 4:81-88.

Young, S., Evermann, G., Kershaw, D., Moore, G., Odell, J., Ollason, D., Povey, D., Valtchev, V., and Woodland, P. (2002). *The HTK Book* (for HTK Version 3.2), Microsoft Corporation, Cambridge University Engineering Department, pages 22-44.

Xu, Y. (2004). Transmitting tone and intonation simultaneously - the parallel encoding and target approximation (PENTA) model. In *Proceedings of the International Symposium on Tonal Aspects of Languages (TAL) - 2004*, pages 215–220.

Wightman, C., and Ostendorf, M. (1994) Automatic labeling of prosodic patterns, *IEEE Transactions on Speech and Audio Processing*, 2(4):469–481.

Simple and Accountable Segmentation of Marked-up Text

Jonathon Read,[*][♠] *Rebecca Dridan,*[♣] *Stephan Oepen*[♣]

[♠] School of Computing, Teesside University, UK

[♣] Department of Informatics, University of Oslo, Norway

`j.read@tees.ac.uk, {rdridan,oe}@ifi.uio.no`

Abstract

Segmenting documents into discrete, sentence-like units is usually a first step in any natural language processing pipeline. However, current segmentation tools perform poorly on text that contains markup. While stripping markup is a simple solution, we argue for the utility of the extra-linguistic information encoded by markup and present a scheme for normalising markup across disparate formats. We further argue for the need to maintain *accountability* when preprocessing text, such that a record of modifications to source documents is maintained. Such records are necessary in order to augment documents with information derived from subsequent processing. To facilitate adoption of these principles we present a novel tool for segmenting text that contains inline markup. By converting to plain text and tracking alignment, the tool is capable of state-of-the-art sentence boundary detection using any external segmenter, while producing segments containing normalised markup, with an account of how to recreate the original form.

Keywords: Accountability, Markup, Normalisation, Sentence Boundary Detection, Traceability.

---

[*] Work carried out at the University of Oslo.

1   Introduction

Attention in Natural Language Processing (NLP) research increasingly focuses on text from the World Wide Web, the so-called 'Web as Corpus' (Kilgarriff and Grefenstette, 2003). This fertile source of language use has enriched the field by greatly expanding the genres and styles of text being analysed by standard NLP techniques, including much information available as user-generated content. One outcome of this recent attention is a host of research showing the degradation of performance on web text when using tools trained on, for example, the venerable Penn Treebank (Marcus et al., 1993). Techniques such as domain adaptation (Foster et al., 2011) and normalisation (Gimpel et al., 2011) have been shown to reduce the impact on performance of tools such as statistical parsers and part-of-speech taggers. One particular aspect that has not had much attention in this regard is sentence segmentation, frequently a fundamental piece of any NLP pipeline, from corpus building to machine translation. In the following sections, we look at a different technique for handling issues at this often-overlooked stage.

While the differences in style and register can have an effect on sentence segmentation, the major impact is from the markup (such as HTML or WikiText) that is present in web-sourced text. Reuse of standard tools is generally desirable, since we can take advantage of previous tuning on plain text, but using tools designed for plain text on text with markup can result in a major loss in recall of sentence boundaries. This occurs when markup elements obscure sentence-ending punctuation (Read et al., 2012b). For instance, in the example given in Figure 1 the sentence terminating full-stop is attached to the closing tag. Thus, any tool that operates under the assumption that full-stops must have whitespace to the right will fail to detect this boundary.

To avoid this problem, markup could be—and often is—stripped and discarded during processing. However, another frequently ignored aspect of preprocessing is *accountability*: the recording of actions taken that alter the text, in order to preserve the link to the original data. Many applications of NLP augment the original document with new information. For example, the ACL Anthology Searchbench (Schäfer et al., 2011) highlights search hits in text from scientific papers—such annotations would also be useful in HTML and other source documents. When unilaterally throwing away markup, it becomes difficult to trace back to the original source and hence one loses some of the utility of the annotations from downstream processing. Alternatively, in corpus creation, discarding information without record can unnecessarily limit future unforeseen uses of the corpus, whereas full accountability leaves open possibilities that cannot be predicted at creation time.

To facilitate the accountability of preprocessing when building corpora from marked-up documents, in Section 2 we present a novel tool[1] for sentence boundary detection of text with inline markup. By tracking alignment while creating a plain text version, the tool is able to utilise any third-party software for sentence segmentation. Our tool then recovers sentence positions in the original, and produces one sentence per line along with an account of how the text corresponds to the original document. While exemplified in application to sentence boundary detection here, this general technique is applicable of course to other processing downstream as well, where it is deemed desirable to invoke off-the-shelf tools that lack support for markup processing (tokenisation, for example).

Another issue with simply stripping markup is that it can be of relevance for natural language processing tasks. For instance, some markup (e.g. block elements such as paragraphs, quotes and list elements) strongly influences sentence segmentation (Read et al., 2012a). Other elements are of

---

[1]The tool is open-source and available to download from www.delph-in.net/deler/.

```
<p>The name <b>Clanfield</b> is derived from the <a>Old English</a>
and means "field clean of weeds".</p><p>Clanfield was historically
a small <a>farming</a> community.</p>
```

Figure 1: A passage illustrating how HTML markup can obscure sentence-ending punctuation.

relevance to part-of-speech tagging and parsing (e.g. italics may indicate foreign language words and links may offer clues to constituent structure). However, exactly which markup elements are relevant for which tasks in natural language processing remains to be explored. In order to answer comprehensively, it is important to normalise the disparate types of markup (such as LaTeX, WikiText, or XML) so that they can be treated generally. For such normalisation we provide options that allow a user to specify how different elements of markup should be treated, including a configurable mapping option. Following previous work (Flickinger et al., 2010; Solberg, 2012), we have used this option to map certain source elements into an abstraction of these markup languages dubbed the Grammar Markup Language (described in Section 3).

In Section 4 we evaluate the tool using two collections of text from blogs, and provide an error analysis. We then summarise our work and outline the future directions for improvements in Section 5.

2   A Generic Approach to Segmenting Text with Inline Markup

In this section we describe our generic approach to sentence boundary detection in text with inline markup. The approach is generic in that it is (a) applicable across other markup formats, (b) operates independently of the strategy for sentence boundary detection, and (c) could conceivably be applied to segmentation at other levels (e.g. tokenisation). The approach is based on the notion that, in order to achieve optimum performance, extant tools for sentence boundary detection must be presented with text that is free from markup. However, as described above, our goal is to obtain sentences with original markup preserved.

A naïve approach one might consider is to conceal markup with whitespace. Then, using a tool which produces character offsets, it would be possible to use such offsets to point back into the original text with markup. However, this is inadvisable because the superfluous whitespace could confound the model employed by the tool. Furthermore, many segmentation tools do not output character offsets, making it difficult to recover sentence positions in the original document.

Instead, our approach (depicted in Figure 2) involves creating a reduced form of the raw original text that is free from markup (♦1A) but replicates the appearance of the rendered document in terms of hard line breaks and paragraph breaks (as represented by double new lines). Since certain markup elements (such as paragraphs, headings and list items) can inform sentence boundary detection, at this stage we force segmentation by inserting paragraph breaks in place of certain sentence-forcing elements.[2] In the case of XML, some characters may be encoded as entities. These can also inform sentence segmentation, so we convert entities into their Unicode equivalents (for example, both `&8230;` and `…` are transformed to '...'). While making the reduction, we record a character-by-character alignment from the reduced form back to the raw (♦1B).

---

[2] As not all tools enforce sentence breaks at the end of paragraphs (Read et al., 2012a) we provide an optional *paragraph-mode*, wherein documents are split into paragraphs (as delimited by double new lines), which are presented separately to the external tool.

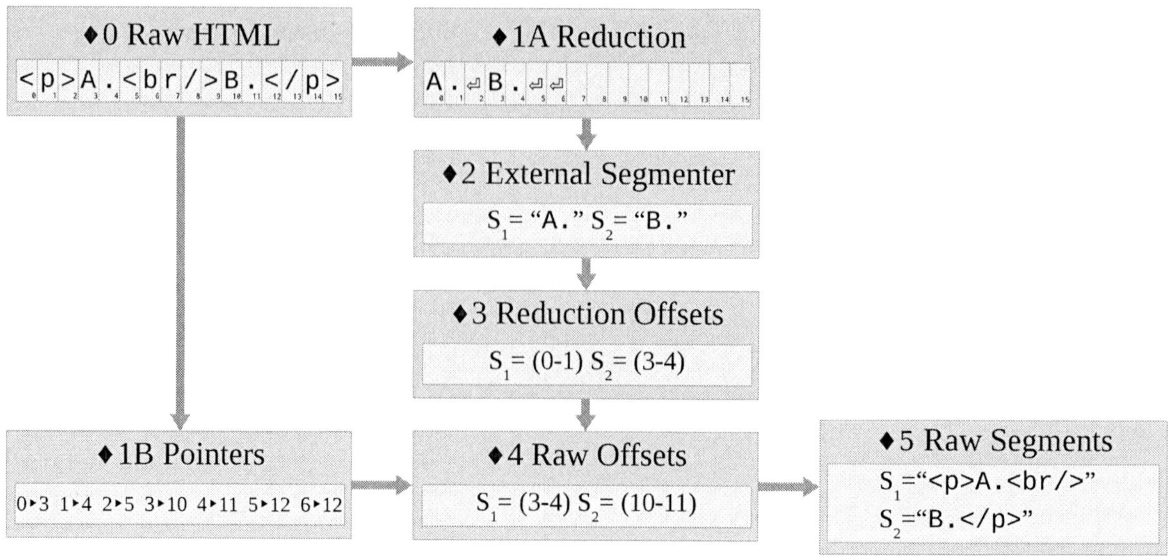

Figure 2: A generic approach for segmenting text with inline markup, with an HTML example.

In the next stage (♦2) one is free to run any tool for sentence boundary detection (assuming its output is mapped to our expectations of a single sentence on each new line). We then find the character offsets of the segments produced by the external tool (♦3), from which we obtain offsets in the raw form (♦4) by following the pointers collected in ♦1B.

Segments in the raw form can be easily obtained using these offsets. However the segments are not yet complete, because it is necessary to recover tags at beginning and end of each (♦5). In the case of HTML we achieve this heuristically—only opening tags should occur at the start of a segment and, conversely, only closing tags should occur at the end of a segment. Thus we expand to the left of a segment until we observe either text or a closing element, and expand to the right until we observe either text or an opening element.

With segmentation complete we can now carry out various normalising actions. As stated above, there is evidence that some elements of markup can be useful to downstream processing tools. For this reason, we provide the mechanism to re-incorporate the markup (optionally in a normalised form) that a user considers potentially relevant. Our intent is to provide a tool that is easily configurable according to the preferences of the user; thus we present a set of normalisation actions but do not make any assertions about how they should be applied:

Map For selected elements, we map the concrete markup element to a normalised equivalent. Grammar Markup Language (GML), described in Section 3, provides one means of normalisation and is the method we use in experimentation.

Strip In other cases one may be certain that the tag is not useful in downstream processing, hence we remove the tag but leave its contents in place.

Mask The textual contents of some markup elements are not easily obtainable or have little linguistic meaning. However, their presence still plays a structural role in the sentence (for

```
The name ⌊*Clanfield*⌋ is derived from the ⌊>Old English>⌋ and means
"field clean of weeds".
Clanfield was historically a small ⌊>farming>⌋ community.
```

Figure 3: Our running example annotated using the Grammar Markup Language (GML), with new line characters to delimit sentences.

example, `code` containing a variable name). We propose replacing such elements with a placeholder (i.e. an empty element) in order to preserve sentence structure.

Purge For some applications one might be confident that certain elements are not useful for downstream processing (tables, for example). For such instances we provide a function to remove the elements and their contents. Note that for efficiency this function is carried out at ♦1A in Figure 2, as it would be wasted effort to attempt to segment content that is only removed later.

Finally we output an account of the segmentation process—a list of sentences with (optionally) normalised markup, each with a series of offsets and lengths that represent deletions and insertions made to the original document.

Note that all the behaviour described above is configurable. For instance, some websites use paragraph elements to force formatting rather than to indicate paragraphs, hence turning off this heuristic for paragraph elements could prevent the generation of spurious sentences.

3 Markup Normalisation

As mentioned previously, the properties of markup can significantly affect subsequent processing. For instance, (Flickinger et al., 2010) observe that italicisation frequently functions like quotation (for example, to indicate use – mention distinctions or foreign language text). To explore the interface between markup and grammar they proposed a Grammar Markup Language (GML) which abstracts away from concrete markup (Flickinger et al., 2010; Solberg, 2012). In this section, we embrace this general idea but propose a refined and extended scheme for this purpose, dubbed GML 2.0.

GML is designed to be a low-impact markup language that promotes compactness and human readability (particularly by those who are unfamiliar with rich mark-up languages such as XML). As such, elements are named with a single character, often using 'unusual' characters,[3] with names selected from Unicode's extended sets in order to promote distinctiveness from the surrounding text. Figure 3 shows our running example with sentences delimited by new line characters, and contains instances of links (>) and bold text (*) as GML annotations. There are only three meta-characters: ⌊ (LEFT FLOOR, U+230A), ⌋ (RIGHT FLOOR, U+230B) and ¦ (BROKEN BAR, U+00A6), respectively serving as left, right and middle delimiters. A GML opening tag is composed of the left delimiter followed by the element name. Conversely the closing tag is the element name followed by the right delimiter. Empty elements are formed of the left delimiter, the element name and the right delimiter (e.g. an image is represented as ⌊✎⌋). Attributes of elements are separated using

---

[3] Using unusual characters means that GML does not require escaping of common ASCII characters (as is the case in, for example, XML), but good Unicode capabilities are a prerequisite for humans to author GML; however, we anticipate that GML texts will typically be produced automatically.

	Linux			NLP		
	Prec	**Rec**	**F$_1$**	**Prec**	**Rec**	**F$_1$**
(1) Markup in place	97.6	91.7	94.6	99.1	91.3	95.1
(2) Markup reduced	98.5	91.4	94.8	98.9	96.3	97.6

Table 1: The performance of two strategies for segmenting marked-up text; (1) segmenting with markup in place and (2), the approach described in this paper, reducing markup to plain text and reintroducing it through character alignment. Note that the gold-standard was derived by manually correcting the segmentation produced by strategy (1), potential biasing the evaluation in its favour.

the middle delimiter and are attached to the closing tag (e.g. second-level headings are specified as ⌊=Title¦2=⌋).

4   Evaluation and Error Analysis

To evaluate our approach we use text from the WeSearch Data Collection, a freely-available corpus of user-generated content (Read et al., 2012b). In this corpus, text was automatically segmented using the sentence splitter from the Stanford CoreNLP Tools, with the HTML-based sentence forcing heuristics described above, but with text being processed by the sentence splitter with HTML in place. Specifically, we use the two mixed source test sections from the blog domain, which are drawn from blogs about Linux (WLB03) and natural language processing (WNB03). The sentence segmentation in these sections was corrected by hand to create a gold-standard resulting in 1,130 sentences in WLB03 and 1,073 sentences in WNB03.

To measure segmentation performance we employ the evaluation script provided by Read et al. (2012a), which calculates precision, recall and F$_1$ by considering *every character*[4] in the text as a potential sentence boundary. Table 1 shows the performance of two methods when segmenting the raw HTML used to generate WLB03 and WNB03; row (1) gives the results of the original automatic procedure, while row (2) gives the results of the reduction approach described in this paper (when coupled with the Stanford CoreNLP sentence splitter). Note that the gold-standard was derived by manually-correcting the original automatic segmentation; this potentially biases the evaluation in favour of the original procedure.

We find that, for Linux blogs, the new approach results in a small improvement in precision and a minor loss in recall. The effect is quite different for natural language processing blogs. There is a strong improvement in segmentation, with a gain of 5% points in recall, with only a minor loss in precision. We performed an analysis of errors made by our approach, in order to acquire an understanding of how to improve the tool.

False negatives account for the largest proportion of the errors. Within these we note two dominating trends: non-standard lists, and non-standard typography—both of which could be considered issues of robustness when dealing with user-generated content. Over half the false negatives relate to character-based list conventions, where list items are not indicated with HTML but instead delimited with characters as bullets (e.g., '*', '-' or 'o'), or 'Q:' or 'A:'. Another quarter of the false negatives could more generally be considered aspects of informal English or author error. These include the lack of end-of-sentence punctuation, sentence-initial capitals or whitespace between sentences. While the list conventions could potentially be handled heuristically by our tool, more general

---

[4]Evaluation of sentence segmentation is often carried out using a small set of potential sentence boundaries (e.g. '!', '.' or '?'), but Read et al. (2012a) argue that this is an oversimplification, with these characters only appearing at the end of 92% of sentences in edited text such as The Wall Street Journal portion of the Penn Treebank.

robustness issues arise from the fact that the splitter appears to be optimised towards edited text. This is a well-known issue that is being dealt with in other tools (Foster et al., 2011). Similar techniques could be applied to sentence splitters, but that is not the focus of this tool.

A smaller proportion of the false negative errors do arise from markup-related issues. In particular, we note a few instances where placement of masked elements (e.g. <code/>) from repeated occurrences hide the end of a sentence. While some of these are obvious errors, others point to possible inconsistencies in the gold standard.

Of the smaller number of false positives, we again find that list conventions account for about half the erroneous instances. One regular pattern was enumerated lists where a full-stop is used to delimit the item from its number (e.g. 1.) which incorrectly led to segmentation after the number. Another trend related to the use of full-stops in bibliographic entries, which was specific to the natural language processing dataset and possibly needs specific handling.

Of greater concern from the perspective of our tool was that there were a few instances where the decision to introduce hard sentence breaks at paragraph and list elements led to false positives. While formally an incorrect use of HTML, occasionally authors will use these elements for their layout properties, rather than their abstract meaning. This could suggest that we should introduce a more nuanced handling of these elements, using heuristics to decide when to enforce breaks. However, in these datasets containing just over 2,000 sentences, this type of error only accounts for four false positives, indicating that the improvement this change would bring could well be offset by the false negatives that would likely occur.

5   Conclusions and Future Work

We have produced a simple tool that, by producing a plain text version that is aligned character-by-character, allows users to make use of previous plain text segmentation research and tools, while also using the *advantages* of the markup. Further, by maintaining accountability of any normalisation actions, this tool facilitates the projection of downstream processing back to the original source, enabling inline annotation in a browser, for example. In addition, by including different handling mechanisms for various aspects of the markup, we provide the option of passing on relevant normalised markup to downstream tools, and present Grammar Markup Language (GML) as a way of abstracting from various different concrete markup schemes.

Our main use of this tool to date has been for sentence segmentation of HTML documents, however it was deliberately designed to be suitable for generic text segmentation of multiple markup styles. Most of the markup handling specifics are defined in a simple external configuration file, but the heuristics for expanding segments to include enclosing markup are handled by a HTML-specific module. Ideally, one would learn the markup conventions that influence sentence segmentation. However, the lack of appropriate training data (and the likelihood of needing data for each new website or content management system) makes a statistical approach impractical. As our previous survey (Read et al., 2012a) indicated that rule-based systems perform best at this task, we have opted for that method in our wrapper.

The error analysis has revealed a number of interesting possibilities for improving the tool. Most significantly, almost half of the false negative errors made on the datasets were due to the use of character-based list conventions, without HTML markup. Such errors could perhaps be fixed simply by forcing breaks when observing sequences of newlines, whitespace and a bullet-like characters, potentially greatly improving the recall of sentence boundaries. Similarly, precision could be improved with a heuristic to remove sentence breaks after the item number of enumerated lists. As mentioned above, there is also potential for improving precision by using soft constraints to decide when to introduce forced breaks at paragraph or list items, however the possibility of missing more sentence breaks in this fashion is a concern that should be tested empirically.

In other future work, we anticipate creating variants of this module for WikiText, and possibly for LaTeX. We intend to run experiments on tokenisation, and possibly other forms of pre-processing where markup could be distracting to off-the-shelf tools, to evaluate the impact of this form of normalisation more generally.

References

Flickinger, D., Oepen, S., and Ytrestøl, G. (2010). Wikiwoods: Syntacto-semantic annotation for English Wikipedia. In *Proceedings of the 7th Conference on International Language Resources and Evaluation*, Valletta, Malta.

Foster, J., Cetinoglu, O., Wagner, J., Le Roux, J., Nivre, J., Hogan, D., and van Genabith, J. (2011). From news to comment: Resources and benchmarks for parsing the language of Web 2.0. In *Proceedings of the 2011 International Joint Conference on Natural Language Processing*, page 893 – 901, Chiang Mai, Thailand.

Gimpel, K., Schneider, N., O'Connor, B., Das, D., Mills, D., Eisenstein, J., Heilman, M., Yogatama, D., Flanigan, J., and Smith, N. A. (2011). Part-of-speech tagging for Twitter: Annotation, features, and experiments. In *Proceedings of the 49th Meeting of the Association for Computational Linguistics*, page 42 – 47, Portland, OR, USA.

Kilgarriff, A. and Grefenstette, G. (2003). Introduction to the special issue on the web as corpus. *Computational Linguistics*, 29(3):333 – 347.

Marcus, M., Santorini, B., and Marcinkiewicz, M. A. (1993). Building a large annotated corpora of English: The Penn Treebank. *Computational Linguistics*, 19:313 – 330.

Read, J., Dridan, R., Oepen, S., and Solberg, L. J. (2012a). Sentence boundary detection: A long solved problem? In *Proceedings of the 24th International Conference on Computational Linguistics*, Mumbai, India.

Read, J., Flickinger, D., Dridan, R., Oepen, S., and Øvrelid, L. (2012b). The WeSearch Corpus, Treebank, and Treecache. A comprehensive sample of user-generated content. In *Proceedings of the 8th International Conference on Language Resources and Evaluation*, Istanbul, Turkey.

Schäfer, U., Kiefer, B., Spurk, C., Steffen, J., and Wang, R. (2011). The ACL Anthology Searchbench. In *Proceedings of the 49th Meeting of the Association for Computational Linguistics System Demonstrations*, page 7 – 13, Portland, OR, USA.

Solberg, L. J. (2012). A corpus builder for Wikipedia. Master's thesis, University of Oslo, Norway.

Statistical Machine Translation with Readability Constraints

Sara Stymne, Jörg Tiedemann, Christian Hardmeier and Joakim Nivre

Uppsala University
Department of Linguistics and Philology
Box 635, 751 26 Uppsala, Sweden

`firstname.lastname@lingfil.uu.se`

ABSTRACT

This paper presents experiments with document-level machine translation with readability constraints. We describe the task of producing simplified translations from a given source with the aim to optimize machine translation for specific target users such as language learners. In our approach, we introduce global features that are known to affect readability into a document-level SMT decoding framework. We show that the decoder is capable of incorporating those features and that we can influence the readability of the output as measured by common metrics. This study presents the first attempt of jointly performing machine translation and text simplification, which is demonstrated through the case of translating parliamentary texts from English to Swedish.

KEYWORDS: Machine Translation, Text Simplification, Readability.

1   Introduction

Typically, statistical machine translation (SMT) focuses on the translation of isolated sentences. However, humans usually emphasize the translation of coherent texts into equally coherent translations targeted at a specific audience. In this paper, we address the problem of including document-wide features into statistical MT that may influence the style of the generated documents in the target language. For this, we adopt the task of producing simplified translations that could be useful, for example, for language learners, dyslectic people or simply for non-experts who want to grasp the major content in highly domain-specific documents written in a foreign language. An example for the latter could be legal texts that often use a very domain-specific terminology and jargon.

Readability and text simplification has been widely studied in the field of computational linguistics and several metrics and approaches have been proposed in the literature. Common readability metrics make use of global text properties such as type/token ratios, lexical consistency, and the proportion of long versus short words as indicators. Our goal is to incorporate these features in machine translation in order to combine text simplification and adequate translation in one system. To the best of our knowledge, this has not been attempted before and represents a novel and challenging idea in the field of MT research.

Global features such as the ones mentioned above require new approaches to the general problem of decoding in SMT. Fortunately, we have recently presented a new document-level decoder, which, contrary to standard SMT decoders, translates documents as a unit instead of sentences in isolation (Hardmeier et al., 2012). This allows us to define document-wide features in the target language to test our ideas. Our application is also a good test case for the capabilities of the decoder and we would like to use our findings in future developments of general user-targeted machine translation.

The contributions of this paper are thus two-fold: (1) We show that document-wide decoding can effectively use global features and (2) we demonstrate that readability features can be used in SMT to produce simplified text translations. The remainder of the paper is organized as follows: First, we introduce important background on document-level decoding and readability. Thereafter, we present our experiments using a set of global features. Finally, we add some information about related work, summarize our findings and give ideas about future work.

2   Document-wide SMT

Most current SMT systems translate sentences individually, assuming independence between the sentences in a text. This independence assumption is exploited in the most popular SMT decoding algorithms, which efficiently explore a very large search space by using dynamic programming (Och et al., 2001). Integrating discourse-wide information into traditional SMT decoders is difficult because of these dynamic programming assumptions. We therefore implement our document-level readability models in the recently published document-level SMT decoder Docent (Hardmeier et al., 2012), which does not have these limitations.

The model implemented by Docent is phrase-based SMT (Koehn et al., 2003). The decoder uses a local search approach whose state consists of a complete translation of an entire document at any time. The initial state is improved by applying a series of operations using a hill climbing strategy to find a (local) maximum of the score function. The three operations used are to change the translation of phrases, to swap the position of two phrases , and to resegment phrases. This setup is not limited by dynamic programming constraints, so we can define scoring functions over the entire document. By initializing the decoder state with the output of a Moses run, which makes it possible to include all models except the ones with document-level dependencies, we ensure that the final hypothesis is no worse than what would have been found by Moses alone.

3 Readability – Metrics and Features

Readability is a complex notion that is related both to properties of texts, and to individual readers and their skills. Chall (1958) defines four elements that she considers significant for a readability criterion: vocabulary load, sentence structure, idea density, and human interest. Mühlenbock and Kokkinakis (2009) map these categories to metrics for readability that can be used in combination in order to capture several readability aspects. Vocabulary load can be measured as word-frequency ratios, or based on the proportion or number of long words. For Swedish, they suggest the commonly used metric *LIX* (Björnsson, 1968), which measures sentence length and proportion of long words and in addition the proportion of *extra long words* (XLW). For sentence structure, parsed text can be used to calculate the proportion of simple versus complex sentences. Such calculations are relatively costly, however, and dependent on the availability of parsers and definitions of sentence types, and they suggest that *average sentence length* (ASL) can be used as a proxy. Idea density can be measured based on lexical variation and the proportion of function vs content words. A common density measure for Swedish is the *Word variation index* (OVIX), a reformulation of *type token ratio* (TTR) that is less sensitive to text length. Another one is *nominal ratio* (NR), which is a ratio based on parts of speech. Finally, human interest can be captured for instance by the proportion of proper names (PN). To cover the four readability aspects, we use all these metrics for evaluation. Their definitions are shown in Eq. 1–6, where $C(x)$ is the count of x.

$$\text{ASL} = \frac{C(\text{tokens})}{C(\text{sentences})} \tag{1}$$

$$\text{LIX} = \text{ASL} + 100 * \frac{C(\text{tokens} > 6 \text{ chars})}{C(\text{tokens})} \tag{2}$$

$$\text{XLW} = 100 * \frac{C(\text{tokens} >= 14 \text{ chars})}{C(\text{tokens})} \tag{3}$$

$$\text{OVIX} = \frac{\log(C(\text{tokens}))}{\log\left(2 - \frac{\log(C(\text{types}))}{\log(C(\text{tokens}))}\right)} \tag{4}$$

$$\text{NR} = \frac{C(\text{nouns}) + C(\text{prepositions}) + C(\text{participles})}{C(\text{pronouns}) + C(\text{adverbs}) + C(\text{verbs})} \tag{5}$$

$$\text{PN} = \frac{C(\text{proper names})}{C(\text{tokens})} \tag{6}$$

In order to couple text simplification with SMT we also need to include features that can capture some aspects of readability into the decoder. While our main focus is on document-level features, we also include some basic sentence level count features used in readability metrics. On the document-level we use features for type token ratio and for lexical consistency. Table 1 gives an overview of the readability features.

Document-level		Sentence-level	
OVIX	Word variation index (Eq. 4)	SL	Sentence length in words
TTR	Type token ratio (Eq. 7)	nLW	Number of long words (> 6 chars)
Qw	Q-value, word level (Eq. 8)	nXLW	Number of extra long words (>= 14 chars)
Qp	Q-value, phrase level (Eq. 8)		

Table 1: Readability features used in the decoder

Lexical consistency has not typically been used as a readability indicator as such, but consistent vocabulary can be considered likely to improve readability. To measure it we chose the Q-value metric, which has been proposed for measuring bilingual term quality (Deléger et al., 2006). It is based on the frequency and consistency in translation of term candidates, as shown in Eq. 8 where $f(st)$ is the frequency of the term pair and $n(s)$ and $n(t)$ are the numbers of different term pairs in which the source and target terms occur respectively. We include a Q-value feature both on word level and on phrase level. On the phrase level we consider the phrases used by the SMT decoder, and on the word level we consider individual source words, and their alignment to $0 - N$ target words.

$$\text{TTR} = \frac{C(\text{tokens})}{C(\text{types})} \tag{7}$$

$$\text{Q-value} = \frac{f(st)}{n(s) + n(t)} \tag{8}$$

4 Experiments

In the following, we show results for our experiments with the Docent decoder that include readability features and compare them to runs without them. The systems are evaluated using both MT and readability metrics.

4.1 Experimental Setup

We evaluate our models on parliamentary texts from Europarl (Koehn, 2005), which contain both complex sentences and a lot of domain-specific terminology. All tests are performed for English–Swedish translation. Our system is trained on 1,488,322 sentences. For evaluation, we extracted 20 documents with a total of 690 sentences from a separate part of Europarl. A document is defined as a complete contiguous sequence of utterances of one speaker. We excluded documents that are shorter than 20 sentences and longer than 79 sentences.

Moses (Koehn et al., 2007) was used for training the translation model and SRILM (Stolcke, 2002) for training the language model. We initialized our experiments with a Moses model that uses standard features of a phrase-based system: a 5-gram language model, five translation model features, a distance-based reordering penalty, and a word counter. These features were optimized using minimum error-rate training (Och, 2003) and the same weights were then used in Docent. Currently, we are developing the optimization procedure in Docent and could not use it in this work. We thus used a grid search approach for choosing weights for the readability-based features with low, medium, and high impact relative to the standard features.

We performed automatic evaluations using a set of common metrics for MT quality and readability. For MT quality we used BLEU (Papineni et al., 2002) and NIST (Doddington, 2002),

Feature	Weight	BLEU↑	NIST↑	LIX↓	ASL↓	OVIX↓	XLW↓	NR↓	PN↑
Reference	–	–	–	50.47	24.65	57.73	3.08	1.055	0.013
Baseline	–	0.243	6.12	51.17	25.01	56.88	2.63	1.062	0.015
OVIX	low	0.243	6.11	51.00	25.09	54.65	2.60	1.069	0.015
	medium	0.228	5.83	49.33	25.45	44.43	2.53	1.063	0.015
	high	0.144	4.41	46.59	29.09	31.65	1.82	0.941	0.013
TTR	low	0.243	6.12	51.04	25.11	55.25	2.60	1.070	0.015
	medium	0.225	5.75	49.86	26.19	45.31	2.44	1.080	0.014
	high	0.150	4.48	48.30	30.54	32.95	1.77	0.975	0.012
Qw	low	0.242	6.10	51.16	25.07	57.16	2.62	1.064	0.015
	medium	0.231	5.90	51.28	25.32	58.90	2.62	1.074	0.015
	high	0.165	4.93	50.92	26.14	60.61	2.63	1.101	0.016
Qp	low	0.243	6.12	51.16	24.99	56.94	2.65	1.061	0.015
	medium	0.229	5.99	49.79	24.14	54.75	2.62	1.060	0.015
	high	0.097	3.90	41.45	21.99	39.22	2.39	1.129	0.015
nLW	low	0.244	6.14	50.96	24.98	56.73	2.63	1.065	0.015
	medium	0.225	5.96	46.72	24.21	55.39	2.72	1.080	0.018
	high	0.106	4.11	30.27	22.18	45.41	1.78	0.899	0.023
nXLW	low	0.241	6.10	51.03	24.96	56.69	1.85	1.060	0.015
	medium	0.225	5.85	50.92	25.09	56.56	0.19	1.070	0.016
	high	0.224	5.84	50.97	25.12	56.55	0.19	1.068	0.016
SL	low	0.242	6.21	51.07	24.22	57.79	2.71	1.058	0.016
	medium	0.211	5.94	50.77	21.61	60.93	3.15	1.040	0.018
	high	0.150	4.38	50.77	18.46	65.37	3.72	1.072	0.021

Table 2: Results of systems with single readability features, compared to the reference and baseline. Arrows indicate the direction of metrics (better MT/more readable). For definitions of metrics and features see Eq. 1–6 and Table 1.

and for readability we used LIX, ASL, OVIX, XLW, NR and PN, explained in section 3. Since we lack a customized evaluation set, the MT metrics were computed against a standard reference set of normal Europarl translations that are not simplified. We can thus expect that simplification leads to a decrease in MT metrics. To further investigate the effects on adequacy and readability, we performed a small human evaluation. We leave more principled optimization and evaluation to future work, where we also plan to use simple dev and test sets.

4.2   Results

In this section we present results on metrics and a small human evaluation. We also exemplify the types of simplifications we can achieve in our setup.

Metrics

Table 2 shows the results when we activate one readability feature at a time using low, medium, and high weights for each feature. We can see that the baseline and reference are quite similar with respect to readability with some interesting differences, for example for extra long words. As expected, giving a high weight to a readability feature usually results in a dramatic decrease in MT quality (with respect to the unsimplified reference translation), but also affects the corresponding readability feature(s) much, in some cases with unreasonably low scores (see e.g., LIX for the nLW feature). Using low or medium weights, on the other hand, can give reasonable MT scores as well as some improvements on several readability metrics. Obviously, the features corresponding directly to a metric affects that metric, such as LIX for nLW and OVIX for OVIX and TTR. Several features also affects other readability metrics, though. For

	BLEU↑	NIST↑	LIX↓	ASL↓	OVIX↓	XLW↓	NR↓	PN↑
Baseline	0.243	6.12	51.17	25.01	56.88	2.63	1.062	0.015
LIX (nLW+SL)	0.214	5.96	46.09	23.02	56.27	2.90	1.061	0.018
OVIX+SL	0.229	5.94	48.86	24.34	44.53	2.63	1.046	0.015
Qp+OVIX+nLW+SL	0.225	5.93	47.77	24.08	43.77	2.65	1.045	0.016
All features	0.235	6.04	49.29	24.34	47.80	1.98	1.046	0.015

Table 3: Results for systems with combinations of readability features (medium weights)

	Preferred system		
	Baseline	Equal	Readability (All)
Adequacy	51	33	16
Readability	33	29	38

Table 4: Preferred system with regard to adequacy and redability in the human evaluation

instance, OVIX and TTR decrease several metrics, but give an increase in sentence length, which is unwanted. For the Q-value, the effect is very different when used on phrase and word level. On the phrase level it decreases most metrics, except NR, which increases, while the effect is small on the readability metrics when used on the word level. We need to analyze these outcomes in more detail in the future.

In Table 3 we show results for some of the possible feature combinations, using medium weights. As expected, the effect on the readability metrics is more balanced in these cases. For the system with all features there are improvements on all readability metrics, except for PN, which is on par with the baseline. The other systems that use some global feature also have a positive effect on most readability metrics, while the LIX system that uses only local features has little effect on OVIX and a negative effect on extra long words. All these systems show only a modest decrease in MT quality, though. We can thus show that the decoder, with global features, managed to simplify translations on aspects corresponding to vocabulary load, idea density, and sentence structure while maintaining a reasonable translation quality.

Human Evaluation

We also performed a small human evaluation of 100 random non-identical sentences from the baseline and the system using all readability features.[1] For each sentence we ranked the output on adequacy, how well the content is translated, and readability, how easy to read the translations are. For annotation we used the Blast interface (Stymne, 2011), which also showed the overlap between the two translations. The evaluation was performed by the four authors, who are either native Swedish speakers, or have a good command of Swedish.

The results are shown in Table 4. It shows that the baseline produces a higher number of adequate translations than the system with readability features, but adequacy is also equal often. For readability there is a small advantage for the system with readability features, which is consistent with the improvement on readability metrics. Overall the output was often very similar, with only few words differing. In several of the cases where the baseline was judged as having better adequacy the cause is a single changed word, which can be more common or shorter, but has the wrong form or part of speech, which means it does not fit into the context. In other cases some non-essential information is removed from the sentence, which

---

[1]177 out of 690 sentences were identical.

while making the translation less adequate, is actually what we want to achieve. There were several cases where essential words have disappeared from the translation as well, though.

This evaluation was small scale, with course-grained judgments, and for only one possible system with readability features. In the future we want to look at several systems in some more detail. We can still see a tendency though, that we can gain a little bit in readability, but we're currently paying a cost as concerns adequacy.

Translation Examples

In Table 5 we show sample translations, in order to exemplify the types of operations our current system is able to perform. One type of successful simplification is to remove words that are not crucial for the main content. In many of the systems with readability constraints, the phrase *the honourable Members* has been simplified, either by removing the adjective and giving only *ledamöterna* ('the members'), or even by using the pronoun *ni* ('you'). Another positive simplification is that of *in such a way that*, which is translated quite literally in the baseline, but simplified into *så att* ('so that') in several of the systems. There are also instances, however, where the changes lead to a loss of information, especially for the shorter translation options. Examples are *handlingsplan* ('action plan'), which is reduced to *plan* ('plan') in the nLW system, and *2003* which is missing in the OVIX and Qp systems. There are several cases where different translations have been chosen for a word or phrase. Sometimes this can lead to a simplification, as in the nLW system where the everyday expression *bli klar* ('finish') is used instead of the more formal *avsluta* ('finish'). In other cases the translation options are of a relatively similar degree of difficulty, such as *vissa/en del/några* ('some'). In some cases a change of translation also lead to a change of part of speech, as for *uppmärksamhet* ('attention') which is often translated as the adjective *uppmärksam* ('attentive'), which unfortunately have led to syntactic problems in these translations. In general, as can be expected of SMT, there are some problems with fluency in all translations, but they tend to get worse in the systems with high-weight readability features.

There are also other types of changes, which are not shown in Table 5. Using the feature for extra long words tend to break long compounds, sometimes successfully, for example, translating the long compound *gemenskapslagstiftningen* ('the community legislation') into the genitive construction *gemenskapens lagstiftning* ('the community's legislation'), which is done in the XLW and All systems. Sometimes this is less successful, however, e.g., when not translating *World Trade Organisation* at all or giving the English-based abbreviation *WTO* instead. There are also cases where the readability features lead to changes in syntactic structure, such as the translation of *the excellent work he has done* into *hans utmärkta arbete* ('his excellent work') in some systems with the Qw feature, instead of a literal translation in the baseline.

5   Related Work

As far as we are aware this is the first work presenting joint machine translation and text simplification. Aziz et al. (2012) investigate the task of translating subtitles where time and space constraints are important, which leads to the task of sentence compression, which is related to our work on simplifying translated texts. They introduce dynamic length penalties which they integrate in a standard SMT decoder. Their model successfully compresses subtitles on three data sets. However, they also show that a similar compression can be achieved with appropriate tuning data that meets the length constraints. There are also a number of studies that use SMT techniques for monolingual paraphrasing (e.g., Ganitkevitch et al., 2011) and

Source	As the honourable Members know - some speakers have mentioned it - the European Council at Lisbon paid particular attention to promoting our efforts to implement risk capital in such a way that the action plan will be finished in 2003.
Baseline	Som de ärade ledamöterna vet - vissa talare har nämnt det - som Europeiska rådet i Lissabon ägnat särskild uppmärksamhet åt att främja våra ansträngningar att genomföra riskkapital på ett sådant sätt att handlingsplanen kommer att vara avslutat år 2003.
All (medium)	Som ledamöterna vet - vissa talare har nämnt det - som Europeiska rådet i Lissabon särskilt uppmärksam på att främja våra insatser för att genomföra riskkapital så att handlingsplanen kommer att vara avslutat 2003.
LIX (medium)	Som ledamöterna vet - vissa talare har nämnt det - Europeiska rådet i Lissabon lagt särskild vikt vid att främja våra ansträngningar att genomföra riskkapital så att handlingsplanen kommer att vara avslutat år 2003.
OVIX+SL (medium)	Som ni vet - vissa talare har nämnt det - som Europeiska rådet i Lissabon särskilt uppmärksam på att främja våra ansträngningar att genomföra riskkapital så att handlingsplanen kommer att avslutas under 2003.
OVIX (high)	Som ledamöter - en del talare har nämnt det - som Europeiska rådet i Lissabon särskilt uppmärksam på att stödja våra insatser för att genomföra av riskkapital, på så sätt att handlingsplanen kommer att vara avslutat i.
Qp (high)	Som de ärade ledamöterna vet, som några talare har nämnt det rådet i Lissabon, ägnat särskild uppmärksamhet åt att vi för att genomföra riskerna i det att handlingsplanen kommer att avslutas med.
nLW (high)	Som ni vet - vissa har sagt det - EU:s möte i Lissabon lagt särskild vikt vid vår för att genomföra risk i så att den plan att bli klar under 2003.
SL (high)	Som ledamöterna vet vissa talare har nämnt - Europeiska rådet i Lissabon särskilt uppmärksammat främja våra ansträngningar att genomföra riskkapital så att handlingsplanen avslutas 2003.

Table 5: Examples of translation output from a sample of systems

sentence compression (e.g., Knight and Marcu, 2000; Specia, 2010). Furthermore, there is a wide range of publications using other methods for monolingual sentence compression and text simplification, (e.g., Daelemans et al., 2004; Cohn and Lapata, 2009).

Readability has also been investigated as an effect of text summarization, as measured by user studies (Margarido et al., 2008) and automatic metrics (Smith and Jönsson, 2011). In these studies the readability was generally better in the summarized texts than in the original texts. Stymne and Smith (2012) showed that SMT is affected by summarization, but found no relation between readability and SMT quality measured by standard evaluation metrics.

There is also related work concerned with the integration of wide contextual features in machine translation, such as lexical consistency. The effect of lexical consistency in translation has been studied by Carpuat (2009) and Carpuat and Simard (2012). Tiedemann (2010) proposed cached models to push consistent translation with some success in the case of domain adaptation. The use of word sense disambiguation in SMT is another example where wide contextual information can be incorporated on the source side (Carpuat and Wu, 2007; Chan et al., 2007)

Another study related to ours is Genzel et al. (2010), who study poetry translation and perform joint translation and poetry creation of news text as well as translation of poems that keep the poetic form. They use features in the decoder such as rhyme and meter. They also introduce constraints over the target language output in order to adapt to the task-specific properties. However, they do not work on the document level, which would be an interesting direction for future work.

6   Conclusion and Future Work

In this article we explore a few readability related features in statistical machine translation. We have shown that these global features can successfully be integrated in a document-level decoder. We have evaluated a test case for English and Swedish using parliamentary texts which illustrates the effect of adding readability constraints. Our results demonstrate that the decoder can easily be influenced in terms of several aspects of readability of its output and that the approach can lead to a number of different types of simplifications. As expected, the translation quality goes down to some extent as measured by MT metrics as the one and only reference translation is not aimed at simplifying the text compared to its original version. The human evaluation also showed that we suffered on adequacy. So far we did not formally evaluate the effect on fluency, but the inspection of sentences showed that there were problems in this respect, which we plan to address in the future, for instance by the use of sequence models based on parts of speech or morphology.

Further directions for future work include the incorporation of additional features. So far, we only use surface features but we could complement them with features based on linguistic annotation such as POS labels and syntactic information. We could capture aspects measured by readability metrics such as NR and PN, or apply features like Q-value only for content words, but also could help to eliminate complex structures such as relative clauses. Another direction could be the task of splitting sentences into simpler ones if necessary. This however, would involve substantial developments in the decoder framework and would require appropriate training data that cover such cases. Finally, we are currently working on the optimization of feature weights within the document-level decoder. In our current experiments, no automatic tuning procedure has been applied for document-level features. We expect that proper weighting will be crucial to optimize the interaction between feature functions.

References

Aziz, W., de Sousa, S. C. M., and Specia, L. (2012). Cross-lingual sentence compression for subtitles. In *Proceedings of the 16th Annual Conference of the European Association for Machine Translation*, pages 103–110, Trento, Italy.

Björnsson, C. H. (1968). *Läsbarhet*. Liber, Stockholm.

Carpuat, M. (2009). One translation per discourse. In *Proceedings of the Workshop on Semantic Evaluations: Recent Achievements and Future Directions (SEW-2009)*, pages 19–27, Boulder, Colorado.

Carpuat, M. and Simard, M. (2012). The trouble with SMT consistency. In *Proceedings of the Seventh Workshop on Statistical Machine Translation*, pages 442–449, Montréal, Canada.

Carpuat, M. and Wu, D. (2007). Improving statistical machine translation using word sense disambiguation. In *Proceedings of the 2007 Joint Conference on Empirical Methods in Natural Language Processing and Computational Natural Language Learning*, pages 61–72, Prague, Czech Republic.

Chall, J. S. (1958). *Readability: An appraisal of research and application*. Columbus : Bureau of Educational Research, Columbus, Ohio, USA.

Chan, Y. S., Ng, H. T., and Chiang, D. (2007). Word sense disambiguation improves statistical machine translation. In *Proceedings of the 45th Annual Meeting of the ACL*, pages 33–40, Prague, Czech Republic.

Cohn, T. and Lapata, M. (2009). Sentence compression as tree transduction. *Journal of Artificial Intelligence Research*, 34:637–674.

Daelemans, W., Höthker, A., and Sang, E. T. K. (2004). Automatic sentence simplification for subtitling in Dutch and English. In *Proceedings of the 4th International Conference on Language Resources and Evaluation (LREC'04)*, pages 1045–1048, Lisbon, Portugal.

Deléger, L., Merkel, M., and Zweigenbaum, P. (2006). Enriching medical terminologies: an approach based on aligned corpora. In *International Congress of the European Federation for Medical Informatics*, pages 747–752, Maastricht, The Netherlands.

Doddington, G. (2002). Automatic evaluation of machine translation quality using n-gram co-occurence statistics. In *Proceedings of the Second International Conference on Human Language Technology*, pages 228–231, San Diego, California, USA.

Ganitkevitch, J., Callison-Burch, C., Napoles, C., and Durme, B. V. (2011). Learning sentential paraphrases from bilingual parallel corpora for text-to-text generation. In *Proceedings of the 2011 Conference on Empirical Methods in Natural Language Processing*, pages 1168–1179, Edinburgh, Scotland.

Genzel, D., Uszkoreit, J., and Och, F. (2010). "Poetic" statistical machine translation: Rhyme and meter. In *Proceedings of the 2010 Conference on Empirical Methods in Natural Language Processing*, pages 158–166, Cambridge, Massachusetts, USA.

Hardmeier, C., Nivre, J., and Tiedemann, J. (2012). Document-wide decoding for phrase-based statistical machine translation. In *Proceedings of the 2012 Joint Conference on Empirical Methods in Natural Language Processing and Computational Natural Language Learning*, pages 1179–1190, Jeju Island, Korea.

Knight, K. and Marcu, D. (2000). Statistics-based summarization — Step one: Sentence compression. In *National Conference on Artificial Intelligence (AAAI)*, pages 703–710, Austin, Texas, USA.

Koehn, P. (2005). Europarl: A parallel corpus for statistical machine translation. In *Proceedings of MT Summit X*, pages 79–86, Phuket, Thailand.

Koehn, P., Hoang, H., Birch, A., Callison-Burch, C., Federico, M., Bertoldi, N., Cowan, B., Shen, W., Moran, C., Zens, R., Dyer, C., Bojar, O., Constantin, A., and Herbst, E. (2007). Moses: Open source toolkit for statistical machine translation. In *Proceedings of the 45th Annual Meeting of the ACL, Demo and Poster Sessions*, pages 177–180, Prague, Czech Republic.

Koehn, P., Och, F. J., and Marcu, D. (2003). Statistical phrase-based translation. In *Proceedings of the 2003 Human Language Technology Conference of the NAACL*, pages 48–54, Edmonton, Alberta, Canada.

Margarido, P., Pardo, T., Antonio, G., Fuentes, V., Aluísio, S., and Fortes, R. (2008). Automatic summarization for text simplification: Evaluating text understanding by poor readers. In *Anais do VI Workshop em Tecnologia da Informação e da Linguagem Humana*, pages 310–315, Vila Velha, Brazil.

Mühlenbock, K. and Kokkinakis, S. J. (2009). LIX 68 revisited – an extended readability. In *Proceedings of the Corpus Linguistics Conference*, Liverpool, UK.

Och, F. J. (2003). Minimum error rate training in statistical machine translation. In *Proceedings of the 42nd Annual Meeting of the ACL*, pages 160–167, Sapporo, Japan.

Och, F. J., Ueffing, N., and Ney, H. (2001). An efficient A* search algorithm for Statistical Machine Translation. In *Proceedings of the ACL 2001 Workshop on Data-Driven Machine Translation*, pages 55–62, Toulouse, France.

Papineni, K., Roukos, S., Ward, T., and Zhu, W.-J. (2002). BLEU: A method for automatic evaluation of machine translation. In *Proceedings of the 40th Annual Meeting of the ACL*, pages 311–318, Philadelphia, Pennsylvania, USA.

Smith, C. and Jönsson, A. (2011). Automatic summarization as means of simplifying texts, an evaluation for Swedish. In *Proceedings of the 18th Nordic Conference on Computational Linguistics (NODALIDA'11)*, Riga, Latvia.

Specia, L. (2010). Translating from complex to simplified sentences. In *Proceedings of the 9th International Conference on Computational Processing of the Portuguese Language, 9th International Conference (PROPOR'10)*, pages 30–39, Porto Alegre, Brazil.

Stolcke, A. (2002). SRILM – an extensible language modeling toolkit. In *Proceedings of the Seventh International Conference on Spoken Language Processing*, pages 901–904, Denver, Colorado, USA.

Stymne, S. (2011). Blast: A tool for error analysis of machine translation output. In *Proceedings of the 49th Annual Meeting of the ACL: Human Language Technologies, Demonstration session*, Portland, Oregon, USA.

Stymne, S. and Smith, C. (2012). On the interplay between readability, summarization and MTranslatability. In *Proceedings of the 4th Swedish Language Technology Conference*, pages 71–72, Lund, Sweden.

Tiedemann, J. (2010). Context adaptation in statistical machine translation using models with exponentially decaying cache. In *Proceedings of the ACL 2010 Workshop on Domain Adaptation for Natural Language Processing (DANLP)*, pages 8–15, Uppsala, Sweden.

Negation Scope Delimitation in Clinical Text Using Three Approaches: NegEx, PyConTextNLP and SynNeg

Hideyuki Tanushi[1], Hercules Dalianis[1], Martin Duneld[1], Maria Kvist[1,2],
Maria Skeppstedt[1], Sumithra Velupillai[1]

(1) Dept. of Computer and Systems Sciences (DSV), Stockholm University
Forum 100, 164 40 Kista, Sweden
(2) Dept. of clinical immunology and transfusion medicine, Karolinska University Hospital
171 76 Stockholm, Sweden

`hide-tan@dsv.su.se, hercules@dsv.su.se, xmartin@dsv.su.se,`

`maria.kvist@karolinska.se, mariask@dsv.su.se, sumithra@dsv.su.se`

ABSTRACT

Negation detection is a key component in clinical information extraction systems, as health record text contains reasonings in which the physician excludes different diagnoses by negating them. Many systems for negation detection rely on negation cues (e.g. *not*), but only few studies have investigated if the syntactic structure of the sentences can be used for determining the scope of these cues. We have in this paper compared three different systems for negation detection in Swedish clinical text (NegEx, PyConTextNLP and SynNeg), which have different approaches for determining the scope of negation cues. NegEx uses the distance between the cue and the disease, PyConTextNLP relies on a list of conjunctions limiting the scope of a cue, and in SynNeg the boundaries of the sentence units, provided by a syntactic parser, limit the scope of the cues. The three systems produced similar results, detecting negation with an F-score of around 80%, but using a parser had advantages when handling longer, complex sentences or short sentences with contradictory statements.

KEYWORDS: clinical text, negation detection, syntactic analysis.

1 Introduction

Clinical text is written by physicians and nurses in patient records. Most of these notes are noisy, written in telegraphic style, containing e.g. incomplete sentences with missing subjects. Moreover clinical text contains much more spelling errors than ordinary text. All this together makes it difficult for ordinary text processing tools to work properly.

In a clinical setting, it is important to record the symptoms and signs of diseases that the patient reports as a base for the following reasoning and speculation of possible diagnoses. Possible diseases that can be ruled out, as well as symptoms that the patient does not experience, are therefore frequently mentioned in the health record narrative. In one study, some of the most frequently used clinical observations were found to be negated the majority of the time (Chapman et al., 2001a). Negation detection in a clinical setting is essential for, e.g., text summarisation of clinical text, or for information retrieval of symptoms and diagnoses. Such systems would be very valuable for clinical decision support, knowledge extraction and supporting clinicians in their daily work.

The aim of this study is to determine if syntactic information is useful for negation scope detection in clinical text, compared to fixed or flexible rule-based scope detection.

Some of the problems with negation detection and determining the scope of what is negated, particularly in clinical texts, are linked with the characteristics mentioned above: the texts are often telegraphic and may contain information dense sentences where negated and affirmed diagnostic expressions are in close proximity, long enumerations, and complex sentences, where current negation detection approaches produce errors. Such problems may be better handled if syntactic information is used.

We therefore compared three different approaches for determining negation delimitation scope of diagnostic expressions:

1. Using the heuristic that the scope of a negation cue is six tokens, that is, if a diagnostic expression is mentioned in the proximity of six tokens from a negation cue it is considered as negated. This heuristic has previously been used for Swedish (Skeppstedt 2011).

2. Using the sentence as the scope for the negation cues, but limiting the scope if a conjunction is present in the sentence. This approach has previously been used for Swedish (Velupillai et al., 2013)

3. Using morphological and syntactic labels provided by a syntactic parser for determining the scope of a negation trigger.

2 Related Research

There are several studies on negation detection in English clinical text, both rule-based methods (e.g. Chapman et al., 2001b, Mutalik et al., 2001) and machine learning based methods (e.g. Rokach et al., 2010). The rule-based studies use a cue phrase that indicates negation, e.g. *not, no, rule out*. The most simple approaches use a heuristically determined scope, negating all symptoms and diseases that occur in close proximity to a cue phrase (Chapman et al., 2001b), whereas there are also approaches using other cue words, such as conjunctions, for limiting the scope of a negation cue phrase (Elkin et al., 2005, Chapman et al., 2011). Morante and Daelemans (2009) have studied the span of the scope to the left and to the right of the negated term in the BioScope Clinical Corpus and found that over 97 percent of the scopes are to the right of the negation and are on average 6.33 tokens long, while the ones to the left are only 4.84 tokens long. Aronow et al. (1999) describe a negation detection system, NegExpander, where they checked the scope of conjunctions to decide scope of negations, i.e. a sort of basic syntactic analysis. In Goryachev et al. (2006) this approach was compared with other approaches such as NegEx (see below) and machine learning based approaches (SVM and Naïve Bayes).

There are also studies in which parsers have been used for detecting the scope of negation cues. The *SEM shared task (Morante and Blanco, 2012) provided a phrase structure parsed literary corpus, annotated for negation cues and their scope, and had as one of the tasks to detect this scope. Most participating groups based the scope detection on machine learning, and the two most successful both used conditional random fields, one with features from the syntactic tree and the other also using lexical features.

In the clinical domain, Huang and Lowe (2007) categorized negation cues, based on their syntactic category and on typical phrase patterns they occur in, and constructed a grammar for how negation is expressed for each category, using phrase structures given by the Stanford syntactic parser. This resulted in a precision of 98.6% and a recall of 92.6% for detecting negated noun phrases in radiology reports.

Another rule-based system, using the dependency parser Minipar, was constructed by Ballesteros et al. (2012). This system determines scope by traversing the dependency graph towards the terminals, starting from the negation cue, if the cue is a verb, and otherwise with the verb that is affected by the negation cue. This system detected negation cues and their scope with a precision of 95.8% and a recall of 90.6% on the clinical part of the BioScope corpus.

Zhu et al. (2010) also used the BioScope corpus and employed techniques developed for shallow semantic parsing for detecting scope. The negation cue was regarded as a predicate and its constituents, i.e. words included in its scope, were found by a machine learning system among candidates given by a phrase structure parser. This approach resulted in a precision of 82.2% and a recall of 80.6% for determining negation scope in the clinical part of BioScope, when using automatic cue and parse tree detection.

Velldal et al. (2012) combined the output of one rule-based and one machine-learning system for detecting scope of negation in the BioScope corpus. For the rule-based system, rules were constructed for determining the scope of the cue, given the output of the dependency parser MaltParser, trained on the Penn Tree-bank. Separate rules were constructed for each cue part-of-speech category, with a special rule for the word *none*. For the machine learning system, a phrase structure grammar was adapted to identify phrase structure constituents identical to those in the annotated scopes. For the scientific texts in the BioScope corpus, this method gave substantially improved results compared to a baseline of using the entire sentence as the scope. For the clinical texts in the corpus, however, the baseline scope detection gave slightly better results with an F-score of 91.4, compared to 90.7 (using gold standard cues). It was found that 40% of the scope errors in the clinical domain were due to parse errors.

3   Method

We here compare three approaches – fixed size context window, lexical cues and syntactic tags – to determine the scope of a negated diagnostic expression in a Swedish clinical corpus. All approaches rely on predefined trigger lists of negation cues. In order to study the effect of scope delimitation in negation detection we have used the same trigger lists for all systems.

3.1 NegEx

NegEx (Chapman et al., 2001b) is a widely used system for negation detection in clinical text that is built on three different lists of cue phrases that trigger negation; pre-negations, post-negations and pseudo-negations. The pre-negation list consists of cue phrases indicating that a clinical condition, i.e. a disease or a symptom, following the cue is negated, whereas the post-negation list consists of cue phrases indicating that a clinical condition preceding them is negated. Pseudo-negation phrases, on the other hand, are phrases that should not trigger a negation of a clinical condition, even though they contain a negation cue, e.g. *not only*. The first version of NegEx uses a heuristically determined number of tokens for the scope of a negation cue. A clinical condition is thus here negated if it is in the range of one to six tokens from a post- or pre-negation trigger. This version of NegEx has been adapted to Swedish, through a translation of English negation cues into Swedish[1], and through retaining the six token heuristics for determining the scope of the triggers used in the English study (Skeppstedt, 2011). Later versions of NegEx for English use a list of termination terms, e.g. conjunctions, to limit the scope of what clinical conditions a negation cue negates.

3.2 PyConTextNLP

PyConTextNLP (Chapman et al. 2011) is an extension of the NegEx algorithm that includes modifications of the scoping rules, how lexical triggers are matched, and more functionalities for defining user- and task-specific rules. It works on a sentence level and takes as input a database containing the texts or sentences to be analyzed, user-defined targets (here: diagnostic expressions) and user-defined lexical triggers. These triggers are represented as four-tuples: a literal (the lexical cue/trigger), a category (what the trigger represents), a regular expression (to capture variants of the trigger) and a rule that defines the direction a trigger modifies a target (forward, backward or bidirectional). For handling scopes, instead of a six-token window, the algorithm operates on the whole sentence, unless it finds user-defined conjunctions. PyConTextNLP has been ported to Swedish (Velupillai et al., 2013).

3.3 SynNeg

SynNeg is a negation scoping tool that uses morphological and syntactic information provided by the MaltParser (Nivre et al., 2007). The MaltParser is a language-independent and data-driven dependency parsing system which relies on inductive learning from treebank data for the analysis of new sentences. In Hassel et al. (2011) it was shown that the MaltParser trained on general Swedish text worked sufficiently on Swedish clinical text (92.4% accuracy for part-of-speech tagging and a labeled attachment score of 76.6% for the syntactic dependency parsing). Therefore, it is likely that the information provided by a parser trained on general Swedish text can be useful also for negation detection in clinical text.

The basic idea of SynNeg is that a negation scope does not cross the boundary of a sentence unit (i.e. subject + verb phrase). It uses a list of negation triggers in order to identify negative expressions in a sentence and tries to delimit a sentence unit to which a negation cue belongs, through finding another sentence unit in the sentence. The MaltParser assigns the ES (= logical subject), FS (= dummy subject) or SS (=other subject) DEPREL (Dependency Relation) tag to a subject of a sentence unit. When a negation cue is found, SynNeg checks the DEPREL

---

[1]This trigger list is used for all three systems. It contains a total of 42 negation cues: five post-negations, nine pseudo-negations and the remaining are pre-negations.

tags of either the following token (pre-negation) or the preceding token (post-negation) from the negation cue to find a subject DEPREL tag. It also checks the part-of-speech (POS) tag for coordinating conjunction (KN), minor delimiter, e.g. comma (MID), and subordinating conjunction (SN) in order to set the negation span boundary position. Every time one of these POS tags is found, the position of the token is stored as a boundary candidate. Once a subject DEPREL tag is found, the nearest boundary candidate from the subject DEPREL tag is set as the negation span boundary.

3.4 Data

A Swedish clinical corpus[2] annotated for uncertainty and negation on a diagnostic expression level was used in these experiments. The corpus consists of assessment entries from a medical emergency ward in a Swedish hospital (Velupillai et al., 2011) and was annotated by a physician. The annotations, originally for six levels of uncertainty and negation, were collapsed into two annotation classes: negated and non-negated. The data set consists of 8874 sentences (average sentence length 9.56 tokens), of which 2189 sentences contain diagnostic expressions (one sentence contains the same diagnostic expression mentioned twice). 421 of these diagnostic expressions were tagged as *negated* during the annotation of this data set, while 1769 were tagged as *non-negated*. The distribution of negation cues in the data set is shown in table 1.

Pre-negation			Post-negation		
Negation cue	n	Percentage	Negation cue	n	Percentage
ingen (no, common gender)	363	21.25%	*negativt* (negative for)	13	0.76%
ej (not)	344	20.14%	*osannolikt* (unlikely)	9	0.53%
inga (no, plural)	240	14.05%	*inget avvikande* (no abnormal)	6	0.35%
inte (not)	209	12.24%			
utan (without)	120	7.03%	*saknas* (absence of)	1	0.06%
utesluta (rule out)	87	5.09%	Pseudo-negation		
inga tecken (no signs of)	76	4.45%	Negation cue	n	Percentage
inget (no, neuter gender)	69	4.04%	*kan inte uteslutas* (cannot be ruled out)	7	0.41%
uteslutas (be ruled out)	27	1.58%			
inte har (not have, reversed word order)	20	1.17%	*inte utesluta* (not rule out)	3	0.18%
kan inte (cannot)	17	1.00%	*ingen förändring* (no change)	2	0.12%
aldrig (never)	13	0.76%			
har inte (not have)	13	0.76%	*vet inte* (do not know)	2	0.12%
icke (non-, not)	13	0.76%			
inte kan (cannot, reversed word order)	13	0.76%			
inget som (nothing that)	12	0.70%			
utan tecken (without sign of)	10	0.59%			
förnekar (denies)	7	0.41%			
inte visar (not demonstrate)	6	0.35%			
avsaknad av (absence of)	4	0.23%			
kunde inte (cannot, past tense)	1	0.06%			
utan några (with no)	1	0.06%			

Table 1: Frequency and percentage of negation cues in the data set. n is the number of instances of each cue. The total number of cues in the data was 1708.

---

[2]This research has been approved by the Regional Ethical Review Board in Stockholm (Etikprövningsnämnden i Stockholm), permission number 2012/1838-31/3.

The MaltParser was used to parse the texts and used directly as input for the SynNeg algorithm. This parsed data was also used to construct data in the input formats used by NegEx and PyConTextNLP, respectively. As the MaltParser requires POS tagged data as input, we first tagged the clinical text with the Granska tagger (Knutsson et al., 2003).

4 Results

Table 2 summarizes the result of negation detection for the three systems. As the data was annotated on a diagnostic expression level, the figures show precision and recall for detecting whether these diagnostic expressions are negated or not. Overall results are very similar for NegEx, PyConTextNLP and SynNeg. NegEx produces slightly higher precision results for *negated* (79.6), while SynNeg results in slightly higher recall (82.9) and F-Score (79.9).

	NegEx	**PyConTextNLP**	**SynNeg**
Precision	79.6	78.1	77.0
Recall	79.6	81.2	82.9
F-Score	79.6	79.6	79.9

Table 2: Results of negation detection for NegEx, PyConTextNLP and SynNeg.

Some examples of how diagnostic expressions are classified by the three systems are presented in figures 1 and 2 and table 3. Figure 1 shows an example where a non-negated instance is within 6 tokens from a negation cue and a conjunction is missing. A sentence with a negated instance beyond a 6-token window is presented in figure 2. Table 3 demonstrates a long sentence containing an adversative expression and a subordinate conjunction.

		Negation cue (pre-negation)							
Swedish	Har	ingen	**hjärtinfarkt**	,	hans	**angina**	har	ökat	.
English	Has	no	**heart attack**	,	his	**angina**	has	increased	.
NegEx			1	2	3	4	5	6	
			negated			*negated*			
PyConTextNLP			*negated*			*negated*			
SynNeg									
DEPREL	ROOT	DT	OO	IK	DT	**SS**	ET	VG	IP
POS-tag	VB	DT	NN	**MID**	PS	NN	VB	VB	MAD
			negated			non-negated			

Figure 1: Sentence with non-negated instance within 6 tokens and lack of conjunction. Negated instances and non-negated instances are illustrated with red-colored italic and green-colored bold, respectively. DEPREL (Dependency Relation) and POS-tag as given by MaltParser and Granska, respectively.

			Negation cue (pre-negation)								
Swedish	Han	har	inte	någon	på	röntgen	synlig	**fissur**	eller	**fraktur**	.
English	He	does	not	have	any	x-ray	visible	fissure	or	fracture	.
NegEx				1	2	3	4	5	6		
								negated		non-negated	
PyConTextNLP											
								negated		*negated*	
SynNeg											
DEPREL	SS	ROOT	NA	DT	ET	PA	AT	CJ	OO	CJ	IP
POS-tag	PN	VB	AB	PN	PP	NN	JJ	NN	KN	NN	MAD
								negated		*negated*	

Figure 2: Sentence with negated instance beyond a 6-token window. Negated instances and non-negated instances are illustrated with red-colored italic and green-colored bold, respectively. DEPREL (Dependency Relation) and POS-tag as given by MaltParser and Granska, respectively.

> Vid ankomst opåv, <u>ingen</u> *astma*, <u>inga</u> hållpunkter för *lunginflammation*, dock UVI och anamnestisk klåda <u>utan</u> att man kan se *urticharia* eller annan *dermatit*.
>
> (At arrival unaff, <u>no</u> *asthma*, <u>no</u> signs of *pneumonia*, but UTI and anamnestical itching <u>without</u> any visible *urticharia* or other *dermatitis*.)

Swedish	English	Annotation	NegEx	PyConTextNLP	SynNeg
astma	asthma	*negated*	*negated*	*negated*	*negated*
lunginflammation	pneumonia	*negated*	*negated*	*negated*	*negated*
UVI	UTI	non-neg	*negated*	non-neg	*negated*
urticharia	urticharia	*negated*	*negated*	*negated*	non-neg
dermatit	dermatitis	*negated*	non-neg	*negated*	non-neg

Table 3: Sentence with an adversative expression and a subordinate conjunction. Negation cue, negated instance and non-negated instance are illustrated with underlined, red-colored italic and green-colored bold, respectively.

5 Discussion

Given the relatively small sample size, the differences in results between the three systems are difficult to draw conclusions from. Employing a simple, rule-based approach with a small amount of negation triggers and a fixed context window for determining scope is very efficient and useful, if results around 80% F-score are sufficient for a given purpose.

However, to better handle sentences such as the examples in figures 1 and 2 and table 3, other approaches are necessary. In the example in figure 1, (*Has no heart attack, his angina has increased.*), the lack of a conjunction makes it difficult to specify a cue phrase for delimiting the scope in PyConTextNLP, while this can be captured through the syntactic rules employed in SynNeg. On the other hand, table 3, (*At arrival unaff, no asthma, no signs of pneumonia, but UTI and anamnestical itching without any visible urticharia or other dermatitis.*), shows an example where PyConTextNLP correctly classifies all instances, while the other two systems produce errors. The scoping window of six tokens in NegEx is problematic (*UTI* incorrectly classified as negated and *dermatitis* incorrectly classified as non-negated), and SynNeg produces an error due to the subordinating conjunction *att* following *utan* (without) (*UTI*, *urthicaria* and *dermatitis*).

Both PyConTextNLP and SynNeg can correctly classify more complex cases, such as sentences with enumerations beyond the 6-token window (see figure 2) and short sentences with conjunctions that contradict instances. For improving the results of PyConTextNLP, it is essential to define lexical cue phrases, such as conjunctions, that delimit the scope of the negation trigger. For SynNeg, on the other hand, no lexical information is needed, only correct Part-of-Speech tags and syntactic labels. The advantage of the latter approach is that it generalizes over lexical terms.

The current version of SynNeg does not utilize the dependency tree produced by the parser, i.e. no traversal is done as in e.g. Ballesteros et al. (2012). This could be useful and will be studied further in the development of SynNeg.

The results for all three systems are in line with previous studies on negation detection for Swedish, e.g. Skeppstedt (2011). The results for most English studies are higher, e.g. Huang and Lowe (2007), but it is difficult to directly compare the findings, for instance given differences in used data.

One limitation in this study is that no evaluation on the performance of the MaltParser on this data has been conducted. A previous study shows that applying the MaltParser on Swedish clinical text yields promising results (Hassel et al., 2011), but that the parser produces errors in sentences with complicated conjunctional, conditional and prepositional constructions. As these are important factors for the correct identification of negation scope, this needs to be studied further.

The fixed context window approach (NegEx) is efficient and simple, but limited in its approach and will not be able to handle longer, complex sentences or short sentences with contradictory statements. With the more flexible approach employed in PyConTextNLP, it is possible to improve results if lexical phrases that define boundaries for the negation scope are defined. However, this approach will be problematic for cases that are ambiguous. Moreover, finding these lexical phrases may be time-consuming, and there is a risk of overfitting. Using syntactic information (SynNeg) instead may prove fruitful, as it is more generalizable. Also, with such an approach, it will be easier to port the system to another domain or language. However, it is crucial that the syntactic parser produces correct labels, and, of course, that a syntactic parser is available for that domain and language.

We plan to further develop SynNeg and evaluate it on larger datasets. In particular, we intend to incorporate information from traversing the dependency tree, in order to handle cases where the current heuristics are limited (double negation is, for example, currently not handled by any of the systems). Ongoing studies on automatically generating trigger terms both for negation and conjunctions for improving PyConTextNLP for Swedish clinical texts will also be of importance, and we will continue to compare the two approaches in order to further understand how well these types of systems can perform, along with comparisons of current state-of-the-art machine learning based approaches. We hypothesize that a combination of lexical- and syntactic-based systems may be very powerful, as they may complement each other.

6 Concluding Remarks

In this study we compare three different approaches for determining negation delimitation scope in Swedish clinical text. The approaches are rule-based, one of them relying on a fixed context window (NegEx) and one relying on full sentences or predefined lexical cue phrases for delimitation (PyConTextNLP). The third approach utilizes Part-of-Speech and syntactic labels (SynNeg). All three systems depend on the same trigger list of negation cues. Results show that although we are at the initial stages of developing SynNeg we achieve similar results compared to established lexical rule-based negation detection approaches: around 80% F-score. Using syntactic information may also prove more generalizable, facilitating porting to other domains or languages.

References

Aronow, D. B., Fangfang, F., and Croft, W. B. (1999). Ad Hoc Classification of Radiology Reports. *J Am Med Inform Assoc*, 5(6):393–411.

Ballesteros, M., Francisco, V., Díaz, A., Herrera, J., and Gervás, P. (2012). Inferring the scope of negation in biomedical documents. In *13th International Conference on Intelligent Text Processing and Computational Linguistics (CICLING 2012)*, New Delhi. Springer, Springer.

Chapman, B., Lee, S., Kang, H., and Chapman, W. (2011). Document-level classification of CT pulmonary angiography reports based on an extension of the ConText algorithm. *J Biomed Inform*, 44(5):728–737.

Chapman, W., Bridewell, W., Hanbury, P., Cooper, G., and Buchanan, B. (2001a). Evaluation of negation phrases in narrative clinical reports. In *Proceedings AMIA*, pages 105–109.

Chapman, W. W., Bridewell, W., Hanbury, P., Cooper, G. F., and Buchanan, B. G. (2001b). A simple algorithm for identifying negated findings and diseases in discharge summaries. *J Biomed Inform*, pages 34–301.

Elkin, P. L., Brown, S. H., Bauer, B. A., Husser, C. S., Carruth, W., Bergstrom, L. R., , and Wahner-Roedler, D. L. (2005). A controlled trial of automated classification of negation from clinical notes. *BMC Med Inform Decis Mak*, 13(5).

Goryachev, A., Sordo, M., Ngo, L., and Zeng, Q. (2006). Implementation and evaluation of four different methods of negation detection. Technical report, DSG.

Harkema, H., Dowling, J. N., Thornblade, T., and Chapman, W. W. (2009). Context: An algorithm for determining negation, experiencer, and temporal status from clinical reports. *J. of Biomedical Informatics*, 42(5):839–851.

Hassel, M., Henriksson, A., and Velupillai, S. (2011). Something Old, Something New – Applying a Pre-trained Parsing Model to Clinical Swedish. In *Proc. 18th Nordic Conf. on Comp. Ling. - NODALIDA '11*.

Huang, Y. and Lowe, H. J. (2007). A Novel Hybrid Approach to Automated Negation Detection in Clinical Radiology Reports. *JAMIA*, 3(14):304–311.

Knutsson, O., Bigert, J., and Kann, V. (2003). A robust shallow parser for Swedish. In *Proc. 14th Nordic Conf. on Comp. Ling. – NODALIDA '03*.

Morante, R. and Blanco, E. (2012). *sem 2012 shared task: resolving the scope and focus of negation. In *Proceedings of the First Joint Conference on Lexical and Computational Semantics - Volume 1: Proceedings of the main conference and the shared task, and Volume 2: Proceedings of the Sixth International Workshop on Semantic Evaluation*, SemEval '12, pages 265–274, Stroudsburg, PA, USA. Association for Computational Linguistics.

Morante, R. and Daelemans, W. (2009). Learning the scope of hedge cues in biomedical texts. In *Proceedings of the Workshop on BioNLP*, pages 28–36.

Mutalik, P., Deshpande, A., and Nadkarni, P. (2001). Use of general-purpose negation detection to augment concept indexing of medical documents a quantitative study using the umls. *JAMIA*, 8(6):598–609.

Nivre, J., Hall, J., Nilsson, J., Chanev, A., Eryigit, G., Kübler, S., Marinov, S., and Marsi, E. (2007). MaltParser: A language-independent system for data-driven dependency parsing. *Natural Language Engineering*, 13(2):95–135.

Rokach, L., Romano, R., and Maimon, O. (2010). Negation recognition in medical narrative reports. *Information Retrieval*, 11(6):499–538.

Skeppstedt, M. (2011). Negation detection in Swedish clinical text: An adaption of NegEx to Swedish. *Journal of Biomedical Semantics*, 2(Suppl 3):S3.

Velldal, E., Øvrelid, L., Read, J., and Oepen, S. (2012). Speculation and negation: Rules, rankers, and the role of syntax. *Comput. Linguist.*, 38(2):369–410.

Velupillai, S., Dalianis, H., and Kvist, M. (2011). Factuality Levels of Diagnoses in Swedish Clinical Text. In Moen, A., Andersen, S. K., Aarts, J., and Hurlen, P., editors, *Proc. XXIII International Conference of the European Federation for Medical Informatics – User Centred Networked Health Care*, pages 559 – 563, Oslo. IOS Press.

Velupillai, S., Skeppstedt, M., Kvist, M., Mowery, D., Chapman, B., Dalianis, H., and Chapman, W. (2013). Porting a rule-based assertion classifier for clinical text from English to Swedish. In *Proc. 4th Louhi 2013*, Sydney, Australia.

Zhu, Q., Li, J., Wang, H., and Zhou, G. (2010). A unified framework for scope learning via simplified shallow semantic parsing. In *Proceedings of the 2010 Conference on Empirical Methods in Natural Language Processing*, EMNLP '10, pages 714–724, Stroudsburg, PA, USA. Association for Computational Linguistics.

Tone restoration in transcribed Kammu: Decision-list word sense disambiguation for an unwritten language

Marcus Uneson

Centre for Languages and Literature, Lund University

`marcus.uneson@ling.lu.se`

Abstract

The RWAAI (Repository and Workspace for Austroasiatic Intangible heritage) project aims at building a digital archive out of existing legacy data from the Austroasiatic language family. One aspect of the project is the preservation of analogue legacy data. In this context, we have at our hands a large number of mostly-phonemic transcriptions of narrative monologues, often with accompanying sound recordings, in the unwritten Kammu language of northern Laos. Some of the transcriptions, however, lack tone marks, which for a tonal language such as Kammu makes them substantially less useful. The problem of restoring tones can be recast as one of word sense disambiguation, or, more generally, lexical ambiguity resolution. We attack it by decision lists, along the lines of Yarowsky (1994), using the tone-marked part of the corpus (120kW) as training data. The performance ceiling of this corpus is uncertain: the stories were all annotated, primarily for human rather than machine consumption, by a single person during almost 40 years, with slowly emerging idiosyncratic conventions. Thus, both inter-annotator and intra-annotator agreement figures are unknown. Nevertheless, with the data from this one annotator as a gold standard, we improve from an already-high baseline accuracy of 95.7% to 97.2% (by 10-fold cross-validation).

Keywords: word sense disambiguation, Kammu, decision lists, lexical ambiguity resolution, tone restoration, legacy data.

1   Introduction

The RWAAI (Repository and Workspace for Austroasiatic Intangible heritage) project aims at building a digital archive out of existing legacy data from the Austroasiatic language family, not only linguistic but also encompassing general cultural heritage (musicological, anthropological, etc). This goal involves digitizing analogue data, converting existing digital formats into modern, non-proprietary if necessary, and providing machine-readable metadata descriptions.

A major part of the project's digitization efforts concerns a large collection on Kammu, an Austroasiatic language spoken in northern Laos. The collection, gathered from the early 70's and on, among other things spots what is for an unwritten language a very sizeable text corpus: a large number of mostly-phonemic transcriptions of spontaneous, narrative monologue, often with the original recording intact. A problem, however, is that four decades of data handling, even by a single person, will inevitably witness varying practices. For instance, there are different spelling conventions; preferably, these should be harmonized. More crucially, the early transcriptions, in contrast to later ones, do not have tones marked, which for a tonal language such as Kammu is essential (especially for computational applications). The present paper deals with inference of the missing tones by word sense disambiguation (WSD), similar to what Yarowsky (1994) applied to restoration of accents in Spanish and French.

The paper is organized as follows. Section 2 describes the data. Thus, we present Kammu in some detail: a few words on the typological properties of the language (2.1); on the work which has produced the data we use (2.2); and finally on the particular content of the transcriptions – namely folk tales in narrative, self-paced monologue (2.3). Section 3 presents the problem as an instance of WSD, the experimental setup, and the outlines of the algorithm; and motivates the choice of decision lists as machine learning approach. Section 4 comments the results and Section 5 concludes with a general discussion of the context of the task, including variant applications of the algorithm.

2   Background

2.1   On Kammu

The following summary is based on Svantesson (1983). The Kammu (or Khmu; ISO 693-3 kjg) is the largest minority language of Laos, spoken by half a million people in the northern regions of the country, as well as in adjacent parts of Vietnam, Thailand and China. It belongs to the Khmuic subgroup of the Austroasiatic languages.

Kammu is predominantly analytic, exhibiting no inflectional morphology. Derivational morphology is productive through reduplication, prefixation and infixation. New words are also coined by compounding. Kammu has no practical orthography; however, practically all Kammu speakers also know Lao, and the younger generation is literate in it.

Kammu is a tonal language. With only slight simplifications[1] every lexical entry is monosyllabic and can be assigned either high or low tone. At type level, the tones are about

---

[1] The simplifications are operationally motivated and phonologically rather than phonetically based. First, we assume that function words carry tone, which is true in a lexical sense but may not be obvious in connected speech (and the transcriber may or may not have marked tones in such cases). Second, we assume that all words are monosyllabic, whereas in reality there are many sesquisyllabic ("one-and-a-half-syllables") words, where a full tonic syllable is preceded by a reduced, "minor" one. In some cases, the minor syllable may carry tone, although

equally common. However, among the most common types (many of them function words), low tone is much more frequent (e.g. 19 out of the 20 most frequent types in our data), and thus low tone is significantly more common at token level (about 71% in our data). In a recent Kammu dictionary (Svantesson et al., in press), there are on the order of a thousand minimal word form pairs with respect to tone.

2.2 The Lindell-Raw Kammu collection

Most of the RWAAI Kammu material was collected by Kristina Lindell (1928-2005) and her most important consultant, transcriber, translator, and general assistant, the native Kammu Kam Raw (1938-2011). Kam Raw moved to Sweden in 1974, where he became a researcher in his own right (then usually known under his Thai name, Damrong Tayanin); he continued documentation of the Kammu language and culture until his death.

The Lindell-Raw collection is very large. It is also somewhat physically dispersed and, in the lamentable absence of its creators, confusingly organized. The collection is very varied with respect to content (linguistic, ethnographical, anthropological, musicological, botanical) as well as physical format (thousands of drawings, figures and photos; thousands of notes, translations, transcriptions written by hand, on typewriter, and on printers of the 80's; hundreds of reel-to-reel tapes and audio cassettes; hundreds of VHS cassettes and super-8 movies; hundreds of floppy disks and zip drives; hundreds of GB of content on portable drives). Before the start of the RWAAI project, only a small fraction of the data had been previously digitized, leaving plenty of excavation sites for the data archaeologist.

2.3 Kammu folk tales

From the point of view of a linguist, including the computational type, the most interesting part of the Lindell-Raw collection is perhaps the many sound recordings of folk tales, ranging from about 1 to 20 minutes in length. The conversational setting is monologic, spontaneous, narrative: the speakers know the general content, but the actual phrasing is mostly improvised. At least 700 such stories are known to have been recorded, by dozens of speakers (although it is not clear at this point that all of the recordings have survived). A sizeable subset (between 300 and 350 have been identified at the time of writing) was transcribed by Raw over the years. English translations of many of these, but by no means all, have been published in six volumes (Lindell et al., 1977, 1980, 1984, 1989, 1995, 1998), with a seventh, unpublished one close to being finished at the time of Raw's death. A small number of the transcriptions also have accompanying interlinear glossings (Figure 1).

As noted above, Kammu is an unwritten language. The transcriptions are in principle phonemic, using IPA, except for common use of capitalization and punctuation. However, as is natural, they also bear some hallmarks of an idiosyncratic, increasingly conventionalized orthography – for instance, when transcribing the Eastern Kammu dialect, where the tonal distinction is missing and instead corresponds to a contrast in voicing (Svantesson, 1989), Raw still marks tone as for the cognate of his native Northern variety.

We currently have a machine-readable corpus of around 175 stories thus transcribed, comprising ≈120kW in total (Section 3.2). This may be tiny for written languages, but it is very

---

it is usually predictable. Third, the parts of a compound each independently carry tone – here, we consider compounds as strings of independent, monosyllabic words.

Yèm   yə̀   húal   snáa   kɔ̀ɔy   prɔ̀ɔm   yɔ̀ tèe.
Time   old   bear   those-two   squirrel   together   each-other

Once upon a time the bear and the squirrel were close friends.

Yə̀h,   tnì   prɔ̀ɔm   yɔ̀ tèe   yɔ̀h   ə̀h   crɔ́,
Well,   there   together   each-other   go   make   weir,

Well, there they went together to make weirs

kɔ̀ɔy   lə̀ə   ə̀h   crɔ́   òm   nɛ̀,
squirrel   then   make   weir   water   small,

The squirrel built a weir in a small brook

húal   lə̀ə   ə̀h   crɔ́   òm   nám.
bear   then   make   weir   water   big.

but the bear built his weir in a big river.

Figure 1: First lines of a (tone-marking) transcription of a recording of the Kammu folktale Lìaŋ húal káp kɔ̀ɔy "The story of the bear and the squirrel", with interlinear glossing.

sizeable as far as unwritten ones go. Although Raw originally intended this corpus as documentation, not as a computational resource, we have already used it (in conjunction with the Kammu dictionary mentioned above) for some basic computational applications, such as simple context-dependent spell checking and interlinear glossing.

Nevertheless, for documentation and computation alike, it is highly desirable to extend the corpus with the remaining transcriptions (after digitization). The main problem in so doing is that the early transcriptions, although well matched in terms of style and genre, are incomplete: they do not mark tones, which makes them significantly less useful for many practical purposes. In the following, we use methods for word sense disambiguation to supply the missing tones with good accuracy, substantially reducing the errors of an already-high baseline.

3   Experiment

3.1   Tone restoration through WSD

Word sense disambiguation (WSD) aims at automatically assigning the most appropriate meaning (or meanings, but usually only one is preferred) to a homonymous or polysemous word, given its context. Early work often targeted a lexical sample, with a small, predefined set of ambiguous words, like *interest* or *bank*. Later, the "all-words" task has become more common, where systems simultaneously disambiguate every single word of an input text, given the different possible senses for each (see Navigli (2009) for an extensive survey, or Agirre and Edmonds (2006) for a monograph). This standard problem phrasing is reasonably accurate also for tone restoration in Kammu, with a few notes:

All-words task Kammu tone restoration is more "all-words" than most: every single lexical entry is associated with either high or low tone; if tone is unmarked in transcription, the word form is usually ambiguous (for instance, in our 120kW corpus, about 70% of word tokens also occur with the other possible tone). Thus, the task also targets function words, which are of less interest to most WSD applications.

Easy supervision and evaluation As noted by Yarowsky (1994) for the similar case of accent restoration in French and Spanish, by stripping the accents (or tones, in our case) from existing transcriptions, we get a gold standard and a fully supervised task, with convenient and objective evaluation. By contrast, in traditional WSD, annotating new training data is expensive, and human inter-annotator agreement is relatively poor even for well-known resources.

Word form required For typological reasons, there is no reasonable way to predict the tone of a Kammu word from its context only. This is different from, say, the accent restoration case, where we sometimes may know the accent of a word without actually knowing the word itself (for instance, in French, we may for syntactic reasons be sure that an omitted word is a participle, and thus has acute accent).

Minimal resources available Compared to most WSD settings, the computational resources for Kammu are few (a small corpus and a dictionary; see next section) – no lemmatizers, thesauri, taggers, parsers, etc. Furthermore, as pointed out above, the few resources there are were produced for the purposes of language and cultural heritage documentation – if they also turn useful for computational applications, this is more of a fortunate but unintended side effect. Just as importantly, qualified transcribers and/or proofreaders of Kammu are very hard to find.[2]

3.2 Resources

The Kammu folktale corpus we have used in the experiments below comprises 119999 words, divided into 10526 sentences and 174 stories. We should note upfront that it does contain a significant number of transcription errors and, in particular, inconsistencies – the transcriptions were never intended primarily for machines. The relatively high error rate unfortunately makes the corpus less useful as a gold standard; among other things, the performance ceiling is unknown. Thus, even if we use the term "accuracy" below, the figures reported are rather agreement rates with respect to corpus annotations (just like they are for Yarowsky (1994)). That is, they can be compared to each other, but do not correspond perfectly to accuracy in an absolute sense and would very likely improve if the gold standard would contain no errors. Similarly, a phrase such as "35% error rate reduction" is really a lower bound – the true figure may well be much higher.

We prepared the corpus as follows. Case was normalized and sentences (or rather utterances) split up at punctuation end marks ([:!.?…]). We used 10-fold cross-validation: from the training data every tenth sentence, starting at sentence 1, 2, … 10 in the different runs, was removed and added to the test corpus. The reported results are the average of these 10 runs. Words with no tone or more than one (typically function words with tone unmarked, and compounds written without separator, respectively; about 3000 tokens,

---

[2]Jan-Olof Svantesson (p.c.) estimates that there are less than 20 people in the world with experience of transcribing Kammu.

or 2.5%) do not conform to either the target classifier's output, nor to current transcription conventions; these were excluded from classifications (although permitted, with tones stripped, in the contexts of other words).

3.3　A tonal classifier

As in most approaches to traditional supervised WSD, our classifier computes, represents, and stores the context for homographs with known classes. When encountering unclassified, ambiguous words, representations for these are similarly computed, and compared to the stored contexts of the training data. In our case, we based the classifier on *decision lists* (Rivest, 1987; Yarowsky, 1994, 1996). Very briefly, in decision lists, each feature-value pair implies a test (like a line in a case statement); as soon as a single test is true, the associated classification is output. We will use the term *rule* for the combination of a test and its associated classification. Crucially, at training time the rules are arranged, and at application time the associated tests are run, in (automatically estimated) descending order of *discrimination power* – a measure of how cleanly a feature assigns an ambiguous item into a single target class, given the item's context.

Decision lists are easy to implement, conceptually simple, and flexible. In particular, they readily accommodate different kinds of information, bypassing the difficult modelling of dependencies between heterogeneous feature sets. Also potentially irrelevant features can be specified, with little performance loss (except training time) – the relevant features float to the top of the ranking anyway.

To be sure, there are many more recent machine learning approaches to WSD, and any one of them would also have been a reasonable choice. However, although we will not pursue the issue very far in this paper, decision lists by design have an additional property which make them well suited for working with a noisy gold standard: every single decision can be attributed to a specific, human-interpretable feature-value pair. This property of "classification accountability" is useful when we wish to trace the reasoning behind a surprising (mis)classification – it may be due to an error in the target class of the training data; but it may also be caused by, say, a spelling error in the feature description. If we are interested in decreasing the noise of the gold standard, both possibilities are worth following up.

We implemented a decision list classifier similar to that of Yarowsky (1994) for binary homonym discrimination with main specifications as follows below (we refer to Yarowsky (1994) for the algorithmic details).[3] An excerpt of a decision list thus learned is given in Fig 1.

Notation　We use w for a word with some unspecified tone; $w^\uparrow$ ($w^\downarrow$) for one with known high (low) tone; $w^?$ for a word whose tone we wish to find out. We write $c(w)$ for the number of occurrences of w in the entire corpus, and similarly $c(w, f_i)$ for the occurrences with feature f_i.

Baseline　We used the most-common sense baseline: $w^? = w^\uparrow$ if $c(w^\uparrow) > c(w^\downarrow)$, else $w^\downarrow$. This baseline is very high (>95%) and can be implemented in few lines of code (for a

---

[3]As a variant, we also applied *interpolated* decision lists to the problem, using the mechanism suggested in Yarowsky (1994). However, as we observed no performance gain whatsoever over ordinary uninterpolated decision lists, for reasons of space we restrict the following report to our experiments with the uninterpolated version, conceptually (and implementationally) much simpler.

score	feature	value	output
5.99	coll+1	pɨan	màan
5.63	coll-1	ləə	màan
5.08	coll-1	priaŋ	máan
5.08	bow	cəə	máan
5.08	coll-1	ma	màan
4.79	coll-1	kɔɔ	màan
...			

Table 1: Beginning of a decision list for the minimal pair máan 'to bury; to fade'/ màan 'pregnant; Burmese' (irrelevant duplicate rules omitted). For instance, if the first test which returns true is the third (that is, maan neither has pɨan to the right (coll+1) nor ləə to the left (coll-1); but does indeed have priaŋ to the left), then classifier output is máan.

comparison, as noted above, the much cruder baseline of always choosing the globally most common low tone will only score about 70.5%). In addition, we can take $\max(c(w^\uparrow), c(w^\downarrow))/c(w)$ as a basic measure of confidence in the baseline decision.

Features We used single-word fixed-width features up to $k = 2$, for which we let 'coll-1' denote the neighbour one step to the left (and similarly: 'coll-2', 'coll+1', 'coll+2'); and single-word non-positional context features ('bag-of-words') up to window-size n; for which we write 'bow-n' (i.e. $\{w|w \in w_{-n}, \ldots, w_{-1}, w_1, \ldots, w_n\}$). As a less off-the-shelf item, we encode a little bit of linguistic insight in a third feature 'onset': certain onsets determine tone unequivocally (Svantesson, 1983). For instance, an empty onset (initial vowel) occurs only with low tone, whereas onsets /d, ʔw, ʔj/ occur only with high. Of course, for words which do occur in the training corpus, we have access to more reliable global frequencies and onsets will add nothing new; but they can be useful for unseen words.

Discrimination power We used the log-likelihood ratio with simple laplace (add-delta) smoothing ($\delta = 0.05$; e.g. Jurafsky and Martin, 2008, p. 134) applied to P:

$$\mathrm{dp}(w, f_i) = \left| \log\left(\frac{P(w^\uparrow|f_i)}{P(w^\downarrow|f_i)} \right) \right|$$

4 Results

The results are given in Table 2. The decision list-based classifier significantly improves on the baseline (0.9722 vs 0.9572, $p \ll 0.001$, paired t-test), an error rate reduction of around 35%. We note that features coll+2 and coll-2 are hardly ever selected, and that the width of the bag-of-words window for our tiny corpus reaches maximum already at 3 words.

The log-likelihood discrimination scores can be used for other purposes than rule ranking. For every word in the test corpus, if present in the training data, some rule will be the first to match, and it will have an associated log-likelihood. We can treat this score as a measure of classifier confidence and rank all classifications accordingly. Figure 2 shows a graph of cumulative accuracy versus algorithm confidence, thus operationalized.

bow-n↓ coll±k→	0	1	2
1	0.9572	0.9654	0.9623
2	0.9690	0.9719	0.9715
3	0.9700	0.9722	0.9705
4	0.9686	0.9705	0.9701
5	0.9670	0.9693	0.9691

Table 2: Decision list tone restoration, accuracy. 10-fold cross-validation. Baseline 0.9572

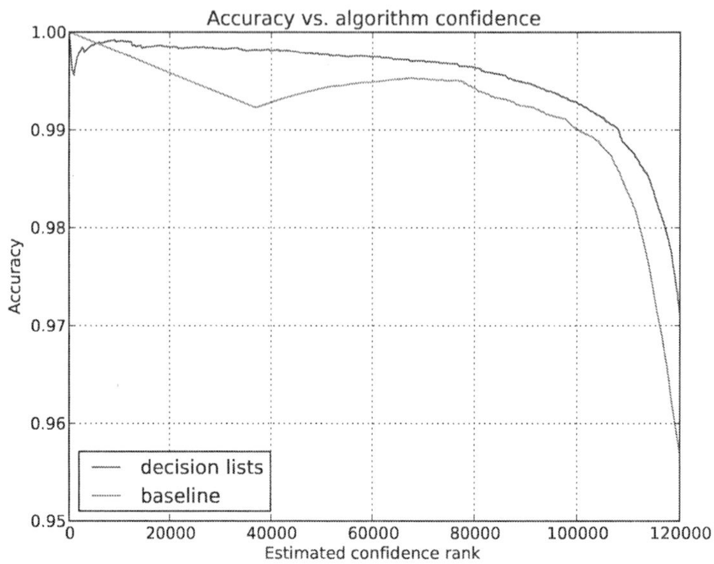

Figure 2: Cumulative accuracy per classification sites ranked after descending classifier confidence (summed results from all cross-validation runs). Decision lists (blue) and most-common baseline (green; see text for definition).

A strategy that lies close at hand is to apply the rules immediately and iteratively – conceptually (if not in implementation) only the most confident decision is applied in each iteration, and its result is allowed to influence future classifications. If the two members of a minimal pair with respect to tone occur in the same (tone-unmarked) context, then it is conceivable that classification accuracy for the pair may be improved if we first can assign tones to that context. As it turns out, this variation made no significant difference at all to our current setup, but we note the possibility for other tasks in the future.

5   Discussion

One might wonder if beating a good baseline with a percentage point or two is worth all the classifier hassle. It is, however. As noted, the Kammu corpus contains a certain amount of errors – typos, omissions, misinterpretations, competing conventions, etc – and qualified Kammu transcribers are in extremely short supply. Fortunately, a few of them are indeed tied to the RWAAI project. However, their time is valuable and needed for many things other than proofreading. In this context a single percentage point may mean 1000 errors less to worry about.

Actually, raw performance aside, the classifier may be even more useful from the more general perspective of managing human resources. If, as may well be the case, proofreading the entire corpus turns out infeasible, then an algorithm which can rank its decisions according to confidence may be used to point out where manual effort is likely to pay off best, in a process somewhat analogous to active learning (Settles, 2009). For instance, when checking automatically tone-annotated data, rather than traversing the corpus linearly, the transcriber/proofreader may check the nodes in ascending order of classifier confidence, as estimated by log-likelihood (cf. Figure 2). If desired, proofreading can be interrupted when the error rate falls below some threshold.

Similarly, it is easy to extract a ranked list over suspected mistakes in the training corpus: predict all tones by cross-validation, identify the miclassifications and sort them by descending order of confidence. With what we termed the accountability of decision lists (Section 3.3), this should be an efficient way of improving the gold standard, finding errors both in targets and in contexts.

On a final note, it should be pointed out that there is a recent Kammu-English dictionary (Svantesson et al., in press). We are currently converting it from presentationally oriented MS Word format into structured XML. Once this (rather painful) conversion is finished, the dictionary will certainly be an important resource. However, for the task at hand, its obvious usage (as a Kammu wordlist, disregarding the definitions) is less helpful than one might expect; its use is mainly restricted to word forms unseen in the corpus. For these, the wordlist can tell us whether they are unambiguous or not: in the former happy (but rare) case, it can output a classification; in the latter, it can at least provide better-coverage statistics on tones conditioned on word features such as onset. Also, for forms which are observed in the corpus with one tone only, the wordlist can possibly tell us that a minimal pair exists; this will not influence the system's guess, but may affect its confidence.

To be sure, there are more ambitious ways of using the dictionary, e.g. exploiting semantic overlap in the English definitions via Wordnet (Miller et al., 1990). Moreover, notwithstanding the desirable properties of decision lists (Section 3.3) for the task at hand, there are several other machine learning methods that could be tried. However, our next step should be to arrange proofreading of a large enough subset of the corpus to estimate the error rate of the gold standard. Any more ambitious attempts to extend the current system make little sense before this has been done, as it may well be the case that 97.2% is approaching the ceiling.

6 Acknowledgement

This work was carried out as part of the infrastructural project 'Digital Multimedia Archive of Austroasiatic Intangible Heritage', funded by the Riksbankens Jubileumsfond (project ID In11-0066:1). We are grateful to Jan-Olof Svantesson, Nicole Kruspe, and three anonymous reviewers for useful comments.

References

Agirre, E. and Edmonds, P. (2006). *Word sense disambiguation: Algorithms and applications*, volume 33. Springer Science+ Business Media.

Jurafsky, D. and Martin, J. H. (2008). *An Introduction to Natural Language Processing, Computational Linguistics, and Speech Recognition*. Prentice-Hall, 2 edition.

Lindell, K., Öjvind Swahn, J., and Tayanin, D. (1977). *A Kammu story-listener's tales*. Number 33 in Scandinavian Institute of Asian Studies Monograph Series. Curzon Press, London.

Lindell, K., Öjvind Swahn, J., and Tayanin, D. (1980). *Folk Tales from Kammu II: A Story-teller's Tales*, volume 40 of *Scandinavian Institute of Asian Studies Monograph Series*. Curzon Press, London.

Lindell, K., Öjvind Swahn, J., and Tayanin, D. (1984). *Folk Tales from Kammu III: Pearls of Kammu Literature*. Number 51 in Scandinavian Institute of Asian Studies Monograph Series. Curzon Press, London.

Lindell, K., Öjvind Swahn, J., and Tayanin, D. (1989). *Folk Tales from Kammu IV: A Master-Teller's Tales*. Number 56 in Scandinavian Institute of Asian Studies Monograph Series. Curzon Press, London.

Lindell, K., Öjvind Swahn, J., and Tayanin, D. (1995). *Folk Tales from Kammu V: A Young Story-Teller's Tales*. Number 66 in Nordic Institute of Asian Studies Monograph series. Curzon Press, London.

Lindell, K., Öjvind Swahn, J., and Tayanin, D. (1998). *Folk Tales from Kammu VI: A Teller's Last Tales*, volume 77 of *Nordic Institute of Asian Studies Monograph series*. Curzon Press, London.

Miller, G. A., Beckwith, R., Fellbaum, C., Gross, D., and Miller, K. (1990). Five papers on WordNet. *International Journal of Lexicography*, 3(4):235–244.

Navigli, R. (2009). Word sense disambiguation: a survey. *ACM Computing Surveys*, 41(2):1–69.

Rivest, R. (1987). Learning decision lists. *Machine learning*, 2(3):229–246.

Settles, B. (2009). Active learning literature survey. Technical Report Computer Sciences Technical Report 1648, University of Wisconsin–Madison.

Svantesson, J.-O. (1983). *Kammu Phonology and Morphology*. PhD thesis, Lund University. Travaux de l'Institut de linguistique de Lund, 18.

Svantesson, J.-O. (1989). Tonogenetic mechanisms in northern mon-khmer. *Phonetica*, 46(1-3):60–79.

Svantesson, J.-O., Tayanin, D., Lindell, K., and Lundström, H. (in press). Kammu yùan-english dictionary.

Yarowsky, D. (1994). Decision lists for lexical ambiguity resolution: Application to accent restoration in spanish and french. In *Proceedings of the 32nd annual meeting on Association for Computational Linguistics*, pages 88–95. Association for Computational Linguistics.

Yarowsky, D. (1996). Homograph disambiguation in text-to-speech synthesis. pages 157–172.

The automatic identification of discourse units in Dutch text

Nynke van der Vliet, Gosse Bouma, Gisela Redeker

University of Groningen, The Netherlands

`n.h.van.der.vliet@rug.nl, g.bouma@rug.nl, g.redeker@rug.nl`

ABSTRACT

The identification of discourse units is an essential step in discourse parsing, the automatic construction of a discourse structure from a text. We present a rule-based algorithm to identify elementary discourse units (EDUs) in Dutch written text. Contrary to approaches that focus on the determination of segment boundaries, we identify complete discourse units, which is especially helpful for the recognition of interrupted EDUs that contain embedded discourse units. We use syntactic and lexical information to decompose sentences into EDUs. Experimental results show that our algorithm for EDU identification performs well on texts of various genres.

KEYWORDS: discourse analysis, elementary discourse units, segmentation.

1 Introduction

Discourse structures can be useful as input for several other tasks, such as automatic summarization (Marcu, 2000; Thione et al., 2004; Bosma, 2008; Louis et al., 2010), question answering (Verberne et al., 2007) and information extraction (Maslennikov and Chua, 2007). However, the manual analysis of discourse relations in a text is a time-consuming task. The use of discourse relations for other applications thus presupposes that these relations can be added to a text automatically with relatively high accuracy.

This paper addresses the first step in automatic discourse analysis, namely the identification of suitable Elementary Discourse Units (EDUs) in a text. This process involves segmenting the text into sentences, and decomposing complex sentences into smaller units (typically clauses) that express states of affairs and form the basis for discourse analysis. The task thus concerns fine-grained discourse segmentation, not to be confused with segmenting a text into paragraph-size chunks reflecting the topic structure (e.g. Hearst (1997) and Eisenstein (2009)), which is also sometimes called discourse segmentation.

We describe a rule-based approach to identify EDUs in Dutch sentences using syntactic and lexical information, and present the results of applying the algorithm to an annotated corpus that contains texts from four different genres.

2 Related work

Several successful segmentation systems have been developed for English (e.g. Tofiloski et al. (2009), Subba and Di Eugenio (2007) and Bach et al. (2012)), German (Lüngen et al., 2006) and French (Afantenos et al., 2010) written text. Tofiloski et al. (2009) show for their English data that good segmentation results can be obtained by a rule-based approach. For English, the RST Discourse Treebank (Carlson et al., 2002), a substantial corpus segmented and manually annotated for discourse structure, has been widely used for the development of machine learning approaches to discourse segmentation for English text (Soricut and Marcu, 2003; Sporleder and Lapata, 2005; Fisher and Roark, 2007; Subba and Di Eugenio, 2007; Sagae, 2009; Hernault et al., 2010; Bach et al., 2012).

For Dutch, there is insufficient annotated data to apply machine learning techniques. In van der Vliet (2010) we present a basic rule-based segmenter that makes use of syntactic information and punctuation for the automatic identification of segment boundaries in Dutch text. This automatic discourse segmentation algorithm uses the common approach of identifying EDUs by determining the segment boundaries in sentences. A well-known complication for this type of approach is the occurrence of embedded discourse units that interrupt an ongoing EDU, as in sentence (1).

(1)   [Echter gedurende de nacht, [die op Mercurius maanden lang kan duren,] daalt de temperatuur tot zo'n -185 graden Celsius,][wat weer tot de laagste in ons zonnestelsel mag worden gerekend.]
[However during the night, [which can last for months on Mercury,] the temperature drops to about -185 degrees Celsius,][which in turn can be counted among the lowest in our solar system.]

In this case the non-restrictive relative clause 'which can last for months on Mercury' is an embedded discourse unit, and the sentence parts before and after this clause together form another discourse unit. As Afantenos et al. (2010) point out, a segmenter that is only able to identify whether there is a boundary or not in the text cannot distinguish between an embedded discourse unit within another discourse unit and three separate subsequent EDUs. Afantenos et al. solve this problem by identifying three types of segment boundaries: boundaries that only start a segment, boundaries that only end a segment and boundaries that do both.

In the segmentation of the RST Discourse Treebank the two parts of an EDU that is split by an embedded EDU are kept as separate units. In the discourse relation annotation process that follows, the two parts of the EDU are linked by the pseudo-relation SAME-UNIT that was introduced by Carlson and Marcu (2001) for this purpose. Carlson and Marcu's approach thus relegates the problem of embedded units to the relational level, which we consider undesirable.[1] In our corpus, discontinuous EDUs are represented as complete EDUs in the segmentation. As explained above, a binary classification algorithm that identifies for each text position whether there is a boundary or not is not sufficient for our purpose. In this paper, we therefore improve on van der Vliet (2010). We identify the EDUs that form the starting point for discourse relation annotation that uses the established set of Rhetorical Structure Theory (RST) relations (originally introduced by Mann and Thompson (1988); see www.sfu.ca/rst). In addition, we add lexical features and apply the algorithm to two more genres, namely popular scientific news texts and advertisements.

3 Principles of segmentation

Our definition of an elementary discourse unit is guided by the question of whether a discourse relation could hold between the unit and another segment. We identify independent clauses, adverbial clauses and non-restrictive relative clauses (separated by a comma) as EDUs. Sentence fragments (subclausal expressions ending with a period and (sub)headings in the text) are also treated as EDUs. If forward conjunction reduction (see (2)) or gapping occurs in clause-level coordination, we consider both parts of the coordination as EDUs. If VP coordination occurs as in (3) we consider this as two separate propositions about the subject and thus distinguish two EDUs.

(2)   [De planeet draait in 58.6 dagen om haar as][en in 88.0 dagen om de zon.]
        [The planet turns around its axis in 58.6 days][and around the sun in 88.0 days.] (EE02)

(3)   [Dankzij een project van Dark & Light Blind Care is deze aandoening vroegtijdig ontdekt][en behandeld.]
        [Thanks to a project of Dark & Light Blind Care this disorder was discovered in time][and treated.] (FL14)

We do not treat restrictive relative clauses, appositives, and complement clauses as separate EDUs. In line with Tofiloski et al. (2009) we do not consider speech parentheticals (e.g. "...", *he said*) as EDUs. For more details about our segmentation principles, see van der Vliet et al. (2011).

4 Implementation

The input for the EDU identification algorithm is a text file containing the text that needs to be segmented. Before applying our segmentation rules we use Alpino (Van Noord et al., 2006), a

---

[1]Borisova and Redeker (2010) show that the identification of SAME-UNIT pseudo-relations in a boundary-segmented corpus can be problematic.

Dutch dependency parser, to segment the input text into sentences and to create a syntactic tree for each sentence of the text.

We then use the syntactic analysis of the sentences to identify the EDUs for each sentence and produce a text file containing all the EDUs of all sentences. For each sentence we start to identify possible EDUs by applying a set of EDU identification rules. We use two types of rules in our system: EDU rules (see below) that are used to recognize the basis for an EDU, and combination rules that are used to build the complete EDU from the basis by combining it for example with punctuation or prepositional phrases.

EDU rules

1. *Main clauses* are identified by the syntactic category tag *@cat='smain'*. The tag *@cat='sv1'* is used for *imperatives* and *yes/no questions*. Text parts with these two tags are identified as EDUs, unless they start with a verb of reported speech.[2] If they do, they are identified as speech parentheticals (which we do not consider as an EDU on its own in our segmentation) and later combined with the preceding EDU using a combination rule.

2. *Infinitival clauses* are only identified as EDUs if they do not function as a complement. The tag *@cat='oti'* is used for *om te* ('to') - clauses. Only if an *om te*-clause is classified as a modifier with the tag *@rel= 'mod'* is it taken as a separate EDU.

3. *Phrases that start with a subordinating conjunction* are identified by the Alpino tag *@cat= 'cp'*. They are only identified as an EDU if they contain a verb and if they are classified as a modifier with the tag *@rel='mod'*.

4. *Relative clauses* are identified in Alpino with the tags *@cat= 'rel'* and *@cat= 'whrel'*. Text parts with these tags are only identified as an EDU if they are preceded by a comma.[3]

5. *Clauses between parentheses or hyphens* are identified as EDUs.

6. *Complement clauses* are not identified as EDUs. The construction *zo..dat* and *zodanig..dat* (both can be translated as 'so..that') forms an exception to this rule. If the text part that precedes the *dat*-clause contains the word *zo* or *zodanig*, the *dat*-clause is identified as a separate EDU.

7. *Verb-final clauses* are identified with the tag *@cat='ssub'*. These clauses often function as complements and are *not* identified as EDUs. Only when a sentence contains two conjoined verb-final clauses as in (4), the second clause is identified as an EDU.

(4)   [Het probleem is echter wel dat Phobos zich onder het minimum van de geschikte synchronisatiehoogte bevindt][en elke eeuw 1.8 meter dichter bij Mars komt te liggen.] *[The problem however is that Phobos is situated under the minimum of appropriate synchronisation hight][and ends up 1.8 meters closer to Mars each century.* (EE02)

The combination rules are used to create complete EDUs by combining the identified EDUs with tokens that directly precede or follow the EDU and should be part of it. For example, punctuation symbols are assigned to the top of the syntactic trees by Alpino; so we use a punctuation rule to combine a punctuation symbol that immediately precedes an EDU with the EDU, and another rule to combine a punctuation symbol that immediately follows an EDU with

---

[2]We used the following list of verbs of reported speech: zeggen (to say), uitleggen (to explain), vinden(to think, find), vertellen (to tell), beweren (to claim), denken (to think), vermoeden (to suspect), concluderen (to conclude), melden (to report). Note that Dutch requires subject-verb inversion in postposed tags.

[3]In our segmentation we only identify *non-restrictive relative clauses* as EDUs, which Dutch punctuation rules require to be preceded by a comma.

414

the EDU. In the same way, complementizers and any remaining prepositional phrases and noun phrases in a sentence are incorporated into an adjacent EDU. A separate combination rule is used to combine speech parentheticals with a preceding EDU.

In the next step the possible EDUs, which are strings of tokens (e.g. words, punctuation), are used to determine the EDUs of the sentence. This is done with a straightforward method:

1. An EDU that spans the whole sentence is added to the list of possible EDUs to make sure that there are no sentence parts left out in the identified EDUs of a sentence.

2. If overlapping EDUs (i.e. two EDUs of which the second EDU starts before the end of the first EDU and ends after the end of the first EDU) or duplicate EDUs occur in the list of possible EDUs, the second EDU is removed from the list.

3. Textual overlap in the EDUs in the list is eliminated by removing tokens from the longer EDUs. For each EDU in the list of EDUs, we check if there are EDUs in the list that fall within the boundaries of the EDU under consideration, i.e. EDUs that start at the same word but end earlier, EDUs that start later but end at the same word, and EDUs that start later and end earlier than the EDU under consideration. We then remove the text tokens of those EDUs from the string of tokens of the longer EDU. For example, if the EDU list consists of the EDUs [1 2 3] and [1 2 3 4 5 6], the list will be transformed in this step to a list containing the EDUs [1 2 3] and [4 5 6].

4. The list of EDUs is sorted by the start positions of the EDUs in the sentence.

The final step is to make the output suitable for discourse relation annotation within the RST framework. The output of the algoritm is a text file containing one EDU per line. The text files can be opened with the O'Donnell's RSTTool3 (O'Donnell, 1997) for annotating the discourse structure. One issue in the production of the text file containing the EDUs is the handling of embedded EDUs. Note that the sorting procedure in step 4 above solves the problem of embedded EDUs by placing the embedded EDU after the EDU inside which it occurs in the text.

5 Data

Our corpus consists of 80 Dutch texts varying in length between a minimum of approximately 190 words and a maximum of approximately 400 words. The corpus consists of 40 expository texts and 40 persuasive texts. The expository subcorpus contains 20 texts from online encyclopedias on astronomy and 20 astronomy news texts from a popular-scientific news website. The persuasive texts are 20 fundraising letters from humanitarian organizations and 20 commercial advertisements from lifestyle and news magazines. Table 1 shows the total number of sentences, EDUs and embedded EDUs in each genre. For more details about the corpus, see van der Vliet et al. (2011) and Redeker et al. (2012)).

Text type	sentences	EDUs	embedded EDUs
Encyclopedia texts	395	618	17
Popular Scientific News	435	585	5
Fundraising letters	467	597	2
Advertisements	410	545	3
Total	1707	2345	27

Table 1: Number of sentences, segments and embedded segments per genre

The texts were segmented by two trained annotators following the segmentation principles established in the project. A kappa value of 0.97 shows a high level of inter-annotator agreement.

6   Evaluation

The performance of a discourse segmentation algorithm can be measured by comparing the output of the system with the manual segmentation of the text. The most widely used evaluation measures for automatic discourse segmentation are precision, recall and F-score. Precision is the number of correct units divided by the total number of units given by the system. Recall is the number of correct units divided by the total number of units in the manual segmentation. F-score is the harmonic mean of precision and recall: F = (2 * precision * recall)/(precision + recall).

When comparing the algorithm's performance with other approaches, it is important to note that automatic segmentation approaches differ in the unit that is used for the computation of these evaluation measures. Some approaches (e.g. Subba and Di Eugenio (2007), Tofiloski et al. (2009) and Sagae (2009)) use sentence-internal discourse boundaries, while others (e.g. Le Thanh et al. (2004),Lüngen et al. (2006), Afantenos et al. (2010)) use elementary discourse units. This leads to differences in the scores. For example, sentence (5) consists of three EDUs that are distinguished by two sentence-internal segment boundaries. Consider the segmentation in sentence (6) as the output of the segmentation algorithm. The precision based on sentence-internal boundaries is then $1/1 = 1$ and the precision based on EDUs $1/2 = 0.5$. Recall is $1/2 = 0.5$ based on inside-sentence boundaries and $1/3 = 0.33$ based on EDUs. The F-score is 0.667 based on sentence-internal boundaries and 0.4 based on EDUs.

(5)   [Als dat te strak wordt,][breekt het magneetveld los van het gas][en krijgt een nieuwe structuur.] *[If that becomes too tight,][the magnetic field breaks from the gas][and gets a new structure.]*

(6)   [Als dat te strak wordt, breekt het magneetveld los van het gas][en krijgt een nieuwe structuur.] *[If that becomes too tight, the magnetic field breaks from the gas][and gets a new structure.]*

The evaluation based on sentence-internal boundaries is problematic for the evaluation of embedded discourse units, because an evaluation based on boundaries cannot distinguish between an EDU that is interrupted by an embedded EDU and three subsequent EDUs. We will thus present our results using precision, recall and F-score based on EDUs.

7   Results

For the development of the segmenter we used a training set of 20 texts from our corpus: 5 texts from each of the four genres. We used the remaining 60 texts (15 texts per genre) for the evaluation of the segmenter. We used precision, recall and F-score based on EDUs as evaluation measures. Table 2 shows the segmentation results on our test set per genre. Although the nature and structure of the text types is quite different, the performance of the segmenter is stable across genres and the results show a reasonable agreement with the manually annotated texts.

Our segmenter makes use of the syntactic parser Alpino to segment the input text into sentences and to produce syntactic trees of the sentences in the text. However, both the tokenization component and the dependency parser can make errors, which could influence the results of the segmentation algorithm. We therefore compared the performance of the segmenter in three different settings. In the first setting (SEG1) we used the Alpino tokenizer and dependency

Genre	EDUs	Precision	Recall	F-score
EE	454	0.832	0.784	0.807
PSN	436	0.814	0.823	0.818
FL	453	0.870	0.859	0.864
AD	383	0.831	0.757	0.792
Total	1726	0.837	0.808	0.822

Table 2: Segmentation results in Encyclopedia Entries (EE), Popular Scientific News (PSN), Fundraising Letters (FL) and Advertisements (AD)

parser for EDU identification. In the second setting (SEG2) we used gold standard sentence tokenization and automatically generated syntactic trees. In the third setting (SEG3) we used gold standard tokenization and gold standard syntactic trees as the input for EDU identification. Table 3 shows the results for EDU identification on a subset of the test set of 20 texts (5 texts per genre) for which we manually corrected the Alpino parse trees. For comparison, the table also contains two baselines. BASE 1 takes every comma in a sentence as the end of an EDU and the start of a new EDU. BASE2 uses only EDU rules 1, 3 and 4 and the combination rules (see section 4) for segmentation.

Segmenter	GS tok.	GS synt.	EDUs	Precision	Recall	F-score
BASE1	X		563	0.654	0.604	0.628
BASE2			563	0.839	0.776	0.806
SEG1			563	0.858	0.826	0.842
SEG2	X		563	0.860	0.831	0.845
SEG3	X	X	563	0.895	0.865	0.880

Table 3: Segmentation results based on EDUs

As can be seen in table 3 our EDU identification algorithm performs better than the two baselines. The EDU identification results are only marginally better when using gold standard tokenization (SEG2) compared to the automatic tokenizer (SEG1). When compared to the results using automatically identified syntactic trees (SEG2), using gold standard syntactic trees (SEG3) leads to an improvement of the results for EDU identification of about 3.5%.

In table 4 we compare the EDU identification algorithm with our earlier work on automatic segmentation (see van der Vliet (2010)). Our previous segmenter inserts segment boundaries but is not able to identify EDUs, so in our comparison we evaluate the segmentation results based on sentence-internal segment boundaries. When applied to our test set of 60 texts (using gold standard tokenization), our new segmenter (SEG2013) performs better than the old one (SEG2010) on each of the evaluation measures.

Segmenter	GS tok.	Boundaries	Precision	Recall	F-score
SEG2010	X	480	0.68	0.66	0.67
SEG2013	X	480	0.77	0.73	0.75

Table 4: Segmentation results based on EDU boundaries

Our EDU identification algorithm performs reasonably well compared to that of segmenters for English. Bach et al. (2012) report an F-score of 0.86 based on EDUs using the Stanford parse trees. Subba and Di Eugenio (2007), Sagae (2009) and Tofiloski et al. (2009) use an evaluation based on sentence-internal boundaries and report F-scores of respectively 0.85, 0.87 and 0.83.

Note however that when we compare the results of these systems we should be aware of the differences in segmentation guidelines that are implemented in these systems.

7.1 A qualitative evaluation

The evaluation measures presented above show only quantitative evaluation results. In this section we present a qualitative evaluation and study the kinds of mistakes that occur when applying our EDU identification algorithm. We analyzed the EDU identification results (using gold standard tokenization and gold standard syntactic analysis) in the test set of 20 texts (5 per genre) and categorized the mistakes. We distinguish three different types of errors: errors concerning breaks in the manual segmentation that are not recognized by the system and lead to EDUs that are too long (34 errors), errors concerning extra breaks inserted by the segmentation algorithm that lead to EDUs that are too short (14 errors), and errors concerning an EDU break by the algorithm that is inserted at the wrong place in the sentence (3 errors).

The majority of errors of the first type occur in conjunction constructions. For example, in (7) there is forward conjunction reduction at clause-level coordination: the subject is elided in the second clause. In the syntactic analysis Alpino assigns the category 'prepositional phrase'to the second part. Generally, ouur EDU identification algorithm should not treat prepositional phrases as EDUs. A more specific rule is needed for a correct EDU identification in sentences like (7).

(7)   [Tijdens de explosie is de kern van de ster in elkaar gestort] [en in de snel ronddraaiende pulsar veranderd].
        [During the explosion the core of the star was collapsed] [and changed into the fast-spinning pulsar]. (PSN08)

Other errors of the first type concern the recognition of non-restrictive relative clauses. Our algorithm only inserts segment boundaries when non-restrictive relative clauses are preceded by a comma, so it does not recognize other non-restrictive relative clauses as in (8).

(8)   [De Oortwolk is een grote wolk met miljarden kometen rondom ons zonnestelsel (inclusief de Kuipergordel)] [die zich uitstrekt tot ongeveer een kwart van de afstand tussen de zon en de dichtstbijzijnde ster.]
        [The Oort cloud is a large cloud with billions of comets surrounding our solar system (including the Kuiper belt)] [which extends to about a quarter of the distance between the sun and the nearest star.] (EE08)

An example of an error of the second type is shown below. In sentence (9) our algorithm wrongly identifies the text part *'doordat de kometen hier maar weinig ondervinden'* (because the comets are here barely affected) as a separate EDU. The text part functions as a complement clause and is therefore not treated as EDU in our manual segmentation. In the syntactic analysis of Alpino it is labeled with *@cat='cp'* and *@rel='mod'* and it contains a verb, so according to our automatic segmentation rules it is identified as an EDU (see EDU rule 3, section 4). This results in an embedded EDU in the segmentation of sentence (9) produced by our segmenter, as shown in (10).

(9)   Dat komt doordat de kometen hier maar weinig ondervinden van de aantrekkingskracht

van de zon.
This is because the comets are here barely affected by the gravitational force of the sun.
(EE08)

(10)   [Dat komt van de aantrekkingskracht van de zon.][doordat de kometen hier maar
        weinig ondervinden]
        [This is by the gravitational force of the sun.][because the comets are barely affected]

Example (12) shows an error of the third type, wrongly placed segment boundary, in combination of errors of the second type, failure to identify a boundary. Our manual segmentation is shown in (11) and the output of our segmenter is shown in (12). The segmenter does not recognize the segment boundaries after *rompslomp,*, after *rekening,* and after *opnemen* (which separate four elliptical clauses in this sentence), but does identify an embedded discourse discourse unit instead. The text part *'waar en wanneer u maar wilt'* is labeled with the tag *@cat='whrel'* in the syntactic analysis and is preceded by a comma, so the segmenter the EDU rule for non-restrictive relative clauses and identifies it as a separate EDU. Note that the segmenter produces an error of the second type in this sentence as well: it fails to identify the boundary after *opnemen*.

(11)   [Dus.. geen papieren rompslomp,][waar en wanneer u maar wilt toegang tot uw
        rekening][en altijd vrij opnemen][en storten.]
        *[So.. no paperwork,][access to your account where and when you want][and always
        freely withdraw][and pay.]*

(12)   [Dus.. geen papieren rompslomp, toegang tot uw rekening en altijd vrij opnemen en
        storten.][waar en wanneer u maar wilt]
        *[So..no paperwork, access to your account and always freely withdraw and pay.][where
        and when you want]*

8   Conclusion

We presented a rule-based algorithm to identify elementary discourse units (EDUs) in Dutch written texts. Our experimental results show that good identification results can be obtained using a relatively simple method. The performance of the EDU identifier is stable across the genres in our data. Together with the work of Tofiloski et al. (2009) and Le Thanh et al. (2004)) our work suggests that for languages for which large corpora annotated with discourse relations are not available, a rule-based approach is a viable alternative to machine learning approaches. In future work we will use the output of the EDU identification algorithm in our experiments on the automatic identification of discourse relations in Dutch text.

Acknowledgments

This work has been supported by grant 360-70-282 of the Netherlands Organization for Scientific Research (NWO) as part of the program Modelling textual organization (http://www.let.rug.nl/mto/).

References

Afantenos, S., Denis, P., Muller, P., and Danlos, L. (2010). Learning recursive segments for discourse parsing. *Arxiv preprint arXiv:1003.5372*.

Bach, N. X., Nguyen, M. L., and Shimazu, A. (2012). A reranking model for discourse segmentation using subtree features. In *SIGDIAL Conference'12*, pages 160–168.

Borisova, I. and Redeker, G. (2010). Same and Elaboration relations in the Discourse Graphbank. In *Proceedings of the 11th annual SIGdial Meeting on Discourse and Dialogue, Tokyo, September 24-25*.

Bosma, W. E. (2008). *Discourse Oriented Summarization*. PhD thesis, University of Twente, Enschede, the Netherlands.

Carlson, L. and Marcu, D. (2001). Discourse tagging reference manual. Technical report, ISI Technical Report ISI-TR-545.

Carlson, L., Okurowski, M. E., and Marcu, D. (2002). *RST discourse treebank*. Linguistic Data Consortium, University of Pennsylvania.

Eisenstein, J. (2009). Hierarchical text segmentation from multi-scale lexical cohesion. In *Proceedings of Human Language Technologies: The 2009 Annual Conference of the North American Chapter of the Association for Computational Linguistics*, pages 353–361.

Fisher, S. and Roark, B. (2007). The utility of parse-derived features for automatic discourse segmentation. In *Proceedings of ACL '07*, pages 488–495.

Hearst, M. (1997). Texttiling: Segmenting text into multi-paragraph subtopic passages. *Computational Linguistics*, 23(1):33–64.

Hernault, H., Bollegala, D., and Ishizuka, M. (2010). A sequential model for discourse segmentation. In *Proceedings of CICLing 2010*, pages 315–326.

Le Thanh, H., Abeysinghe, G., and Huyck, C. (2004). Automated discourse segmentation by syntactic information and cue phrases. In *Proceedings of the IASTED International Conference on Artificial Intelligence and Applications (AIA 2004), Innsbruck, Austria*.

Louis, A., Joshi, A., and Nenkova, A. (2010). Discourse indicators for content selection in summarization. In *Proceedings of the 11th Annual Meeting of the Special Interest Group on Discourse and Dialogue*, pages 147–156.

Lüngen, H., Puskàs, C., Bärenfänger, M., Hilbert, M., and Lobin, H. (2006). Discourse segmentation of German written text. In *Proceedings of the 5th International Conference on Natural Language Processing (FinTAL 2006)*.

Mann, W. C. and Thompson, S. A. (1988). Rhetorical structure theory: Toward a functional theory of text organization. *Text*, 8(3):243–281.

Marcu, D. (2000). *The theory and practice of discourse parsing and summarization*. The MIT Press.

Maslennikov, M. and Chua, T. (2007). A multi-resolution framework for information extraction from free text. In *Proceedings of the 45th Annual Meeting of the Association of Computational Linguistics*, pages 592–599.

O'Donnell, M. (1997). RST-Tool: An RST analysis tool. In *Proc. of the 6th European Workshop on Natural Language Generation, Duisburg*.

Redeker, G., Berzlánovich, I., van der Vliet, N., Bouma, G., and Egg, M. (2012). Multi-Layer discourse annotation of a Dutch text corpus. In *Proceedings of LREC 2012, Istanbul, May 21-27*, pages 2820–2825.

Sagae, K. (2009). Analysis of discourse structure with syntactic dependencies and data-driven shift-reduce parsing. In *Proceedings of the 11th International Conference on Parsing Technologies*, pages 81–84.

Soricut, R. and Marcu, D. (2003). Sentence level discourse parsing using syntactic and lexical information. In *Proceedings of HLT/NAACL 2003*, pages 228–235.

Sporleder, C. and Lapata, M. (2005). Discourse chunking and its application to sentence compression. In *Human Language Technology Conference and the Conference on Empirical Methods in Natural Language Processing (HLT-EMNLP)*, pages 257–264.

Subba, R. and Di Eugenio, B. (2007). Automatic Discourse Segmentation using Neural Networks. In *Proc. of the 11th Workshop on the Semantics and Pragmatics of Dialogue*, pages 189–190.

Thione, G., Van Den Berg, M., Polanyi, L., and Culy, C. (2004). Hybrid text summarization: Combining external relevance measures with structural analysis. In *Proceedings ACL Workshop Text Summarization Branches Out. Barcelona*.

Tofiloski, M., Brooke, J., and Taboada, M. (2009). A syntactic and lexical-based discourse segmenter. In *Proceedings of the ACL-IJCNLP 2009 Conference Short Papers*, pages 77–80.

van der Vliet, N. (2010). Syntax-based discourse segmentation of Dutch text. In Slavkovik, M., editor, *Proceedings of the 15th Student Session, ESSLLI*, pages 203–210.

van der Vliet, N., Berzlánovich, I., Bouma, G., Egg, M., and Redeker, G. (2011). Building a Discourse-annotated Dutch Text Corpus. In Dipper, S. and Zinsmeister, H., editors, *Bochumer Linguistische Arbeitsberichte 3*, pages 157–171.

Van Noord, G. et al. (2006). At last parsing is now operational. In *Verbum ex machina: actes de la 13e conférence sur le traitement automatique des langues naturelles (TALN 2006): Leuven, 10-13 avril 2006*, page 20.

Verberne, S., Boves, L., Oostdijk, N., and Coppen, P. (2007). Discourse-based answering of why-questions. *Traitement Automatique des Langues (TAL), special issue on "Discours et document: traitements automatiques"*, 47(2):21–41.

Example-Based Treebank Querying with GrETEL
– now also for Spoken Dutch

Liesbeth Augustinus, Vincent Vandeghinste, Ineke Schuurman,
and Frank Van Eynde

Centre for Computational Linguistics, University of Leuven

`{liesbeth,vincent,ineke,frank}@ccl.kuleuven.be`

ABSTRACT

Although several syntactically annotated corpora (or treebanks) exist for Dutch, they are seldomly used for descriptive linguistic research because there are no easy-to-use exploitation tools available. This demonstration paper describes *GrETEL*, a linguistic search engine (`http://nederbooms.ccl.kuleuven.be/eng/gretel`) that enables non-technical users to consult treebanks in a user-friendly way. Instead of a formal search expression, a natural language example is used as input to the system, allowing users to search for similar constructions as the example they provide. In the first version of GrETEL, only written Dutch (LASSY) was included. Based on user requests we have now included the Spoken Dutch Corpus (CGN) as well.

KEYWORDS: Dutch, treebank, querying, example-based.

1 Introduction

Within CLARIN (**C**ommon **L**anguage **R**esources and Technology **I**nfrastructure), a European research infrastructure project, researchers in language and speech technology aim at making it easy for researchers in the humanities and social sciences to work with digital language data.[1] For linguists those language data could be annotated corpora, such as treebanks. While several syntactically annotated corpora (or treebanks) exist for Dutch, they are seldomly used for descriptive linguistic research up till now.

Talking with (descriptive) linguists about using treebanks, the same problems pop up over and over again: on the one hand the limited user-friendliness of the query languages and search tools, and on the other hand the lack of standardisation in both treebanks and query languages. This is unfortunate, since treebanks could be very useful for them, especially when they are looking for (possibly) discontinuous constructions. In order to overcome the querying problems, the linguistic search engine GrETEL (**Gr**eedy **E**xtraction of **T**rees for **E**mpirical **L**inguistics) was developed.[2] GrETEL was created as a part of the Nederbooms project, a CLARIN project funded by the Flemish Community.

Instead of developing yet another query language or designing yet another GUI, we present a query engine which does not ask for any formal input query. As input, the tool takes something linguists are familiar with: natural language. Since linguists tend to start their research from example sentences, the methodology of example-based querying allows users to search for similar constructions as the example they provide. How similar is for the user to decide.

A first version of GrETEL (1.0), which is optimized for the Dutch LASSY treebank (van Noord et al., 2013), is described in Augustinus et al. (2012). In a more refined version (GrETEL 1.1), the Spoken Dutch Corpus (CGN) (Oostdijk et al., 2002) is also supported. For the next release (GrETEL 2.0), we will make the tool less dependent on particular XML formats. Moreover, we will enable much larger treebanks to be queried compared to the ones that are supported at the moment.

2 Methodology and Design

As an example, we look for collective noun constructions, such as *een aantal mensen* 'a number of people' and *een school vissen* 'a school of fish'. In Dutch, such constructions consist of a determiner (e.g. *een* 'a'), a noun denoting the kind of collection (e.g. *aantal* 'number'), and a noun denoting the entities in the collection (e.g. *mensen* 'people'). As we want to find discontinous examples as well, such as *een school kleine vissen* 'a school of small fish', a treebank is the obvious resource to use, rather than a corpus just annotated for part of speech. The construction in mind may also determine which treebank is consulted. The LASSY treebank contains written Dutch, whereas the CGN treebank contains (transcribed) spoken language. For this example, we will use CGN, as case studies on the LASSY treebank were already described in previous work (Augustinus et al., 2012). We will furthermore indicate the differences between the updated version of GrETEL and the previous release.

Work related to our approach is the now deceased Linguist's Search Engine (Resnik and Elkiss, 2005), a tool that also used example-based querying; and the TIGER Corpus Navigator (Hellmann et al., 2010), which is a SemanticWeb system used to classify and retrieve sentences from the TIGER corpus on the basis of abstract linguistic concepts.

---

[1] http://www.clarin.eu
[2] http://nederbooms.ccl.kuleuven.be/eng/gretel

Natural language example The user provides a relevant natural language example, containing the syntactic construction (s)he is looking for. After presenting an input construction (in this case: *een aantal mensen gaan naar huis* 'a number of people go home') to the system, GrETEL returns the sentence to the user in the *sentence parts selection matrix*, cf. Figure 1.

Selection The user can indicate for each word whether (s)he is interested in the short part of speech (pos), the extended pos, the lemma or the token.[3] For general non-lexical similarities, **pos** should be selected. To take into account more detailed information, such as agreement or number, **extended pos** should be selected. The **lemma** button should be indicated to abstract over word forms, and the **token** button should be selected for retrieving specific word forms. Mind that token is a case sensitive feature, while lemma is case insensitive (except for proper nouns).

If the input contains words that are not part of the target construction, the **optional nodes** button should be used. Note that both the dependency relation and the syntactic category of all relevant nodes are taken into account,[4] cf. the XPath expression (1) describing the subtree depicted in Figure 2b. Instead of marking certain words as optional, one could also use a sentence part as input (such as *een aantal mensen*).

sentence		Een	aantal	mensen	gaan	naar	huis
relevant nodes	pos	◉	◉	○	○	○	○
	extended pos	○	○	◉	○	○	○
	lemma	○	○	○	○	○	○
	token	○	○	○	○	○	○
optional nodes		○	○	○	◉	◉	◉

Figure 1: Sentence Parts Selection Matrix

We indicated **pos** for both *een* 'a' and *aantal* 'number', since we are looking for any determiner, followed by a noun. For *mensen* 'people', we indicated **extended pos**, as this wil return matches not merely with the same part of speech, but also with the same number (we are looking for plural nouns).

XPath expression GrETEL turns the information from the matrix into an XPath expression[5] (1), which can be used to query the treebank. In addition, the parse tree of the input sentence is presented, along with the subtree containing the construction the user is looking for, cf. Figure 2. Users can optionally adapt the XPath query in order to refine or generalize the search instruction. The user also has the option to search a complete treebank or to select one or more subcorpora. In the case of CGN, one could for example only query the Flemish part of the corpus.

---

[3]The short pos tags are different in LASSY and CGN. The LASSY treebank contains both the tags assigned by the Alpino parser (van Noord, 2006) (e.g. *noun, verb*) and the (extended) CGN/D-COI tags (e.g. N(soort,mv,basis), WW(pv,tgw,ev)) (Van Eynde, 2004). CGN only contains the CGN/D-COI tags, so the shortened versions of the CGN/D-COI tags (e.g. *n, ww*) are used as pos tags.

[4]The list of all dependency relations and syntactic categories can be found in Hoekstra et al. (2003) for CGN and in van Noord et al. (2011) for LASSY.

[5]http://www.w3.org/TR/xpath

(1) //node[@cat="np" and node[@rel="det" and @cat="np" and node[@rel="det" and
     @pt="lid"] and node[@rel="hd" and @pt="n"]] and node[@rel="hd" and @pt="n" and
     @postag="N(soort,mv,basis)"]]

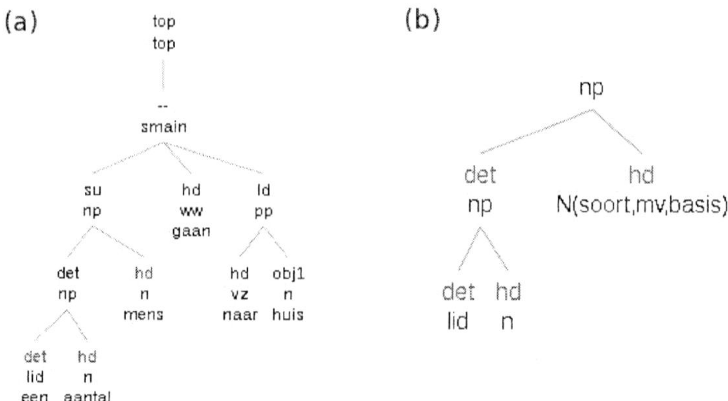

Figure 2: Parse tree (a) and subtree (b) of the input example

Results In the last phase the search results are presented, i.e. the sentences containing the
construction at hand. The user can inspect the tree and/or or the source XML of all results.
It is also possible to download the results in text format. For the query in (1), we found 594
matches in the complete CGN treebank (130k sentences, 1M tokens). Some examples are given
in (2). Note that 2b is discontinuous.

(2) a. heb je   gezien dat in de frigo dat er   daar **een pakje**   **pralines** stond?
         have you seen   that in the fridge that there there a   packet-DIM chocolats stood

         'Did you see there was a box of chocolats in the fridge?' [fva400282__2]

     b. ik heb hier nog **een hele   reut** ouwe **boeken** staan.
         I have here still a   whole lot   old   books   stand
         'I still have a whole lot of old books here.' [fnc008006__344]

Search options Besides adding the extended pos option to the *selection matrix*, we added
some other options in GrETEL 1.1. It is now possible to include some context in the search
results, to ignore the syntactic properties of the dominating node in the subtree, and to split up
the extended pos tags. Due to limitations of space, we are not able to discuss the options here.

3 Technical description

GrETEL is accessible online, which means that users do not have to install any treebanks or
specific software (e.g. a parser) locally.[6] Drupal is used as content management system.[7] Figure
3 presents GrETEL's general architecture, which consists of three tiers: the presentation layer,
the search layer, and the data layer.

Presentation tier In the first tier we interact with the user, resulting in an information flow
to and from the search layer. This is done using PHP and HTML.

---

[6]The user is adviced to access the tool via Mozilla Firefox (http://www.mozilla.org), as that browser supports
W3C standards very well.

[7]http://drupal.org

Search tier This tier is used to process information coming from the presentation layer, and to interact with the data layer. The (Alpino) parser (van Noord, 2006) is addressed using PHP, while the *Subtree Finder* and *XPath Generator* are implemented as perl scripts. For the treebank search PHP, SQL, and XPath are used.

Data tier In the current implementation (cf. 'version 1' in Figure 3) the data is stored into a PostgreSQL database.[8] The data format of the treebanks is Alpino XML.[9]

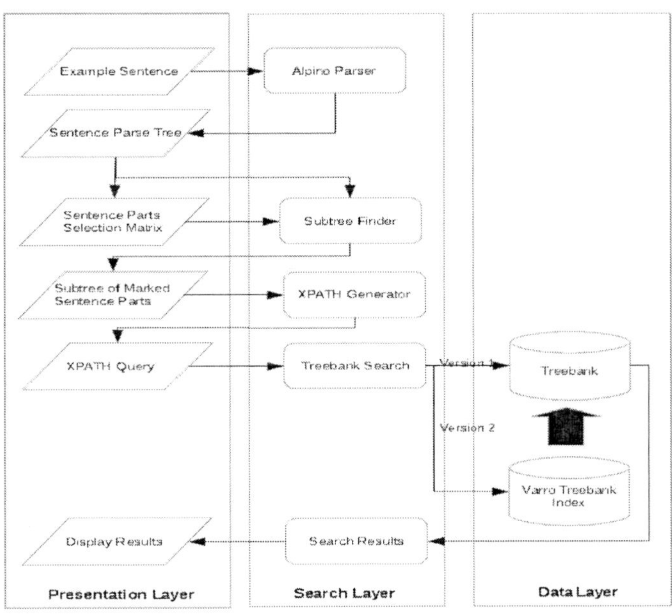

Figure 3: GrETEL's 3-tier architecture

4 Conclusion and Future Work

Thanks to the positive response to GrETEL 1.0, we can now implement GrETEL 2.0, which will be able to deal with larger treebanks, and which will also be able to deal with XML formats other than Alpino XML.

We plan to make the various layers less intertwined to make adaptation for other languages, treebanks, and/or data formats possible.

The major challenge, however, is making the system usable for very large treebanks, such as the LASSY large corpus (500M tokens). In the next implementation the PostgreSQL database will be replaced by a native XML database, such as BaseX,[10] and we will make use of the *Varro Treebank Indexer*, cf. 'version 2' in Figure 3.

Varro (Martens and Vandeghinste, 2010), (Martens, 2011) is a toolkit and algorithm for indexing regular structures in treebanks. Subtrees are listed in the Varro Treebank Index, which indicates where they are located and what their frequency is.

With this preprocessing step we intend to allow for faster treebank mining and, we hope, to query large (huge) treebanks in a timespan acceptable for the intended users, i.e. descriptive linguists.

---

[8]http://www.postgresql.org/
[9]http://www.let.rug.nl/vannoord/Lassy/alpino_ds.dtd
[10]http://basex.org

References

Augustinus, L., Vandeghinste, V., and Van Eynde, F. (2012). Example-Based Treebank Querying. In *Proceedings of the 8th International Conference on Language Resources and Evaluation (LREC 2012)*, Istanbul.

Hellmann, S., Unbehauen, J., Chiarcos, C., and Ngomo, A.-C. N. (2010). The TIGER Corpus Navigator. In *Proceedings of TLT-9*, pages 91–102, Tartu, Estonia.

Hoekstra, H., Moortgat, M., Renmans, B., Schouppe, M., Schuurman, I., and van der Wouden, T. (2003). *CGN Syntactische Annotatie*. http://nederbooms.ccl.kuleuven.be/documentation/sa-man_cgn.pdf.

Martens, S. (2011). *Quantifying Linguistic Regularity*. PhD thesis, KU Leuven, Leuven, Belgium.

Martens, S. and Vandeghinste, V. (2010). An Efficient, Generic Approach to Extracting Multi-Word Expressions from Dependency Trees. In *Proceedings of the CoLing Workshop: Multiword Expressions: From Theory to Applications (MWE 2010)*, Beijing, China.

Oostdijk, N., Goedertier, W., Van Eynde, F., Boves, L., Martens, J.-P., Moortgat, M., and Baayen, H. (2002). Experiences from the Spoken Dutch Corpus Project. In *Proceedings of the 3rd International Conference on Language Resources and Evaluation (LREC'02)*, pages 340–347, Las Palmas, Spain.

Resnik, P. and Elkiss, A. (2005). The Linguist's Search Engine: An Overview. In *Proceedings of the ACL Interactive Poster and Demonstration Sessions*, pages 33–36, Ann Arbor.

Van Eynde, F. (2004). *Part of Speech Tagging en Lemmatisering van het Corpus Gesproken Nederlands*. www.ccl.kuleuven.be/Papers/POSmanual_febr2004.pdf.

van Noord, G. (2006). At Last Parsing Is Now Operational. In *TALN 2006*, pages 20–42.

van Noord, G., Bouma, G., Van Eynde, F., de Kok, D., van der Linde, J., Schuurman, I., Tjong Kim Sang, E., and Vandeghinste, V. (2013). Large Scale Syntactic Annotation of Written Dutch: Lassy. In *Essential Speech and Language Technology for Dutch: Resources, Tools and Applications*. Springer.

van Noord, G., Schuurman, I., and Bouma, G. (2011). *Lassy Syntactische Annotatie, Revision 19455*. www.let.rug.nl/vannoord/Lassy/sa-man_lassy.pdf.

Korp and Karp – a bestiary of language resources: the research infrastructure of Språkbanken

Malin Ahlberg, Lars Borin, Markus Forsberg, Martin Hammarstedt, Leif-Jöran Olsson, Olof Olsson, Johan Roxendal, Jonatan Uppström

Språkbanken, Dept. of Swedish, University of Gothenburg, Sweden

```
{malin.ahlberg,lars.borin, markus.forsberg, martin.hammarstedt,
    leif-joran.olsson, olof.olsson.2, johan.roxendal,
        jonatan.uppstrom}@svenska.gu.se
```


Abstract

A central activity in Språkbanken, an R&D unit at the University of Gothenburg, is the systematic construction of a research infrastructure based on interoperability and widely accepted standards for metadata and data. The two main components of this infrastructure deal with text corpora and with lexical resources. For modularity and flexibility, both components have a backend, or server-side part, accessed through an API made up of a set of well-defined web services. This means that there can be any number of different user interfaces to these components, corresponding, e.g., to different research needs. Here, we will demonstrate the standard corpus and lexicon search interfaces, designed primarily for linguistic searches: *Korp* and *Karp*.

Keywords: Swedish, corpora, lexical resources, research infrastructure.

1 The research infrastructure of Språkbanken

Språkbanken <http://spraakbanken.gu.se/eng/start> is a research and development unit at the University of Gothenburg, and a node in a cross-disciplinary research collaboration at the University of Gothenburg and Chalmers University of Technology formalized under the name of Centre for Language Technology <http://www.clt.gu.se>. Språkbanken was established with government funding already in 1975 as a national centre. The main focus of Språkbanken's present-day activities is the development and refinement of language resources and language technology (LT) tools, and their application to research in language technology, in linguistics, and in several other disciplines, notably text-based research in the humanities, social sciences, medicine and health sciences.

The larger context of these activities is the systematic construction of a research infrastructure based on interoperability and widely accepted standards for metadata and data. The two main components of this infrastructure deal with text corpora and with lexical resources. For modularity and flexibility, both components have a backend, or server-side part, accessed through an API made up of set of well-defined web services. This means that there can be any number of different user interfaces to these components, corresponding, e.g., to different research needs. Here, we will focus on the standard corpus and lexicon search interfaces *Korp* and *Karp* – designed primarily for linguistic searches – but the same backend web services are also used, e.g., in a corpus-driven grammar and vocabulary exercise generator (Volodina et al., 2012).

2 The search interface of Korp

The search interface of Korp (Borin et al., 2012b; <http://http://spraakbanken.gu.se/korp>) has been inspired by corpus search interfaces such as SketchEngine (Kilgarriff et al., 2008), Glossa (Nygaard et al., 2008), and DeepDict (Bick, 2009).

At first glance, the search interface of Korp is a concordance tool that displays search results in the standard KWIC (*keywords in context*) layout (figure 1), here with the example word *svininfluensa (noun)* 'swine flu'. This basic functionality is extended by various visualisations of statistical data, such as the basic table (figure 2) and and interactive trend diagram (figure 4) plotting relative frequency over time. Furthermore, the interface features so called word pictures that provides an overview of a selected set of syntactic relations for a word (figure 3). The purpose is to quickly gain an understanding of the contexts in which a word most commonly appears.

We are also working on increasing the diachronic coverage of the corpora, by including Swedish texts from the 19th century back to the 13th century. Ultimately, our goal is to develop tools for all types of text, at various levels of annotation, such as part-of-speech, morphosyntactic information, and dependency parses (Borin et al., 2010; Borin and Forsberg, 2011; Adesam et al., 2012). Our primary source material for Old Swedish (ca 1225–1526) comes from *Fornsvenska textbanken*,<http://project2.sol.lu.se/fornsvenska> a 3 MW collection of around 160 digitized texts, mainly from the 13th to the 16th century. Further, a 1 MW corpus of medieval letters from the Swedish National Archives <http://riksarkivet.se> is available. Work in progress concerns newspaper texts (17th–19th century) and a collection of law texts (13th century – present).

A number of issues are problematic for annotation of historical texts. For example, sentence splitting cannot be handled with standard tools, as sentence boundaries are often not marked by punctuation or uppercase letters. Compared to modern Swedish texts, the Old Swedish texts have a different vocabulary and richer morphology, show a more free word order, and Latin and German influences. Finally, the lack of a standardized orthography results in a wide variety of spellings for the same word.

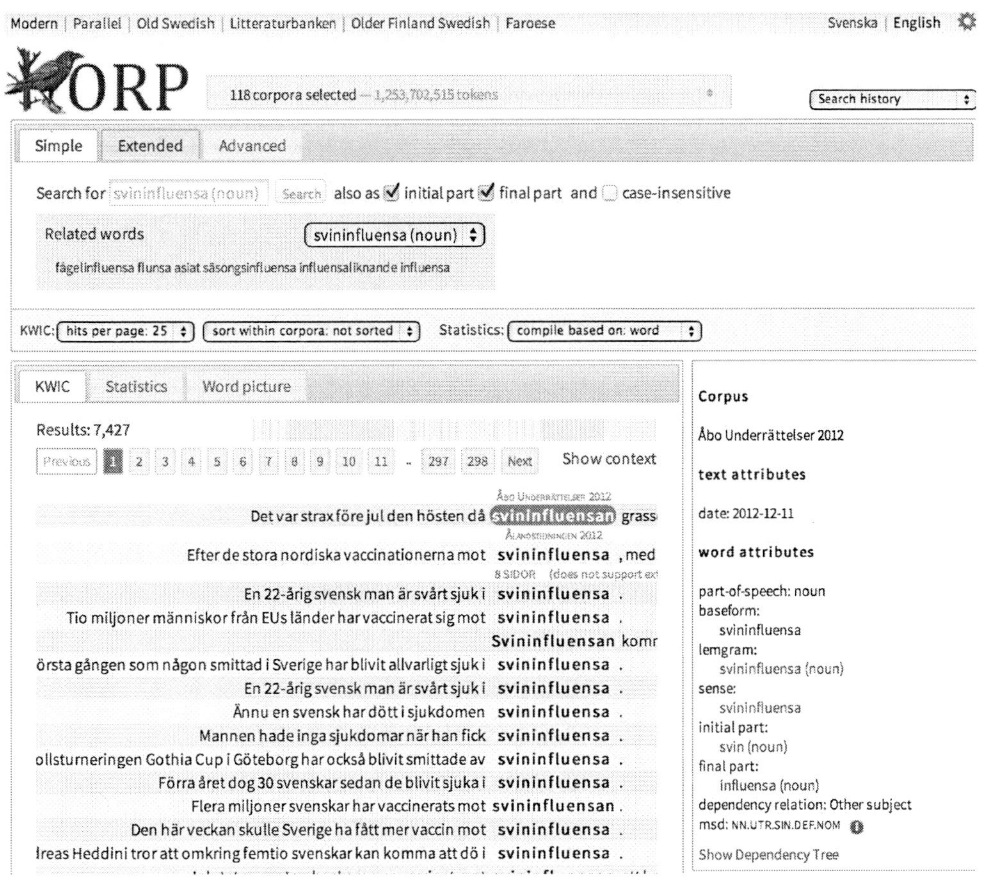

Figure 1: The Korp KWIC view of *svininfluensa (noun)* 'swine flu'

Hit		Total	Åbo Und...	Åbo Und...	Astra No...	Ålandsti...	8 SIDOR	Bloggmix...	Bloggmi
Σ		5.9 (7,427)	0.8 (1)			1.0 (1)	100.2 (68)		19.4 (8)
svininfluensan		3.0 (3,818)	0.8 (1)				47.1 (32)		9.7 (4)
svininfluensa		1.4 (1,785)				1.0 (1)	45.7 (31)		4.8 (2)
Svininfluensan		0.7 (878)					7.4 (5)		2.4 (1)
Svininfluensa		0.3 (416)							
svininfluensavaccinet		0.1 (95)							
svininfluensavaccin		0.0 (51)							
svininfluensans		0.0 (49)							2.4 (1)
svininfluensaviruset		0.0 (26)							
SVININFLUENSAN		0.0 (22)							
Svininfluensans		0.0 (17)							
svininfluensavirus		0.0 (16)							
svininfluensasprutan		0.0 (15)							

Figure 2: The Korp statistics of *svininfluensa (noun)* 'swine flu' (including compounds)

3 The search interface of Karp

The interface of Karp (Borin et al., 2012a; <http://http://spraakbanken.gu.se/karp>) supports searching and editing lexical resources. It currently hosts 21 lexical resources, some of which have been created from scratch using existing free resources, both external and in-house. The resources have been converted to the Lexical Markup Framework format (ISO, 2008) to ensure uniformity and interchangeability. The infrastructure has one primary lexical resource, SALDO (Borin and Forsberg,

Preposition		Pre-Modifier svininfluensa		Post-Modifier		Svininfluensa verb		Verb svininfluensa	
1. mot	818	1. mexikansk	9	1. i Sverige	22	1. sprida	59	1. få	157
2. om	381	2. aktuell	8	2. med argument	5	2. sprida sig	25	2. ha	158
3. av	593	3. jävla	8	3. i Norge	7	3. vara	228	3. vaccinera	9
4. kring	54	4. dödlig	4	4. för panikartad	3	4. härja	13	4. skita	9
5. för	244	5. ny	18	5. på vis	5	5. drabba	14	5. kalla	14
6. på grund av	19	6. eventuell	4	6. i län	5	6. smitta	9	6. stoppa	11
7. upp mot	8	7. farlig	4	7. i land	7	7. nå	17	7. dra på sig	4
8. pga	8	8. bli kvitt	2	8. som vara	15	8. slå	20	8. dra på	4
9. utav	6	9. resistent	2	9. som smitta	3	9. mutera	7	9. slippa	6
10. inför	14	10. kvitt	2	10. i höst	4	10. klassa	8	10. undvika	5
11. för hand	3	11. oförarglig	2	11. under pandemi	2	11. komma	44	11. ta	17
12. angående	5	12. sibirisk	2	12. till influensa	2	12. skörda	7	12. smitta	3
13. för sig	7	13. livsfarlig	2	13. som sprida	3	13. fortsätta	13	13. diskutera	6
14. emot	6	14. inrikes	2	14. på gris	2	14. influensa	4	14. sprida	5
15. p.g.a.	1	15. jäkla	3	15. i Halland	3	15. bryta ut	6	15. hantera	4

Figure 3: The word picture of *svininfluensa (noun)* 'swine flu'

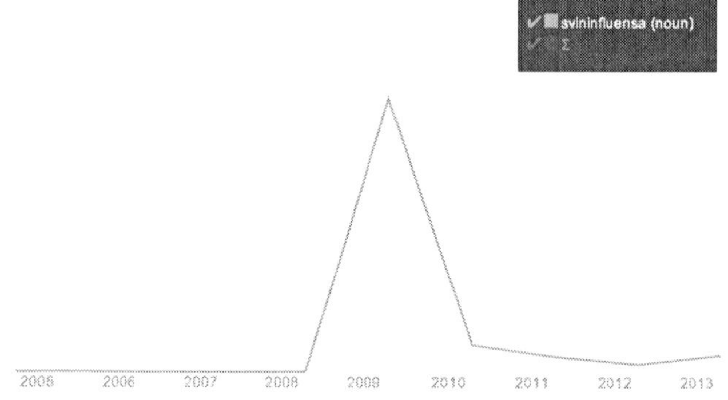

Figure 4: The trend diagram of *svininfluensa (noun)* 'swine flu'

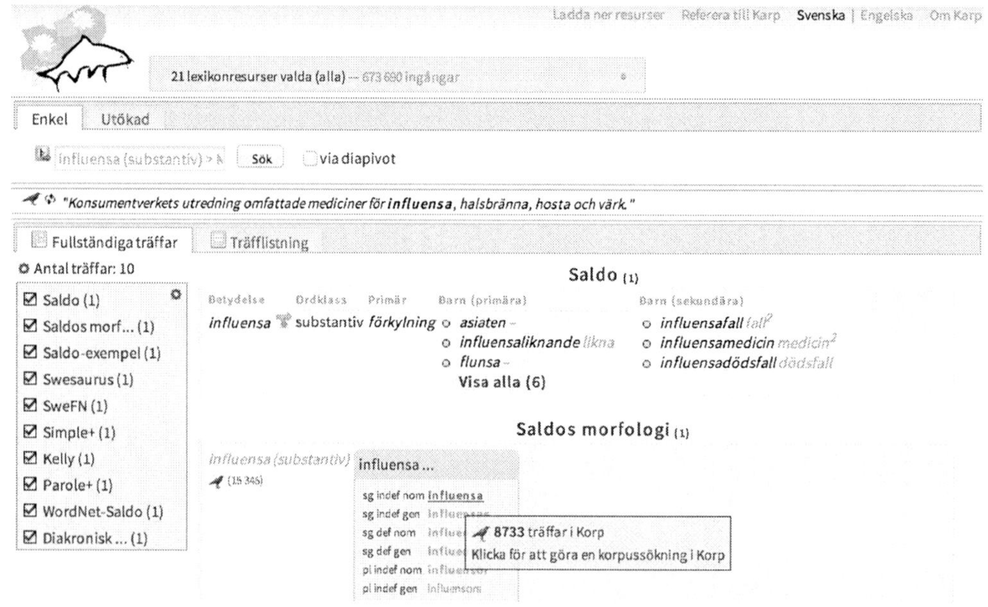

Figure 5: The search result of *influensa* 'flu'

2009), which acts as a pivot to which all other modern resources are linked. SALDO is a large freely available morphological and lexical-semantic lexicon for modern Swedish. Moreover, there is a diachronic pivot resource with links between the modern and the historical morphologies.

In the simple search a user can input either a word form, a lemgram (a form unit), or a sense unit, and the interface will render all information associated to all sense units related to the input. E.g., figure 5 displays the search result of the lemgram *influensa (noun)* 'flu'. In the extended search the user can combine available filters from drop down boxes which are translated to SRU/CQL expressions. E.g. a word form as reglular expression and a certain part of speech type.

In addition, the interface supports full text search in the textual parts of the lexical resources, such as examples and definitions. The full text search, beyond extending the search capabilities, also makes the lexical information not linked to SALDO discoverable.

References

Adesam, Y., Ahlberg, M., and Bouma, G. (2012). *bokstaffua, bokstaffwa, bokstafwa, bokstaua, bokstawa…* Towards lexical link-up for a corpus of Old Swedish. In *Proceedings of LTHist 2012*.

Bick, E. (2009). A graphical corpus-based dictionary of word relations. In *Proceedings of NODALIDA 2009. NEALT Proceedings Series Vol. 4*, Odense. NEALT.

Borin, L. and Forsberg, M. (2009). All in the family: A comparison of SALDO and WordNet. In *Proceedings of the Nodalida 2009 Workshop on WordNets and other Lexical Semantic Resources – between Lexical Semantics, Lexicography, Terminology and Formal Ontologies*, Odense. NEALT.

Borin, L. and Forsberg, M. (2011). A diachronic computational lexical resource for 800 years of Swedish. In *Language technology for cultural heritage*, pages 41–61. Springer, Berlin.

Borin, L., Forsberg, M., and Kokkinakis, D. (2010). Diabase: Towards a diachronic blark in support of historical studies. In *Proceedings of LREC 2010*.

Borin, L., Forsberg, M., Olsson, L.-J., and Uppström, J. (2012a). The open lexical infrastructure of Språkbanken. In *Proceedings of LREC 2012*, pages 3598–3602, Istanbul. ELRA.

Borin, L., Forsberg, M., and Roxendal, J. (2012b). Korp – the corpus infrastructure of Språkbanken. In *Proceedings of LREC 2012*, pages 474–478, Istanbul. ELRA.

ISO (2008). Language resource management – lexical markup framework (lmf). International Standard ISO 24613:2008.

Kilgarriff, A., Rychlý, P., Smrž, P., and Tugwell, D. (2008). The Sketch Engine. In Fontenelle, T., editor, *Practical Lexicography: A Reader*, pages 297–306. Oxford University Press, Oxford.

Nygaard, L., Priestley, J., Nøklestad, A., and Johannessen, J. B. (2008). Glossa: a multilingual, multimodal, configurable user interface. In *Proceedings of the Sixth International Language Resources and Evaluation Conference (LREC'08)*, Marrakech. ELRA.

Volodina, E., Borin, L., Loftsson, H., Arnbjörnsdóttir, B., and Leifsson, G. Ö. (2012). Waste not, want not: Towards a system architecture for icall based on nlp component re-use. In *Proceedings of the SLTC 2012 workshop on NLP for CALL, Lund, 25th October, 2012*, pages 47–58.

A Grammar Sparrer for Norwegian

Lars Hellan[1], Tore Bruland[2], Elias Aamot[3], Mads H. Sandøy[4]

(1,3,4) Department of Language and Communication Studies, NTNU, N-7491 Trondheim
(2) Department of Informatics, NTNU, N-7491 Trondheim

lars.hellan@ntnu.no, torebrul@idi.ntnu.no, eliasaa@stud.ntnu.no,
mads_h_s@hotmail.com

ABSTRACT

We demonstrate an on-line tool for grammatical error detection for Norwegian with freely chosen inputs, and error-messages informing the user about possible mistakes; the system also generates grammatically correct alternatives for ill-formed input strings. The system is built as an extension to a general-purpose large HPSG grammar of Norwegian, with special 'mal'-rules identifying a set of 40 types of errors. The system is still a prototype.

KEYWORDS: Computer Assisted Language Learning, HPSG, LKB, error message, mal-rules

1   Introduction

The ***Norwegian Online Grammar Sparrer*** is an interactive online Grammar Tutor with freely chosen written inputs, with error-messages informing the user about possible mistakes, and generated grammatically correct alternatives for some ill-formed input strings. The system is developed at NTNU, and was first taken into use in 2011. It is built as an extension to a general-purpose large HPSG grammar of Norwegian (see below).

2   Functionalities of the system

The main functionalities can be illustrated as follows. A user writes a putative Norwegian sentence into a window, as shown in FIGURE 1;[1] if grammatical, the system responds that the sentence is grammatical, while if ungrammatical, the system informs the user in what respect the string is ungrammatical. FIGURE 1 shows how, for the ungrammatical string "Mannet smiler", one gets the feedback *The word "mannet" is of masculine gender, not neuter*.

FIGURE 1:   Illustration of *Error Information* display

In addition to the slot for error message(s), the window provides three buttons: *Info* takes one to a detailed instruction about the tool,[2] *More description* takes one to succinct information about the relevant aspect of Norwegian grammar,[3] and by pushing *Generate*, one can get an example of how the intended sentence should be written, as illustrated in FIGURE 2 for the same string:

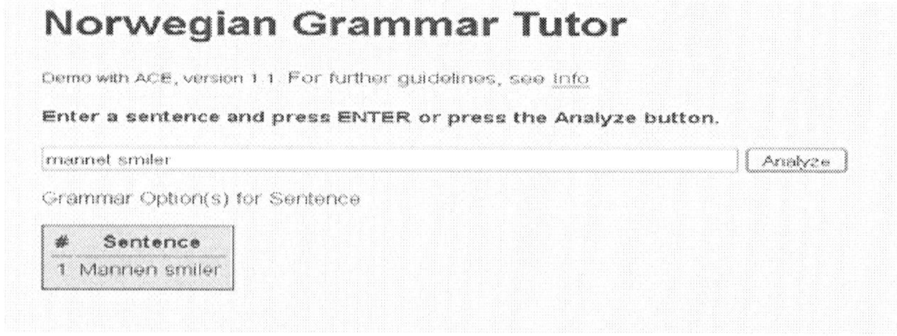

FIGURE 2:   Illustration of *Correct Option* generation

---

[1]   http://regdili.idi.ntnu.no:8080/studentAce/parse

[2]   http://typecraft.org/tc2wiki/Classroom:Norwegian_Grammar_Checking

[3]   In the relevant case, http://typecraft.org/tc2wiki/The_Noun_Phrase_-_Norwegian.

We call the system 'grammar sparring' to highlight the circumstance that the system immediately responds to each move by the user. While the interface shown above is for this interaction, a more general wiki interface is being hosted at *TypeCraft*[4], with instructions and pages supplementing those accessed by the buttons *Info* and *More description* mentioned above.[5]

3   The system architecture

The system builds on the computational grammar **NorSource** of Norwegian, developed at NTNU,[6] and is an implemented HPSG grammar (Pollard and Sag 1994) based on the development platform LKB (Copestake 2002). LKB grammars are purely *declarative*, in that they define what are possible structures in a language, while the status of *un*grammatical for a given string resides in its not being included in this set of structures; thus, such a grammar contains no negative statements. NorSource uses the architecture of the *HPSG Grammar Matrix* (Bender 2010, 2012), which includes the semantic representation formalism *Minimal Recursion Semantics* (*MRS*; Copestake et al. 2005); such a representation accompanies any parse produced by the grammar, and from it, sentences of the language can be generated (such a grammar is thus both 'analyzing' and 'generating'). This generation capacity is crucial in the *recommendation* capacity illustrated in Figure 2, the recommended sentence being generated from the MRS of the input string.

With Norsource as a so-called 'bon-grammar', a 'mal-apparatus' is built onto the 'bon'-grammar, with 'mal-rules' accommodating a predefined set of grammatical errors. Norsource and the 'mal-apparatus together constitute the full system named **NorMal**, all parts of Norsource thus being used in NorMal, while NorMal includes files not used in Norsource. When an illformed string is parsed, with an error type which has been assigned a mal-rule, the set of syntactic rules accepting the string will include a mal-rule. The strategy enabling generation of recommendations is to let mal-rules and mal-lexical entries introduce into the MRS exactly the same EP(s) as their 'bon'-counterparts generally introduce, whereby generation can produce well-formed strings coming very close to the intended form.

Norsource currently has close to 200 phrasal combinatory rules, and verb- and adjective lexicons with approximately 10,000 entries each. A noun lexicon with about 50,000 entries is also available, but not used in the Grammar Sparrer, as it induces too much parse ambiguity at the present point. The number of MRSs from a parsed sentence generally depends on the strictness of the rules of the grammar, but even with the fairly strict format presently used, a given parse – especially with mal-rules involved – will be associated with many MRSs. While it is in many cases impossible to predict the intended grammatical sentence of the user, a qualified guess is still possible. In this regard, it is essential that the relevant MRS can be automatically chosen, and for this purpose we use the parse ranker Velldal (2008) implemented with treebanking in [tsdb++] (Oepen et al. 1998, 2002), a tool in the LOGON system (Oepen et al. 2004). A number of sentences representative of the expected input of our system are treebanked and a ranking model is trained, using Rob Malouf's Toolkit for Advanced Discriminative Modeling (http://tadm.sourceforge.net/). The model is loaded with the grammar and it sorts the MRSes

---

[4]   http://typecraft.org
[5]
     http://typecraft.org/tc2wiki/Feedback_messages,
     http://typecraft.org/tc2wiki/Grammar_sparring_phenomena
[6]   http://typecraft.org/tc2wiki/Norwegian_HPSG_grammar_NorSource

according to the ranking model. For the selection of MRS for a given parse, the system will choose the first MRS in the list.

Such selection is particularly important in cases where parses with alternative mal-rules – or sets of mal-rules – are produced in a parse. It is similarly essential if one wants to deploy the large noun lexicon: in Norwegian, there are very many noun stems homophonous with verb stems, and only systematic tree-banking can 'relegate' the noun options below the verb option on the parse ranking.

From the outset, parsing in the system has been done in processing system PET[7], and generation in LKB. During the last year we have taken into use the system ACE[8], integrated for both purposes, thereby increasing speed by a significant factor.

4   Pedagogical development and outlook

We originally based our mal-rule development on a corpus of common errors among L2 learners of Norwegian at NTNU. The set of phenomena covered in this corpus has proved adequate for the system so far, but we will soon face the need for increasing the phenomena range.[9]

With a running log of sentences processed by the Sparrer, we get continuous feedback on the number of use interactions (approximately 3000 per month, currently), and on the behavior of the system regarding correct identification of grammatical vs. ungrammatical, and delivery and correctness of error messages. The Sparrer is in addition a recommended facility in the Norwegian L2 course NoW hosted at NTNU,[10] an environment in which more systematic pedagogical developments of the tool can be tried out and tested in the future.

In the general context of Computer Assisted Language Learning, the present system follows a type of architecture envisaged in Schneider, D. and K. McCoy (1998), and situated relative to LKB systems in Bender et al. (2004). Relative to the overview of CALL systems presented in Heift et al. (2007), the system is 'rule based' rather than 'constraint-based' (despite HPSG as a framework being commonly called 'constraint-based'). Among CALL systems implemented with LKB, to our knowledge the only other system in current use is a system based on the English grammar ERG (cf. Flickinger 2010), used in primary school teaching, with a more closed pedagogical architecture, and with a significantly broader scope.

What the present type of system perhaps most interestingly demonstrates is the way in which a fully 'generic' grammar – i.e., a domain- and purpose-neutral grammar – can be seamlessly extended into a working pedagogical system. This aspect is particularly interesting in view of the fact that there are currently 8-10 fairly large grammars based on the Grammar Matrix format, and thus using the same formalism as Norsource: an architecture made operative for one of them can relatively easily be applied to others as well. In addition to the rapid avenue to a multi-lingual system of grammar checkers thereby opening, the circumstance that the grammars in all of their modules use largely the same formalism opens for the possibility of creating parallel repositories of language information, and thereby the build-up of parallel pedagogical resources.

---

7   http://moin.delph-in.net/PetTop
8   http://moin.delph-in.net/AceTop
9   See footnote 5 for links to overview of phenomena.
10   http://www.ntnu.edu/now

References

Bender, E. M., D. Flickinger, S. Oepen and A. Walsh (2004). "Arboretum: Using a precision grammar for grammar checking in CALL," in Proceedings of the InSTIL/ICALL Symposium 2004, Venice, Italy.

Bender, E.M., Scott Drellishak, Antske Fokkens, Laura Poulson. and S. Saleem. 2010. Grammar Customization. In *Research on Language & Computation*, Volume 8, Number 1, 23-72.

Bender, E.M., Sumukh Ghodke, Timothy Baldwin and Rebecca Dridan. 2012. From Database to Treebank: On Enhancing Hypertext Grammars with Grammar Engineering and Treebank Search. In Sebastian Nordhoff (ed) *Electronic Grammaticography*. Pp179-206.

Copestake, A. (2002). *Implementing Typed Feature Structure Grammars*. CSLI Publications, Stanford.

Copestake, A., D. Flickinger, C. Pollard, and I. Sag. (2005). Minimal Recursion Semantics: an Introduction. *Research on Language and Computation* 3(4): 281—332.

Heift, T., and M. Schulze. (2007). *Errors and Intelligence in Computer-Assisted Language Learning: Parsers and Pedagogues.* Routledge, New York.

Flickinger, D. (2010). Prescription and Explanation -- Using an HPSG implementation to teach writing skills. Invited talk, HPSG Conference 2010.

Heift, T., and M. Schulze. (2007). *Errors and Intelligence in Computer-Assisted Language Learning: Parsers and Pedagogues.* Routledge, New York.

Oepen, S. and D. Flickinger (1998). Towards systematic grammar profiling. test suite technology ten years after. Journal of Computer Speech and Language 12(4), 411 - 436.

Oepen, S., K. Toutanova, S. Shieber, C. Manning, D. Flickinger, and T. Brants (2002). The lingo redwoods treebank: Motivation and preliminary applications. In Proceedings of the 19th international conference on Computational linguistics-Volume 2, pp. 1 - 5. Association for Computational Linguistics.

Oepen, S., H. Dyvik, J. T. Lønning, E. Velldal, D. Beermann, J. Carroll, .n Flickinger, L. Hellan, J. B. Johannessen, P. Meurer, T. Nordgård, and V. Rosén (2004). Som å kapp-ete med trollet? Towards MRS-based Norwegian-English Machine Translation. In Proceedings of the 10th International Conference on Theoretical and Methodological Issues in Machine Translation, pp. 11 - 20. Baltimore, MD.

Schneider, D. and K. McCoy (1998). "Recognizing Syntactic Errors in the Writing of Second Language Learners," in Proceedings of Coling-ACL, pp. 1198-1204. Montreal.

Velldal, E. (2008). Empirical realization ranking. Ph. D. thesis, The University of Oslo.

Finite state applications with Javascript

Mans Hulden[1] *Miikka Silfverberg*[1] *Jerid Francom*[2]

(1) University of Helsinki
(2) Wake Forest University

`mans.hulden@email.arizona.edu, miikka.silfverberg@helsinki.fi, francojc@wfu.edu`

ABSTRACT

In this paper we present a simple and useful Javascript application programming interface for performing basic online operations with weighted and unweighted finite-state machines, such as word lookup, transductions, and least-cost-path finding. The library, *jsfst*, provides access to frequently used online functionality in finite-state machine-based language technology. The library is technology-agnostic in that it uses a neutral representation of finite-state machines into which most formats can be converted. We demonstrate the usefulness of the library through addressing a task that is useful in web and mobile environments—a multilingual spell checker application that also detects real-word errors.

KEYWORDS: Finite-state technology, Javascript, spell checking, perceptrons.

1   Introduction

Finite-state machine (FSM) technology is widely used in language-processing and FSMs are applied in many contexts ranging from text processing to more complex tasks. Currently, several high-quality toolkits exist for the manipulation and construction of weighted and unweighted finite-state machines, such as *foma* (Hulden, 2009), *HFST* (Lindén et al., 2009), *OpenFST* (Allauzen et al., 2007), *SFST* (Schmid, 2006), and *xfst* (Beesley and Karttunen, 2003), to name a few. These toolkits, once compiled, also provide programming interfaces for the real-time use of automata in language processing tasks. However, for online and mobile applications, the use of finite-state machines is complicated by the unavailability of generic application interfaces for applying the finite-state machines built with any of the above toolkits. In the following, we demonstrate a simple Javascript API that allows one to take advantage of finite-state technology in a toolkit-agnostic environment. The API can take advantage of any FSM represented in the AT&T toolkit format (to which all of the above tools can export). We demonstrate its real-world usefulness with a Javascript spell checking application that offers both traditional spell checking functionality—marking of incorrectly spelled words using a simple unweighted automaton—and more advanced real-word error (RWE) correction, implemented through a perceptron algorithm and encoded as weighted finite automata.

2   The *jsfst* API

The *jsfst* API allows basic operations on FSMs, both weighted and unweighted. These include: checking whether a word (string) is accepted by an automaton, performing a string transduction by a transducer, and finding, given an input string, the least-cost path through a weighted automaton.

It is assumed that the user has stored the required FSMs as a compressed string representation (see below), after which the FSM may be expanded in memory and subsequently used in applications through the API. We also provide a tool for converting FSMs from the widely-used AT&T textual format (Mohri et al., 1997) into a compressed Javascript format discussed below. The workflow is simple; the user defines one or several compressed FSM variables, after which operations on the FSMs can be performed through the API:

```
<script type='text/javascript' src='./jsfst.js'></script>
<script type='text/javascript' src='./my_automaton.js'></script>
// my_automaton.js: var mycompressedFSM = "moomoom4se8us7loo9s7goo9|4FEBC|9280" ;
...
// Uncompress
var myNet = jsfst_uncompress_unweighted(mycompressedFSM);
...
// Check if a word is accepted by the machine
var accept = jsfst_apply_unweighted_automaton(myNet, myString);
...
```

2.1   Compression of FSMs for online use

When dealing with online and mobile applications, memory restrictions tend to be more severe than under other environments. This calls for compression of finite-state networks during transmission and storing. Often, Javascript code is transferred from server to client in a *gzip*-compressed format which offers some compaction; however, this can be much improved upon by judicious encoding of the finite-state machines. In the current work, we rely on a

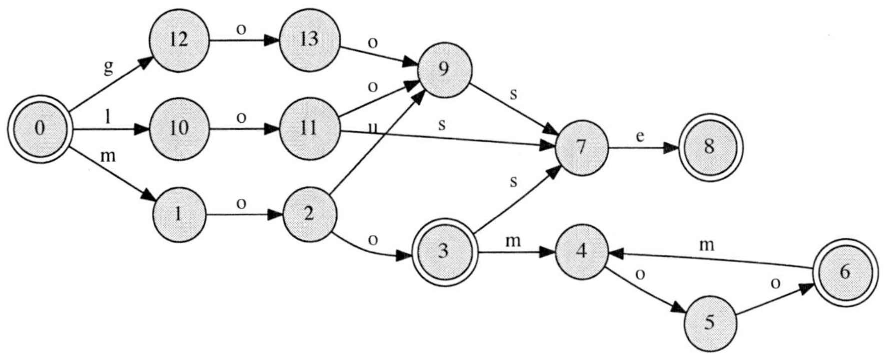

Figure 1: *Finite state machine represented as the string:* `moomoom4se8us7loo9s7goo9|4FEBC|9280`.

string representation of FSMs that, together with standard compression methods (*gzip*), yields compression ratios of about 1:10 compared with completely uncompressed material, and about 1:3 compared with other textual formats which are compressed, such as the widely used AT&T FSM format followed by *gzip*.

We represent the FSMs as a string in three parts, **A|B|C**. The string encodes the result of printing out a depth-first-search through an FSM, where states are only mentioned when strictly necessary for its later reconstruction. Similar methods have been used successfully in other circumstances where space has been at a premium (Karttunen, 1990). The parts encode the following information:

- Part A: represents a depth-first-search through the automaton. Each arc is mentioned once whenever it is encountered. A state number is given every time a backtrack occurs during the DFS, or at the end. States not mentioned are assumed to be constructed in ascending numerical order, one for each transition that is not followed by a backtrack.

- Part B: a sequence of bits, 1 for each arc that is the last one in the source state, otherwise 0, converted into hexadecimal symbols, 4 bits in each symbol.

- Part C: a sequence of bits, 1 for each state that is final, otherwise 0, converted into hexadecimal, 4 bits in each symbol.

For example, in our compressed format, the FSM in figure 1, which encodes the regular expression `/(moo)*|(mo(o|u)se|goose|loo?se)/`, is represented as the concatenation of the three strings:

(A)   `moomoom4se8us7loo9s7goo9`   (is a DFS path)
(B)   `4FEBC`   (is 0100 1111 1110 1011 11(00) in binary)
(C)   `9280`   (is 1001 0010 1000 00(00) in binary)

Transducers are encoded similarly, but differing input-output pairs are separated by a colon. Weighted machines additionally have the weight specified in parentheses after each transition. Likewise, weighted machines have their final weight (in **C**) given explicitly, instead of in the bit-encoded format. Note that the original state numbering of any given FSM may change when this encoding is performed by a DFS, as states are assigned running numbers in the order they

Language	.cmp.gz	.cmp	.att.gz	.att
Basque	797K	2.1M	2.3M	8.2M
English	632K	1.3M	1.9M	6.1M
Finnish	1.3M	2.9M	3.7M	13M
German	8.2M	23M	22M	84M
Spanish	194K	415K	591K	2.0M
Swedish	433K	994M	1.3M	4.0M

Table 1: *File sizes of some morphologies from which word-surface forms have been extracted in different formats for use in a online spell-checking application. Here **.cmp** represents the string format FSM compression, **.gzip** a gzipped file, and **.att** the AT&T file format.*

Javascript FST + Perceptron spell checker demo

Figure 2: *Screenshot of combined standard and RWE spell checker in Spanish: incorrectly spelled words are marked interactively in red, while real-word errors are marked in orange.*

are encountered. This allows for a very compact encoding of sets of words and FSMs in general. For example, the basic acyclic Spanish morphological dictionary used in subsequent examples contains 571,129 words. Represented as an FSM encoded in our compressed format, and then gzipped, it occupies 198,904 bytes. This is equivalent to 2.79 bits per word. Table 1 shows the size of various morphological transducers, converted into automata by extracting only the valid word-forms, and then encoded in various compressed and uncompressed formats.

3   Example application: spell checking

A classic byproduct of encoding a morphological analyzer as an FSM is the ability to quickly implement spell checking tools. This involves extracting the domain or range of the morphological transducer, yielding an automaton that (presumably) contains only valid surface forms of words. This automaton can then be consulted for checking correctness of words—usually with much larger coverage than word lists can provide. For our experiments, we have done so using morphological transducers for Basque (Agirre et al., 1992), English, Finnish (Pirinen, 2011), German (Schmid et al., 2004), Spanish (Carreras et al., 2004), and Swedish. As is seen from table 1, except for the German transducer which encodes many circumfixation phenomena and is rather large to begin with, the compressed sizes of the automata are small enough to be used and integrated into, for instance, web-based text editing environments. [1]

3.1   Real-word errors with perceptrons encoded as weighted automata

To demonstrate more advanced usage, we have implemented a real-word-error-aware spell checker using weighted automata. Catching real-word spelling errors is a difficult problem

---

[1] Performance is also reasonable. When using a determinized automaton, we can check correctness of an average of 49,000 words/s using the Javascript API (vs. 1,400,000 words/s in a C implementation using the *foma* API).

(see Hirst and Budanitsky (2005) for an overview). However, in restricted domains, fairly high accuracies can be achieved (Yarowsky, 1994). One of these is the detection of diacritic placement errors in Romance languages. We focus here on Spanish, as it is arguably at the easier end of the spectrum, and a comfortable level of certainty in error marking can be achieved.

When restoring diacritics, we divide words into three classes: (1) words whose correct orthographic form has no diacritics, for example "para" (for); (2) words whose correct form has diacritics, but there is only one possible form, for example "según" (according to); (3) words that have two orthographically correct forms with and without diacritics, for example "que" (that) and "qué" (what).

In the unambiguous cases, a list of correct forms is sufficient for restoring the diacritics. For ambiguous words, one of the forms for example "qué" is the diacritized form and the other one, "que", is the non-diacritized form. It is possible to train a binary classifier based on contextual features, which decides whether the form should be diacritized or not. The contextual features that are used in the classifier are: (1) the word form itself, for example $WORD = que$; (2) the neighboring words, for example $NEIGHBOR = por$; and (3), whether the word occurs at a sentence boundary $NEIGHBOR = \#\#$. These features are usually sufficient to choose between alternative forms. For example, in a case like '... para él.' the ambiguity of 'el' (article) vs. 'él' (he/him) is resolved by the presence of a sentence boundary.

We use a logistic classifier to classify ambiguous words. Model parameters are estimated using the averaged perceptron algorithm (Collins, 2002) and all features whose parameters are non-zero are compiled into a weighted FSM. Using the word lists and the classifier, the system achieves 99.4% accuracy when determining whether a form should be diacritized or not.[2]

To reduce the size of the resulting FSM, it is useful to filter features. For training data consisting of approximately 14M words, we filtered out features for words occurring less than 60 times. This reduced the accuracy of the system from 99.4% to 99.1%, while the size of the feature FSM was reduced from 4.7M to 1.4M in AT&T text format. The size is further reduced to 141K by representing the transducer in compressed format as explained in section 2.1. The performance of the RWE detection is similar to that of checking a word against an automaton, as the perceptron is encoded as a deterministic weighted automaton (30,000 lookups/s). However, for each word to be checked, three separate lookups are needed (one for each feature). The combined use of both a basic spell checker and an RWE error checker is shown in figure 2.

4 Conclusion

Javascript-based tools have already demonstrated their usability: there are now Javascript-based WYSIWYG text editors and PDF readers, for example. As we have demonstrated, it is also possible to create Javascript-based language technology tools that are sufficiently fast and compact for heavy use even in, for example, mobile devices.

It is possible to encode a variety of machine learning and language modeling paradigms as FSMs, which means that a general, efficient Javascript API for FSMs provides access to a broad swathe of cutting-edge technology. Since Javascript is widely supported, tools using such an API are also easy to insert in a variety of applications. This, in turn, offers the potential to promote the creation of tools with a much wider coverage of languages, including less-resourced minority languages.

---

[2]We use a section of the Spanish GigaWord corpus (Graff, 2011) for training data, from which 10% was held out for tuning, and another 10% set aside to be used as evaluation data.

References

Agirre, E., Alegria, I., Arregi, X., Artola, X., de Ilarraza, A. D., Maritxalar, M., Sarasola, K., and Urkia, M. (1992). Xuxen: A spelling checker/corrector for Basque based on two-level morphology. In *Proceedings of the third conference on Applied natural language processing*, pages 119–125. Association for Computational Linguistics.

Allauzen, C., Riley, M., Schalkwyk, J., Skut, W., and Mohri, M. (2007). OpenFst: A general and efficient weighted finite-state transducer library. In *Implementation and Application of Automata*, pages 11–23. Springer.

Beesley, K. R. and Karttunen, L. (2003). *Finite state morphology*. CSLI, Stanford.

Carreras, X., Chao, I., Padró, L., and Padró, M. (2004). Freeling: An open-source suite of language analyzers. In *Proceedings of the 4th LREC*, volume 4.

Collins, M. (2002). Discriminative training methods for hidden Markov models: theory and experiments with perceptron algorithms. In *Proceedings of EMNLP '02*, pages 1–8.

Graff, D. (2011). Spanish Gigaword Third Edition (LDC2011T12). *Linguistic Data Consortium, University of Pennsylvania, Philadelphia, PA*.

Hirst, G. and Budanitsky, A. (2005). Correcting real-word spelling errors by restoring lexical cohesion. *Natural Language Engineering*, 11(01):87–111.

Hulden, M. (2009). Foma: a finite-state compiler and library. In *Proceedings of the 12th Conference of the European Chapter of the Association for Computational Linguistics: Demonstrations Session*, pages 29–32. Association for Computational Linguistics.

Karttunen, L. (1990). Binary encoding format for finite-state networks. *Technical Report, Palo Alto Research Center*, (P90-00019).

Lindén, K., Silfverberg, M., and Pirinen, T. (2009). HFST tools for morphology–an efficient open-source package for construction of morphological analyzers. In *State of the Art in Computational Morphology*, pages 28–47. Springer.

Mohri, M., Pereira, F., Riley, M., and Allauzen, C. (1997). AT&T FSM library-finite state machine library. *AT&T Labs-Research*.

Pirinen, T. (2011). Modularisation of Finnish finite-state language description—towards wide collaboration in open source development of morphological analyser. In *Proceedings of NoDaLiDa*, volume 18.

Schmid, H. (2006). A programming language for finite state transducers. *Lecture Notes in Computer Science*, 4002.

Schmid, H., Fitschen, A., and Heid, U. (2004). SMOR: A German computational morphology covering derivation, composition and inflection. In *Proceedings of LREC 2004*, pages 1263–1266. Citeseer.

Yarowsky, D. (1994). Decision lists for lexical ambiguity resolution: Application to accent restoration in Spanish and French. *Proceedings of the 32nd annual meeting on Association for Computational Linguistics*, pages 88–95.

HPC-ready Language Analysis for Human Beings

Emanuele Lapponi[1], *Erik Velldal*[1], *Nikolay A. Vazov*[2], *Stephan Oepen*[1]

(1) Language Technology Group, Department of Informatics, University of Oslo
(2) Research Support Services Group, University Center for Information Technology, University of Oslo

`{emanuel|erikve|oe}@ifi.uio.no, n.a.vazov@usit.uio.no`

ABSTRACT

This demonstration presents a first operable pilot of the Language Analysis Portal (LAP), an ongoing project within the Norwegian CLARINO initiative that aims at providing easy access to Language Technology (LT) tools running on a powerful High-Performance Computing (HPC) cluster. The system is built on top of the Galaxy framework, giving users an on-line platform where they can design experiments using an array of processors. These processors can be combined into complex workflows using a visual editor. The current implementation functions as a testbed for further development, hosting a limited collection of tools addressing common use-cases in the LT-realm; the long-term goal for LAP is to reach beyond the field and be an enabling platform for LT-powered research in the humanities and social sciences.

KEYWORDS: research infrastructure, High-Performance Computing, web portal, CLARINO.

1   Introduction

This demonstration will be showcasing ongoing work within the CLARINO[1] project on building a web portal for natural language analysis. The effort is carried out at the University of Oslo (UiO) jointly by the Language Technology Group (LTG) and the Research Computing group at the University Center for Information Technology (USIT).

An important part of the overall mission of CLARINO is to facilitate the use of language technology (LT) in the social sciences and humanities. In the same vein, the construction of the Language Analysis Portal (LAP) aims to boost the availability and usability of large-scale language analysis for researchers both within and outside the field of LT itself. Currently, many common LT tools can appear rather daunting to use, requiring a lot of technical knowledge on the side of the user. Apart from the challenge of orienting oneself in the fragmented ecosystem of available tools, many potential users, especially from less technically oriented disciplines, might not be comfortable with command-line interfaces or having to wrestle with difficult and poorly documented installation procedures, or might lack the required knowledge about annotation formats or other dependencies. Many researchers might also not have access to the computing power necessary to process larger data sets. LAP aims to eliminate such obstacles. The goal is to maintain a large repository of LT tools that are easily accessible through a web portal, offering a uniform graphical interface and ensuring a low bar of entry for users, while at the same time enabling execution of complex workflows to be run on a high-performance computing (HPC) cluster, also ensuring scalability to very large data sets. LAP's HPC-centric design also sets it apart from other abstractly similar infrastructure projects such as WebLicht[2] within CLARIN-D, in that all the tools will be hosted locally and adapted to work with the national grid infrastructure.

While the LAP development is still in its early stages, an operable pilot is already available for testing and demonstration purposes. The remaining part of the paper is structured analogously to the interactive demonstration, viz. providing a walk-through of a representative use case—touching on everything from user authentication and data set management to workflow design and viewing results—commenting on technical details along the way.

2   LAP Pilot

The long-term goal for LAP is to reach beyond the field and be an enabling platform for LT-powered research in the humanities and social sciences. At this early stage of development, however, the pilot use case is centered around the needs of LT researchers and in particular students, as their level of proficiency strikes a good balance between non programming-savvy historians and seasoned programmers. This allows us to make certain assumptions that facilitate the initial development stage—we assume the users have a certain knowledge of what the installed tools do—while at the same time providing test candidates that can truly benefit from the system.

The pilot system serves several purposes: Most importantly it will act as a *proof-of-concept*, assessing the viability of involved software as well as ideas before extending the implementation to a larger set of tools and support for a larger set of features. The most important part of this, in turn, is assessing the suitability of the *Galaxy platform* (Giardine et al., 2005;

---

[1]The Norwegian branch of the pan-European CLARIN project (Common Language Resources and Technology Infrastructure). For more information see; `http://clarin.b.uib.no/`

[2]The WebLicht website: `http://weblicht.sfs.uni-tuebingen.de/weblichtwiki/`

Blankenberg et al., 2010; Goecks et al., 2010), a web-based workflow management system initially developed for data-intensive research in genomics and bioinformatics , which is a core component of the current pilot implementation.[3] Another important use of the pilot will be as a *demonstrator*; for reaching out to tool developers, to illustrate use cases for potential user groups in the humanities and social sciences, and as a foundation for further surveying user-requirements. The pilot is only meant to support a minimal selection of LT tools and will be evaluated in part by a group of test users consisting of master students of the study program *Informatics: Language and Communication* at the University of Oslo.

In this context, a typical use case is that of annotating natural language text with syntactic analyses, e.g. annotating a collection of newspaper articles or a novel with dependency graphs. The completion of this task would ordinarily require the user to install the relevant software packages and execute the tools that satisfy the dependencies of the parser; minimally a sentence-segmenter, a tokenizer and a POS-tagger. Furthermore, the user in question could be interested in producing dependency annotations generated using different parsers, that are in turn invoked with part of speech tags that originate from different upstream annotators. These actions typically require at least basic Unix-shell proficiency; wrapping the execution in a small, parameterizable program that allows the user to effectively try out different settings further raises the entry-bar for this kind of experimental process. Additionally, different tools in the chain might use different representations—tab-separated columns or nested XML, say—requiring the user to further pre-process the data at each step. Lack of in-depth technical knowledge, perhaps in combination with lack of good documentation, might make each of these steps difficult for many potential users, especially for those from less technically oriented disciplines. Access to the necessary computing power might itself also be a barrier, depending on the complexity of the task or the size of the dataset in question.

The LAP pilot includes enough tools and functionality to enable this kind of computation with a few mouse-clicks, allowing users to visually design complex tool-chains, store results and experiment with different tool-configurations and datasets on any platform that can run a modern web-browser. After logging into the system via Feide, users are presented with the Galaxy *workspace*, as shown in Figure 1. The left panel displays the installed processing tools; clicking on tool-names displays general information and configuration options in the center panel. In order to be integrated in the LAP tool-chain, existing tools are 'wrapped' inside scripts that decode the LAP-internal format, present the tool itself with its expected input and finally re-encode the output so that it is compatible with the next processing step. For LAP's system-internal representation, we are at the moment looking into both TCF (Text Corpus Format, Heid et al., 2010) (the format used within WebLicht, which comes with a full, albeit closed-source API) and our own in-house JSON-based LTON format (Language Technology Object Notation) which is still currently under development.

Additionally, the wrapper handles the submission of the job to the Abel cluster, a shared resource for research computing boasting more than 600 machines, totaling more than 10.000 cores (CPUs).[4] The HPC connection is a very important feature, as Language technology can be computationally quite expensive, often involving sub-problems where known best solutions

---

[3]For more information about Galaxy, please see `http://wiki.galaxyproject.org/`

[4]At the time of writing, the cluster ranks at position 134 on the `http://www.top500.org` list of top supercomputers world- wide. Among its frequent users, besides the language technology group, we find researchers from the life sciences, astrophysics, geophysics, and chemistry.

Figure 1: A screenshot of the current implementation of LAP within Galaxy. The left panel displays the installed tools, the center panel shows the currently selected function and the right panel hosts the file history.

have exponential worst-case complexity. At the same time, typical language analysis tasks can be trivially parallelized, as processing separate documents (and for many tasks also individual sentences) constitute independent units of computation. The fact that the portal will submit the sub-tasks of a workflow to an underlying HPC cluster—without the need for user knowledge about job scheduling etc.—means that the user will be able to perform analyses that might otherwise not be possible (and faster and on larger data sets).

Returning to Figure 1, the right panel contains so-called *histories*, where files associated with different experiments are collected and persistently stored across sessions. Users can add datasets to a history by uploading local files, providing a URL to the dataset location, or by pasting the relevant text using the 'Get Data' tool. The simplest action achievable with this pilot consists of adding a dataset to a history and running one of the processing tools. The processing job then starts and the annotated dataset is added to the same history; users can then select it and run other annotators. The resulting datasets can either be inspected within LAP or downloaded (the system also allows for full histories to be downloaded as compressed archives).

Most importantly, users can also compose workflows using the workflow editor, where experimental tool-chains such as the one sketched previously can be designed using a simple graphical interface; Figure 2 shows an example of workflow design within the editor, here with a workflow with four endpoints. To build the chain, users invoke GUI elements representing tool instances to the center panel and link inputs to outputs, guiding the data flow across tools. Workflows can then be saved and shared with all or selected LAP users. When running a workflow, the system populates the history with a version of the dataset for each processing point, so that the user can return to the partially processed data and run (or re-run) relevant tools without re-starting the whole workflow.

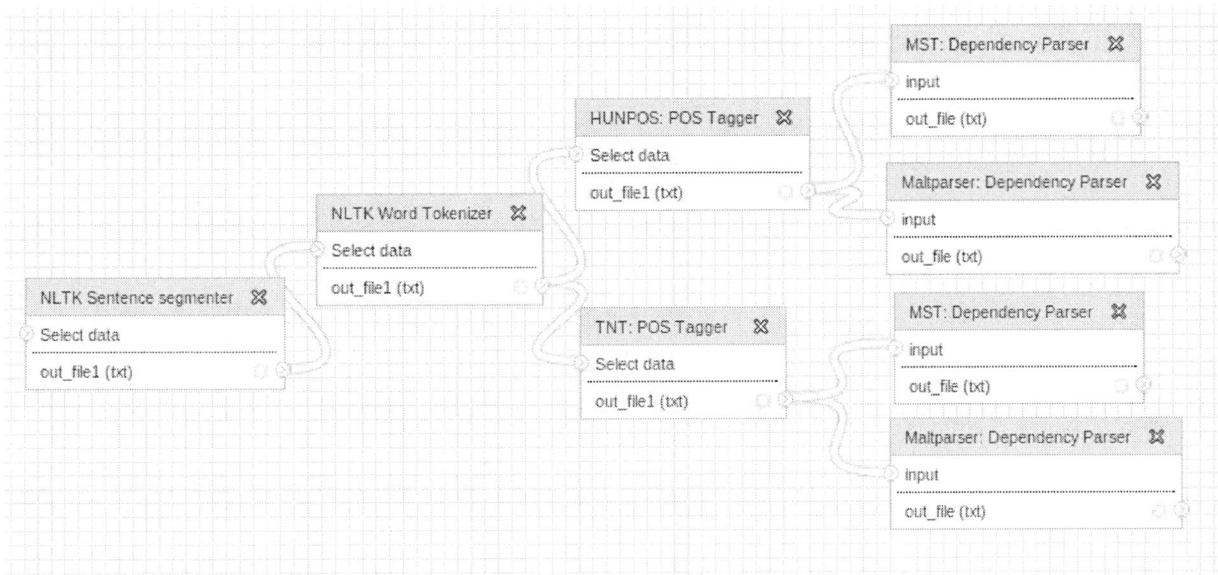

Figure 2: A user-defined LAP workflow with four endpoints. The data processing starts with unannotated text and ends with four datasets containing different annotations.

3   Conclusion and Outlook

In this demonstration we presented the current pilot implementation of the Language Analysis Portal (LAP), an in-development web-portal for natural language processing. LAP, developed under the umbrella of the CLARINO initiative, aims to facilitate the use of LT-tools for non-programmers by letting users create complex experimental setups visually, and allowing them to run large-scale processes on the national grid infrastructure for HPC computing. Further discussion of the technical details of the pilot can be found in (Lapponi et al., 2013).

While the long-term goal for the portal is to also address the language processing needs of researchers outside the field, the current implementation focuses on a typical use case within the LT realm, allowing users to quickly and simply combine processing tools into complex workflows and collect the results. Future releases of the systems will feature a larger array of tools, and further work starting after the release of the final pilot will address the challenge of shaping LAP into a useful research tool for the humanities and the social sciences, investigating possible use cases and surveying user-requirements from active researchers from these fields.

References

Blankenberg, D., Kuster, G. V., Coraor, N., Ananda, G., Lazarus, R., Mangan, M., Nekrutenko, A., and Taylor, J. (2010). Galaxy: a web-based genome analysis tool for experimentalists. *Current Protocols in Molecular Biology*, pages 19.10.1–19.10.21.

Giardine, B., Riemer, C., Hardison, R. C., Burhans, R., Elnitski, L., Shah, P., Zhang, Y., Blankenberg, D., Albert, I., Taylor, J., Miller, W., Kent, W. J., and Nekrutenko, A. (2005). Galaxy: a platform for interactive large-scale genome analysis. *Genome Research*, 15(10):1451–5.

Goecks, J., Nekrutenko, A., Taylor, J., and Team, T. G. (2010). Galaxy: a comprehensive approach for supporting accessible, reproducible, and transparent computational research in the life sciences. *Genome Biology*, 11(8):R86.

Heid, U., Schmid, H., Eckart, K., and Hinrichs, E. (2010). A corpus representation format for linguistic web services: The D-SPIN Text Corpus Format and its relationship with ISO standards. In *Proceedings of the 7th International Conference on Language Resources and Evaluation*, pages 494–499, Malta.

Lapponi, E., Velldal, E., Vazov, N. A., and Oepen, S. (2013). Towards large-scale language analysis in the cloud. In *Proceedings of the Workshop on Nordic Language Research Infrastructure at the 19th Nordic Conference of Computational Linguistics*, Oslo, Norway.

The INESS Treebanking Infrastructure

*Paul Meurer[2], Helge Dyvik[1,2], Victoria Rosén[1,2], Koenraad De Smedt[1],
Gunn Inger Lyse[1], Gyri Smørdal Losnegaard[1], Martha Thunes[1]*

(1) University of Bergen, Norway
(2) Uni Computing, Bergen, Norway

`paul.meurer@uni.no, helge.dyvik@uib.no, victoria@uib.no, desmedt@uib.no,`
`gunn.lyse@lle.uib.no, gyri.losnegaard@lle.uib.no, martha.thunes@lle.uib.no`

ABSTRACT

This paper briefly describes the current state of the evolving INESS infrastructure in Norway which is developing treebanks as well as making treebanks more accessible to the R&D community. Recent work includes the hosting of more treebanks, including parallel treebanks, and increasing the number of parsed and disambiguated sentences in the Norwegian LFG treebank. Other recent improvements include the presentation of metadata and license handling for restricted treebanks. The infrastructure is fully operational and accessible, but will be further improved during the lifetime of the INESS project.

KEYWORDS: treebanks, research infrastructure, parsed corpora, metadata, IPR, INESS, META-NORD, CLARIN, CLARINO.

1   Introduction

This short paper sketches the current state of the *Infrastructure for the Exploration of Syntax and Semantics* (INESS) (Rosén et al., 2012a). The implementation and operation of this infrastructure is carried out by the University of Bergen (Norway) and Uni Computing (a division of Uni Research, Bergen), and is funded by the Research Council of Norway and the University of Bergen (2010–2016).

INESS is aimed at providing access to treebanks to the R&D community in the language sciences. One of the project's main activities is the development of a large, deep parsebank for Norwegian with a wide coverage grammar and lexicon based on the Lexical-Functional Grammar (LFG) formalism (Bresnan, 2001). The other is the implementation and operation of a comprehensive open treebanking environment for building, hosting and exploring treebanks, thereby overcoming problems of maintenance and fragmentation due to treebanks being scattered and dependent on various platform-dependent software.

The project has recently cooperated with META-NORD (Vasiļjevs et al., 2012) (2011–2013), in the Information and Communication Technologies Policy Support Programme (CIP ICT-PSP), aimed at creating an open infrastructure to promote the accessibility and reuse of language resources and technologies (LRT). The META-NORD consortium included organizations from all the Nordic and Baltic countries. Among its recent results has been the documentation, rights clearance, licensing and sharing of many language resources, including treebanks, via the META-SHARE[1] catalogue and repository, thereby making LRT more readily available to R&D.

While the details of this cooperation are presented elsewhere,[2] the present paper will summarize the present state of the INESS infrastructure with a focus on functionality and usability.

2   Hosting treebanks in the INESS infrastructure

INESS currently provides the most comprehensive web-based treebanking services available. A normal web browser is sufficient as a client platform for accessing, searching and downloading treebanks, and also for the annotation of LFG-based parsebanks, including computer-aided manual disambiguation, text cleanup and handling of unknown words (Rosén et al., 2009, 2012b). The search functionality has recently been extended and simplified (Meurer, 2012). Search, visualization, resource management and cataloguing have been streamlined and work in similar ways for treebanks in several different paradigms (LFG, constituency and various dependency formats), thus simplifying access to a variety of resources.

For these reasons, INESS has become an attractive service for research groups who have developed or want to develop treebanks, but who cannot or do not want to invest in their own suite of web services for treebanking. Since the project start in 2010, INESS has been hosting an increasing number of treebanks, small and large. Among the larger treebanks developed by others and made available through INESS are the Icelandic Parsed Historical Corpus (IcePaHC, 73,014 sentences) (Wallenberg et al., 2011), the German Tiger treebank (50,472 sentences with dependency annotation, 9,221 with LFG annotation) (Brants et al., 2002) and the dependency part of the Bulgarian BulTreeBank (11,900 sentences) (Simov and Osenova, 2004). There is also a collection of sizable treebanks for Northern Sami (in total more than 1.7 million sentences, although not manually checked).

---

[1] http:/meta-share.tilde.lv

[2] A paper about the cooperation between INESS and META-NORD has been accepted for the Workshop on *Nordic Language Resources Infrastructure (NoLaReIn)* at NoDaLiDa 2013.

Figure 1: Choosing treebanks in INESS with the parallel treebanks setting.

The INESS infrastructure also offers tools for the development and exploitation of *parallel* corpora. Two parallel corpora aligned at sentence level were recently constructed and documented in cooperation with META-NORD. One of these is based on excerpts of a number of translations of the novel *Sofies Verden* (*Sophie's World*) (Gaarder, 1991), annotated for different languages and various formalisms, amounting to 26 aligned language pairs. Annotations of translations of a document from the Acquis communautaire were also aligned, currently yielding 21 pairs.

The ParGram project (Butt et al., 2002) has recently started using INESS as a testbed for semi-automatically aligning several LFG treebanks at phrase level. For treebanks constructed with parallel LFG grammars, the technology developed in the XPAR project (Dyvik et al., 2009) makes it possible to automatically align c-structure phrases based on manually indicated translational equivalences between f-structures. The resulting parallel treebanks are currently too small for exploitation, but their construction and exploration is an important proof of concept and a test of the parallel grammar construction endeavor in ParGram.

A screenshot with an overview of the treebank selection interface, with the option of choosing parallel treebanks, is shown in Figure 1. This figure also shows the 30 languages for which there are currently treebanks in the INESS infrastructure.

3   Accessing treebanks in the INESS interface

When accessing treebanks, users may want to identify treebanks and their provenance, for instance to correctly cite the materials. Access to many resources also requires that users be authenticated and authorized to use the materials under specified conditions. In recent joint work with META-NORD more attention has therefore been paid to the documentation and licensing of treebanks in INESS.

Relevant information is presented in the user interface after login. By way of example, Figure 2 shows how information on the Sofie Estonian treebank is presented the first time an authenticated user accesses this resource in INESS. A text describing the terms of the license and other metadata is presented to the user. The user can then choose to accept this license by clicking on the "Accept" button. This procedure is only necessary for treebanks with restrictions; in many cases the restrictions amount to no more than the requirement of attribution.

Resource: META-NORD Sofie Estonian Treebank

Description:

The Estonian part of the META-NORD Sofie Parallel Treebank.

This is a syntactically annotated parallel corpus based on the first chapters of the novel "Sofies verden" (Sophie's World) by Jostein Gaarder, published by Aschehoug forlag. The treebank consists of grammatical annotations of extracts from the Estonian translation of the novel, originally created as part of the Nordic Treebanking Network and now included in the extended META-NORD Sofie Parallel Treebank. The Estonian translation is published by Koolibri Publishing House. For more information, see the metadata description of the META-NORD Sofie Parallel Treebank.

ACCESS TO THE TREEBANK

The following terms hold for the use of the treebank:

The IPR holdership remains with Jostein Gaarder, who kindly permits INESS to distribute the "Sofie analyses" outside the project under the following terms of use:

a. The "Sofie analyses" can only be used for language technology research and development.

b. The users of the "Sofie analyses" are not allowed to redistribute or to publish the "Sofie analyses", only the knowledge and work that has been made on the basis of the "Sofie analyses",

c. The users of the "Sofie analyses" will ensure appropriate acknowledgement/references to the author of the original text, Jostein Gaarder, to Aschehoug Publishing House, Koolibri Publishing House and to the project INESS.

The alignments in the META-NORD Sofie Parallel Treebank are available under a CC-BY license (http://creativecommons.org/licenses/by/3.0/).

Attribution text:

"Alignments provided by the project INESS (www.iness.uib.no) in cooperation with META-NORD (http://www.meta-nord.eu/)."

Availability: available-restrictedUse

License: See «Description» for details
  Restrictions of use: Treebank creators and IPR holders must be attributed, see «Description» for details.
  Access medium:
  Can be used for academic and commercial purposes.

By accepting the terms of the license you will be granted access to the resource.

Accept

Funding project (Nordic Treebank Network)
  Project URL: http://w3.msi.vxu.se/~nivre/research/nt.html
  Project funded by: the Nordic Language Technology Program
  Project start date: , end date:

Language: Estonian (*ISO code:* et)

Figure 2: Presentation of documentation and user license, Sofie Estonian treebank.

4 The INESS Norwegian treebank

One of the main activities of the INESS project is the development of a large treebank for Norwegian, obtained by parsing automatically with an LFG grammar on the XLE parsing platform. The Norwegian treebank is growing and consists of a number of different genres in fiction and non-fiction. Part of the treebank is being efficiently manually disambiguated with the LFG PARSEBANKER (Rosén et al., 2009) Currently 4568 Norwegian sentences (46735 words) have been manually (at least partially) disambiguated; of these, 3602 sentences (35450) have been fully disambiguated. Based on the increasing number of manually disambiguated and quality controlled sentences, a stochastic disambiguator has been implemented which currently operates on the fly for any new sentences that are added.

(1) *Men det var helt   umulig.*
     But it   was completely impossible.

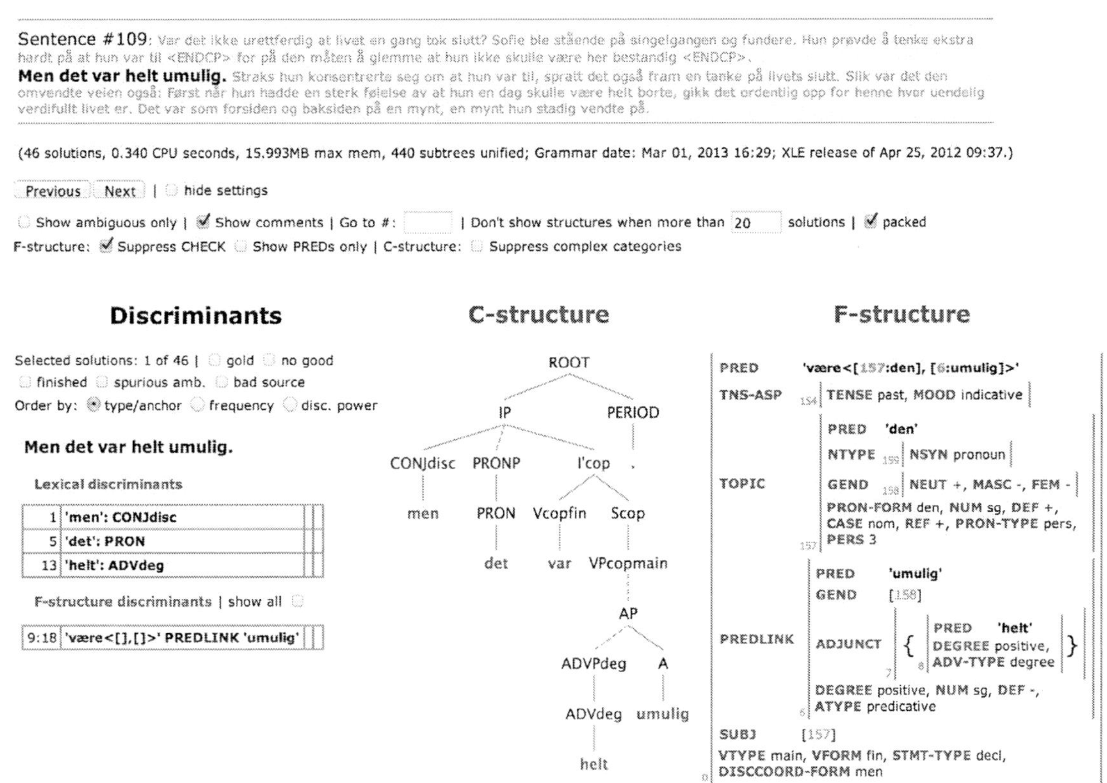

Figure 3: Screenshot of a disambiguated sentence in the INESS Norwegian treebank.

Figure 3 shows the manually disambiguated analysis of the sentence in example 1. Parsing resulted in 46 analyses for this sentence, and 211 discriminants were calculated (see Rosén et al. (2007) for the use of discriminants in LFG). Of these 211, only four were chosen in order to select the intended analysis.

5 Conclusion and outlook

INESS is becoming established as an infrastructure hosting a variety of existing treebanks as well as actively promoting the development of new treebanks. The infrastructure provides added value to existing treebanks through an increasing number of services, now including streamlined documentation and metadata, cataloguing information, access and licensing procedures, search, visualization and download. The INESS infrastructure is fully functional.

In the future, access will be further improved through user authentication by means of single sign-on via federated identity servers (eduGain) and through the use of persistent identifiers to identify resources (including also complex resources and possibly parts of resources). The resources and services in INESS will also be catalogued and linked in CLARINO (the Norwegian part of the CLARIN network) and in the *Language Technology Resource Collection for Norwegian – Språkbanken*, hosted at the National Library of Norway.

Acknowledgments

The reported work has been funded by the Research Council of Norway, the University of Bergen, and the European Commission under CIP-ICT-PSP grant agreement no. 270899.

References

Brants, S., Dipper, S., Hansen, S., Lezius, W., and Smith, G. (2002). The TIGER treebank. In *Proceedings of the 1st Workshop on Treebanks and Linguistic Theories*, pages 24–41.

Bresnan, J. (2001). *Lexical-Functional Syntax*. Blackwell, Malden, MA.

Butt, M., Dyvik, H., King, T. H., Masuichi, H., and Rohrer, C. (2002). The Parallel Grammar project. In *Proceedings of COLING-2002 Workshop on Grammar Engineering and Evaluation, Taipei, Taiwan*.

Dyvik, H., Meurer, P., Rosén, V., and De Smedt, K. (2009). Linguistically motivated parallel parsebanks. In Passarotti, M., Przepiórkowski, A., Raynaud, S., and Van Eynde, F., editors, *Proceedings of the Eighth International Workshop on Treebanks and Linguistic Theories*, pages 71–82, Milan, Italy. EDUCatt.

Gaarder, J. (1991). *Sofies verden: roman om filosofiens historie*. Aschehoug, Oslo, Norway.

Meurer, P. (2012). INESS-Search: A search system for LFG (and other) treebanks. In Butt, M. and King, T. H., editors, *Proceedings of the LFG '12 Conference*, LFG Online Proceedings, pages 404–421, Stanford, CA. CSLI Publications.

Rosén, V., De Smedt, K., Meurer, P., and Dyvik, H. (2012a). An open infrastructure for advanced treebanking. In Hajič, J., De Smedt, K., Tadić, M., and Branco, A., editors, *META-RESEARCH Workshop on Advanced Treebanking at LREC2012*, pages 22–29, Istanbul, Turkey.

Rosén, V., Meurer, P., and De Smedt, K. (2007). Designing and implementing discriminants for LFG grammars. In King, T. H. and Butt, M., editors, *The Proceedings of the LFG '07 Conference*, pages 397–417. CSLI Publications, Stanford.

Rosén, V., Meurer, P., and De Smedt, K. (2009). LFG Parsebanker: A toolkit for building and searching a treebank as a parsed corpus. In Van Eynde, F., Frank, A., van Noord, G., and De Smedt, K., editors, *Proceedings of the Seventh International Workshop on Treebanks and Linguistic Theories (TLT7)*, pages 127–133, Utrecht. LOT.

Rosén, V., Meurer, P., Losnegaard, G. S., Lyse, G. I., De Smedt, K., Thunes, M., and Dyvik, H. (2012b). An integrated web-based treebank annotation system. In Hendrickx, I., Kübler, S., and Simov, K., editors, *Proceedings of the Eleventh International Workshop on Treebanks and Linguistic Theories (TLT11)*, pages 157–167, Lisbon, Portugal. Edições Colibri.

Simov, K. and Osenova, P. (2004). BulTreeBank Stylebook. BulTreeBank Project Technical Report 5, Bulgarian Academy of Sciences.

Vasiļjevs, A., Forsberg, M., Gornostay, T., Haltrup Hansen, D., Jóhannsdóttir, K., Lyse, G., Lindén, K., Offersgaard, L., Olsen, S., Pedersen, B., Rögnvaldsson, E., Skadiņa, I., De Smedt, K., Oksanen, V., and Rozis, R. (2012). Creation of an open shared language resource repository in the Nordic and Baltic countries. In Calzolari, N., Choukri, K., Declerck, T., Doğan, M. U., Maegaard, B., Mariani, J., Odijk, J., and Piperidis, S., editors, *Proceedings of the Eighth Conference on International Language Resources and Evaluation (LREC'12)*, pages 1076–1083, Istanbul, Turkey. European Language Resources Association (ELRA).

Wallenberg, J., Ingason, A. K., Sigurðsson, E. F., and Rögnvaldsson, E. (2011). Icelandic Parsed Historical Corpus (IcePaHC) version 0.9.

Building gold-standard treebanks for Norwegian

Per Erik Solberg

National Library of Norway, P.O.Box 2674 Solli, NO-0203 Oslo, Norway

`per.solberg@nb.no`

ABSTRACT

Språkbanken at the National Library of Norway is currently building up gold-standard Dependency Grammar treebanks for Norwegian Bokmål and Nynorsk. The treebanks are manually annotated for morphological features, syntactic functions and dependency relations. This paper explains the choice of texts and format of the treebanks, some key aspects of the morphological and syntactic annotation, and it is illustrated how the treebanks can be used.

KEYWORDS: Treebanking, Dependency Grammar, Morphology, Syntax, Norwegian.

1 Introduction

Data-driven NLP tools such as part-of-speech taggers and syntactic parsers require sufficiently large manually annotated corpora for training and testing, so-called gold-standard corpora (Brants (2000), Nivre et al. (2006a)). Språkbanken has decided to provide gold-standard Dependency Grammar treebanks for the two written standards of Norwegian - Bokmål and Nynorsk. The treebanks are manually annotated for morphological features, syntactic functions and dependency relations.

The project was initiated in October 2011, and beta versions of the tree-banks are released at irregular intervals at Språkbanken's web page (see `http://www.nb.no/English/Collection-and-Services/Spraakbanken/Available-resources/Text-Resources`). Stable versions will be released in October 2013.

This paper and the system demonstration at NoDaLiDa 2013 present some important features of the treebanks: Section 2 describes the format, size and choice of texts, and section 3 lays out traits of the morphological analysis. Section 4 explains some key aspects of the syntactic annotation, and section 5 exemplifies how the treebanks can be used.

2 Choice of texts and format

At the time of writing (April 2013), the Bokmål treebank consists of approximately 204 000 tokens and the Nynorsk treebank of around 156 000 tokens. These numbers will increase significantly during the the last months before the final release. The size of the two treebanks will also be leveled out.

Comparable treebanks for other languages, such as the TIGER treebank and Prague Dependency Treebank, contain, to a large extent, newspaper text (Brants et al. (2004), Böhmová et al. (2003)). The Norwegian treebanks also contain a significant amount of text of this genre, taken from Norsk aviskorpus, a corpus of Norwegian newspaper articles from the last 15 years (`http://avis.uib.no/om-aviskorpuset/english`). Other types of factual prose, such as government reports and transcripts of parliament debates, are also included. In order to include texts in a more colloquial style, we have received permission from individual bloggers to use selected posts from their blogs.

The distribution of texts in the treebanks is currently as follows:

Newspaper text	79%
Government reports	9%
Parliament debates	6%
Blogs	6%

Table 1: Distribution of texts in the treebanks

The texts are morphologically tagged, using the *Oslo-Bergen Tagger* (OBT), (Johannessen et al. (2011)) and subsequently checked and corrected. For the syntactic preprocessing, we use the MaltParser, trained on an earlier version of the treebanks ((Nivre et al. (2006a)). The output of the syntactic parsing is checked and corrected using the annotation software TrEd (`http://ufal.mff.cuni.cz/tred/`). Most texts are syntactically annotated by one annotator, but the two annotators working in the project regularly perform double annotations to check that their annotations are consistent.

The treebanks are released in the CONLL format (Nivre et al. (2007)). The CONLL format is a 10 column tab-separated table, where each new line represents a token. The columns, from right to left, are token index, word form, lemma, coarse-grained part-of-speech (POS) tag, fine-grained POS tag, morphological features, index of head, dependency relation, and two columns which are left blank in our treebanks. We do not distinguish between coarse-grained POS tags and fine-grained POS tags in our annotations, and these columns therefore always contain the same information. In the final release, the treebanks will also be available in Prague Markup Language, the XML-based format used in the Prague Dependency Treebank.

3   Morphological annotation

The lemmatization and the morphological tagset are mostly the same for OBT and Språbanken's treebanks, although we have added a few additional morphological tags (cf. Kinn et al. (2013, 7-16)), the most important being the tag *unorm*, explained below. The lemmas are taken from *Norsk ordbank*, a lexicographic database for Norwegian (http://www.edd.uio.no/prosjekt/ordbanken). In addition to this, OBT generates lemmas for compounds and for adjectives formed on the basis of participial forms of verbs. The morphological tagset of OBT is rather rich: In addition to features pertaining to the inflection of words, it also contains information on whether the token belongs to a particular sub-class of a POS: Pronouns are marked as demonstrative, personal, reflexive, reciprocal, question-forming etc., determiners as demonstrative, quantifying, possessive and so on. For users of the treebanks who need a distinction between coarse- and fine-grained POS tags, it should be relatively easy to make a conversion scheme based on these tags.

A phenomenon which OBT cannot handle, is spelling variants and inflectional forms which do not comply with the official norm for Bokmål and Nynorsk, and non-compounds which do not have an entry in Norsk ordbank. In such cases, the annotators manually add a lemma and the correct morphological tags, and mark the token as not complying with the norm, using the morphological tag *unorm*, (i.e. *unormert*, 'non-standard').

4   Syntactic annotation

While the morphological analyses are based on OBT, the syntactic annotation guidelines for the treebanks have been developed specifically for this project (see Kinn et al. (2013)). The formalism for the syntactic annotation is Dependency Grammar. The sentence in example (1) and its analysis in FIGURE 1 illustrates some key features of the syntactic annotation.

(1)   *Den   kinesiske   ledelsen   har   tydeligvis   innsett   alvoret.*
      the   Chinese   administration   has   evidently   realized   seriousness+the
      'The Chinese administration has evidently realized the seriousness.'

One token serves as head for the whole sentence. In (1), the finite auxiliary verb *har* heads the sentence and carries the root-function for finite sentences FINV. Each of the other tokens are annotated for syntactic functions and unique dependency relations to another token in the sentence. The subject is dependent on the finite verb, as subjects usually only occur in finite constructions. Other arguments and modifiers, such as the object *alvoret* and the adverb *tydeligvis* in example (1), are, however, dependents on the lexical verb. While there might be cases where it would be adequate to make e.g. an adverbial dependent on the

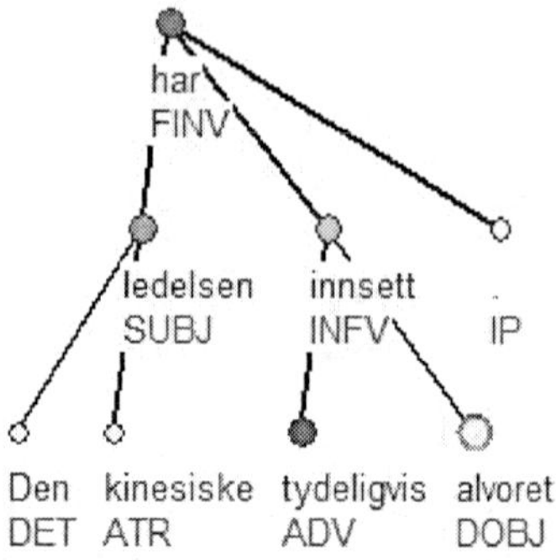

Figure 1: Analysis of (1)

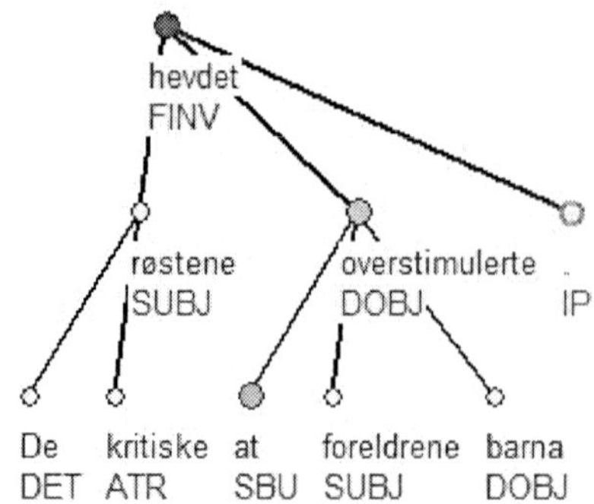

Figure 2: Analysis of (2)

auxiliary, we have chosen this analysis to ensure annotations which are as consistent and uniform as possible.

Finite subordinate clauses are always headed by the finite verb in our treebanks. Example (2) and its analysis in FIGURE 2 illustrates this.

(2) *De   kritiske   røstene   hevdet   at   foreldrene   overstimulerte   barna.*
     the   critical   voices   claimed   that   parents+the   overstimulated   children+the
     'The critical voices claimed that the parents overstimulated the children.'

The complement clause in (2) is headed by the verb *overstimulerte*, which receives the function DOBJ (*direct object*). An alternative analysis would be to make the subjunction head. In Norwegian, the subjunction can quite often be dropped in both relative and complement clauses. If all finite subordinate clauses are headed by the finite verb, it is quite simple to make queries for all subordinate clauses of a specific type, regardless of whether a subjunction is present. In the alternative analysis where the subjunction serves as head, a different analysis would have to be found for clauses lacking a subjunction, and some queries would be much more difficult to perform.

5   Use

The treebanks are mainly intended as testing and training material for data-driven NLP tools, both morphological and syntactic. Such resources have been lacking for Norwegian[1]. For example, there have been no suitable treebank for testing and training data-driven dependency parsers. To illustrate how the gold-standard treebanks can be used for this purposes, I parsed a 15 000 token text in Bokmål both with the MaltParser, and compared the results to a manually annotated version of the text, using the *CONLL-X shared task evaluation script* (http://ilk.uvt.nl/conll/software.html). The MaltParser was trained on the current version of the Bokmål treebank. I used the Covington's non-projective parsing algorithm and the Liblinear learning algorithm, but didn't try to optimize the parser any further (Nivre et al. (2006a), Covington (2001), Fan et al. (2008)). the MaltParser gave a

---

[1]But see also the INESS project at the University of Bergen: http://iness.uib.no/

labeled attachment score (LAS; the percentage of tokens for which both the dependency relation and the syntactic function is correct) of 85.77 %. In comparison, Nivre et al. (2006b) obtained a LAS of 84.58 % for Swedish and 84.77 % for Danish using the MaltParser, the best results for those languages in the 2006 CoNLL-X shared task on Multilingual Dependency Parsing (Buchholz and Marsi (2006)).

While the treebanks are primarily developed for NLP research and development, they can also be interesting tools for researchers within other linguistic disciplines, such as morphology, lexicography and syntax. A treebank can be used to query very specific constructions, which cannot be found in corpora with a less detailed annotation. For example, Julien (2009), who studied main clause word order in subordinate clauses in Mainland Scandinavian, wasn't able to search for fronted non-subjects in subordinate clauses in the corpora she used (Julien (2009, 5)). This could have been retrieved easily from the gold-standard treebanks, using e.g. PML Tree Query (Pajas and Štěpánek (2009)). A query in the treebanks can also immediately give all lemmas occurring e.g. as indirect object, while this kind of information is much harder to retrieve in corpora without syntactic annotation. A downside to manually annotated treebanks when used for such purposes, is that they are usually much smaller than corpora with a more shallow annotation, and it might therefore be difficult to find infrequent constructions.

6 Conclusion

This paper has presented Språkbanken's gold-standard treebanks for Norwegian Bokmål and Nynorsk, two Dependency Grammar treebanks which are manually annotated for morphological features, syntactic functions and dependency relations. The treebanks have primarily been developed with the testing and training of data-driven NLP tools in mind. Norwegian treebanks containing detailed syntactic annotation can, however, be useful and interesting resources for other purposes too, such as syntactic and lexicographic research.

Acknowledgments

Språkbanken's gold-standard treebanks are built up in close collaboration with the Text Laboratory at the University of Oslo. I would also like to thank Lilja Øverlid and Arne Skjærholt at the Department of Informatics at the University of Oslo for their valuable advice and for helping us set up a more effective syntactic preprocessing. Inquiries regarding the treebanks can be sent to *sprakbanken@nb.no*.

References

Böhmová, A., Hajič, J., Hajičová, E., and Hladká, B. (2003). The Prague Dependency Treebank. In *Treebanks*, pages 103–127. Springer, Netherlands.

Brants, S., Dipper, S., Eisenberg, P., Hansen-Schirra, S., König, E., Lezius, W., Rohrer, C., Smith, G., and Uszkoreit, H. (2004). Tiger: Linguistic interpretation of a german corpus. *Research on Language and Computation*, 2(4):597–620.

Brants, T. (2000). Tnt: a statistical part-of-speech tagger. In *Proceedings of the sixth conference on Applied natural language processing*, pages 224–231, Seattle, WA.

Buchholz, S. and Marsi, E. (2006). Conll-x shared task on multilingual dependency parsing. In *Proceedings of the Tenth Conference on Computational Natural Language Learning*, pages 149–164, New York, NY.

Covington, M. A. (2001). A fundamental algorithm for dependency parsing. In *Proceedings of the 39th annual ACM southeast conference*, pages 95–102, Athens, GA.

Fan, R.-E., Chang, K.-W., Hsieh, C.-J., Wang, X.-R., and Lin, C.-J. (2008). Liblinear: A library for large linear classification. *The Journal of Machine Learning Research*, 9:1871–1874.

Johannessen, J. B., Hagen, K., Nøklestad, A., and Lynum, A. (2011). Obt+ stat: Evaluation of a combined cg and statistical tagger. *Constraint Grammar Applications*, pages 26–34.

Julien, M. (2009). Embedded clauses with main clause word order in mainland scandinavian. *Published on LingBuzz:(http://ling. auf. net/lingBuzz/000475)*.

Kinn, K., Solberg, P. E., and Eriksen, P. K. (2013). Retningslinjer for morfologisk og syntaktisk annotasjon i Språkbankens gullkorpus. Manuscript. Språkbanken, National Library of Norway. URL: `http://www.nb.no/Tilbud/Forske/Spraakbanken/Tilgjengelege-ressursar/Tekstressursar`. [last visited on 05/04/2013].

Nivre, J., Hall, J., Kübler, S., McDonald, R., Nilsson, J., Riedel, S., and Yuret, D. (2007). The conll 2007 shared task on dependency parsing. In *Proceedings of the CoNLL Shared Task Session of EMNLP-CoNLL*, pages 915–932, Toulouse, France.

Nivre, J., Hall, J., and Nilsson, J. (2006a). Maltparser: A data-driven parser-generator for dependency parsing. In *Proceedings of LREC*, volume 6, pages 2216–2219.

Nivre, J., Hall, J., Nilsson, J., Eryiit, G., and Marinov, S. (2006b). Labeled pseudo-projective dependency parsing with support vector machines. In *Proceedings of the Tenth Conference on Computational Natural Language Learning*, pages 221–225, New York, NY.

Pajas, P. and Štěpánek, J. (2009). System for querying syntactically annotated corpora. In *Proceedings of the ACL-IJCNLP 2009 Software Demonstrations*, pages 33–36, Suntec, Singapore.